· HUGH ·
JOHNSON'S
POCKET ENCYCLOPEDIA OF
WINE 1996

A Fireside Book
Published by Simon & Schuster Inc.
New York London Toronto
Sydney Tokyo Singapore

Key to Symbols

r	red
p	rosé
w	white
br	brown
(r)	denotes less important wine
dr	dry (assume wine is dry when dr or sw not indicated)
sw	sweet
s/sw	semi-sweet
sp	sparkling
*	plain, everyday quality
**	above average
***	well known, highly reputed
****	grand, prestigious à expensive
▓▓	usually particularly good value in its class
85 88 etc	recommended years which may be currently available
90' etc	vintage regarded as particularly successful for the property in question
87 etc	Years in **bold** should be ready for drinking (the others should be kept). Where both reds and whites are indicated the red is intended unless otherwise stated.
89 etc	Vintages in colour are the ones to choose first for drinking in '95. They should be à point. **NB** German vintages are codified by a different system. See note on page 106.
(93) etc	provisional rating
DYA	drink the youngest available
NV	Vintage not normally shown on label. In Champagne, means a blend of several vintages for continuity.
SMALL CAPS	properties, areas or terms cross-referred within the section.

See page 5 for extra explanation.
A quick-reference vintage chart appears on page 224.

Fireside
Simon & Schuster Inc
Rockefeller Center
1230 Avenue of the Americas
New York, New York 10020

© Mitchell Beazley International Ltd 1977–1995
Text © Hugh Johnson 1977–1995
Maps © Mitchell Beazley International Ltd 1977–1995
First edition published 1977
Revised editions published 1978, 1979, 1980, 1981, 1982, 1983, 1984, 1985, 1986, 1987, 1988, 1989, 1990, 1991, 1992, 1993, 1994, 1995

ISBN 0-684-80181-7
ISSN 0893-259X

The author and publishers will be grateful for any information which will assist them in keeping future editions up to date. Although all reasonable care has been taken in the preparation of this book, neither the publishers nor the author can accept any liability for any consequences arising from the use thereof, or from the information contained herein.

Editor Susan Keevil
Executive Editor Anne Ryland
Production Juliette Butler
Maps Lovell Johns
Produced by Mandarin Offset
Printed and bound in China

Contents

Foreword

The wine world in 1996 has expanded again; at least if this minimalist annual précis is anything to go by. It takes eight more pages than last year to shoehorn in all the information you might need. I just hope you can follow the shorthand.

This, though, is the essay page, where I can allow myself whole sentences to celebrate successes or voice concerns. After many years of trench warfare against health fascists and puritans it seems that we are beginning to see the dawn of reason. The senior medical associations of the world are at last prepared to admit what their individual members have known (and practised) all along; that wine is not only life-enhancing, it can be and often is also life-preserving. In 1994 the American Medical Association stated that 'generalized messages to abstain from alcohol are no more responsible than generalized recommendations to drink it'. I do not recommend that you drink alcohol; I merely offer my view that wine taken moderately is good for body and soul.

Two other discernible current trends seem to me to be very much for the good. One is the planting of a much wider range of grape varieties, bringing into use the diverse traditions and flavours of the whole of Europe; experiments going far beyond the me-too 'classics' which have been a depressing feature of the last 20 years.

The other is increasing use of vineyard names for top-quality wines in regions where the only means of identification used to be the brand. It is the inevitable dividend of experience. For years intelligent growers, especially in California, have been observing where certain varieties produce consistently better wine. They have, in fact, been doing exactly what Europeans have done over centuries. It used to the be the fashion to decry appellations contrôlées and their equivalents as restrictive. How interesting it is to see self-imposed appellations slowly taking shape. The dominance of varietal wines is certainly not at an end; but its end is in sight – distant as it may be.

As always, my aim in this book is to compress the essence of this ever-changing world into your pocket. My information is gleaned from many sources, through visits, tastings and never-ending correspondence. Revision is constant. I shall have a much-scribbled on proof for 1997 before you even read this.

The book is designed to take the panic out of buying. You are faced with a daunting restaurant wine list, or mind-numbing shelves of bottles in a store. Your mind goes blank. Out comes your little book. Just establish which country a wine comes from, then look up the principal words on the label in that country's section. You should find enough information to guide your choice – and often a great deal more: the cross-references are there to help you delve further. Even after 19 editions I find I can browse for hours...

How to use this book

The top line of most entries consists of the following information:

1   Which part of the country in question the wine comes from.

2   Whether it is red, rosé or white (or brown/amber), dry, sweet or sparkling, or several of these (and which is most important).

3   Its general standing as to quality: a necessarily rough and ready guide based on its current reputation as reflected in its prices.

     *   plain, everyday quality

     **   above average

     ***   well-known, highly reputed

     **** grand, prestigious, expensive

     So much is more or less objective. Additionally there is a subjective rating: shading around the stars of any wine which in my experience is usually particularly good within its price range. There are good everyday wines as well as good luxury wines. The shading system helps you find them.

4   Vintage information: which of the recent vintages that may still be available can be recommended; of these, which are ready to drink this year, and which will probably improve with keeping. Your choice for current drinking should be one of the vintage years printed in **bold** type. Buy light-type years for further maturing.

Vintages printed in colour are the ones you should choose first for drinking in 1996. Consult the Bordeaux introduction (page 58) for more on this.

The German vintages work on a different principle again: see page 106.

...and my thanks

This store of detailed recommendations comes partly from my own notes and partly from those of a great number of kind friends. Without the generous help and cooperation of innumerable winemakers, merchants and critics, I could not attempt it. I particularly want to thank the following for help with research or in the areas of their special knowledge.

Burton Anderson	Richard Mayson
Colin Anderson MW	Maggie McNie MW
Fritz Ascher	Eszter Molnár
Martyn Assirati	Adam Montefiore
Jean-Claude Berrouet	Vladimir Moskvan
Michael Broadbent MW	Christian Moueix
John Cossart	Douglas Murray
Stelios Damianou	Nobuko Nishioka
Marc Dubernet	Judy Peterson-Nedry
Len Evans	Stuart Pigott
Dereck Foster	John and Erica Platter
François Gaignet	Carlos Read
Howard G Goldberg	Jan and Maite Read
Grahame Haggart	Rory Ross
James Halliday	Michael, Prinz zu Salm
Russell Hone	Peter A Sichel
Susan Keevil	Stephen Skelton
Andreas Keller	Steven Spurrier
Gabriel Lachmann	Charles and Philippa Sydney
Tony Laithwaite	Paul Symington
Miles Lambert-Gócs	Bob Thompson
Christopher Lindlar	Peter Vinding-Diers
John Livingstone-Learmonth	Rebecca Wassermann-Hone
Giles MacDonogh	Julia Wilkinson
Andreas März	David Wolfe

Grape Varieties

In the past ten years a major change has come about in such importing countries as the USA, Britain and Germany. Suddenly the names of a handful of grape varieties have become the ready reference to wine. In the senior wine countries, above all France and Italy (which between them still produce nearly half the world's wine), more complex traditions prevail. Wine is known by its origin, not just the particular fruit-juice that fermented.

For the present the two notions are in rivalry. Eventually the primacy of place over fruit will become obvious, at least for wines of quality. But for now, for most people, grape tastes are the simplistic reference-point – despite the fact that they are often confused by the added taste of oak. If grape flavours were really all that mattered this would be a very short book.

But of course they do matter, and a knowledge of them both guides you to flavours you enjoy and helps comparisons between regions. Hence the originally Californian term 'varietal wine' – meaning, in principle, one grape variety.

At least seven varieties – Cabernet, Pinot Noir, Riesling, Sauvignon Blanc, Chardonnay, Gewürztraminer and Muscat – have tastes and smells distinct and memorable enough to form international categories of wine. To these you can add Merlot, Syrah, Sémillon, Chenin Blanc, Pinots Blanc and Gris, Sylvaner, Nebbiolo, Sangiovese, Tempranillo.... The following are the best and/or commonest wine grapes. Abbreviations used in the text are in brackets.

Grapes for white wine

Albariño The Spanish name for N Portugal's Alvarinho, emerging as excellently fresh and fragrant wine in Galicia.

Aligoté Burgundy's second-rank white grape. Crisp (often sharp) wine, needs drinking in 1–3 yrs. Perfect for mixing with cassis (blackcurrant liqueur) to make a 'Kir'. Widely planted in E Europe, esp Russia.

Blanc Fumé Alias of SAUV BL, referring to its reputedly 'smoky' smell, particularly from the Loire (Sancerre and Pouilly). In California used for oak-aged Sauv and reversed to 'Fumé Blanc'. But the smoke is oak.

Bual Makes top quality sweet madeira wines.

Chardonnay (Chard) The white burgundy grape, the white champagne grape, and the best white grape of the New World, partly because it is one of the easiest to grow and vinify. All regions are trying it, mostly aged (or fermented) in oak to reproduce the flavours of burgundy. Australia and California make classics. Those of Italy, Spain, New Zealand, South Africa, New York State, Bulgaria, Chile, Hungary and the Midi are all coming on strong. Called Morillon in Austria.

Chasselas A prolific early-ripening grape with little aroma, also grown for eating. Best known as Fendant in Switzerland (where it is supreme), Gutedel in Germany.

Chenin Blanc (Chenin Bl) Great white grape of the middle Loire (Vouvray, Layon etc). Wine can be dry or sweet (or very sweet), but always retains plenty of acidity – hence its long life and use in California, where it can make fine wine, but is rarely so used. See also Steen.

Clairette A low-acid grape formerly widely used in the S of France as a vermouth base. Being revived.

Colombard Slightly fruity, nicely sharp grape, hugely popular in California, now gaining ground in SW France, South Africa, California, etc.

Fendant See Chasselas.

Folle Blanche High acid/little flavour make this ideal for brandy. Called Gros Plant in Brittany, Picpoul in Armagnac. Respectable in California.

Fumé Blanc (Fumé Bl) See Blanc Fumé.

Furmint A grape of great character: the trademark of Hungary both as the principal grape in Tokay and as vivid vigorous table wine with an appley flavour. Called Sipon in Slovenia. Some grown in Austria.

Gewürztraminer, alias Traminer (Gewürz) One of the most pungent grapes, distinctively spicy with aromas like rose petals and grapefruit. Wines are often rich and soft, even when fully dry. Best in Alsace; also good in Germany, E Europe, Australia, California, Pacific NW, New Zealand.

Grauburgunder See Pinot Gris.

Grechetto or Greco Ancient grape of central and S Italy: vitality and style.

Grüner Veltliner Austria's favourite (almost half her vineyards). Around Vienna and in the Wachau and Weinviertel (also in Moravia) it can be delicious: light but dry and lively. The best age 5 years or so.

Italian Riesling Grown in N Italy and E Europe. Much inferior to Rhine RIES, with lower acidity, best in sweet wines. Alias Welschriesling, Olaszrizling (no longer legally labelled simply 'Riesling').

Kerner The most successful of many recent German varieties, mostly made by crossing RIES and SILVANER (but in this case RIES x (red) Trollinger). Early-ripening flowery (but often too blatant) wine with good acidity. Popular in Pfalz, Rheinhessen etc.

Macabeo The workhorse white grape of N Spain, widespread in Rioja (alias Viura) and in Catalan cava country.

Malvasia Known as Malmsey in Madeira, Malvasia in Italy, Malvoisie in France. Alias Vermentino (esp in Corsica). Also grown in Greece, Spain, W Australia, E Europe. Makes rich brown wines or soft whites, ageing magnificently with superb potential not often realized.

Marsanne Principal white grape (with Roussanne) of the N Rhône (eg Hermitage, St-Joseph, St-Péray). Also good in Australia, California and (as Ermitage Blanc) the Valais. Soft full wines age v well.

Müller-Thurgau (Müller-T) Dominant in Germany's Rheinhessen and Pfalz and too common on the Mosel; a cross between RIESLING and SILVANER. Ripens early to make soft aromatic wines for drinking young. Makes good sweet wines but usually dull, often coarse, dry ones.

Muscadelle Adds aroma to many white Bordeaux, esp Sauternes.

Muscadet, alias Melon de Bourgogne Makes light, very dry wines with a seaside tang round Nantes in Brittany. They should not be sharp, but faintly salty and very refreshing. (California 'Pinot Bl' is this grape.)

Muscat (Many varieties; the best is Muscat Blanc à Petits Grains.) Universally grown, easily recognized, pungent grapes, mostly made into perfumed sweet wines, often fortified (as in France's vins doux naturels). Superb in Australia. Rarely (eg Alsace) made dry.

Palomino, alias Listan Makes all the best sherry but poor table wine.

Pedro Ximénez, alias PX Makes very strong wine in Montilla and Málaga. Used in blending sweet sherries. Also grown in Argentina, the Canaries, Australia, California, South Africa.

Pinot Blanc (Pinot Bl) A cousin of PINOT N; not related to CHARD, but with a similar, milder character: light, fresh, fruity, not aromatic, to drink young; good for eg Italian spumante. Grown in Alsace, N Italy, S Germany, E Europe. Weissburgunder in Germany. See also Muscadet.

Pinot Gris (Pinot Gr) At best makes rather heavy, even 'thick', full-bodied whites with a certain spicy style. Known (formerly) as Tokay in Alsace; Ruländer (sweet) or Grauburgunder (dry) in Germany; Tocai or Pinot Grigio in Italy and Slovenia (but much thinner wine).

Pinot Noir (Pinot N) Superlative black grape (See Grapes for red wine) used in Champagne and occasionally elsewhere (eg California, Australia) for making white, sparkling, or very pale pink 'vin gris'.

Riesling (Ries) Germany's great grape, and at present the world's most underrated. Wine of brilliant sweet/acid balance, either dry or sweet, flowery in youth but maturing to subtle oily scents and flavours. Unlike CHARD it does not need high alcohol for character. Very good (usually dry) in Alsace (but absurdly nowhere else in France), Austria, Australia (widely grown), Pacific NW, Ontario, California, South Africa. Often called White-, Johannisberg- or Rhine Riesling. Subject to 'noble rot'.

Ruländer German name for PINOT GRIS used for sweeter wines.

Sauvignon Blanc (Sauv Bl) Makes v distinctive aromatic grassy – or gooseberry – sometimes rank-smelling wines; best in Sancerre. Blended with SEM in B'x. Can be austere or buxom. Pungent success in New Zealand, now overplanted everywhere. Also called Fumé Bl or vice versa.

Scheurebe Spicy-flavoured German RIES x SYLVANER, very successful in Pfalz, esp for Auslesen. Can be weedy in dry wines.

Sémillon (Sém) Contributes the lusciousness to Sauternes; subject to 'noble rot' in the right conditions but increasingly important for Graves and dry white Bordeaux too. Grassy if not fully ripe, but can make soft dry wine of great ageing potential. Formerly called 'Riesling' in parts of Australia. Old Hunter Valley Sém can be great wine.

Sercial Makes the driest madeira; (where myth says it is really RIESLING!).

Seyval Blanc (Seyval Bl) French-made hybrid of French and American vines. V hardy and attractively fruity. Popular and reasonably successful in eastern States and England but banned by EC from 'quality' wines.

Steen South Africa's most popular white grape: good lively fruity wine. Said to be the CHENIN BL of the Loire.

Silvaner, alias Sylvaner Germany's former workhorse grape: wine rarely fine except in Franken where it is savoury and ages admirably, and in Rheinhessen and Baden, where it is enjoying a renaissance. Good in the Italian Tyrol and useful in Alsace. Very good (and powerful) as 'Johannisberg' in the Valais, Switzerland.

Tokay See Pinot Gris. Also a table grape in California and a supposedly Hungarian grape in Australia. The wine Tokay is made of FURMINT.

Traminer See Gewürztraminer.

Trebbiano Important but mediocre grape of central Italy, used in Orvieto, Chianti, Soave, etc. Also grown in S France as Ugni Bl, and Cognac as St-Emilion. Thin, neutral wine; really needs blending.

Ugni Blanc (Ugni Bl) See Trebbiano.

Verdejo The grape of Rueda in Castile, potentially fine and long-lived.

Verdelho Madeira grape making excellent medium-sweet wine; in Australia, fresh soft dry wine of great character.

Verdicchio Gives its name to good dry wine in central-eastern Italy.

Vermentino See Malvasia.

Vernaccia Grape grown in central and S Italy and Sardinia for strong smooth lively wine, sometimes inclining towards sherry.

Viognier Rare grape of the Rhône, grown at Condrieu for v fine fragrant wine. Much in vogue in the Midi, California, etc, but still only a trickle.

Viura See Macabeo.

Weissburgunder See Pinot Blanc.

Welschriesling See Italian Riesling.

Grapes for red wine

Aleatico Dark Muscat variety, alias Aglianico, used the length of W Italy for fragrant sweet wines.

Barbera Most popular of many productive grapes of N Italy, esp Piedmont, giving dark, fruity, often sharp wine. Gaining prestige in California.

Brunello S Tuscan form of SANGIOVESE, splendid at Montalcino.

Cabernet Franc, alias Bouchet (Cab F) The lesser of two sorts of Cab grown in Bordeaux but dominant (as 'Bouchet') in St-Emilion. The Cab of the Loire, making Chinon, etc, and rosé.

Cabernet Sauvignon (Cab S) Grape of great character: spicy, herby, tannic, with characteristic 'blackcurrant' aroma. The first grape of the Médoc, also makes most of the best Californian, Australian, S American and E European reds. Its wine almost always needs ageing; usually benefiting from blending with eg MERLOT, CAB F or SYRAH. Makes very aromatic rosé.

Carignan By far the commonest grape of France, covering hundreds of thousands of acres. Prolific with dull but harmless wine. Best from old vines in Corbières. Also common in N Africa, Spain, California.

Cinsaut Common bulk-producing grape of S France; in S Africa crossed with PINOT N to make PINOTAGE. Pale wine, but quality potential.

Dolcetto Source of soft seductive dry red in Piedmont. Now high fashion (though low budget).

Gamay The Beaujolais grape: light, very fragrant wines, at their best young. Makes even lighter wine on the Loire, in central France, and in Switzerland and Savoie. Known as 'Napa Gamay' in California.

Gamay Beaujolais Not GAMAY but a poor variety of PINOT N in California.

Grenache, alias Garnacha, Alicante, Cannonau Useful grape for strong fruity but pale wine: good rosé and vin doux naturel. Grown in S France, Spain, California. Usually blended (eg Châteauneuf-du-Pape).

Grignolino Makes one of the good everyday table wines of Piedmont.

Kadarka, alias Gamza Makes healthy sound agreeable reds in Hungary, Bulgaria etc.

Lambrusco Productive grape of the lower Po Valley, giving quintessentially Italian, cheerful sweet and fizzy red.

Malbec, alias Cot Minor in Bordeaux, major in Cahors (alias Auxerrois) and Argentina. Dark, dense and tannic wine capable of real quality.

Merlot Adaptable grape making the great fragrant and plummy wines of Pomerol and (with CAB F) St-Emilion, an important element in Médoc reds, soft and strong in California, Washington and Australia, lighter but often good in N Italy, Italian Switzerland, Slovenia, Argentina, etc.

Montepulciano Confusingly, a major central-eastern Italian grape of high quality, as well as a town in Tuscany.

Mourvèdre, alias Mataro Excellent dark aromatic tannic grape used mainly for blending in Provence (especially in Bandol) and the Midi. Enjoying new interest in eg S Australia, California.

Nebbiolo, alias Spanna and Chiavennasca One of Italy's best red grapes; makes Barolo, Barbaresco, Gattinara, Valtellina. Intense, nobly fruity and perfumed wine but very tannic, taking years to mature.

Petit Verdot Excellent but awkward Médoc grape now largely superseded.

Pinot Noir (Pinot N) The glory of Burgundy's Côte d'Or, with scent, flavour, and texture unmatched anywhere. Less happy elsewhere; makes light wines rarely of much distinction in Germany, Switzerland, Austria, Hungary. The great challenge to California and Australia (and recently S Africa). Shows exciting promise in California's Carneros and Central Coast, Oregon, Ontario, Yarra Valley, Adelaide Hills, Tasmania and NZ.

Pinotage Singular S African grape (PINOT N x CINSAUT). Can be very fruity and age interestingly, but often jammy.

Sangiovese (or Sangioveto) The main red grape of Chianti and much of central Italy. BRUNELLO is the Sangiovese Grosso.

Saperavi Makes good sharp very long-lived wine in Georgia, Ukraine etc. Blends very well with CABERNET (eg in Moldova).

Spätburgunder German for PINOT N, but a very pale shadow of burgundy.

Syrah, alias Shiraz The great Rhône red grape, with tannic purple peppery wine which can mature superbly. Very important as Shiraz in Australia, increasingly successful in the Midi and California.

Tempranillo The pale aromatic fine Rioja grape, called Ull de Lebre in Catalonia, Cencibel in La Mancha. Early ripening.

Zinfandel (Zin) Fruity adaptable grape peculiar to California with blackberry-like, and sometimes metallic, flavour. Can be gloriously lush, but also makes 'blush' white wine.

Wine & Food

Our attitudes to pairing wine and food range from the slapdash to the near-neurotic. Oddly, the subject has attracted very little ink until only recently: it is fertile ground for experiment. Few combinations can be dismissed outright as 'wrong', but generations of tradition and error have produced certain working conventions that certainly do no harm.

The following are ideas intended to help you make quick decisions. Any of the groups of recommended wines could be extended at will. In general I have stuck to wines that are widely available, at the same time trying to ring the changes so that the same wines don't come up time and time again – as they tend to do in real life. Remember that in a restaurant that is truly regional (Provençal, Basque, Tuscan, Catalan, Austrian...) there is a ready-made answer – the wine of the region in question.

Before the meal – aperitifs

The conventional aperitif wines are either sparkling (epitomized by champagne) or fortified (epitomized by sherry in Britain, port in France, vermouth in Italy etc). A glass of white or rosé table wine before eating is presently in vogue. It calls for something light and stimulating, fairly dry but not acid, with a degree of character; rather Riesling or Chenin Blanc than Chardonnay.

Warning:
Avoid peanuts; they destroy wine flavours.

Olives are also too piquant for most wines; they need sherry or a Martini. Eat almonds, pistachios or walnuts, plain crisps or cheese straws instead.

First courses

Aïoli A thirst-quencher is needed for its garlic heat. Rhône (*→**), Provence rosé, Minervois, Verdicchio. And marc, too, for courage.

Antipasto in Italy Dry or medium white (**): Italian (Arneis, Soave, Pinot Grigio, Greco di Tufo); light red (Dolcetto, Franciacorta or young ** Chianti).

Artichoke vinaigrette Young red (*): Bordeaux, Côtes du Rhône; or a rather blunt white, eg Côtes du Rhône.
    hollandaise Full-bodied dry or medium white (* or **): Mâcon Blanc, Pfalz, or a California Chardonnay (**).

Asparagus A difficult flavour for wine, so the wine needs plenty of its own. Sémillon beats Chardonnay, esp from Australia. Alsace Pinot Gris, even dry Muscat can be good, or Jurançon Sec.

Avocado with prawns, crab, etc Dry to medium or slightly sharp white (**→***): Rheingau or Pfalz Kabinett, Sancerre, Pinot Grigio; Sonoma or Australian Chard or Sauvignon, Cape Steen, or dry rosé.
    vinaigrette Light red (*), or manzanilla sherry.

Bisques Dry white with plenty of body (**): Pinot Gris, Chardonnay. Fino or dry amontillado sherry, or Montilla. Australian Semillon.

Boudin (blood sausage) Local Sauvignon or Chenin – esp in the Loire.

Bouillabaisse Very dry white (*→**): Dry rosé of Provence or Corsica, or Cassis, Verdicchio, California Blanc Fumé.

Caesar Salad California (Central Coast) Chardonnay.

Carpaccio, beef Seems to work well with the flavour of most wines, incl
★★★ reds. Top Tuscan vino da tavola is appropriate. But fine Chards
are good. So is vintage champagne. (See also Carpaccio under fish.)
salmon Chardonnay (★★→★★★), or champagne.

Caviar Iced vodka. Champagne, if you must, full-bodied (eg Bollinger, Krug).

Ceviche California or Australian Chardonnay (★★), NZ Sauvignon Blanc.

Chabrot The end of a bowl of vegetable soup; add equal quantity of young red.

Charcuterie Young Beaujolais-Villages or ★★ Bordeaux Blanc, Arbois
rouge, Oregon Pinot N.

Cheese fondue Dry white (★★): Fendant or Johannisberg du Valais, Grüner
Veltliner, Alsace Riesling or Pinot Gris.

Chowders Big-scale white (★★), not necessarily bone dry: Pinot Gris, Rhine
Spätlese. Or fino sherry, dry madeira or Marsala.

Clams As for oysters.

Consommé Medium-dry sherry (★★→★★★), dry madeira, Marsala Vergine.

Crostini Morellino di Scansano, Montepulciano d'Abruzzo, Valpolicella.

Crudités Light red or rosé (★→★★, no more): Côtes du Rhône, Minervois,
Chianti, Zinfandel; or fino sherry.

Dim-Sum Classically, tea: Oolong or Bo-Li. For fun: fried **Dim-Sum**
Sauvignon Blanc or Riesling, **steamed** Light red (Chianti, Bardolino).

Eggs (See also Soufflés.) These present difficulties: they clash with most
wines and spoil good ones. So ★→★★ of whatever is going. As a last
resort I can bring myself to drink champagne with scrambled eggs.

Escargots White Mâcon-Villages or young Beaujolais-Villages. In the Midi,
vg Petits-Gris go with local white or red. In Alsace, Pinot Bl or Gewurz.

Fish terrine Pfalz Riesling Spätlese Trocken, Chablis, Washington or
Australian Semillon, Sonoma Chardonnay; or fino sherry.

Foie gras White (★★★→★★★★). In Bordeaux they drink Sauternes. Others
prefer a late-harvest Riesling (incl New World) or Gewürztraminer, or
Alsace Pinot Gris. Old dry amontillado can be sublime. But not Chard.

Gazpacho A glass of fino before and after.

Goat's cheese, grilled or fried (warm salad) Chilled Chinon or Saumur-
Champigny or Provence rosé. Or strong red: Ch Musar, Greek, Turkish.

Grapefruit If you must start a meal with grapefruit try port, madeira or
sweet sherry with (or in) it.

Gravlax Akvavit or iced sake. Or Grand Cru Chablis, or ★★★ California,
Washington or Australian Chardonnay.

Guacamole California Chardonnay (★★) or Mexican beer.

Haddock, smoked, mousse of A wonderful dish for showing off any stylish
full-bodied white, incl Grand Cru Chablis or top Pouilly Fuissé.

Ham, raw or cured (See also Prosciutto.) Alsace Grand Cru Pinot Gris.

Herrings, raw or pickled Dutch gin (young, not aged) or Scandinavian
akvavit, and cold beer.

Hors d'oeuvres (See also Antipasto.) Clean, fruity, sharp white (★→★★★):
Sancerre or any Sauvignon, Grüner Veltliner, Muscadet, Cape Steen;
or young light red Bordeaux, Rhône or Corbières. Or fino sherry.

Mackerel, smoked An oily wine-destroyer. Manzanilla sherry, or
schnapps, peppered or bison-grass vodka. Or good lager.

Mayonnaise Adds richness that calls for a contrasting bite in the wine.
Côte Chalonnaise whites (eg Rully) are good. Try NZ Sauvignon Blanc,
Verdicchio or a Spätlese trocken from the Pfalz.

Melon Needs a strong sweet wine (if any): port (★★), Bual madeira, Muscat
de Frontignan, oloroso sherry or vin doux naturel.

Minestrone Red (★): Grignolino, Chianti, Zinfandel, Shiraz, etc. Or fino.

Mushrooms à la Grecque Greek Verdea or Mantinia, or any hefty dry
white, or fresh young red.

Omelettes See Eggs.

Oyster stew California, Long Island or Australian ★★ Chardonnay.

Oysters White (★★→★★★): NV champagne, Chablis or (better) Chablis Premier
Cru, Muscadet, white Graves, Sancerre. Guinness or Scotch and water.

Pasta Red or white (*→**) according to the sauce or trimmings:
    cream sauce Orvieto, Frascati, Italian Chardonnay.
    meat sauce Montepulciano d'Abruzzo, Montefalco d'Arquata, Merlot.
    pesto (basil) sauce Barbera, NZ Sauvignon Blanc.
    seafood sauce (vongole, eg) Verdicchio, Soave, Pomino, Sauv Bl.
    tomato sauce Barbera, Sicilian or S Italian red, Zinfandel.
Pâté According to constituents and quality:
    chicken livers Call for pungent white, a smooth red like a light Pomerol, or even amontillado sherry.
    with simple pâté A ** dry white: Mâcon-Villages, Graves, Fumé Blanc.
    with duck pâté Coteaux du Languedoc, Chianti Classico or Franciacorta.
Pimentos, roasted NZ Sauvignon, Raimat (Spanish) Chardonnay; or Valdepeñas.
Pizza Any ** dry Italian red or ** Rioja, Australian Shiraz or California Zinfandel. Corbières or Roussillon or red Bairrada.
Prawns or shrimps Dry white (**→***): burgundy, Bordeaux, Chard, Riesling – even fine mature champagne.
    Indian-, Thai- or Chinese-style rich Australian Chardonnay. ('Cocktail sauce' kills wine, and I suspect, in time, people.)
Prosciutto (also with melon, pears or figs) Full-bodied dry or medium white (**→***): Orvieto, Frascati, Pomino, Fendant or Grüner Veltliner, Alsace or California Gewürztraminer, Australian Riesling or Jurançon Sec.
Quiches Dry white with body (*→***): Alsace, Graves, Sauvignon, Rheingau dry; or young red (Beaujolais-Villages), according to the ingredients. Never a fine-wine dish.
Ravioli (See pasta.)
    with wild mushrooms Dolcetto or Nebbiolo d'Alba, Oregon Pinot Noir.
Risotto primavera Pinot Grigio (Collio), Frascati.
    squid ink young Valpolicella.
Saffron sauces (eg on fish) Pungent or full-bodied white (esp Chardonnay) or Provence Rosé.
Salade niçoise Very dry, **, not too light or flowery white or rosé: Provençal, Rhône or Corsican; Catalan white; Dâo; California Sauv Bl.
Salads As first course, especially with blue cheese dressing, any dry and appetizing white wine. After a main course: no wine.
    NB Vinegar in salad dressings destroys the flavour of wine. If you want salad at a meal with fine wine, dress the salad with wine or a little lemon juice instead of vinegar.
Salami Very tasty red or rosé (*→***): Barbera, young Zinfandel, Tavel or Ajaccio rosé, Vacqueyras, young Bordeaux, Toro, or Chilean Cabernet Sauvignon.
Salmon, smoked A dry but pungent white: fino sherry, Alsace Pinot Gris, Chablis Grand Cru, Pfalz Riesling Spätlese, vintage champagne. Or vodka, schnapps or akvavit.
Seafood salad Fresh N Italian Chardonnay or Pinot Grigio. Australian Marsanne or Clare Riesling.
Shark's fin soup Add a teaspoon of cognac. Sip amontillado.
Soufflés As show dishes these deserve **→*** wines.
    fish Dry white: *** burgundy, Bordeaux, Alsace, Chardonnay, etc.
    cheese *** Red burgundy or Bordeaux, Cabernet Sauvignon, etc.
    spinach (tougher on wine) Mâcon-Villages, St-Véran.
Taramasalata A rustic southern white with personality; not necessarily Retsina. Fino sherry works well. Try Australian Chard or Semillon.
Terrine As for pâté, or equivalent red: Mercurey, Beaujolais-Villages, fairly young St-Emilion (**), California Cab or Zinfandel, Bulgarian or Chilean Cabernet.
Thai-style dishes (seasoned with lemon-grass, coconut milk, ginger etc) Riesling Spätlesen (Pfalz or Austrian) or pungent Sauvignon.

Warning notice:

Tomatoes (with anything) The acidity of tomatoes is no friend to fine wines. Red (**) will do. Try Chianti. Try skipping tomatoes.

Tortilla Rioja crianza.

Trout, smoked Sancerre, California or NZ Fumé Blanc. Or Rully.

Vegetable terrine Not a great help to fine wine, but California and Australian Chardonnays make a fashionable marriage.

Fish

Abalone Dry or medium white (**→***): Sauvignon Blanc, Chardonnay, Pinot Grigio, Muscadet sur Lie.

Bass, striped or sea Weissburgunder from Baden or Pfalz. Vg for any fine/delicate white, eg Coonawarra dry Riesling.

Beurre blanc, fish with A top-notch Muscadet sur Lie, a Sauvignon/Sémillon blend, or a Rheingau Charta wine.

Carpaccio of salmon or tuna Puligny-Montrachet or (***) Australian Chardonnay. (See also First courses.)

Cod A good neutral background for fine dry or medium whites: **→*** Chablis, Meursault, cru classé Graves or dryish Vouvray; German Kabinett, or dry Spätlesen and their equivalents.

Coquilles St Jacques See Scallops.

Crab, cioppino Sauvignon Blanc; but West Coast friends say Zinfandel.

    cold, with salad Pfalz Riesling Kabinett or Spätlese, dry California or Australian Riesling, or Viognier from Condrieu.

    softshell *** Chardonnay or top quality German Riesling Spätlese.

    Chinese, baked with ginger and onion Hungarian Furmint.

    with Black Bean sauce A big Shiraz or Syrah.

Eel, jellied NV champagne or a nice cup of (Ceylon) tea.

    smoked Strong/sharp wine: fino sherry, Bourgogne Aligoté. Schnapps.

Fish and chips, fritto misto (or tempura) Chablis, ** white Bordeaux, Sauvignon Blanc, Alsace Riesling, Fiano, Montilla, Koshu, tea...

Fish pie (with creamy sauce) Napa Chardonnay, Pinot Gris d'Alsace.

Haddock Rich dry white (**→***): Meursault, California or Australian Chard.

Hake Sauv Bl or any freshly fruity white: Pacherenc, Tursan, white Navarra.

Herrings Need a white with some acidity to cut their richness. Bourgogne Aligoté, Gros Plant from Brittany, dry Sauvignon Blanc. Or cider.

Kippers A good cup of tea, preferably Ceylon (milk, no sugar). Scotch?

Lamproie à la Bordelaise 5-yr-old St-Emilion or Fronsac: **→***.

Lobster, richly sauced Vintage champagne, fine white burgundy, cru classé Graves, California or Australian Chard, Pfalz Spätlese, Hermitage Bl.

    salad White (**→****): NV champagne, Alsace Riesling, Chablis Premier Cru, Condrieu, Mosel Spätlese.

Mackerel Hard or sharp white (**): Sauvignon Blanc from Bergerac or Touraine, Gros Plant, vinho verde, white Rioja. Or Guinness.

Mullet, red A chameleon, adaptable to gd white or red (but avoid the liver).

Mussels Muscadet sur lie, Chablis Premier Cru, *** Chardonnay.

    stuffed, with garlic See Escargots.

Perch, Sandre Exquisite fishes for finest wines: Puligny-Montrachet Premiers Crus or noble Mosels. Top Swiss Fendant or Johannisberg.

Salmon, fresh Fine white burgundy (***): Puligny- or Chassagne-Montrachet, Meursault, Corton-Charlemagne, Chablis Grand Cru; Condrieu, California, Idaho or Australian Chard, Rheingau Kabinett/Spätlese, California Riesling or equivalent. Young Pinot Noir can be perfect, too.

Sardines, fresh grilled Very dry white (*→**): vinho verde, Dão, Muscadet.

Sashimi If you are prepared to forego the wasabi, sparkling wines, incl California's; or California or Australian Chardonnay, Chablis Grand Cru, Rheingau Riesling Halbtrocken. Otherwise, iced sake or beer.

Scallops An inherently slightly sweet dish, best with medium-dry whites.

    in cream sauces German Spätlese (***) or a -Montrachet.

    grilled or fried Hermitage Blanc, Gewürztraminer, Grüner Veltliner, Bergerac Blanc, Australian Riesling or champagne.

Shad White Graves (**→***) or Meursault or Hunter Semillon.

Shellfish Dry (***) white with plain boiled shellfish, richer wines with richer sauces.

Shrimps, potted Fino sherry, (***) Chablis, Gavi or New York Chardonnay.

Skate with black butter White (**) with some pungency (eg Alsace Pinot Gr) or a clean straightforward one like Muscadet or Entre-Deux-Mers.

Snapper Serious Sauvignon Blanc country.

Sole, plaice, etc – plain, grilled or fried An ideal accompaniment for fine wines: ***→***** white burgundy, or its equivalent.

    with sauce Depending.on the ingredients: sharp dry wine for tomato sauce, fairly rich for sole véronique, etc.

Sushi Hot wasabi is usually hidden in every piece. German QbA trocken wines or simple Chablis are good enough. Or of course sake.

Swordfish Dry (**) white of whatever country you are in. Nothing grand.

Trout Delicate white wine, eg *** Mosel (esp from Saar), Alsace Pinot Bl.

    smoked A full-flavoured **→*** white: Gewürztraminer, Alsace Pinot Gr, Rhine Spätlese, Pinot Bl from Italy or Australian Hunter white.

Tuna, grilled White, red or rosé (**) of fairly fruity character; a top Côtes du Rhône would be fine.

Turbot Your best rich dry white: *** Meursault or Chassagne-Montrachet or its California, Australian or NZ equivalent. Condrieu. Mature Rheingau, Mosel or Nahe Spätlese or Auslese (not trocken).

For key to grape variety abbreviations, see pages 6–9.

Meat, poultry etc

Barbecues Red (**) with a slight rasp, therefore young: Shiraz, Chianti, Navarra, Zinfandel, Turkish Buzbag. Bandol for a real treat.

Beef, boiled Red (**): Bordeaux (Bourg or Fronsac), Roussillon, Australian Shiraz. Or good Mâcon-Villages white. Or top-notch beer.

    roast An ideal partner for fine red wine: **→**** red of any kind.

Beef stew Sturdy red (**→***): Pomerol or St-Emilion, Hermitage, Cornas, Barbera, Shiraz, California/Oregon Pinot Noir, Torres Gran Coronas.

Beef Stroganoff Dramatic red (**→***): Barolo, Brunello, Valpolicella Amarone, Hermitage, late-harvest Zin – even Moldovan Negru de Purkar.

Cabbage, stuffed Hungarian Cabernet Franc/Kadarka, Bulgarian Cabernet.

Cajun food Côtes de Brouilly. With gumbo: amontillado or Mexican beer.

Cassoulet Red (**) from SW France (Madiran, Cahors, Corbières), or Barbera or Zinfandel or Shiraz.

Chicken/turkey/guinea fowl, roast Virtually any wine, incl very best bottles of dry/medium white and finest old reds (esp burgundy). The meat of fowl can be adapted with sauces to match almost any fine wine (eg coq au vin: red burgundy). Avoid sauces which include tomato if you want to taste any good bottles.

Chicken casserole Lirac, St-Joseph, Crozes-Hermitage, or ** Bordeaux.

    Kiev Alsace Riesling, Bergerac Rouge.

Chilli con carne Young red (*→***): Barbera, Beaujolais, Navarra, Zinfandel.

Chinese food, Canton or Peking style Dry to medium-dry white (**→***) – Sauvignon Blanc or (better) Riesling – can be good throughout a Chinese banquet. Dry sparkling (esp cava) is good for cutting the oil. Eschew sweet/sour dishes but try an 89/90 St-Emilion ** or St-Estèphe cru bourgeois, or Châteauneuf-du-Pape with duck. I often serve both white and red wines concurrently through Chinese meals.

    Szechuan style Muscadet, Alsace Pinot Blanc or v cold beer.

Wine & Food

Choucroute garni Alsace, Pinot Blanc, Pinot Gris or Riesling or beer.

Cold meats Generally taste better with full-flavoured white wine than red. Mosel Spätlese or Hochheimer are very good. And so is Beaujolais.

Confit d'oie Young tannic red Bordeaux Cru Bourgeois (★★→★★★) helps cut the richness. Alsace Tokay-Pinot Gris or Gewurztraminer matches it.

Coq au vin Red burgundy (★★→★★★★). In an ideal world one bottle of Chambertin in the dish, two on the table.

Corned beef hash Zinfandel, Chianti, Côtes du Rhône red: (★★).

Curry Medium-sweet white (★→★★), very cold: Orvieto abboccato, California Chenin Bl, Slovenian Traminer, Indian sparkling. Or emphasize the heat with a tannic Barolo or Barbaresco, or deep-flavoured reds such as St-Emilion, Cornas, Shiraz-Cabernet or Valpolicella Amarone.

Duck or goose Rather rich white (★★★): Pfalz Spätlese or Alsace réserve exceptionelle; or ★★★ Bordeaux or burgundy. With oranges or peaches, the Sauternais propose Sauternes, others a top Loire red.
    Peking See Chinese food.
    wild duck Big-scale red (★★★): Hermitage, Châteauneuf-du-Pape, Cornas, Bandol, California or S African Cabernet, Australian Shiraz.
    with olives Top-notch Chianti or Tuscan VdT.

Frankfurters German (★→★★★), New York Riesling, Beaujolais. Or Budweiser.

Game birds, young birds plain roasted The best red wine you can afford.
    older birds in casseroles ★★→★★★ red (Gevrey-Chambertin, Pommard, Santenay, Grand Cru St-Emilion, Napa Cabernet).
    well-hung game Vega Sicilia, great red Rhône, Château Musar.
    cold game Mature vintage champagne.

Game pie, hot Red wine (★★★); **cold** equivalent white or champagne.

Goulash Strong young red (★★): Zinfandel, Bulgarian Cabernet or Mavrud, Hungarian Kadarka, young Australian Shiraz.

Grouse See Game birds – but push the boat right out.

Guinea Fowl See Chicken.

Ham Fairly fresh red burgundy (★★→★★★): Volnay, Savigny, Beaune; Chinon or Bourgueil; slightly sweet German white (Rhine Spätlese); Czech Müller-Thurgau; Tuscan red; lightish Cabernet (eg Chilean).

Hamburger Young red (★→★★★): Beaujolais, Corbières or Minervois, Chianti, Zinfandel, Kadarka from Hungary. Or Coke or Pepsi.

Hare Jugged hare calls for ★★→★★★ flavourful red: not-too-old burgundy or Bordeaux, Rhône (eg Gigondas), Bandol, or a fine Rioja reserva. The same for saddle. Australia's Grange would be an experience.

Kebabs Vigorous red (★★): Greek Nemea or Naoussa, Turkish Buzbag, Bulgarian or Chilean Cabernet, Zinfandel.

Kidneys Red (★★→★★★): St-Emilion, Cornas, Barbaresco, Rioja, California, Spanish or Australian Cabernet, Portuguese Bairrada.

Lamb, cutlets or chops As for roast lamb, but a little less grand.
    roast One of the traditional and best partners for very good red Bordeaux – or its Cabernet equivalents from the New World. In Spain, the partner of the finest old Rioja reservas.

Liver Young (★★) red: Beaujolais-Villages, St-Joseph, Médoc, Italian Merlot, Breganze Cabernet, Zinfandel, Oregon Pinot Noir.

Meatballs Red (★★→★★★): Mercurey, Crozes-Hermitage, Madiran, Rubesco, Dão, Bairrada, Zinfandel or Cabernet.

Mixed grill A fairly light, easily swallowable red: ★★ Bordeaux from Bourg, Fronsac or Premières Côtes; Côtes de Buzet; Coteaux du Languedoc; Chianti; Chilean Cabernet; or a Cru Beaujolais such as Juliénas.

Moussaka Red or rosé (★→★★): Naoussa from Greece, Chianti, Corbières, Côtes de Provence, Ajaccio or Patrimonio, California 'Burgundy'.

Oxtail or osso bucco Rather rich red (★★→★★★): St-Emilion or Pomerol, Nuits-St-Georges, Barolo or Chianti Classico, Rioja reserva, California or Coonawarra Cabernet; or a dry Riesling Spätlese.

Paella Young (★★) Spanish red, dry white or rosé: Penedès or Rioja.

Partridge, pheasant See Game birds.

15

Pigeons or squab Red Burgundy (**→****): Beaune, Savigny; Chianti Classico, California/Australian Pinot. Silvaner Spätlese from Franken.

Pork, roast A good rich neutral background to a fairly light red or rich white. It deserves *** treatment – Médoc is fine. Portugal's famous sucking pig is eaten with Bairrada garrafeira, Chinese is good with Beaujolais.

Quail As for pigeon. But does not harm finer reds.

Rabbit Young Italian red (*→***), Chinon, Saumur-Champigny, Rhône rosé.

Ris de veau See Sweetbreads.

Risotto Pinot Gr from Friuli, Gavi, youngish Sém, Dolcetto, or Barbera d'Alba.

  with mushrooms Cahors, Madiran, Barbera.

  with Fungi porcini Finest mature Barolo or Barbaresco.

Satay Australian Cabernet-Shiraz or Alsace Pinot Gris or Gewurztraminer.

Sauerkraut Lager or stout. (But see also Choucroute garni.)

Sausages The British banger requires a 2½-yr-old NE Italian Merlot (or a red wine, anyway). See also Frankfurters, Salami.

Shepherd's Pie Rough and ready red (*→**) seems most appropriate eg Barbera, but beer or dry cider is the real McCoy.

Spare Ribs Gigondas or St-Joseph, or Australian Shiraz, or Zinfandel.

Steak, au poivre A fairly young *** Rhône red or Cabernet.

  tartare Vodka or ** light young red: Beaujolais, Bergerac, Valpolicella.

  Korean Yuk Whe (the world's best steak tartare) Sake.

  filet or tournedos Any *** red (but not old wines with béarnaise sauce).

  T-bone Reds of similar bone structure (**→****): Barolo, Hermitage, Australian Cabernet or Shiraz.

  fiorentina (bistecca) Chianti Classico Riserva or Brunello.

Steak and kidney pie or pudding Red Rioja reserva or mature **→**** B'x.

Stews and casseroles A lusty full-flavoured red: young Côtes du Rhône, Corbières, Barbera, Shiraz, Zinfandel, etc.

Sweetbreads A grand dish, so grand wine: Rhine Riesling (***) or Franken Silvaner Spätlese, well-matured B'x or burgundy, depending on sauce.

Tandoori chicken Sauvignon Blanc, or young ** red Bordeaux.

Thai food, Ginger and lemon grass call for Gewürztraminer.

  coconut curries Hunter Valley Chard; Alsace Pinot Bl for refreshment.

Tongue Good for any red or white of abundant character, esp Italian.

Tripe Red (*→**), eg Corbières, Roussillon or rather sweet white (eg German Spätlese). Better: W Australian 'White Burgundy'.

Veal, roast A good neutral background dish for any fine old red which may have faded with age (eg a Rioja reserva) or a *** German white.

Venison Big-scale red (***): Rhône, Bordeaux or California Cab of a mature vintage; or rather rich white (Pfalz Spätlese or Alsace Tokay-Pinot Gr).

Vitello tonnato Light red (Valpolicella, Beaujolais) served cool.

Wiener Schnitzel Light red (**→****) from Austria or the Médoc; Austrian Ries, Grüner Veltliner or Gumpoldskirchener.

Vegetarian dishes

Bean salad Red Rioja reserva.

Bean stew Bairrada from Portugal, Toro from Spain.

Cabbage (including 'bubble-and-squeak') Beer or stout.

Choucroute (See also Sauerkraut.) Alsace Pinot Gris or Sylvaner.

Couscous Young red with a bite: Shiraz, Corbières, Minervois, etc.

Fennel-based dishes Pouilly-Fumé or Beaujolais.

'Meaty' aubergine, lentil or mushroom bakes Corbières, Zinfandel.

Mushrooms (in most contexts) Fleshy red; eg *** Pomerol, California Merlot, Australian Shiraz.

  on toast Your best claret.

  wild mushrooms (cèpes are best for wine) Barbaresco, Pauillac or St-Estèphe.

Onion/leek tart Fruity dry white (*→***): Alsace Pinot Gr or Gewurz. Mâcon-Villages, Jurançon, California/Australian Ries. Or Beaujolais or Loire red.

Peppers or aubergines (eggplant), stuffed Vigorous red (**): Chianti, Dolcetto, Zinfandel, Bandol, Vacqueyras.

Ratatouille Vigorous young red (**): Chianti, Zinfandel, Bulgarian, young red Bordeaux or young Côtes du Rhône or Coteaux du Languedoc.

Spinach/pasta bakes Valpolicella (its bitterness helps); Greco di Molise, or Sicilian/Sardinian white.

Desserts

Apple pie or strudel Sweet (**→***) German, Austrian, Hungarian white.

Apples, Cox's Orange Pippins Vintage port (55 60 63 66 70 75 82).

Bread and butter pudding 10-yr-old Barsac from a good château.

Cakes Bual or Malmsey madeira, oloroso or cream sherry.

Cheesecake Sweet white from Vouvray or Anjou, but nothing special.

Chocolate cake, mousse, soufflés Bual madeira, Huxelrebe Auslese, California orange Muscat, Beaumes-de-Venise. Or a tot of good rum.

Christmas pudding, mince pies Tawny port, cream sherry, Asti or Vinsanto.

Creams, custards, fools Sauternes, Loupiac, Ste-Croix-du-Mont, Monbazillac.

Crème brûlée ***→**** Sauternes or Rhine Beerenauslese, best madeira or Tokay. (With concealed fruit, a more modest sweet wine.)

Crêpes Suzette Sweet champagne or Asti Spumante.

Fruit, fresh Sweet Coteaux du Layon, light sweet or liqueur Muscat.

stewed, ie apricots, pears, etc Sweet Muscatel: Muscat de Beaumes-de-Venise, Moscato di Pantelleria or dessert Tarragona.

Fruit flans Sauternes, Monbazillac or sweet Vouvray or Anjou: ***.

Fruit salads, orange salad A fine sweet sherry.

Nuts Oloroso sherry, Bual madeira, vintage or tawny port, Vin Santo.

Oranges, caramelized Experiment with old Sauternes.

Pears in red wine A pause before the port.

Raspberries (no cream, little sugar) Excellent with fine reds that themselves taste of raspberries: young Juliénas, Regnié.

Rice Pudding Liqueur Muscat, Moscatel de Valencia, or Loupiac.

Sorbets, ice-creams Asti, or (better) Moscato d'Asti Naturale. Amaretto liqueur with vanilla; rum with chocolate.

Strawberries, wild (no cream) Serve with *** red B's poured over them.

Strawberries and cream Sauternes (***) or similar sweet Bordeaux, or Vouvray Moelleux (1990).

Summer pudding Fairly young Sauternes of a good vintage (82 83 85 86).

Sweet soufflés Sauternes or Vouvray moelleux. Sweet champagne.

Tiramisu Vin Santo, young tawny port, Beaumes-de-Venise.

Trifle Should be sufficiently vibrant with its internal sherry.

Walnuts Nature's match for finest port, madeira, oloroso sherry.

Zabaglione Light gold Marsala.

Urgent notice: sherry, port, madeira and food

By a quirk of fashion the wines of sherry, madeira and to some extent port are currently being left on the sidelines by a world increasingly hypnotized by a limited range of 'varietal' wines. Yet all three include wines with every quality of 'greatness', and far more gastronomic possibilities than anyone seems to remember. It is notorious that for the price of eg a bottle of top-class white burgundy you can buy three of the very finest fino sherry, which with many dishes (see above) will make an equally exciting accompaniment. Mature madeiras give the most lingering farewell of any wine to a splendid dinner. Tawny port is a wine of many uses, especially wonderful at sea. Perhaps it is because the New World cannot rival these Old World classics that they are left out of the headlines.

Wine & Cheese

Matching cheese and wine is not easy. 'Red wine with cheese' is outdated, inadequate, even wrong, for many cheeses are better with white. And two cheeses of the same name may differ as much in flavour and texture as two clarets: Château Quotidien and Château Latour.

Principles to remember, despite exceptions, are first: the harder the cheese the more tannin the wine can have. And the creamier the cheese the more acidity is needed in the wine. The main exception constitutes a third principle – wines and cheeses of a region go together.

Cheese is classified by its texture and the nature of its rind. So its appearance is a guide to the type of wine to match it. Individual cheeses mentioned below are only examples from the hundreds sold in good cheese shops.

Fresh, no rind: cream cheese, crème fraîche, Mozzarella, Mascarpone (not layered with blue) Light crisp white – Côtes de Duras, Bergerac, Vinho Verde; or pink – Anjou, Rhône; or very light, very young, very fresh red Bordeaux, Bardolino or Beaujolais.

Hard cheeses, waxed or oiled, often showing marks from cheese cloth – Gruyère family, Manchego and many other Spanish cheeses, Parmesan, Cantal, old Gouda, Cheddar and most 'traditional' English cheeses Particularly hard to generalize here; Gouda, Gruyère, some Spanish and a few English complement fine claret or Cabernet Sauvignon and great Shiraz/Syrah wines, but strong cheeses need less refined wines, preferably local. Sugary, granular old Dutch red Mimolette is perhaps the best cheese of old for finest mature Bordeaux.

Blue cheeses Roquefort is wonderful with Sauternes, but don't extend the idea to other blues. It is the saltiness of Sauternes, especially old, which complements the saltiness of the cheese. Stilton and port, preferably tawny, is a classic. Intensely flavoured old oloroso, dry amontillado, Madeira, dry Marsala and other fortified wines, go with most blues.

Natural rind (mostly goat's cheese), with bluish-grey mould. The rind becomes wrinkled with maturity, and is sometimes dusted with ash: St-Marcellin Sancerre, Valençay, light fresh Sauvignon, Jurançon, Savoy, Soave, Italian Chardonnay.

Bloomy rind soft cheeses, pure white rind if pasteurized, or dotted with red: Brie, Camembert, Chaource, Bougon (goat's milk 'Camembert') Full dry white Burgundy or Rhône if cheese is white and immature; if matured, powerful, fruity – St-Emilion, red East European Pinot Noir, young Australian (or Rhône) Shiraz/Syrah.

Washed-rind soft cheeses, with rather sticky orange-red rind: Langres, mature Epoisses, Maroilles, Carré de l'Est, Milleens Local reds, especially for Burgundy cheeses; vigorous Languedoc, Cahors, Côtes du Frontonnais, Corsican, southern Italian, Sicilian, Bairrada.

Semi-soft cheeses, grey pink thickish rind – Livarot, Pont l'Evêque, Reblochon, Tomme de Savoie, St-Nectaire Powerful white Bordeaux, Chardonnay, Alsace Pinot Gris, dryish Riesling, southern Italian and Sicilian white, aged white Rioja, dry oloroso sherry. But the strongest of these cheeses kill most wines.

The 1994 Vintage

It is easy to use a snapshot of harvest weather to form a vintage judgement. Easy, but risky. After a memorably fine summer in most of Europe hopes were high in 1994 of a return to the glory days of 1989 and 1990. Then the pattern of '93 repeated itself with a vengeance. In the second week of September rain arrived in Western France. In Bordeaux it was incessant, in Burgundy more patchy. Like '93, it was a year when those eliminating rotten grapes made wine to be proud of; the rest, not.

In Bordeaux '94 is certainly the best vintage since '90. Some growers believe it will be comparable; especially in Pomerol and St-Emilion. Dry white wines picked early will be excellent; sweet ones, picked late, will not be better than fair.

In Burgundy the picture is similar. White grapes came in in better shape than red (the reverse of the situation in '93).

No part of France was spared the rain except the extreme south. The Loire brought home a small crop (frost caught the vines in April) but a ripe one, with the chance of great sweet wines. The Rhône, roasted in the summer, was under umbrellas at vintage time. In Provence the story was the same. Only the Midi had most of its grapes in the cellar before rain arrived.

Champagne is not likely to produce any vintage wine. In Alsace Gewurztraminer survived to make some fine late-harvest wines. But by the time the rain-clouds reached the Rhine they had lightened; German growers had the chance to make fine wines, especially in the Pfalz and Franken, and above all in the Mosel-Saar-Ruwer, where sun after rain made great Auslesen possible. Austria also reports another excellent vintage.

Northern Italy shared the experience of most of France; rain diluting mid-season grapes. But in Piedmont the late-ripening Nebbiolo of Barolo came in in sunshine. To the east Friuli and Collio have very good whites. Central Italy had a fine early harvest: Tuscan and Umbrian wines should be excellent.

For Spain, problems arose not at vintage time, but in spring when frosts savaged the vines. But Rioja's reduced crop ripened perfectly, to give what may be an exceptional vintage. Penedès and Ribera del Duero seem equally well pleased. And in Portugal port-makers are almost certain of a vintage year.

California's summer was without extremes, leading to the slow ripening that benefits fruit flavours. Some growers were still picking in November. The consensus is that reds did best, especially Pinot Noir. Washington and Oregon both had an excellent early vintage, while the ever-increasing eastern industry had the benefit of a fine summer and early harvest.

The multifarious climates of Australia's vineyards conspired to produce a small, generally late crop overall, but excellent quality, especially for Hunter Valley Semillon, red varieties in the Adelaide region and Coonawarra, and especially Cabernet in much of Victoria. Western Australia claimed a great vintage. Alas for booming export sales, though, the '95 vintage came in with only about half the grapes needed to keep up with demand.

South Africa in '94 found itself with the same problem; much less wine than it wanted, although very good.

France

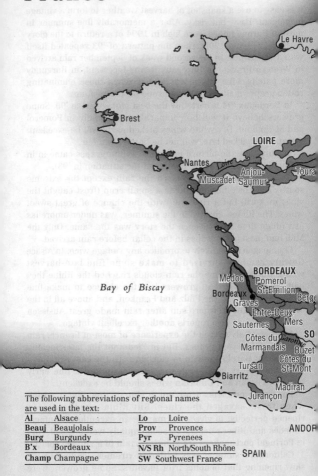

The following abbreviations of regional names are used in the text:

Al	Alsace	Lo	Loire
Beauj	Beaujolais	Prov	Provence
Burg	Burgundy	Pyr	Pyrenees
B'x	Bordeaux	N/S Rh	North/South Rhône
Champ	Champagne	SW	Southwest France

Each year hears louder voices challenging France's pole position in the wine world. Yet no-one has displaced her by definitively bettering even one of her many wine styles. Tens of thousands of properties make wine of all complexions over a large part of her surface. This is a guide to the names, types, producers and vintages.

All France's best wine regions have appellations contrôlées, which may apply to a single small vineyard or to a large district. The system varies with region, Burgundy on the whole having the smallest and most precise appellations, Bordeaux the widest and most general. In between lies an infinity of variations.

An appellation contrôlée is a guarantee of origin, production method, grape varieties and quantities produced, but not really one of quality. All AC wines are officially tasted, but too many of

NETHERLANDS

BELGIUM

GERMANY

LUXEMBOURG

Lille

Reims

CHAMPAGNE

Paris

Seine

Strasbourg

ALSACE

Marne

Chablis

ncerre

Pouilly-
Fumé

Loire

Cher

Dijon

Saône

Côte d'Or

BURGUNDY

JURA

SWITZERLAND

AUSTRIA

Côte
Chalonnaise

Mâconnais

Geneva

Beaujolais

Bugey

Lyon

SAVOIE

Côte Rôtie

Condrieu

St-Joseph

RHÔNE

Grenoble

ITALY

Cornas

Hermitage

Crozes Hermitage

hors

Côtes du
Rhône-Villages

Beaumes-
de-Venise

Rhône

Châteauneuf-
du-Pâpe

T

Gaillac

Tarn

LANGUEDOC

ntonnais

Montpellier

PROVENCE

Nice

use

St-Chinian

rvois

Corbières

Marseille

Bandol

ILLON

Fitou

Rivesaltes

Perpignan

Banyuls

Mediterranean

Bastia

CORSICA

Ajaccio

shoddy quality get through the net. The AC is the first thing to look for on a label. But the next is the name of the maker. The best growers' and merchants' names are a vital ingredient of these pages. Regions without the overall quality and traditions required for an appellation can be ranked as vins délimités de qualité supérieure (VDQS), a shrinking category as its members gain AC status. Their place is being taken by the relatively new and highly successful vins de pays. Vins de pays are almost always worth trying. They include some brilliant originals and often offer France's best value for money – which still means the world's.

Recent vintages
of the French classics

Red burgundy

Côte d'Or Côte de Beaune reds generally mature sooner than the bigger wines of the Côte de Nuits. Earliest drinking dates are for lighter commune wines, eg Volnay, Beaune; latest for the biggest wines of eg Chambertin, Romanée. But even the best burgundies are much more attractive young than the equivalent red Bordeaux.

1994 As in Bordeaux, but less rain. Success rate probably similar.
1993 Emerging as a great vintage – in the right hands.1998–2010.
1992 Ripe, plump, pleasing. No great concentration. Start to drink. Now–2005.
1991 Very good to poor. Depends on date of harvest: before/after rain. Best like 89s.
1990 A great vintage to rival 88: perfect weather compromised only by drought on some slopes and over-production in some v'yds. Long life ahead.
1989 A yr of great charm, not necessarily for v long maturing, but will age. Now–2015.
1988 Exceptional quality; a great vintage. now–2020?
1987 Small crop with promising ripe fruit flavours esp in Côte de Beaune. Now–2010.
1986 A v mixed bag – aromatic but rather dry: generally lacks flesh. Now–2000.
1985 At best a great vintage. Concentrated wines will be splendid. Now–2010.
1984 Lacks natural ripeness; tends to be dry and/or watery. Now – if at all.
1983 Powerful, vigorous, tannic and attractive vintage, compromised by rot. The best are splendid, but be careful. Now–2000.
1982 Big vintage, pale but round and charming. Best in Côte de Beaune. Drink up.
1981 A small crop, ripe but picked in rain.
1980 A wet yr, but v attractive wines from best growers who avoided rot. Côte de Nuits best. Drink.
1979 Big, generally good, ripe vintage with weak spots. Drink up.
1978 A small vintage of outstanding quality. The best will live to 2000+.
1976 Hot summer, excellent vintage. As usual great variations, but the best (esp Côte de Beaune) tannic, rich and long-lived – to 2000.
1971 V powerful and impressive wines, not as long-lasting as they first appeared. Drink.
Older fine vintages: 69 66 64 62 61 59 (all mature).

Beaujolais 94 is vg; drink or keep. 93: Crus to keep. 92: good primeur wines; not keepers. 91: small crop, Crus excellent, now. 90 was a lusciously ripe vintage; drink top Crus. 89 was v fine, drink soon. 88 is entirely ready. 87 and 86 wines should be finished. 85 was a wonderful vintage some Moulin-à-Vent will have stayed, but only the Crus will keep.

White burgundy

Côte de Beaune Well-made wines of good vintages with plenty of acidity as well as fruit will improve and gain depth and richness for some years – anything up to 10. Lesser wines from lighter vintages are ready for drinking after 2 or 3 years.

1994 Patchy; top growers made v fine wines.
1993 September rain on ripe grapes. Easy wines, high potential but v variable. Now–2005.
1992 Ripe, aromatic and charming. Will develop beautifully. Now–2010.
1991 Mostly lack substance. Frost problems. For early drinking. Now–97.
1990 Very good, even great, but with a tendency to fatness. Now–2000+.
1989 Revealing itself as a model. At best ripe, tense, structured and long. Now–2005.
1988 Extremely good, some great wines but others more dilute. Now–2000.
1987 Mainly disappointing, though a few exceptions have emerged.
1986 Powerful wines; most with better acidity and balance than 85. Now–97.
1985 V ripe; those that still have balance are ageing v well. Now–2000.
1984 Most lean or hollow. Avoid.
1983 Potent wines; some exaggerated, some faulty, but the best splendid. Drink soon.
1982 Fat, tasty but delicate whites of low acidity. Drink up.
1981 A sadly depleted crop with great promise. But time to drink up.
1980 A weak, but not bad, vintage. Should be finished.
1979 Big vintage. Overall good and useful, not great. Drink up.
1978 Vg wines, firm and well-balanced. Keep only the best.

The white wines of the Mâconnais (Pouilly-Fuissé, St-Véran, Mâcon-Villages) follow a similar pattern, but do not last as long. They are more appreciated for their freshness than their richness.

Alsace 94 was a general success, if not a triumph. 93 was good, fruity, not for long keeping. 92 was splendid; 91 admirable. 90 was the third outstanding vintage in succession. 89 and 88 both made wines of top quality (though rain spoiled some 88s). 87s should be drunk soon and 86s finished. Top 85s and 83s may be drunk or kept even longer.

FRANCE

Chablis Grand Cru Chablis of vintages with both strength and acidity can age superbly for up to 10 years; Premiers Crus proportionately less.

1994 Downpours on a ripe vintage. Delicious easy wines to 2000+.
1993 Fair to good quality; nothing great. Now—2001.
1992 Ripe and charming wines. Grands Crus splendid. Now—2005 at least.
1991 Generally better than Côte d'Or. Useful wines. Now—97.
1990 Grands Crus will be magnificent; other wines may lack intensity and acidity. Now—2000.
1989 Excellent vintage of potent character. Now—2000.
1988 Almost a model: great pleasure now in store. Now—2000.
1987 Rain at harvest. Wines for the short term. Drink up.
1986 A splendid big vintage. Now or soon.
1985 Good but often low-acid wines. The best Grands Crus are ready.

Red Bordeaux

Médoc/red Graves For some wines bottle-age is optional: for these it is indispensable. Minor châteaux from light vintages need only 2 or 3 yrs, but even modest wines of great years can improve for 15 or so, and the great châteaux of these years need double that time.

1994 Hopes of a supreme vintage; then heavy rain. At least good; some v fine.
1993 Ripe grapes but a drenching vintage. Under the circumstances, remarkably good.
1992 Rain at flowering, in August and at vintage. A huge crop; some good early drinking. Now—2005.
1991 Frost in April halved crop and rain interrupted vintage. Difficult; but keep an open mind. Now—2005?
1990 A paradox: a drought year with a threat of over-production. Self-discipline was essential. Its results are magnificent. To 2020.
1989 Early spring and splendid summer. The top wines will be classics of the ripe dark kind with elegance and length. Small ch's are uneven. To 2020.
1988 Generally excellent; ripe, balanced, for long keeping. To 2020.
1987 Much more enjoyable than seemed likely. Not for long keeping. Now or soon.
1986 Another splendid, huge, heatwave harvest. Superior to 85 in Pauillac and St-Julien. Now—2020.
1985 Very good vintage, in a heatwave. V fine wines already accessible. Now—2010.
1984 Poor. Little Merlot but good ripe Cabernet. No charm. Originally overpriced. Drink up.
1983 A classic vintage, esp in Margaux: abundant tannin with fruit to balance it. To 2010.
1982 Made in a heatwave. Huge, rich, strong wines which promise a long life but are developing unevenly. Most châteaux are now ready. Now—2010.
1981 Admirable despite rain. Not rich, but balanced and fine. Now—2005.
1980 Small late harvest ripe but rained-on. Some delicious light wines. Drink up.
1979 Abundant harvest of above average quality. Now—2000.
1978 A miracle vintage: magnificent long warm autumn. Some excellent wines. Now—2000.
1976 Excessively hot, dry summer; rain just before vintage. Generally vg; now ready.
1975 A v fine vintage. For long keeping, but some may not improve now; many have lost their fruit.
1973 A huge vintage, attractive young but fading fast.
1971 Small crop. Less fruity than 70 and less consistent. Most have faded away.
1970 Big, excellent vintage with scarcely a failure. Now—2005.
Older fine vintages: 62 61 64 59 55 53 52 50 49 48 47 45 29 28.

St-Emilion/Pomerol
1994 Less compromised by rain than Médoc. Very good.
1993 As in the Médoc, but probably better, esp in Pomerol; good despite terrible vintage weather.
1992 Exceptionally dilute but some charming wines to drink quickly. Now or soon.
1991 A sad story. Terrible frost and little chance to recover. Many wines not released.
1990 Another chance to make great wine or a lot of wine. Now—2020.
1989 Large, ripe, early harvest; an overall triumph. To 2020.
1988 Generally excellent; ideal conditions. But some overproduced. Now—2000+.
1987 Some v adequate wines (esp in Pomerol) but for drinking soon.
1986 A prolific vintage; but top St-Emilions have long life ahead.
1985 One of the great yrs, with a long future. To 2010.
1984 A sad story. Most of the crop wiped out in spring. Avoid.
1983 Less impressive than it seemed. Drink soon.
1982 Enormously rich and concentrated wines, most excellent. Now—2000+.
1981 A vg vintage, if not as great as it first seemed. Now or soon.
1979 A rival to 78, but not developing as well as hoped. Now or soon.
1978 Fine wines, but some lack flesh. Drink soon.
1976 V hot, dry summer, but vintage rain. Some excellent. Drink soon.
1975 Most St-Emilions good, the best superb. Pomerol made splendid wine. Now—2000.
1971 On the whole better than Médocs, but now ready.
1970 Beautiful wines with great fruit and strength. V big crop. Now.
Older fine vintages: 67 66 64 61 59 53 52 49 47 45.

23

Abel-Lepitre Brut NV; Brut 85 86 88; Cuvée 134 Bl de Blancs NV; Réserve Crémant Bl de Blancs Cuvée 'C' 83 85 86 88 90; Rosé 83 85 86 88 CHAMPAGNE house, also owning GOULET and St-Marceaux. Luxury Cuvée: Cuvée Reserve Abel-Lepitre 85.

Abymes Savoie w * DYA Hilly little area nr Chambéry; light mild Vin de Savoie AC from the Jacquère grape has alpine charm.

Ackerman-Laurance Vg classic method sparkling house of the Loire, at SAUMUR, said to be the oldest in the region. Fine CREMANT DE LOIRE.

Ajaccio Corsica r p w *→*** 89' 90' 91 92 93 94 The capital of CORSICA. AC for some vg SCIACARELLO reds. Top grower: Peraldi.

Aligoté Second-rank burgundy white grape and its wine. Should be pleasantly tart and fruity with local character when young. BOUZERON is the one commune to have an all-Aligoté appellation. Its wine is richer, but try others from good growers. NB PERNAND-VERGELESSES.

Aloxe-Corton Burg r w **→*** 78' 85' 87 88' 89' 90' 91 92 93' 94 Village at N end of COTE DE BEAUNE famous for its two GRANDS CRUS: CORTON (red), CORTON-CHARLEMAGNE (white). Village wines much lighter but can be good value.

Alsace Al w (r sp) **→*** 85' 88 89 90' 91 92 93 94 Aromatic, fruity, often strong, rather Germanic dry white from eastern foothills of Vosges Mts, bordering the River Rhine. Generally dry but increasingly made sweet (see Vendange Tardive and Sélection des Grains Nobles). Sold by grape variety (Pinot Bl, Ries, GEWURZ, etc). Matures well up to 5, even 10 yrs; GRAND CRU even longer. Also good quality and value CREMANT, but red wines (Pinot N) offer little to non-natives.

Alsace Grand Cru w ***→**** 76 83 85 86 88 89' 90 91 92 93 94 AC restricted to 50 of the best named v'yds (1,400 acres) and noble grapes (Ries, Pinot Gr ('Tokay'), GEWURZ and MUSCAT). Not without controversy.

Ampeau, Robert Exceptional grower and specialist in MEURSAULT; also POMMARD, etc. Perhaps unique in only releasing long matured bottles.

André, Pierre Négociant with growing reputation at Ch Corton-André, ALOXE-CORTON; 95 acres of v'yds in CORTON, SAVIGNY, GEVREY-CHAMBERTIN etc. Also owns REINE PEDAUQUE.

d'Angerville, Marquis Famous burgundy grower with immaculate 30-acre estate in VOLNAY. Top wines: Champans and Clos des Ducs.

Anjou Lo r p w (sw dr sp) *→*** Loire AC embracing wide spectrum of styles. Esp good red (Cab) ANJOU-VILLAGES, strong dry SAVENNIERES, luscious COTEAUX DU LAYON Chenin Bl whites.

Anjou-Coteaux de la Loire Lo w dr sw **→*** AC for some forceful Chenin Bl whites. Only 100 acres; mostly sweet or v sweet.

Anjou-Villages Lo r *→*** 89 90 93 94 AC for reds (mainly Cab F) from less limited zone than SAUMUR-CHAMPIGNY. Potentially juicy and good value wines.

Appellation Contrôlée (AC or AOC) Government control of origin and production of all the best French wines (see France Introduction).

Apremont Savoie w ** DYA One of the best villages of SAVOIE for pale delicate whites, mainly from Jacquère grapes, recently incl CHARD.

Arbin Savoie r ** Deep-coloured lively red from MONDEUSE grapes, rather like a good Loire Cabernet. Ideal après-ski wine. Drink at 1–2 yrs.

Arbois Jura r p w (sp) **→*** Various good and original light but tasty wines; speciality is VIN JAUNE. On the whole DYA.

l'Ardèche, Coteaux de Central France r p (w) *→*** DYA Bargain country reds; best from Syrah, Gamay and recently Cab. Also powerful, almost burgundy-like CHARD 'Ardèche' from LOUIS LATOUR (keep 1–3 yrs). (Choose this rather than too-oaky 'Grand Ardèche'.)

l'Arlot, Domaine de Outstanding producer of supreme NUITS ST GEORGES, esp Clos de l'Arlot, red and white. Owned by AXA Insurance.

Armagnac Region of SW France and its often excellent brandy, a fiery spirit of rustic character. The outstanding red of the area is MADIRAN. See Côtes de Gascogne for region's other still wines.

Aube Southern extension of CHAMPAGNE region. See Bar-sur-Aube.

Aujoux, J-M Substantial grower/merchant of BEAUJOLAIS. Swiss-owned.

Auxey-Duresses Burg r w **→*** 78 83 85 87 88 89 90' 91 92 93 94 Second-rank (but v pretty) COTE DE BEAUNE village: affinities with VOLNAY, MEURSAULT. Best estates: Diconne, HOSPICES DE BEAUNE (Cuvée Boillot), LEROY, M Prunier, R Thévenin. Drink whites in 4–5 yrs. Top white: Leroy's Les Boutonniers.

Avize Champ **** One of the top Côte des Blancs villages. All CHARDONNAY.

Ay Champ **** One of the best Pinot N-growing villages of CHAMPAGNE.

Ayala NV; Demi-Sec NV; Brut 89; Château d'Ay 82 83 85; Grande Cuvée 82 83 85 88; Bl de Blancs 82 83 88; Brut Rosé NV Once-famous Ay-based old-style CHAMPAGNE firm. Deserves more notice for fresh appley wines.

Bachelet, Denis Brilliant young grower of GEVREY-CHAMBERTIN. Top wine: CHARMES-CHAMBERTIN.

Bahuaut, Donatien Leading Loire-wine merchants and distributors of Ch de la Cassemichère, MUSCADET.

Bandol Prov r p (w) *** 73 79 82 83 85' 86 87' 88 89 90 91 92 93 Little coastal region near Toulon producing Provence's best wines; splendid vigorous tannic reds from the Mourvèdre grape; esp DOM OTT, Dom de Pibarnon, Ch Pradeaux, Mas de la Rouvière, DOM TEMPIER, Ch Vannières.

Banyuls Pyr r sw **→*** One of the best VINS DOUX NATURELS, made chiefly of Grenache (a Banyuls GRAND CRU is over 75% Grenache, aged for 2 yrs+). Technically a distant relation of port. Best wines are RANCIOS eg from Domaine des Hospices, Dom du Mas Blanc (***), Dom Vial Magnères (Blanc), at 10–15 yrs old. Also cheap NV wines for bars.

Bar-sur-Aube Champ w (p) ** Important secondary CHAMPAGNE region 100 miles SE of R Marne, Epernay etc – ie, half-way to CHABLIS. Some good lighter wines and excellent ROSE DES RICEYS.

Barancourt Brut Réserve NV; Rosé NV; Bouzy Grand Cru 81 83 85; Rosé GC 85 Grower at BOUZY making full-bodied CHAMPAGNE. New owners Champagne Vranken; now esp Bouzy Rouge and Rosé Grand Cru.

Barrique The Bordeaux (and Cognac) term for an oak barrel holding 225 litres (eventually 300 bottles). Barrique-ageing to flavour almost any wine with oak was the craze of the late '80s, with some sad results.

Barsac B'x w sw **→**** 70 71' 75 76' 78 79' 80' 81 82 83' 85 86' 88' 89' 90' 91 93 Neighbour of SAUTERNES with similar superb golden wines, generally less rich and more racy. Richly repays ageing. Top ch'x: CLIMENS, COUTET, DOISY-DAENE, DOISY-VEDRINES.

Barton & Guestier BORDEAUX shipper since 18th C, now owned by Seagram.

Bâtard-Montrachet Burg w **** 78 79 83 85 86' 87 88 89' 90' 91 92 93 94 Larger (55-acre) neighbour of MONTRACHET. Should be v long-lived with intense flavours and rich texture. Bienvenues-Bâtard-M is a separate adjacent 9-acre GRAND CRU with 15 owners, thus no substantial bottlings and v rare. Top growers incl BOUCHARD PERE, J-M Boillot, Carillon, DROUHIN, Gagnard, LOUIS LATOUR, LEFLAIVE, Lequin-Roussot, MOREY, RAMONET, SAUZET.

Baumard, Domaine des Leading grower of ANJOU wine, esp SAVENNIERES and COTEAUX DU LAYON (Clos Ste-Catherine).

Baur, Léon Small but vigorous ALSACE family firm at Eguisheim. Esp for Ries: Elisabeth Stumpf; also oaked Pinot. Don't confuse with LEON BEYER.

Baux-en-Provence, Coteaux des Prov r p *→*** Neighbour of COTEAUX D'AIX, also gathering speed. NB the excellent DOMAINE DE TREVALLON (Cab and Syrah) and Mas de Gourgonnier.

Béarn SW France r p w *→** DYA Wide-spread low-key AC of growing local (Basque) interest, esp wines of coop Sallies de Béarn-Bellocq. Rosés began post-war as instant Paris hit. Also the AC for red JURANCON, white and rosé MADIRAN.

Beaujolais Beauj r (p w) * DYA   The simple AC of the v big Beaujolais region: light short-lived fruity red from Gamay grapes. Beaujolais Supérieur means little different.

Confusingly, the best wines of the Beaujolais region are not identified as Beaujolais at all on their labels. They are known simply by the names of their 'crus': Brouilly, Chénas, Chiroubles, Côte de Brouilly, Fleurie, Juliénas, Morgon, Moulin-à-Vent, Regnié, Saint-Amour. See entries for each of these. The Confrérie des Compagnons du Beaujolais offers a 'Beaujolais Grumé' label to selected wines from the region with ageing potential.

Beaujolais de l'année The BEAUJOLAIS of the latest vintage, until the next.

Beaujolais Primeur (or Nouveau) Same as above, made in a hurry (often only 4–5 days fermenting) for release at midnight on the third Wednesday in November. Ideally soft, pungent, fruity and tempting; often crude, sharp, too alcoholic. BEAUJ-VILLAGES should be a better bet.

Beaujolais-Villages Beauj r ** 93 94   Wines from better (N) half of BEAUJOLAIS; should be much tastier than plain BEAUJOLAIS. The 10 (easily) best 'villages' are the 'CRUS': FLEURIE etc (see note above). Of the 30 others the best lie around Beaujeu. Crus cannot be released EN PRIMEUR before December 15th. Best kept until spring (or longer).

Beaumes-de-Venise S Rh br (r p) **→*** DYA   Generally France's best dessert MUSCAT, from S CÔTES DU RHÔNE; can be high-flavoured, subtle, lingering (eg from CHAPOUTIER, Dom de Coyeux, Dom Durban, JABOULET, VIDAL-FLEURY). Red and rosé from Ch Redortier and the coop are also gd.

Beaune Burg r (w) *** 78' 83 85' 87 88 89' 90' 91 92 93 94   The historic wine capital of Burgundy, a walled town hollow with cellars. Wines are middle-rank classic burgundy. Many fine growers. Négociants' CLOS wines (usually PREMIER CRU) are often best; eg DROUHIN's superb Clos des Mouches, JADOT's Clos des Ursules. Beaune du Château is a (good) BOUCHARD PÈRE brand. Best v'yds: Bressandes, Fèves, Grèves, Marconnets, Teurons.

Becker, Caves J Proud old family firm at Zellenberg, ALSACE. Classic Ries Hagenschlauf and GRAND CRU Froehn MUSCAT. Second label: Gaston Beck.

Bellet Prov p r w ***   Fashionable much above average local wines from nr Nice. Serious producers: Ch'x de Bellet and CREMAT. Pricey.

Bergerac Dordogne r w dr sw **→*** 90' 92' 93' 94   Lightweight, often tasty, BORDEAUX-style. Drink young, the white v young. See also Monbazillac, Côtes du Montravel, Pécharmant, Saussignac. Top growers incl Courts-les-Muts, JAUBERTIE, CH DE MONTAIGNE, Ch de Panisseau, Tiregand.

Besserat de Bellefon Grande Tradition NV; Cuvée des Moines Brut and Rosé NV; Grande Cuvée NV; Brut and Rosé 82 85 89   Reims CHAMPAGNE house for light wines, esp CREMANT. Owned by MARNE ET CHAMPAGNE.

Beyer, Léon Ancient ALSACE family firm at Eguisheim making forceful dry wines that need ageing at least 3–5 yrs. Comtes d'Eguisheim Gewürz is renowned, and 'Cuvée Particulière' Ries of GRAND CRU Pfersigberg is esp fine. Beyer is militant against Grand Cru restrictions.

Bichot, Maison Albert One of BEAUNE's biggest growers and merchants. V'yds (32-acre Dom du Clos Frantin is excellent) in CHAMBERTIN, RICHEBOURG, CLOS DE VOUGEOT, etc, and Dom Long-Depaquit in CHABLIS; also many other brand names.

Billecart-Salmon NV; Rosé NV; Brut 85 86; Bl de Blancs 83 85 86; Grande Cuvée 82   One of the best small CHAMPAGNE houses, founded in 1818, still family-owned. Fresh-flavoured wines incl a v tasty rosé. New CUVÉES: Nicolas François Billecart (88), Elisabeth Salmon Rosé (88).

NB Vintages in colour are those you should choose first for drinking in 1996.

Bize, Simon Admirable red burgundy grower with 35 acres at SAVIGNY-LES-BEAUNE. Usually model wines, racy and elegant.

Blagny Burg r w ****→****** (w) 83 85 86' 88 89 90' 91 92 93 94   Hamlet between MEURSAULT and PULIGNY-MONTRACHET: whites have affinities with both (sold under each AC), reds with VOLNAY (sold as AC Blagny). Good ones need age; esp AMPEAU, Jobard, LATOUR, LEFLAIVE, Matrot, G Thomas.

Blanc de Blancs Any white wine made from white grapes only, esp CHAMPAGNE (usually both red and white). Not an indication of quality.

Blanc de Noirs White (or slightly pink or 'blush') wine from red grapes.

Blanck, Marcel Versatile ALSACE grower at Kientzheim. Good Pinot Bl, and GRANDS CRUS Furstentum (GEWURZ, Pinot Gr, esp Ries), Schlossberg (Ries).

Blanquette de Limoux Midi w sp ******   Good bargain sparkler from nr Carcassonne with long local history. V dry and clean; increasingly tasty as more CHARD and Chenin Bl is added, esp in new AC Crémant de Limoux. Normally NV.

Blaye B'x r w *** 88 89 90 93 94**   Your daily BORDEAUX from E of the Gironde. PREMIERES COTES DE BLAYE is the AC of the better wines.

Boisset, Jean-Claude Far and away the biggest burgundy merchant/grower, at NUITS-ST-GEORGES. Owns BOUCHARD-AINE, Lionel Bruck, F Chauvenet, Delaunay, JAFFELIN, Morin Père et Fils, de Marcilly, Pierre Ponnelle, Thomas-Bassot, VIENOT. Generally high commercial standards.

Bollinger NV 'Special Cuvée'; Grande Année 69 70 73 75 76 79 82 83 85 88; Rosé 81 82 83 85   Top CHAMPAGNE house, at AY. Dry, very full-flavoured style, needs ageing. Luxury wines: RD (73 75 76 79 81 82), Vieilles Vignes Françaises (69 70 75 79 80 81 82 85 88) from ungrafted Pinot vines. Pioneered Charter of Quality ('91). Investor in Petaluma, Australia.

Bonneau du Martray, Domaine Biggest grower (with 27 acres) of CORTON-CHARLEMAGNE of the highest quality; also red GRAND CRU CORTON. Cellars at PERNAND-VERGELESSES. Whites often outlive reds.

Bonnes-Mares Burg r *****→******* 69 71 76 78' 79 80 83 85' 86 87 88 89 90' 91 92 93 94   37-acre GRAND CRU between CHAMBOLLE-MUSIGNY and MOREY-ST-DENIS. V sturdy long-lived wines, less fragrant than MUSIGNY; can rival CHAMBERTIN. Top growers: DUJAC, Groffier, JADOT, MUGNIER, ROUMIER, DOM DES VAROILLES, de VOGUE.

Bonnezeaux Lo w sw ******* 76' 78 81 83 85' 86 88' 89' 90' 91 92 93' 94 Unusual rich tangy wine from Chenin Bl grapes, the best of COTEAUX DU LAYON. Esp Ch de Fesles, Dom du Petit Val. Ages well – but v tempting young.

Bordeaux B'x r w (p) *** 88 89 90 92 93 94** (for ch'x see pages 58–79) Catch-all AC for low-strength B'x wine. Not to be despised: it may be light but its flavour cannot be imitated. If I had to choose one daily wine this would be it.

Bordeaux Supérieur *→*** As above, with slightly more alcohol.

Borie-Manoux Admirable BORDEAUX shippers and château-owners, owned by the Castéja family. Ch'x incl BATAILLEY, BEAU-SITE, DOMAINE DE L'EGLISE, HAUT-BAGES-MONPELOU, TROTTEVIEILLE.

Bouchard Aîné Long-est (1750) burgundy shipper/grower in BEAUNE, MERCUREY, etc. Bought in '93 by BOISSET.

Bouchard Père et Fils Important burgundy shipper (est 1731) and grower with 209 acres of excellent v'yds, mainly in the COTE DE BEAUNE, and cellars at the Château de Beaune. Now ('95) controlled by HENRIOT. Recent wines mostly v well made; some whites outstanding.

Bouches-du-Rhône Prov r p w *****   VINS DE PAYS from Marseille environs. Robust reds from southern varieties, Cab S, Syrah and Merlot.

Bourg B'x r (w) **** 85' 86' 88' 89' 90' 93 94**   Un-fancy claret from E of the Gironde. For châteaux see Côtes de Bourg.

Bourgogne Burg r w (p) **** 90' 91 92 93 94**   Catch-all Burgundy AC, with higher standards than basic B'x. Light, often gd flavour, best at 2–4 yrs. Top growers make bargain beauties from fringes of Côte d'Or villages; do not despise. BEAUJOLAIS CRUS can also be labelled Bourgogne.

Bourgogne Grand Ordinaire Burg r (w) ★ DYA Lowest B AC, also allowing GAMAY. Rare. White may incl ALIGOTE, Pinot Bl, Melon de Bourgogne.

Bourgogne Passe-Tout-Grains Burg r (p) ▮ Age 1–2 yrs Junior burgundy: minimum 33% Pinot N, the balance GAMAY, mixed in the vat. Often enjoyable. Not as heady as BEAUJOLAIS.

Bourgueil Lo r ★★★ 76' 83' 85 86' 88 89' 90' 91 92 93' 94 Normally delicate fruity Cab red from TOURAINE. Deep-flavoured, long-lasting in best yrs, ageing like Bordeaux. ST-NICOLAS-DE-BOURGUEIL often lighter. Esp from Audebert, Billet, Caslot, Cognard, Druet, Jamet, Lamé-Delille-Boucard.

Bouvet-Ladubay The major producer of sparkling SAUMUR, controlled by TAITTINGER. Excellent CREMANT DE LOIRE. 'Saphir' is vg vintage wine. Deluxe 'Trésor' is oak-fermented, with 2 yrs age.

Bouzeron Village of the COTE CHALONNAISE distinguished for the only single-village AC ALIGOTE. Top grower: de Villaine. Also NB BOUCHARD PERE.

Bouzy Rouge Champ r ★★★ 85 88 89 90 91 Still red of famous red-grape CHAMPAGNE village. Like v light burgundy, ageing early but can last well.

Brédif, Marc One of the most important growers and traders of VOUVRAY, owned by LADOUCETTE.

Bricout Brut NV (Réserve, Prestige, Cuvée Spéciale Arthur Bricout); Rosé NV; Brut 82 85 86 Small CHAMPAGNE house at AVIZE making light wines. Owned by Kupferberg of Mainz.

Brouilly Beauj r ▮▮ 92 93 94 Biggest of the 10 CRUS of BEAUJOLAIS: fruity, round, refreshing wine, can age 3–4 yrs. CH DE LA CHAIZE is largest estate. Top growers: Michaud, Dom de Combillaty, Dom des Grandes Vignes.

Bruno Paillard Brut Première Cuvée NV; Rosé Première Cuvée NV; Chard Réserve Privée NV, Brut 79 81 83 85 89 Small but prestigious young CHAMPAGNE house: excellent silky vintage and NV; fair prices.

Brut Term for the driest wines of CHAMPAGNE.

Bugey Savoie r p w sp ★→▮▮ DYA VDQS district for light sparkling, still or half-sparkling wines. Grapes incl Roussette (or Roussanne) and good CHARD. Best from Cerdon and Montagnieu.

Buxy Burg w ▮▮ Village in AC MONTAGNY with good coop for CHARD.

Buzet SW France r (w) ★→▮▮ 86 88 89' 90' 92' 93 94 Good BORDEAUX-style wines, reputedly 'pruney', from just SE of Bordeaux. Good value area with well-run cooperative: best are barrel-aged Tradition, Carte d'Or, Cuvée Baron d'Ardeuil and firm, ageable Ch de Gueyze. Also Ch'x de Frandat, Matelot and Sauvagnères, and Dom de Versailles.

Cabardès Midi r (p w) ★→▮▮ 85 86 88 89 90 91 92 93 94 Newcomer VDQS region north of Carcassonne, CORBIERES, etc. MIDI and BORDEAUX grapes show promise at Ch Rivals, Ch Rayssac, Ch Ventenac, Coops de Conques sur Orbiel.

Cabernet See Grapes for red wine (pages 8–9).

Cabernet d'Anjou Lo p ★→★★ DYA Delicate, grapey, usually rather sweet rosé.

Cabrières Midi p (r) ▮▮ DYA COTEAUX DU LANGUEDOC.

Cahors SW France r ★→▮▮ 82 83 85 86' 88 89' 90' 92' 93 94 Historically 'black' and tannic from Malbec grapes, now made like BORDEAUX: full-bodied and distinct or much lighter. Top growers: Clos Triguedina (esp 'Prince Probus'), Ch'x de Caïx, La Caminade, de Cayrou, de Chambert, Latuc, Pech de Jammes; Clos la Coutale, Dom Eugénie (v traditional), Clos de Gamot, Jouffreau, Vigouroux (esp Ch de Haute-Serre). Lighter wines from coop, Caves d'Olt.

Cairanne S Rh r p w ▮▮ 86 88 89 90 91 92 93 One of best COTES DU RHONE-VILLAGES: solid, robust esp from Doms Brusset, l'Oratoire St-Martin, Rabasse-Charavin.

Calvet Famous old shippers of BORDEAUX and burgundy, now owned by Allied-Hiram Walker. Some reliable standard wines, esp from Bordeaux.

Canard-Duchêne Brut NV; Demi-Sec NV; Rosé NV; Charles VII NV; Brut 83 85 88 Quality CHAMPAGNE house owned by VEUVE-CLICQUOT, ie, the same group as Moët-Hennessy. Fair prices for lively, Pinot N-tasting wines.

Canon-Fronsac B'x r ★★–★★★★ 82 83' 85' 86 88 89' 90' 92 93 94 Full tannic reds of increasing quality from small area W of POMEROL. Need less age than formerly. Eg Ch'x: CANON, CANON DE BREM, CANON-MOUEIX, Coustolle, Junayme, Mazeris-Bellevue, Moulin-Pey-Labrie, Toumalin, La Truffière, Vraye-Canon-Boyer. See also Fronsac.

Cantenac B'x r ★★★ Village of HAUT-MÉDOC entitled to the AC MARGAUX. Top châteaux include BRANE-CANTENAC, PALMER, etc.

Cap Corse Corsica w br ★★–★★★ CORSICA's wild N cape. Splendid Muscat from Clos Nicrosi, Rogliano, and rare soft dry Vermentino white. Vaut le détour, if not le voyage.

Caramany Pyr r (w) ▮ 88 89 90 91 92 93 Notionally superior new AC for part of CÔTES DU ROUSSILLON-VILLAGES.

Cassis Prov w (r p) ★★ DYA Seaside village E of Marseille known for lively dry white wine, one of the best in PROVENCE (eg Domaine du Paternel). Not to be confused with cassis, a blackcurrant liqueur made in Dijon.

Cave Cellar, or any wine establishment.

Cave coopérative Wine-growers' cooperative winery. Coops now account for 55% of all French production (4 out of 10 growers are members). Almost all now well-run, well-equipped and their wine is good value.

Cellier des Samsons BEAUJOLAIS/MÂCONNAIS coop at Quincié with 2,000 grower-members. Widely distributed.

Cépage Variety of vine, eg CHARDONNAY, Merlot.

Cérons B'x w dr sw ▮▮ 83' 85' 86' 88' 89' 90 91 92 93 94 Neighbour of SAUTERNES with some good sweet wine châteaux, eg de Cérons et de Calvimont, Grand Enclos, Haura. Ch Archambeau makes vg dry GRAVES.

Chablis

There is no better expression of the all-conquering Chardonnay than the full but tense, limpid but stony wines it makes on the heavy limestone soils of Chablis. The Chablis terroir divides cleanly into three quality levels with remarkable consistency. The best makers use very little or no new oak to mask the precise definition of variety and terroir. These makers include: J-M Brocard, J Collet, D Dampt, R Dauvissat, B, Det E, and J Defaix, Droin, Durup, Fèvre, Geoffroy, J-P Grossot, Laroche, Long-Depaquit, Dom des Malandes, Michel, Pic, Pupillon, Raveneau, G Robin, Tribut, Vocoret. Simple unqualified 'Chablis' may be thin; best is premier or grand cru (see below). The coop, La Chablisienne, has high standards and many different labels (it makes one in every three bottles).

Chablis Burg w ★★–★★★★ 90 92 93 94 Unique full-flavoured dry minerally wine of N Burgundy, CHARD only, from 10,000 acres (doubled since '85).

Chablis Grand Cru Burg w ★★★–★★★★★ 78 83 85 86 88 89 90 91 92 93 94 In maturity a match for greatest white burgundy: forceful but often dumb in youth, at best almost SAUTERNES-like with age. 7 v'yds: Blanchots, Bougros, Clos, Grenouilles, Preuses, Valmur, Vaudésir. See Moutonne.

Chablis Premier Cru Burg w ★★★ 85 86 88 89 90 91 92 93 94 Technically second-rank but at best excellent, more typical of CHABLIS than its GRANDS CRUS. Often outclasses more expensive MEURSAULT and other CHARDS. Best v'yds incl Côte de Lechet, Fourchaume, Mont de Milieu, Montée de Tonnerre, Montmains, Vaillons. See above for producers.

Chai Building for storing and maturing wine, esp in BORDEAUX.

Chambertin Burg r ★★★★ 69 71 76 78' 79 80 82 83 85' 87 88 89 90' 91 92 93 94 32-acre GRAND CRU for some of the meatiest, most enduring, best red burgundy, 15 growers, incl BOUCHARD, Camus, Damoy, DROUHIN, Mortet, PONSOT, Rebourseau, Rossignol-Trapet, ROUSSEAU, Tortochot, TRAPET.

Chambertin-Clos de Bèze Burg r ★★★★ 69 71 76 78' 79 80 82 83 85 87 88 89 90' 91 92 93 94 37-acre neighbour of CHAMBERTIN. Similarly splendid wines. May legally be sold as Chambertin. 10 growers incl B CLAIR, CLAIR-DAU, Damoy, DROUHIN, Drouhin-Laroze, FAIVELEY, JADOT, ROUSSEAU.

Chambolle-Musigny Burg r (w) ***→**** 78' 82 83 85' 87 88 89 90' 91 92
93 94 420-acre COTE DE NUITS village with fabulously fragrant, complex,
never heavy wine. Best v'yds: Les Amoureuses, part of BONNES-MARES,
Les Charmes, MUSIGNY. Growers to note: Barthod, DROUHIN, FAIVELEY,
Hudelot-Noëllat, JADOT, Moine-Hudelot, Mugneret, MUGNIER, RION,
ROUMIER, Serveau, DE VOGUE.

Champagne Sparkling wine of Pinots N and Meunier and/or CHARD, and its
region (70,000+ acres 90 miles E of Paris); made by METHODE CHAM-
PENOISE. Wines from elsewhere, however good, cannot be 'champagne'.

Chandon de Briailles, Domaine Small burgundy estate at SAVIGNY. Makes
wonderful CORTON (and Corton Blanc) and vg PERNAND-VERGELESSES.

Chanson Père et Fils Old family firm of growers (with 125 acres) and
négociants at BEAUNE. Esp for BEAUNE Clos des Fèves, SAVIGNY, PERNAND-
VERGELESSES, CORTON. Fine quality.

Chantovent Major brand of VIN DE PAYS, largely from MINERVOIS.

Chapelle-Chambertin Burg r *** 78' 82 83 85 87 88 89' 90' 91 92 93 94
13-acre neighbour of CHAMBERTIN. Wine more 'nervous', not so meaty.
Top producers: Damoy, JADOT, Rossignol-Trapet, TRAPET.

Chapoutier Long-est'd growers and traders of top-quality, full-bodied
Rhônes. Best are CHATEAUNEUF Barbe Rac and HERMITAGE Le Pavillon.

Charbaut, A et Fils Brut NV; Bl de Blancs Brut NV; Brut Rosé NV; Brut 79
82 85 87 88; Certificate Bl de Blancs 82 85; Certificate Rosé 79 82 85
Substantial Epernay CHAMPAGNE house. Clean light wines. Good rosé.
New CUVEE launched '93: Grand Evénement Brut NV.

Chardonnay See Grapes for white wine (pages 6–8). Also the name of a
MACON-VILLAGES commune. Hence Mâcon-Chardonnay.

Charmes-Chambertin Burg r *** 71 76 78' 79 83 85' 87 88 89' 90' 91 92
93 94 76-acre neighbour of CHAMBERTIN, incl AC MAZOYERES-CHAMBERTIN.
Wines more 'supple', rounder. Growers incl BACHELET, Castagnier,
DROUHIN, DUJAC, LEROY, ROTY, ROUSSEAU.

Chartron & Trebuchet Young co (founded '84): some delicate harmonious
white burgundies, esp Dom Chartron's PULIGNY-MONTRACHET, Clos de la
Pucelle. Also BATARD- and CHEVALIER-MONTRACHET. Good ALIGOTE, too.

Chassagne-Montrachet Burg r w ***→**** r (***) 78' 82 83 85 87 88 89'
90' 91 92 93 94; w 78' 83 85 86 88 89' 90 91 92 93 94 750-acre COTE
DE BEAUNE village with excellent rich dry whites and sterling hefty
reds. Whites rarely have the extreme finesse of PULIGNY next door but
often cost less. Best v'yds include part of MONTRACHET, BATARD-
MONTRACHET, Boudriottes (r w), Caillerets, CRIOTS-BATARD-MONTRACHET,
Morgeot (r w), Ruchottes, CLOS ST-JEAN (r). Growers incl Amiot-Bonfils,
Colin-Deleger, Delagrange-Bachelet, DROUHIN, J-N Gagnard, GAGNARD-
DELAGRANGE, Lamy-Pillot, MAGENTA, Ch de la Maltroye, MOREY, Niellon,
RAMONET-PRUDHON.

Chasseloir, Dom du HQ of the firm of Chéreau-Carré: makers of several
excellent AC-leading domaine MUSCADETS (esp Ch du Chasseloir).

Château

*Means an estate, big or small, good or indifferent, particularly in
Bordeaux (see pages 58–79). Elsewhere in France château tends to mean
literally, castle or great house, as in most of the following entries. In
Burgundy 'Domaine' is the usual term.*

Château d'Arlay Major JURA estate; 160 acres in skilful hands with wines
incl vg VIN JAUNE, VIN DE PAILLE, Pinot N and MACVIN.

Château de Beaucastel S Rh r w *** 78 79 81 83 85 86' 87 88 89' 90' 91
92 93' One of the biggest (173 acres), best-run CHATEAUNEUF-DU-PAPE
estates. Deep-hued, complex wines for at least 12 yrs ageing. Small
amount of wonderful Roussanne white to keep 5–10 yrs. Also leading
COTES DU RHONE Coudoulet de Beaucastel (red and white). New interest:
Beaucastel Estate, California.

Château de la Chaize Beauj r ✳✳✳ 91 92 93 94 Best-known BROUILLY estate.

Château Corton-Grancey Burg r ✳✳✳ 78 82 83 85 88 89 90 91 92 93 Famous ALOXE-CORTON estate; property of LOUIS LATOUR: benchmark wines.

Château de Crémat Prov r p w ✳✳→✳✳✳ Prestigious little estate in BELLET nr Nice. Light but long-lived red, adequate rosé, excellent origial white.

Château Fortia S Rh r (w) ✳✳✳ 78 81 83 85 86 88 89 90 91 92 93 Traditional 72-acre CHATEAUNEUF property. Owner's father, Baron Le Roy, also fathered the APPELLATION CONTROLEE system in the '20s. Good, but not at the v top today.

Château Fuissé Burg w ✳✳✳ The ultimate POUILLY-FUISSE estate. Its PF VIEILLES VIGNES is ✳✳✳✳, and sumptuous with age.

Château de la Jaubertie English- ('Rystone'-) owned top BERGERAC estate. Sumptuous luxury Sauv, Cuvée Mirabelle. Equally fine Réserve red.

Château de Meursault Burg r w ✳✳✳ 100-acre estate owned by PATRIARCHE with good v'yds and wines in BEAUNE, MEURSAULT, POMMARD, VOLNAY. Splendid cellars open to the public for tasting.

Château de Mille Prov r p w ✳✳ Leading star of advancing COTES DU LUBERON.

Château de Montaigne Dordogne w (sw) ✳✳ Home of the great philosopher Michel de M (outside HAUT-MONTRAVEL), now making sweet COTES DE MONTRAVEL, also sharing a part-owner with CH PALMER (MARGAUX).

Château La Nerthe S Rh r (w) ✳✳✳ 78' 79 81 85 86 88 89 90 91 92 93 Renowned imposing CHATEAUNEUF 222-acre estate. Solid modern-style wines, esp special CUVEES Cadettes (r) and Beauvenir (w).

Château du Nozet Lo w ✳✳✳ 90 91' 92' 93' 94 Biggest, best-known estate of POUILLY (FUME) -SUR-LOIRE. Luxury Baron de L, can be wonderful (at a price).

Château Rayas S Rh r (w) ✳✳✳ 78' 79 81 85 86 88 89 90 91 92 93 Famous old-style property of only 37 acres in CHATEAUNEUF-DU-PAPE. Concentrated wines are entirely Grenache, yet can age superbly. Pignan is second label. Also vg Ch Fonsalette, COTES DU RHONE (NB Cuvée Syrah and long-lived whites).

Château de Selle Prov r p w ✳✳→✳✳✳ 100-acre estate of OTT family nr Cotignac, Var. Pace-setters for PROVENCE. Cuvée Spéciale is largely Cab.

Château Simone Prov r p w ✳✳ Age 2–6 yrs Famous old property in Palette; the only one with a name in this AC nr Aix-en-Provence. The red is best: smooth but herby and spicy. White is catching up.

Château Val-Joanis Prov r p w ✳✳✳ Impressive estate making outstanding full-blooded COTES DU LUBERON. Don't miss them.

Château Vignelaure Prov r ✳✳✳ 82' 83' 85 86 87 88 89 90 91 92 93 94 135-acre Provençal estate nr Aix: exceptional more-or-less B'X-style wine with Cab, Syrah and Grenache grapes. Bought in '94 by Rystone.

Château-Chalon Jura w ✳✳✳ Not a CHATEAU but an area/appellation with unique strong dry yellow wine, like sharpish fino sherry. Usually ready when bottled (at about 6 yrs). A curiosity.

Château-Grillet N Rh w ✳✳✳✳ 89 90 91 92 94 9-acre v'yd: one of France's smallest ACs. Intense, fragrant, absurdly over-expensive, but showing signs of revival in the '90s. Drink young.

Châteaumeillant Lo r p w ✳ DYA Tiny VDQS area nr SANCERRE. Light Gamay and Pinot N. Good pale rosé.

Châteauneuf-du-Pape S Rh r (w) ✳✳✳ 78' 79 81 83 85 86 88 89 90 91 92 93 94 8,200 acres nr Avignon with core of 30 or so domaines for v fine wines (quality more variable over remaining 90). Best are dark, strong, exceptionally long-lived. Whites either fruity and zesty or rather heavy: mostly now 'DYA'. Top growers incl ch'x DE BEAUCASTEL, FORTIA, MONT-REDON, LA NERTHE, RAYAS; Doms de Beaurenard, Le Bosquet des Papes, les Cailloux; Clos du Mont-Olivet, Clos des Papes, VIEUX TELEGRAPHE, etc.

Châtillon-en-Diois Rh r p w ✳ DYA Small AC of mid Rhône. Adequate largely Gamay reds; white (some ALIGOTE) mostly made into CLAIRETTE DE DIE.

Chauvenet, F Substantial modern firm in NUITS; buys grapes on contract from good growers for wide range of much-appreciated COTE D'OR wines, incl CORTON-CHARLEMAGNE, CHARMES-CHAMBERTIN, etc. Assoc with J-C BOISSET.

Chave, Gérard To many the superstar grower of HERMITAGE, with 25 acres. V long-lived red and white (esp vg red ST-JOSEPH), and also VIN DE PAILLE.

Chavignol Village of SANCERRE with famous v'yd, Les Monts Damnés. Chalky soil gives vivid wines that age 4–5 yrs. Also fromage de chèvre.

Chénas Beauj r ✱✱✱ 90 91 92 93 94 Smallest BEAUJOLAIS CRU and one of the weightiest; neighbour to MOULIN-A-VENT and JULIENAS. Growers incl Benon, Braillon, Champagnon, Charvet, Ch Chèvres, DUBOEUF, Robin, coop.

Chenin Blanc See Grapes for white wine (pages 6–8).

Chenonceau, Ch de Lo ✱✱ Architectural jewel of the Loire now makes excellent AC Touraine Sauv Bl, Cab, Cot (Malbec) and ✱✱✱ Chenin.

Chevalier-Montrachet Burg w ✱✱✱✱ 78 83 85' 86 88 89' 90 91 92 93 17-acre neighbour of MONTRACHET making similar luxurious wine, perhaps less powerful. Incl 2.5-acre Les Demoiselles. Growers incl LATOUR, JADOT, BOUCHARD PÈRE, CHARTRON, Deleger, LEFLAIVE, Niellon, PRIEUR.

Cheverny Lo r p w (sp) ✱—✱✱✱ DYA Loire AC nr Chambord. Dry crisp whites from Sauv Bl. Also Gamay, Pinot N or Cab reds; generally light but tasty. 'Cour Cheverny' uses the local Romorantin grape.

Chevigny, Pascal Producer of fine VOSNE-ROMANEE: neighbour to LA TACHE.

Chevillon, R 21-acre estate at NUITS-ST-GEORGES; outstanding winemaking.

Chignin Savoie w ✱ DYA Light soft white from Jacquère grapes for Alpine summers. Chignin-Bergeron is best and liveliest.

Chinon Lo r ✱✱✱ 76 83' 85 86' 88 89' 90' 91' 92 93' Juicy, variably rich Cab F from TOURAINE. Drink cool, young; treat exceptional yrs like B'X. Growers: Baudry, Couly-Dutheil (Clos de l'Echo), Druet, Joguet, Mabileau, Raffault. Cave Rabelais coop is prolific with wine to drink young.

Chiroubles Beauj r ✱✱✱ 91 92 93 94 Good but tiny BEAUJOLAIS CRU next to FLEURIE; freshly fruity silky wine for early drinking (1–3 yrs). Growers incl Bouillard, Cheysson, DUBOEUF, Fourneau, Passot, Raousset, coop.

Chorey-lès-Beaune Burg (w) ✱✱ 85 87 88 89 90' 91 92 93 Minor AC on flat land N of BEAUNE: 2 fine growers: Germain (Ch de Chorey), TOLLOT-BEAUT.

Chusclan S Rh r p w ✱—✱✱ 89 90 91 92 93 94 Village of COTES DU RHONE-VILLAGES with able coop. Labels incl Cuvée de Marcoule, Seigneurie de Gicon. Also special CUVEES from André Roux, incl good white.

Cissac HAUT-MEDOC village just west of PAUILLAC.

Clair, Bruno Recent little domaine at MARSANNAY. Vg wines from there and GEVREY-CHAMBERTIN (esp CLOS DE BEZE), FIXIN, MOREY-ST-DENIS, SAVIGNY.

Clairet Very light red wine, almost rosé. Bordeaux Clairet is an AC.

Clairette Traditional white grape of the MIDI. Its low-acid wine was a vermouth base. Revival by Terrasses de Landoc is full and zesty.

Clairette de Bellegarde Midi w ✱ DYA AC nr Nîmes: plain neutral white.

Clairette de Die Rh w dr s/sw sp ✱✱ NV Popular dry or (better) semi-sweet MUSCAT-flavoured sparkling wine from E Rhône; or straight dry CLAIRETTE white, surprisingly ageing well 3–4 yrs. Worth trying.

Clairette du Languedoc Midi w ✱ DYA Neutral white from nr Montpellier, but watch for improvements. Ch La Condamine Bertrand looking good.

Clape, La Midi r p w ✱—✱✱ AC to note of COTEAUX DU LANGUEDOC. Full-bodied wines from limestone hills between Narbonne and the sea. Red gains character after 2–3 yrs, Bourboulenc white after even longer. Vg rosé. Esp from Ch'x Rouquette-sur-Mer, Pech-Redon, Dom de l'Hospitalet.

Claret Traditional English term for red BORDEAUX.

Climat Burgundian word for individual named v'yd, eg BEAUNE Grèves.

Clos A term carrying some prestige, reserved for distinct, usually walled, v'yds, often in one ownership. Frequent in Burgundy and ALSACE. Les Clos is CHABLIS' Grandest Cru.

Clos de Bèze See Chambertin-Clos de Bèze.

Clos des Lambrays Burg r ✱✱✱ 83 85' 87 88 89' 90' 91 92 93 94 15-acre GRAND CRU v'yd at MOREY-ST-DENIS. Changed hands in '79 after a shaky period. Now, after replanting, looking good (for a v long life).

Clos des Mouches Burg r w ✱✱✱ Splendid PREMIER CRU BEAUNE v'yd, largely owned by DROUHIN. White and red, spicy and memorable – and consistent.

Clos de la Roche Burg r ✹✹✹ 72 78' 82 83 85' 86 87 88 89' 90 91 92 93' 94
38-acre MOREY-ST-DENIS GRAND CRU. Powerful complex, like CHAMBERTIN.
Esp BOUCHARD P, BOUREE, CASTAGNIER, DUJAC, Lignier, PONSOT, REMY, ROUSSEAU.

Clos du Roi Burg r ✹✹✹ Part of GRAND CRU CORTON. Also a BEAUNE PREMIER CRU.

Clos St-Denis Burg r ✹✹✹ 76 78 79 82 83 85' 87 88 89' 90' 91 92 93' 94
16-acre GRAND CRU at MOREY-ST-DENIS. Splendid sturdy wine growing
silky with age. Growers incl DUJAC, Lignier, PONSOT.

Clos Ste Hune Al w V fine austere Ries from TRIMBACH; perhaps ALSACE's
best. Needs 5 yrs age to reveal potential; doesn't need GRAND CRU status.

Clos St-Jacques Burg r ✹✹✹ 78' 80 82 83 85' 86 87 88 89' 90' 91 92 93' 94
17-acre GEVREY-CHAMBERTIN PREMIER CRU. Excellent powerful velvety, often
better (and dearer) than some of GRANDS CRUS. Main grower: ROUSSEAU.

Clos St-Jean Burg r ✹✹✹ 78 83 85' 87 88 89' 90' 91 92 93 94   36-acre
PREMIER CRU of CHASSAGNE-MONTRACHET. Vg red, more solid than subtle,
from eg Ch de la Maltroye. NB Domaine RAMONET.

Clos de Tart Burg r ✹✹✹ 85' 87 88' 89' 90' 92 93 94   GRAND CRU at MOREY-ST-
DENIS, owned by MOMMESSIN. At best wonderfully fragrant, young or old.

Clos de Vougeot Burg r ✹✹✹ 78 83 85' 87 88 89' 90' 91 92 93 94 124-acre
COTE DE NUITS GRAND CRU with many owners. Variable, occasionally
sublime. Maturity depends on the grower's philosophy, technique and
position on hill. Top growers incl CLAIR-DAU, DROUHIN, Drouhin-Laroze,
ENGEL, FAIVELEY, GRIVOT, Gros, Hudelot-Noëllat, JADOT, LEROY, Chantal
Lescure, MEO-CAMUZET, Mugneret, Rebourseau, ROUMIER.

Coche-Dury 16-acre MEURSAULT domaine (and 1 acre+ of CORTON-CHARLEMAGNE)
with sky-high reputation for oak-perfumed wines. Also vg ALIGOTE.

Cognac Town and region of the Charentes, W France, and its brandy.

Collines Rhodaniennes S Rh r w p ✶ Popular Rhône VIN DE PAYS. Mainly
reds. Merlot, Syrah, Gamay. Some VIOGNIER and CHARD in white.

Collioure Pyr r ✹✹ 85 86 88 89 90 91 92 93 94 Strong dry red from BANYULS
area. Tiny production. Top growers include Cellier des Templiers, Les
Clos de Paulilles, Cave L'Etoile, Dom du Mas Blanc, Dom de la
Rectorie, La Tour Vieille, Vial-Magnères.

Comté Tolosan SW r p w Regional VDP for Midi and Pyrenees. Mostly red
from trad varieties. Esp from Coop de Fronton (COTES DU FRONTONNAIS).

Condrieu N Rh w ✹✹✹✹ DYA Soft fragrant white of great character (and
price) from the VIOGNIER grape. Can be outstanding but rapid growth
of v'yd (now 222 acres) has made quality outside top names variable.
Best growers: DELAS, Dumazet, GUIGAL, André Perret, Pinchon, Vernay
(esp Coteau de Vernon). CHATEAU-GRILLET is similar. Don't try ageing it.

Corbières Midi r (p w) ✹✹→✹✹✹✹ 88 89 90 91 92 93 94 Vigorous bargain
reds. Best growers incl Ch'x Aiguilloux, de Cabriac, des Ollieux, Les
Palais, de Quéribus, de la Voulte Gasparet, Dom de Villemajou; Coops
de Embrès et Castelmaure, Camplong, St-Laurent-Cabrerisse, etc.

Cordier, Ets D Important BORDEAUX shipper and château-owner: wonderful
track-record but troubled present. Incl Ch'x CANTEMERLE, GRUAUD-LAROSE,
LAFAURIE-PEYRAGUEY, MEYNEY, TALBOT, and also SANCERRE, Clos de la Poussie.

Cornas N Rh r ✹✹→✹✹✹✹ 78' 79 80 81 83' 85' 86 88 89 90 91 92 93' Sturdy v
dark Syrah wine of unique quality, from steep-sloping v'yds S of
HERMITAGE. Needs 5–15 yrs' ageing. Top are Allemand, de Barjac,
Clape, DELAS, Lionnet, JABOULET, Noël Verset.

Corsica (Corse) Strong wines of all colours. Better ACs incl AJACCIO, CAP
CORSE, PATRIMONIO, Sartène. VIN DE PAYS: ILE DE BEAUTE!

Corton Burg r ✹✹✹→✹✹✹✹ 78' 83 85' 86 87 88 89' 90' 91 92 93 94 The only
GRAND CRU red of the COTE DE BEAUNE. 200 acres in ALOXE-C incl CLOS DU ROI,
Les Bressandes. Rich powerful, should age well. Many good growers.

Corton-Charlemagne Burg w ✹✹✹✹ 78' 79 82 83 85' 86' 87 88 89' 90' 91 92
93 94 The white section (one-third) of CORTON. Rich spicy lingering
wine, behaves like a red and ages magnificently. Top growers:
BONNEAU DU MARTRAY, Chapuis, COCHE-DURY, Delarche, Dubreuil-
Fontaine, FAIVELEY, HOSPICES DE BEAUNE, JADOT, LATOUR, Rapet.

Costières de Nîmes Midi r p w *→*** DYA   Large new AC of improving quality from the Rhône delta. Formerly Costières du Gard. NB Ch de Nages, Ch de la Tuilerie ('Dinettes et Croustilles').

Côte(s) Means hillside; generally a superior v'yd to those on the plain. Many ACs are prefixed by either 'Côtes' or 'Coteaux', meaning the same. In ST-EMILION distinguishes valley slopes from higher plateau.

Côte de Beaune Burg r w **→****   Used geographically: the southern half of the COTE D'OR. Applies as an AC only to parts of BEAUNE itself.

Côte de Beaune-Villages Burg r w ** 85 88 89' 90' 91 92 93   Regional APPELLATION for secondary wines of classic area. Cannot be labelled 'Côte de Beaune' without either '-Villages' or village name appended.

Côte de Brouilly Beauj r ** 90 91 92 93 94   Fruity rich vigorous BEAUJOLAIS CRU. One of best. Esp from: Dom de Chavanne, G Cotton, Ch Delachanel, J-C Nesme, Ch Thivin.

Côte Chalonnaise Burg r w sp **→****   V'yd area between BEAUNE and MACON. See also Givry, Mercurey, Montagny, Rully. Alias 'Région de Mercurey'.

Côte de Nuits Burg r (w) **→****   N half of COTE D'OR. Mostly red wine.

Côte de Nuits-Villages Burg r (w) ** 88 89 90 91 92 93 94   A junior AC for extreme N and S ends of Côte; well worth investigating for bargains.

Côte d'Or Département name applied to the central and principal Burgundy v'yd slopes, consisting of the COTE DE BEAUNE and COTE DE NUITS. The name is not used on labels.

Côte Rôtie N Rh r ***→**** 78 79 80 82 83' 85' 86 87 88' 89 90' 91 92 94   Potentially the finest Rhône red, from S of Vienne; can achieve rich, complex, almost B'x-like finesse with age. Top growers incl Barge, Burgaud, Champet, CHAPOUTIER, DELAS, GUIGAL (long cask-ageing, different and fuller in style), JABOULET, Jamet, Jasmin, Rostaing, VIDAL-FLEURY.

Coteaux d'Aix-en-Provence Prov r p w **→****   AC on the move. Est'd CH VIGNELAURE now challenged by Ch'x Commanderie de la Bargemone and Fonscolombe. See also Baux-en-Provence.

Coteaux d'Ancenis Lo r p w * DYA   Light Cab and Gamay reds and rosés, sharpish whites, from MUSCADET country.

Coteaux de l'Ardèche See l'Ardèche.

Coteaux de l'Aubance Lo p w sw ** DYA   Light ANJOU wines: sweet, and only from Chenin Bl. Best are MOELLEUX; demi-sec in lesser yrs. Esp from Dom Richou, Dom des Rochettes (to age, not DYA).

Coteaux des Baronnies S Rh r p w *   Rhône VIN DE PAYS. Syrah, Merlot, Cab, CHARD, plus trad grapes. Promising. Dom du Rieu-Frais worth noting.

Coteaux Champenois Champ r w (p) *** DYA (whites)   The AC for non-sparkling CHAMPAGNE. Vintages (if mentioned) follow those for Champagne. Do not pay inflated prices.

Coteaux du Giennois Lo r p w * DYA   Loire VDQS surrounding POUILLY. Light Gamay and Pinot, Sauv à la SANCERRE. Top grower: Balland-Chapuis.

Coteaux du Languedoc Midi r p w **   Scattered well-above-ordinary MIDI AC areas. Best reds (eg CABRIERES, LA CLAPE, FAUGERES, St-Georges-d'Orques, Quatourze, ST-CHINIAN, St-Saturnin) age for 2–4 yrs. Now also some good whites. Follow with increasing interest.

Coteaux du Layon Lo w s/sw ** 79 82 85' 86 88' 89 90' 91 92 93'   The heart of ANJOU, S of Angers: sweet Chenin with admirable acidity, ageing almost forever, excellent aperitif or dessert. Since '93 new AC SELECTION DES GRAINS NOBLES (cf ALSACE). Top ACs: BONNEZEAUX, C du Layon-Chaume. Incl Dom d'Ambinos, Douet, des Forges, TOUCHAIS.

Coteaux du Loir Lo r p w dr sw ** 78 82 83 85 86 88' 89' 90' 91 92 93'   Small region N of Tours. Occasionally fine Chenin Bl, Gamay, Cab. Best v'yd: JASNIERES. Top grower: Gigon. Loir is a tributary of the Loire.

For key to grape variety abbreviations, see pages 6–9.

Coteaux de la Loire See Anjou-Coteaux de la Loire.

Coteaux du Lyonnais Beauj r p (w) ✸ DYA   Junior BEAUJOLAIS. Best EN PRIMEUR.

Coteaux de Peyriac Midi r p ✶ DYA   One of the most-used VIN DE PAYS names of the Aude département. Huge quantities.

Coteaux de Pierrevert S Rh r p w sp ✸ DYA   Minor southern VDQS nr Manosque. Well-made coop wine, mostly rosé, with fresh whites.

Coteaux de Saumur Lo w dr sw ✶✶→✶✶✶ 89 90   Rare, potentially fine semi-sweet Chenin. Creamy-sweet (MOELLEUX) at best.

Coteaux du Tricastin S Rh r p w ✶✶ 88 89 90 91 92 93   Fringe COTES DU RHONE of increasing quality. Attractive PRIMEUR red. Dom de Grangeneuve, Dom St-Luc and Ch La Décelle among the best.

Coteaux Varois Prov r p w ✶→✶✶   Substantial new AC zone: California-style Dom de St-Jean de Villecroze makes vg red.

Coteaux du Vendômois Lo r p w ✶ DYA   Fringe Loire from N of Blois with VDQS rank. Mainly Gamay and Pineau d'Aunis (for rosé).

Côtes d'Affreux Centre r ✶   Aspiring to VDP. Shd perhaps use grapes as base.

Côtes d'Auvergne Central France r p (w) ✶ DYA   Flourishing small VDQS. Red (at best) like light BEAUJOLAIS. Corent is rosé.

Côtes de Blaye B'x w ✶ DYA   Run-of-the-mill BORDEAUX white from BLAYE.

Côtes de Bordeaux Saint-Macaire Bx w dr sw ✶ DYA   Every-day BORDEAUX white from E of SAUTERNES.

Côtes de Bourg B'x r ✶→✶✶ 82' 83 85' 86' 88' 89' 90 92 93 94   Appellation used for many of the better reds of BOURG. Ch'x incl DE BARBE, La Barde, DU BOUSQUET, Brûlesécaille, La Croix de Millorit, Falfas, Font Guilhem, Grand-Jour, de la Grave, La Grolet, Guerry, Guionne, Haut-Maco, Lalibarde, Lamothe, Mendoce, Peychaud, Rousset, Tayac, de Thau.

Côtes de Castillon B'x r ✶→✶✶ 86' 88' 89' 90' 92 93 94   Flourishing region just E of ST-EMILION. Similar but lighter wines. Ch'x incl Beauséjour, La Clarière-Laithwaite, Fonds-Rondes, Haut-Tuquet, Lartigue, Moulin-Rouge, PITRAY, Rocher-Bellevue, Ste-Colombe, Thibaud-Bellevue.

Côtes de Duras Dordogne r w ✸ 90' 92 93 94   Neighbour to BERGERAC, dominated by two v competent coops (Landerrouat and Berticot). Similar light wines.

Côtes du Forez Central France r p ✸ DYA   Fashionable light Beaujolais-style Gamay red, can be good in warm yrs. VDQS status.

Côtes de Francs B'x r w ✶✶ 85 86' 88' 89' 90' 92 93 94   Fringe BORDEAUX from E of ST-EMILION. Increasingly attractive tasty wines, esp from Ch'x de Belcier, La Claverie, de Francs, Lauriol, PUYGUERAUD, La Prade.

Côtes du Frontonnais SW France r p ✶→✶✶ DYA   Local wines of Toulouse, gaining admirers everywhere. Two distinct styles: CdF-Fronton good from coop, Ch du Roc and Ch Bellevue-la-Forêt (250 acres, outstanding silky red and rosé 'l'Allégresse'), CdF-Villaudric is bolder (esp from Ch La Colombière and Dom Caze).

Côtes de Gascogne SW w (r) ✶→✶✶ DYA   VIN DE PAYS branch of ARMAGNAC. Esp deliciously floral Sauv whites, Ugni Bl, Colombard and Gros Manseng blends, all in bountiful supply; also full fruity reds. Top growers: Dom de Biau, Grassa, Coop de Plaimont, Dom de Papolle. Also Floc de Gascogne (red or white, like PINEAU DE CHARENTE).

Côtes du Haut-Roussillon SW France br sw ✶→✶✶ NV   Area for VINS DOUX NATURELS N of Perpignan.

Côtes du Jura Jura r p w (sp) ✶ DYA   Various light tints/tastes. ARBOIS is better.

Côtes du Lubéron S Rh r p w sp ✶→✶✶ 88 89 90 93 94   Spectacularly improving country wines from N PROVENCE. Actors and media magnates among owners. Stars are CH DE MILLE, CH VAL-JOANIS, with vg largely Syrah red, and whites as well. Others incl good coop and Ch de la Canorgue.

Côtes de la Malepère Midi r ✸ DYA   Rising star VDQS on frontier of MIDI and SW, nr Limoux. Watch for fresh eager reds.

Côtes du Marmandais Dordogne r p w ✶ DYA   Light wines from SE of BORDEAUX. The coops at Cocumont and Beaupuy make most of the best.

Côtes de Montravel Dordogne w dr sw ▩ DYA Part of BERGERAC; traditionally medium-sweet, now often quite dry. Good from Ch Laroque and Dom de Libarde. Montravel Sec is dry, HAUT MONTRAVEL sweet.

Côtes de Provence Prov r p w ★→★★★ Wines of Provence; revolutionized by new attitudes and investment. Dom Bernarde, Castel Roubine, Commanderie de Peyrassol, Dom de la Courtade, DOM OTT, Dom des Planes, Dom Rabiéga, Dom Richeaume are leaders. 60% is rosé, 30% red. See also Coteaux d'Aix, Bandol, etc.

Côtes du Rhône S Rh r p w ★→★★ 90 93 94 Basic AC of the Rhône Valley. Best drunk young – even as PRIMEUR. Wide variations of quality due to grape ripeness: tending to rise with alcohol %. See C du R -Villages.

Top Côtes du Rhône producers: Cave Jaume, Caveau Chantecôtes (Ste-Cecile); Châteaux La Courançonne, Estagnol, Grand Moulas, Grand Prébois, St-Estève; Domaines Gramenon, Réméjeanne, Vieux Chêne, also Coudoulet de Beaucastel, Guigal, Jaboulet; and Coops Puyméras, Villedieu.

Côtes du Rhône-Villages S Rh r p w ★→★★ 88 89 90 91 92 93 Wine of 17 best S Rhône villages. Substantial and on the whole reliable. S'times delicious. See Beaumes-de-Venise, Cairanne, Chusclan, Laudun, Rasteau, Séguret, St-Gervais, etc.

Côtes Roannaises Central France r ▩ DYA New ('94) AC for Gamay, between Lyon and the Loire. At best (from R Serol) like good Beaujolais.

Côtes du Roussillon Pyr r p w ★→★★ 88 89 90 91 93 94 E Pyrenees AC. Hefty CARIGNAN reds best. Some whites are sharp VINS VERTS.

Côtes du Roussillon-Villages Pyr r ★★→★★★ 86 88 89 90 91 92 93 94 The region's best reds, from 28 communes incl CARAMANY, LATOUR DE FRANCE. Best labels: Coop Baixas, Cazes Frères, Dom des Chênes, Gauby, Ch de Jau, Coop Lesquerde, Dom Piquemal, Coop Les Vignerons Catalans. Some now choose to renounce AC status and make varietal VINS DE PAYS.

Côtes de St-Mont SW France r w p ▩ Promising Gers VDQS, not unlike lighter MADIRAN. The same coop as COTES DE GASCOGNE: esp for Les Hauts de Bergelle range and Ch de Sabazan; Ch de Bergalasse also good.

Côtes de Thongue Midi r w ▩ DYA Popular VIN DE PAYS from the HERAULT. Some good wines coming. Esp from Doms Arsolle, COUSSERGUES, Croix Belle, Montmarin.

Côtes de Toul E France p r w ★ DYA Very light VDQS wines from Lorraine; mainly VIN GRIS (rosé).

Côtes du Ventoux S Rh r p (w) ★★ 90' 91 92 93 94 Booming (17,000-acre) AC between the Rhône and PROVENCE for tasty reds (from café-style to much deeper flavours), and easy rosés. La Vieille Ferme, owned by J-P Perrin of CH DE BEAUCASTEL, is top producer; Domaine Anges, Ch'x Pesquié and Valcombe are good too.

Côtes du Vivarais Prov r p w ★ DYA Pleasant country wines from south Massif Central VDQS. Like light COTES DU RHONE: eg Dom de Belvezet.

Coulée de Serrant Lo w dr sw ★★★ 73 76' 78 79' 81 82 83' 85' 86 88 89' 90' 91 92 93 10-acre Chenin Bl v'yd on Loire's N bank at SAVENNIERES run on ferociously organic principles. Intense strong fruity/sharp wine, good aperitif. Ages almost for ever.

Coussergues, Domaine de Midi r w p ▩ DYA Large estate in formerly notorious territory nr Beziers. CHARD, Syrah etc are bargains.

Crémant In CHAMPAGNE means 'creaming' (half-sparkling). Since '75 an AC for quality classic method sparkling from ALSACE, Loire, BOURGOGNE and most recently LIMOUX – often a bargain. Term phasing out in Champagne.

Crémant de Loire w sp ★★→★★★ NV High quality sparkling wine from ANJOU, esp SAUMUR, TOURAINE and Pays Nantais.

Crépy Savoie w ★★ DYA Light soft Swiss-style white from S shore of Lake Geneva. 'Crépitant' has been coined for its faint fizz.

Criots-Bâtard-Montrachet Burg w ★★★ 78' 79 83 85 86 88 89 90 91 92 93 94 4-acre neighbour to BATARD-M. Similar wine without extreme pungency.

Crozes-Hermitage N Rh r (w) ✹✹ 85 86 88 89 90 91 92 93 94 Nr HERMITAGE: larger v'yds, wine with fewer dimensions. Some is fruity, early-drinking (drink at 2+yrs); some cask-aged (wait 5–8 yrs). Good examples from Belle, Ch Curson Combier, Desmeure, Dom des Entrefaux, Fayolle et Fils, Alain Graillot, Dom de Thalabert of JABOULET. Jaboulet's Mule Blanche is good white.

The Bourgeoisie and other classes

Cru Growth, as in first growth/classed growth – meaning v'yd. Also, in BEAUJOLAIS, one of the top 10 villages.

Cru Bourgeois General term for MEDOC châteaux below CRU CLASSE. There are 250-odd in the Syndicat, covering 7,000 acres, with an annual competition. Others who use the term are prosecuted. In '94 a Paris merchant was jailed for a year.

Cru Bourgeois Supérieur (Cru Grand Bourgeois) One rank better than the last – must be barrel-aged. Being phased out by typically unhelpful Brussels decree from '93.

Cru Classé Classed growth. One of the first five official quality classes of the MEDOC, classified in 1855. Also any growth of another district (eg GRAVES, ST-EMILION, SAUTERNES) named in its local classification.

Cru Exceptionnel Rank above CRU BOURGEOIS SUPÉRIEUR, immediately below CRU CLASSE. Cru Bourgeois divisions are being phased out as of '93. Now officially suppressed by Brussels – but memories are long.

Cruse et Fils Frères Senior BORDEAUX shipper. Owned by Pernod-Ricard. The Cruse family (not the company) owns CH D'ISSAN.

Cussac Village S of ST-JULIEN. (AC HAUT-MEDOC.) Top ch's: BEAUMONT, LANESSAN.

Cuve Close Short-cut method of making sparkling wine in a tank. Sparkle dies away in glass much quicker than with METHODE TRADITIONELLE wine.

Cuvée Wine contained in a cuve or vat. A word of many uses: 'blend' (as in CHAMPAGNE); in Burgundy interchangeable with 'CRU'. Often just refers to a 'lot' of wine.

De Castellane Brut NV; Brut 85 89; Cuvée Royale 82 88; Prestige Florens de Castellane 82 86; Cuvée Commodore Brut 85 88 Long-established Epernay CHAMPAGNE house, now part-owned by LAURENT-PERRIER. Good rather light wines incl Maxim's house champagne.

De Luze, A & Fils BORDEAUX shipper owned by Rémy-Martin of COGNAC.

Degré alcoolique Degrees of alcohol, ie percent by volume.

Deiss, Marcel Fine ALSACE grower at Bergheim with 50 acres, wide range incl splendid Ries (GRAND CRU Schoenenberg), GEWURZ (Altenburg at Bergheim), good SELECTION DES GRAINS NOBLES and VIN DE PAILLE.

Delamotte Brut, Bl de Bls (85), Cuvée Nicolas Delamotte Fine small CHARD-dominated CHAMPAGNE house at Le Mesnil, owned by LAURENT-PERRIER.

Delas Frères Old and worthy firm of Rhône wine specialists with v'yds at CONDRIEU, COTE ROTIE, HERMITAGE. Top wines: Condrieu, Marquise de Tourette Hermitage (red and white). Owned by ROEDERER.

Delbeck Small fine CHAMPAGNE house reborn '91. Plenty of Pinot N in blend.

Delorme, André Leading COTE CHALONNAISE merchants and growers. Specialists in CREMANT DE BOURGOGNE and excellent RULLY etc.

Demi-Sec Half-dry: in practice more than half sweet. (Eg of CHAMPAGNE.)

Deutz Deutz Brut Classic NV; Rosé NV; Brut 79 81 82 85 88 90; Rosé 82 85 88; Bl de Bls 81 82 85 88 89 90 One of better small CHAMPAGNE houses. Flavourful wines. Luxury brands: Cuvée William Deutz (79 82 85 88), Rosé (85). V successful branches in California, NZ. Also Sekt in Germany.

Dirler, Jean-Pierre ALSACE producer of Kessler, Saering and Spiegel GRAND CRUS: each esp for Ries.

Dom Pérignon, Cuvée 71 73 75 76 78 82 83 85 88; Rosé 78 82 85 Luxury CUVÉE of MOET & CHANDON (launched 1936), named after the legendary Abbey cellarmaster who 'invented' CHAMPAGNE. Astonishing consistent quality, esp with 10–15 yrs bottle-age.

Domaine Property, particularly in Burgundy and the south.

Dopff & Irion Another excellent Riquewihr (ALSACE) business. Esp MUSCAT les Amandiers, Ries de Riquewihr, Ries Les Murailles, Gewurz Les Sorcières, Pinot Gr Les Maquisards: long-lived. Good Crémant d'Alsace.

Dopff au Moulin Ancient top-class family wine house at Riquewihr, ALSACE. Best: Gewurz Eichberg, Ries Schoenenbourg, Sylvaner de Riquewihr. Pioneers of sparkling wine in Alsace; good CUVEES: Bartholdi and Julien.

Doudet-Naudin SAVIGNY burgundy merchant and grower. V'yds incl BEAUNE-CLOS DU ROI, Redrescul. Dark long-lived wines, supplied to Berry Bros & Rudd of London, eventually come good. Lighter style recently.

Dourthe Frères B'X merchant with wide range: good CRUS BOURGEOIS, incl BELGRAVE, MAUCAILLOU, TRONQUOY-LALANDE. Beau-Mayne is well-made brand.

Doux Sweet.

Drappier, André Leading Aube region CHAMPAGNE house, esp for Bl de Noirs.

DRC See Romanée-Conti, Domaine de la.

Drouhin, J & Cie Deservedly prestigious Burgundy grower (130 acres) and merchant with highest standards. Cellars in BEAUNE; v'yds in Beaune, CHABLIS, CLOS DE VOUGEOT, MUSIGNY, etc, and Oregon, USA. Top wines incl BEAUNE-CLOS DES MOUCHES, CHABLIS LES CLOS, CORTON-CHARLEMAGNE, GRIOTTE-CHAMBERTIN, PULIGNY-MONTRACHET Les Folatières. Majority share now held by Tokyo co.

Duboeuf, Georges The grand fromage of BEAUJOLAIS. Top-class merchant at Romanèche-Thorin. Leader of the region in every sense, with a huge range of admirable wines. Also MOULIN-A-VENT untypically aged in new oak, and white MACONNAIS, etc.

Dubos High-level BORDEAUX négociant.

Duclot BORDEAUX négociant; top-growth specialist. Linked with J-P MOUEIX.

Dujac, Domaine Burgundy grower (Jacques Seysses) at MOREY-ST-DENIS with v'yds in that village, BONNES-MARES, ECHEZEAUX, GEVREY-CHAMBERTIN, etc. Splendidly vivid and long-lived wines. Now also in MEURSAULT, and planting Cab in COTEAUX VAROIS.

Dulong Highly competent BORDEAUX merchant. Breaks all the rules with unorthodox Rebelle blends. Also VIN DE PAYS.

Durup, Jean One of the biggest CHABLIS growers with 140 acres, including Domaine de l'Eglantiere and admirable Ch de Maligny.

Duval-Leroy Coteaux Champenois r w; Brut; Bl de Blancs Brut NV; Fleur de Champagne Brut NV and Rosé NV; Cuvée des Rois Rosé NV; Fleur de Champagne Brut 88; Cuvée des Rois Brut 86   Large progressive Vertus producer with high standards.

Echézeaux Burg r ******* 78' 82 83 85' 87 88 89' 90' 91 92 93 94   74-acre GRAND CRU between VOSNE-ROMANEE and CLOS DE VOUGEOT. Can be superlative, fragrant, without great weight, eg Confuron-Cotetidot, ENGEL, Gouroux, Grivot, A F Gros, MONGEARD-MUGNERET, Mugneret, DRC.

Lah-la, lah-la, la-la-la-la-lah-la

The Confrérie des Chevaliers du Tastevin is the wine fraternity of Burgundy: the world's most famous of its kind. It was founded in 1933 by a group of Burgundian patriots, led by Camille Rodier and Georges Faiveley, to rescue their beloved region from a period of slump by promoting its inimitable wines. Today it regularly holds banquets, with elaborate and sprightly song and ceremonies, for 600 guests, at its headquarters, the Cistercian château in the Clos de Vougeot, above all at 'Les Trois Glorieuses', the November weekend of the Hospices de Beaune auction (see page 41). The Confrérie has branches in many countries and members among lovers of wine all over the world. See also Tastevin, page 55.

Edelzwicker Alsace w ***** DYA Modest blended light white: often fruity, good.

Eguisheim, Cave Vinicole d' Vg ALSACE coop: fine GRAND CRUS Hatchbourg, Hengst, Ollwiller and Spiegel. Owns WILLM. Top label: Wolfberger (65% of production). Grande Réserve and Sigillé ranges best. Good CREMANT.

Engel, R Top-class grower of CLOS DE VOUGEOT, ECHEZEAUX, GRANDS ECHEZEAUX, VOSNE-ROMANEE.

Entre-Deux-Mers B'x w ★→★★★ DYA Improving standard dry white BORDEAUX from between the Garonne and Dordogne rivers. Often a good buy, as techniques improve. Esp ch'x BONNET, Gournin, Latour-Laguens, Moulin de Launay, Séguin, Thieuley, Turcaud etc.

L'Estandon The everyday wine of Nice (AC COTES DE PROVENCE) in all colours.

l'Etoile Jura w dr sp (sw) ★★ Subregion of the Jura known for stylish whites, incl VIN JAUNE, similar to CHATEAU-CHALON; good sparkling.

Faiveley, J Family-owned growers and merchants at NUITS-ST-GEORGES, with v'yds (150 acres) in CHAMBERTIN-CLOS DE BEZE, CHAMBOLLE-MUSIGNY, CORTON, MERCUREY, NUITS (44 acres). Consistent high quality. For serious ageing.

Faller, Théo Top ALSACE grower at Domaine Weinbach, Kaysersberg. Concentrated firm dry wines needing unusually long ageing, up to 10 yrs. Esp GRAND CRUS Geisburg (Ries), Kirchberg de Ribeauvillé (Gewurz).

Faugères Midi r (p w) ★★ 88 89 90 91 92 93 94 Isolated COTEAUX DU LANGUEDOC village with above-average wine. Gained AC status in '82. Best growers: Dom Alquier, Dom des Estanilles, Ch La Liquière.

Fessy, Sylvain Dynamic BEAUJOLAIS merchant with wide range.

Fèvre, William Excellent CHABLIS grower with the biggest GRAND CRU holding (40 acres). But spoils some of his top wines with new oak. One whimsy wine he calls Napa Vallée de France. His label is Dom de la Maladière.

Fiefs Vendéens Lo r p w ★ DYA Up-and-coming VDQS for light wines from the Vendée, just S of MUSCADET on the Atlantic coast.

Fitou Midi r ★★ 85 86 88 89 90 91 92 93 94 Superior CORBIERES red; powerful, ages well. Best from coops at Cascastel, Paziols and Tuchan. Interesting experiments with Mourvèdre grapes in Leucate.

Fixin Burg r ★★ 78' 83 85' 88' 89' 90' 91 92 93 94 Worthy and undervalued northern neighbour of GEVREY-CHAMBERTIN. Often splendid reds. Best v'yds: Clos du Chapitre, Les Hervelets, Clos Napoléon. Growers incl Bertheau, CLAIR, FAIVELEY, Gelin, Gelin-Moulin, Guyard.

Fleurie Beauj r ★★★ 90 91 92 93 94 The epitome of a BEAUJOLAIS CRU: fruity, scented, silky, racy. Top wines from Chapelle des Bois, Chignard, Després, DUBOEUF, Ch de Fleurie, the coop.

Fortant de France Midi r p w ★→★★ Brand (dressed to kill) of fair quality single-grape wines from the neighbourhood of Sète. See Skalli.

Frais Fresh or cool.

Frappé Ice-cold.

Froid Cold.

Fronsac B'x r ★→★★★ 82 83 85' 86' 88' 89' 90' 92 93 94 Picturesque area of increasingly fine tannic reds just W of ST-EMILION. Ch'x incl de Carles, DALEM, LA DAUPHINE, Fontenil, Mayne-Vieil, Moulin-Haut-Laroque, LA RIVIERE, La Rousselle, La Valade, La Vieille Cure, Villars. Give them time. See also smaller Canon-Fronsac.

Frontignan Midi br sw ★ NV Strong sweet liquorous MUSCAT of ancient repute. Best growers: Châteaux Stony and La Peyrade.

Gagnard-Delagrange, Jacques Estimable small (13-acre) grower of CHASSAGNE-MONTRACHET, including some MONTRACHET.

Gaillac SW France r p w dr sw sp ★→★★ mostly DYA Ancient area coming to life. Reds in three styles: DYA Classique, selected-grape/short aged and new-oak-aged. Slightly fizzy perlé is value. Méthode Gaillacoise trad sparkling. Ch Larroze is the best known; other good growers Dom des Hourtets, Dom de Labarthe, Dom de Perches, Mas d'Aurel and Robert Plageoles. Important coops: Labastide de Lévis (with fruity wines from local Mauzac grapes incl top Gaberlé perlé), La Cave Técou (quality, esp successful wood-aged 'Passion').

Gamay See Grapes for red wine (pages 8–9).

Gard, Vin de Pays du The Gard département at the mouth of the Rhône is a centre of good VINS DE PAYS; incl Coteaux Flaviens, Pont du Gard, SABLES DU GOLFE DU LION, Salaves, Uzège and Vaunage. Watch this area.

Geisweiler et Fils Big Burgundy merchant and grower. Now owned by the Rehs of the Mosel. Cellars and 50 acres at NUITS-ST-GEORGES, also 150 acres at Bevy in HAUTES-COTES DE NUITS and 30 in the COTE CHALONNAISE.

Gevrey-Chambertin Burg r *** 83 85' 87 88 89' 90' 91 92 93 94 The village containing the great CHAMBERTIN and its Grand Cru cousins and many other noble v'yds (eg PREMIERS CRUS Cazetiers, Combe aux Moines, CLOS ST-JACQUES, Clos des Varoilles), as well as much more commonplace land. Growers incl BACHELET, Boillot, Damoy, DROUHIN, FAIVELEY, JADOT, Leclerc, LEROY, MORTET, ROTY, Roumier, ROUSSEAU, TRAPET, DOM DES VAROILLES.

Gewurztraminer Speciality grape of ALSACE: one of 4 allowed for specified GRAND CRU wines. Perfumed like old roses, often tasting like grapefruit.

Gigondas S Rh r p ■■ 78 79 83 85 86 88 89' 90 91 92 93 94 Worthy neighbour to CHATEAUNEUF-DU-PAPE. Strong, full-bodied, sometimes peppery wine, largely Grenache; eg Dom du Cayron, Les Goubert, Gour de Chaule, Dom les Pallières, Dom du Pesquier, Dom Raspail-Ay, Dom St-Gayan, Dom des Travers, Ch du Trignon.

Ginestet Long-established B'x négociant now owned by Jacques Merlaut, said to be second in turnover. Merlaut's empire incl Ch'x CHASSE-SPLEEN, HAUT-BAGES-LIBERAL, LA GURGUE, FERRIERE.

Gisselbrecht, Louis High quality ALSACE shippers at Dambach-la-Ville. Ries and Gewurz best. Cousin Willy Gisselbrecht's wines are v competitive.

Givry Burg r w ■■ 85' 88' 89' 90' 91 92 93 94 Underrated COTE CHALONNAISE village: light but tasty and typical burgundy from eg DELORME, Dom Joblot, L Latour, T Lespinasse, Clos Salomon, BARON THENARD.

Gosset Brut NV; Rosé NV; Brut 81 82 83 85 86 88; Grande Réserve; Grand Millésime Brut 79 82 83 85; Grand Rosé 85 88 Small, v old CHAMPAGNE house at AY. Excellent full-bodied wine (esp Grand Millésime). Now linked with PHILIPPONNAT.

Goulaine, Château de The ceremonial showplace of MUSCADET; a noble family estate and its appropriate wine.

Goulet, George NV; Rosé NV High quality Reims CHAMPAGNE house. Luxury brand: Cuvée du Centenaire (79 82 83 85) now replaced by Cuvée Veuve Goulet.

Goût Taste, eg goût anglais: as the English like it (ie, dry, or, in CHAMPAGNE, well-aged).

Grand Cru One of top Burgundy v'yds with its own appellation contrôlée. Similar meaning in recent ALSACE law, but more vague elsewhere. In ST-EMILION the third rank of ch'x, incl about 200 properties.

Grande Champagne The AC of the best area of COGNAC.

Grande Rue, La Burg r *** 89' 90' 91 92 93 94 Recently-promoted GRAND CRU in VOSNE-ROMANEE, neighbour to ROMANEE-CONTI. Owners, the Lamarche family, are trying harder.

Grands-Echézeaux Burg r **** 69' 76 78' 82 83 85' 87 88' 89' 90' 91' 92 93 94 Superlative 22-acre GRAND CRU next to CLOS DE VOUGEOT. Wines not weighty but aromatic. Viz: DROUHIN, ENGEL, MONGEARD-MUGNERET, DOM DE LA ROMANEE-CONTI.

Gratien, Alfred and Gratien & Meyer Brut NV; Cuvée Paradis Brut; Cuvée Paradis Rosé; Brut 79 82 83 85' Excellent smaller family CHAMPAGNE house with top traditional standards. (Fine v dry long-lasting wine.) Also its counterpart at SAUMUR. (Vg Cuvée Flamme.)

Graves B'x r w **→**** Large region S of Bordeaux city with excellent soft earthy reds, and dry whites (Sauv Bl-Sém) reasserting star status.

Graves de Vayres B'x r w * DYA Part of ENTRE-D-M; no special character.

Griotte-Chambertin Burg r **** 78' 83 85' 87 88' 89' 90' 91 92 93 94 14-acre GRAND CRU adjoining CHAMBERTIN. Similar wine, but less masculine, more 'tender'. Growers incl DROUHIN, PONSOT.

Grivot, Jean 25-acre COTE DE NUITS domaine, in 5 ACs incl RICHEBOURG, NUITS PREMIERS CRUS, VOSNE-ROMANEE, CLOS DE VOUGEOT, etc. Top quality.

Gros Plant du Pays Nantais Lo w * DYA Junior VDQS cousin of MUSCADET, sharper, lighter; from the COGNAC grape, aka Folle Blanche, Ugni Bl, etc.

Guffens-Heynen Belgian POUILLY-FUISSE grower. Minute quantity, fine quality. Also heady Gamay and COTE D'OR wine from bought-in grapes. To follow.

Guigal, E and M Celebrated growers and merchants of CONDRIEU, COTE ROTIE and HERMITAGE. Since '85 owners of VIDAL-FLEURY. By ageing single-v'yd Côte Rôtie (La Landonne, La Mouline, La Turque) over 3 years in new oak Guigal breaks local tradition. His standard wines are good value, esp red COTES DU RHONE. Special CONDRIEU CUVEE La Doriane (since '95).

Guyon, Antonin Considerable domaine at ALOXE-CORTON with adequate wines from CHAMBOLLE-MUSIGNY, CORTON, etc, and HAUTES-COTES DE NUITS.

Haut Poitou Lo w (r) ★★★★ DYA Up-and-coming young VDQS S of ANJOU. Vg whites (CHARD, Sauv) from coop. Has rejected restrictions of AC status.

Haut-Benauge B'x w ★ DYA AC for a limited area in ENTRE-DEUX-MERS.

Haut-Médoc B'x r ★★→★★★ 70 75 78 81' 82' 83' 85' 86' 87 88' 89' 90' 92 93 94 Big AC including all the best parts of the MEDOC. Most of the zone has communal ACs (eg MARGAUX, PAUILLAC). Some excellent châteaux (eg LA LAGUNE) are simply AC HAUT-MEDOC.

Haut-Montravel Dordogne w sw ★ 90' 93 Rare BERGERAC, like MONBAZILLAC.

Hautes-Côtes de Beaune Burg r w ★★ 85 88 89' 90' 91 92 93 94 Appellation for a dozen villages in the hills behind the COTE DE BEAUNE. Light wines, worth investigating. Top growers: Cornu, Mazilly.

Hautes-Côtes de Nuits Burg r w ★★ 85 88 89' 90' 91 92 93 94 As above, for COTE DE NUITS. An area on the way up. Top growers: C Cornu, Jayer-Gilles, M Gros. Also has large BEAUNE coop; good esp from GEISWEILER.

Heidsieck, Charles Brut Réserve NV; Brut 79 81 83 85; Rosé 81 83 85 Major Reims CHAMPAGNE house, now controlled by Rémy Martin; also incl Trouillard, de Venoge. Luxury brands: Cuvée Champagne Charlie (81 82 83, then withdrawn), Bl des Millénaires (83 85). Fine quality recently; NV a real bargain. See also Piper-Heidsieck.

Heidsieck, Monopole Brut NV; Rosé NV Important CHAMPAGNE merchant and Reims grower now owned by Seagram and made by MUMM. Luxury brands of note: Diamant Bleu (76 79 82 85), Diamant Rosé (82 85 88).

Henriot Brut Souverain NV; Bl de Bls de Chard NV; Brut 79 82 85 88; Brut Rosé 81 83 85 88; Cuvée des Enchanteleurs 85 Old family CHAMPAGNE house regained independence in '94. Fresh fine style: luxury CUVEES (eg Baron Philippe de Rothschild) withdrawn.

Hérault Midi Biggest v'yd département in France with 980,000 acres of vines. Chiefly VIN DE TABLE but some good AC COTEAUX DU LANGUEDOC, and, more interestingly, pioneering Vins de Pays de l'Hérault.

Hermitage N Rh r w ★★★→★★★★ 61 66 70 72 78' 79 80 82 83' 84 85 86 87 88 89 90' 91' 92 93 94 'Manliest' wine of France: dark powerful and profound. Truest example of the Syrah grape. Needs long ageing. White is heady and golden; now usually made for early drinking, though best wines mature for up to 25 yrs. Top makers: CHAPOUTIER, CHAVE, DELAS, Faurie, Grippat, GUIGAL, JABOULET, Sorrel.

Hospices de Beaune Historic hospital in BEAUNE, with excellent v'yds (known by 'CUVEE' names) in BEAUNE, CORTON, MEURSAULT, POMMARD, VOLNAY. Wines are auctioned on the third Sunday of each November.

Hugel et Fils The best-known ALSACE growers and merchants; founded at Riquewihr in 1639 and still in the family. 'Johnny' H (ret'd '94) is the region's beloved spokesman. Quality escalates with Cuvée Tradition and then Jubilée Réserve ranges. SELECTIONS DES GRAINS NOBLES: Hugel pioneered this style in Alsace. Many are sweet, but not all.

Ile de Beauté Name given to VINS DU PAYS from CORSICA. Mostly red.

Impériale BORDEAUX bottle holding 8.5 normal bottles (6.4 litres).

Irancy ('Bourgogne Irancy') Burg r (p) ★★ 85 88 89 90 91 92 93 94 Good light red made nr CHABLIS from Pinot N and the local César. The best vintages are long-lived and mature well. To watch. Growers incl Colinot.

Irouléguy SW France r p (w) ★★ DYA Agreeable local wines of the Basque country. Mainly rosé; also dark dense Tannat/Cab reds to keep 5 yrs+. Good from Doms Ilarria, Brana and coop. A future MADIRAN?

Jaboulet, Paul Old family firm at Tain, leading growers of HERMITAGE (esp La Chapelle ▓▓▓▓), and merchants of other Rhône wines – esp CORNAS, COTES DU RHONE Parallèle 45.

Jaboulet-Vercherre & Cie Burgundy merchant house with v'yds (34 acres) in POMMARD, etc, and cellars in BEAUNE. Should try harder.

Jacquart Brut NV (Tradition and Selection); Brut Rosé NV; Brut 85 87 Relatively new ('62) coop-based CHAMPAGNE marque; in quantity the sixth largest. Fair quality. Luxury brands: Cuvée Nominée Blanc 85, CN Rosé 85. Vg Mosaïque Bl de Blancs 86, Mosaïque Rosé 86.

Jacquesson Small quality Epernay CHAMP house. Several good luxury CUVEES.

Jadot, Louis Much-respected top quality Burgundy merchant house with v'yds (150 acres) in BEAUNE, CORTON etc. Incl former estate of CLAIR-DAU. Wines to bank on.

Jaffelin Independent quality négociant, bought in '92 from DROUHIN by BOISSET.

Jardin de la France Lo r w p One of the four regional VINS DE PAYS. Covers Loire Valley: Gamay and Sauv Bl wines (slightly more red than white), mostly single grape. Top vin de pays de zone: Marches de Bretagne.

Jasnières Lo w (r p) *** 76 78 79 83 85 86 88' 89' 90' 91 92 93' V rare dry rather VOUVRAY-like wine of N TOURAINE.

Jaubertie, Château de la Jayer, Henri See Rouget, Emmanuel.

Jeroboam In BORDEAUX a 6-bottle bottle (holding 4.5 litres) or triple magnum; in CHAMPAGNE a double magnum.

Joseph Perrier Cuvée Royale Brut NV; Cuvée Royale Bl de Blancs NV; Cuvée Royale Rosé NV; Brut 76 79 82 83 85 89 Family-run CHAMPAGNE house with considerable v'yds at Châlons-sur-Marne. Light fruity style, best in prestige CUVEE (since '89) Cuvée Joséphine 82 85.

JosMeyer Family house at Wintzenheim, ALSACE. Vg long-ageing wines, esp GEWURZ and Pinot Bl. Fine Ries from Hengst GRAND CRU. Wide range of grape varieties, labels and locations.

Juliénas Beauj r *** 90 91 92 93 94 Leading CRU of BEAUJOLAIS: vigorous fruity wine to keep 2–3 yrs. Growers incl Ch'x du Bois de la Salle, des Capitans, de Juliénas, des Vignes; Dom Bottière, Dom R Monnet, coop.

Jura See Côtes de Jura.

Jurançon SW France w sw dr ▓▓→▓▓▓▓ 78 82 83 85' 86 88' 89' 90' 91 93 94 Rare high-flavoured long-lived speciality of Pau in Pyrenean foothills, at best like wild-flower SAUTERNES. Not to be missed. Both sweet and dry should age. Top growers: Barrère, Dom du Bellegarde, Gaillot, Guirouilh, Lamouroux, Lapeyre, Larredya, de Rousse, Dom Cauhapé. Also coop's dry Grain Sauvage, Brut d'Ocean and Peyre d'Or.

Kaefferkopf Alsace w dr sw *** Ammerschwihr v'yd famous for blends rather than single-grape wines; growers are not happy with restrictions of GRAND CRU status.

Kientzheim-Kayserberg Important ALSACE coop for quality as well as style. Esp for GEWURZ, Ries (Schlossburg GRAND CRU) and Crémant d'Alsace.

Kientzler, André Fine ALSACE Ries specialist in Geisburg GRAND CRU, esp VENDANGE TARDIVE and SELECTION DES GRAINS NOBLES. Equally good from GCs Kirchberg de Ribeauvillé for Gewurz and Osterberg for occasional 'vins de glaces' (Eisweins).

Kreydenweiss Fine ALSACE grower with 24 acres at Andlau, esp for Pinot Gr (vg from Moenchberg GRAND CRU), Pinot Bl and Ries. Top wine: Kastelberg (Ries ages 20 yrs+); also fine Auxerrois 'Kritt Klevner' and good VENDANGE TARDIVE. One of first in Alsace to use new oak. Good Ries-Pinot Gr blend 'Clos du Val d'Eléon'.

Kriter Popular sparkler processed in Burgundy by PATRIARCHE.

Krug Grande Cuvée; 79 81 82 85; Rosé; Clos du Mesnil (Bl de Blancs) 79 80 81 82 83 85; Krug Collection 62 64 66 69 71 73 76 Small but supremely prestigious CHAMPAGNE house. Dense full-bodied v dry wines, superlative quality. Owned by Rémy-Cointreau (but no-one would know).

Kuentz-Bas Top-quality ALSACE grower/merchant at Husseren-les-Châteaux, esp for Pinot Gr (Tokay d'Alsace), GEWURZ. Also good VENDANGES TARDIVES.

Labouré-Roi Outstandingly reliable merchant at NUITS. Mostly whites. Many fine domaine wines, esp René Manuel's MEURSAULT, Chantal Lescure's Nuits, CLOS DE VOUGEOT. Vg CHABLIS. Also VOLNAY-SANTENOTS.

Ladoix-Serrigny Burg r (w) ** Northernmost village of COTE DE BEAUNE below hills of CORTON. To watch for bargains.

Ladoucette, de Leading producer of POUILLY-FUME, based at CH DE NOZET. Luxury brand: Baron de L. Also SANCERRE Comte Lafond (and PIC CHABLIS).

Lafarge, Michel 23-acre COTE DE BEAUNE estate, with outstanding VOLNAYS.

Lafon, Domaine des Comtes 32-acre quality Burgundy estate in MEURSAULT, LE MONTRACHET, VOLNAY. Glorious intense wines; extraordinary dark reds.

Laguiche, Marquis de Largest owner of LE MONTRACHET. Magnificent wines made by DROUHIN.

Lalande de Pomerol B'x r ** 82 83 85 86' 88' 89' 90' 92 93 94 Neighbour to POMEROL. Wines similar, but less mellow. Top ch'x: Les Annereaux, DE BELAIR, Belles-Graves, Bertineau-St-Vincent, La Croix Bellevue, La Croix-St-André, Les Hauts-Conseillants, Les Hauts-Tuileries, Moncets, SIAURAC, TOURNEFEUILLE.

Langlois-Château SAUMUR sp house (esp CREMANT) controlled by BOLLINGER.

Lanson Père & Fils Black Label NV; Rosé NV; Brut 88 89 Important CHAMPAGNE house with cellars at Reims. Luxury brand: Noble Cuvée (81 85 88). Black Label is a reliable fresh (sometimes thin) NV. New CUVEE: Bl de Blancs 83 89.

Laroche Important grower (238 acres) and dynamic CHABLIS merchant, incl Domaines La Jouchère and Laroche. Top wines: Blanchots and Clos 'Vieilles Vignes'. Also blends good non-regional CHARD.

Latour, Louis Famous Burgundy merchant and grower with v'yds (120 acres) in BEAUNE, CORTON, etc. Among the v best for white: CHEVALIER-MONTRACHET Les Demoiselles, CORTON-CHARLEMAGNE, MONTRACHET, gd value MONTAGNY and ARDECHE CHARD, etc. Developing Pinot N in the Var.

Latour de France r (w) *→** 88 89 90 91 92 93 94 New AC in COTES DE ROUSSILLON-VILLAGES.

Latricières-Chambertin Burg r *** 78' 83 85' 88' 89' 90' 91 92 93 94 17-acre GRAND CRU neighbour of CHAMBERTIN. Similar wine but lighter and 'prettier' eg from FAIVELEY, LEROY, PONSOT, TRAPET.

Laudun S Rh w (r p) * Village of COTES DU RHONE-VILLAGES. Attractive wines from the coop incl fresh whites. Dom Pelaquié is best, esp white.

Laugel, Michel One of the biggest ALSACE merchant houses at Marlenheim: esp good Cuvée Jubilaire range and CREMANT.

Laurent-Perrier Brut NV; Rosé NV; Brut 78 79 81 82 85 88 Excellent dynamic highly successful family-owned CHAMPAGNE house at Tours-sur-Marne. Luxury brands: Cuvée Grande Siècle (NV and 81-82-85 blend), CGS Alexandra Brut Rosé (82). Ultra Brut is bone dry. Owns SALON, DELAMOTTE, DE CASTELLANE.

Leflaive, Domaine Sometimes considered the best of all white burgundy growers, at PULIGNY-MONTRACHET. Best v'yds: Bienvenue- and Chevalier-Montrachet, Clavoillons, Pucelles. Increasingly organic methods.

Leflaive, Olivier Négociant at PULIGNY-MONTRACHET since '84, now with 22 acres of his own, nephew of the above. Reliable whites and reds, incl less famous ACs, have upgraded seriously since '90.

Léognan B'x r w ***→***** Top village of GRAVES with its own AC: PESSAC-LEOGNAN. Best ch'x: DOM DE CHEVALIER, HAUT-BAILLY, MALARTIC-LAGRAVIERE.

Leroy Important NEGOCIANT-ELEVEUR at AUXEY-DURESSES with a growing domaine and the finest stocks of old wines in Burgundy. Part-owners of DOM DE LA ROMANEE-CONTI. In '88 bought the 35-acre Noëllat estate in CLOS VOUGEOT, NUITS, ROMANEE-ST-VIVANT, SAVIGNY, etc. Leroy's range (from AUXEY whites to CHAMBERTIN and neighbours) is simply magnificent.

Lichine, Alexis & Cie BORDEAUX merchants (once of the late Alexis Lichine). No connection with CH PRIEURE LICHINE.

Lie, sur On the lees. MUSCADET is often bottled straight from the vat, without racking or filtering, for maximum freshness and character.

Limoux Pyr r w ** Burgeoning AC, formerly for BLANQUETTE DE LIMOUX sparkling, now good for CHARD and Pinot N as well as trad grapes. Also a good claret-like red from the coop: Anne des Joyeuses.

Lirac S Rh r p (w) ** 88' 89' 90 91 92 93 94 Next to TAVEL. Approachable soft red (best needs 5yrs age). Red is overtaking rosé, esp Doms Maby, de la Mordorée, Sabon, St-Roch, Ch de Ségriès. Good whites too.

Listel Midi r p w *→*** DYA Vast (4,000-acre+) historic estate on sandy beaches of the Golfe du Lion. Owned by giant Salins du Midi salt co and VAL D'ORBIEU group. Pleasant light 'vins des sables' incl sparkling, Dom du Bosquet-Canet is a fruity Cab, Dom de Villeroy fresh BLANC DE BLANCS SUR LIE, and CHARD since '89. Also fruity almost non-alcoholic PETILLANT, Ch de Malijay COTES DU RHONE, Abbaye de Ste-Hilaire COTEAUX VAROIS, Ch La Gordonne COTES DE PROVENCE.

Listrac-Médoc B'x r **→*** Village of HAUT-MEDOC next to MOULIS. Best ch'x: CLARKE, FONREAUD, FOURCAS-DUPRE, FOURCAS-HOSTEN.

Livinière, La Midi r (p w) *→*** High quality MINERVOIS CRU. Best growers: Abbaye de Tholonies, Combe Blanche, Ch de Gourgazaud, Laville Bertrous, Dom Maris, Dom Ste Eulalie, Coop La Livinière.

Long-Depaquit Vg CHABLIS domaine (esp MOUTONNE), owned by BICHOT.

Lorentz Two small quality ALSACE houses at Bergheim: Gustave L and Jerome L, have same management. Esp GEWURZ and Ries from Altenberg de Bergheim and Kanzlerberg.

Loron & Fils Big-scale grower and merchant at Pontanevaux; specialist in BEAUJOLAIS and sound VINS DE TABLE.

Loupiac B'x w sw ** 76 79' 83 85 86' 88' 89 90 91 93 Across the River Garonne from SAUTERNES. Top châteaux: Clos-Jean, Haut-Loupiac, LOUPIAC-GAUDIET, RICAUD, Rondillon.

Lugny See Mâcon-Lugny.

Lupé-Cholet & Cie Once famous merchants/growers at NUITS-ST-GEORGES, now controlled by BICHOT. Estate wines: Clos de Lupé and Ch Gris.

Lussac-St-Emilion B'x r ** 82 85 86' 88' 89' 90' 92 93 94 NE neighbour to ST-EMILION. Top ch'x incl Barbe Blanche, Bel Air, DU LYONNAT, Tour de Grenat, Villadière. Coop (at PUISSEGUIN) makes pleasant Roc de Lussac.

Macération carbonique Traditional technique of fermentation with whole bunches of unbroken grapes in a closed vat. Fermentation inside each grape eventually bursts it, giving vivid fruity mild wine, not for ageing. Esp in BEAUJOLAIS; now much used in the MIDI and elsewhere.

Machard de Gramont BURGUNDY family estate: cellars in Premeaux and v'yds in BEAUNE, NUITS, POMMARD, SAVIGNY. Well-made reds.

The Mâconnais

The hilly zone just north of Beaujolais has outcrops of limestone where Chardonnay gives full, if not fine, wines. The village of Chardonnay here may (or may not) be the home of the variety. Granite soils give strong Gamay reds. The top Mâconnais AC is Pouilly-Fuissé, then St-Véran, then Mâcon-Villages with a village name. The potential is here to produce lower priced, richly typical Chardonnays to out-do the New World (and indeed the south of France). Currently most wines are less than extraordinary.

Mâcon Burg r w (p) ** 89' 90' 91 92 93 94 Sound, usually unremarkable reds (Gamay best), tasty dry (CHARD) whites.

Mâcon-Lugny Burg r w sp ** 89 90 91 92 93 Village next to VIRE with huge and vg coop (4M bottles). Les Genevrières is sold by LOUIS LATOUR.

Mâcon-Villages Burg w **→*** 89 90 91 92 93 94 Increasingly well-made typical white burgundies (when not over-produced). Named for their villages, eg M-CHARDONNAY, -Clessé, -Lugny, -Prissé, -Viré, -Uchizy. Best coop is probably Prissé, biggest Lugny. Top grower: Thevenet of Clessé.

Mâcon-Viré Burg w ** 91 92 93 94 One of the best white wine villages of MACON. Esp A Bonhomme, Clos du Chapitre, JADOT, Ch de Viré, coop.

Macvin Jura w sw ** AC for 'traditional' MARC and grape juice aperitif.

Madiran SW France r *** 82 85' 86' 88 89' 90' 92 93 94 Dark vigorous red from ARMAGNAC, like hard but fruity MEDOC with a fluid elegance of its own. Ages 5–10 yrs, but 'barriques' are changing it, not necessarily for the better: now light and heavy schools. Top growers: Ch'x d'Arricau-Bordes, d'Aydié, Barréjat, Bouscassé, Dom Capmartin, Laplace (esp Ch d'Aydie), Montus, Peyros. White is AC PACHERENC.

Magenta, Duc de Recently revamped Burgundy estate (30 acres) based at CHASSAGNE-MONTRACHET, managed by JADOT.

Magnum A double bottle (1.5 litres).

Mähler-Besse First-class Dutch négociants in B'X, with a share in CH PALMER and owners of Ch Michel de Montaigne. Brands incl Cheval Noir.

Mailly-Champagne Top CHAMPAGNE coop. Luxury wine: Cuvée des Echansons.

Maire, Henri The biggest grower/merchant of JURA wines, with half of the entire AC. Some top wines, many cheerfully commercial. To visit.

Maranges Burg r ** New ('89) AC for 600-odd acres of S COTE DE BEAUNE, beyond SANTENAY, one-third PREMIER CRU. Top/first négociant: JAFFELIN.

Marc Grape skins after pressing; also the strong-smelling brandy made from them (see Italian 'Grappa').

Marcillac SW France r p *→** DYA Promoted to AC in '90. Violet-hued with grassy red-fruit character. Good from coop Cave de Valady (rustic) , Dom du Cros and J-M Revel.

Margaux B'x r **→**** 70 75 78 79 81 82' 83' 85 86' 87 88' 89 90' 91 92 93 94 Village of the HAUT-MEDOC making some of the most 'elegant' red BORDEAUX. AC incl CANTENAC and several other villages. Top ch'x incl MARGAUX, RAUSAN-SEGLA, LASCOMBES, etc.

Margnat Major producer of everyday VIN DE TABLE.

Marne et Champagne, Ste Recent but huge-scale CHAMPAGNE house, owner (since '91) of LANSON and many smaller brands, incl BESSERAT DE BELLEFON.

Marque déposée Trademark.

Marsannay Burg p w (r) *** 85 88' 89' 90' 91 92 93 (rosé DYA) Village with fine light red and delicate Pinot N rosé. Incl villages of Chenôve, Conchey. Growers: Charlopin, CLAIR, Dijon University, JADOT, Quillardet, TRAPET.

Mas de Daumas Gassac Midi r w p *** 80 81 82 83 85 86 87 88 89 90 91 92 93 94 The one 'first-growth' estate of the LANGUEDOC, producing potent largely Cab wines on apparently unique soil. Sensational quality. Also Rosé Frisant and a sumptuous white of blended CHARD, Viognier, Petit Manseng, etc. Now also a vg quick-drinking red, Les Terrasses de Guilhem, from a nearby coop and trad Languedoc varietals (Clairette, Cinsaut, Aramon etc) from v old vines under Terrasses de Landoc label. VIN DE PAYS status.

Maufoux, Prosper Old firm of burgundy merchants at SANTENAY, now with NY owners. Reliable wines, esp whites, keep well. Alias Marcel Amance.

Maury Pyr r sw ** NV Red VIN DOUX NATUREL of Grenache from ROUSSILLON. Taste the terroir. Much recent improvement.

Mazis (or Mazy) Chambertin Burg r *** 78' 83 85' 87 88' 89' 90' 91 92 93 94 30-acre GRAND CRU neighbour of CHAMBERTIN, sometimes equally potent. Best from FAIVELEY, HOSPICES DE BEAUNE, LEROY, ROTY.

Mazoyères-Chambertin See Charmes-Chambertin.

Médoc B'x r ** 82' 83 85 86' 87 88' 89' 90' 92 93 94 AC for reds of the less good (northern) part of BORDEAUX's biggest and best district. Flavours tend to earthiness. HAUT-MEDOC is much better. Top châteaux incl LA CARDONNE, GREYSAC, LOUDENNE, LES ORMES-SORBET, POTENSAC, LA TOUR-DE-BY.

Meffre, Gabriel The biggest S Rhône estate, based at GIGONDAS. Variable quality. Often in French supermarkets. Also bottles and sells for small CHATEAUNEUF-DU-PAPE domaines, eg Guy Jullian, Dom de Baban.

Menetou-Salon Lo r p w ** DYA Attractive similar wines from W of SANCERRE: Sauv Bl white, Pinot N red. Top grower: Clément.

Méo-Camuzet V fine domaine in CLOS DE VOUGEOT, NUITS, RICHEBOURG, VOSNE-ROMANEE. HENRI JAYER oversees winemaking. Esp: V-R Cros Parantoux.

Mercier & Cie, Champagne Brut NV; Brut Rosé NV; Brut 81 82 83 85 86 88 90 One of the biggest CHAMPAGNE houses at Epernay. Controlled by MOET & CHANDON. Good commercial quality, sold mainly in France. Bulle d'Or and Reserve de l'Empereur CUVEES no longer produced.

Mercurey Burg r w ✯✯→✯✯✯✯ 85 88' 89' 90' 91 92 93 94 Leading red wine village of COTE CHALONNAISE. Good middle-rank burgundy incl more and improving whites. Growers incl Ch de Chamirey, Chanzy, FAIVELEY, M Juillot, Dom de Suremain.

Mercurey, Région de The up-to-date name for the COTE CHALONNAISE.

Métaireau, Louis The ringleader of a group of top MUSCADET growers. Expensive well-finished wines.

Méthode champenoise The traditional laborious method of putting bubbles into CHAMPAGNE by refermenting the wine in its bottle. Must be referred to as 'classic method' or 'méthode traditionelle' when used outside the region. Not mentioned on champagne labels.

Méthode traditionelle See entry above.

Meursault Burg w (r) ✯✯✯→✯✯✯✯ 78' 83 85 86 88 89' 90' 91 92 93 94 COTE DE BEAUNE village with some of the world's greatest whites: savoury, dry but nutty and mellow. Best v'yds: Charmes, Genevrières, Perrières; also: Goutte d'Or, Meursault-Blagny, Poruzots, Narvaux, Tillets. Producers incl AMPEAU, J-M Boillot, M Bougereau, CH DE MEURSAULT, COCHE-DURY, Delagrange, P Javillier, Jobard, LAFON, LATOUR, O Leflaive, LEROY, MAGENTA, Manuel, Matrot, Michelot-Buisson, P MOREY, G ROULOT. See also Blagny.

Meursault-Blagny See Blagny.

Michel, Louis CHABLIS domaine with model, unoaked, v long-lived wines, incl superb LES CLOS, vg MONTEE DE TONNERRE.

Midi General term for the south of France west of the Rhône delta. Improving reputation, brilliant promise. Many top wines based on grape variety rather than APPELLATION. A melting-pot.

Minervois Midi r (p w) br sw ✯→✯✯✯ 85 86 88 89 90 91 92 93 94 Hilly AC region for good MIDI wines: lively, full of flavour, esp from Ch du Donjon, Dom Laurent Fabre, LA LIVINIERE, Coop Pouzols. See also St-Jean de Minervois.

Mis en bouteille au château/domaine Bottled at the château, property or estate. NB dans nos caves (in our cellars) or dans la région de production (in the area of production) are often used but mean little.

Moelleux Creamy sweet. Used of the sweet wines of VOUVRAY, etc.

Moët & Chandon Brut NV; Rosé 81 82 85 86 88 90; Brut Imperial 76 78 81 82 83 85 86 88 90 Much the biggest CHAMPAGNE merchant and grower, with cellars in Epernay, and branches in Argentina, Australia, Brazil, California, Germany and Spain. Consistent quality, esp in Vintage wines. Coteaux Champenois 'Saran' can be disappointing. Prestige CUVEE: DOM PERIGNON. Links with CLICQUOT, MERCIER, POMMERY, RUINART, etc and Cognac Hennessy.

Moillard Big family firm (Domaine Thomas-Moillard) of growers and merchants in NUITS-ST-GEORGES, making full range incl dark and v tasty wines, eg CLOS DU ROI, CLOS DE VOUGEOT, CORTON, etc.

Mommessin, J Major BEAUJOLAIS merchant, merged with THORIN. Owner of CLOS DE TART. White wines less successful than red.

Monbazillac Dordogne w sw ✯✯ 75 76 79 83' 85 86' 88' 89' 90' 92 93 94 Golden SAUTERNES-style wine from BERGERAC, gradually gaining typicité. Can age well. Ch Monbazillac and Ch Septy are best known; also good are La Borderie, Haut-Brie, La Fage. The peripatetic British winemaker Hugh Ryman operates at the Cave Coop de Monbazillac.

Mondeuse Savoie r ✯✯ DYA Red grape of SAVOIE. Good vigorous deep-coloured wine. Perhaps NE Italy's Refosco.

France entries also cross-refer to Châteaux of Bordeaux section, pages 58–79.

Mongeard-Mugneret 50+-acre VOSNE-ROMANEE estate. Very fine ECHEZEAUX, RICHEBOURG, SAVIGNY, VOSNE PREMIER CRU, VOUGEOT, etc.

Monopole V'yd under single ownership.

Mont-Redon, Ch de S Rh r (w) ★★★ 85 86 88 89 90 92 93 94 Outstanding 235-acre CHATEAUNEUF-DU-PAPE estate. Reliable early-maturing reds and fresh (early-drinking) whites.

Montagne-St-Emilion B'x r ▓▓ 82' 83 85 86' 88' 89' 90' 93 94 NE neighbour and largest 'satellite' of ST-EMILION: similar wines and AC regulations; becoming more important each year. Top ch'x: St-André-Corbin, Calon, Faizeau, Haut-Gillet, Roudier, Teyssier, DES TOURS, VIEUX-CH-ST-ANDRE.

Montagny Burg w (r) ▓▓ 89' 90 91 92 93 94 COTE CHALONNAISE village. Between MACON and MEURSAULT, both geographically and gastronomically. Top producers: Cave Coop de Buxy, LOUIS LATOUR, Michel, Ch de la Saule.

Montée de Tonnerre Burg w ★★★ 86 88 89 90 91 92 93 94 Famous excellent CHABLIS PREMIER CRU. Growers incl Duplessis, L Michel, Raveneau, Robin.

Monthélie Burg r (w) ★★→★★★ 78 83 85 87 88' 89' 90' 91 92 93 94 Little-known neighbour, s'times almost equal of VOLNAY. Excellent fragrant reds. Growers incl BOUCHARD PERE, COCHE-DURY, COMTE LAFON, DROUHIN, Garaudet, Ch de Monthélie (de Suremain), Monthélie-Douhairet.

Montlouis Lo w dr sw (sp) ★★→★★★ 75 76 78 82 83' 85' 86 88' 89 90' 91 92 93' 94 Neighbour of VOUVRAY. Similar sweet or dry long-lived wine. Top growers: Berger, Deletang, Levasseur, Taille aux Loups.

Montrachet Burg w ★★★★ 69' 71 78 79 82 83 85' 86' 88 89' 90 91 92 93 94 (Both 't's in the name are silent.) 19-acre GRAND CRU v'yd in both PULIGNY- and CHASSAGNE-MONTRACHET. Potentially the greatest white burgundy: strong, perfumed, intense, dry yet luscious. Top wines from LAFON, LAGUICHE (DROUHIN), RAMONET, DOM DE LA ROMANEE-CONTI, THENARD.

Montravel See Côtes de Montravel.

Moreau & Fils CHABLIS merchant and grower with 187 acres. Also major table wine producer. Best wine: Clos des Hospices (GRAND CRU).

Morey, Domaines 50 acres in CHASSAGNE-MONTRACHET. Vg wines made by family members, incl BATARD-MONTRACHET.

Morey-St-Denis Burg r ▓▓ 78 82 83 85' 86 87 88 89' 90' 91 92 93 94 Small village with four GRANDS CRUS between GEVREY-CHAMBERTIN and CHAMBOLLE-MUSIGNY. Glorious wine often overlooked. Incl Amiot, Bryczek, Castagnier, DUJAC, Groffier, Lignier, Moillard-Grivot, PONSOT, ROUSSEAU, Serveau.

Morgon Beauj r ▓▓ 85 88 89 90 91 92 93 94 The 'firmest' CRU of BEAUJOLAIS, needing time to develop its rich, savoury flavour. Growers incl Aucoeur, Ch de Bellevue, Desvignes, Lapierre, Ch de Pizay. DUBOEUF excellent.

Moueix, J-P et Cie Legendary leading proprietor and merchant of ST-EMILION, POMEROL and FRONSAC. Châteaux incl LA FLEUR-PETRUS, MAGDELAINE and part of PETRUS. Now also in California: see Dominus.

Moulin-à-Vent Beauj r ★★★ 85 88 89 90 91 92 93 94 The 'biggest' and best wine of BEAUJOLAIS: powerful, meaty and long-lived, eventually can even taste like fine Rhône or burgundy. Many good growers, esp Ch du Moulin-à-Vent, Ch La Tour du Bief, Ch des Jacques.

Moulis B'x r ★★→★★★ H-MEDOC village with several CRUS EXCEPTIONNELS: CHASSE-SPLEEN, MAUCAILLOU, POUJEAUX (THEIL), etc. Good hunting ground.

Mousseux Sparkling.

Mouton Cadet Popular brand of blended red and white BORDEAUX.

Moutonne CHABLIS GRAND CRU honoris causa (between Vaudésir and Preuses), owned by BICHOT.

Mugnier, J-F 10-acre Ch de Chambolle estate with first-class delicate CHAMBOLLE-MUSIGNY Les Amoureuses and MUSIGNY. Also BONNES-MARES.

Mumm, G H & Cie Cordon Rouge NV; Mumm de Cramant NV; Cordon Rouge 79 82 85 88; Rosé NV Major CHAMPAGNE grower and merchant owned by Seagram. Luxury brands: René Lalou (79 82 85), Grand Cordon (85; launched '91), Grand Cordon Rosé 85. Cordon Rouge is pretty tasteless. Also in Napa, California.

Muré, Clos St-Landelin Fine ALSACE merchant at Rouffach with v'yds in GRAND CRU Vorbourg. Full-bodied wines: ripe (unusual) Pinot N, big Ries and Muscat VENDANGES TARDIVES.

Muscadet Lo w ** DYA Popular, good value, often delicious v dry wine from around Nantes. Should never be sharp but should have an iodine tang. Perfect with fish. The best are bottled SUR LIE – on their lees.

Muscadet Côte de Grand Lieu New AC ('95) for slightly superior MUSCADET, from eg Luc Choblet.

Muscadet de Sèvre-et-Maine Wine from the central (best) part of the area.

Muscat Distinctively perfumed grape and its (usually sweet) wine, often fortified as VIN DOUX NATUREL. Made dry in ALSACE.

Muscat de Beaumes-de-Venise See Beaumes-de-Venise.

Muscat de Frontignan Midi br sw ** DYA Sweet MIDI MUSCAT. Quality improving. See Frontignan.

Muscat de Lunel Midi br sw ** NV Ditto. A small area but good, making real recent progress.

Muscat de Mireval Midi br sw ** NV Ditto, from nr Montpellier.

Muscat de Rivesaltes Midi br sw ** NV Sweet MUSCAT from large zone near Perpignan. Good from Cazes Frères, Ch de Jau.

Musigny Burg r (w) **** 69 76 78 79 82 83 85' 86 87 88' 89' 90' 91 92 93 94 25-acre GRAND CRU in CHAMBOLLE-MUSIGNY. Can be the most beautiful, if not the most powerful, of all red burgundies (and a little white). Best growers: DROUHIN, JADOT, LEROY, MUGNIER, ROUMIER, DE VOGUE.

Nature Natural or unprocessed – esp of still CHAMPAGNE.

Négociant-éleveur Merchant who 'brings up' (ie matures) the wine.

Nicolas, Ets Paris-based wholesale and retail wine merchants controlled by Castel Frères. One of the biggest in France and one of the best.

Burgundy: growers and merchants
The image of Burgundy négociants' wines is the family car, Detroit end of the business. In contrast, buying from growers can feel like driving a sports car. There are arguments for both.

Nuits-St-Georges r **→*** 69 71 76 78' 82 83 85' 86 87 88' 89' 90' 91 92 93 94 Important wine town: wines of all qualities, typically sturdy and relatively tannic, needing time. Name often shortened to 'Nuits'. Best v'yds incl Les Cailles, Clos des Corvées, Les Pruliers, Les St-Georges, Vaucrains, etc. Many growers and merchants esp DOM DE L'ARLOT, CHAUVENET, Chevillon, FAIVELEY, Gouges, GRIVOT, LEROY, MACHARD DE GRAMONT, Michelot, RION.

d'Oc Midi r p w *→** Regional VIN DE PAYS for Languedoc and ROUSSILLON. Esp single-grape wines and VINS DE PAYS PRIMEURS. Tremendous technical advances recently. Top growers: VAL D'ORBIEU, SKALLI, Jeanjean.

Oisly & Thesée, Vignerons de Go-ahead coop in E TOURAINE (Loire), with good Sauv, Cab and CHARD. Blends labelled Baronnie d'Aignan. Value.

Orléanais, Vin de l' Lo r p w * DYA Small VDQS for light but fruity wines.

Ostertag Little ALSACE domaine at Epfig. Uses new oak for good Pinot N and makes the best Ries and Pinot Gr of GRAND CRU Muenchberg. Gewurz from lieu-dit Frönholz is worth ageing.

Ott, Domaines Top high-quality producer of PROVENCE, incl CH DE SELLE (rosé, red), Clos Mireille (white), BANDOL and Ch de Romassan.

Pacherenc du Vic-Bilh SW France w dr sw *→** NV Rare minor speciality of ARMAGNAC region, trad from currently-shunned Arrufiac grape. Doms Capmartin and Mauréou are some of the best. Red is MADIRAN.

Palette Prov r p w ** Near Aix-en-Provence. Aromatic reds and vg rosés from CH SIMONE.

Parigot-Richard Producer of vg CREMANT DE BOURGOGNE at SAVIGNY.

Pasquier-Desvignes V old firm of BEAUJOLAIS merchants nr BROUILLY.

Patriarche One of the bigger firms of burgundy merchants. Cellars in BEAUNE; also owns CH DE MEURSAULT (100 acres), sparkling KRITER, etc.

Patrimonio Corsica r w p ****→***** 90 91 92 93 94   Wide range from dramatic chalk hills in N CORSICA. Fragrant reds, crisp whites, fine VINS DOUX NATURELS. Top grower: Gentile.

Pauillac B'x r ****→****** 66' 70' 75 78' 79 81' 82' 83' 85' 86' 87 88' 89' 90' 91 92 93 94   The only BORDEAUX (HAUT-MEDOC) village with 3 first-growths (CHATEAUX LAFITE, LATOUR, MOUTON) and many other fine ones, famous for high flavour; v varied in style.

Pécharmant Dordogne r ****** 89 90 92 93 94   Usually better-than-typical BERGERAC: more 'meat'. Best: Doms des Bertranoux and du Haut-Pécharmant, Ch de Tiregand.

Pelure d'oignon 'Onion skin' – tawny tint of certain rosés.

Perlant or Perlé Very slightly sparkling.

Pernand-Vergelesses Burg r (w) ******* 78' 83 85 87 88' 89' 90 91 92 93 94   Village next to ALOXE-CORTON containing part of the great CORTON and CORTON-CHARLEMAGNE v'yds and one other top v'yd: Ile des Vergelesses. Growers incl BONNEAU DU MARTRAY, CHANDON DE BRIAILLES, CHANSON, Delarche, Dubreuil-Fontaine, JADOT, LATOUR, Rapet.

Perrier-Jouët Brut NV; Blason de France NV; Blason de France Rosé NV; Brut 76 79 82 85 86 88   Excellent CHAMPAGNE-growers at Epernay, the first makers of dry CHAMPAGNE and once the smartest name of all, now owned by Seagram. Luxury brands: Belle Epoque (79 82 83 85 86 88) in a painted bottle. Also Belle Epoque Rosé (79 82 85 86 88).

Pessac-Léognan Relatively recent AC for part of N GRAVES, incl the area of most of the GRANDS CRUS.

Pétillant Slightly sparkling.

Petit Chablis Burg w ****** DYA   Wine from fourth-rank CHABLIS v'yds. Not much character but can be pleasantly fresh. Best wines are from coop La Chablisienne.

Pfaffenheim Top ALSACE coop with 500 acres. Strongly individual wines of all varieties incl good Sylvaner and vg Pinots (N, Gr, Bl). GRANDS CRUS: Goldert, Steinert. Hartenberger Crémant d'Alsace is vg.

Philipponnat NV; Rosé NV; Réserve Spéciale 82 85 88; Grand Blanc Vintage 76 81 82 85 86 88; Clos des Goisses 76 78 79 82 85 86   Small family-run CHAMPAGNE house: well-structured, wines, esp remarkable single v'yd Clos des Goisses, charming rosé. Owners: Marie Brizard. Since '92 also Le Reflet Brut NV.

Piat Père & Fils Important merchants of BEAUJOLAIS and MACON wines at Mâcon, now controlled by Grand Met. V'yds in MOULIN-A-VENT, also CLOS DE VOUGEOT. BEAUJOLAIS, MACON-VIRE in special Piat bottles maintain a fair standard. Piat d'Or is something else.

Pic, Albert Fine CHABLIS producer, controlled by DE LADOUCETTE.

Picpoul de Pinet Midi w ***→**** AC exclusively for the old variety Picpoul. Best growers: Dom Gaujal, Coop Pomérols.

Pineau de Charente Strong sweet aperitif made from white grape juice and COGNAC.

Pinot See Grapes for white and red wine (pages 6–9).

Piper-Heidsieck Brut NV; Brut Rosé NV; Brut 76 79 82 85   CHAMPAGNE-makers of old repute at Reims, now owned by Rémy-Cointreau. Rare (76 79 85 88) and Brut Sauvage (79 82 85) are far ahead of their other, rather light wines. See also Piper Sonoma, California.

Pol Roger Brut White Foil NV; Brut 73 75 76 79 82 85 86 88; Rosé 75 79 82 85 86 88; Blanc de Chardonnay 79 82 85 86 88   Top-ranking family-owned CHAMPAGNE house at Epernay. Esp good NV White Foil, Rosé, Réserve PR (86 88) and CHARD. Sumptuous luxury CUVÉE: 'Sir Winston Churchill' (75 79 82 85 86).

Pomerol B'x r ****→****** 70 75' 81' 82' 83 85 86 88 89' 90' 92 93 94   Next village to ST-EMILION: similar but more plummy and creamy wines, maturing sooner, reliable and delicious. Top châteaux: CERTAN-DE-MAY, L'EVANGILE, LA FLEUR, LA FLEUR-PETRUS, LATOUR-A-POMEROL, PETRUS, TROTANOY, VIEUX CH CERTAN, etc.

Pommard Burg r ✱✱✱ 69 71 72 78' 82 83 85' 86 87 88' 89' 90 91 92 93 94 The biggest COTE D'OR village. Few superlative wines, but many potent and distinguished ones to age 10 yrs+. Best v'yds: Epenots, HOSPICES DE BEAUNE CUVEES, Rugiens. Growers incl Comte Armand, G Billard, Billard-Gonnet, J-M Boillot, de Courcel, Gaunoux, LEROY, MACHARD DE GRAMONT, de Montille, Mussy, Ch de Pommard, Pothier-Rieusset.

Pommery Brut NV; Rosé NV; Brut 82 83 85 87 89 Very big CHAMPAGNE growers and merchants at Reims, bought by Möet-Hennessy in '91. Wines are much improved. The luxury Louise Pommery (81 82 83 85 87 88), is outstanding. Louise Pommery Rosé (82 83 85 88 89).

Ponsot, J M 25-acre MOREY-ST-DENIS estate. Many GRANDS CRUS including CHAMBERTIN, CHAPELLE-C, LATRICIERES-C, CLOS DE LA ROCHE, CLOS ST-DENIS. V high quality.

Pouilly-Fuissé Burg w ✱✱→✱✱✱ 89' 90' 91 92 93 The best white of the MACON region. At its best (eg Ch Fuissé VIEILLES VIGNES) outstanding, but usually over-priced compared with (eg) CHABLIS. Good growers: Ferret, GUFFENS-HEYNEN, Luquet, Noblet, Vincent.

Pouilly-Fumé Lo w ✱✱→✱✱✱ 89 90' 91' 92' 93' 94 'Gun-flinty', fruity, often sharp white from upper Loire, nr SANCERRE. Grapes must be Sauv. Best CUVEES improve 5–6 yrs. Top growers incl Bailly, Blondelet, Dagueneau, Figeat, LADOUCETTE, Redde, Renaud, Saget, Tinel, Ch de Tracy.

Pouilly-Loché Burg w ✱✱ POUILLY-FUISSE's neighbour. Similar, much cheaper, but scarce.

Pouilly-sur-Loire Lo w ✱ DYA Inferior wine from the same v'yds as POUILLY-FUME but different grapes (Chasselas). Rarely seen today.

Pouilly-Vinzelles Burg w ✱✱ 88 89 90 91 92 Neighbour of POUILLY-FUISSE. Similar wine, worth looking for. Value.

Pousse d'Or, Domaine de la 32-acre estate in POMMARD, SANTENAY and esp VOLNAY, where its MONOPOLES Bousse d'Or and Clos des 60 Ouvrées are powerful, tannic, and justly famous.

Premier Cru First-growth in BORDEAUX, but the second rank of v'yds (after GRAND CRU) in Burgundy.

Premières Côtes de Blaye B'x r w ✱→✱✱ 82 85 86 88' 89' 90' 92 93 94 Restricted AC for better wines of BLAYE, greater emphasis on reds. Ch'x include Barbé, LE BOURDIEU, Charron, l'Escadre, Haut-Sociondo, Le Menaudat, La Rose-Bellevue, Segonzac, La Tonnelle.

Premières Côtes de Bordeaux B'x r w (p) dr sw ✱→✱✱ Large hilly area E of GRAVES across the R Garonne: a good bet for quality and value, upgrading sharply. Largely Merlot. Châteaux incl Bertinerie (esp), Carsin, La Croix de Roche, Fayau, Fontenil, Gardera, HAUT-BRIGNON, du Juge, Laffitte (sic), Lamothe, Peyrat, Plaisance, REYNON, Tanesse. An area to watch.

Prieur, Domaine Jacques Splendid 35-acre estate all at top Burgundy sites, incl PREMIER CRU MEURSAULT, VOLNAY, PULIGNY- and even LE MONTRACHET. Now 50% owned by RODET and quality rejuvenated, esp since '89.

Primeur 'Early' wine for refreshment and uplift; esp BEAUJOLAIS; VINS DE PAYS too. Wine sold 'En Primeur' is offered for sale still in barrel for future delivery.

Prissé See Mâcon-Villages.

Propriétaire-récoltant Owner-manager.

Provence See Côtes de Provence.

Puisseguin St-Emilion B'x r ✱✱ 82 85 86 88' 89' 90' 92 93 94 Eastern neighbour of ST-EMILION, its smallest 'satellite'; wines similar – not so fine or weighty but often good value. Ch'x incl La Croix de Berny, LAURETS, Puisseguin, Soleil, Teyssier, Vieux-Ch-Guibeau. Also Roc de Puisseguin from coop.

To decipher codes, please refer to symbols key at front of book, and to 'How to use this book' on page 5.

Puligny-Montrachet Burg (r) **** 78' 83' 85' 86' 88 89' 90' 91 92 93 94
Bigger neighbour of CHASSAGNE-MONTRACHET with potentially even finer,
more vital and complex rich dry whites. Apparent finesse can also be
the result of over-production. Best v'yds: BATARD-MONTRACHET, Bienvenues-
Bâtard-Montrachet, Champ-Canet, CHEVALIER-MONTRACHET, Clavoillon,
Les Combettes, MONTRACHET, Pucelles, etc. Top growers incl Amiot-
Bonfils, AMPEAU, J-M Boillot, BOUCHARD PERE, L Carillon, CHARTRON, H
Clerc, DROUHIN, JADOT, LATOUR, DOM LEFLAIVE, O LEFLAIVE, Pernot, SAUZET.

Quarts de Chaume Lo w sw *** 75 76 78' 79' 82 85' 86 88' 89' 90' 91 92
93' 94   Famous COTEAUX DU LAYON plot. Chenin grapes. Immensely
long-lived intense rich golden wine. Esp Beaumard, Bellerive, Suronde.

Quatourze Midi r w (p) * 89 90 91 92 93 94   Minor AC area nr Narbonne.
Best from Dom Notre Dame du Quatorze.

Quincy Lo w ** DYA   Small area: v dry SANCERRE-style wine of Sauv. Worth
trying. Growers: Domaine Mardon, Cave Romane de Brinay, Sorbe.

Ramonet, Domaine Leading estate in CHASSAGNE-MONTRACHET with 34 acres,
incl some MONTRACHET. Vg whites, and red CLOS ST-JEAN.

Rancio Term for the much-appreciated nutty tang of brown wood-aged
fortified wine, esp BANYULS and other VDN. A fault in table wines.

Rasteau S Rh r br sw (p w dr) ** 85' 86 88 89 90 92 93 94   Village for sound,
robust reds, esp Cave des Vignerons, Doms Charavin, Corinne Couturier,
St-Gayan, Soumade. Strong sweet dessert wine is (declining) speciality.

Ratafia de Champagne Sweet aperitif made in CHAMPAGNE of 67% grape
juice and 33% brandy. Not unlike PINEAU DE CHARENTE.

Récolte Crop or vintage.

Regnié Beauj r ** 91 92 93 94   BEAUJ village between MORGON and BROUILLY,
promoted to CRU in '88. About 1,800 acres. Try DUBOEUF's or Aucoeur's.

Reine Pédauque, La Long-established Burgundy growers and merchants
at ALOXE-CORTON with growing reputation, esp in duty-free. V'yds in
ALOXE-CORTON, SAVIGNY etc, and COTES DU RHONE. Owned by Pierre André.

Remoissenet Père & Fils Fine burgundy merchant (esp for whites) with a
tiny BEAUNE estate. Give his reds time. Also broker for NICOLAS wine
shops. Some of his best wines are from DOM THENARD.

Rémy Pannier Important Loire wine merchant at SAUMUR.

Reuilly Lo w (r p) ** DYA   Neighbour of QUINCY with similar wine, gaining in
reputation. NB New Chai de Reuilly. Also good Pinot Gr.

Riceys, Rosé des Champ p *** DYA   Minute AC in S CHAMPAGNE for a
notable Pinot N rosé. Principal producer: A Bonnet.

Richebourg Burg r **** 69' 71 72 76 78' 80' 82 83 85' 86 87 88' 89' 90'
91 92 93' 94   19-acre VOSNE-ROMANEE GRAND CRU. Powerful perfumed
fabulously expensive wine, among Burgundy's very best. Top growers:
BICHOT, GRIVOT, J Gros, LEROY, MEO-CAMUZET, DOM DE LA ROMANEE-CONTI.

Riesling See Grapes for white wine (pages 6–8).

Rion, Daniel et Fils 36-acre domaine in Prémeaux (NUITS). Excellent VOSNE-
ROMANEE (Les Chaumes, Les Beaumonts), Nuits PREMIER CRU Les Vignes
Rondes and CHAMBOLLE-MUSIGNY-Les Charmes. NB Also Patrice Rion.

Rivesaltes Midi r w br dr sw ** NV   Fortified wine of east Pyrenees. A
tradition v much alive, if struggling these days. Top producers:
Château de Calce, Dom Cazes, Château de Jau.

Roche-aux-Moines, La Lo w sw *** 75 76' 78 79 82 83 85' 86 88' 89' 90'
91 92' 93' 94   60-acre v'yd in SAVENNIERES, ANJOU. Intense strong
fruity/sharp wine, needs long ageing or drinking fresh.

Rodet, Antonin Substantial quality burgundy merchant with large (375-
acre) estate, esp in MERCUREY (Ch de Chamirey). See also Prieur. Now
owned by LAURENT-PERRIER.

Roederer, Louis Brut Premier NV; Rich NV; Brut 71 73 75 76 78 79 81 83
85 86 88 90; Bl de Blancs 88 90; Brut Rosé 75 83 85 86 88 91   One of
best CHAMPAGNE-growers and merchants at Reims. Reliable NV, plenty
of flavour. Luxury brand: velvety Cristal Brut (79 82 83 85 86 88), in
white glass bottles, needs time. See California, Australia (Tasmania).

Romanée, La Burg r **** 78' 82 83 85' 86 87' 88' 89' 90' 91 92 93 94 2-acre GRAND CRU in VOSNE-ROMANEE, just uphill from ROMANEE-CONTI. Monopole of Liger-Belair, sold by BOUCHARD PERE.

Romanée-Conti Burg r **** 66' 76 78' 80' 82 83 84 85' 86 87 88' 89' 90' 91 92 93' 4.3-acre MONOPOLE GRAND CRU in VOSNE-ROMANEE; 450 cases pa. The most celebrated and expensive red wine in the world, with reserves of flavour beyond imagination. 85 88 90 are astonishing. See next entry.

Romanée-Conti, Domaine de la (DRC) The grandest estate in Burgundy. Includes the whole of ROMANEE-CONTI and LA TACHE and major parts of ECHEZEAUX, GRANDS ECHEZEAUX, RICHEBOURG and ROMANEE-ST-VIVANT. Also v small parts of MONTRACHET and VOSNE-ROMANEE. Crown-jewel prices. Keep top DRC wines for decades.

Romanée-St-Vivant Burg r **** 76 78' 80' 82 83 85' 86 87 88' 89' 90' 91 92 93' 23-acre GRAND CRU in VOSNE-ROMANEE. Similar to ROMANEE-CONTI but lighter and less sumptuous. Top growers: DRC and LEROY.

Ropiteau Burgundy growers at MEURSAULT. Merchant business bought '94 by BOISSET.

Rosé d'Anjou Lo p * DYA Pale slightly sw rosé. CAB D'ANJOU should be better.

Rosé de Loire Lo p *→** DYA AC for dry Loire rosé (ANJOU is sweet).

Roty, Joseph Small grower of classic GEVREY-CHAMBERTIN, esp CHARMES- and MAZIS-CHAMBERTIN. Long-lived wines.

Rouget, Emmanuel Inheritor (nephew) of the legendary 13-acre estate of Henri Jayer in ECHEZEAUX, NUITS, VOSNE-ROMANEE. Top wine: V-R Cros Parantoux. Jayer (ret'd '88) still consults here and at DOM MEO-CAMUZET.

Roumier, Georges 35-acre domaine with exceptional BONNES-MARES, CLOS DE VOUGEOT, MUSIGNY, etc. High standards. Long-lasting reds.

Rousseau, Domaine A Major burgundy grower famous for CHAMBERTIN, etc, of v highest quality. Wines are intense, long-lived and mostly GRAND CRU.

Roussette de Savoie Savoie w ** DYA Tastiest of the fresh whites from S of Lake Geneva.

Roussillon Midi Largest producer of VDNS (often 'Grands Roussillons'). Lighter MUSCATS taking over from darker heavier wines. See Côtes du R.

Ruchottes-Chambertin Burg r *** 78' 80 83 85' 86 87 88' 89' 90' 91 92 93' 94 7.5-acre GRAND CRU neighbour of CHAMBERTIN. Similar splendid lasting wine of great finesse. Top growers: LEROY, Mugneret, ROUMIER, ROUSSEAU.

Ruinart Père & Fils 'R' de Ruinart Brut NV; 'R' de Ruinart Rosé NV; 'R' de Ruinart Brut 86 88 90 The oldest CHAMPAGNE house, now owned by Moët-Hennessy, with notably fine crisp wines, esp the luxury brands: Dom Ruinart Blanc de Blancs (81 82 83 85 86 88), Dom Ruinart Rosé (81 82 83 85 86). NB the vg mature Rosé. Good value.

Rully Burg r w (sp) ** 88' 89' 90' 91 92 93 COTE CHALONNAISE village famous for CREMANT. Still white and red are light but tasty, gd value, esp whites. Growers incl DELORME, FAIVELEY, Dom de la Folie, Jacquesson, A RODET.

Sables du Golfe du Lion Midi p r w * DYA VIN DE PAYS from Mediterranean sand-dunes: esp GRIS DE GRIS from Carignan, Grenache and Cinsaut. Dominated by LISTEL.

Sablet S Rh r w (p) ** 89 90 91 92 93 94 Admirable, improving COTES DU RHONE village, esp Dom de Boissan, Piaugier, Ch du Trignon, Dom de Verquière. Whites to try, too.

St-Amour Beauj r ** 91 92 93 94 Northernmost CRU of BEAUJOLAIS: light, fruity, irresistible. Growers to try: Janin, Patissier, Revillon.

St-André-de-Cubzac B'x r w *→** 88' 89' 90' 92' 93 94 Town 15 miles NE of BORDEAUX, centre of the minor Cubzaguais region. Sound reds have AC BORDEAUX SUPERIEUR. Incl: Domaine de Beychevelle, Ch du Bouilh, CH DE TERREFORT-QUANCARD, CH TIMBERLAY.

St-Aubin Burg w (r) ** 85' 86' 88 89' 90 91 92 93 94 Little-known neighbour of CHASSAGNE-MONTRACHET, up a side-valley. Several PREMIERS CRUS: light firm quite stylish wines at fair prices. Also sold as COTE DE BEAUNE-VILLAGES. Top growers: Clerget, JADOT, J Lamy, LAMY-PILLOT, H Prudhon, Roux, Thomas.

St-Bris Burg w (r) ✱ DYA Village west of CHABLIS known for fruity ALIGOTE, but chiefly for SAUVIGNON DE ST-BRIS. Also good CREMANT.

St-Chinian Midi r ✱→✱✱✱ 88 89 90 91 92 93 94 Hilly area of growing reputation in COTEAUX DU LANGUEDOC. AC since '82. Tasty southern reds, esp at Berlou.

St-Emilion B'x r ✱✱→✱✱✱✱ 70' 75 79' 81 82' 83' 85' 86' 88 89' 90' 92 93 94 The biggest top-quality BORDEAUX district (13,000 acres); solid rich tasty wines from hundreds of châteaux, incl AUSONE, CANON, CHEVAL BLANC, FIGEAC, MAGDELAINE, etc. Also a good coop.

St-Estèphe B'x r ✱✱→✱✱✱✱ 75 78' 79 81 82' 83' 85' 86 87 88' 89' 90' 91' 92 93 94 N village of HAUT-MEDOC. Solid, structured, sometimes superlative wines. Top châteaux: COS D'ESTOURNEL, MONTROSE, CALON-SEGUR, etc, and more notable CRUS BOURGEOIS than any other HAUT-MEDOC commune.

Apples into milk

Malolactic (or secondary) fermentation sometimes happens after the first (alcoholic) fermentation. It is the natural conversion of excess malic (sharp) acid in the wine into (milder) lactic acid. It is generally desirable in cool, high-acid wine regions, not in warm regions where a touch of sharpness is a balancing attribute. It can be encouraged or prevented. Where the acidity can be spared 'malo' adds 'complexity' to flavours.

St-Gall Brut NV; Extra Brut NV; Brut Blanc de Blancs NV; Brut Rosé NV; Brut Bl de Blancs 88; Cuvée Or Pale 85 Brand name used by Union-Champagne, the vg CHAMPAGNE-growers' coop at AVIZE. Style is usually softer than true BRUT.

St-Georges-St-Emilion B'x r ✱✱ 82 83' 85' 86' 88' 89' 90' 92 93 94 Part of MONTAGNE-ST-EMILION with high standards. Best châteaux: Belair-Montaiguillon, Marquis-St-G, ST-GEORGES, Tour du Pas-St-G.

St-Gervais S Rh r (w) ★ West bank S Rhône village. Sound coop, excellent Dom Ste-Anne reds (marked Mourvèdre flavours); whites incl a VIOGNIER.

St-Jean de Minervois Min w sw ✱✱→✱✱✱ Perhaps the best French MUSCAT: sweet and fine, esp from Dom de Barroubio, Michel Sige, Coop St-Jean de Minervois. Vg recent progress.

St-Joseph N Rh r (p w) ✱✱ 83 85 86 88 89 90 93 94 AC stretching the whole length of N Rhône (40 miles). Delicious, fruit-packed wines at its core, around Tournon; elsewhere quality variable. Often better than CROZES-HERMITAGE, esp from CHAPOUTIER, CHAVE, Chèze, Coursodon, Gaillard, B Gripa, Grippat, JABOULET, Paret, Trollat. Good whites.

St-Julien B'x r ✱✱✱→✱✱✱✱✱ 70' 75 78' 79 81' 82' 83' 85' 86 87' 88' 89' 90' 91 92 93 94 Mid-MEDOC village with a dozen of BORDEAUX's best châteaux, incl three LEOVILLES, BEYCHEVELLE, DUCRU-BEAUCAILLOU, GRUAUD-LAROSE, etc. The epitome of well-balanced, fragrant and savoury red wine.

St-Nicolas-de-Bourgueil Lo r ✱✱ 82 83 85' 86 88 89' 90' 91 92 93' 94 The next village to BOURGUEIL: the same lively and fruity Cab F red. Top growers: Amirault, Cognard, Jamet, Mabilleau, Taluau.

St-Péray N Rh w sp ✱✱ NV Rather heavy Rhône white, much of it sparkling. A curiosity worth trying once. Top names: J-F Chaboud, J-L Thiers.

St-Pourçain-sur-Sioule Central France r p w ★→✱✱ DYA Light but venerable local wine of Vichy. Red and rosé made from Gamay and/or Pinot, white from Tressalier and/or CHARD or Sauv. Recent vintages improved but still pricey. Top growers: Ray, Dom de Bellevue and good coop.

St-Romain Burg r w ✱✱ (w) 86' 88 89' 90' 91 92 93 94 Overlooked village just behind the COTE DE BEAUNE. Value, esp for firm fresh whites. Reds have a clean 'cut'. Top growers: FEVRE, Jean Germain, Gras, LATOUR, LEROY, Thévenin-Monthélie.

St-Véran Burg w ✱✱ 90 91 92 93 94 Next-door AC to POUILLY-FUISSE. Similar but better value: real character from the best slopes of MACON-VILLAGES. Try DUBOEUF's, Dom des Deux Roches, Demessey, CH FUISSE and Dom des Valanges.

Ste-Croix-du-Mont B'x w sw ** 75 76' 82 83 86' 88' 89 90 91 92 93
Neighbour to SAUTERNES with similar golden wine. No superlatives but
well worth trying, esp Clos des Coulinats, Ch Loubens, Ch Lousteau
Vieil, Ch du Mont. Often a bargain, esp with age.

Salon 71 73 76 79 82 The original Blanc de Blancs CHAMPAGNE, from Le
Mesnil in the Côte de Blancs. Superlative intense v dry wine with long
keeping qualities in tiny quantities. Bought in '88 by LAURENT-PERRIER.

Sancerre Lo w (r p) *** 89 90' 91 92' 93' 94 Very fragrant and fresh Sauv
Bl, almost indistinguishable from POUILLY-FUME, its neighbour across
the Loire. Top wines can age 5 yrs+. Also light Pinot N red (best drunk
at 2–3 yrs) and rosé. Occasional vg VENDANGES TARDIVES. Top growers
incl Bailly, Bourgeois, Ch de Sancerre, CORDIER, Cotat, Crochet, Gitton,
Jolivet, Laporte, Pinard, Reverdy and Vacheron.

Santenay Burg r (w) *** 78' 82 83 85' 87 88' 89' 90 91 92 93 94 Sturdy
reds from village S of CHASSAGNE. Best v'yds: La Comme, Les Gravières,
Clos de Tavannes. Top growers: Lequin-Roussot, MOREY, POUSSE D'OR.

Saumur Lo r p w sp *→** Versatile district in ANJOU. Fresh fruity whites, vg
CREMANT (producers incl BOUVET-LADUBAY), pale rosés and increasingly
good Cab F (see next entry).

Saumur-Champigny Lo r 82 85 86' 88 89' 90' 91 92 93' 94 Flourishing
10-village AC for fresh Cab F ageing remarkably in sunny yrs. Look for
Ch'x de Chaintres, du Hureau, Dom Filliatreau, Ruault, coop St-Cyr.

Saussignac Dordogne w sw AC ('82) for almondy sweet wines only, like
MONBAZILLAC. Top grower Ch Court-les-Mûts.

Sauternes B'x w sw **→**** 67' 71' 75 76' 78 79' 80' 81 82 83' 85 86' 88'
89' 90' 91 92 District of 5 villages (incl BARSAC) which make France's
best sweet wine, strong (14%+ alcohol), luscious and golden,
demanding to be aged. Top châteaux are D'YQUEM, CLIMENS, COUTET,
GUIRAUD, SUDUIRAUT, etc. Dry wines cannot be sold as Sauternes.

Sauvignon Blanc See Grapes for white wine (pages 6–8).

Sauvignon de St-Bris Burg w ** DYA A baby VDQS cousin of SANCERRE, from
nr CHABLIS. To try. 'Dom Saint Prix' from Dom Bersan is good.

Sauvion & Fils Ambitious and well-run MUSCADET house, based at the Ch de
Cléray. Top wine: Cardinal Richard.

Sauzet, Etienne Top-quality white burgundy estate at PULIGNY-MONTRACHET.
Clearly-defined, well-bred wines, at best superb.

Savennières Lo w dr sw *** 75 76' 78' 82 83 85 86' 88 89' 90' 93 94 Small
ANJOU district of pungent long-lived whites, incl Clos du Papillon,
COULEE DE SERRANT, Ch d'Epiré, ROCHE-AUX-MOINES.

Savigny-lès-Beaune Burg r (w) *** 78' 85' 87 88' 89' 90' 91 92 93 94
Important village next to BEAUNE, similar balanced mid-weight wines,
often deliciously lively, fruity. Top v'yds: Dominode, Les Guettes,
Marconnets, Serpentières, Vergelesses; growers: BIZE, Camus, CHANDON
DE BRIAILLES, CLAIR, Ecard, Girard-Vollot, LEROY, Pavelot, TOLLOT-BEAUT.

Savoie E France r w sp ** DYA Alpine area with light dry wines like some
Swiss or minor Loires. APREMONT, CREPY and SEYSSEL are best-known
whites, ROUSSETTE is more interesting. Also good MONDEUSE red.

Schaller, Edgard ALSACE grower (dry style wines) in Mandelburg GRAND CRU,
Mittelwihr; esp for Ries 'Mambourg Vieilles Vignes' (needs time) and
'Les Amandiers' (younger-drinking).

Schlumberger ALSACE grower-merchants at Guebwiller. Unusually rich
wines incl luscious Kessler and Kitterlé GRAND CRU GEWURZ (also SGN
and VT). Fine Kitterlé and Saering Ries. Also good Pinot Gr.

Schoffit, Domaine Colmar ALSACE house with Grand Cru Rangen Pinot Gris,
Gewurz of top quality. Chasselas is unusual daily delight.

Schröder & Schÿler Old BORDEAUX merchants, owners of CH KIRWAN.

Sciacarello Red grape of CORSICA's best red and rosé, eg AJACCIO, Sartène.

For key to grape variety abbreviations, see pages 6–9.

Sec Literally means dry, though CHAMPAGNE so-called is medium-sweet (and better at breakfast, tea-time and weddings than BRUT).

Séguret S Rh r w ✳ Good S Rhône Village, nr GIGONDAS. Peppery, quite full red, rounded clean white. Esp Ch La Couran015çonne, Dom de Cabasse.

Sélection des Grains Nobles (SGN) Description coined by HUGEL for ALSACE equivalent to German Beerenauslese. Grains nobles are individual grapes with 'noble rot' (see page 77).

Sèvre-et-Maine The département containing the best v'yds of MUSCADET.

Seyssel Savoie w sp ✳✳ NV Delicate pale dry Alpine white, making very pleasant sparkling wine.

Sichel & Co Two famous merchant houses. In BORDEAUX Peter A Sichel runs Maison Sichel and owns CH D'ANGLUDET and part of CH PALMER, with interests in VAL D'ORBIEU. In Germany, Peter M F Sichel (of New York) runs Sichel Söhne, makers of BLUE NUN and respected merchants.

Silvaner See Grapes for white wine (pages 6–8).

Sipp, Jean and Louis Ribeauvillé GRAND CRU ALSACE producers competing to make finest Ries (in Kirchberg): Jean's with youthful elegance (smaller v'yd, own vines only), Louis' finer when mature.

Sirius Serious oak-aged blended BORDEAUX from Maison SICHEL.

Skalli Dynamic producer of top VINS DE PAYS D'OC from Cab, Merlot, CHARD, etc etc, at Sète in the Languedoc. FORTANT DE FRANCE is standard brand; style and value.

Sparr, Pierre Sigolsheim ALSACE grower/producer, as good at CUVÉES of several grapes (eg Symphonie) as rich GRANDS CRUS.

Sur Lie See Lie and Muscadet.

Syrah See Grapes for red wine (pages 8–9).

Tâche, La Burg r ✳✳✳✳ 69' 76 78' 80' 82 83 85' 86 87 88' 89' 90' 91 92 93' 15-acre (1,500 case) GRAND CRU of VOSNE-ROMANÉE and one of best v'yds on earth: dark perfumed luxurious wine. See DOM DE LA ROMANÉE-CONTI.

Taittinger Brut NV; Rosé NV; Brut 73 75 76 78 79 80 82 83 85 86 88 89; Collection Brut 78 81 82 83 85 86 88 Fashionable Reims CHAMPAGNE growers and merchants with a light flowery touch. Luxury brand: Comtes de Champagne Blanc de Blancs (79 81 82 83 85 86 88), also vg Rosé (79 83 85 86). Also owns Champagne Irroy. See also Domaine Carneros, California.

Tastevin, Confrérie des Chevaliers du Burgundy's colourful successful promotion society. Wine with their Tastevinage label has been approved by them and is usually of a fair standard. A tastevin is the traditional shallow silver wine-tasting cup of Burgundy. See also page 18.

Tavel Rh p ✳✳✳ DYA France's most famous, though not her best, rosé: strong and dry. Best growers: Ch d'Aquéria, Bernard, Dom Corne-Loup, Maby, Dom de la Mordorée, Ch de Trinquevedel. Drink v young.

Tempier, Domaine Top grower of BANDOL, with noble reds and rosé.

Thénard, Domaine The major grower of GIVRY, but best known for his substantial portion (4+ acres) of LE MONTRACHET. Could still try harder with this jewel.

Thorin, J Grower and major merchant of BEAUJOLAIS, owner of the Château des Jacques, MOULIN-A-VENT.

Thouarsais, Vin de Lo r w ✳ DYA Light Gamay and Sauv VDQS S of SAUMUR.

Tokay d'Alsace See under Pinot Gris (Grapes for white wine – pages 6–8).

Tollot-Beaut Stylish burgundy grower with 50+ acres in the CÔTE DE BEAUNE, incl Beaune Grèves, CORTON, SAVIGNY- (Les Champs Chevrey) and at his CHOREY-LES-BEAUNE base.

Touchais, Moulin Extraordinary luscious COTEAUX DU LAYON from remarkable old stocks of the Touchais family. Vintages back to the '20s are like creamy honey and not over-priced.

Touraine Lo r p w dr sw sp ✳→✳✳✳ Big mid-Loire province with immense range, incl dry white Sauv, dry and sweet Chenin (eg VOUVRAY), red CHINON and BOURGUEIL, light red Cabs, Gamays, rosés; often bargains. Amboise, Azay-le-Rideau and Mesland are sub-sections of the AC.

Trapet Two domaines in GEVREY-CHAMBERTIN, both good; esp R Trapet.

Trévallon, Domaine de Provence r *** Fashionable estate at LES BAUX with rich intense Cab-Syrah blend to age.

Trimbach, F E Distinguished ALSACE grower and merchant at Ribeauvillé. Best wines include the austere Ries CLOS STE-HUNE, GRAND CRU Geisberg and Cuvée Frédéric-Emile (Ries from GC Osterberg). Also Gewurz.

Turckheim, Cave Vinicole de Perhaps the best coop in ALSACE. Many fine wines incl GRANDS CRUS from 900+ acres, eg vg Pinot Gr from GC Hengst.

Tursan SW France r p w * DYA Emerging VDQS in Landes. Sound red (light, holiday-drinking) and white. Ch de Bachen (***), owned by the *** chef Michel Gérard, guarantees notoriety and suggests an AC on the way.

Vacqueyras S Rh r ** 85 86 88 89 90 91 92 93 94 Neighbour to GIGONDAS and often cheaper. Try JABOULET's version, Ch de Montmirail, Ch des Tours, Dom des Amouriers or Pascal Frères.

Val d'Orbieu, Vignerons du Association of some 200 top growers and coops in CORBIERES, COTEAUX DU LANGUEDOC, MINERVOIS, ROUSSILLON etc, with Maison SICHEL marketing a first-class range of selected MIDI AC wines.

Valençay Lo w * DYA VDQS neighbour of CHEVERNY: similar pleasant sharpish.

Vallée du Paradis Midi r w p * Popular VINS DE PAYS of local red varieties.

Vallouit, Louis de N Rhône family co mixing v'yd ownership (biggest in COTE ROTIE; esp Les Roziers, ST-JOSEPH Les Anges) with négociant business.

Valréas S Rh r (p w) ** 88 90 92 93 94 COTES DU RHONE village with big coop. Good mid-weight reds, improving whites. Esp Romain Bouchard, Dom des Grands Devers.

Varichon & Clerc Principal makers and shippers of SAVOIE sparkling wines.

Varoilles, Domaine des Burgundy estate of 30 acres, principally in GEVREY-CHAMBERTIN. Tannic wines with great keeping qualities.

Vaudésir Burg w **** 78' 83' 85' 86 88 89' 90 91 92 93 94 Arguably the best of 7 CHABLIS GRANDS CRUS (but then so are the others).

VDQS Vin Délimité de Qualité Supérieure (see page 21).

Vendange Harvest.

Vendange Tardive Late harvest. In ALSACE equivalent to German Auslese, but stronger and frequently less fine.

Veuve Clicquot Yellow label NV; White Label Demi-Sec NV; Gold Label 76 78 79 82 83 (since '85 called Vintage Réserve: 85 88); Rosé Reserve 83 85 Historic CHAMPAGNE house of highest standing, now owned by LVMH. Full-bodied, almost rich: one of Champagne's surest things. Cellars at Reims. Luxury brand: La Grande Dame (79 83 85 88).

Vidal-Fleury, J Long-established shippers of top Rhône wines and grower of COTE ROTIE. Bought in '85 by GUIGAL.

Vieilles Vignes Old vines – therefore the best wine. Used by many, esp by BOLLINGER, DE VOGUE and CH FUISSE.

Viénot, Charles Grower-merchant of good burgundy, owned by BOISSET at NUITS-ST-GEORGES. 70 acres in CORTON, Nuits, RICHEBOURG, etc.

Vieux Télégraphe, Domaine du S Rh r (w) *** 78' 79 81 82 83 85 86 88 89 90 91 92 93 A leader in fine, vigorous, modern red CHATEAUNEUF-DU-PAPE, and fresh whites. New second wine: Vieux Mas des Papes. Second domaine: de la Roquette.

Vignoble Area of vineyards.

Vin de l'année This year's wine. See Beaujolais, Beaujolais-Villages.

Vin Doux Naturel (VDN) Sweet wine, fortified with wine alcohol, so the sweetness is 'natural', not the strength. The speciality of ROUSSILLON. A vin doux liquoreux is several degrees stronger.

Vin de garde Wine that will improve with keeping. The serious stuff.

Vin Gris 'Grey' wine is v pale pink, made of red grapes pressed before fermentation begins, unlike rosé which ferments briefly before pressing. Oeil de Perdrix means much the same; so does 'blush'.

NB Vintages in colour are those you should choose first for drinking in 1996.

Vin Jaune Jura w *** Speciality of ARBOIS: odd yellow wine like fino sherry. Normally ready when bottled (at at least 7 yrs old). Best is CH-CHALON.

Vin nouveau See Beaujolais Nouveau.

Vin de paille Wine from grapes dried on straw mats, consequently v sweet, like Italian passito. Esp in the JURA. See also Chave.

The vin de pays revolution

The junior rank of country wines. No one should overlook this category, the most dynamic in France today. More than 140 vins de pays names have come into active use recently, mainly in the Midi. They fall into three categories: regional (eg Vin de Pays d'Oc for the whole Midi); departmental (eg Vin de Pays du Gard for the Gard département near the mouth of the Rhône), and vins de pays de zone, the most precise, usually with the highest standards. Single-grape vins de pays and vins de pays primeurs (reds and whites, all released on the third Thursday in November) are especially popular. Well-known zonal vins de pays include Coteaux de l'Uzège, Côtes de Gascogne, Val d'Orbieu. Don't hesitate. There are some real gems among them, and many charming trinkets.

Vin de Table Standard everyday table wine, not subject to particular regulations about grapes and origin. Choose VINS DE PAYS instead.

Vin Vert Very light acidic refreshing white wine, a speciality of ROUSSILLON (and v necessary in summer in those torrid parts).

Vinsobres S Rh r (p w) ** 85 86 88 89 90 92 93 94 Contradictory name of good S Rhône village. Potentially substantial reds, but many ordinary. Best producers incl Dom les Aussellons, Dom du Moulin.

Viré See Mâcon-Viré.

Visan S Rh r p w ** 88 89 90 93 94 Village for far better reds than whites.

Viticulteur Wine-grower.

Vogüé, Comte Georges de ('Dom les Musigny') First-class 30-acre domaine at CHAMBOLLE-MUSIGNY. At best the ultimate BONNES-MARES and MUSIGNY.

Volnay Burg r *** 78 83 85' 87 88' 89' 90' 91 92 93 94 Village between POMMARD and MEURSAULT: often the best reds of the COTE DE BEAUNE, not dark or heavy but structured and silky. Best v'yds: Caillerets, Champans, Clos des Chênes, Clos des Ducs, etc. Best growers: D'ANGERVILLE, J Boillot, HOSPICES DE BEAUNE, LAFARGE, LAFON, de Montille, POUSSE D'OR, M ROSSIGNOL.

Volnay-Santenots Burg r *** Excellent red wine from MEURSAULT is sold under this name. Indistinguishable from Premier Cru VOLNAY.

Vosne-Romanée Burg r ***→**** 78' 83 85' 86 87 88' 89' 90' 91 92 93 94 Village with Burgundy's grandest CRUS (ROMANEE-CONTI, LA TACHE, etc). There are (or should be) no common wines in Vosne. Many good growers incl Arnoux, Castagnier, CHEVIGNY, ENGEL, GRIVOT, Gros, JAYER, LATOUR, LEROY, MEO-CAMUZET, MONGEARD-MUGNERET, Mugneret, RION, DRC.

Vougeot See Clos de Vougeot.

Vouvray Lo w dr sw sp **→**** 76' 78' 79 82 83 85' 86 88 89' 90' 91 92 93 94 Small district of TOURAINE with v variable wines, increasingly good, reliable, at their best intensely sweet, almost immortal. Good dry sparkling. Best producers: Allias, BREDIF, Brisebarre, Champalou, Foreau, Fouquet, Ch Gaudrelle, Huet, Ch Moncontour, Poniatowski.

Willm, A N ALSACE grower at Barr, with vg GEWURZ Clos Gaensbronnel.

'Y' (pronounced 'ygrec') 78' 79' 80' 84 85 86 87 88 89 Dry wine produced occasionally at CH D'YQUEM. Most interesting with age.

Ziltener, André Swiss burgundy grower/mail-order merchant with entertaining cellars at Ch Ziltener, CHAMBOLLE MUSIGNY. Wide range; sound wines.

Zind-Humbrecht 64-acre ALSACE estate in Thann, Turckheim, Wintzenheim. First-rate single-v'yd wines (esp Clos St-Urbain Ries), and v fine from GRANDS CRUS Goldert (GEWURZ and MUSCAT), Hengst and Rangen.

Châteaux of Bordeaux

The golden years of the 1980s are still with us. It was perhaps the greatest decade for ripe vintages Bordeaux has ever known. Those who bought the wines of '81, '82, '83, '85, '86, '88, '89 or '90 when they were young either have treasured bottles and appreciating assets, or at least sweet memories. Earlier years are now drinking, with increasing sweetness as their maturity approaches. The great trio of '88, '89, '90 are starting to try our patience as their wines move through adolescence. They are not to be hurried.

Meanwhile we have the lean years of '91 and '92 to pick among for bargains – they certainly exist – and the almost twin pair of '93 and '94 to contemplate for the future. The '94 vintage repeated the pattern of '93 with sadistic accuracy, heavy harvest rain on ripe grapes drowning the very real prospect of another '90. Many growers feel that their best vats of '94 were little affected by the rain. Grape-skins were thick, the juice inside concentrated and sweet. 1976 was a similar vintage: hot, then wet. 20 years later you can detect the dilution – but only just.

As in last year's edition I have picked out in colour the vintages which proprietors themselves will be serving this year as first choices: their own wines in the state of maturity they prefer. Their choices remind us that there are no absolutes in wine – least of all in the glorious diversity of Bordeaux.

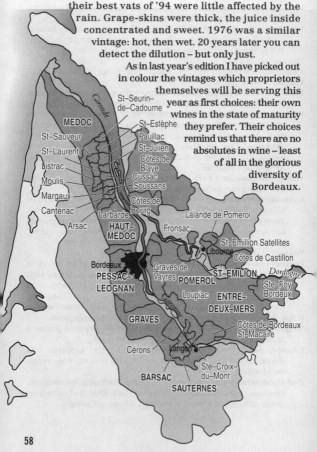

- Gironde
- St-Seurin-de-Cadourne
- MEDOC
- St-Estèphe
- St-Sauveur
- Pauillac
- St-Laurent
- St-Julien
- Côtes de Blaye
- Listrac
- Cussac
- Moulis
- Soussans
- Margaux
- Côtes de Bourg
- Cantenac
- Larbarde
- Lalande de Pomerol
- Arsac
- HAUT-MEDOC
- Fronsac
- St-Emilion Satellites
- Libourne
- Côtes de Castillon
- Bordeaux
- Graves de Vayres
- ST-EMILION
- PESSAC-LEOGNAN
- POMEROL
- Dordogne
- Ste-Foy Bordeux
- Loupiac
- ENTRE-DEUX-MERS
- GRAVES
- Côtes de Bordeaux St-Macaire
- Cérons
- Langon
- Ste-Croix-du-Mont
- BARSAC
- SAUTERNES

> *Vintages shown in light type should only be opened now out of curiosity to gauge their future. Vintages shown in bold type are deemed (usually by their makers) to be ready for drinking. Remember though that the French tend to enjoy the vigour of young wines, and that many 82s, 83s, 85s and 86s have at least another decade of development in front of them. Vintages marked thus ' are regarded as particularly successful for the property in question. Vintages in colour are the special selection for '96.*

d'Agassac H-Méd r ★★ 82' 83' 85' 86 88 89' 90' 91 92 93 94 Sleeping Beauty 14th-C moated fort. 86 acres v nr Bordeaux suburbs. Same owners as châteaux CALON-SEGUR and DU TERTRE. Lively wine much drunk in Holland.

d'Alesme Mar r ★★ 81 82 83 85 86 88' 89 90 94 Tiny (17-acre) third-growth, formerly 'Marquis-d'Alesme'. A lost CRU CLASSE, once highly regarded. Potential.

Andron-Blanquet St-Est r ★★ 82 85' 86 88 89' 90 92 93 94 Sister château to COS-LABORY. 40 acres. Wines lack charm.

L'Angélus St-Em r ★★★ 79' 81 82 83' 85' 86 87' 88 89' 90' 92 93 94' Well-sited 57-acre classed-growth on ST-EMILION COTES. A recent star.

d'Angludet Cant-Mar r ★★–★★★ 70' 76' 78' 79 80 81' 82 83 85 86 87 88' 89' 90 91 92 93 94 75-acre CRU EXCEPTIONNEL of classed-growth quality owned by Peter A Sichel. Lively fragrant MARGAUX of great style. Value.

d'Archambeau Graves r w dr (sw) ★★ (r) 85 86 88 89 90 91 92 93 94 (w) 88 90' 92' 93 Up-to-date 54-acre property at Illats. Vg fruity dry white; since '85 fragrant barrel-aged reds (planned to be ¾ of v'yard).

d'Arche Saut w sw ★★ 81 82 83' 85 86' 88' 89' 90 93 94 Classed-growth of 88 acres rejuvenated since '80. Modern methods. Rich juicy wines.

d'Arcins Central Méd r ★★ 86 88 89 90 93 94 185-acre Castel family property (Castelvin is a well-known VIN DE TABLE). Sister to next-door Barreyres (160 acres).

d'Armailhac Pau r ★★★ 78' 79 81 82' 83 85 86' 87 88 89 90' 91 92 93 94' New name ('91) for CH MOUTON-BARONNE-PHILIPPE. Substantial fifth growth nurtured by the late Baron Philippe de Rothschild. 125 acres: wine less rich and luscious than MOUTON-ROTHSCHILD, but outstanding in its class.

l'Arrosée St-Em r ★★★ 79 81 82 83 85' 86' 87 88 89' 90' 93 94' 24-acre COTES estate. Name means watered, but wine is top-flight: opulent, structured. Modern cuvier; 100% new barrels.

Ausone St-Em r ★★★★ 75 76 78' 79 81 82' 83' 85 86' 87 88 89 90 91 92 93 94 First-growth with 17 acres (about 2,500 cases) in the best position on the COTES with famous rock-hewn cellars. The most expensive ST-EMILION, but far behind CHEVAL BLANC or FIGEAC in performance. See also Ch Belair.

Bahans-Haut-Brion Graves r ★★★ NV and 82 83 85 86' 87 88 89' 90 91 92 93 94 The second-quality wine of CH HAUT-BRION. Wine worthy of its noble origin.

Balestard-la-Tonnelle St-Em r ★★ 81 83 85 86' 87 88' 89 90' 92 93 94 Historic 30-acre classed-growth on the plateau. Big flavour; more finesse since '85. New chai in '95.

de Barbe Côtes de Bourg r (w) ★★ 85 86 88 89 90 92 93 94 The biggest (148 acres), best-known château of BOURG. Light fruity Merlot.

Baret Pessac-L r w ★★ (r) 83 85 86 88 89' 90' Famous name recovered from a lull. Now run by BORIE-MANOUX. White well-made, too.

The following abbreviations of regional names are used in the text:

B'x	Bordeaux	Méd	Médoc	St-Em	St-Emilion
E-Deux-Mers	Entre-Deux-Mers	Pau	Pauillac	St-Est	St-Estèphe
		Pessac-L	Pessac-Léognan	St-Jul	St-Julien
H-Méd	Haut-Médoc			Saut	Sauternes
Mar	Margaux	Pom	Pomerol		

Bastor-Lamontagne Saut w sw ****** 76 79 82 83 85 86 87 88' 89' 90' 94 Large Bourgeois Preignac château with same owners as CH BEAUREGARD. Classed-growth quality; excellent rich wines. Second label: Les Remparts de Bastor (92 93). Also Ch St-Robert at Pujols: red and white GRAVES. 10,000 cases.

Batailley Pau r ******* 70 75' 78' 79' 81 82' 83' 85' 86 87 88' 89' 90' 91 92 93 94 The bigger of the famous pair of fifth-growths (with HAUT-BATAILLEY) on the borders of PAUILLAC and ST-JULIEN. 110 acres. Fine, firm, strong-flavoured wine. Home of the Castéja family of BORIE-MANOUX.

Beaumont Cussac (H-Méd) r ****** 82 85 86' 88 89' 90' 91 92 93' 94 200-acre+ CRU BOURGEOIS, well-known in France for easily enjoyable and improving wines from maturing vines. Second label: Ch Moulin d'Arvigny. 35,000 cases. In the same hands as CH BEYCHEVELLE since '87.

Beauregard Pom r ******* 82' 83 85 86 87 88 89' 90' 92 93 94' 42-acre v'yd; fine 17th-C château nr LA CONSEILLANTE owned by a bank. Top-rank rich wines. Advice from M Rolland. Second label: Benjamin de Beauregard.

Beau-Séjour-Bécot St-Em r ****** 75 82' 83 85 86' 88' 89' 90' 91 92 93 94 The other half of BEAUSÉJOUR-DUFFAU-LAGAROSSE; 45 acres. Controversially demoted in class in '85 but much revved-up since. The Bécots also own CH GRAND-PONTET.

Beau-Site St-Est r ****** 75' 78' 79 81 82 83 85 86' 87 88 89' 90 92 93 55-acre CRU BOURGEOIS EXCEPTIONNEL in same hands as CH BATAILLEY etc. Quality and substance typical of ST-ESTEPHE.

Beauséjour-Duffau-Lagarosse St-Em r ******* 82 83 85 86 88 89' 90' 93 94 Part of the old Beau-Séjour Premier Grand Cru estate on W slope of the COTES. 17 acres in old family hands; firm-structured, concentrated.

de Bel-Air Lalande de Pom r ****** 82' 85 86 88' 89' 90 92 93 94' The best-known estate of L de P, just N of POMEROL. Pomerol-style wine. 37 acres.

Bel-Air-Marquis-d'Aligre Soussans-Mar r ****** 79' 81 82' 85 86 88 89 90 Organically-run CRU EXCEPTIONNEL with 42 acres of old vines giving only 3,500 cases. The owner likes gutsy wine.

Bel-Orme-Tronquoy-de-Lalande St-Seurin-de-Cadourne (H-Méd) r ****** 81 82 83 85 86 87 88 89 90 92 93 94 60-acre CRU BOURGEOIS N of ST-ESTEPHE. Old v'yd producing tannic wines. More effort; new manager.

Belair St-Em r ******* 75' 78 79' 82' 83' 85' 86' 88' 89' 90' 92 93 94 Sister château/neighbour of AUSONE. Wine a shade easier, less tight. V high standard recently. Also NV Roc-Blanquant (magnums only).

Belgrave St-Laurent r ****** 81 82 83 85 86' 87 88 89 90' Obscure fifth growth in ST-JULIEN's back-country. 107 acres. Managed by DOURTHE since '79. Second label: Diane de Belgrave.

Bellegrave Listrac r ****** 82 83 85 86 88 89 90 92 93 38-acre CRU BOURGEOIS making full-flavoured wine with advice from PICHON-LALANDE.

Berliquet St-Em r ****** 78 81 82 83 85 86 88 89' 90 91 92 93 94 23-acre Grand Cru Classé recently v well-run (sold by the ST-EMILION coop).

Bertineau St-Vincent Lalande de Pom r ****** 10 acres owned by top oenologist Michel Rolland (see also Le Bon Pasteur).

Beychevelle St-Jul r *****→******* 70' 78 81 82' 83 85 86' 87 88 89' 90 91 92 93 94' 170-acre fourth growth with MEDOC's finest mansion. Owned by an insurance company since '85. Wine of elegance and power, just below top-flight ST-JULIEN. Second wine: Amiral de Beychevelle.

Biston-Brillette Moulis r ****** Another attractive MOULIS. 7,000 cases.

Le Bon Pasteur Pom r ******* 70 75 76 81 82 83 85 86' 87 88 89' 90' 92 93 94' Excellent small property on ST-EM boundary, owned by consultant oenologist Michel Rolland. Concentrated, s'times even creamy wines.

Bonalgue Pom r ****** Ambitious 2,500-case estate to watch. Les Hautes-Tuileries is sister château. Wines built to age.

Bonnet E-Deux-Mers r w ****** (r) 90 92 93 94 (w) DYA Big-scale producer (600 acres!) of some of the best ENTRE-DEUX-MERS.

Le Boscq St-Est r ****** 82 83 85 86 87 88 89' 90 92 93 Leading CRU BOURGEOIS giving excellent value in tasty ST-ESTEPHE ('Vieilles Vignes').

Le Bourdieu-Vertheuil H-Méd r ** 81 82 83 85 86 88 89 90' 92 93' 94
Vertheuil CRU BOURGEOIS with sister château, Victoria, (134 acres in all);
well-made ST-ESTEPHE-style wines. New owners, equipment and effort
since '90.

Bourgneuf Pom r ** 81 82 83 85' 86 88 89' 90 92 93   22-acre v'yd on
chalky clay soil, making fairly rich wines with typically plummy
POMEROL perfume. 5,000 cases. Alias Bourgneuf-Vayron.

Bouscaut Graves r w ** 81 82' 83 85 86' 88 89 90 92 93   Classed-growth
at Cadaujac bought in '80 by Lucien Lurton of CH BRANE-CANTENAC etc.
75 acres red (largely Merlot); 15 acres white. Never yet brilliant, but
slowly getting there.

du Bousquet Côtes de Bourg r ** 82 83 85 86 88 89 90' 92 93   Reliable
estate with 148 acres making attractive solid wine.

Boyd-Cantenac Mar r *** 78' 81 82' 83' 85 86' 88 89 90 91 92 93 94'
44-acre third growth often producing attractive wine, full of flavour,
if not of third-growth class. See also Ch Pouget.

Branaire-Ducru St-Jul r *** 75' 79' 81 82' 83 85 86 87 88 89' 90' 91 92 93
Fourth growth of 125 acres, producing notably spicy and flavoury
wine in the '70s. The late '80s saw a full-scale revival. New owners in
'88. Second label: Duluc.

Brane-Cantenac Cantenac-Mar r *** 75' 78' 79 81 82' 83 85 86' 87 88
89 90   Big (211-acre) second growth. Rich, even gamey wines of
strong character. Same owners as CH'X BOUSCAUT, CLIMENS, DURFORT-
VIVENS, VILLEGEORGE, etc. Second labels: Ch'x Baron de Brane, Notton.

du Breuil Cissac r ** 88 89 90 92 93   Abandoned historic château bought
by owners of CISSAC and restored. To follow.

Brillette Moulis r ** 81' 82 83 85' 86 88 89' 90 91 92 93   70-acre CRU
BOURGEOIS. Reliable and attractive. Second label: Berthault Brillette.

La Cabanne Pom r ** 79 81 82' 83 85 86 87 88' 89' 90' 92 93 94   Well
regarded 25-acre property nr the great TROTANOY. Recently modernized.
Second wine: Dom de Compostelle. See also CH HAUT-MAILLET.

Cadet-Piola St-Em r ** 75' 78 81 82 83' 85' 86 87 88 89' 90 91 92 93' 94'
Distinguished little property just N of the town of ST-EMILION. 3,000 cases
of tannic wine. CH FAURIE-DE-SOUCHARD has same owner; less robust.

Caillou Saut w sw ** 75 76 78 81 82 83 85 86 87 88' 89' 90' 91 92 94   Well-
run second-rank 37-acre BARSAC v'yd for firm fruity wine. Private
Cuvée (81 83 85 86 88 89') is a top selection.

Calon-Ségur St-Est r *** 78 79 81 82' 83 85' 86 87 88' 89' 90 91 92 93 94
Big (123-acre) third growth of great reputation for fruity hearty
wines; less stylish than very top ST-ESTEPHES but currently on good
form. Second label: Marquis de Ségur.

Cambon-la-Pelouse H-Méd r ** 82 85 86 87 88 89 90 92 93   Big accessible
CRU BOURGEOIS. A sure bet for fresh typical MEDOC without wood-ageing.

Camensac St-Laurent r ** 81 82' 85 86' 87 88 89 90 92 93 94'   149-
acre fifth growth. Good lively if not exactly classic wines. New vat-
house in '94. Second label: La Closerie de Camensac.

Canon Canon-Fronsac r **→→→→ 82 83 85 86' 88 89' 90 92   Tiny property
of Christian MOUEIX. Long-ageing wine.

Canon St-Em r *** 79' 81 82' 83 85' 86 87 88' 89' 90' 92 93 94   Famous
first-classed-growth with 44+ acres on the plateau W of the town.
Conservative methods with modern kit; v impressive wine, among ST-
EMILION's best. Second label (in '91): Clos J Kanon.

Canon-de-Brem Canon-Fronsac r ** 81 82' 83 85 86 88 89' 90 92 93   One
of the top FRONSAC v'yds for vigorous wine. MOUEIX property.

Canon-la-Gaffelière St-Em r ** 82 83 85 86' 87 88' 89 90' 92 93 94   47-acre
classed-growth on lower slopes of COTES. German owners. Total
renovation in '85. Stylish, meaty, impressive wines.

Châteaux entries also cross-refer to France section, pages 20–57.

Canon-Moueix Canon-Fronsac r ** 82 83 85 86 87 88 89' 90 91 92 93 94
The latest MOUEIX investment in this rising AC. V stylish wine. NB also sister-châteaux CANON-DE-BREM, Canon-Milary.

Cantegril Graves r ** 88 89 90 Good earthy red from CH DOISY-DAENE.

Cantemerle Macau r *** 61 78 81 82 83' 85 87 88 89' 90 91 92 93
Romantic S MEDOC estate, a château in a wood with 150 acres of vines. Officially fifth growth; potentially much higher for its harmony of flavours. Problems in late '70s, but a new broom (CORDIER) since '81 has restored to potential. New cellars and oak vats in '90. Second label: Villeneuve de Cantemerle.

Cantenac-Brown Cantenac-Mar r **→*** 70 78 79 81 82 83 85 86' 87 88 89 90' 91 92 93 94   Formerly old-fashioned 77-acre third growth. New owners (same as PICHON-LONGUEVILLE) investing heavily; direction from J-M Cazes and v promising recent vintages. Big wines. Second label: Canuet.

Cap-de-Mourlin St-Em r ** 79' 81 82' 83 85 86 87 88 89 90 92 93   Well-known 37-acre property of the Cap-de-Mourlin family, owners of CH BALESTARD and CH ROUDIER, MONTAGNE-ST-EM. Rich tasty ST-EMILION.

Capbern-Gasqueton St-Est r ** 81 82 83 85 86 88 89 90 92 93 94   Good 85-acre CRU BOURGEOIS; same owner as CALON-SEGUR.

Carbonnieux Graves r w *** 82 83 85 86' 87 88 89' 90' 91 92 93 94
Historic estate at LEOGNAN making rather light reds (since '85 much better). The whites, 50% Sémillon (eg 87 88 89 90 91 92' 93 94'), have the structure to age 10 yrs. Ch'x Le Pape and Le Sartre are also in the family. Second label: La Tour-Léognan.

Cardaillan Graves r **   The trusty red wine of the distinguished CH DE MALLE (SAUTERNES).

La Cardonne Blaignan (Méd) r ** 86 88 89 90 91 92 93 94   Large (300-acre+) CRU BOURGEOIS of the northern MEDOC. Rothschild-owned 1973–90. Big changes since. Fairly simple fruity Médoc, best when young.

Les Carmes-Haut-Brion Graves r ** 81' 82' 83 85 86 87 88' 89 90' 91 92 93' 94   Small (11-acre) neighbour of HAUT-BRION with higher than Bourgeois standards. Old vintages show its potential. Only 1,500 cases.

Caronne-Ste-Gemme St-Laurent r **→*** 81 82' 83 85 86 87 88 89' 90 91 92 93' 94'   CRU BOURGEOIS EXCEPTIONNEL (100 acres). Steady stylish quality repays patience. At minor CRU CLASSE level.

Carteau-Côtes-Daugay St-Em **   Emerging 5,000-case GRAND CRU; to follow for full-flavoured wines maturing fairly early.

du Castéra Méd r ** 85 86 88 89 90' 91 92 93 94'   Historic property at St-Germain (N MEDOC). Recent investment; tasty but not tannic wine.

Certan-Giraud Pom r ** 75 79 81 82 83' 85 86 87 88 89' 90' 92 93' 94
Small (17-acre) property next to PETRUS. Good, but one expects more.

Certan-de-May Pom r *** 70 75 78 79 81 82' 83' 85' 86 87 88' 89' 90' 91 92 93 94   Neighbour of VIEUX CHATEAU CERTAN. Tiny property (1,800 cases) with full-bodied, rich, tannic wine, consistently flying v high.

Chambert-Marbuzet St-Est r ** 70 76 78 79 81 82 83 85 86 87 88 89' 90' 91 92 93 94'   Tiny (20-acre) sister château of HAUT-MARBUZET. Vg predominantly Cab wine, aged v tastily in new oak. The owner, Monsieur Duboscq, likes it well hung.

Chantegrive Graves r w **   215-acre estate, half white, half red; modern GRAVES of high quality. Cuvée Caroline is top white selection (89 90 92 93 94), Cuvée Edouard top red (82 83 85 87 88). Other labels incl Mayne-Lévêque, Bon-Dieu-des-Vignes.

Chasse-Spleen Moulis r *** 75' 76 78' 79 81' 82' 83' 85 86 87 88 89' 90' 91 92 93 94   180-acre CRU EXCEPTIONNEL of classed-growth quality. Consistently good, usually outstanding, long-maturing wine. Second label: Ermitage de C-S. One of the surest things in Bordeaux. See also La Gurgue.

Chéret-Pitres Graves r w *→**   Substantial estate in the up-and-coming village of Portets. Drink young or keep.

Cheval Blanc St-Em r ✯✯✯✯ 64 70 71 75' 76 78 79 80 81' 82' 83' 85' 86 87 88 89 90' 91 92 93 94' This and AUSONE are the 'first growths' of ST-EMILION. Cheval Blanc is consistently richer, more full-blooded, intensely vigorous and perfumed, from 100 acres. Delicious young and lasts a generation. Second wine: Le Petit Cheval.

Chevalier, Domaine de Graves r w ✯✯✯✯ 66' 70' 78' 79 81' 82 83' 84 85 86' 87 88' 89' 90' 91 92 93 94' Superb small estate of 36 acres at LEOGNAN. The red is stern at first, richly subtle with age. The white matures slowly to rich flavours (81 82 83' 85' 87' 88 89 90' 91 92 93' 94). Also the little Domaine de la Solitude, PESSAC-LEOGNAN.

Cissac Cissac r ✯✯ 70' 75' 76 78' 79 81 82' 83' 85 86' 87 88 89 90 91 92 93 94' Pillar of the bourgeoisie. 80-acre CRU GRAND BOURGEOIS EXCEPTIONNEL: steady record for tasty, v long-lived wine. Second wine: Les Reflets du Ch Cissac. Also, since '87, CH DU BREUIL.

Citran Avensan (H-Méd) r ✯✯ 82 85 86 87 88 89' 90' 91 92 93 94' CRU GRAND BOURGEOIS EXCEPTIONNEL of 178 acres, bought by Japanese in '87. Major works. 89 is turbo-charged. Second label: Moulins de Citran. To watch.

View from the Médoc…
'White wine is what you drink before you drink red wine.'
Bruno Prats, Château Cos d'Estournel.

Clarke Listrac r (p w) ✯✯ 82 83 85' 86' 87 88 89' 90 91 92 93 94 Huge (350-acre) CRU BOURGEOIS Rothschild development, incl visitor facilities and neighbouring Ch'x Malmaison and Peyrelebade. Also a unique sweet white 'Le Merle Blanc du Ch Clarke'.

Clerc-Milon Pau r ✯✯✯ 78' 81 82' 83 85 86' 87 88 89' 90' 91 92 93 94 Once-forgotten fifth growth bought by the late Baron Philippe de Rothschild in '70. Now 73 acres. Not thrilling in the '70s (except 70), but vg 85, 86 (esp), and now a top performer, weightier than ARMAILHAC.

Climens Saut w sw ✯✯✯✯ 71' 75' 76 78 79 80' 81 82 83' 85' 86' 88' 89 90' 74-acre BARSAC classed-growth making some of the world's most stylish wine (but not the v sweetest) for a good 10 yrs' maturing. (Occasional) second label: Les Cyprès. Same owner as CH BRANE-CANTENAC etc.

Clinet Pom r ✯✯✯ 81 82 83 85 86 87 88' 89' 90' 91 92 93 17-acre property in central POMEROL making intense wines from old vines. Since '86 one of the models for POMEROL.

Clos l'Eglise Pom r ✯✯✯ 75 81 83 85 86 88 89 90' 92 93 94 14-acre v'yd on one of the best sites in POMEROL. Fine wine without great muscle or flesh. The same family owns CH PLINCE.

Clos Floridène Graves r w ✯✯ (r) 90' 91 92 93' 94 (w) 89' 90 92 93 94 A sure thing from one of the best white-wine-makers of Bordeaux, Denis Dubourdieu. Oak-fermented Sauv-Sém to keep 5 yrs, and fruity red. See also Ch Reynon.

Clos Fourtet St-Em r ✯✯✯ 78 79 81 82' 83 85 86 88 89 90 Well-placed 42-acre first growth on the plateau, cellars almost in town. Back on form after a middling patch: André Lurton is now winemaker; more changes to come. Same owners as BRANE-CANTENAC, CLIMENS etc. Second label: Dom de Martialis.

Clos Haut-Peyraguey Saut w sw ✯✯ 76 79 80 83 85 86' 87 88' 89 90' 93 94 Tiny production of good medium-rich wine. Haut-Bommes is the second label.

Clos des Jacobins St-Em r ✯✯ 75' 78 79 81 82' 83' 85 86 87 88' 89' 90' 92 93 Well-known and well-run little (18-acre) classed-growth owned by the shipper CORDIER. Wines of notable depth and style.

Clos du Marquis St-Jul r ✯✯–✯✯✯✯ 81 82 83 85 86' 87 88 89' 90 91 92 93 94 The second wine of LEOVILLE-LAS-CASES, cut from the same cloth.

Clos René Pom r ✯✯ 75 81 82' 83 85 86 87 88 89 90 93 94 Leading château west of POMEROL. 38 acres. Increasingly concentrated wines. Alias Ch Moulinet-Lasserre.

La Closerie-Grand-Poujeaux Moulis r ** 85 86 88 89 90 91 92 93 94'
Small but respected middle-MEDOC property modernized in '92/'93.
Also owners of neighbouring ch'x Bel-Air-Lagrave and Haut-Franquet.

La Clotte St-Em r ** 82 83' 85 86 88 89 90' 92 93' 94 Tiny COTES GRAND CRU:
pungent supple wine. Drink at owners' restaurant, Logis de la Cadène,
in ST-EM. Second label: Clos Bergat Bosson (91).

Colombier-Monpelou Pau r ** 82 83 85 86' 87 88 89 90' 91 92 93 94
Reliable small CRU BOURGEOIS made to a fair standard.

La Conseillante Pom r **** 70' 75' 76 79 81' 82' 83 84 85 86 87 88 89 90'
91 92 93 94 29-acre historic property on the plateau between PETRUS
and CHEVAL BLANC. Some of the noblest and most fragrant POMEROL,
worthy of its superb position; drinks well, young or old.

Corbin (Giraud) St-Em r ** 75 79 81 82' 83 85 86 88 89 90' 92 93 94 28-acre
classed-growth in N ST-EMILION where a cluster of Corbins occupy the
plateau edge. Top vintages are v rich. Same owner as CERTAN-GIRAUD.

Corbin-Michotte St-Em r ** 81 82 83 85 88 89' 90 93 94' Well-run
modernized 19-acre property; 'generous' POMEROL-like wine.

Cordeillan-Bages Pau r ** A mere 1,000 cases of full-blooded PAUILLAC
from the château-hotel of J-M Cazes (see Lynch-Bages).

Cos-d'Estournel St-Est r **** 70 75' 76' 78' 79 81' 82' 83' 84 85' 86' 87
88' 89' 90' 91 92 93' 94 140-acre second growth with eccentric
chinoiserie tower overlooking CH LAFITE. The most refined ST-ESTEPHE.
Regularly one of best in the MEDOC. Second label: CH DE MARBUZET.

Cos-Labory St-Est r ** 82 83 85 86 87 88 89' 90' 91 92 93 94 Little-known
fifth growth neighbour of COS-D'ESTOURNEL with 37 acres. Efforts since
'85 have raised it steadily to classed-growth form (esp 90). ANDRON-
BLANQUET is sister château.

Coufran St-Seurin-de-Cadourne (H-Méd) r ** 81 82' 83 85 86' 87 88 89 90
91 92 93 94 Coufran and CH VERDIGNAN, on the northernmost hillock of
the HAUT-MEDOC are co-owned. Coufran has mainly Merlot vines; soft
supple wine. 148 acres. CH SOUDARS is another, smaller sister.

Couhins-Lurton Graves w ** 85 86' 88 89 90 91 92 93 94 Tiny quantity of
v fine oaky Sauv for maturing. Classed-growth château being restored.

Coutet Saut w sw *** 71' 75' 76 81' 82 83' 85 86' 87 88' 89' 90' (no 93 or 94)
Traditional rival to CH CLIMENS; 91 acres in BARSAC. Usually slightly less
rich; at its best equally fine. Cuvée Madame is a v rich selection of the
best. A dry GRAVES is sold under the same name.

Couvent des Jacobins St-Em r ** 75 78 79' 81 82' 83 85 86 87 88 89 90
92 93 94 Well-known 22-acre v'yd on E edge of town. Among the
best of its kind. Splendid cellars. Second label: Ch Beau-Mayne.

Le Crock St-Est r ** 79 81 82 83 85 86 87 88 89 90' 92 93 Outstanding CRU
BOURGEOIS of 74 acres in the same family as CH LEOVILLE-POYFERRE.
Among the best Crus Bourgeois of the commune.

La Croix Pom r ** 75' 76 79' 81 82 83 85' 86 87 88 89 90 91 92 93 94
Well-reputed property of 32 acres. Appealing plummy POMEROL with a
spine; matures well. Also La C-St-Georges, La C-Toulifaut, Castelot,
Clos des Litanies and HAUT-SARPE (St-Em).

La Croix-de-Gay Pom r *** 81 82' 83' 85 86 88' 89 90 91 92 93 94' 30 acres
in best part of the commune. Recently on fine form. Has underground
cellars (rare in POMEROL). LA FLEUR-DE-GAY is the best selection.

Croizet-Bages Pau r ** 82' 83 85 86 87 88 90' 91 92 93 94 52-acre fifth
growth (lacking a château or a reputation). Same owners as CH RAUZAN-
GASSIES. Only a flicker of life, but new manager in '94.

Croque-Michotte St-Em r ** 75 78 81 82' 83 85 86 87 88 89' 90' 93 94
35-acre classed-growth on the POMEROL border. New equipment.

de Cruzeau Graves r w ** (r) 86 88 89 90 91 92 93 94 100-acre GRAVES-
LEOGNAN v'yd recently developed by André Lurton of LA LOUVIERE etc. V
high standards; to try. Oak-fermented white: keeps 2–5 years.

Curé-Bon-la-Madeleine St-Em r ** 75 78 81 82' 83 85 86 88 89 90 Tiny
little-known (12-acre) property between AUSONE and CANON.

64

BORDEAUX/Clo–Eva

To decipher codes, please refer to symbols key at front of book, and to 'How to use this book' on page 5.

Dalem Fronsac r ✱✱ 82 83 85 86 87 88 89 90 92 93 94 Leading full-blooded FRONSAC. 36 acres: 85% Merlot.

Dassault St-Em r ✱✱ 82 83 85 86 88 89 90 92 93 94 Consistent, early-maturing middle-weight GRAND CRU. 58 acres.

La Dauphine Fronsac ✱✱ 85 86 87 88 89' 90' 91 92 93 94 Old star rejuvenated by J-P MOUEIX.

Dauzac Labarde-Mar r ✱✱→✱✱✱ 82' 83' 85' 86 87 88' 89' 90' 92 93' 94 120-acre fifth growth nr the river south of MARGAUX; underachiever for many years. New owner (insurance company) in '89; direction since '92 by André Lurton. New cuvier in '94. 2nd wine: La Bastide Dauzac.

Desmirail Mar r ✱✱ 82 83' 85 86 87 88 89 90 Third growth, now 45 acres. A long-defunct name revived in '81 by Lucien Lurton of BRANE-CANTENAC. So far wines for drinking fairly young.

Doisy-Daëne Barsac w (r) sw dr ✱✱✱ 76' 78 79 80 81 82 83 85 86 88' 89' 90' 91 94 Forward-looking, even experimental, 34-acre estate for crisp oaky dry white and red CH CANTEGRIL as well as notably fine (and long-lived) sweet BARSAC. L'Extravagance (90) was a super-cuvée.

Doisy-Dubroca Barsac w sw ✱✱✱ 75' 76 78 79 81 83 85 86 87 88' 89 90' Tiny (8.5-acre) BARSAC classed-growth allied to CH CLIMENS.

Doisy-Védrines Saut w sw ✱✱✱ 70 75' 76' 78 79 80 81 82' 83' 85 86 88' 89' 90 92 93 50-acre classed-growth at BARSAC, nr CLIMENS and COUTET, recently re-equipped. Delicious, sturdy, rich: for keeping. NB the 89.

La Dominique St-Em r ✱✱ 78 79 81 82' 83 86' 87 88' 89' 90' 92 93 94 45-acre classed-growth next to CH CHEVAL BLANC making every effort. Second label: St Paul de Dominique (91).

Ducluzeau Listrac r ✱✱ Tiny sister property of DUCRU-BEAUCAILLOU. 10 acres, unusually 90% Merlot.

Ducru-Beaucaillou St-Jul r ✱✱✱✱ 61 62 66' 70' 75' 76 78' 79 80 81 82' 83' 84 85' 86' 87 88 89 90 91 92 93 94 Outstanding second growth; 120 acres overlooking the river in stone cellar under château. M Borie makes classic cedar-scented claret for long ageing. See also Grand-Puy-Lacoste, Haut-Batailley, Lalande-Borie.

Duhart-Milon-Rothschild Pau r ✱✱✱ 78 79 80 81 82' 83 85 86 87 88 89 90 91 92 93 Fourth growth neighbour of LAFITE, under the same management. Maturing vines; increasingly fine quality. 110 acres. Second label: Moulin de Duhart.

Duplessis-Fabre Moulis r ✱✱ 82 83 85 86 87 88' 89 90 92 93 Former sister château of FOURCAS-DUPRE; since '89 owned by DOURTHE. To watch.

Durfort-Vivens Mar r ✱✱✱ 78' 79' 81 82' 83 85' 86 87 88' 89' 90 Relatively small (49-acre) second growth owned by M Lurton of BRANE-CANTENAC. Recent wines have structure (lots of Cab S) and class.

Dûtruch-Grand-Poujeaux Moulis r ✱✱ 79 81 82' 83 85 86 87 88 89 90 91 92 93 94 One of the leaders of MOULIS making full-bodied and tannic wines. 60 acres.

de l'Eglise, Domaine Pom r ✱✱ 79' 81 82' 83 85 86 88 89 90 92 93 Small property: stylish resonant wine distributed by BORIE-MANOUX.

L'Eglise-Clinet Pom r ✱✱✱ 70 71' 75 76 78 79 81 82' 83' 84 85' 86 87 88' 89 90' 91 92 93' 94 11 acres. Ranked v nr top; full fleshy wine. Changed hands in '82; 86 90 noble. 1,700 cases. Second label: La Petite Eglise.

L'Enclos Pom r ✱✱✱ 70 75 79 82' 83 85 86 87 88 89' 90' 91 92 93 Respected 26-acre property on west side of POMEROL, nr CLOS RENE. Big well-made long-flavoured wine.

L'Evangile Pom r ✱✱✱→✱✱✱✱ 75' 78 79 82' 83' 85' 86 87 88' 89' 90' 92 93 33 acres between PETRUS and CHEVAL BLANC. Deep-veined but elegant style. In the same area and class as LA CONSEILLANTE. Bought in '90 by Domaines (LAFITE) Rothschild.

65

de Fargues Saut w sw ✱✱✱ 70' 71' 75' 76' 78 79 80 81 83 85' 86 87 88 89 90 25-acre v'yd by ruined château in same ownership as CH D'YQUEM. Fruity and extremely elegant wines, maturing earlier than Yquem.

Faurie-de-Souchard St-Em r ✱✱ 82 83 85 86 **88** 89 90 91 92 93 94 Small Grand Cru Classé on the COTES tightening its grip. See also Château Cadet-Piola.

de Ferrand St-Em ✱✱→✱✱✱ 85 86 87 88 89 90 92 93 Big (75-acre) plateau estate. Rich, oaky wines, sometimes too tannic.

Ferrande Graves r (w) ✱✱ 81 82 83 **85** 86 88 89 90 91 **92** 93 94 Major estate of Castres: 100+ acres. Easy enjoyable red and good white wine, best at 1–4 yrs.

Ferrière Mar r ✱✱ 92 93 94 Until '92 a phantom third growth; only 10+ acres; part of LASCOMBES. Now in same capable hands as CHASSE-SPLEEN.

Feytit-Clinet Pom r ✱✱ 75' 79 81 82' 83 85' **86** 87 88' 89' 90' 92 93 94 Little property near LATOUR-A-POMEROL. Fine lightish wines. Managed by J-P MOUEIX.

Fieuzal Graves r (w) ✱✱✱ 75 79 81 82' 83 85' 86' 87 88 89 90' 91 92 93 94 75-acre classed-growth at LEOGNAN. Finely made, memorable wines of both colours esp since '84. Classic whites since '85 are 4–10-yr keepers (esp 85 90 92 93). New owners in '94. Ch Le Bonnat is sister-château vinified at Fieuzal.

Figeac St-Em r ✱✱✱✱ 59 64 70' 78 81 82' 83 84 85' 86' 87 88 89' 90' 92 93 94' First growth neighbour of CHEVAL BLANC. 98-acre gravelly v'yd gives one of Bordeaux's most stylish, rich but elegant wines, lovely to drink relatively quickly but lasting indefinitely. Second label: Grangeneuve.

Filhot Saut w sw dr ✱✱ 75 76' 82' 83' 85 86' **87** 88 89 90' 91 92 93 94 Second-rank classed-growth with splendid château, 148-acre v'yd. Lightish rather simple (Sauv) sweet wines for fairly early drinking, a little dry, and red. Vg 'Crème de Tête' (90 extremely rich).

La Fleur St-Em r ✱✱ 75 78 81 82' 83 85 86 88 89' 90' 92 93 94 16-acre COTES estate; increasingly fruity wines. Now managed by J-P MOUEIX.

La Fleur-de-Gay 1,000-case super-CUVEE of CH LA CROIX DE GAY.

La Fleur-Pétrus Pom r ✱✱✱✱ 70 75' 78 79 81' 82 83' 85 86 87 88' 89' 90' 92 18-acre v'yd flanking PETRUS and under same management. Exceedingly fine plummy wines; POMEROL at its most stylish.

Fombrauge St-Em r ✱✱ 81 82' 83 85 86 87 88' 89 90 92 93 94' 120-acres at St-Christophe-des-Bardes, E of ST-EMILION; Danish connections. Reliable mainstream St-Emilion making great efforts. Second label: Ch Maurens.

Fonbadet Pau r ✱✱ 70 **76** 78 79 81' 82' 83 85 86 87 88 89 90' 91 92 93 94 CRU BOURGEOIS of solid reputation. 38 acres next to PONTET-CANET. Old vines; wine needs long bottle-age. Recent building work. Value.

Fonplégade St-Em r ✱✱ 75 78 81 82' 83 85 86 **87** 88 89 90' 93 94 48-acre Grand Cru Classé on the COTES W of ST-EMILION in the Armand Moueix group. Firm and long-lasting.

Fonréaud Listrac r ✱✱ 78' 79 81 82' 83 85' 86' 87 88 89 90 91 92 93 One of the bigger (96 acres) and better CRUS BOURGEOIS of its area. New broom (and barrels) since '83. Now also 5 acres of white: Le Cygne, barrel-fermented. See also Ch Lestage.

Fonroque St-Em r ✱✱✱ 70 75' 78 79 81 82 83' 85' **86** 87 88 89' 90' 92 93 94 48 acres on the plateau N of ST-EMILION. J-P MOUEIX property. Big deep dark wine: drink or (better) keep.

Les Forts de Latour Pau r ✱✱✱ 70' 75 78' 79 80 81 82' 83 84 85 86' 87 88 90' 91 92 93 94 The second wine of CH LATOUR; well worthy of its big brother. For long unique in being bottle-aged at least 3 yrs before release; since '90 offered EN PRIMEUR as well. Specially fine 82 and 90.

Fourcas-Dupré Listrac r ✱✱ 70' 75 78' 79 81 82' 83' 85' 86' 87 88 89' 90 91 92 93 Top-class 100-acre CRU BOURGEOIS EXCEPTIONNEL making consistent and elegant wine. To follow. Second label: Ch Bellevue-Laffont.

Fourcas-Hosten Listrac r ****→****** 70 75 78' 79 81 82' 83' 85 86' 87 88 89 90 91 92 93 96-acre CRU BOURGEOIS currently considered the best of its (underestimated) commune. Firm wine with a long life.

Franc-Mayne St-Em r ****** 85 86 87 88 89' 90' 91 92 93 94 '89 acquisition of AXA Insurance. 18 acres run by J-M Cazes (LYNCH-BAGES). High standards. Ch'x La Fleur-Pourret and Petit-Figeac (19 acres) are in same stable.

de France Pessac-L r w ****** Well-known GRAVES, 65 acres red, 10 white, recently replanted. Recent reds notable.

La Gaffelière St-Em r ******* 70 75 82' 83' 85 86' 87 88' 89' 90' 92 93 94 61-acre first growth at the foot of the CÔTES below CH BEL-AIR. Elegant, not rich wines; worth its rank since '82, after a bad patch.

Why do the Châteaux of Bordeaux have such a large section of this book devoted to them? The reason is simple: collectively they form by far the largest supply of high-quality wine on earth. A single typical Médoc château with 150 acres (some have far more) makes approximately 26,000 dozen bottles of identifiable wine each year – the production of two or three California 'boutique' wineries.

The tendency over the last two decades has been to buy more land. Many classed-growths have expanded very considerably since their classification in 1855. The majority has also raised its sights and invested the good profits of the past decade in better technology.

Galius St-Em r ******* 85 86 88 89 90 92 93 94 Oak-aged selection from ST-EMILION coop, to a high standard. Formerly Haut Quercus.

La Garde Graves r (w) ****** 81 82' 83' 84 85 86 88 89 90 91 92 93 94 Substantial property making reliably sound red.

Le Gay Pom r ******* 70 75' 76' 78 79 82' 83' 85 86 88 89' 90' 92 Fine 14-acre v'yd on N edge of POMEROL. Same owner as CH LAFLEUR; under J-P MOUEIX management since '85.

Gazin Pom r ******* 81 82 83 85 86 87' 88 89' 90' 91 92 93 94' Large property (for POMEROL) with 58 acres next to PETRUS. Inconsistent up to '85; now back on top form. Distributed (except tiny '91 crop) by J-P MOUEIX. Second label: Ch l'Hospitalet.

Gilette Saut w sw ******* 37 49 53 55 59 61 62 70 Extraordinary small Preignac château stores its sumptuous wines in cask to a great age. Only about 5,000 bottles of each. Ch Les Justices is the sister château (83 85 86).

Giscours Labarde-Mar r ******* 70 71' 75' 76 78' 79' 81' 82' 83' 85 86 87 88 89' 90 91 92 93 Splendid 182-acre third growth south of CANTENAC. Dynamically run with excellent vigorous wine in '70s; '80s less sure-footed. Second labels: Ch'x Cantelaude, Grand Goucsirs (!). Ch La Houringue is baby sister.

du Glana St-Jul r ****** 81 82' 83 85 86 88 89 90 91 92 93 94 Big CRU BOURGEOIS in centre of ST-JULIEN. Undemanding; undramatic; value. Second wine: Ch Sirène.

Gloria St-Jul r ****→***** 70' 75 76 81 82 83 85 86 88 89 90 92 93 94 Outstanding CRU BOURGEOIS making wine of vigour and finesse. 110 acres. In '82 the owner, the late Henri Martin, bought CH ST-PIERRE. Recent return to long-maturing style. Second label: Peymartin.

Grand-Barrail-Lamarzelle-Figeac St-Em r ****** 82' 83 85 86 88 89 90 91 92 93 94 48-acre property S of FIGEAC, incl Ch La Marzelle. Well-reputed and popular, if scarcely exciting.

Grand-Corbin-Despagne St-Em r ****→***** 70 75 76 78 79 81 82' 83 85 86 88 89 90' 91 92 93 94 One of biggest and best GRANDS CRUS on CORBIN plateau. A new generation (of the founding Despagne family, since 1812) in '93. Also owns Ch Maison Blanche, MONTAGNE ST-EMILION.

Grand-Mayne St Em ****** 82 83 85 86 87 88 89' 90' 93 94 40-acre Grand Cru Classé on W CÔTES. To watch for rich tasty wines.

Grand-Pontet St-Em r ✶✶ 82' 83 85 86' 87 88 89 90' 91 92 93 94   35 acres beside CH BEAU-SEJOUR-BECOT; both revitalized since '85. To follow.

Grand-Puy-Ducasse Pau r ✶✶✶ 79 81 82' 83 85 86 87 88 89' 90 91 92 93 94   Well-known fifth growth enlarged to 90 acres under expert management. Recent wines less steady. Second label: Ch Artigues-Arnaud.

Grand-Puy-Lacoste Pau r ✶✶✶ 70' 75 78' 79' 81' 82' 83 85' 86' 87 88' 89' 90' 91 92 93 94   Leading fifth growth famous for excellent full-bodied vigorous PAUILLAC. 110 acres among the 'Bages' châteaux, owned by the Borie family of DUCRU-BEAUCAILLOU. Second label: Lacoste-Borie.

Gravas Saut w sw ✶✶ 83' 85 86 88 89' 90' 92 93   Small BARSAC property; impressive firm sweet wine. NB Cuvée Spéciale.

La Grave, Domaine Graves r w ✶✶ 89' 90' 91 92 93 94   Innovative little estate with lively reds; delicious oak-aged whites (w 91 92 93 94). Made at CH DE LANDIRAS by Peter Vinding-Diers.

La Grave-Trigant-de-Boisset Pom r ✶✶✶ 75' 76' 78 79 81' 82' 83 85 86' 87 88 89' 90 92 93 94   Verdant château with small but first-class v'yd owned by CHRISTIAN MOUEIX. Elegant beautifully structured POMEROL.

Gressier-Grand-Poujeaux Moulis r ✶✶→✶✶✶✶ 70 75' 78 79' 81 82 83' 85 86 87 88 89 90 91 92 93   Good CRU BOURGEOIS, neighbour of CHASSE-SPLEEN. Fine firm wine with good track record for repaying patient cellaring.

Greysac Méd r ✶✶ 81' 82 83 85 86 88 89 90 91 92 93 94   Elegant 140-acre property. Easy early-maturing wines popular in US.

Gruaud-Larose St-Jul r ✶✶✶ 70 75 76 78' 79 81 82' 83 85 86 87 88' 89 90' 91 92 93 94   One of the biggest and best-loved second growths. 189 acres. Smooth rich stylish claret, year after year. Bought '94 by Alcatel Co but same CORDIER management. New equipment '94. Vg second wine: Sarget de Gruaud-Larose.

Guadet-St-Julien St-Em ✶✶ 75 81 82 83 85 86 87 88 89 90' 92 93   Extremely well-made wines from v small Grand Cru Classé.

Guiraud Saut w (r) sw (dr) ✶✶✶ 67 79 80 81 82 83' 84 85 86' 87 88' 89' 90' 92 93 94   Restored classed-growth of top quality. 250+ acres. At best excellent sweet wine of great finesse, and a small amount of red and dry white. The 88, 89 and 90 will be superb in time.

Guiteronde du Hayot Saut ✶✶ 75-acres in BARSAC; known for finesse and value.

La Gurgue Mar r ✶✶ 81 82 83' 85' 86 87 88 89' 90 91 92 93 94   Small, well-placed 30-acre property, for MARGAUX of the fruitiest sort. From owners of CHASSE-SPLEEN and HAUT-BAGES-LIBERAL. To watch.

Hanteillan Cissac r ✶✶ 82' 83 85' 86 87 88' 89 90' 91 92 93 94   Large vineyard: v fair Bourgeois wine, conscientiously made. Ch Laborde is second quality.

Haut-Bages-Averous Pau r ✶✶ 82' 83 85' 86 87 88 89' 90 91 92 93 94   The second wine of CH LYNCH BAGES. Delicious tasty drinking.

Haut-Bages-Libéral Pau r ✶✶ 78 82' 83 85 86' 87 88 89 90' 91 92 93 94'   Lesser-known fifth growth of 64 acres (next to LATOUR) in same stable as CHASSE-SPLEEN. Results are excellent, full of PAUILLAC vitality.

Haut-Bages-Monpelou Pau r ✶✶ 81 82' 83 85 86 88 89' 90 91 92 93   25-acre CRU BOURGEOIS stable-mate of CH BATAILLEY on former DUHART-MILON land. Good minor PAUILLAC.

Haut-Bailly Graves r ✶✶✶ 70' 78 79' 81' 82 83 85' 86 87 88' 89' 90' 92 93' 94   70-acres+ at LEOGNAN, Belgian-owned. Since '79 some of the best ripe, round, intelligently-made red GRAVES. Second label is La Parde de Haut-Bailly.

Haut-Batailley Pau r ✶✶✶ 66 70' 75' 78 79 81 82' 83 85 86 87 88 89' 90' 91 92 93 94   Smaller part of fifth growth BATAILLEY: 49 acres. Often gentler than sister château, GRAND-PUY-LACOSTE. Second wine: La Tour-d'Aspic.

Haut-Bergey Pessac-L r ✶✶   40 acres, largely Cab; fragrant delicate GRAVES.

Haut-Bommes See Clos Haut-Peyraguey.

Haut-Brignon Premières Côtes r w ✶   Big producer of standard wines at Cénac, owned by major CHAMPAGNE coop. Do not confuse with the next!

Haut-Brion Pessac (Graves) r (w) **** 61 64 70' 71' 75' 76 78' 79' 80 81 82' 83' 84 85' 86' 87 88' 89' 90' 91 92 93 94 The oldest great château of BORDEAUX and only non-MEDOC first growth of 1855. 108 acres. Beautifully harmonious, never aggressive wine. Particularly good (and modestly priced) since '75. A little full dry white in 78 81 82 83 85 87 88 89' 90 91 92 93 94. See Bahans-Haut-Brion, La Mission-Haut-Brion.

Haut-Maillet Pom ** 82 83 85 86 88 89 90 91 92 93 12-acre sister château of LA CABANNE. Well-made gentle wines.

Haut-Marbuzet St-Est r **→**** 70 75' 76 78' 81 82' 83' 85' 86' 87 88 89' 90' 91 92 93' 94 The best of many good ST-ESTEPHE CRUS BOURGEOIS. Monsieur Dubosq has reassembled the ancient Dom de Marbuzet, in total 175 acres. Haut-M is 60% Merlot. See also CHAMBERT-MARBUZET, MACCARTHY, MacCarthy-Moula, Tour de Marbuzet. New oak gives them classic style.

Haut-Pontet St-Em r ** Reliable 12-acre v'yd of the COTES deserving its GRAND CRU status. 2,500 cases.

Haut-Sarpe St-Em r ** 79 81 82 83' 85 86 87 88 89 90' 91 92 93 94 Grand Cru Classé (6,000 cases) with elegant château and park, 70% Merlot. Same owner as CH LA CROIX, POMEROL.

Hortevie St-Jul r ** 81 82 83 85' 86 87 88 89' 90' 91 92 93 94 One of the few ST-JULIEN CRUS BOURGEOIS. This tiny v'yd and its bigger sister TERREY-GROS-CAILLOU are shining examples.

Houissant St-Est r ** 82 83 85 86 87 88 89' 90' 91 92 93 94 Typical robust well-balanced ST-ESTEPHE CRU BOURGEOIS also called Ch Leyssac; well-known in Denmark.

d'Issan Cantenac-Mar r *** 70 75' 78 79 81 82' 83' 85 86 87 88 89 90' 91 92 93 94 Beautifully restored moated château with 75-acre third growth vineyard; fragrant, virile, delicate wine. Second label: Ch de Candale.

Kirwan Cantenac-Mar r *** 70 78 81 82' 83' 85 86 87 88 89' 90' 91 92 93' 94 Well-run 86-acre third growth; majority owned by insurance co La Gan. Mature v'yds giving ever tastier wines. New consultant (Michel Rolland) since '92.

Labégorce Mar r ** 75' 78 79 81' 82' 83' 85 86 87 88 89' 90' 91 92 93 94 Substantial 69-acre property N of MARGAUX producing long-lived wines of true Margaux quality. New owner since '89.

Labégorce-Zédé Mar r **→**** 75' 78 81' 82' 83' 85 86' 87 88 89' 90' 91 92 93 94 Outstanding CRU BOURGEOIS on road N from MARGAUX. 62 acres. Typically delicate, fragrant; truly classic since '81. Same family as VIEUX CH CERTAN. Second label: Dom Zédé. Also 23 acres of AC Bordeaux: 'Z'.

Lacoste-Borie The second wine of CH GRAND-PUY-LACOSTE.

Lafaurie-Peyraguey Saut w sw *** 78 80 81' 82 83' 85 86' 87 88' 89' 90' Fine classed-growth of only 49 acres at Bommes, belonging to CORDIER. After a lean patch, good, rich and racy wines in late '80s.

Lafite-Rothschild Pau r **** 59 75' 76' 78 79 81' 82' 83 84 85 86' 87 88' 89' 90' 91 92 93 94 First growth of fabulous style and perfume in its great vintages, which keep for decades. Resplendent since '76. Amazing circular cellars opened '87; joint ventures in Chile ('88), California ('89), Portugal ('92). Second wine: Carruades de Lafite. 225 acres. Also owns CH'X DUHART-MILON, L'EVANGILE, RIEUSSEC.

Lafleur Pom r **** 70' 75' 78 79' 81 82' 83 85' 86' 88' 89' 90' 92 93 94 Superb 12-acre property just N of PETRUS. Resounding wine of the tannic, less 'fleshy' kind. Same owner as LE GAY. Second wine: Pensées de Lafleur.

NB The vintages printed in colour are the ones you should choose first for drinking in 1996.

Lafleur-Gazin Pom r ✹✹ 75' 79 81 82' 83 85' 86 87 88' 89 90 92 93 94
Distinguished small J-P MOUEIX estate on the NE border of POMEROL.

Lafon-Rochet St-Est r ✹✹ 70' 79 81 82 83' 85 86 87 88' 89' 90' 91 92 93 94
Fourth growth neighbour of COS D'ESTOURNEL, restored in '60s and again
recently. 110 acres. Rather hard dark full-bodied ST-ESTEPHE, reluctant
to 'give'. Same owner as CH PONTET-CANET. Second label: Numéro 2.

Lagrange Pom r ✹✹ 70' 75' 78 81 82' 83 85' 86 87 88 89' 90' 92 93 94
20-acre v'yd in the centre of POMEROL run by the ubiquitous house of J-
P MOUEIX. Rising profile for flavour/value.

Lagrange St-Jul r ✹✹✹ 70 82 83 84 85' 86' 87 88' 89' 90' 91 92 93 94
Formerly run-down third growth inland from ST-JULIEN, bought by
Suntory ('83). 280 acres now in tiptop condition. A property to follow.
2nd wine: Les Fiefs de Lagrange (83 85 86 87 88 89 90 91 92 93 94).

La Lagune Ludon r ✹✹✹ 70' 75' 76' 78' 79 81 82' 83' 85 86' 87 88' 89' 90' 91
92 93 94   Well-run ultra-modern (new chais '93) 160-acre third
growth in the extreme S of the MEDOC. Attractively rich wines with
marked oak; steadily v high quality. Owned by CHAMPAGNE AYALA.

Lalande-Borie St-Jul r ✹✹ 81 82 83 85 86 87 88 89 90' 91 92 93 94   A baby
brother of the great DUCRU-BEAUCAILLOU created from part of the former
v'yd of CH LAGRANGE.

Lamarque Lamarque (H-Méd) r ✹✹ 82 83' 85 86' 87 88 89 90' 91 92 93 94
Splendid medieval fortress in central MEDOC with 113 acres giving
admirable wine of high Bourgeois standard. 2nd wine: Donjon de L.

Lamothe Bergeron H-Méd r ✹✹   150 acres at CUSSAC making 25,000 cases
of reliable claret. Run by GRAND-PUY-DUCASSE.

Landiras Graves w r ✹✹→✹✹✹ (w) 90 91 92 93' 94   Medieval ruin in S
GRAVES replanted in '80s by Peter Vinding Diers. 50 acres Sém, 15 red
(88 89 90' 91 92 93 94). See also Domaine La Grave. Second label:
Notre Dame de Landiras (B'x AC).

Lanessan Cussac (H-Méd) r ✹✹→✹✹✹ 78' 79 81 82 83 85 86' 87 88' 89' 90'
91 92 93 94   Distinguished 108-acre CRU BOURGEOIS EXCEPTIONNEL just S
of ST-JULIEN. Fine rather than burly but ages v well. Same family owns
châteaux de Ste-Gemme, Lachesnaye, La Providence.

Langoa-Barton St-Jul r ✹✹✹ 70' 75' 76 78' 79 81 82' 83 85 86' 87 88' 89'
90' 91 92 93 94'   49-acre third growth sister château to LEOVILLE-
BARTON. V old family property with impeccable standards, and value.
Second wine: Lady Langoa.

Larcis-Ducasse St-Em r ✹✹ 66 78 79 81 82' 83 84 85 86 87 88' 89' 90' 91
92 93 94   Top property of St-Laurent, eastern neighbour of ST-EMILION,
on COTES next to CH PAVIE. 30 acres in a fine situation. Long-lived wines
in keeping.

Larmande St-Em r ✹✹✹ 75' 78 79 81 82 83' 85 86 87 88' 89' 90' 91 92 93 94
Substantial 54-acre property related to CAP-DE-MOURLIN. Replanted, re-
equipped and now making rich strikingly scented wine. Second label:
Ch des Templiers.

Laroque St-Em r ✹✹ 75' 81 82' 83 85 86 88 89 90 91 92 93 94   Important
108-acre v'yd on the ST-EMILION COTES in St-Christophe.

Larose-Trintaudon St-Laurent r ✹✹ 82 85 86 87 88 89 90' 91 92 93 94'
The biggest v'yd in the MEDOC: 425 acres. Modern methods make
reliable fruity and charming CRU BOURGEOIS wine to drink young. New
management in '89 and second label Larose St-Laurent.

Laroze St-Em r ✹✹ 82 83 85 86 87 88' 89' 90' 91 92 93 94   Big vineyard
(74 acres) on western COTES. Fine lightish wines from sandy soil;
soon enjoyable.

Larrivet-Haut-Brion Graves r (w) ✹✹ 75' 81 82' 83 85 86 87 88 89 90 91 92
93 94   Little LEOGNAN property with perfectionist standards. Also 500
cases of fine barrel-fermented white (87 88 89 90 91 92 93 94).

Châteaux entries also cross-refer to France section, pages 20–57.

Lascombes Mar r (p) *** 70' 75' 82 83 85 86 **87 88**' 89' 90' 91 92 93 94
240-acre second growth owned by British brewers Bass-Charrington,
lavishly restored. After a poor patch, new vigour since '86. A second
growth needs the severest standards. Second wine: Ch Segonnes.

Latour Pau r **** 59 61 62 64 66 67 70' 73 75' 76 78' **79 80** 81 82' 83 84
85 86 87 88' 89' 90' 91' 92 93 94'   First growth considered the
grandest statement of the MEDOC. Rich, intense, almost immortal
wines in great years; classical and pleasing even in weak ones. 150
acres sloping to the R Gironde. Latour always needs time to show its
hand. British-owned from '63 to '93, now again in (private) French
hands. Second wine: LES FORTS DE LATOUR.

Latour-Martillac Graves r w ** (r) 82' 83 85' 86 **87 88**' 89 90 91 92 93 94
Small but serious property at Martillac. 10 acres of white grapes; 37
of black. The white can age admirably (86 87 88 89 90 91 **92** 93' 94').
The owner is resurrecting the neighbouring Ch Lespault.

Latour-à-Pomerol Pom r **** 70' 71 75 **76** 78 79 81 82 83 85' **86** 87 88' 89'
90' 92 93 94   Top growth of 19 acres under MOUEIX management.
POMEROL of great power and perfume, yet also ravishing finesse.

des Laurets St-Em r ** 82 83 85 **86 88 89**' 90' 92 93 94   Major property in
PUISSEGUIN-ST-EMILION and MONTAGNE-ST-EMILION (to the E) with 160 acres
of v'yd on the COTES (40,000 cases). Sterling wines sold by J-P MOUEIX.

Laville-Haut-Brion Graves w **** 82 85' **86** 87' 88 89' 90 91 92 93' 94
A tiny production of one of the v best white GRAVES for long succulent
maturing, made at CH LA MISSION-HAUT-BRION.

Léoville-Barton St-Jul r *** 70' 75' **76** 78' 81 82' 83 85' 86' 87 88' 89' 90'
91 92 93 94'   90-acre portion of the great second growth Léoville v'yd
in Anglo-Irish hands of the Barton family for over 150 years. Powerful
classic claret; traditional methods, v fair prices. Major investment has
raised already v high standards. See also Langoa-Barton.

Médoc: the class system

*The Médoc has 60 crus classés, ranked in 1855 in five classes. In a
separate classification it has 18 Crus Grands Bourgeois Exceptionnels, 41
Crus Grands Bourgeois (which must age their wine in barrels), and 68 Crus
Bourgeois. (The terms Grand Bourgeois and Exceptionnel are not
acceptable to the EC, and are therefore no longer used on labels.)*

*Apart from the first growths, the five classes of 1855 are now considerably
jumbled in quality, with some second growths at fifth growth level and vice
versa. They also overlap in quality with the Crus Exceptionnels. (Besides
the official 18, another 13 châteaux are unofficially acknowledged as
belonging to this category.) The French are famous for logic.*

Léoville-Las-Cases St-Jul r **** 66' 70 75' **76** 78' 79 81' 82' 83' 84 85' 86'
87 88 89' 90' 91 92 93' 94   Largest LEOVILLE. Next to LATOUR; 210 acres.
One of highest reputations in B'x. Elegant complex powerful austere
wines, for immortality. Second label CLOS DU MARQUIS also outstanding.

Léoville-Poyferré St-Jul r *** 81 82' 83' 84 **85** 86' 87 88 89' 90' 91 92
93 94   For years the least outstanding of the LEOVILLES; since '80 again
living up to the great name. Now advised by M Rolland. 156 acres.
Second label: Ch Moulin-Riche.

Lestage Listrac r ** 82' 83 85 86' 87 88 89' 90' 91 92 93 94   130-acre CRU
BOURGEOIS in same hands as CH FONREAUD. Light, quite stylish wine aged
in oak since '85. Second wine: Ch Caroline. Also white: La Mouette.

Lilian-Ladouys St-Est ** 89 90 91 92 93 94   Recent creation: a 50-acre CRU
BOURGEOIS with high ambitions and real early promise. To watch.

Liot Barsac w sw ** 75' 76 82 83 85 86 88 89' 90' 92 94   Consistent fairly
light golden wines from 50 acres.

Liversan St-Sauveur r ** 82' 83 85 86' 87 88' 89' 90' 91 92 93 94   116-acre
Grand Cru Bourgeois inland from PAUILLAC. Since '84 the Polignac
family has greatly improved standards. Second wine: Ch Fonpiqueyre.

Livran Méd r ** 82' 83 85 86 88' 89' 90' 91 92 93 94' Big CRU BOURGEOIS at St-Germain in the N MEDOC. Consistent round wines (half Merlot).

Loudenne St-Yzans (Méd) r ** 82' 83 85 86' 87' 88 89' 90 91 92 93 Beautiful riverside château owned by Gilbeys since 1875. Well-made CRU BOURGEOIS red and an increasingly delicious dry Sauvignon white from 120 acres. The white is best at 2–4 yrs (90 91 92' 93 94).

Loupiac-Gaudiet Loupiac w sw ** 85 86 87 88 89 90 91 92 93 94 Reliable source of value 'almost-SAUTERNES', just across R Garonne. 7,500 cases.

La Louvière Graves r w *** (r) 81 82' 83 85 86' 87 88' 89' 90' 91 92 93' 94' (w) 86 88 89' 90' 91 92 93' 94 Noble 135-acre LEOGNAN estate restored by the ubiquitous Lurtons. Excellent white, and classed-growth standard red.

de Lussac St-Em r ** 82 83 85 86 88 89' 90 91 92 93 94 One of the best estates in LUSSAC-ST-EMILION (to the NE).

Lynch-Bages Pau r (w) ***→***** 61' 66 70 75' 78' 79 81 82' 83' 84 85' 86' 87 88' 89' 90' 91 92 93' 94 Always popular, now a regular star. 200 acres. Rich robust wine: deliciously dense, brambly; aspiring to greatness. See also Haut-Bages-Averous. From '90, intense oaky white. Owner J-M Cazes also directs CH PICHON-LONGUEVILLE etc for AXA Insurance.

Lynch-Moussas Pau r ** 81 82 83 85 86 87 88 89 90' 91 92 93 94 Fifth growth restored by the director of CH BATAILLEY since '69. Now 60+ acres are making serious wine, gaining depth as the young vines age.

du Lyonnat Lussac-St-Em r ** 82 83 85 86' 88 89 90' 91 92 93 94 120-acre estate with well-distributed reliable wine.

MacCarthy St-Est r ** The second label of CHAMBERT-MARBUZET.

Macquin-St-Georges St-Em r ** 85 86' 88 89 90' 91 92 93 94 Steady producer of delicious 'satellite' ST-EMILION at ST-GEORGES.

Magdelaine St-Em r *** 70' 71' 75 78 79 81 82' 83' 85 86 88 89' 90' 92 93 94 Leading COTES first-growth: 28 acres next to AUSONE owned by J-P MOUEIX. Beautifully balanced subtle wine: not normally the richest. Substantial rebuilding ('92) promises even better things.

Magence Graves r w ** Go-ahead 45-acre property in S GRAVES. Sauv Bl-flavoured dry white and fruity red. Both age well 2–6 yrs.

Malartic-Lagravière Graves r (w) *** (r) 81 82' 83 85 86' 87 88 89 90' 91 92 93' 94 (w) 85 87' 88 89 90 91 92 93 94 Well-known LEOGNAN classed-growth of 53 acres. Well-structured rather hard red and a v little long-ageing Sauvignon white. Austere wines that need cellaring. Perhaps the style will change with new owners (LAURENT-PERRIER ('90).

Malescasse Lamarque (H-Méd) r ** 82 83 85 86 88 89 90 91 92 93 94 Renovated CRU BOURGEOIS with 100 acres in good situation. Second label: Le Tana de Malescasse. New (corporate) owners in '92, same as GRUAUD-LAROSE. To watch.

Malescot-St-Exupéry Mar r *** 70 75 82' 83' 85 86 87 88 89 90' 91 92 93 94 Third growth of 84 acres. Often tough when young, eventually fragrant and stylish MARGAUX. New consultant from '90 augurs well.

de Malle Saut w r sw dr *** (w sw) 75 76 78 79 80 81' 82' 83 85 86' 87 88 89' 90' 91 94 Beautiful château with Italian gardens at Preignac. 124 acres. Vg SAUTERNES (second label: Ste Hélène 93); also dry white (90), and red (GRAVES) CH DU CARDAILLAN (**) (88 89).

de Malleret H-Méd r ** 82 83 85 86 88 89' 90 92 93 94 An aristocrat's domaine. The Marquis du Vivier makes 25,000 cases of fine gentlemanly claret at Le Pian, among forests just N of Bordeaux.

de Marbuzet St-Est r ** Second label of COS-D'ESTOURNEL: equally reliable.

Margaux Mar r (w) ****61' 78' 79 80 81' 82' 83' 84 85' 86' 87 88' 89' 90' 91 92 93' 94 First growth (209 acres), the most penetrating and fabulously perfumed of all in its (v frequent) best vintages. Pavillon Rouge (81 82' 83 85 86 87 88 89 90' 91 92 93 94) is second wine. Pavillon Blanc is best white (Sauv) of MEDOC (85 86 87 88 89 90 91 92 93 94).

Marquis-d'Alesme See d'Alesme.

Marquis-de-Terme Mar r **→*** 81' 82 83' 85 86' 87 88' 89' 90' 91 92 93 Renovated fourth growth of 84 acres. Fragrant, fairly lean style has developed since '85, with more Cab S and more flesh.

Martinens Mar r ** 81 82 83 85 86 88 89 90 91 92 93 94' Worthy 75-acre CRU BOURGEOIS of the mayor of CANTENAC; new barrels since '89.

Maucaillou Moulis r ** 75' 79 81 82 83' 85' 86' 87 88' 89' 90' 91 92 93 94' 130-acre CRU BOURGEOIS with CRU CLASSE standards, property of DOURTHE family. Richly fruity Cap de Haut-Maucaillou is second wine.

Mazeyres Pom r ** Consistent, useful lesser POMEROL. 5,000 cases.

Méaume B'x Supérieur r ** Englishman's domaine, N of POMEROL. Since '80 has built solid reputation for vg daily claret to age 4–5 yrs. 7,500 cases.

Meyney St-Est r **→*** 75' 78' 79 81 82' 83 85 86' 87 88' 89' 90' 91 92 93 94 Big (125-acre) riverside property next door to CH MONTROSE with a superb situation; one of the best of many steady CRUS BOURGEOIS in ST-ESTEPHE. Owned by CORDIER. Second label: Prieur de Meyney.

Millet Graves r w (p) ** (r) 82 83 85 86 88 89 90' 92 93 94 Useful GRAVES. 2nd label, Clos Renon: drink young. Cuvée Henri is new oak-aged white.

La Mission-Haut-Brion Graves r **** 61 64 66' 75' 78' 79 80 81 82' 83 84 85' 86 87 88 89' 90' 91 92 93 94' Neighbour and long-time rival to CH HAUT-BRION; since '84 in same hands. New equipment in '87. Serious grand old-style for long maturing; usually 'bigger' wine than H-B. 30 acres. White is LAVILLE-H-B.

Monbousquet St-Em r ** 78' 79' 81 82 83 85' 86 88' 89' 90' 93 94 Attractive early-maturing wine from deep gravel soil: lasts well. Second label: Ch Caperot 91 92'.

Monbrison Arsac-Mar r ** 81 82 83 84 85 86 87 88' 89' 90 91 92 93 94 A new name to watch. Top Bourgeois standards. 4,000 cases plus 2,000 of second label, Ch Cordet.

Montrose St-Est r *** 61 64 66 70' 75' 76 78' 79 81 82' 83 84 85 86' 87 88 89' 90' 91 92 93 94 158-acre family-run second growth well-known for deeply coloured forceful old-style claret. Vintages 79–85 (except 82) were lighter, but recent Montrose is almost ST-ESTEPHE's answer to CH LATOUR. Second wine: La Dame de Montrose.

Moulin du Cadet St-Em r p ** 75' 81 82' 83 85 86 88 89' 90' 92 93 Little v'yd on the COTES, owned by J-P MOUEIX. Fragrant medium-bodied wines.

Moulin-à-Vent Moulis r ** 81 82' 83 85' 86 87 88 89' 90' 91 92 93 94 60-acre property in the forefront of this booming AC. Lively forceful wine. LA TOUR-BLANCHE (MEDOC) has the same owners.

Moulinet Pom r ** 82 83 85 86 87 88 89' 90 92 93 94 One of POMEROL's bigger châteaux, 45 acres on lightish soil; wine lightish too.

Mouton-Baronne-Philippe See d'Armailhac.

Mouton-Rothschild Pau r **** 59 61 62' 66' 70' 75' 76 78 81 82' 83' 85' 86' 87 88' 89' 90' 91 92 93 94 Officially a first growth since '73, though for 40 yrs worthy of the title. 175 acres (87% Cab S) make majestic rich wine (also, from '91, white Aile d'Argent). Also the world's greatest museum of art relating to wine. Baron Philippe, the foremost champion of the MEDOC, died in '88. His daughter Philippine now reigns. See also Opus One, California.

Nairac Saut w sw ** 73 75 76' 79 80 81 82 83' 85 86' 87 88 89 90' 91 92 93 94 Perfectionist BARSAC classed-growth château. Wines to lay down for a decade.

Nenin Pom r ** 70' 75' 76 78 82 83 85' 86 87 88' 89 90 93' 94 Well-known 66-acre estate; on a (v necessary) but slow upswing since '85 (esp 93).

d'Olivier Graves r w *** (r) 82 83 84 85 86 87 88 89' 90' 91 92 93 94 (w) 89 90 91 92 93 94 90-acre classed-growth, surrounding a moated castle at LEOGNAN. 9,000 cases red, 6,000 white. New broom in '89 is upgrading quality.

Les Ormes-de-Pez St-Est r **→*** 75' 78 79 81' 82' 83' 85 86' 87 88 89' 90' 91 92 94 Outstanding 72-acre CRU BOURGEOIS owned by CH LYNCH-BAGES. Increasingly notable full-flavoured ST-ESTEPHE.

73

Les Ormes-Sorbet Méd r ****** 78 81 82' 83 85' 86' 87 88 89 90' 91 92 93 94
Emerging 10,000-case producer of good stylish red aged in new oak
at Couquèques. A leader of the N MEDOC. Second label: Ch de Conques.

Palmer Cantenac-Mar r **** 61' 62 66' 70 71' 75' 76 78' 79' 80 81 82 83'
84 85 86' 87 88' 89 90 91 92 93 94   The star of CANTENAC: a third
growth often of nearly first growth quality. Wine of power, flesh,
delicacy and much Merlot. 110 acres with Dutch, British (Peter A
Sichel) and French owners. Second wine: Réserve du Général.

Pape-Clément Graves r (w) *** 70 75' 82 83 85 86' 87 88' 89' 90' 92 93' 94'
Ancient v'yd at PESSAC with record of seductive, scented, not
ponderous reds. Early '80s not so good: dramatic new resolve (and
more white) since '85.

de Parenchère r (w) ** 89 90 93 94   Steady supply of useful AC Ste-Foy
Bordeaux from handsome château with 125 acres.

Patache d'Aux Bégadan (Méd) r ** 82' 83' 85 86 88 89' 90' 91 92 93 94
90-acre CRU BOURGEOIS of the N MEDOC. Fragrant largely Cab wine with
the earthy quality of its area.

Paveil (de Luze) Mar r ** 81 82' 83' 85 86' 87 88' 89' 90 91 92 93 94   Old
family estate at SOUSSANS. Small but highly regarded.

Pavie St-Em r *** 78 79' 81 82' 83' 85 86' 87 88' 89' 90' 92 93' 94 Splendidly-
sited first growth; 92 acres mid-slope on the COTES. Rich and tasty and
on top form since '82. PAVIE-DECESSE and La Clusière in same family.

Pavie-Decesse St-Em r **→*** 82 83 85 86 87 88 89 90 92 93 94   24 acres
seriously challenging their big brother (above).

Pavie-Macquin St-Em r **→*** 82 83 85' 86 87 88 89 90 91 92   Another
PAVIE challenge; this time the neighbours up the hill. 25-acre COTES v'yd
E of ST-EMILION. Fine organic winemaking by a son of VIEUX CH CERTAN.
Second label: Les Chênes.

Pavillon Rouge (Blanc) du Château Margaux See Ch Margaux.

Pedesclaux Pau r ** 81 82' 83 85 86 87 88 89 90' 91 92 93 94   50-acre
fifth growth on the level of a good CRU BOURGEOIS. Solid strong wines
that Belgians love. Second labels: Bellerose, Grand-Duroc-Milon.

Petit-Village Pom r *** 75' 78 79 81 82' 83 85' 86 87 88 89' 90' 91 92 93 94
Top property revived. 26 acres next to VIEUX CHATEAU CERTAN, same
owner (AXA) as CH PICHON-LONGUEVILLE since '89. Powerful plummy wine.

Pétrus Pom r **** 61 62 64 66 67 70' 71' 73 75' 76 78 79' 80 81 82' 83 84
85' 86 87 88' 89' 90 92 93 94   The great name of POMEROL. 28 acres of
gravelly clay giving massively rich and concentrated wine. 95%
Merlot vines. Each vintage adds lustre (NB no 91). The price too is
legendary.

Peyrabon St-Sauveur r ** 79 81 82' 83 85 86' 87 88 89' 90' 91 92 93 94
Serious 132-acre CRU BOURGEOIS popular in the Low Countries. Also La
Fleur-Peyrabon (only 12 acres).

Peyre-Labade Listrac ** Second label of CH CLARKE.

Peyreau St-Em r **   Sister château of Clos l'Oratoire.

de Pez St-Est r *** 64 70' 75' 76 78' 79 81 82' 83 85 86' 87 88 89 90' 91
92 93' 94   Outstanding CRU BOURGEOIS of 60 acres. As reliable as any of
the classed-growths of the village if not as fine.

Phélan-Ségur St-Est r ** 75' 81 82' 85 86 87 88' 89' 90' 91 92 93 94   Big
and important CRU BOURGEOIS (125 acres): some fine old vintages. 83 84
had to be withdrawn, but from '86 has gone from strength to strength.

Pibran Pau r ** 87 88 89' 90' 91 92 93 94   Small CRU BOURGEOIS allied to
PICHON-LONGUEVILLE. V classy wine with real PAUILLAC drive.

Pichon-Lalande (formerly Pichon-Longueville, Comtesse de Lalande)
Pau r **** 61 62 66 70' 75' 76 78' 79' 81 82' 83' 84 85' 86' 87 88' 89'
90' 91 92 93 94   'Super-second' growth neighbour to CH LATOUR. 148
acres. Consistently among v top performers; long-lived wine of
fabulous breed for those who like it luscious, even in lesser yrs.
Second wine: Réserve de la Comtesse. Rivalry across the road (next
entry) is worth watching.

Pichon-Longueville (formerly Baron de Pichon-Longueville) Pau r **** 78 79' **81** 82' 83 85 86' 87 88' 89' 90' 91 92 93 94' 77-acre second growth: wines have varied widely. Since '87 owned by AXA Insurance, run by J-M Cazes (LYNCH-BAGES). Revitalized winemaking matches aggressive building works. Second label: Les Tourelles de Longueville.

Le Pin Pom r **** 81 82 83 **85** 86 87 88 89 90' 92 93 94 A mere 500 cases of Merlot, with same owners as VIEUX CHATEAU CERTAN. A perfectionist miniature.

Pindefleurs St-Em r ** 82' **83** 85 86 88 89 90' 92 93' 94 Steady 23-acre v'yd on light soil. Second label: Clos Lescure.

St-Emilion: the class system

St-Emilion has its own class system, revised in 1985. At the top are two Premiers Grands Crus Classés 'A': Châteaux Ausone and Cheval Blanc. Then come nine Premiers Grands Crus Classés 'B'. 63 châteaux were elected as Grands Crus Classés. Another 170-odd are classed simply as Grands Crus, a rank renewable each year after official tastings. St-Emilion Grand Cru is therefore the very approximate equivalent of Médoc Crus Bourgeois and Grand Bourgeois.

Pique-Caillou Graves r (w dr) ** 85' 86 88' 89 90' 91 92 93 94 Nr Bordeaux airport. Refurbished. Ripe seductive GRAVES, and white since '93. Also next-door Ch Chênevert.

de Pitray Castillon r ** 82 83 85 86 87 88 89 90 91 92 93 94 Large (62-acre) v'yd on COTES DE CASTILLON E of ST-EM. Good flavoursome chewy wines.

Plagnac Méd r ** 82 83 85 86 88 89' 90' 91 92 93 94 CRU BOURGEOIS at Bégadan restored by CORDIER. To follow.

Plince Pom r ** 75 79 81 82 83 85 86 88 89' 90 92 93 94 Reputable 20-acre property nr Libourne. Attractive lightish wine from sandy soil.

La Pointe Pom r **→*** 82 83' 85 86 88 89' 90' 92 93 94 Prominent 63-acre estate; well-made wines, but relatively spare of flesh. New consultant in '86. LA SERRE is in the same hands.

Pontac-Monplaisir Graves r (w) ** 87 89 90 91 92 93 94 Another GRAVES property offering delicious white and fragrant light red.

Pontet-Canet Pau r *** 81 82' 83 85 86' 87 88 89' 90' 91 92 93 94 182-acre neighbour to MOUTON-ROTHSCHILD. Dragged its feet for many yrs. Owners (same as LAFON-ROCHET) have done better since '85. Should make v fine wines, but hardness (lack of selection in big v'yd?) has been the problem. Second label: Les Hauts de Pontet.

Pontoise-Cabarrus H-Méd r ** Useful and improving 60-acre CRU BOURGEOIS at ST-SEURIN. Wines need 5–6 yrs.

Potensac Méd r ** 78' 81' 82' 83 85' 86 87 88 89' 90' 91 92 93 94 Best-known CRU BOURGEOIS of N MEDOC. Neighbouring ch'x Lassalle, Gallais-Bellevue and LEOVILLE-LAS-CASES all owned by Delon family. Class shows.

Pouget Mar ** 78 81 82' 83 85 86 87 88 89 90 91 92 93 94 19-acres attached to BOYD-CANTENAC. Sharing owners since 1906. Similar, rather lighter wines.

Poujeaux (Theil) Moulis r ** 70' 75' 76 78 79' 81 82' 83' 85' 86 87 88' 89' 90' 91 92 93' 94' Family-run CRU EXCEPTIONNEL of 120 acres. 20,000-odd cases of characterful tannic and concentrated wine for a long life. Second label: La Salle de Poujeaux. Also Ch Arnauld.

Prieuré-Lichine Cantenac-Mar r *** 70 75 78' 82' 83' 85 86' 87 88 89' 90' 91 92 93 94' 143-acre fourth growth brought to the fore by the late Alexis Lichine. Excellent full fragrant MARGAUX. Second wine: Clairefont.

Puy-Blanquet St-Em r ** 75' 82' 83 85 86 88 89' 90' 92 93 The major property of St-Etienne-de-Lisse, E of ST-EMILION, with over 50 acres. Early-maturing in early '80s; now firming up well.

Puygueraud Côte de Francs r ** 85 86 88 89' 90 92 93 94 Leading château of this rising district. Wood-aged wines of surprising class. Ch Laclaverie and Les Charmes-Godard follow the same lines.

Rabaud-Promis Saut w sw ** 83' 85 86' 87 88' 89' 90   74-acre classed-growth at Bommes. Keep under observation.

Rahoul Graves r w ** (r) 82 83 85 86 88 89' 90' 91 92 93 94   37-acre v'yd at Portets making particularly good wine in the '80s from maturing vines; 80% red. White (90 91) also oak-aged.

Ramage-la-Bâtisse H-Méd r ██ 82 83' 85 86 88 89' 90 91 92 93 94   Potentially outstanding CRU BOURGEOIS of 130 acres at ST-SAUVEUR, N of PAUILLAC. Increasingly good since '85. Ch Tourteran is second wine.

Rausan-Ségla Mar r ██ 70' 82 83' 84 85 86' 88' 89' 90' 91 92 93 94'   106-acre second growth famous for its fragrance; a great MEDOC name trying successfully to regain its rank since '82. New owners in '89 and again in '94. Second wine Ségla. This should be the top second-growth. Ancient vintages can be superb.

Rauzan-Gassies Mar r ** 75' 79 82 83 85 86 88 89' 90' 91 92 93 94   75-acre second-growth neighbour of the last with little excitement to report for two decades, now perking up – but still far to go.

Raymond-Lafon Saut w sw ███ 75' 76 78 79 80' 81 82 83' 85 86' 87 88 89' 90' 91 92 93 94   Serious SAUTERNES estate of 44 acres run by the ex-manager of YQUEM. Splendid wines for long ageing. Among the top Sauternes.

de Rayne-Vigneau Saut w sw ** 76' 83 85 86' 88 89 90' 91 92 94   164-acre classed-growth at Bommes. Standard sweet wine and dry Rayne Sec.

Respide-Médeville Graves w (r) ** (w) 87 88 89 90 91 92' 93 94   One of the better unclassified white wine châteaux. Full-flavoured wines for ageing. (NB Cuvée Kauffman.) Drink the reds at 4–6 yrs.

Reynon Premières Côtes r w ██   100 acres for fragrant white from old Sauv vines (VIEILLES VIGNES) (92 93' 94); serious red (85 86 88' 89 90 91 92 93 94). 2nd wine (red): Ch Reynon-Peyrat. See also Clos Floridène.

Reysson Vertheuil (H-Méd) r ** 82' 83 85 86 87 88 89' 90'   Recently replanted 120-acre CRU BOURGEOIS in Japanese hands.

Ricaud Loupiac w sw (r dr) ██ (w) 81 82 83' 85 86' 88 89 90 91 92 94   Substantial grower of almost SAUTERNES-like wine just across the river. New owners are working hard. It ages well.

Rieussec Saut w sw *** 67 71' 75' 79 81 82 83' 85 86' 87 88' 89' 90' 91 92 93 94   Worthy neighbour of CH D'YQUEM with 136 acres in Fargues, bought in '84 by the (LAFITE) Rothschilds. Not the sweetest; can be exquisitely fine. Also dry 'R' and super-wine Crème de Tête.

Ripeau St-Em r ** 81 82 83 85 86 87 88 89 90 93 94   Steady GRAND CRU in the centre of the plateau. 40 acres.

La Rivière Fronsac r ** 82 83 85' 86 87 88' 89 90   The biggest and most impressive FRONSAC property with a Wagnerian castle. Tannic but juicy wines win prizes in youth and stay young for a decade.

de Rochemorin Graves r (w) ** 82 83 85 86 87 88 89' 90' 91 92 93   An important restoration at Martillac by CH LA LOUVIÈRE's owner: 165 acres of maturing vines promise great things. Oaky whites to keep 4–5 yrs.

Romer Saut w sw   Classed-growth with its name under legal dispute.

de Roquetaillade-la-Grange Graves r w ** 86 88 89 90 91 92 93 94   Substantial estate: fine red (southern) GRAVES and well-made white. See Cap de Mourlin.

Rouget Pom r ** 75' 76' 78 79 81 82' 83 85' 86 88 89' 90 92 93 94   Attractive old estate on the northern edge of POMEROL. Good, without polish; needs age.

Royal St-Emilion Brand name of the important and dynamic growers' coop. See also Berliquet, Galius.

Ruat-Petit-Poujeaux Moulis r ** 82 85 86 88 89 90 91 92 93 94   45-acre v'yd gaining in reputation for vigorous wine, to drink in 5–6 yrs.

St-André-Corbin St-Em r ██ 81 82' 83 85' 86 88 89 90 92 93 94   54-acre estate in MONTAGNE- and ST-GEORGES-ST-EMILION: above average wines.

St-Bonnet Méd r ** 82 85 86 88 89 90 91 92 93 94   Big N MEDOC estate at St-Christoly. V flavoury wine.

St-Estèphe, Marquis de St-Est r ✴ 82 86 88 89 90 93 94   The growers' coop; bigger but not as interesting as formerly.

St-Georges St-Georges-St-Em r ✴✴ 82 83 85' 86 87 88' 89' 90' 92 93 94   Noble 18th-C château overlooking the ST-EMILION plateau from the hill to the north. 125 acres. Vg wine sold direct to the public.

St-Georges-Côte-Pavie St-Em r ✴✴ 82 83' 85' 86 88' 89' 90' 92 93 94   Perfectly placed little v'yd on the COTES. Run with dedication.

St-Pierre St-Jul r ✴✴✴ 70' 78' 81' 82' 83' 85 86' 88' 89' 90' 91 92 93 94   Small (42-acre) fourth growth bought in '82 by the late Henri Martin of CH GLORIA. V stylish and consistent classic ST-JULIEN.

de St-Pierre Graves w (r) ✴✴   Main-line white of notable character and flavour to drink young or keep. Also red.

de Sales Pom r ✴✴✴ 75' 82' 83 85 86 88 89' 90' 92 93 94   Biggest v'yd of POMEROL (116 acres), attached to grandest château. Rarely poetry, but good lucid prose. Second labels: ch'x Chantalouette, du Delias.

Saransot-Dupré Listrac r (w) ✴✴ 86 88 89 90 92 93 94   Small property performing well since '86. Also one of LISTRAC's growing band of whites.

Sénéjac H-Méd r (w) ✴✴ 78 81 82' 83' 85 86' 87 88 89' 90' 91 92 93 94   60-acre CRU BOURGEOIS in S MEDOC, run with zeal by a New Zealander. All-Sém white, to age (90 91 92 93 94). Second label: Dom de l'Artigue.

La Serre St-Em r ✴✴ 75 81 82 83 85 86 88' 89 90 92 93 94   Small GRAND CRU, same owner as LA POINTE. Reliably tasty.

Siaurac Lalande de Pom r ✴✴   Substantial, consistent; nr POMEROL. 57 acres.

Sigalas-Rabaud Saut w sw ✴✴✴ 76' 79 80 81 82 83 85 86 87 88' 89' 90' 91 92   The smaller part of the former RABAUD estate: 34 acres in Bommes making first-class sweet wine in a rich grapey style.

Rotting with style

Botrytis cinerea (French pourriture noble, German Edelfäule, English noble rot) is a form of mould that attacks the skins of ripe grapes in certain vineyards in warm and misty autumn weather.

Its effect, instead of rotting the grapes, is to wither them. The skin grows soft and flaccid, the juice evaporates through it, and what is left is a super-sweet concentration of everything in the grape except its water content.

The world's best sweet table wines are all made of 'nobly rotten' grapes. They occur in good vintages in Sauternes, the Rhine and the Mosel (where wine made from them is called Trockenbeerenauslese), in Tokaji in Hungary, in Burgenland in Austria, and elsewhere – California and Australia included. The danger is rain on pulpy grapes already far gone in botrytis. All too often the growers' hopes are dashed by the weather.

Siran Labarde-Mar r ✴✴ 70 75' 78' 81 82' 83 85 86 88 89' 90' 93 94   74-acre property approaching CRU CLASSE quality. Recent investment.

Smith-Haut-Lafitte Graves r (w p) ✴✴→✴✴✴ (r) 82' 85 86 89' 90' 91 92 93 94; (w) 92 93 94   Classed-growth at Martillac: 122 acres (14 of white). New ambitious owners in '90. Formerly light wines now much more concentrated. Second label: Les Hauts de Smith.

Sociando-Mallet H-Méd r ✴✴ 82' 83 85' 86' 88' 89' 90' 91 92 93 94   Splendid CRU GRAND BOURGEOIS at ST-SEURIN. 65 acres. Conservative big-boned wines to lay down for yrs. Second wine: Lartigue-de-Brochon.

Soudars H-Méd r ✴✴   Sister to COUFRAN; new CRU BOURGEOIS doing v well.

Soutard St-Em r ✴✴✴ 70' 71 78' 79 81 82' 83 85' 86 88' 89' 90' 91 92 93 94   Excellent 48-acre classed-growth, 60% Merlot. Potent; long-lived, exciting young to French palates. Second label: Clos de la Tonnelle.

Suduiraut Saut w sw ✴✴✴ 67 70 75 76' 78 79' 81 82' 83' 84 85 86 88' 89' 90' 94   One of the best SAUTERNES, in its best vintages supremely luscious. 173 acres potentially of top class. Now in AXA control. See Pichon-Longueville. Selection: Cuvée Madame (82 83 86 89).

du Tailhas Pom r ✴✴   5,000 cases. POMEROL of the lighter kind, near FIGEAC.

Taillefer Pom r ✱✱ 82 83 85 86 88' 89 90 92 93 94 28-acres on the edge of POMEROL in the Armand Moueix family (see also Fonplégade).

Talbot St-Jul r (w) ✱✱✱ 78' 79 81 82' 83' 84 85' 86' 87 88' 89' 90 91 92 93 94 Important 240-acre fourth growth, sister to GRUAUD-LAROSE. Wine similarly attractive: rich, satisfying, reliable and gd value. Vg second label: Connétable Talbot. White is 'Caillou Blanc'.

Tayac Soussans-Mar r ✱✱ 82 83 85 86 87 88 89 90 92 93 94 MARGAUX's biggest CRU BOURGEOIS. Reliable if not noteworthy.

de Terrefort-Quancard B'x r w ✱✱ Huge producer of good value wines at ST-ANDRE-DE-CUBZAC on the road to Paris. Rocky subsoil contributes to surprising quality. 33,000 cases. Drink at 5–10 yrs. Several other châteaux owned by Cheval-Quancard.

Terrey-Gros-Caillou St-Jul ✱✱ 82' 83 85 86' 88 89 90 91 92 93 94 Sister-château to HORTEVIE; at best equally noteworthy and stylish.

du Tertre Arsac-Mar r ✱✱ 70' 79' 81 82' 83' 85 86 88' 89' 90' 91 92 93 94 Fifth growth isolated S of MARGAUX; restored by the owner of CALON-SEGUR. Fragrant and long-lived.

Tertre-Daugay St-Em r ✱✱✱ 82' 83' 85 86 88' 89' 90' 92 93 94 Small, spectacularly sited GRAND CRU. Restored to proper rank by owner of LA GAFFELIERE.

Le Tertre-Rôteboeuf St-Em ✱✱→✱✱✱ 85 86 87 88' 89' 90' 91 92 93 94 A new star making concentrated, even dramatic, largely Merlot wine since '83. The 'roast beef' of the name gives the idea.

Thieuley E-Deux-Mers r p w ✱✱ Substantial supplier esp of clairet (rosé) and grapey Sauv. But reds are aged in oak.

Timberlay B'x r (w) ✱ 185 acres at ST-ANDRE-DE-CUBZAC. Pleasant light wines to age 2–5 yrs. Same owners as VILLEMAURINE.

Toumilon Graves r w ✱✱ Little château in St-Pierre-de-Mons to note. Fresh and charming red and white.

La Tour-Blanche Saut w (r) sw ✱✱✱ 81' 82 83' 85 86 87 88' 89' 90' 91 92 93 94 Historic leader of SAUTERNES, now a government wine college. Coasted in '70s; hit historic form again in '88.

La Tour-de-By Bégadan (Méd) r ✱✱ 81 82' 83 85' 86 87 88' 89' 90' 91 93 94 V well-run 182-acre CRU BOURGEOIS in N MEDOC steadily increasing its reputation for sturdy, impressively good wine; yet instantly appealing wine.

La Tour-Carnet St-Laurent r ✱✱ 82 83 85 86 88 89' 90 91 92 93' 94' Fourth growth with medieval fortress, long neglected. Light wine; bolder since '86. Second wine: Sire de Comin.

La Tour-Figeac St-Em r ✱✱ 79 81 82' 83 85 86 87 88 89' 90' 93 94' 34-acre GRAND CRU between CH FIGEAC and POMEROL. Californian ideas since '94.

La Tour-Haut-Brion Graves r ✱✱✱ 70 78 79 81 82' 83 85 86 87 88 89 90 91 92 93 94 Formerly second label of CH LA MISSION-HAUT-BRION. Up to '83 a plainer, v tannic wine for long life. Now a separate v'yd: easier wines.

La Tour-Haut-Caussan Méd r ✱✱ Ambitious small (23-acre) estate at Blaignan attracting admiration.

La Tour-du-Haut-Moulin Cussac (H-Méd) r ✱✱ 75 76 81 82' 83 84 85' 86' 87 88' 89' 90' 91 92 93 94 Conservative producer of intense wine: top CRU BOURGEOIS.

La Tour-de-Mons Soussans-Mar r ✱✱ 70' 82' 83 85 86' 88' 89' 90' 91 92 93 94 Famous CRU BOURGEOIS of 87 acres, 3 centuries in the same family. A long dull patch but new wines look better.

Tour du Pas St-Georges St-Em r ✱✱ Wine from 40 acres of ST-GEORGES-ST-EMILION made by AUSONE winemaker. V stylish; to follow.

La Tour-du-Pin-Figeac St-Em r ✱✱ 26-acre GRAND CRU worthy of restoration.

La Tour-du-Pin-Figeac-Moueix St-Em r ✱✱ 81 82 83 85 86 88' 89' 90' 92 93 94 Another 26-acre section of the same old property, owned by the Armand Moueix family. Splendid site; powerful wines.

For key to grape variety abbreviations, see pages 6–9.

La Tour-St-Bonnet Méd r ★★ 82' 83 85 86 87 88 89' 90' 91 92 93 94
  Consistently well-made potent N MEDOC from St-Christoly. 100 acres.

Tournefeuille Lalande de Pom r ★★ 81' 82' 83' 85 86 88 89 90' 91 92 93 94
  Best-known château of NEAC. 43 acres; sound wine. Also Ch de Bourg.

des Tours Montagne-St-Em r ★★ 82 85 86 88 89 90 92 93 94 Spectacular
  château with modern 170-acre v'yd. Sound easy wine.

Toutigeac, Domaine de E-Deux-Mers r (w) ★ 89 90' 91 92 93 94' Enormous
  producer of useful Bordeaux at Targon.

Tronquoy-Lalande St-Est r ★★ 70 79 81 82' 83 85 86 88 89 90 92 93 94
  40-acre CRU BOURGEOIS: typical high-coloured, ageable ST-ESTEPHE.
  DOURTHE-distributed.

Troplong-Mondot St-Em r ★★→★★★ 82' 83 85' 86 87 88' 89' 90' 92 93 94
  70 acres well-sited on the COTES above CH PAVIE (and in same family).
  Now run with passion and new barrels. To follow. 2nd wine: Mondot.

Trotanoy Pom r ★★★★ 61' 70' 71' 75' 76' 78 79 81 82 83 84 85' 86 87 88 89
  90' 92 93 94 Usually the second POMEROL, after PETRUS, from the same
  stable. Only 27 acres; but at best a glorious fleshy perfumed wine.

Trottevieille St-Em r ★★★ 79' 81 82' 83 85' 86 87 88 89' 90 92 93 94 GRAND
  CRU of 27 acres on the COTES. Dragged its feet for yrs. Same owners as
  BATAILLEY have raised their sights since '85. To watch.

Le Tuquet Graves r w ★★ Big estate at Beautiran Light fruity wines to
  drink young; the white better. (Cuvée Spéciale oak-aged.)

Verdignan Méd r ★★ 81 82 83 85 86 87 88 89' 90' 91 92 Substantial
  Bourgeois sister to CH COUFRAN. More Cab than Coufran.

Vieux Château Certan Pom r ★★★ 70 78 79 81 82' 83' 85 86' 87 88' 89 90'
  92 93 94 Traditionally rated close to PETRUS in quality, but totally
  different in style; almost HAUT-BRION build. 34 acres. Same (Belgian)
  family owns LABEGORCE-ZEDE and tiny POMEROL, LE PIN. See also Château
  Puygueraud.

Vieux-Château-St-André St-Em r ★★ 82' 83 85' 86 87 88' 89' 90' 91 92
  93' 94' Small v'yd in MONTAGNE-ST-EMILION owned by the winemaker of
  PETRUS. To follow. 2,500 cases.

Villegeorge Avensan r ★★ 82 83' 85 86 87' 88 89 90 92 93 94 24-acre CRU
  BOURGEOIS N of MARGAUX; same owner as BRANE-CANTENAC. Enjoyable
  rather tannic wine. Sister château: Duplessis (Hauchecorne).

Villemaurine St-Em r ★★ 82' 83 85' 86 87 88 89 90 92 93 94 Small
  GRAND CRU with splendid cellars well-sited on the COTES by the town.
  Firm wine with a high proportion of Cab.

Vray-Croix-de-Gay Pom r ★★ 75' 82' 83 85 86 87 88 89 90 92 93 94 V small
  ideally situated v'yd in the best part of POMEROL. Needs devotion.

Yon-Figeac St-Em r ★★ 81 82 83 85 86 88 89 90 92 93 94 59-acre GRAND
  CRU to follow for savoury supple wine.

d'Yquem Saut w sw (dr) ★★★★ 67' 71' 73 75' 76' 77 78 79 80' 81' 82' 83' 84
  85 86' 87 88' 89' (90' 91 93 94 to come) The world's most famous
  sweet-wine estate. 250 acres; only 500 bottles per acre of v strong
  intense luscious wine, kept 4 yrs in barrel. Most vintages improve
  for 15 yrs+. Also make dry Ygrec ('Y') in 78 79 80 84 85 (86 v little) 87
  88 89 91 92.

More Bordeaux châteaux are listed under Canon-Fronsac, Côtes de Bourg,
Côtes de Castillon, Côtes de Francs, Fronsac, Lalande de Pomerol, Loupiac,
Premières Côtes de Blaye, Premières Côtes de Bordeaux, St-André-de-
Cubzac, Ste-Croix-du-Mont in the A–Z of France, pages 20–57.

Italy

FRANCE

SWITZERLAND

L. Co

VALLE
D'AOSTA   L. Maggiore

Milar

LOMBA

Turin   Po
PIEDMONT

Gen

LIGURIA

The Italian wine industry still lives
in a state of genial chaos that can
easily mask its real qualities and values.
1992 seemed to be the turning point in its
reputation and fortunes. January 23 that
year saw the enactment of a completely
revised version of the seriously discredited
DOC legislation, which for 30 years has caused
confusion among consumers and militated
against both quality and innovation.

'Law 164' was intended to end all the old
anomalies, but especially that by which a vino
da tavola, officially the lowest grade of wine classification,
was frequently a much better (and more expensive) wine than
one made within the statutory requirements of a DOC – or even
a DOCG, formerly the most elevated appellation available.

Eventually (this at least is the theory) the new laws will bring
Italian appellations very close in spirit to those of France, where
all the stress is on geography – or 'terroir'. They are also
intended (like the French laws) to discourage the marketing of
high quality wines simply by grape variety name.

Law 164 is most graphically represented by a pyramid, whose
base is the humble vino da tavola. No geographical (or varietal,
or even vintage) claims can be made at this level: only a brand
name. Next is a new institution, intended to mirror the French vin
de pays and known as IGT (Indicazione Geografica Tipica). As
planned, IGTs will use a geographical name and can also use the
name of a grape. So far, however, no IGT has materialized. Will
they ever? Above IGTs come DOCs and DOCGs. These can label
information as specific as the vineyard (vigna) name – but only
by producing less: sacrificing quantity for quality.

Thus the highest rank in the pyramid will be a vigna wine
from a DOCG zone. But whereas the rank of DOCG was formerly
limited to a dozen famous areas, it now becomes the right of any
DOC which has performed well enough for five years.
Conversely a DOC which functions half-heartedly will lose its
rank. Even more radically, an outstanding proprietorial wine
'which does honour to Italy' may be eligible for its own DOCG
status. Some are already well on the way.

A clear advantage of the pyramid system is that producers
can decide at vintage time how high they are going to pitch their
wine. Self-discipline can give them the right to the top appellation;
high yields and lower concentration will demote them down the
pyramid. The control is by provincial Chambers of Commerce.

There is much more detail to the new Law, and much that
only experience will determine. It is a convincingly brave attempt
to sort out the minestrone of the old system. In the political
chaos of Italy, though, who knows what may happen?

Meanwhile, as always, the best advice is to be bold. Do not
cling limply to familiar names. This section is packed with new
creations: some thrillingly good – some (Italy is Italy) merely
cosmetic. But quality in Italy is by no means an automatic bargain.

The following abbreviations are used in the text:

Ab	Abruzzi	**F-VG**	Friuli– Venezia Giulia	**Sar**	Sardinia	
Ap	Apulia			**Si**	Sicily	
Bas	Basilicata	**Lat**	Latium	**T-AA**	Trentino- Alto Adige	
Cal	Calabria	**Lig**	Liguria	**Tus**	Tuscany	
Cam	Campania	**Lom**	Lombardy	**Umb**	Umbria	
E-R	Emilia- Romagna	**Mar**	Marches	**VdA**	Valle d'Aosta	
		Pie	Piedmont	**Ven**	Veneto	
				fz	frizzante	
				pa	passito	

Abbazia di Rosazzo ★★★ A leading estate of COLLI ORIENTALI. White Ronco delle Acacie and R di Corte and red R dei Roseti are vg single-v'yd wines.

Abboccato Semi-sweet.

Adanti ★★→★★★ Umbrian maker of good red SAGRANTINO DI MONTEFALCO, VDT BIANCO D'ARQUATA and Rosso d'Arquata (a vg BARBERA-Canaiolo-MERLOT blend). Also good CAB S. Value.

Aglianico del Vulture Bas DOC r dr (s/sw sp) ★★★ 82 85 86 87 88 90 91 92 93 Among the best wines of S Italy. Ages well to rich aromas. Called vecchio after 3 yrs, RISERVA after 5. Top growers: D'ANGELO (also makes vg pure Aglianico VDT Canneto) and Paternoster.

Alba Major wine centre of PIEDMONT, on R Tanaro, S of Turin.

Albana di Romagna E-R DOCG w dr s/sw (sp) ★★(★) DYA Italy's first DOCG for white wine, though it is hard to see why. Albana is the grape. Cold fermentation usually robs it of what little character it had. FATTORIA PARADISO makes some of the best. AMABILE is usually better than dry. ZERBINA's botrytis-sweet PASSITO is outstanding. Also try Romandiola.

Albola, Castello d' Old CHIANTI CLASSICO estate owned by ZONIN. Average.

Alcamo Si DOC w ✳ Soft neutral whites. Rapitalà is the best brand.

Aleatico Excellent red Muscat-flavoured grape, for sweet, aromatic, strong dessert wines, chiefly of the south. Aleatico di Puglia DOC (best grower, Candido) is better and more famous than A di Gradoli (Lat) DOC.

Alezio Ap DOC p (r) ★★ DYA Recent DOC at Salento, esp for delicate rosé. Top grower: Calò Michele (who also makes gd barrel-aged NEGROAMARO VDT, Vigna Spano).

Allegrini ★★★ Top quality producer of Veronese wines, incl fine VALPOLICELLA from prime new v'yds and vg AMARONE.

Altare ★★★ Small producer of good modern BAROLO and BARBERA VDT Vigna Larigi.

Altesino ★★ Producer of BRUNELLO DI MONTALCINO and VDT Palazzo Altesi.

Alto Adige T-AA DOC r p w dr sw sp ★→★★★ DOC covering 20 different wines, usually named by their grapes, in 33 German-speaking villages around Bolzano. Best are white. Region often called Südtirol.

Ama, Castello di, (or Fattoria di Ama) ★★★★ One of the best, most consistent modern CHIANTI CLASSICO estates, nr Gaiole. San Lorenzo, Bertinga, La Casuccia and Bellavista are top single-v'yd wines. Also good VDTS, CHARD, SAUV, MERLOT (Vigna L'Apparita), PINOT N (Il Chiuso).

Amabile Means semi-sweet, but usually sweeter than ABBOCCATO.

Amaro Bitter. When prominent on label, content is not wine but 'bitters'.

Amarone della Valpolicella (alias Recioto della Valpolicella Amarone) Ven DOC r ★★★→★★★★ 80 83 84 85 86 88 90 (91) (93) (94) Dry version of RECIOTO DELLA VALPOLICELLA, potent, concentrated, long-lived and impressive; from air-dried grapes. Best from Serègo Alighieri, ALLEGRINI, BERTANI, Brigaldara, Brunelli, Corte Sant Alda, Aleardo Ferrari, Fornaser, DAL FORNO, GUERRIERI-RIZZARDI, LE RAGOSE, MASI, QUINTARELLI, San Rustico, Le Salette, Speri, TEDESCHI, Vantini, Venturini, Viviani.

Anghelu Ruju ★★★ Port-like version of Sardinian CANNONAU wine from SELLA & MOSCA. To try.

Anselmi, Roberto ★★★ A leader in SOAVE with his single-v'yd Capitel Foscarino and exceptional sweet dessert RECIOTO dei Capitelli.

Antinori, Marchesi L & P ★→★★★ Immensely influential long-established Florentine house of the highest repute, now wholly owned by Piero A, producing first-rate CHIANTI CLASSICO (esp PEPPOLI, Tenute Marchese Antinori, Villa Antinori and Badia a Passignano), Umbrian (CASTELLO DELLA SALA) and PIEDMONT (PRUNOTTO) wines. The first pioneer of new VDT, eg TIGNANELLO, SOLAIA (Tuscany), CERVARO DELLA SALA (Umbria). Marchese Piero A was the Voice of Italy in world wine circles in the 1970s and '80s. See also Prunotto.

Aquileia F-VG DOC r w ★★ (r) 88 90 93 94 12 single-grape wines from around town of Aquileia on border of Slovenia. Good REFOSCO.

Argiano ★★★ Top MONTALCINO producer, owned by Noemi Marone Cinzano.

Argiolas, Antonio ✶✶ Important Sardinian producer with astonishing quality. Vg: CANNONAU, NURAGUS, VERMENTINO and red VDT Turriga.

Arneis Pie w ✶✶ DYA At last a good white from BAROLO country: the revival of an ancient grape to make fragrant light wine. Now DOC as Roero Arneis, a zone N of Alba, and Langhe Arneis. Good from Almondo, Bel Colle, Correggia, Deltetto, BRUNO GIACOSA, Malvirà, Negro, Rabino and Gianni Voerzio (Roero A); Castello di Neive (Langhe A).

Artimino Tusc r ✶✶✶ Ancient hill-town W of Florence. Fattoria di Artimino produces top DOCG CARMIGNANO.

Assisi Umb r (w) ✶✶ DYA VDT Rosso and Bianco di A: v attractive. Drink cool.

Asti Major wine centre of PIEDMONT.

Asti (Spumante) Pie DOCG w sp ✶✶✶–✶✶✶✶ NV Immensely popular sweet and v fruity Muscat sparkling wine, now updated to DOCG with raised standards. V low in alcohol. Can be delicious with dessert. Top producers: Barbero-Secondino, BERA, Caudrina, CINZANO, FONTANAFREDDA, GANCIA, MARTINI & ROSSI, and Vignaioli di Santo Stefano Belbo.

Attems, Conti Famous old COLLIO estate with range of good typical wines (esp PINOT GRIGIO). Now run by Collavini.

Avignonesi ✶✶✶→✶✶✶✶ MONTEPULCIANO house with v fine range: VINO NOBILE, blended red Grifi, top CHARD, SAUV, MERLOT and superlative VIN SANTO.

Azienda agricola/agraria A farm producing crops, often incl wine.

Azienda/casa vinicola Wine firm using bought-in grapes and/or wines.

Azienda vitivinicola A (specialized) wine estate.

Badia a Coltibuono ✶✶→✶✶✶ Fine CHIANTI-maker in an old abbey at Gaiole with a restaurant and collection of old vintages. Also VDT SANGIOVETO.

Banfi (Castello or Villa) ✶✶→✶✶✶ Space-age CANTINA of biggest US importer of Italian wine. Huge plantings at MONTALCINO, mostly SANGIOVESE, but also Syrah, PINOT N, CAB, CHARD, SAUV etc, are part of a drive for quality plus quantity. BRUNELLO is good but 'Poggio all'Oro' is ✶✶✶✶. Centine is ROSSO DI MONTALCINO. In PIEDMONT Banfi produces vg sparkling Banfi Brut, Principessa GAVI, BRACCHETTO D'ACQUI, PINOT GR. See also NE USA.

Barbacarlo Lom r dr sw sp ✶✶ Traditional light wines with typical bitter-almond taste, from OLTREPO PAVESE.

Barbaresco Pie DOCG r ✶✶✶→✶✶✶✶ 85' 86 87 88' 89' 90' 93' Neighbour of BAROLO from the same grapes. Perhaps marginally less sturdy. At best palate-cleansing, deep, subtle and fine. At 4 yrs becomes RISERVA. Producers incl CERETTO, CIGLIUTI, GAJA, BRUNO GIACOSA, Marchesi di Gresy, MOCCAGATTA, Fiorenzo Nada, Giorgio Pelissero, PIO CESARE, Produttori del B, PRUNOTTO, Alfredo Roagna, BRUNO ROCCA, Sottimano.

Barbatella, Cascina La ✶✶✶ Top producer of BARBERA D'ASTI: excellent single-v'yd Sonvico and dell'Angelo.

Barbera Dark acidic red grape, the second most planted in Italy after SANGIOVESE; a speciality of PIEDMONT also used in Lombardy, Emilia-Romagna and other northern provinces. Its best wines follow...

Barbera d'Alba Pie DOC r ✶✶✶→✶✶✶✶ 85' 86 87 88' 89' 90' 91 92 93' 94 Tasty tannic fragrant red. SUPERIORE can age 7+ yrs. Round ALBA, NEBBIOLO is sometimes added to make a VDT (some barrique-aged 100% BARBERA is also vdt). Top producers: CIGLIUTI, CLERICO, Elvio Cogno, A and G CONTERNO, CONTERNO-FANTINO, E GRASSO, Silvio Grasso, Manzone, G MASCARELLO, OBERTO, PARUSSO, Pianpolvere Soprana, PRUNOTTO, BRUNO ROCCA, Scavino, Aldo Vajra, Eraldo Viberti, VIETTI, Gianni Voerzio, R VOERZIO. See also Gaja.

Barbera d'Asti Pie DOC r ✶✶✶→✶✶✶✶ 85' 86 87 88' 89' 90' 91 92 93' 94 For real BARBERA-lovers: solely Barbera grapes, tangy and appetizing, drunk young or aged up to 7 yrs or longer. Top growers incl La Barbatella, Bava, Bertelli, BOFFA, BRAIDA, Brema, Cascina Castlét, Chiarlo, COPPO, SCARPA, Trinchero, Viarengo.

Barbera del Monferrato Pie DOC r ✶→✶✶✶ DYA Easy-drinking BARBERA from Alessandria and ASTI. Pleasant, slightly fizzy, s'times sweetish.

Barberani ** Leading ORVIETO producer; Calcaia is botrytis-sweet wine.

Barbi, Fattoria dei ** Traditional producer of BRUNELLO DI MONTALCINO.

Barco Reale Tus DOC r ** DOC for junior wine of CARMIGNANO; same grapes.

Bardolino Ven DOC r (p) ** DYA Pale summery slightly bitter red from E shore of Lake Garda. Bardolino CHIARETTO is even paler and lighter. Top makers: GUERRIERI-RIZZARDI, Fratelli Zeni.

Barolo Pie DOCG r ***→**** 82' 85' 86 88' 89' 90' 93' Small area S of ALBA with one of Italy's supreme reds: rich, tannic, alcoholic (min 13°), dry but wonderfully deep and fragrant (also crisp and clean) in the mouth. From NEBBIOLO grapes. Ages for up to 15 yrs (RISERVA after 5).

Top Barolo producers incl Altare, Azelia, Cappellano, Cavallotto, Ceretto, Clerico, Aldo Conterno, Giacomo Conterno, Conterno-Fantino, Corino, Gaja, Giacosa, Elio Grasso, Silvio Grasso, G Manzone, Marengo-Marenda, Marcarini, Bartolo Mascarello, Guiseppe Mascarello, Mauro Molino, Monfalletto, A Oberto, Oddero, Parusso, Pio Cesare, Prunotto, Ratti, Rocche dei Manzoni, Sandrone, Scavino, Fratelli Seghesio, Viberti, Vietti, Gianni Voerzio, Roberto Voerzio.

Bellavista **→*** FRANCIACORTA estate with brisk sparkling. Also Crémant. Good VDT reds from CAB and PINOT N.

Bera, Fratelli **→*** Family estate. Vg MOSCATO D'ASTI.

Berlucchi, Guido Italy's biggest producer of sparkling METODO CLASSICO, at FRANCIACORTA. Quality steady.

Bertani ** Well-known producers of quality Veronese wines (VALPOLICELLA, AMARONE, SOAVE, etc).

Bertelli *** Good small PIEDMONT producer: BARBERA D'ASTI, VDT CAB, CHARD.

Biancara, La *** Top quality GAMBELLARAS (vg RECIOTO and late-harvest VENDEMMIA TARDIVA). (ZONIN is number one in quantity.)

Bianco White.

Bianco d'Arquata Umb w ** DYA See Adanti.

Bianco di Custoza Ven DOC w (sp) *→*** DYA Twin of SOAVE from the other side (west) of Verona.

Bianco di Pitigliano Tus DOC w * DYA Usually v dull dry white from nr Grosseto.

Biancolella ISCHIA's best white. A VDT from D'AMBRA.

Bigi, Luigi & Figlio Famous producers of ORVIETO and other wines of Umbria and TUSCANY. Their TORRICELLA v'yd produces vg dry Orvieto.

Biondi-Santi **→**** The original producer of BRUNELLO DI MONTALCINO, from 45-acre Il Greppo vineyard. Prices are absurd, but the old vintages are unique.

Boca Pie DOC r ** 85 88 89 90 93 From same grape as BAROLO (NEBBIOLO) in N of PIEDMONT. Look for Poderi ai Valloni.

Boffa, Alfiero Small property for top BARBERA D'ASTI. Esp single-v'yd wines.

Bolgheri Tus DOC r p w (sw) **→*** On the coast south of Livorno. Incl 7 types of wine: BIANCO, VERMENTINO, SAUVIGNON, ROSSO, ROSATO, VIN SANTO OCCHIO DI PERNICE and (since '94) SASSICAIA (****).

Bolla Famous Verona firm producing VALPOLICELLA, SOAVE, etc. Top wines: Castellaro (one of the v best SOAVES), Creso (red and white), Jago.

Bonarda Minor red grape (alias Croatina) widely grown in PIEDMONT, Lombardy, Emilia-Romagna and blended with BARBERA.

Bonarda (Oltrepò Pavese) Lom DOC r ** Soft fresh often FRIZZANTE red from S of Pavia.

Borgo del Tiglio *** FRIULI estate for one of NE Italy's top MERLOTS: VDT Rosso della Centa; also good are COLLIO CHARD, TOCAI and BIANCO.

Boscaini Ven ** Verona producer of VALPOLICELLA, AMARONE, SOAVE.

Boscarelli, Poderi *** Small estate with vg VINO NOBILE DI MONTEPULCIANO, barrel-aged VDT Boscarelli and good ROSSO DI M.

Brachetto d'Acqui Pie DOC r sw (sp) ** DYA Sweet sparkling red with enticing Muscat scent.

Bramaterra Pie DOC r ** 85 88 89 90 93   Neighbour to GATTINARA. NEBBIOLO grapes predominate in a blend. Good producers: Perazzi, SELLA.

Breganze Ven DOC *→*** (r) 88 89 90 91 93 94   A catch-all for many varieties around Vicenza. CAB and PINOT BL are best. Top producers: B Bartolomeo, MACULAN.

Bricco Term for a high (and by implication vg) ridge v'yd in PIEDMONT.

Bricco del Drago Pie vdt 88 89 90 93 94   Original long-lived blend of DOLCETTO and NEBBIOLO from Cascina Drago.

Bricco Manzoni Pie r *** 82' 85' 88' 89' 90' 91 92 93' 94   V successful blend of NEBBIOLO and BARBERA from Monforte d'Alba.

Bricco dell'Uccellone Pie r *** 85' 88' 89' 90' 91 92 93' 94   Barrique-aged BARBERA from the firm of the late Giacomo Bologna. Bricco della Bigotta and Ai Suma are others.

Brindisi Ap DOC r **   Strong NEGROAMARO. Esp Patriglione (***) from Taurino.

Brolio, Castello di After a sad period in foreign hands, the Ricasoli family has taken this legendary estate in hand again. The near future will show the results.

Brunello di Montalcino Tus DOCG r ***→****   82' 85' 86 88' 90' 91 92 93 With BAROLO, Italy's most celebrated red: strong, full-bodied, high-flavoured, tannic and long-lived. 4 yrs' ageing, after 5 becomes RISERVA. Montalcino is 25 miles S of Siena.

Good Brunello di Montalcino producers include Altesino, Argiano, Banfi, Fattoria dei Barbi, Biondi-Santi, Caparzo, Casanova di Neri, Case Basse, Cerbaiona, La Chiesa di Santa Restituta, Col d'Orcia, Costanti, Eredi Fuligni, Lisini, Siro Pacenti, Ciacci Piccolomini, Poggio Antico, Poggione, Salvioni-Cerbaiola, Talenti. See also Rosso di Montalcino (value).

Brusco dei Barbi Tus r ** 88 89 90 91 92 93 94   Lively variant on BRUNELLO using old CHIANTI GOVERNO method.

Bukkuram Celebrated MOSCATO DI PANTELLERIA from De Bartoli.

Cà del Bosco *** FRANCIACORTA estate making some of Italy's v best sparkling wine, CHARD, and excellent reds (see Zanella).

Cabernet Sauvignon Much used in NE Italy and new (esp in VDT) in TUSCANY, PIEDMONT and the south.

Cacchiano, Castello di *** First-rate CHIANTI CLASSICO estate at Gaiole, owned by RICASOLI cousins. Outstanding RISERVA 'Millenio'.

Cafaggio, Villa **→*** CHIANTI CLASSICO estate. Solid red VDT: Solatio Basilica.

Caldaro or Lago di Caldaro T-AA DOC r *→** DYA   Alias KALTERERSEE. Light soft slightly bitter-almond red from SCHIAVA grapes. From a huge area. CLASSICO from a smaller area is better.

Caluso Passito Pie DOC w sw (fz) **   Made from Erbaluce grapes; delicate scent, velvety taste. Tiny production. Best from Bianco, Ferrando.

Candido, Francesco ** Top grower of Salento, Puglia; good reds: Duca d'Aragona, Cappello del Prete, SALICE SALENTINO; vg dessert wine: ALEATICO DI PUGLIA.

Cannonau di Sardegna Sar DOC r (p) dr s/sw ** 89 90 91 92 93 94 Cannonau (Grenache) is Sardinia's basic red grape. Wines range from v potent to fine and mellow.

Cantalupo, Antichi Vigneti di *** Top GHEMME wines – esp single-vineyard Breclemae and Carellae.

Cantina Cellar or winery.

Cantina Sociale (CS) Growers' coop.

Capannelle *** Good producer of VDT (formerly CHIANTI CLASSICO), nr Gaiole.

Caparzo, Tenuta *** MONTALCINO estate with excellent BRUNELLO La Casa; also vg ROSSO DI MONTALCINO (look for La Caduta), red blend Ca'del Pazzo and white blend Le Grance.

Capezzana, Tenuta di (or Villa) **→*** The Tuscan estate (W of Florence) of the Contini Bonacossi family. Excellent CHIANTI Montalbano and CARMIGNANO. Also vg Bordeaux-style red, GHIAIE DELLA FURBA.

Capri Cam DOC r p w *→** Famous island with widely abused name. Only interesting wines from La Caprense.

Carema Pie DOC r **→*** 85' 88' 89' 90' (91) (92) 93' Old speciality of N PIEDMONT. Best from Luigi Ferrando (or the CANTINA SOCIALE).

Carignano del Sulcis Sar DOC r p **→*** 87' 88' 90 91 93 94 Well-structured red with capacity for ageing. Best: Terre Brune from CANTINA SOCIALE di Santadi.

Carmignano Tus DOCG r *** 85' 86 88' 90' 91 93' 94' Region of Florence. CHIANTI grapes plus 10% CAB make distinctive, reliable, even excellent reds. Good producers: Ambra, ARTIMINO, CAPEZZANA, Poggiolo.

Carpenè Malvolti Leading producer of classic PROSECCO and other sparkling wines at Conegliano, Veneto.

Carpineto Producer of CHIANTI CLASSICO in N part of region.

Carso F-VG DOC r w **→*** 88 90 93 94 DOC nr Trieste incl good MALVASIA. Terrano del C is a REFOSCO red. Top grower: Edi Kante.

Casa fondata nel... Firm founded in...

Casalte, Fattoria Le *** Good VINO NOBILE DI MONTEPULCIANO; also ROSSO and white VDT Celius.

Casanova di Neri *** BRUNELLO DI MONTALCINO (and vg ROSSO DI M) from the Neri family; better every year.

Cascina Castlet **→*** Concentrated BARBERA PASSITO, VDT Passum, vg BARBERA D'ASTI.

Case Basse *** Small estate with v impressive BRUNELLO and VDT Intistieti.

Case Bianche, Le ** Reliable estate nr Conegliano (Ven) for PROSECCO, SAUV and surprising red Wildbacher (from ancient Austrian grape).

Castel del Monte Ap DOC r p w ** (r) 91 92 93 94 Dry fresh well-balanced southern wines. The red is RISERVA after 3 yrs. Rosé most widely known. RIVERA's Il Falcone stands out.

Castell'in Villa *** Vg CHIANTI CLASSICO estate.

Castellare **→*** Small but admired CHIANTI CLASSICO producer with first-rate SANGIOVESE VDT I Sodi di San Niccoló and sprightly GOVERNO del Castellare: old-style CHIANTI up-dated.

Castello Castle. (See under name: eg Albola, Castello d'.)

Castelluccio **→*** Best SANGIOVESE of Emilia-Romagna: VDT Ronco dei Cigliegi and Ronco della Simia.

Cavalleri **→*** Vg and reliable producer of FRANCIACORTA wines; sparkling are top.

Cavallotto **→*** Reliable BAROLO estate: esp Barolo Vigna San Giuseppe.

Càvit (Cantina Viticoltori) Group of quality coops near Trento. Wines incl MARZEMINO, CAB, PINOTS N, BL and GR, NOSIOLA. Top wines: Brume di Monte (red and white) and sparkling Graal and Firmato.

Cerasuolo Ab DOC p ** The ROSATO version of MONTEPULCIANO D'ABRUZZO.

Cerasuolo di Vittoria Si r ** 92 93 94 Cherry-red from southern Sicily: best from Avide and COS, Giuseppe Coria's is a fine matured non-DOC version.

Ceretto *** Vg grower of BARBARESCO (Bricco Asili), BAROLO (Bricco Rocche), top BARBERA D'ALBA (Piana), CHARD (La Bernardina), DOLCETTO and ARNEIS.

Cervaro See Castello della Sala.

Chardonnay Has recently joined permitted varieties for several N Italian DOCs (eg T-AA, FRANCIACORTA, F-VG). Some of the best (eg from ANTINORI, FELSINA, GAJA, LUNGAROTTI) are still only VDT.

Chianti Tus DOCG r *→** 93 94' The lively local wine of Florence and Siena. Fresh fruity and tangy, still sometimes sold in straw-covered flasks. Mostly made to drink young. Of the subdistricts, RUFINA and Colli Fiorentini can make CLASSICO-style RISERVAS. Montalbano, Colli Senesi, Aretini and Pisani make lighter wines.

To decipher codes, please refer to symbols key at front of book, and to 'How to use this book' on page 5.

Chianti Classico Tus DOCG r **→**★★★★ 88 90 **91 92** 93 94 (Riserva) 83 85 86 88 90 93 94   Senior CHIANTI from the central area. Its old pale astringent style is becoming rarer as top estates opt for either darker tannic wines or softer and fruitier ones. Some are among the best wines of Italy. Members of the Consorzio use the badge of a black rooster, but several top firms do not belong.

Outstanding Chianti Classico producers incl Ama, Bibbiano, Cacchiano, Capaccia, Casa Emma, Castel Ruggero, Castellare, Castell'in Villa, Coltibuono, Felsina, Le Filigare, Fonterutoli, Fontodi, Isole e Olena, Querciabella, Lilliano, La Massa, Le Masse di San Leolino, Palazzino, Paneretta, Poggerino, Rampolla, Riecine, Rocca di Castagnoli, Rodano, San Fabiano Calcinaia, San Felice, San Giusto, Valtellina, Vecchie Terre di Montefili, Verrazzano, Vignamaggio, Volpaia.

Chianti Putto Tus DOCG r ★→★★ DYA   From a league of producers outside the CLASSICO zone. The neck-label, a pink cherub, is now rarely seen.

Chiaretto Rosé (the word means 'claret') produced esp around Lake Garda. See Bardolino, Riviera del Garda.

Chiesa di Santa Restituta ★★★   Estate for admirable BRUNELLO DI MONTALCINO, vg ROSSO DI M and red VDT Pian de Cerri. Links with GAJA.

Chionetti ★★→★★★   Makes best DOLCETTO DI DOGLIANI (look for Briccolero).

Ciacci Piccolomini ★★★   Vg BRUNELLO DI MONTALCINO (best is Vigna di Pianrosso) and ROSSO DI M.

Cigliuti, Renato ★★★   Small top estate for BARBARESCO.

Cinqueterre Lig DOC w dr sw pa ★★   Fragrant fruity white from steep coast nr La Spezia. PASSITO is known as SCIACCHETRA (★★→★★★). Good from De Batte, Coop Agricola di Cinqueterre, Forlini & Cappellini, F Giusti.

Cinzano Major Vermouth company also known for its ASTI from PIEDMONT and Florio MARSALA. Now owned by Grand Met.

Cirò Cal DOC r (p w) ★★→★★★ 87' 88 89 90' 91 92 93 94   V strong red from Gaglioppo grapes; fruity white (DYA). Best from LIBRANDI (Duca San Felice), San Francesco (Donna Madda and Ronco dei Quattroventi) and Caparra & Siciliani.

Classico Term for wines from a restricted area within the limits of a DOC. By implication, and often in practice, the best of the district. Applied to sparkling wines it denotes the classic method (as for champagne).

Clerico, Domenico ★★★   Constantly evolving PIEDMONT wines; the aim is for international flavour. Esp good for BAROLO.

Col d'Orcia ★★★   Top estate of MONTALCINO with interesting VDT. Best wine is BRUNELLO (look for Poggio al Vento).

Colle Picchioni ★★   Estate S of Rome making the best MARINO white; also red (CAB-MERLOT) VDT, Vigna del Vassallo, perhaps Latium's best.

Colli Hills. Occurs in many wine-names.

Colli Berici Ven DOC r p w ★★   Hills S of Vicenza. CAB is the best wine. Top producer is Villa Dal Ferro.

Colli Bolognesi E-R DOC r p w ★★ (w) DYA   SW of Bologna. 8 wines, 5 grape varieties. TERRE ROSSE is top estate (★★★).

Colli Euganei Ven DOC r w dr s/sw (sp) ★→★★ DYA   A DOC SW of Padua for 7 wines. Red is adequate; white and sparkling soft and pleasant. Best producers: Vignalta (★★★), Cà Lustra.

Colli Orientali del Friuli F-VG DOC r w dr sw ★★→★★★ 88 90 93 94   20 different wines (18 named after their grapes) on hills E of Udine. Whites esp are vg. Top producers: ABBAZIA DI ROSAZZO, BORGO DEL TIGLIO, DORIGO, Livon, RONCO DEL GNEMIZ, Torre Rosazza, VOLPE PASINI.

Colli Piacentini E-R DOC r p w ★→★★ DYA   DOC incl traditional GUTTURNIO and Monterosso Val d'Arda among 11 types grown S of Piacenza. Good fizzy MALVASIA. Most wines FRIZZANTE.

Colli Romani The wooded hills S of Rome: ancient summer resort and source of FRASCATI etc.

Colli del Trasimeno Um DOC r w ★→★★ 90 **91** 93 94 Often lively wines from Perugia. Best from: La Fiorita, Marella, MARTINI & ROSSI, Morolli.

Colline Novaresi Pie DOC r w ★→★★ New DOC for old region in Novara province. 7 different wines: BIANCO, ROSSO, NEBBIOLO, BONARDA, Vespolina, Croatina and BARBERA. Incl declassified BOCA, GHEMME, FARA and SIZZANO.

Collio F-VG DOC r w ★★→★★★★ 88 **90** 93 94 19 wines, 17 named after their grapes, from a small area on the Slovenian border. Vg whites, esp SAUV, PINOT BIANCO and PINOT GRIGIO. Best from: La Castellada, L FELLUGA, GRAVNER, JERMANN, Primosic, Radikon, SCHIOPETTO, VILLA RUSSIZ.

Coltassala Tus r ★★★ Notable VDT red of SANGIOVESE from the ancient CHIANTI CLASSICO estate of CASTELLO DI VOLPAIA at Radda.

Conterno, Aldo ★★★★ Legendary grower of BAROLO, etc, at Monforte d'Alba. Good GRIGNOLINO, FREISA, vg CHARD 'Printanier' and 'Bussia d'Oro'. Best BAROLOS are Cicala and Colonello. Barrel-aged NEBBIOLO VDT 'Favot' vg.

Conterno, Giacomo ★★★★ Top grower of BAROLO etc at Monforte d'Alba. Monfortino Barolo is long-aged, rare, outstanding.

Conterno-Fantino ★★★ 3 young families for vg BAROLO etc at Monforte d'Alba.

Contini, Attilio ★→★★★ Famous producer of VERNACCIA DI ORISTANO; best is vintage blend 'Antico Gregori'.

Contratto ★★ PIEDMONT firm known for ASTI, BAROLO, etc.

Contucci, Conti ★★→★★★ Ancient esteemed makers of VINO NOBILE DI MONTEPULCIANO.

Copertino Ap DOC r (p) ★★ 89 90 91 92 93 94 Savoury ageable red wine of NEGROAMARO from the heel of Italy. Look for the CANTINA SOCIALE'S RISERVA.

Coppo Ambitious producers of BARBERA D'ASTI (eg 'Pomorosso').

Cordero di Montezemolo-Monfalletto ★★ Tiny maker of good BAROLO.

Cortese di Gavi See Gavi. (Cortese is the grape.)

Corzano & Paterno, Fattoria di ★★→★★★ Dynamic CHIANTI Colli Fiorentini estate. Vg RISERVA, red VDT Corzano and outstanding VINSANTO.

Costanti, Conti ★★★ Tiny estate for top quality BRUNELLO DI MONTALCINO.

D'Ambra ★★ Top producer of ISCHIA wines, esp excellent white BIANCOLELLA ('Piellero' and single-v'yd 'Frassitelli').

D'Angelo ★★ Leading producers of admirable DOC AGLIANICO DEL VULTURE. Barrel-aged Aglianico VDT Canneto also vg.

Dal Forno, Romano ★★★★ Very high quality VALPOLICELLA and AMARONE from perfectionist grower, bottling only best: 8,000 bottles from 20 acres.

Darmagi Pie r ★★★★ 82 85 88 89 90 91 92 93 94 CAB S from GAJA in BARBARESCO is one of PIEDMONT's most discussed (and expensive) VDT reds.

Decugnano dei Barbi Top ORVIETO estate with an ABBOCCATO known as 'Pourriture Noble', and a good red VDT.

Di Majo Norante ★★→★★★ Lone star of Molise on the Adriatic with vg Biferno DOC MONTEPULCIANO and white Falanghina 'Ramitello'. Also lighter, more aromatic Molí. Fine value. To watch for new ideas.

Dolce Sweet.

Dolceacqua See Rossese di Dolceacqua.

Dolcetto ★→★★★ PIEDMONT's earliest ripening grape, for v attractive everyday wines: dry, young-drinking, fruity, fresh, with deep purple colour. Gives its name to several DOCs: D d'Acqui, D d'Alba, D di Diano d'Alba (also Diano DOC), D di Dogliani (CHIONETTI and Pecchenino are top growers) and D di Ovada (best from Abbazia di Vallechiara). Dolcetto is made by most BAROLO and BARBARESCO growers.

Donnafugata Si r w ★★ Zesty Sicilian whites (best are Vigna di Gabri, Damaskino). Also sound red. Was VDT, now in DOC Contessa Entellina.

Donnaz VdA DOC ★★ 85 88 89 **90** 93 A mountain NEBBIOLO: fragrant pale and faintly bitter. Aged for a statutory 3 yrs. Now part of the VALLE D'AOSTA regional DOC.

Dorigo, Girolamo ★★★ Top COLLI ORIENTALI DEL FRIULI producer for outstanding white VDT 'Ronc di Juri', CHARD, dessert VERDUZZO and PICOLIT, red Pignolo, REFOSCO, Schioppettino, and VDT Montsclapade.

Duca Enrico See Duca di Salaparuta.

Duca di Salaparuta ★★→★★★ Popular Sicilian wines. Sound dry reds, pleasant soft whites. Excellent barrique red called Duca Enrico (★★★) is one of Sicily's best.

Elba Tus r w (sp) ★ DYA The island's white is drinkable with fish.

Enfer d'Arvier VdA DOC r ★★ 90 93 Alpine speciality (see Donnaz); pale pleasantly bitter light red.

Enoteca Wine library. There are many, the impressive original being the Enoteca Italiana of Siena. Also used for wine shops or restaurants.

Erbaluce di Caluso See Caluso Passito.

Est! Est!! Est!!! Lat DOC w dr s/sw ★ DYA Unextraordinary white from Montefiascone, N of Rome. Trades on its odd-ball name.

Etna Si DOC r p w ★→★★ (r) 90 91 92 93 94 Wine from volcanic slopes. Red is warm, full, balanced and can age well; white is distinctly grapey.

Falchini ★★ Producer of good DOCG VERNACCIA DI SAN GIMIGNANO and the best reds of the district, eg VDT Campora.

Falerno del Massico Cam DOC r w ★★ 88 89 90 92 93 94 As Falernum, the best-known wine of ancient times. Times change. Strong red from AGLIANICO, fruity white from Falanghina. Good producer: VILLA MATILDE.

Fara Pie DOC r ★★ 85 88 89 90 93 Good NEBBIOLO from Novara, N PIEDMONT. Fragrant; worth ageing; esp Dessilani's Caramino.

Farneta, Tenuta ★★→★★★ Nr Siena but outside CHIANTI CLASSICO, an estate for pure SANGIOVESE VDT: eg Bongoverno (★★★) and Bentivoglio (★★★).

Farnetella, Castello di ★★ Estate nr MONTEPULCIANO where Giuseppe Mazzocolin of FELSINA makes vg SAUV and Chianti Colli Senesi.

Faro Si DOC r ★★ 90 91 92 93 94 Strong Sicilian red from the Straits of Messina. Made only (and rather well) by Bagni.

Fattoria Tuscan term for a wine-growing property, traditionally noble.

Favorita Pie w ★→★★ DYA Dry fruity white wine making friends in BAROLO country. From eg Negro, VOERZIO.

Fazi-Battaglia Well-known producer of VERDICCHIO, etc. White Le Moie VDT is pleasant. Also owns Fassati (producer of VINO NOBILE DI MONTEPULCIANO), Val di Suga (BRUNELLO) and San Leonino (CHIANTI CLASSICO).

Felluga Brothers Livio and Marco (RUSSIZ SUPERIORE) have separate companies in COLLIO and COLLI ORIENTALI. Both are highly esteemed.

Felsina-Berardenga ★★★→★★★★ CHIANTI CLASSICO estate with famous RISERVA Vigna Rancia and VDT Fontalloro.

Ferrari Cellars making some of Italy's best dry sparkling wines nr Trento, TRENTINO-ALTO ADIGE. Giulio Ferrari RISERVA is best.

Fiano di Avellino Cam w ★★→★★★ 93 94 (DYA) Considered the best white of Campania, esp MASTROBERARDINO'S Vignadora. Also good from Vadiaperti, Feudi di S Gregorio, Struzziero, Vega.

Florio The major volume producer of MARSALA, controlled by CINZANO.

Foianeghe T-AA vdt r (w) ★★ 88 89 90 93 TRENTINO CAB-MERLOT red to age 7–10 yrs. White is PINOT BL-CHARD-TRAMINER. Esp Conti Bossi Fedrigotti.

Folonari Large run-of-the-mill merchant of Lombardy. See also GIV.

Fontana Candida One of the biggest producers of FRASCATI. Single-v'yd Santa Teresa stands out. See also GIV.

Fontanafredda ★★ Big historic producer of PIEDMONT wines on former royal estates, incl BAROLO from single v'yds and a range of ALBA DOCs. Also very good DOCG ASTI and SPUMANTE Brut.

Fonterutoli High quality (★★★→★★★★) CHIANTI CLASSICO estate at Castellina with noted VDT Concerto and RISERVA Ser Lapo (★★★).

Le Fonti, Fattoria ★★ CHIANTI estate of 30 acres at Panzano. Still uses ancient 'promiscuo' mixed cultivation.

Fontodi ★★★★ Top CHIANTI CLASSICO estate at Panzano producing highly regarded RISERVA, red VDT Flaccianello and white vdt 'Meriggio' (a PINOT BIANCO-SAUV-TRAMINER blend).

Franciacorta Pinot Lom DOC w (p sp) ★★→★★★ Pleasant soft white and some vg sparkling wines made of PINOTS BL, N or GR and CHARD. CA'DEL BOSCO is outstanding. BELLAVISTA, CAVALLERI and Monte Rossa also vg.

Franciacorta Rosso Lom DOC r ∗∗ 90 91 93 94   Lightish red of mixed CAB and BARBERA from Brescia.

Frascati Lat DOC w dr s/sw sw (sp) ∗→∗∗ DYA   Best-known wine of Roman hills: should be soft, ripe, golden, tasting of whole grapes. Most is disappointingly neutral today: look for Conte Zandotti, Villa Simone, or Santa Teresa from FONTANA CANDIDA. Sweet is known as Cannellino.

Freisa Pie r dr s/sw sw (sp) ∗∗ DYA   Usually v dry (except nr Turin), often FRIZZANTE red, said to taste of raspberries and roses. With enough acidity can be highly appetizing, especially with salami. Good from: CIGLIUTI, CONTERNO, Cozzo, Gilli, PARUSSO, Pecchenino, Pelissero, Sebaste, Trinchero, VAJRA, VOERZIO.

Frescobaldi ∗∗∗   Ancient noble family, leading pioneers of CHIANTI at NIPOZZANO, E of Florence. Also white POMINO and PREDICATO SAUV BL (Vergena) and CAB (Mormoreto). See also Montesodi. Now also owns Castelgiocondo, a big MONTALCINO estate for BRUNELLO and vg VDT MERLOT Lamaione.

Friuli-Venezia Giulia The NE region on the Slovenian border. Many wines; the DOCs COLLIO and COLLI ORIENTALI include most of the best.

Friuli vintages	
1994	Wet spring and September, hot between. Whites can lack acidity, reds better.
1993	A windy vintage reduced quantities but produced highly concentrated healthy grapes. Top quality whites, but harvest rains compromised the reds.
1992	August rains not so bad in Friuli: an excellent year for whites, and good reds too.

Frizzante (fz) Semi-sparkling. Used to describe wines such as LAMBRUSCO.

Gaja ∗∗∗∗   Old family firm at BARBARESCO under meteoric direction of Angelo G. Top quality – and price – PIEDMONT wines, esp BARBARESCO (single v'yds SORI Tildin, Sorì San Lorenzo, Costa Russi) and BAROLO Sperss (since '88). Also setting trends with excellent CHARD (Gaja & Rey).

Galestro Tus w ∗   V light white from eponymous shaley soil in CHIANTI country. Current moves to upgrade.

Gambellara Ven DOC w dr s/sw (sp) ∗→∗∗ DYA   Neighbour of SOAVE. Dry wine similar. Sweet (known as RECIOTO DI GAMBELLARA) nicely fruity. Also VINSANTO. Outstanding producer, LA BIANCARA (∗∗∗).

Gancia Famous ASTI house also producing vermouth and dry sparkling. New Torrebianco estate in Apulia is making good VDT whites: CHARD, SAUV, PINOT BL, also vg single-v'yd BAROLO, 'Cannubi', since '89.

Garganega Principal white grape of SOAVE and GAMBELLARA.

Garofoli, Gioacchino ∗∗→∗∗∗   Quality leader of the Marches (nr Ancona). Notable style in VERDICCHIO Macrina and Serra Fiorese; also vg sparkling. ROSSO CONERO Piancarda and vg Grosso Agontano (∗∗∗).

Gattinara Pie DOCG r ∗∗→∗∗∗ 82 85 86 88 89 90 93   V tasty BAROLO-type red (from NEBBIOLO, locally known as Spanna). Best are Monsecco and single-v'yd wines from Antoniolo. Others incl Nervi, Travaglini.

Gavi (or Cortese di Gavi) Pie w ∗∗→∗∗∗ DYA   At (rare) best subtle dry white of Cortese grapes. LA SCOLCA is best known, La Giustiniana, Tenuta San Pietro, Castello di Tassarolo and Villa Sparina are v fair. But high prices are rarely justified.

Ghemme Pie DOC r ∗∗→∗∗∗∗ 82 85 86 88 89 90 93   Neighbour of GATTINARA, rival in quality but rare. Best is Antichi Vigneti di Cantalupo.

Ghiaie della Furba Tus r ∗∗∗ 88 90 93   Bordeaux-style VDT CAB blend from the admirable TENUTA DI CAPEZZANA, CARMIGNANO.

Giacosa, Bruno ∗∗∗   Inspired loner: outstanding BARBARESCO, BAROLO and PIEDMONT wines at Neive. Remarkable ARNEIS white, PINOT N sparkling.

GIV (Gruppo Italiano Vini) Complex of coops and wineries, apparently Europe's largest (60 million bottles). Sells 12% of all Italian wine, incl eg BIGI, Conti Serristori, FOLONARI, FONTANA CANDIDA, LAMBERTI, Macchiavelli, MELINI, Negri, Santi...

Goldmuskateller Aromatic ALTO ADIGE grape made into irresistible dry white, esp by TIEFENBRUNNER.

Governo Old Tuscan custom, enjoying mild revival with some producers, in which dried grapes or must are added to young wine to induce secondary fermentation and give a slight prickle – sometimes instead of using must concentrate to increase alcohol.

Gradi Degrees (of alcohol), ie percent by volume.

Grappa Pungent spirit made from grape pomace (skins etc after pressing).

Grasso, Elio *** Hard-working, reliable, quality producer at Monforte d'Alba: outstanding BAROLO (look for Gavarini and Casa Maté), potent barrel-aged BARBERA D'ALBA Vigna Martina, DOLCETTO, etc.

Grattamacco *** Top Tuscan producer on coast outside classic centres (nr SASSICAIA S of Bolgheri). Vg Grattamacco SANGIOVESE-CAB blend.

Grave del Friuli F-VG DOC r w ** (r) 88 90 93 94 DOC covering 15 different wines, 14 named after their grapes, from nr the Slovenian border. Good MERLOT and CAB. Best producers: Borgo Magredo, Di Lenardo, Le Fredis, PIGHIN, Teresa Raiz, Vigneti Le Monde.

Gravner, Josko **** Together with MARIO SCHIOPETTO, spiritual leader of COLLIO: estate with range of excellent whites, led by CHARD and SAUV.

Grechetto White grape with more flavour than the ubiquitous TREBBIANO, increasingly used in Umbria.

Greco di Bianco Cal DOC w sw ** An original smooth and fragrant dessert wine from Italy's toe; worth ageing. Best from Ceratti. See Mantonico.

Greco di Tufo Cam DOC w (sp) **→*** 93 94 (DYA) One of the best white wines of the south: fruity and slightly 'wild' in flavour. A character. MASTROBERARDINO makes single-v'yd Vignadangelo. Also vg from Vadiaperti, Di Meo, Feudi di S Gregorio.

Grignolino d'Asti Pie DOC r * DYA Lively standard light red of PIEDMONT.

Grumello Lom DOC r ** 85 88 89 90 93 NEBBIOLO wine from VALTELLINA. Can be delicate (or meagre).

Guerrieri-Gonzaga **→*** Top producer in TRENTINO; esp VINO DA TAVOLA San Leonardo, a *** CAB-MERLOT blend.

Guerrieri-Rizzardi **→*** Top producer of AMARONE, BARDOLINO, SOAVE and VALPOLICELLA from various family estates.

Gutturnio dei Colli Piacentini E-R DOC r dr (s/sw) ** 90 91 92 93 94 BARBERA-BONARDA blend from the hills of Piacenza, often FRIZZANTE.

Haas, Franz ** Very good ALTO ADIGE MERLOT and PINOT NERO.

Hauner, Carlo *** Island estate for marvellous MALVASIA DELLE LIPARI.

Inferno Lom DOC r ** 85 88 89 90 93 Similar to GRUMELLO and, like it, classified as VALTELLINA SUPERIORE.

Ischia Cam DOC w (r) *→*** DYA Wine of the island off Naples. Slightly sharp white SUPERIORE is best of DOC. But top producer D'AMBRA makes better VDT whites BIANCOLELLA and Forestera and red PER'E PALUMMO.

Isole e Olena ***→**** Top CHIANTI CLASSICO estate with fine red VDT Cepparello. Vg VINSANTO, and L'Eremo Syrah.

Isonzo F-VG DOC r w *** (r) 88 90 93 94 DOC covering 19 wines (17 varietals) in the NE. Best whites and CAB compare with neighbouring COLLIO wines. Best from Borgo Conventi, Francesco Pecorari, Pierpaolo Pecorari, Ronco del Gelso, VIE DI ROMANS, Villanova.

Jermann, Silvio *** Family estate in COLLIO: top white VDT, incl singular VINTAGE TUNINA oak-aged white blend and lighter Vinnae. Also fresh Capo Martino (91) and CHARD 'Where the dreams have no end...'

Kalterersee German name for LAGO DI CALDARO.

Kante, Edi *** Lone star of CARSO with outstanding DOC CHARD, SAUV, MALVASIA and vg red Terrano.

Lacryma (or Lacrima) Christi del Vesuvio Cam r p w dr (sw fz) *→** DYA Famous but ordinary range of wines in great variety from Vesuvius. (DOC Vesuvio.) MASTROBERARDINO produces the only good example.

Lageder, Alois *→*** The lion of Bolzano (ALTO A). DOCs: SANTA MADDALENA, etc. Exciting wines, incl oak-aged CHARD and CAB Löwengang. Single-v'yd SAUV is Lehenhof, PINOT BL Haberlehof, PINOT GR Benefizium Porer.

Lago di Caldaro See Caldaro.

Lagrein, Südtiroler, T-AA DOC r p **→**** 85 86 88 89 90 91 93 94
A Tyrolean grape with a bitter twist. Good fruity wine – at best very appetizing. The rosé is 'Kretzer', the dark 'Dunkel'. Best from Gojer, Gries, Kössler, Maddalena, Niedermayr, Rottensteiner, Schwanburg.

Lamberti Large producers of SOAVE, VALPOLICELLA, BARDOLINO, etc at Lazise on the E shore of Lake Garda. NB LUGANA and VDT Turà. See also GIV.

Lambrusco E-R DOC (or not) r p dr s/sw **→**** DYA Popular fizzy red, best known in industrial s/sw version. Top is SECCO, traditional is with second fermentation in bottle (yeast sediment on bottom). DOCs are L Grasparossa di Castelvetro, L Salamino di Santa Croce and, perhaps best, L di Sorbara. Vg from: Baldini, Barbolini, Bellei, Graziano.

Langhe The hills of central PIEDMONT, home of BAROLO, BARBARESCO, etc. Has become name for recent DOC (r w **→****) for 8 different wines: ROSSO, BIANCO, NEBBIOLO, DOLCETTO, FREISA, ARNEIS, FAVORITA and CHARDONNAY. Barolo and Barbaresco can now be declassified to DOC Langhe Nebbiolo previously only allowed VDT status.

Latisana F-VG DOC r w **→**** (r) 90 93 94 DOC for 13 varietal wines from 50 miles NE of Venice. Esp good TOCAI FRIULANO.

Leone de Castris ** Large producer of Apulian wines. Estate at SALICE SALENTINO, near Lecce.

Lessona Pie DOC r ** 85 86 88 89 90 93 Soft dry claret-like wine from the province of Vercelli. NEBBIOLO, Vespolina and BONARDA grapes.

Librandi **→**** Top Calabria producer. Vg red CIRO (RISERVA Duca San Felice is ***) and VDT Gravello (v interesting value CAB-Gaglioppo blend).

Lilliano, Castello di *** Old CHIANTI CLASSICO estate pulling its weight again.

Liquoroso Means strong and usually sweet (whether fortified or not).

Lisini *** Small estate for some of the finest recent vintages of BRUNELLO.

Loazzolo Pie DOC w sw *** 90 91 92 93 94 New DOC for MOSCATO dessert wine from botrytised air-dried grapes: expensive and sweet. Esp from Borgo Maragliano, Borgo Moncalvo, Borgo Sambui, Bricchi Mej, Luja.

Locorotondo Ap DOC w (sp) * DYA Pleasantly fresh southern white. To try.

Lugana Lom and Ven DOC w (sp) **→**** DYA Whites of S Lake Garda: can be fragrant, smooth, full of body and flavour. Good from Cà dei Frati, Ottella, Roveglia, Zenato.

Lungarotti **→**** The leading producer of TORGIANO wine, with cellars, hotel and wine museum nr Perugia. Also some of Italy's best CHARD (Miralduolo and Vigna I Palazzi) and PINOT GR. See Torgiano.

Maculan *→**** The top producer of DOC BREGANZE. Also Torcolato, dessert VDT (***) and Prato di Canzio (CHARD, PINOT BL and PINOT GR).

Malvasia An important grape of chameleon character: white or red wines, sparkling or still, strong or mild, sweet or dry, aromatic or rather neutral, often as VDT, sometimes as DOC. White, dry to sweet, strong concentrated: **M di Cagliari** Sar DOC ** (eg Meloni); red fragrant grapey sweet, somtimes sparkling: **M di Casorzo d'Asti** Pie DOC ** (eg Bricco Mondalino); red aromatic sparkling: **M di Castelnuovo** Don Bosco Pie DOC ** (eg Gilli); white rich strong, long-living: M delle Lipari Si DOC *** (eg Colosi, Hauner); white dry to semi-sweet, deep bouquet, long-lived: M de Nus VdA DOC *** (eg La Crotta de Vegnerons). See also Torricella.

Manduria (Primitivo di) Ap DOC r s/sw (dr sw fz) ** 88 89 90 91 92 93 94 Heady red, naturally strong but often fortified. From nr Taranto. Esp Vinicola Savese's.

Mantonico Cal w dr sw fz ** 88 89 90 91 92 93 94 Fruity deep amber dessert wine from Reggio Calabria. Can age remarkably well. Good from Ceratti. See also Greco di Bianco.

NB Vintages in colour are those you should choose first for drinking in 1996.

Marino Lat DOC w dr s/sw (sp) ★→★★★ DYA A neighbour of FRASCATI with similar wine; often a better buy. Look for COLLE PICCHIONI brand.

Marsala Si DOC br dr s/sw sw fz ★★→★★★★ NV Sherry-type wine invented by the Woodhouse Brothers from Liverpool in 1773; excellent aperitif or for dessert, but mostly used in the kitchen for Zabaglione etc. The dry ('virgin'), sometimes made by the solera system, must be 5 yrs old. Top producers: FLORIO, Pellegrino, Rallo, VECCHIO SAMPERI.

Martini & Rossi Well-known vermouth and sparkling wine house (now controlled by Bacardi group), also famous for its splendid wine-history museum in Pessione, nr Turin.

Marzemino (Trentino) T-AA DOC r ★→★★★ 93 94 Pleasant local red. Fruity; slightly bitter. Esp from Bossi Fedrigotti, Casata Monfort, CAVIT, De Tarczal, Gaierhof, Letrari, Simoncelli, Vallarom, Vallis Agri.

Mascarello The name of 2 top producers of BAROLO, etc: Bartolo M and Giuseppe M & Figli. Look for the latter's BAROLO Monprivato (★★★★).

Masi, Agricola Well-known, conscientious and reliable specialist producers of VALPOLICELLA, AMARONE (★★★), RECIOTO, SOAVE, etc, incl fine red Campo Fiorin. Also look for excellent new red VDT Toar.

Mastroberardino ★★★ The leading wine producer of Campania, at Avellino. Wines incl FIANO DI AVELLINO, GRECO DI TUFO, LACRYMA CHRISTI and TAURASI (look for Radici).

Melini Long-est'd producers of CHIANTI CLASSICO at Poggibonsi. Good quality/price ratio; look for single-v'yd C Classico Selvanella. See also GIV.

Meranese di Collina T-AA DOC r ★ DYA Light red of Merano, known in German as Meraner Hügel.

Merlot Adaptable red B'x grape widely grown in N (esp) and central Italy. Merlot DOCs are abundant. Best growers are: HAAS, SCHRECKBICHL and Baron Widman in T-AA, Torre Rosazza (L'Altromerlot) and BORGO DEL TIGLIO in F-VG and the Tuscan Super-VDTS of AMA (L'Apparita), AVIGNONESI and ORNELLAIA (Masseto).

Metodo classico or tradizionale Now the mandatory terms to identify classic method sparkling wines. 'Metodo Champenois' banned since '94 and now illegal. (See also Classico.)

Moccagatta ★★→★★★ Specialist in impressive single-v'yd BARBARESCO: Basarin, Bric Balin (★★★) and Vigna Cole.

Monferrato Pie DOC r w sw p ★★ The hills between the River Po and the Apennines give their name to a new DOC that includes ROSSO, BIANCO, CHIARETTO, DOLCETTO, Casalese and FREISA CORTESE.

Monica di Sardegna Sar DOC r ★ DYA Monica is the grape. An ordinary dry light red.

Monsanto ★★→★★★★ Esteemed CHIANTI CLASSICO estate, esp for Il Poggio v'yd.

Montalcino Small town in the province of Siena, TUSCANY, famous for its deep red BRUNELLO and younger ROSSO DI MONTALCINO.

Monte Vertine ★★★→★★★★ Top estate at Radda in CHIANTI. VDT Le Pergole Torte (100% SANGIOVESE) is one of TUSCANY's best. Also Sodaccio (Sangioveto plus Canaiolo) and fine VINSANTO.

Montecarlo Tus DOC w r ★★ DYA (w) White wine area in N TUSCANY: smooth delicate blend of TREBBIANO with a range of better grapes. Now applies to a CHIANTI-style red too (eg Rosso di Cercatoia). Good producers: Buonamico, Carmignani, Michi.

Montefalco (Rosso di) Umb DOC r ★★ 90 91 92 93 Common SANGIOVESE-TREBBIANO-SAGRANTNO blend. ADANTI's Rosso d'Arquata VDT stands out.

Montefalco Sagrantino Umb DOCG r dr sw ★★★ 90 91 92 93 Strong, v interesting SECCO or sweet PASSITO red from Sagrantino grapes only. Good from: ADANTI, Antano, Antonelli, Val di Maggio, Villa Antica.

Montellori, Fattoria di ★★→★★★★ Tuscan father-son team producing admirable SANGIOVESE-CAB VDT blend 'Castelrapiti Rosso', Viognier VDT 'Bonfiglio', Chardonnay VDT 'Castelrapiti Bianco' and vg SPUMANTE.

Montepulciano An important red grape of central-east Italy as well as the famous Tuscan town (see next entries).

Montepulciano d'Abruzzo Ab DOC r p **→**** 85 87 88 90 91 92 93 94 Happens rarely, but when it's at its best, one of Italy's tastiest reds, full of flavour and warmth, from the Adriatic coast round Pescara. Good from: VALENTINI (No 1), Barone Cornacchia, Filomusi-Guelfi, Illuminati, Cataldi Madonna, Masciarelli, Montori, Nicodemi, Castello di Salle, Tenuta del Priore and Zaccagnini. See also Cerasuolo.

Montepulciano, Vino Nobile di See Vino Nobile di Montepulciano.

Montesodi Tus r *** 83 85 86 88 90 93 94 Tip-top CHIANTI RUFINA RISERVA from FRESCOBALDI.

Morellino di Scansano Tus DOC r **→**** 88 90 93 94 Local SANGIOVESE of the Maremma, the S Tuscan coast. Cherry-red, lively and tasty young or matured. Fattorie Le Pupille, Moris Farms, E Banti are good.

Moscadello di Montalcino Tus DOC w sw (sp) →** DYA Traditional wine of MONTALCINO, much older than BRUNELLO. Sweet white fizzy, and sweet to high-octane PASSITO MOSCATO. Good producers: BANFI, POGGIONE.

Moscato Fruitily fragrant ubiquitous grape for a diverse range of wines: sparkling or still, light or full-bodied, but always sweet. Most famous is **M d'Asti** Pie DOCG (**→***): light, aromatic, sparkling and delicious from BERA, Dogliotti, Gatti, RIVETTI, Saracco and Vignaioli di Santo Stefano. Italy's best is from the island of Pantelleria off the Tunisian coast, with top wines from De Bartoli, Murana. And rare but prestigious is **Moscato di Trani** (s'times fortified), best from Nugnes.

Müller-Thurgau Makes wine to be reckoned with in TRENTINO-ALTO ADIGE and FRIULI, esp TIEFENBRUNNER's Feldmarschall.

Nasco di Cagliari Sar DOC w dr sw (fz) ** Sardinian speciality with light bitter taste, high alcohol content. Good from Meloni.

Nebbiolo The best red grape of PIEDMONT and Lombardy.

Nebbiolo d'Alba Pie DOC r dr (s/sw sp) ** 88 89 90 93 From ALBA (but not BAROLO, BARBARESCO). Sometimes like lightweight Barolo; can be easier to enjoy than the powerful classic wine. Best from Correggia, MASCARELLO, PRUNOTTO, RATTI, Roagna. See also Roero.

Negroamaro Literally 'black bitter'; Apulian red grape with potential for quality. See Copertino and Salice Salentino.

Nipozzano, Castello di *** FRESCOBALDI estate east of Florence making MONTESODI CHIANTI. The most important outside the CLASSICO zone.

Nittardi ** Up-coming little CHIANTI CLASSICO estate.

Nosiola (Trentino) T-AA DOC w dr sw ** DYA Light fruity white from dried Nosiola grapes. Also good VINSANTO. Best from Pravis: Le Frate.

Nozzole **→*** Famous estate, owned by RUFFINO, in the heart of CHIANTI CLASSICO, N of Greve. Also good CAB.

Nuragus di Cagliari Sar DOC w ∗ DYA Lively Sardinian white.

Oberto, Andrea ** Hardworking small La Morra producer with top BAROLO and BARBERA D'ALBA.

Oliena, Nepente di Sar r ** Strong fragrant CANNONAU red; a touch bitter.

Oltrepò Pavese Lom DOC r w dr sw sp *→** DOC applicable to 14 wines produced in the province of Pavia, mostly named after their grapes. Top growers incl Cabanon, Doria, Mairano, Tenuta Mazzolino, Monsupello, Montelio.

Ornellaia Tus *** New 130-acre estate of LODOVICO ANTINORI nr Bolgheri on the Tuscan coast. To watch for CAB-MERLOT and SAUV called Poggio delle Gazze. Also Masseto, vg straight Merlot, and blend La Volte (since '91).

Orvieto Umb DOC w dr s/sw **→*** DYA The classical Umbrian golden white: smooth and substantial; formerly rather dull but recently more interesting, esp in sweet versions. Orvieto CLASSICO is better. Only the finest examples (eg BARBERANI, BIGI, DECUGANO DEI BARBI) age well. But see Castello della Sala.

Pagadebit di Romagna E-R DOC w dr s/sw * DYA Pleasant traditional 'payer of debts' from around Bertinoro.

Palazzino, Podere Il ★★★ Small estate with admirable CHIANTI CLASSICO and VDT Grosso Sanese.

Panaretta, Castello della ★★→★★★ An estate to follow: v interesting CHIANTI CLASSICO.

Panizzi ★★ Makes top class VERNACCIA DI SAN GIMIGNANO.

Paradiso, Fattoria ★★★ Old family estate near Bertinoro (E-R). Good ALBANA and PAGADEBIT and unique red Barbarossa. Vg SANGIOVESE.

Parrina Tus r w ★ 90 93 94 Light red and white from Maremma, S TUSCANY.

Parusso ★★★ Tiziana and Marco Parusso are making BAROLO at the highest level (eg single-v'yd Bussia, Mariondino), also vg BARBERA D'ALBA and DOLCETTO, etc.

Pasolini Dall'Onda Noble family with estates in CHIANTI Colli Fiorentini and Romagna, producing fine traditional-style wines.

Passito (pa) Strong sweet wine from grapes dried on the vine or indoors.

Pelaverga Pie r ★★ (DYA) Pale red with spicy perfume, from Verduno. Good producers: Alessandria, Bel Colle, Castello di Verduno.

Peppoli ★★★ Estate owned by ANTINORI, producing excellent CHIANTI CLASSICO in a full round youthful style – first vintage 85.

Per'e Palummo Cam r ★ Appetizing light tannic red from island of ISCHIA.

Piave Ven DOC r w ★→★★ (r) 90 93 94 (w DYA) Flourishing DOC NW of Venice covering 8 wines, 4 red and 4 white, named after their grapes. CAB, MERLOT and RABOSO reds can all age. Good from Molon-Traverso.

Picolit (Colli Orientali del Friuli) F-VG DOC w s/sw sw ★★→★★★ 88 90 93 94 Delicate sweet dessert wine with exaggerated reputation. A little like Jurançon. Ages up to 6 yrs, but wildly overpriced. Best from DORIGO, Dri, LIVIO FELLUGA, Livon, Rodaro, RONCO DEL GNEMIZ.

Piedmont (Piemonte) The most important Italian region for top quality wine. Turin is the capital, ASTI and ALBA the wine centres. See Barbaresco, Barbera, Barolo, Dolcetto, Grignolino, Moscato, etc.

Piedmont vintages

1994 Hot summer; but vintage rains prevented excellence.

1993 Hot summer, good Dolcetto and Barbera, but September rains disrupted Nebbiolo harvest and severe selection was necessary for Barolo and Barbaresco.

1992 An extremely difficult year due to incessant rainfall. Whites good. Nebbiolo wines not so lucky.

1991 Cold April and suddenly v hot in July, harvest then interrupted by rain: some elegant Barolo, Barbaresco and Barbera; Dolcetto and whites fine.

Pieropan ★★★ Outstanding producer of SOAVE and RECIOTO that for once deserves its fame.

Pigato Lig DOC w DOC under Riviera Ligure di Ponente. Often outclasses VERMENTINO as Liguria's finest white, with rich texture and structure. Good from: Anfossi, Colle dei Bardellini, Feipu, Lupi, TERRE ROSSE, Vio.

Pighin, Fratelli Solid producers of COLLIO and GRAVE DEL FRIULI.

Pinocchio Tusc r w ★ Long-established brand notable for variable nose.

Pinot Bianco (Pinot Bl) Popular grape in NE for many DOC wines. Best from ALTO ADIGE T-AA ★★ (top growers: CS St-Michael, LAGEDER, Elena Walch), COLLIO F-VG ★★ (vg from Keber, Mangilli, Picech, Princic) and COLLI ORIENTALI F-VG ★★→★★★ (best from Rodaro and Vigne dal Leon).

Pinot Grigio (Pinot Gr) Tasty low-acid white grape popular in NE. Best from DOCs ALTO ADIGE (LAGEDER, Kloster Muri-Gries, Schwanburg) and COLLIO (Caccese, SCHIOPETTO). AMA in TUSCANY makes vg VDT Pinot Gr.

Pinot Nero T-AA DOC r ★★→★★★ 90 91 92 94 Pinot Nero (Noir) is planted in much of NE Italy, incl TRENTINO and esp ALTO ADIGE. Vg results from Castelfeder, HAAS, Niedrist and SCHRECKBICHL. Also fine sparkling. Promising trials elsewhere, eg AMA, FONTODI, Pancrazi and RUFFINO in TUSCANY, Casotte Bellavista in Lombardy.

Pio Cesare A producer of top-quality red wines of PIEDMONT, incl BAROLO.

Podere Tuscan term for a wine-farm; smaller than a FATTORIA.

Poggio Antico (Montalcino) ★★★→★★★★ Admirably consistent top level BRUNELLO, ROSSO and red VDT Altero.

Poggione, Tenuta Il ✱✱✱ Perhaps the most reliable estate for BRUNELLO and ROSSO DI MONTALCINO.

Pojer & Sandri ✱✱✱ Top TRENTINO producers: reds and whites, incl SPUMANTE.

Poliziano ✱✱✱ Federico Carletti makes top VINO NOBILE DI MONT (esp Asinone, Caggiole), VDT Elegia (CAB, SANGIOVESE) and wonderful VINSANTO. Vg value.

Pomino Tus DOC w (r br) ✱✱✱ 88 90 93 94 Fine white, partly CHARD (Il Benefizio is 100%), and a SANGIOVESE-CAB-MERLOT-PINOT N blend. Also VINSANTO. Esp from FRESCOBALDI.

Predicato Name for 4 kinds of VDT from central TUSCANY, illustrating the current headlong rush from tradition. P del Muschio is CHARD and PINOT BL; P del Selvante is SAUV BL; P di Biturica is CAB with SANGIOVESE, P di Cardisco is Sangiovese straight. Esp RUFFINO's Cabreo brand wines.

Primitivo Vg red grape, perhaps related to Zinfandel. Of few producers, Coppi, Sava, Savese are best.

Primitivo di Apulia See Manduria.

Prosecco White grape for light dry sparkling popular in Venice. Next is better.

Prosecco di Conegliano-Valdobbiadene Ven DOC w s/sw sp (dr) ✱✱ DYA Slight fruity bouquet, the dry pleasantly bitter, the sweet fruity; the best are known as Superiore di Cartizze. CARPENE-MALVOLTI is most renowned producer, now challenged by Adami, Bisol, Bortolotti, Canevel, CASE BIANCHE, Collalto, Nino Franco, Foss Marai, Ruggeri, Zaredetto.

Prunotto, Alfredo Very serious ALBA company with top BARBARESCO (esp Montestefano, ✱✱✱✱), BAROLO (esp ✱✱✱✱ single-v'yd Bussia and Cannubi), NEBBIOLO, etc. Now controlled by ANTINORI.

Querciabella ✱✱✱ Up-coming CHIANTI CLASSICO estate with excellent red VDT Camartina and a dream of a white VDT, Bâtard Pinot (BL and GR).

Quintarelli, Giuseppe ✱✱✱✱ True artisan producer of VALPOLICELLA, RECIOTO and AMARONE, at the top in both quality and price.

Raboso del Piave (now DOC) Ven r ✱✱ 88 90 93 94 Powerful sharp interesting country red; needs age. Look for Molon-Traverso.

Ragose, Le ✱✱✱ Family estate, one of VALPOLICELLA's best. AMARONE and RECIOTO top quality; CAB and Valpolicella vg too.

Ramandolo See Verduzzo Colli Orientali del Friuli.

Ramitello See Di Majo Norante.

Rampolla, Castello dei ✱✱✱ Top CHIANTI CLASSICO estate at Panzano; also excellent CAB-based VDT Sammarco.

Ratti, Renato ✱✱→✱✱✱ Maker of vg BAROLO and other ALBA wines. The late Signor Ratti (d '88) was a highly respected local wine scene leader.

Recioto Wine made of half-dried grapes. Speciality of Veneto since the days of Venetian empire; has roots in famous Roman wine, Raeticus.

Recioto di Gambellara Ven DOC w sw (sp s/sw DYA) ✱ Mostly half-sparkling and industrial. Best is strong and sweet. Look for LA BIANCARA (✱✱✱).

Recioto di Soave Ven DOC w s/sw (sp) ✱✱✱ 87 88 90 91 92 93 SOAVE made from selected half-dried grapes: sweet fruity fresh, slightly almondy; high alcohol. Outstanding from ANSELMI and PIEROPAN.

Recioto della Valpolicella Ven DOC r s/sw sp ✱✱✱ 80 83 85 86 88 90 93 Strong late-harvest red, sparkling. Vg from ALLEGRINI, Brigaldara, MASI, LE RAGOSE, Le Salette, San Rustico, Speri, TEDESCHI.

Recioto della Valpolicella Amarone See Amarone.

Refosco r ✱✱ 88 90 93 94 Interesting full-bodied dark tannic red, needs ageing. Said to be the same grape as the Mondeuse of Savoie (France). It tastes like it. Best comes from F-VG DOC COLLI ORIENTALI, GRAVE and CARSO (where R is called Terrano). Vg from DORIGO, EDI KANTE, Le Fredis, Livon, Villa Belvedere.

Regaleali ✱✱✱ Owned by the noble family Tasca D'Almerita, perhaps the best Sicilian producer; situated between Palermo and Caltanissetta to the SE. Vg VDT red, white and pink 'Regaleali', red 'Rosso del Conte' (✱✱✱) and CAB.

Ribolla (Colli Orientali del Friuli and Collio) F-VG DOC w *→** DYA
Thin NE white. The best comes from COLLIO. Top estates: La Castellada,
GRAVNER, Krapez, Radikon, Venica & Venica, VILLA RUSSIZ.

Ricasoli *→*** Famous Tuscan family, 'inventors' of CHIANTI, whose
CHIANTI CLASSICO is named after their Brolio estate and castle, now
again under family direction.

Riecine Tus r (w) *** First-class CHIANTI CLASSICO estate at Gaiole, created
by an Englishman, John Dunkley. Also VDT La Gioia di Riecine.

Riesling Formerly used to mean Italian Ries (Ries Italico or
Welschriesling). German (Rhine) Ries, now ascendant, is Ries
Renano. Best are DOC ALTO ADIGE ** (esp coop Kurtatsch, Ignaz
Niedrist, coop La Vis, Elena Walch) and DOC OLTREPO PAVESE Lom **
(Brega, Cabanon, Doria, Frecciarossa, coop La Versa), also
astonishing from Ronco del Gelso (DOC ISONZO).

Ripasso VALPOLICELLA re-fermented on AMARONE grape skins to make a more
complex, longer-lived and fuller wine. Best is MASI's Campo Fiorin.

Riserva Wine aged for a statutory period, usually in barrels.

Riunite One of the world's largest coop cellars, nr Reggio Emilia, producing
huge quantities of LAMBRUSCO and other wines.

Rivera Reliable winemakers at Andria, near Bari, with good red Il Falcone
and CASTEL DEL MONTE rosé. Also Vigna al Monte label.

Rivetti, Giorgio (La Spinetta) *** First success with MOSCATO, then with
reds. Top Moscato d'Asti, vg BARBERA, v interesting VDT Pin (blend of
Barbera and NEBBIOLO).

Riviera del Garda Bresciano Lom DOC w p r (sp) *→** Simple, sometimes
charming cherry-pink CHIARETTO, and neutral white from SW Garda.
Good producers: Cà dei Frati, Comincioli, Costaripa, Monte Cigogna.

Rocca, Bruno *** Young producer with admirable BARBARESCO (Rabajà).

Rocca di Castagnoli **→*** Recent producer of vg CHIANTI CLASSICO (best:
Capraia, RISERVA Poggio a'Frati), also vg VDT Stielle and Buriano
(blends of CAB and SANGIOVESE).

Rocca delle Macìe Large CHIANTI CLASSICO maker nr Castellina.

Rocche dei Manzoni, Podere *** Go-ahead estate at Monforte d'Alba.
Excellent BAROLO (best: Vigna Big), BRICCO MANZONI (outstanding
NEBBIOLO-BARBERA blend VDT), ALBA wines, CHARD (L'Angelica) and
Valentino Brut sparkling.

Roero DOC r ** DYA New name for a drink-me-quick NEBBIOLO from ALBA.
Can be delicious. Good from: Correggia, Deltetto, Malabaila, Malvirà.

Ronco Term for a hillside v'yd in FRIULI-VENEZIA GIULIA.

Ronco del Gnemiz *** Tiny property with outstanding COLLI ORIENTALI
DOCs and VDT CHARD made in barriques.

Rosa del Golfo Ap p ** DYA An outstanding VDT rosé of ALEZIO.

Rosato Rosé.

Rosato del Salento Ap p ** DYA From nr Brindisi and v like BRINDISI,
COPERTINO and SALICE SALENTINO ROSATOS; can be strong, but often really
fine and fruity. See Brindisi, Copertino, Salice Salentino for producers.

Rossese di Dolceacqua Lig DOC r ** DYA Well-known fragrant light red
of the Riviera. Good from Cane, Giuncheo, Guglielmi, Lupi, Perrino,
Terre Bianche.

Rosso Red.

Rosso Cònero Mar DOC r **→*** 85 88 90 93 94 Some of the best
MONTEPULCIANO (varietal) reds of Italy, eg GAROFOLI's Grosso Agontano,
Moroder's RC RISERVA, UMANI RONCHI's Cumaro and San Lorenzo.

Rosso di Montalcino Tus DOC r **→*** 88 90 93 94 DOC for younger
wines from BRUNELLO grapes. Still variable but potentially a winner if
the many good producers are not greedy over prices. For growers see
Brunello di M.

For key to grape variety abbreviations, see pages 6–9.

Rosso di Montepulciano Tus DOC r ** 93 94   Equivalent of the last for junior VINO NOBILE, recently introduced and yet to establish a style. For growers see Vino Nobile di M.

Rosso Piceno Mar DOC r *→*** 90 91 93 94   Stylish Adriatic red. SUPERIORE from classic zone near Ascoli. Best include Cocci Grifoni, Villamagna.

Rubesco The excellent popular red of LUNGAROTTI; see Torgiano.

Ruchè (also Rouchè or Rouchet) A rare old grape (French origin) giving fruity, fresh, rich bouqueted red wine (s/sw). Ruchè di Castagnole Monferrato is recent DOC, with Piero Bruno best producer. Rouchet Briccorosa is dry and excellent (***) from SCARPA.

Ruffino *→*** Well known CHIANTI merchants, at Pontassieve. RISERVA Ducale and Santedame are the top wines. NB new PREDICATO wines (red and white Cabreo) and CAB Il Pareto.

Rufina *→*** Important subregion of CHIANTI in the hills E of Florence. Best wines from Castello Nipozzano (FRESCOBALDI), SELVAPIANA.

Russiz Superiore (Collio) See Felluga, Marco.

Sagrantino di Montefalco See Montefalco.

Sala, Castello della *** ANTINORI's estate at ORVIETO. Borro is the regular white. Top wine is Cervaro della Sala: CHARD and GRECHETTO aged in oak. Muffato della S is one of Italy's best botrytis wines.

Salice Salentino Ap DOC r **→*** 85 87 88 89 90 93 94   Resonant red from NEGROAMARO grapes. RISERVA after 2 yrs; smooth when mature. Top makers: Candido, De Castris, Taurino, Vallone.

San Felice **→*** Rising star in CHIANTI with fine CLASSICO Poggio Rosso. Also red VDT Vigorello and PREDICATO di Biturica.

San Giusto a Rentennano One of the best CHIANTI CLASSICO producers (***). Delicious but v rare VINSANTO. Excellent VDT red Percarlo.

San Guido, Tenuta **** See Sassicaia.

San Polo in Rosso, Castello di *** CHIANTI CLASSICO estate with first-rate red VDT Cetinaia (aged in big casks, not barriques).

Sandrone, Luciano *** Exponent of new-style BAROLO vogue with vg B Cannubi Boschis, DOLCETTO and BARBERA.

Sangiovese or Sangioveto Principal red grape of Italy. Top performance only in TUSCANY, where its many forms incl CHIANTI, VINO NOBILE, BRUNELLO, MORELLINO, etc. Sometimes good also in ROSSO PICENO. V popular is S di Romagna (E-R DOC r *→**), a pleasant standard red. Vg from Cesari, Conti, PARADISO, Trerè, ZERBINA. Outstanding *** VDTS Ronco dei Cigliegi and Ronco delle Ginestre from CASTELLUCCIO, and VDT Nespoli (***) from Podere dal Nespoli. S'times good from ROSSO PICENO.

Santa Maddalena (or St-Magdalener) T-AA DOC r * DYA   Typical SCHIAVA Tyrolean red, lightish with bitter aftertaste. Best from: Cantina Sociale St-Magdalena, CS Girlan, Gojer, Thurnhof.

Santa Margherita *→*** Large Veneto-based (Portogruaro) merchants of Veneto (Torresella), ALTO-ADIGE (Kettmeir), Tuscan (Lamole di Lamole) and Lombardy (CA'DEL BOSCO) wines.

Sassella (Valtellina Superiore) Lom DOC r *** 85 88 89 90 93   Considerable NEBBIOLO wine, tough when young. Known since Roman times; mentioned by Leonardo da Vinci. Neighbour to INFERNO, etc.

Sassicaia Tus r **** 75' 82' 83' 85' 86 88' 89 90' 91 92 93 94   Outstanding pioneer CAB, Italy's best, from the Tenuta San Guido of the Incisa family, at Bolgheri nr Livorno. Promoted from SUPER-TUSCAN VDT to DOC BOLGHERI in '94.

Sauvignon Sauvignon Blanc is working v well in the northeast, best from DOCs TERLANO, ALTO ADIGE, ISONZO, COLLIO and COLLI ORIENTALI.

Sauvignon (Colli Orientali del Friuli) F-VG DOC w **→*** 91 92 93 94   Top producers: Torre Rosazza, Vigne dal Leon.

Sauvignon (Collio) F-VG DOC w **→*** 91 92 93 94   Top wines from La Castellada, GRAVNER, Primosic, SCHIOPETTO, VILLA RUSSIZ.

Sauvignon (Isonzo) F-VG DOC w **→*** 91 92 93 94   V full fruity white, increasingly good quality. Top producers: Pecorari, VIE DI ROMANS.

Savuto Cal DOC r p ** 92 93 94 Fragrant juicy wine from the provinces of Cosenza and Catanzaro. Best producer is Odoardi.

Scarpa Old-fashioned house with full-bodied smooth BARBERA D'ASTI (La Bogliona is ***), rare Rouchet (***), vg DOLCETTO, BAROLO, BARBARESCO.

Schiava High-yielding red grape of TRENTINO-ALTO ADIGE with characteristic bitter aftertaste, used for LAGO DI CALDARO, SANTA MADDALENA, etc.

A question of attitude

US and Italian law both require that a warning be printed on each wine label (or back label). The American warning concerns the use of sulphur dioxide as a preservative in wine and its possible – however unlikely – danger to health, and sternly enjoins that pregnant women should spurn all alcohol. The Italian warning reads 'Non disperdere nell'ambiente', or 'Don't throw this bottle away where it can muck up the environment'.

Schioppetto, Mario **** Legendary COLLIO pioneer with brand-new 20,000-case winery; vg DOC SAUV, PINOT GR, TOCAI, VDT blend 'Bl de Rosis', etc.

Schreckbichl (or Colterenzio CS) No 1 Südtirol Cantina Sociale. Admirable ALTO ADIGE CAB S, Gewürz, PINOT N, (look for Schwarzhaus RISERVA), CHARD, PINOT BL, PINOT GR, SAUV (look for Lafoa), red VDT Cornelius, etc.

Sciacchetrà See Cinqueterre

Scolca, La *** Famous estate in GAVI for top Gavi and SPUMANTE (look for Extra Brut Soldati La Scolca).

Secco Dry.

Sella & Mosca ** Major Sardinian growers and merchants at Alghero. Their port-like Anghelu Ruju (***) is excellent. Also pleasant white TORRATO and delicious light fruity VERMENTINO Cala Viola (DYA).

Selvapiana *** CHIANTI RUFINA estate. Top wine is RISERVA Bucerchiale.

Sforzato Lom DOC r **→*** 82 83 85 86 88 89 90 93 VALTELLINA equivalent of RECIOTO AMARONE made with partly dried grapes. Velvety, strong, ages remarkably well. Also called Sfursat. See Valtellina.

Sizzano Pie DOC r ** 88 89 90 93 Full-bodied red from Sizzano, Novara; mostly NEBBIOLO. Ages up to 10 yrs. Esp from: Bianchi, Dessilani.

Soave Ven DOC w *→*** DYA Famous mass-produced Veronese white. Should be fresh with v attractive texture. Standards rising (at last). S CLASSICO is more restricted and better. Esp from ANSELMI, PIEROPAN.

Solaia Tus r **** 82 83 85 88 90 93 94 V fine Bordeaux-style VDT of CAB S and a little SANGIOVESE from ANTINORI; first made in '78. Extraordinarily influential in shaping VDT (and Italian) philosophy.

Solopaca Cam DOC r w ** 92 93 94 Up-and-coming, nr Benevento. Rather sharp when young; white soft and fruity. Esp Antica Masseria Venditti.

Sorì Term for a high S, SE or SW oriented v'yd in PIEDMONT.

Spanna See Gattinara.

Spumante Sparkling, as in sweet ASTI or many good dry wines, incl both METODO CLASSICO (best from TRENTINO, A ADIGE, FRANCIACORTA, PIEDMONT, some vg also from TUSCANY and Veneto) and tank-made cheapos.

Stravecchio Very old.

Südtirol The local name of German-speaking ALTO ADIGE.

Super-Tuscans Term coined for high-price novelties from TUSCANY, usually involving CAB and barriques, and frequently fancy bottles.

Superiore Wine that has undergone more ageing than normal DOC and contains 0.5–1% more alcohol.

Taurasi Cam DOC r *** 87 88 90 92 93 94 The best Campanian red, from MASTROBERARDINO of Avellino. Harsh when young. RISERVA after 4 yrs. Radici (since '86) is Mastroberardino's top estate bottling.

Tedeschi, Fratelli V reliable and vg producer of VALPOLICELLA, AMARONE (***), RECIOTO and SOAVE. Vg Capitel San Rocco red and white VDT.

Terlano T-AA DOC w **→*** DYA DOC for eight whites from BOLZANO province, named after their grapes, esp SAUV. Terlaner in German. Good growers: Cantina Sociale Andrian, CS Terlan, LAGEDER, Niedrist.

Teroldego Rotaliano T-AA DOC r p **✱✱→✱✱✱** 90 91 92 93 94   Attractive blackberry-scented red; slight bitter aftertaste; can age v well. Esp Foradori's.

Terre di Ginestra Si w ✱✱   Good VDT from Cataratto, SW of Palermo.

Terre Rosse ✱✱✱   Distinguished small estate nr Bologna. Its CAB, CHARD, SAUV BL, PINOT GR, RIES, even Viognier, etc, are the best of the region.

Teruzzi & Puthod (Fattoria Ponte a Rondolino) ✱✱✱   Innovative top producers of San Gimignano with vg VERNACCIA DI SAN G, white VDTS 'Terre di Tufi' and 'Carmen'.

Tiefenbrunner ✱✱✱   Leading grower of some of the very best ALTO ADIGE white and red wines at Schloss Turmhof, Kurtatsch (Cortaccio).

Tignanello Tus r ✱✱✱✱ 82 83 85 88 90 93 94   Pioneer and still leader of the new style of Bordeaux-inspired Tuscan reds, made by ANTINORI.

Tocai Mild smooth NE white (no relation of Hungarian or Alsace Tokay). DOC also in Ven and Lom (✱→✱✱✱), but producers are most proud of it in F-VG (esp COLLIO and COLLI ORIENTALI): (✱✱→✱✱✱). Best producers: BORGO DEL TIGLIO, Keber, Picech, Princic, Raccaro, Ronco del Gelso, RONCO DI GNEMIZ, SCHIOPETTO, Scubla, Specogna, Castello di Spessa, Toros, Venica & Venica, VILLA RUSSIZ, VOLPE PASINI.

Torbato di Alghero Sar w (pa) **✱✱** DYA   Good N Sardinian table wine. Top maker: SELLA & MOSCA.

Torgiano Umb DOC r w p (sp) **✱✱→✱✱✱** and **Torgiano, Rosso Riserva** Umb DOCG r ✱✱✱ 85 87 88 90 93 94 (3 yrs ageing)   Creation of Lungarotti family. Excellent red from nr Perugia, comparable with top CHIANTI CLASSICO. Rubesco is standard. RISERVA Vigna Monticchio is (✱✱✱✱); keep 10 yrs. VDT San Giorgio involves CAB to splendid effect. White Torre di Giano, of TREBBIANO and GRECHETTO, also ages well. See also Lungarotti.

Torricella Tus w **✱✱** 88 90 93 94   Remarkable aged, soft, buttery MALVASIA dry white from Brolio. Produced by BARONE RICASOLI.

Toscana See Tuscany.

Tuscany vintages

1994 Dry summer, showers in September; good to very good.

1993 A hot summer was followed by heavy October rains; despite these Chianti Classico generally good, Brunello and Vino Nobile di Montepulciano vg.

1992 Promise of a top quality vintage dispelled for reds by rain. Whites had better luck and are vg.

1991 A difficult vintage: wines to drink quickly, without many positive surprises.

Traminer Aromatico T-AA DOC w ✱✱→✱✱✱ DYA   (German: Gewürz) Delicate, aromatic, soft. Best from: CS Girlan/Cornaiano, CS St-Michael, CS SCHRECKBICHL/ COLTERENZIO, Hofkellerei, Paterbichl, TIEFENBRUNNER.

Trebbiano Principal white grape of TUSCANY, found all over Italy. Ugni Blanc in French. Sadly a waste of good v'yd space, with v rare exceptions.

Trebbiano d'Abruzzo Ab DOC w ✱→✱✱ DYA   Gentle neutral slightly tannic. From round Pescara. VALENTINI is much the best producer (also of MONTEPULCIANO D'ABRUZZO).

Trentino T-AA DOC r w dr sw ✱→✱✱✱   DOC for as many as 20 different wines, mostly named after their grapes. Best are CHARD, PINOT BL, MARZEMINO, TEROLDEGO. The region's capital is Trento.

Tuscany Toscana. Italy's central wine region, incl DOC CHIANTI, MONTALCINO, MONTEPULCIANO etc.

Umani Ronchi ✱→✱✱✱   Leading merchant of quality wines of the Marches; notably VERDICCHIO (Casal di Serra and Villa Bianchi) and ROSSO CONERO (Cumaro and San Lorenzo).

Uzzano, Castello di Famous old CHIANTI CLASSICO estate at Greve. Below par.

Vajra, Giuseppe Domenico ✱✱✱   Vg consistent BAROLO producer, esp for BARBERA, Barolo, DOLCETTO, etc.

Valcalepio Lom DOC r w ✱→✱✱   From nr Bergamo. Pleasant red; lightly scented fresh white. Good from: Bonaldi, Il Calepino, Tenuta Castello.

Valdadige T-AA DOC r w dr s/sw ✱   Name for the simple wines of the ADIGE VALLEY – in German 'Etschtaler'. Top producer: Armani.

Valentini, Edoardo ** Perhaps the best traditionalist maker of TREBBIANO and MONTEPULCIANO D'ABRUZZO.

Valgella Lom DOC r ** 88 89 90 93 One of the VALTELLINA NEBBIOLOS: good dry red. RISERVA at 4 yrs. See Valtellina.

Valle d'Aosta VdA DOC **→*** Regional DOC for 15 Alpine wines incl DONNAZ. A mixed bag. Vg from monastery-run Institut Agricole Régional, Charrère, Crote de Vegnerons, Grosjean.

Valle Isarco (Eisacktal) T-AA DOC w ** DYA A DOC applicable to 5 varietal wines made NE of Bolzano. Good MULLER-T, Silvaner. Top producers are CS Eisacktaler, Kloster Neustift, Kuenhof.

Vallechiara, Abbazia di **→*** New PIEDMONT estate, owned by actress Ornella Muti, with astonishingly high quality wines, eg DOC Dolcetto di Ovada and DOLCETTO-based VDTS Due Donne and Torre Albarola.

Valpolicella Ven DOC r *→*** 93 94 Attractive light red from nr Verona; best young. Delicate nutty scent, slightly bitter taste. (None of this is true of junk Valpolicella sold in litre and bigger bottles.) CLASSICO more restricted; SUPERIORE has 12% alcohol and 1 yr of age. Good esp from ALLEGRINI, Brigaldara, Brunelli, Corte Sant Alda, Aleardo Ferrari, Fornaser, GUERRIERI-RIZZARDI, LE RAGOSE, MASI, Le Salette, San Rustico, Speri, Vantini, Venturini. DAL FORNO and QUINTARELLI make the best (***). Interesting VDTS on the way to a new Valpolicella style are Toar (***) from MASI and La Poja (***) from ALLEGRINI.

Valtellina Lom DOC r **→*** 88 89 90 93 A DOC for tannic wines made mainly from Chiavennasca (NEBBIOLO) grapes in Alpine Sondrio province, N Lombardy. V SUPERIORE are GRUMELLO, INFERNO, SASSELLA, VALGELLA. Best from: Conti Sertoli-Salis, Fay, La Castellina, Triacca.

Vecchio Samperi Si *** MARSALA-like VDT from outstanding estate. The best is barrel-aged 20 years, not unlike amontillado sherry. The owner, Marco De Bartoli, also makes top DOC Marsalas.

Vendemmia Harvest or vintage.

Venegazzù Ven r w sp *** 88 89 90 93 94 Remarkable rustic B'x-style red produced from CAB grapes nr Treviso. Rich bouquet, soft warm taste. 'Della Casa' and 'Capo di Stato' are best quality. Also sparkling.

Verdicchio dei Castelli di Jesi Mar DOC w (sp) *→*** DYA Ancient pleasant fresh pale white from nr Ancona, dating back to the Etruscans. Also CLASSICO. Trad in amphora-shaped bottles. Esp from Belelli, Brunori, Bucci, Coroncino, GAROFOLI, Mancinelli, Moncaro, Monteschiavo, Sartarelli, UMANI RONCHI, Zaccagnini; also FAZI-BATTAGLIA.

Verdicchio di Matelica Mar DOC w (sp) ** DYA Similar to the last, though bigger, less well-known. Esp Belisario, Castiglioni-Bisci, La Monacesca.

Verona Capital of the Veneto region (home of VALPOLICELLA, BARDOLINO, SOAVE etc) and seat of Italy's splendid annual April Wine fair Vinitaly.

Verduzzo (Colli Orientali del Friuli) F-VG DOC w dr s/sw sw **→*** 88 89 90 91 92 93 94 Full-bodied white from a native grape. The best sweet is called Ramandolo. Top makers: Dario Coos, DORIGO, Giovanni Dri.

Verduzzo (del Piave) Ven DOC w * DYA A dull little white.

Vermentino Lig w DOC ** DYA Best seafood white of Riviera: from Pietra Ligure and San Remo. DOC is Riviera Ligure di Ponente. See Pigato. Esp from: Anfossi, Cascina dei Peri, Colle dei Bardellini, Lambruschi, Lupi.

Vermentino di Gallura Sar DOC w ** DYA Soft dry strong white of N Sardinia. Esp from CS di Gallura, CS Giogantinu, CS Del Vermentino.

Vernaccia di Oristano Sar DOC w dr (sw fz) *** 75 78' 81 83 85' 87 88 91 92 93 94 Sardinian speciality, like light sherry, a touch bitter, full-bodied and interesting. SUPERIORE with 15.5% alcohol and 3 yrs of age. Top producer Contini also makes ancient solera wine Antico Gregori.

Vernaccia di San Gimignano Tus DOCG w ** DYA Once Michelangelo's favourite, then ordinary tourist wine. Rapid improvement in last few yrs, now newly DOCG with tougher production laws. Best from FALCHINI, Palagetto, PANIZZI, Rampa di Fugnano, San Quirico, TERUZZI & PUTHOD.

Vernatsch German for SCHIAVA.

Verrazzano, Castello di ★★ Important CHIANTI CLASSICO estate near Greve.

Vicchiomaggio CHIANTI CLASSICO estate near Greve.

VIDE An association of better-class Italian producers for marketing their estate wines from many parts of Italy.

Vie di Romans ★★★→★★★★ A young wine genius, Gianfranco Gallo, has built up his father's ISONZO estate to top FRIULI status within a few years. Unforgettable CHARD and SAUV; excellent TOCAI and PINOT GR.

Vietti Excellent small producer of characterful PIEDMONT wines, including BAROLO and BARBARESCO (both ★★★→★★★★). At Castiglione Falletto in Barolo region.

Vigna A single vineyard – see Introduction, page 80.

Vignamaggio ★★★ Historic, beautiful and vg CHIANTI CLASSICO estate nr Greve.

Villa Matilde ★★ Top Campania producer. Vg FALERNO and white Falanghina.

Villa Russiz ★★★ Impressive white DOC COLLIO from Gianni Menotti: eg, SAUV (look for 'de la Tour'), PINOT BL, TOCAI, etc.

Vin Santo Toscano Tus w s/sw ★★→★★★ Aromatic rich and smooth. Aged in v small barrels called caratelli. Can be as astonishing as expensive, but a good one is v rare and top producers are always short of it. Best from AVIGNONESI, Cacchiano, CAPEZZANA, CONTUCCI, CORZANO & PATERNO, POLIZIANO, SAN GIUSTO A RENTENNANO, SELVAPIANA.

Vino da arrosto 'Wine for roast meat', ie good robust dry red.

Vino Nobile di Montepulciano Tus DOCG r ▄▄▄ 85 86 88 90 91 93 94 Impressive SANGIOVESE red with bouquet and style, rapidly making its name and fortune. RISERVA after 3 yrs. Best estates incl AVIGNONESI, Bindella, BOSCARELLI, La Calonica, Canneto, LE CASALTE, Casella, Fattoria del Cerro, CONTUCCI, Dei, Innocenti, Macchione, Paterno, POLIZIANO, Talosa, Trerose, Valdipiatta, Vecchia Cantina (look for the RISERVA). Nobile is so far very reasonably priced.

Vino novello Italy's equivalent of France's primeurs (as in Beaujolais).

Vino da tavola (vdt) 'Table wine': intended to be the humblest class of Italian wine, with no specific geographical or other claim to fame, but also category to watch (with reasonable circumspection and a wary eye on the price) for top-class wines not conforming to DOC regulations. New laws introduced in '92 should phase out this situation (see Introduction, page 80).

Vinsanto or Vin(o) Santo Term for certain strong sweet wines esp in TUSCANY: usually PASSITO. Can be v fine, esp in Tuscany and TRENTINO.

Vintage Tunina F-VG w ★★★ A notable blended white from JERMANN estate.

Voerzio, Roberto ★★★ Young BAROLO pace-setter: Brunate is new-style best.

Volpaia, Castello di ★★ First-class CHIANTI CLASSICO estate at Radda, with elegant, rather light Chianti. VDT red Balifico contains CAB; COLTASSALA is all SANGIOVESE.

Volpe Pasini ★★★ Ambitious COLLIO ORIENTALI estate, esp for good SAUV.

VQPRD Often found on the labels of DOC wines to signify Vini di Qualità Prodotti in Regioni Delimitate.

Zanella, Maurizio Creator of CA'DEL BOSCO. His name is on his top CAB-MERLOT blend, one of Italy's best.

Zerbina, Fattoria ★★→★★★ New leader in Romagna with best ALBANA DOCG to date (a rich PASSITO), good SANGIOVESE and a barrique-aged Sangiovese-CAB VDT called Marzeno di Marzeno.

Zibibbo Si w sw ★★ Fashionable MOSCATO from the island of Pantelleria. Good producer: Murana.

Zonin One of Italy's biggest privately owned estates and wineries, based at GAMBELLARA, with DOC VALPOLICELLA, etc. Others are at ASTI and in CHIANTI, San Gimignano and FRIULI. Also at Barboursville, Virginia, USA.

Germany

The German wine industry is only now beginning to recover from over two decades of drift and demoralization that began with the catastrophic Wine Laws of 1971. They encouraged low standards, over-production and confusing (not to say misleading) labelling. Demoralization, greed and fraud made matters worse. And so did the weather: 20 years with only four really good vintages.

Now quality is reasserting itself. The world is aware once more that Germany's wines reach unassailable levels – when made of the right grapes. Above all, of Riesling. Six fine vintages have been matched by new determination among a new generation of winemakers. Germany's best growers (mostly young) have at last resolved to ignore laws that encourage inflation of quantity and dilution of quality, and make the best wine they can. Sugar-watery wines are still made in vast ignoble quantities – largely for the British market. But today a large number are being made dry or close to dry, with sweetness reserved as the exception, for Spätlesen and Auslesen, and not always for these. Experiments with oak-ageing (though not of Riesling) open up new stylistic possibilities. On the home market, in restaurants, these dry wines are all the rage: abroad they have yet to be fully appreciated.

Officially, all German wines are classified according to grape ripeness. Most wines (like most French) need sugar added before fermentation to make up for missing sunshine. But unlike in France, German wine from grapes ripe enough not to need extra sugar is made and sold as a separate product: Qualitätswein mit Prädikat, or QmP. Within this top category, natural sugar content is expressed by traditional terms in ascending order of ripeness: Kabinett, Spätlese, Auslese, Beerenauslese, Trockenbeerenauslese.

Qualitätswein bestimmter Anbaugebiete (QbA), the second level, is for wines that needed additional sugar before fermentation. The third level, Tafelwein, has no pretensions to quality.

Though there is much more detail in the laws, this is the gist of the quality grading. It differs completely from the French system in ignoring geographical difference. There are (at least presently) no Grands Crus, no Premiers Crus. And in theory all any German vineyard has to do to make the best wine is to grow the ripest grapes – even of inferior grape varieties – which is patent rubbish.

The law distinguishes only between degrees of geographical exactness. In labelling quality wine growers or merchants are given a choice. They can (and generally do) label the relatively small quantities of their best wine with the name of the precise vineyard or Einzellage. Germany has about 2,600 Einzellage names. Obviously only a relative few are famous enough to help sell the wine. Therefore the 1971 law created a second class of vineyard name: the Grosslage. A Grosslage is a group of Einzellagen of supposedly similar character. Because there are fewer Grosslage names, and far more wine from each, they have the advantage of familiarity – a poor substitute for hard-earned fame.

Thirdly, growers or merchants may choose to sell their wine under a regional or Bereich name. To cope with the demand for 'Bernkasteler', 'Niersteiner' or 'Johannisberger' these world-

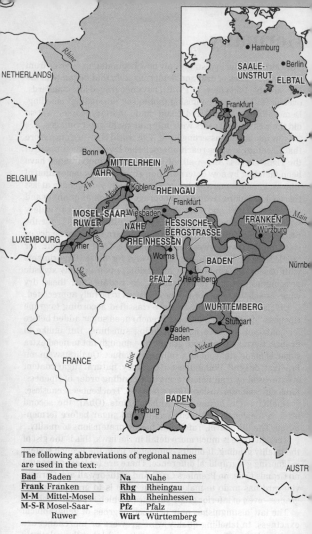

The following abbreviations of regional names are used in the text:

Bad	Baden	**Na**	Nahe
Frank	Franken	**Rhg**	Rheingau
M-M	Mittel-Mosel	**Rhh**	Rheinhessen
M-S-R	Mosel-Saar-	**Pfz**	Pfalz
	Ruwer	**Würt**	Württemberg

famous names were made legal for large districts. 'Bereich Johannisberg' is the whole of the Rheingau. Beware the Bereich.

More growers are now simplifying labels to avoid confusion and clutter. Some use the village name only, or indeed sell top wines under a brand name alone as in Italy. But before German wine can fully recover its rightful place, two things are needed: the banning of inferior grapes from top areas, and a thorough classification of which those areas are. A start has at last been made in classifying 'First-class vineyards' – though unofficially, not by the inert government. They are named here and mapped (for the first time) in the 4th edition of The World Atlas of Wine. It is after all (in Germany above all) the vineyard and producer that count.

Recent vintages

Mosel-Saar-Ruwer

Mosels (including Saar and Ruwer wines) are so attractive young that their keeping qualities are not often enough explored and wines older than about 8 years are unusual. But well-made Riesling wines of Kabinett class gain from at least 5 years in bottle – often much more – Spätlese from 10 to 20, and Auslese and Beerenauslese, anything from 10 to 30 years.

As a rule, in poor years the Saar and Ruwer make sharp thin wines, but in the best years, above all with botrytis, they can surpass the whole world for elegance and thrilling steely 'breed'.

1994 Another v good vintage, mostly QmP with many Auslese, BA, TBA. Rich fruit and high acidity. Try to resist: they have a glorious future.

1993 A v small vintage of excellent quality with lots of Auslese/botrytis and nr perfect harmony.

1992 A very large crop, threatened by cold and rain in October. Mostly good QbA, but 30% QmP, some exceptional, esp in Mittelmosel. Start to taste.

1991 A diverse vintage. Bad frost damage in Saar and Ruwer, but many fine Spätlesen. Start to drink.

1990 Superb vintage, though small. Many QmP wines were the finest for 20 years. Try to resist drinking too soon.

1989 Large and outstandingly good, with noble rot giving many Auslesen etc. Saar best; Mittelmosel overproduced. Mostly ready to drink.

1988 Excellent vintage. Much ripe QmP, esp in Mittelmosel. For long keeping.

1987 Rainy summer but warm Sept/Oct. 90% QbA wines, crisp and lively, to drink soon.

1986 Fair Riesling year despite autumn rain: 13% QmP wines, mostly Kabinett. For drinking.

1985 A modest summer but beautiful autumn. 40% of harvest was QmP. Riesling vintage from best v'yds, incl Fiswein. Many still need keeping.

1983 The best between 76 and 88; 31% Spätlese; Auslesen few but fine. No hurry to drink.

1982 A huge ripe vintage marred by rain which considerably diluted the wines. Most is plain QbA but good sites made Kabinett, Spätlese and Auslese. Drink up.

1981 A wet vintage but some good Mittelmosels up to Spätlese. Also Eiswein. Drinking well.

1979 A patchy vintage after bad winter damage. But many excellent Kabinetts and better. Light but well-balanced wines should be drunk up.

1976 Vg small vintage, with some superlative sweet wines and almost no dry. Most wines ready; only the best will keep.

1971 Superb, with perfect balance. At its peak – but no hurry for best wines.

Older fine vintages: 69 64 59 53 49 45.

Rheinhessen, Nahe, Pfalz, Rheingau

Even the best wines can be drunk with pleasure when young, but Kabinett, Spätlese and Auslese Riesling gain enormously in character by keeping for longer. Rheingau wines tend to be longest-lived, improving for 15 years or more, but wines from the Nahe and Pfalz can last as long. Rheinhessen wines usually mature sooner, and dry Franken wines are best at 3–6 years.

1994 Good vintage, mostly QmP, abundant fruit and firm structure. Need time to develop. Best in Pfalz where finest vintage since '90.

1993 A small vintage of v good to excellent quality. Plenty of Spätlese and Auslese.

1992 Very large vintage, would have been great but for October cold and rain. A third QmP wines of rich stylish quality. Start to taste.

1991 A good middling vintage in most regions, though light soils in Pfalz suffered from drought. Some fine wines are emerging. Start to taste.

1990 Small but exceptionally fine. High percentage of QmP will keep well beyond 2000.

1989 Summer storms reduced crop in Rheingau. Vg quality elsewhere, up to Auslese level. Try now.

1988 Not quite so outstanding as the Mosel, but comparable with 83. Drinking well.

1987 Good average quality: lively round and fresh. 80% QbA, 15% QmP. Now drinking well.

1986 Well-balanced Rieslings, mostly QbA but some Kabinett and Spätlese, esp in Rheinhessen and Nahe. Good botrytis wines in Pfalz. Now drinking well.

1985 Sadly small crops, of variable quality, esp Riesling. Average 65% QmP. Keep the best.

1983 Vg Rieslings, esp in the Rheingau and central Nahe. Generally about half QbA, but plenty of Spätlesen, now excellent to drink.

1982 A colossal vintage gathered in torrential rain. All 82s should be drunk up.

1981 Rheingau poor, Nahe and Rheinhessen better, Pfalz best. Drink up.

1976 The richest vintage since 21 in places. Very few dry wines. Generally mature.

1971 A superlative vintage, now at its peak.

Older fine vintages: 69 67 64 59 53 49 45.

Vintage notes after entries in the German section are given in a different form from those elsewhere, to show the style of the vintage as well as its quality. Three styles are indicated:

Bold type (eg **93**) indicates classic, super-ripe vintages with a high proportion of natural (QmP) wines, including Spätlese and Auslese.

Normal type (eg 92) indicates 'normal' successful vintages with plenty of good wine but no great preponderance of sweeter wines.

Italic type (eg *91*) indicates cool vintages with generally poor ripeness but a fair proportion of reasonably successful wines, tending to be over-acid. Few or no QmP wines, but correspondingly more selection in the QbA category. Such wines sometimes mature better than expected.

Where no mention is made the vintage is generally not recommended, or most of its wines have passed maturity.

Achkarren Bad w (r) ▧▧   Village on the KAISERSTUHL, known esp for RULANDER. Best site: Schlossberg. Good wines: DR HEGER and coop.

Adelmann, Graf ✶✶→✶✶✶ Aristocratic grower with 37 acres at Kleinbottwar, WURTTEMBERG. Uses the name 'Brussele'. LEMBERGER reds best.

Ahr Ahr r ✶→✶✶ **76** 83 85 *87* 88 89 90 *91* *92* 93 94   Germany's best-known red wine area, south of Bonn. Very light, pale SPATBURGUNDER, esp from Deutzerhof, Kreuzberg, MEYER-NAKEL, STATE DOMAIN.

Amtliche Prüfungsnummer See Prüfungsnummer.

Anheuser, Paul NAHE grower (✶✶) at BAD KREUZNACH.

APNr Abbreviation of AMTLICHE PRUFUNGSNUMMER.

Assmannshausen Rhg r ✶→✶✶✶ 71 75 76 83 85 *87* 88 89 90 *91* *92* 93 94   RHEINGAU village known for its usually pale, light reds. Top v'yd: Höllenberg. Grosslagen: Steil and Burgweg. Growers incl AUGUST KESSELER, Robert König, VON MUMM, and the STATE DOMAIN at ELTVILLE.

Auslese Specially selected wine with high natural sugar; the best affected by 'noble rot' (Edelfäule) and correspondingly unctuous in flavour.

Avelsbach M-S-R (Ruwer) w ✶✶✶ 71 75 76 83 85 *87* 88 89 90 *91* 92 93 94   Village nr TRIER. At (rare) best, lovely delicate wines. Esp BISCHOFLICHE WEINGUTER, Staatliche Weinbaudomäne (see Staatsweingut). Grosslage: Römerlay.

Ayl M-S-R (Saar) w ▧▧▧ 71 75 76 83 85 *87* 88 89 90 91 92 93 94   One of the best villages of the SAAR. First-class v'yd: Kupp. Grosslage: SCHARZBERG. Growers incl BISCHOFLICHE WEINGUTER, Lauer, DR WAGNER.

Bacchus Modern, perfumed, even kitsch, grape. Best for KABINETT wines.

Bacharach ▧▧▧→▧▧▧   District name for southern MITTELRHEIN v'yds downstream from RHEINGAU. Now amalgamated with RHEINBURGENGAU as the new BEREICH 'LORELEY'. Racy RIESLINGS, some v fine. Growers incl FRITZ BASTIAN, TONI JOST, Randolph Kauer, RATZENBERGER.

Bad Dürkheim Pfz w (r) ✶✶→✶✶✶ 76 83 85 86 *87* 88 89 90 *91* 92 93 94   Main town of MITTELHAARDT, with the world's biggest barrel (converted into a tavern) and an ancient September wine festival, the 'Wurstmarkt'. Top v'yds: Michelsberg, Spielberg. Grosslagen: Feuerberg, Hochmess, Schenkenböhl. Growers: Kurt Darting, FITZ-RITTER, Karst, Karl Schäfer.

Bad Kreuznach Nahe w ✶✶→✶✶✶ 75 76 79 83 85 86 *87* 88 89 90 *91* 92 93 94   Town of many fine v'yds, First-class: Brückes, Kahlenberg, Krötenpfuhl. Grosslage: Kronenberg. Growers incl ANHEUSER, Finkenauer, PLETTENBERG.

Baden Huge SW area of scattered v'yds, but rapidly growing reputation. Style is substantial, generally dry, relatively low in acid, good for mealtimes. Fine Pinots, SPATBURGUNDER, RIES. Best areas: KAISERSTUHL, ORTENAU.

Badische Bergstrasse/Kraichgau (Bereich) Widespread district of N BADEN. WEISSBURGUNDER and RULANDER make best wines.

Badischer Winzerkeller Current name for the former ZBW, Germany's (and Europe's) biggest coop, at BREISACH; 25,000 members with 12,000 acres, producing almost half of BADEN's wine at all quality levels.

Badisches Frankenland See Tauberfranken.

Barriques Some growers are experimenting with modish new-oak ageing; a quick route to notoriety and higher prices. It can add style to SPATBURGUNDER, WEISSBURGUNDER or GRAUBURGUNDER, but not RIES.

Bassermann-Jordan ★★★ 117-acre MITTELHAARDT family estate with many of the best v'yds in DEIDESHEIM, FORST, RUPPERTSBERG, etc. 100% RIES and a formidable track-record.

Bastian, Weingut Fritz 12 acre BACHARACH estate. Racy RIESLINGS with MOSEL-like delicacy, best from the First-class Posten v'yd.

Becker, J B ★★→★★★ Dedicated family estate and brokerage house at WALLUF. 30 acres in ELTVILLE, MARTINSTHAL, Walluf. Specialist in dry RIES.

Beerenauslese Extremely sweet and luscious wine from selected exceptionally ripe individual berries, their sugar and flavour usually concentrated by 'noble rot'. Rare and expensive.

Bensheim See Hessische Bergstrasse.

Bercher KAISERSTUHL estate; 40 acres of white and red Pinots at Burkheim. Good dry whites and some of Germany's best reds.

Warning notice:

Bereich District within an Anbaugebiet (region). The word on a label should should be treated as a flashing red light. Do not buy. See Introduction and under Bereich names, eg Bernkastel (Bereich).

Bernkastel M-M w ★→★★★★ 71 75 76 79 83 *84* 85 86 *87* 88 89 90 *91* 92 93 94 Top wine town of the MITTELMOSEL; the epitome of RIES. Great First-class v'yd: Doctor, 8 acres (★★★★); First-class v'yds: Graben, Lay. Grosslagen: Badstube (★★★) and Kurfürstlay (★). Top growers incl FRIEDRICH WILHELM GYMNASIUM, HERIBERT KERPEN, LAUERBURG, DR LOOSEN, DR PAULY-BERGWEILER, J J PRUM, Studert-Prüm, THANISCH, WEGELER-DEINHARD.

Bernkastel (Bereich) Wide area of deplorably dim quality but hopefully flowery character. Mostly MULLER-T. Includes all the MITTELMOSEL. Avoid.

Biffar, Josef ★★ Rising star DEIDESHEIM estate. 40 acres (also WACHENHEIM) of RIES. Intense classic wines.

Bingen Rhh w ★★→★★★ 71 75 76 83 85 *87* 88 89 90 *91* 92 93 94 Rhine/NAHE town; fine v'yds: First-class: Scharlachberg. Grosslage: St Rochuskapelle.

Bingen (Bereich) District name for west RHEINHESSEN.

Bischöfliche Weingüter ★★★ Famous M-S-R estate at TRIER, a union of the cathedral properties with 2 other charities, the Bischöfliches Priesterseminar and the Bischöfliches Konvikt. 260 acres of top v'yds, esp in SAAR and RUWER. After recent disappointments there are signs of improvement. Ruwer wines currently best (esp EITELSBACH, KASEL).

Blue Nun Famous but fading brand of LIEBFRAUMILCH, from SICHEL.

Bocksbeutel Flask-shaped bottle used for FRANKEN wines.

Bodenheim Rhh w ★★ Village nr NIERSTEIN with full earthy wines, esp from First-class v'yds Hoch and Silberberg. Top grower: Kühling-Gillot.

Bodensee (Bereich) Minor district of S BADEN, on Lake Constance.

Braun, Weingut Heinrich 60-acre NIERSTEIN estate. Elegant dry and sweet RIES from First-class v'yds and First-class v'yds.

Brauneberg M-M w ★★★★ 71 75 76 83 85 86 87 88 89 90 91 92 93 94 Top M-S-R village nr BERNKASTEL (750 acres), unbroken tradition for excellent full-flavoured RIES. 'Grand Cru' if anything on the Mosel is. Great First-class v'yd: Juffer-Sonnenuhr. First-class v'yd is Juffer. Grosslage: Kurfürstlay. Growers: FRITZ HAAG, WILLI HAAG, Paulinshof, M F RICHTER.

Breisach Bad Frontier town on RHINE nr KAISERSTUHL. Seat of the largest German coop, the BADISCHER WINZERKELLER.

Breisgau (Bereich) Minor BADEN district. Esp v pale pink WEISSHERBST.

Breuer, Weingut G ★★★ Family estate of 36 acres in RUDESHEIM, a CHARTA leader, with 6 acres of Berg Schlossberg, and 12.5-acre monopole RAUENTHALER Nonnenberg. Fine quality and new ideas, incl sparkling (87) RIES-Pinot Bl-Pinot Gr.

Buhl, Reichsrat von **→*** Historic PFALZ family estate, below historic form. 160 acres (DEIDESHEIM, FORST, RUPPERTSBERG...). Now leased by Japanese firm.

Bundesweinprämierung The German State Wine Award, organized by DLG (see below): gives great (Grosse), silver or bronze medallion labels.

Bürgerspital zum Heiligen Geist **→*** Ancient charitable estate at WURZBURG. 333 acres in Würzburg, RANDERSACKER, etc; often magnificent rich dry wines, esp from SILVANER and RIES.

Bürklin-Wolf, Dr ***→**** Famous PFALZ family estate. 222 acres in FORST, DEIDESHEIM, RUPPERTSBERG and WACHENHEIM. Vg 89s and 93s.

Castell'sches, Fürstlich Domänenamt **→*** Historic 142-acre princely estate in STEIGERWALD. Noble FRANKEN wines: SILVANER, RIESLANER. Also SEKT.

Chardonnay A small acreage of Chard has been experimentally, and sometimes illegally, planted – it is now legal in PFALZ and BADEN-WURTTEMBERG.

Charta Organization of top RHEINGAU estates making forceful medium-dry RIES to far higher standards than dismally permissive laws require.

Christoffel, J J ** Tiny domaine in ERDEN, GRAACH, URZIG, WEHLEN. Polished RIES.

Clevner (or Klevner) Synonym in WURTTEMBERG for Blauer Frühburgunder red grape, supposedly a mutation of Pinot N or Italian Chiavenna (early-ripening black Pinot). Also ORTENAU (BADEN) synonym for TRAMINER.

Crusius ****→**** 30-acre family estate in TRAISEN, NAHE. Vivid RIES from Bastei, Rotenfels and SCHLOSSBOCKELHEIM. Top wines age v well. Also good SEKT and freshly fruity SPATBURGUNDER dry rosé.

Deidesheim Pfz w (r) ****→**** 71 75 76 83 85 86 *87* 88 89 90 91 92 93 94 Biggest top-quality wine village of PFALZ (1,000 acres). Rich high-flavoured lively wines. Also Sekt. First-class v'yds are Grainhübel, Hohenmorgen, Kalkofen, Kieselberg, Langenmorgen, Leinhöhle. Grosslagen: Mariengarten (***), Hofstück (**). Esp BASSERMANN-JORDAN, BIFFAR, VON BUHL, BURKLIN-WOLF, DEINHARD, Kimmich.

Deinhard **→*** Famous old Koblenz merchants and growers of high quality wines in RHEINGAU, MITTELMOSEL, RUWER and PFALZ (see Wegeler-Deinhard), also makers of vg SEKT (eg Lila). Leaders in new ideas. Their Heritage range is of single-village (DEIDESHEIM, HOCHHEIM, JOHANNISBERG, etc) TROCKEN wines which are well-made but singularly austere.

Deinhard, Dr *** Fine 62-acre family estate: many of DEIDESHEIM's best v'yds.

Deutsche Weinstrasse Tourist road of S PFALZ, Bockenheim to SCHWEIGEN.

Deutscher Tafelwein Officially the term for v humble German wines. Now confusingly the flag of convenience for some top novelties as well (eg BARRIQUE wines). As in Italy, the law will have to change.

Deutsches Weinsiegel A quality seal (ie neck label) for wines which have passed a statutory tasting test. Seals are: yellow for dry, green for medium-dry, red for medium-sweet.

Diabetiker Wein Wine with minimal residual sugar (less than 4 grams per litre); thus suitable for diabetics – or those who like <u>very</u> dry wine.

Diel auf Burg Layen, Schlossgut *** Fashionable 30-acre NAHE estate; known for ageing RULANDER and WEISSBURGUNDER in French BARRIQUES. Also fine traditional RIES. Impressive AUSLESE and EISWEIN.

DLG (Deutsche Landwirtschaftgesellschaft) The German Agricultural Society at Frankfurt. Awards national medals for quality – generously.

Dom German for 'cathedral'. Wines from the famous TRIER cathedral properties have 'Dom' before the v'yd name.

Domäne German for 'domain' or 'estate'. Sometimes used alone to mean the 'State domain' (STAATLICHE WEINBAUDOMANE).

Dönnhoff, Weingut Hermann ** 23-acre NAHE estate with exceptionally fine RIES from NIEDERHAUSEN, Oberhausen, etc.

Dornfelder New red grape making deep-coloured everyday wines in PFALZ.

To decipher codes, please refer to symbols key at front of book, and to 'How to use this book' on page 5.

Durbach Baden w (r) ✼✼→✼✼✼✼ 76 83 85 *87* 88 89 90 *91* 92 93 94   Village with 775 acres of BADEN's best v'yds. Top growers: A LAIBLE, H Männle, SCHLOSS STAUFENBERG, WOLFF-METTERNICH. Choose their KLINGELBERGERS (RIES) and CLEVNERS (TRAMINER). Grosslage: Fürsteneck.

Edel Means 'noble'. Edelfäule means 'noble rot': see page 77.

Germany's quality levels

The official range of qualities in ascending order are as follows:

(1) *Deutscher Tafelwein: sweetish light wine of no special character. (Unofficially, can be very special.)*

(2) *Landwein: dryish Tafelwein with some regional style.*

(3) *Qualitätswein: dry or sweetish wine with sugar added before fermentation to increase its strength, but tested for quality and with distinct local and grape character.*

(4) *Kabinettwein: dry or dryish natural (unsugared) wine of distinct personality and distinguishing lightness. Can be very fine.*

(5) *Spätlese: stronger, often sweeter than Kabinett. Full-bodied. The trend today is towards drier or even completely dry Spätlese.*

(6) *Auslese: sweeter, sometimes stronger than Spätlese, often with honey-like flavours, intense and long.*

(7) *Beerenauslese. v sweet and usually strong, intense; can be superb.*

(8) *Eiswein: (Beeren- or Trockenbeerenauslese) concentrated, sharpish and very sweet. Extraordinary and everlasting.*

(9) *Trockenbeerenauslese: intensely sweet and aromatic; alcohol slight.*

Egon Müller zu Scharzhof ✼✼✼✼ Top SAAR estate of 32 acres at WILTINGEN. Its rich and racy SCHARZHOFBERGER RIESLINGS in AUSLESEN vintages are among the world's greatest wines. The best are given gold capsules. 89s, 90s and 93s are sublime, honeyed, immortal. Le Gallais is a second estate in WILTINGER Braune Kupp.

Eiswein V sweet wine made from frozen grapes with the ice (ie water content) discarded, thus v concentrated in flavour and sugar – of BEERENAUSLESE ripeness or more. But alcohol content can be as low as 5.5%. High acidity gives them v long life. Rare and v expensive. Sometimes made as late as January or February following the vintage.

Eitelsbach M-S-R (Ruwer) w ✼✼→✼✼✼✼ 71 75 76 83 85 *87* 88 89 90 *91* 92 93 94   RUWER village now part of TRIER, incl superb Great First-class KARTHAUSERHOFBERG estate. Grosslage: Römerlay.

Elbe The wine-river of eastern Germany. See Sachsen.

Elbling Traditional grape widely grown on upper MOSEL. Can be sharp and tasteless; but capable of real freshness and vitality in the best conditions (eg at Nittel or SCHLOSS THORN in the OBERMOSEL).

Eltville Rhg w ✼✼→✼✼✼✼ 71 75 76 83 85 86 *87* 88 89 90 *91* 92 93 94   Major wine town with cellars of RHEINGAU STATE DOMAIN, FISCHER and VON SIMMERN estates. First-class v'yd: Sonnenberg. Grosslage: Steinmächer.

Enkirch M-M w ✼✼→✼✼✼✼ 71 76 83 85 *87* 88 89 90 91 93 94   Minor MITTELMOSEL village, often overlooked but with lovely light tasty wine. Grosslage: Schwarzlay. Top v'yds: Battterieberg, Zeppwingert.

Erbach Rhg w ✼✼✼→✼✼✼✼ 71 76 83 85 86 *87* 88 89 90 *91* 92 93 94   Top RHEINGAU area: powerful perfumed wines, incl from superb First-class v'yds Hohenrain, MARCOBRUNN, Siegelsberg, Steinmorgen, Schlossberg. Major estates: SCHLOSS REINHARTSHAUSEN, SCHLOSS SCHONBORN. Also BECKER, KNYPHAUSEN, VON SIMMERN, etc.

Erben Word meaning 'heirs', often used on old-established estate labels.

Erden M-M w ✼✼→✼✼✼✼ 71 75 76 83 *84* 85 86 *87* 88 89 90 *91* 92 93 94   Village between Urzig and Kröv: noble full-flavoured vigorous wine (different in style so without the high repute of neighbouring BERNKASTEL and WEHLEN). Great First-class v'yds: Prälat, Treppchen. Grosslage: Schwarzlay. Growers incl BISCHOFLICHE WEINGUTER, JJ CHRISTOFFEL, Stefan Ehlen, DR LOOSEN, Meulenhoff, Nicolay.

Erstes Gewächs Literally 'first growth'. A new ('94) classification for the top vineyards of the RHEINGAU. Applies from '92 vintage.

Erzeugerabfüllung Bottled by producer. Being replaced by 'GUTSABFULLUNG'.

Escherndorf Frank w **→***** 76 83 *87* 88 *89* 90 *91* 92 93 94 Important wine town near WURZBURG. Similar tasty dry wine. Top v'yd: First-class Lump. Grosslage: Kirchberg. Growers incl JULIUSSPITAL, Egon Schäffer.

Eser, Weingut August ▨▨▨ 20-acre RHEINGAU estate at OESTRICH. V'yds also in HALLGARTEN, RAUENTHAL (esp Gehrn, Rothenberg), WINKEL. Model wines.

Eser, Hans Hermann ▨▨▨ JOHANNISBERG family estate. 45 acres. RIESLINGS that justify the great Johannisberg name.

Remember that vintage information for German wines is given in a different form from the ready/not ready distinction applying to other countries. Read the explanation at the top of page 106.

Filzen M-S-R (Saar) w **→▨▨▨ 76 83 85 *87* 88 89 90 *91* 92 93 94 Small SAAR village nr WILTINGEN. First-class v'yd: Pulchen. Grower to note: Piedmont.

Fischer, Weingut Dr ** 60-acre OCKFEN, WAWERN estate: variable quality (83 vg, 90 good).

Fischer Erben, Weingut *** 18-acre RHEINGAU estate at ELTVILLE with highest traditional standards. Long-lived classic wines.

Fitz-Ritter *** Reliable BAD DURKHEIM estate. 54 acres, fine RIES.

Forschungsanstalt See Hessische Forschungsanstalt.

Forst Pfz w **→***** 71 75 76 83 85 86 *87* 88 89 90 91 92 93 94 MITTELHAARDT village with 500 acres of Germany's best v'yds. Ripe, richly fragrant, full-bodied but subtle wines. First-class vineyards: Jesuitengarten, Kirchenstück, Pechstein, Ungeheuer. Grosslagen: Mariengarten, Schnepfenflug. Top growers include BASSERMANN-JORDAN, DEINHARD, GEORG MOSBACHER, Eugen Müller, Spindler, Werlé.

Franken Franconia. Region of excellent distinctive dry wines, esp SILVANER, always bottled in round-bellied flasks (BOCKSBEUTEL). The centre is WURZBURG. Bereich names: MAINDREIECK, STEIGERWALD. Top producers: BURGERSPITAL, CASTELL, JULIUSSPITAL, WIRSCHING, etc.

Freiburg Baden w (r) *→** DYA Wine centre in BREISGAU, N of MARKGRAFLERLAND. Good GUTEDEL.

Freinsheim Pfz w r ▨▨ Well-known village of MITTELHAARDT with high proportion of RIES. Aromatic spicy wines. Top grower: LINGENFELDER.

Friedrich Wilhelm Gymnasium Important 111-acre charitable estate based in TRIER with v'yds in BERNKASTEL, GRAACH, OCKFEN, TRITTENHEIM, ZELTINGEN, etc, all M-S-R. 90 91 92 should have been better.

Fuhrmann See Pfeffingen.

Gallais Le See Egon Müller.

Geheimrat 'J' Brand-name of good very dry RIES SPATLESE from WEGELER-DEINHARD, OESTRICH, since '85. Epitomizes new RHEINGAU thinking.

Geisenheim Rhg w **→***** 71 76 83 85 86 *87* 88 89 90 *91* 92 93 94 Village famous for Germany's best-known wine school and fine aromatic wines. First-class v'yds are Kläuserweg, Rothenberg. Grosslagen: Burgweg, Erntebringer. Many top growers (eg SCHLOSS SCHONBORN) have v'yds here.

Gemeinde A commune or parish.

Gewürztraminer (or Traminer) 'Spicy' grape, speciality of Alsace, used a little in Germany, esp in PFALZ, RHEINHESSEN and BADEN.

Gimmeldingen Pfz w *→** 76 83 85 *87* 88 89 90 *91* 92 93 94 Village just S of MITTELHAARDT. At their best, similar wines. Grosslage: Meerspinne.

Graach M-M w **→▨▨▨ 71 75 76 83 *84* 85 86 *87* 88 89 90 *91* 92 93 94 Small village between BERNKASTEL and WEHLEN. First-class v'yds: Domprobst, Himmelreich, Josephshöfer. Grosslage: Münzlay. Many top growers, eg: KESSELSTATT, DR LOOSEN, J J PRUM, WILLI SCHAEFER, SELBACH-OSTER, WEINS-PRUM.

Grans-Fassian ** Fine 25-acre MOSEL estate at Leiwen. V'yds there and in PIESPORT, TRITTENHEIM.

Grauburgunder Synonym of RULANDER or Pinot Gris.

Grosser Ring Group of top (VDP) MOSEL-SAAR-RUWER estates, with annual September auction.

Grosslage See Introduction, pages 103–104.

Gunderloch ✱✱✱ Excellent 30-acre NACKENHEIM estate, one of the best in RHEINHESSEN today. 70% RIES. Best from N Rothenberg, but all are vg.

Guntersblum Rhh w ✱→✱✱ 76 83 85 88 89 90 *91* 92 93 94 Big wine town S of OPPENHEIM. First-class v'yds: Bornpfad, Himmeltal. Grosslagen: Krötenbrunnen, Vogelsgärten. Top grower: RAPPENHOF.

Guntrum, Louis ✱✱→✱✱✱ Fine 164-acre family estate in NIERSTEIN, OPPENHEIM, etc, and reliable merchant house. Fine SILVANERS and GEWURZTRAMINER as well as RIESLING.

Gutedel German word for the Chasselas grape, used in S BADEN.

Gutsabfüllung Estate-bottled. A new term limited to qualified estates.

Gutsverwaltung Estate administration.

Haag, Weingut Fritz ✱✱✱ 12-acre top estate in BRAUNEBERG run by Wilhelm Haag, president of GROSSER RING. MOSEL RIES of crystalline purity and racy brilliance for long ageing.

Haag, Weingut Willi ✱✱→✱✱✱ Tiny 7-acre BRAUNEBERG estate. Full, 'old-style' RIES. Some fine AUSLESE.

Haart, Reinhold ✱✱ Small estate, the best in PIESPORT. Refined aromatic wines, capable of long ageing.

Halbtrocken Medium-dry (literally 'semi-dry'). Containing less than 18 but more than 9 grams per litre unfermented sugar. An increasingly popular category of wine intended for mealtimes, usually better balanced than TROCKEN. All CHARTA wines are halbtrocken.

Hallgarten Rhg w ✱✱→✱✱✱ 71 76 83 85 86 *87* 88 89 90 *91* 92 93 94 Small wine town behind HATTENHEIM. Robust full-bodied wines, mysteriously seldom seen. Dominated by coops (unusual for Rhg). Weingut Fred Prinz is top estate.

Hattenheim Rhg w ✱✱→✱✱✱✱ 71 75 76 83 85 87 88 89 90 91 92 93 94 Superlative 500-acre wine town. First-class v'yds are Engelmannsberg, Mannberg, Pfaffenberg, STEINBERG (ORTSTEIL). Vg others incl Nussbrunnen, Wisselbrunnen. Grosslage: Deutelsberg. MARCOBRUNN lies on ERBACH boundary. Many fine estates incl KNYPHAUSEN, RESS, SCHLOSS SCHONBORN, VON SIMMERN, STATE DOMAIN, etc.

Heger, Dr ✱✱ Some of BADEN's best SPATBURGUNDER reds come from old vines on this 28-acre ACHKARREN estate. Also fine GRAUBURGUNDER.

Heilbronn Würt w r ✱→✱✱ 85 *87* 88 89 90 *91* 92 93 94 Wine town with many small growers and a big coop. Best wines are RIESLINGS. Seat of DLG competition. Top growers: Amalienhof, Drautz-Able, Heinrich.

Hessen, Prinz von ✱✱✱ Famous 75-acre estate in JOHANNISBERG, KIEDRICH and WINKEL. Despite gold medals, some recent wines raw or sharp.

Hessische Bergstrasse Rhg w ✱✱→✱✱ 76 83 85 *87* 88 89 90 *91* 92 93 94 Smallest wine region in western Germany (1,000 acres), N of Heidelberg. Pleasant RIES from STATE DOMAIN v'yds at Bensheim, Bergstrasser Coop, Heppenheim and Stadt Bensheim.

Hessische Forschungsanstalt für Wein-Obst-& Gartenbau Famous wine school and research establishment at GEISENHEIM, RHEINGAU. Good wines incl reds. The name on the label is Forschungsanstalt.

Heyl zu Herrnsheim Leading 72-acre NIERSTEIN estate, 60% RIES. An excellent record, recently patchy. Now part-owned by VALCKENBERG.

Hochgewächs A superior level of QBA RIES, esp in MOSEL-SAAR-RUWER.

Hochheim Rhg w ✱✱→✱✱✱ 71 75 76 79 83 *84* 85 86 *87* 88 89 90 *91* 92 93 94 600-acre wine town 15 miles E of main RHEINGAU area, once thought of as best on Rhine. Similar fine wines with an earthy intensity and fragrance of their own. Top v'yds: Domdechaney, Hölle, Kirchenstück, Königin Viktoria Berg (12-acre monopoly of Hupfeld of OESTRICH, sold only by DEINHARD). Grosslage: Daubhaus. Growers incl ASCHROTT, Hupfeld, FRANZ KUNSTLER, RESS, SCHLOSS SCHONBORN, STAATSWEINGUT, WERNER.

Hock Traditional English term for Rhine wine, derived from HOCHHEIM.

Hoensbroech, Weingut Reichsgraf zu ★★★ Top KRAICHGAU estate. 37 acres. Excellent dry WEISSBURGUNDER, GRAUBURGUNDER and SILVANER wines, eg Michelfelder Himmelberg. Some of BADEN's best wines.

Hohenlohe-Oehringen, Weingut Fürst zu Noble 47-acre estate in Oehringen, WÜRTTEMBERG. Substantial dry RIES and powerful reds from SPATBURGUNDER and LEMBERGER.

Hövel, Weingut von ★★ Very fine SAAR estate at OBERMOSEL (Hütte is 12-acre monopoly) and in SCHARZHOFBERG.

Huxelrebe Modern very aromatic grape variety, mainly for dessert wines.

Ihringen Bad r w ▓▶▶▶▓ 83 85 86 87 88 89 90 91 92 93 94 One of the best villages of the KAISERSTUHL, BADEN. Proud of its SPATBURGUNDER red, WEISSHERBST and vg SILVANER. Top growers: DR HEGER, Stigler.

Ilbesheim Pfz w ▓▶▶▓ 88 89 90 91 92 93 94 Base of vast growers' coop of SÜDLICHE WEINSTRASSE 'Deutsches Weintor'. See also Schweigen.

Ingelheim Rhh r w ★ 85 88 89 90 91 92 93 94 Town opposite the RHEINGAU historically known for SPATBURGUNDER. First-class v'yds: Horn, Pares, Sonnenberg, Steinacker.

Iphofen Frank w ★★→★★★ 75 76 79 83 85 87 88 89 90 91 92 93 94 Village nr WÜRZBURG. Superb First-class v'yds: Julius-Echter-Berg, Kalb. Grosslage: Burgweg. Growers: JULIUSSPITAL, Ruck, STAATLICHER HOFKELLER, WIRSCHING.

Jahrgang Year – as in 'vintage'.

Johannisberg Rhg w ★★→★★★★ 71 75 76 83 85 86 87 88 89 90 91 92 93 94 260-acre village with superlative subtle RIES. Top v'yds incl Goldatzel, Klaus. First-class: Hölle, SCHLOSS JOHANNISBERG. Grosslage: Erntebringer. Many good growers. Beware 'Bereich Johannisberg' wines (next entry).

Johannisberg (Bereich) District name for the entire RHEINGAU. Avoid.

Johner, Karl-Heinz ★★★ Tiny BADEN estate at Bischoffingen, in the front line for new-look SPATBURGUNDER and oak-aged WEISSBURGUNDER.

Josephshöfer Fine v'yd at GRAACH, the sole property of VON KESSELSTATT.

Jost, Toni ★★→★★★ Perhaps the top estate of the MITTELRHEIN. 25 acres, mainly RIES, in BACHARACH and also in the RHEINGAU.

Juliusspital ★★★→★★★★ Ancient WÜRZBURG religious charity with 374 acres of top FRANKEN v'yds and many top wines. Look for its SILVANERS and RIES.

Kabinett The term for the lightest category of natural, unsugared (QMP) wines. Low in alcohol (RIES averages 7–9%) but capable of sublime finesse. Do not hurry to drink Riesling Kabinetts.

Kaiserstuhl (Bereich) One of the top BADEN districts, with notably warm climate and volcanic soil. Villages incl ACHKARREN, IHRINGEN. Grosslage: Vulkanfelsen.

Kallstadt Pfz w (r) ★★→★★★ 76 83 85 86 87 88 89 90 91 92 93 94 Village of N MITTELHAARDT. Fine rich wines are frequently underrated. First-class v'yd: Saumagen. Grosslagen: Feuerberg, Kobnert. Growers incl Henninger, KOEHLER-RUPRECHT, Schüster.

Kammerpreismünze See Landespreismünze.

Kanzem M-S-R (Saar) w ▓▓▓ 71 75 76 83 85 87 88 89 90 91 92 93 94 Small neighbour of WILTINGEN. First-class v'yd: Altenberg. Grosslage: SCHARZBERG. Growers incl Othegraven, Reverchon. Best is J P Reinert.

Karthäuserhofberg ★★★★ Top RUWER estate of 46 acres at Eitelsbach. Easily recognized by bottles with only a neck-label. Recently back on top form, esp with standard wines.

Kasel M-S-R (Ruwer) w ▓▶▶▶▓ 71 75 76 83 85 86 87 88 89 90 91 92 93 94 Stunning flowery light Römerlay wines. First-class v'yds: Kehrnagel, Nies'chen. Top growers: KARLSMUHLE, VON KESSELSTATT, WEGELER-DEINHARD.

Keller Wine cellar.

Kellerei Winery.

Kerner Modern aromatic grape variety, earlier-ripening than RIES, of fair quality but without the inbuilt harmony of Riesling.

Kerpen, Weingut Heribert ★★ Tiny estate in BERNKASTEL, GRAACH, WEHLEN.

Kesseler, Weingut August 35-acre estate making the best SPATBURGUNDER reds in ASSMANNSHAUSEN. Also good off-dry RIES.

Kesselstatt, von ▓▓▓ The biggest private MOSEL estate, 600 yrs old. Some 150 acres in GRAACH, KASEL, PIESPORT, WILTINGEN, etc, plus substantial rented or managed estates, producing aromatic, generously fruity MOSELS. Now belongs to Günther Reh (of Leiwen). Excellent wines made esp since '88.

Kesten M-M w *→*** 71 75 76 83 85 86 *87* 88 89 90 *91* 92 93 94 Neighbour of BRAUNEBERG. Best wines (from Paulinshofberg v'yd) similar. Grosslage: Kurfürstlay. Top grower: Paulinshof.

Kiedrich Rhg w **→**** 71 76 83 85 86 87 88 89 90 91 92 93 94 Neighbour of RAUENTHAL; almost as splendid and high-flavoured. First-class v'yd: Gräfenberg, Wasseros. Grosslage: Heiligenstock. Growers incl FISCHER, KNYPHAUSEN, STATE DOMAIN. R WEIL now top estate.

Klingelberger ORTENAU (BADEN) term for RIESLING, esp at DURBACH.

Kloster Eberbach Glorious 12th-century Cistercian Abbey in the forest at HATTENHEIM, RHEINGAU. Its monks planted the STEINBERG. Now STATE DOMAIN property and HQ of the German Wine Academy.

Klüsserath M-M w **→**▓▓▓ 76 83 85 88 89 90 *91* 92 93 94 Minor MOSEL village, good years are well worth trying. Best vineyard: Bruderschaft. Grosslage: St-Michael. Top growers are FRIEDRICH WILHELM GYMNASIUM and Kirsten.

Knyphausen, Weingut Freiherr zu *** Noble 50-acre estate on former Cistercian land (see Kloster Eberbach) in ELTVILLE, ERBACH, HATTENHEIM, KIEDRICH and MARCOBRUNN. Top RHEINGAU wines, many dry.

Koehler-Ruprecht **→*** Highly-rated little (22-acre) estate; top grower in KALLSTADT. Ultra-traditional winemaking; v long-lived dry RIESLING from K Saumagen is memorable. Now for outstanding burgundy-style Pinot N.

How strong is it?

The alcohol content of wine varies from as little as 7% by volume to as much as 16%, depending on the sugar content of the grapes (and the possible addition of sugar, or 'chaptalisation', before fermentation).

Low strength does not mean low quality; nor vice versa. Finest Mosel Rieslings can balance alcoholic lightness with brilliant fruit-acid intensity. On the other hand a basic over-produced red at 10 or 11% will taste feeble.

Most top-quality wines, red or white, made in the French style contain between 11.5 and 13%. Above this figure the risk is an over-'heady' smell, unless it is balanced by great intensity of flavour or sweetness. Fortified wines vary from 17 to 18% (fino sherry) to about 20% (vintage port).

Königin Viktoria Berg See Hochheim.

Kraichgau Small BADEN region S of Heidelberg. Top grower: HOENSBROECH.

Kreuznach District name for the entire northern NAHE, now united with SCHLOSSBOCKELHEIM to form BEREICH 'NAHETAL'. See also Bad Kreuznach.

Kröv M-M w *→*** 88 89 90 91 92 93 94 Popular tourist resort famous for its Grosslage name: Nacktarsch, or 'bare bottom'. Be very careful.

Künstler, Franz *** Outstanding 12.5-acre HOCHHEIM estate, esp for H Hölle and H Kirchenstück and good CHARTA wines.

Laible, Weingut Andreas 10-acre DURBACH estate. Fine sweet and dry RIES, SCHEUREBE and GEWURZ from First-class Plauelrain v'yd.

Landespreismünze Prizes for quality at state, rather than national, level.

Landwein A category of better quality TAFELWEIN (the grapes must be slightly riper) from 20 designated regions. It must be TROCKEN or HALBTROCKEN. Similar in intention to France's vin de pays.

Lauerburg *** One of the 4 owners of the famous Doctor v'yd, with 10 acres, all in BERNKASTEL. Often excellent racy wines.

Leitz, J ** Fine little RUDESHEIM family estate for elegant dry RIES. A rising star.

Lemberger Red grape imported from Austria where it is known as Blaufränkisch. Gives deep-coloured, tannic wines.

Liebfrauenstift 26-acre v'yd in city of Worms; origin of 'LIEBFRAUMILCH'.

Liebfraumilch Much abused name, accounting for 50% of all German wine exports – to the detriment of Germany's better products. Legally defined as a QBA 'of pleasant character' from RHEINHESSEN, PFALZ, NAHE or RHEINGAU, of a blend with at least 51% RIESLING, SILVANER, KERNER or MULLER-T. Most is mild, semi-sweet wine from Rheinhessen and Pfalz. Rules now say it must have more than 18 grams per litre unfermented sugar. S'times v cheap and of inferior quality, depending on brand or shipper. Its definition makes a mockery of the legal term 'Quality Wine'.

Lieser M-M w ★→▒▒ 71 76 83 85 86 *87* 88 89 90 *91* 92 93 94 Little-known neighbour of BERNKASTEL. Lighter wines. First-class v'yd: Niederberg-Helden. Grosslage: Kurfürstlay.

Lingenfelder, Weingut ★★★ Small, innovative Grosskarlbach (PFALZ) estate: excellent dry and sweet SCHEUREBE, full-bodied RIES, etc.

Loosen, Weingut Dr ▒▒▒ 24-acre St-Johannishof estate in BERNKASTEL, ERDEN, GRAACH, URZIG, WEHLEN. Deep intense RIESLINGS from old vines in Great First-class v'yds. Superlative quality since '90.

Lorch Rhg w (r) ★→★★ 71 76 83 85 *87* 88 89 90 *91* 92 93 94 At extreme W of the RHEINGAU. Some fine light MITTELRHEIN-like RIESLING. Best grower: von Kanitz.

Loreley (Bereich) New BEREICH name for RHEINBURGENGAU and BACHARACH.

Löwenstein, Fürst ★★★ 66-acre FRANKEN estate: classic dry powerful wines. 45-acre HALLGARTEN property is rented by MATUSCHKA-GREIFFENCLAU. V mixed quality since '91.

Maindreieck (Bereich) District name for central FRANKEN, incl WURZBURG.

Marcobrunn Historic RHEINGAU v'yd; one of Germany's v best. See Erbach.

Markgräflerland (Bereich) District S of FREIBURG, BADEN. Typical GUTEDEL wine can be delicious refreshment when drunk v young, but best wines are the -BURGUNDERS: WEISS-, GRAU- and SPAT-. Also Sekt.

Martinsthal Rhg w ★★→▒▒ 71 75 76 83 85 86 *87* 88 89 90 *91* 92 93 94 Little-known neighbour of RAUENTHAL. First-class v'yd: Langenberg; also gd: Wildsau. Grosslage: Steinmächer. Growers incl BECKER, Diefenhardt.

Matuschka-Greiffenclau, Graf Erwein Owner of ancient SCHLOSS VOLLRADS and tenant of WEINGUT FURST LOWENSTEIN at HALLGARTEN. A principal spokesman for German wine, esp dry, and its combination with food.

Maximin Grünhaus M-S-R (Ruwer) w ★★★★ 71 75 76 79 83 85 86 87 88 89 90 *91* 92 93 94 Supreme RUWER estate of 80 acres at MERTESDORF. Wines of firm elegance to mature 20 yrs+.

Mertesdorf See Maximin Grünhaus and Karlsmühle.

Meyer-Näkel, Weingut 15-acre AHR esate. Fine SPATBURGUNDERS in Dernau and Bad Neuenahr exemplify modern oak-aged German reds.

Mittelhaardt The north-central and best part of PFALZ, incl DEIDESHEIM, FORST, RUPPERTSBERG, WACHENHEIM, largely planted with RIESLING.

Mittelhaardt-Deutsche Weinstrasse (Bereich) District name for the northern and central parts of PFALZ.

Mittelheim Rhg w ★★ 71 75 76 83 85 86 *87* 88 89 90 *91* 92 93 94 Relatively minor village between WINKEL and OESTRICH.

Mittelmosel The central and best part of the MOSEL, incl BERNKASTEL, PIESPORT, WEHLEN, etc. Its top sites are (or should be) entirely RIESLING.

Mittelrhein Northern Rhine area of domestic importance, incl BACHARACH and Boppard. Some attractive steely RIESLING.

Morio-Muskat Stridently aromatic grape variety now on the decline.

Mosbacher, Weingut Georg 23-acre estate for some of best dry and sweet RIES of FORST. Three stars on label indicate superior 'Reserve' bottlings.

Mosel The TAFELWEIN name of the area. All quality wines from the Mosel must be labelled MOSEL-SAAR-RUWER. (Moselle is the French – and English – spelling for this beautiful river.)

Mosel-Saar-Ruwer (M-S-R) 31,000-acre QUALITATSWEIN region between TRIER and Koblenz. Incl MITTELMOSEL, RUWER, SAAR areas. Natural home of RIES.

Moselland, Winzergenossenschaft Biggest M-S-R coop, at BERNKASTEL, incl Saar-Winzerverein at WILTINGEN. Its 5,200 members produce 25% of M-S-R wines (incl classic method SEKT), but little above average.

Müller zu Scharzhof, Egon See Egon Müller.

Müller-Catoir, Weingut ★★★★ Outstanding 40-acre NEUSTADT estate. V aromatic powerful RIESLING, SCHEUREBE, RIESLANER, GRAUBURGUNDER and MUSKATELLER. Consistent quality; dry/sweet always equally impressive.

Müller-Thurgau Fruity early-ripening, usually low-acid grape; commonest in PFALZ, RHEINHESSEN, NAHE, BADEN and FRANKEN; increasingly planted in all areas, incl MOSEL. Should be banned from all top v'yds by law.

Mumm, von ★★→★★★ 173-acre estate in JOHANNISBERG, RUDESHEIM, etc. Under the same control as SCHLOSS JOHANNISBERG, but v variable quality.

Munchausen Rhh r w ★ Unlikely v'yd situation. Einzellagen: Märchen, Lüge. Insubstantial wines.

Münster Nahe w ████████ 71 75 76 83 85 86 87 88 89 90 91 92 93 94 Best village of N NAHE, with fine delicate wines. First-class vineyards: Dautenpflänzer, Felseneck, Kapellenberg, Pittersberg, Schlossberg. Grosslage: Schlosskapelle. Top growers: Kruger-Rumpf, STATE DOMAIN.

Muskateller Perfumed white grape with crisp acidity. A rarity in PFALZ, BADEN and WURTTEMBERG, where it is mostly made dry.

Nackenheim Rhh w ★→████ 76 83 85 86 87 88 89 90 91 92 93 94 Neighbour of NIERSTEIN, both have top Rhine terroir. Best wines (esp First-class Rothenberg v'yd) similar. Grosslagen: Spiegelberg (★★), Gutes Domtal (★). Best grower: GUNDERLOCH.

Nahe Tributary of the Rhine and high quality wine region. Balanced fresh clean but full-, even earthy-flavoured wines; RIES best. BEREICH: NAHETAL.

Nahetal (Bereich) DERICH name for amalgamated KREUZNACH and SCHLOSS-BOCKELHEIM districts.

Neckerauer, Weingut Klaus ★★ Interesting, out-of-the-way 40-acre estate at Weissenheim-am-Sand, on sandy soil in N PFALZ. Impressive but unpredictable range.

Neef M-S-R w ★→███ 71 76 83 85 87 88 89 90 91 92 93 94 Village of lower MOSEL with one fine v'yd: Frauenberg.

Neipperg, Graf von ★★★ Noble 70-acre estate in Schwaigern, WURTTEMBERG: elegant dry RIES and TRAMINER, and trad style reds, esp from LEMBERGER.

Neumagen-Dhron M-M w ★★ Neighbour of PIESPORT: fine but sadly neglected.

Neustadt Central town of PFALZ with a famous wine school.

Niederhausen Nahe w ★★→★★★★ 71 75 76 83 85 86 87 88 89 90 91 93 94 Neighbour of SCHLOSS BOCKELHEIM and HQ of the NAHE STATE DOMAIN. Wines of grace and power. First-class v'yds include Felsensteyer, Hermannsberg, Hermannshöhle. Grosslage: Burgweg. Top growers: CRUSIUS, DONNHOFF, Hehner-Kilz, STATE DOMAIN.

Nierstein Rhh w ★→★★★★ 71 75 76 83 85 86 87 88 89 90 91 92 93 94 Famous but treacherous name. 1,300 acres incl superb First-class v'yds: Bruderberg, Glöck, Heiligenbaum, Hipping, Kranzberg, Oelberg, Orbel, Pettenthal, and their Grosslagen: Auflangen, Rehbach, Spiegelberg. Ripe aromatic wines with great 'elegance'. But beware Grosslage Gutes Domtal: a supermarket deception. Growers to choose include H BRAUN, GUNDERLOCH, GUNTRUM, HEYL ZU HERRNSHEIM, ST-ANTONY, G A Schneider, Seebrich, Strub, Wehrheim.

Nierstein (Bereich) Large E RHEINHESSEN district of ordinary quality.

Nierstein Winzergenossenschaft The leading NIERSTEIN coop, with far above average standards. (Formerly 'Rheinfront'.)

Nobling New white grape: light fresh wine in BADEN, esp MARKGRAFLERLAND.

Norheim Nahe w ★→★★★ 71 76 79 83 85 86 87 88 89 90 91 92 93 94 Neighbour of NIEDERHAUSEN. First-class v'yds: Delchen, Kafels, Kirschheck; Klosterberg comes next. Grosslage: Burgweg. Growers: ANHEUSER, CRUSIUS.

Oberemmel M-S-R (Saar) w ★★→★★★ 71 75 76 83 85 86 87 88 89 90 91 92 93 94 Next village to WILTINGEN. V fine wines from First-class v'yd Hütte, also Karlsberg, etc. Grosslage: SCHARZBERG. Esp VON HOVEL, VON KESSELSTADT.

Obermosel (Bereich) District name for the upper MOSEL above TRIER. Generally uninspiring wines from the ELBLING grape, unless v young.

Ockfen M-S-R (Saar) w ★★→★★★ 71 75 76 83 85 86 *87* 88 89 90 *91* 92 93 94 Superb fragrant austere. Top v'yd: Bockstein. Grosslage: SCHARZBERG. Growers: DR FISCHER, FRIEDRICH WILHELM GYMNASIUM, WAGNER, ZILLIKEN.

Oechsle Scale for sugar content of grape juice (see page 219).

Oestrich Rhg w ★★→★★★ 71 75 76 83 85 86 *87* 88 89 90 *91* 92 93 94 Big village; variable but capable of splendid RIES AUSLESE. First-class v'yds are Doosberg, Lenchen; Klosterberg is also good. Grosslage: Gottesthal. Major growers: AUGUST ESER, WEGELER-DEINHARD.

Offene weine Wine by the glass: the way to order it in wine villages.

Oppenheim Rhh w ★→★★★ 71 75 76 83 85 86 *87* 88 89 90 *91* 92 93 94 Town S of NIERSTEIN with a spectacular 13th-C church. Best wines from First-class Herrenberg and Sackträger v'yds. Grosslagen: Guldenmorgen (★★★), Krötenbrunnen (★). Growers incl GUNTRUM, Carl Koch, Kühling-Gillot. None currently up to full potential.

Ortenau (Bereich) District just S of Baden-Baden. Good KLINGELBERGER (RIES), SPATBURGUNDER and RULANDER. Top village: DURBACH.

Ortsteil Independent part of a community allowed to use its estate v'yd name without the village name, eg SCHLOSS JOHANNISBERG, STEINBERG.

Palatinate English for PFALZ.

Pauly-Bergweiler, Dr ★★★ Fine 27-acre BERNKASTEL estate. V'yds there and in WEHLEN, etc. 'Peter Nicolay' wines from URZIG and ERDEN are best.

Perlwein Semi-sparkling wine.

Pfalz 56,000-acre v'yd region S of RHEINHESSEN (see Mittelhaardt and Südliche Weinstrasse). Grapes ripen to relatively high degrees. The classics are rich wines, with TROCKEN and HALBTROCKEN increasingly fashionable and well made. Biggest RIES area after M-S-R. Was known as 'Rheinpfalz'.

Pfeffingen, Weingut ███ Messrs Fuhrmann and Eymael make outstanding RIES and SCHEUREBE on 26 acres of UNGSTEIN.

Piesport M-M w ★★→★★★★ 71 75 76 83 85 86 *87* 88 89 90 *91* 92 93 94 Tiny village with famous vine amphitheatre, at best glorious gentle fruity RIES. Great First-class v'yd: Goldtröpfchen. Treppchen, on flatter land, far inferior. Grosslage: Michelsberg (mainly MULLER-T; avoid). Esp R HAART, Kurt Hain, KESSELSTATT, Reuscher-Haart, Weller-Lehnert.

Plettenberg, von ★★ 100-acre estate at BAD KREUZNACH. Wines recently poor.

Portugieser Second-rate red-wine grape now often used for WEISSHERBST.

Prädikat Special attributes or qualities. See QmP.

Prüfungsnummer The official identifying test-number of a quality wine.

Prüm, J J ★★★★ Superlative and legendary 34-acre MOSEL estate in BERNKASTEL, GRAACH, WEHLEN, ZELTINGEN. Delicate but long-lived wines, esp in WEHLENER SONNENUHR: 81 KABINETT is still young.

Qualitätswein bestimmter Anbaugebiete (QbA) The middle quality of German wine, with sugar added before fermentation (as in French 'chaptalisation'), but controlled as to areas, grapes, etc.

Qualitätswein mit Prädikat (QmP) Top category, incl all wines ripe enough to be unsugared (KABINETT to TROCKENBEERENAUSLESE). See pages 103–104.

Randersacker Frank w ★★→★★★ 76 *83* 86 88 89 90 91 92 93 94 Leading village for distinctive dry wine. First-class v'yds: Marsberg, Pfülben. Grosslage: Ewig Leben. Growers incl BURGERSPITAL, Martin Göbel, STAATLICHER HOFKELLER, JULIUSSPITAL, Robert Schmitt, Schmitt's Kinder.

Ratzenberger, Weingut Jochen 17-acre estate making racy dry and off-dry RIES in BACHARACH, best from First-class Posten and Steeger St-Jost v'yds.

Rauenthal Rhg w ███→★★★★ 71 75 76 83 85 86 *87* 88 89 90 *91* 92 93 94 Supreme village: spicy complex wine. First-class v'yds: Baiken, Gehrn, Nonnenberg, Rothenberg, Wülfen. Grosslage: Steinmächer. Growers: BREUER, ESER, S REINHARTS HAUSEN, S SCHONBORN, VON SIMMERN, STATE DOMAIN.

Rebholz Top SUDLICHE WEINSTRASSE grower. Many varieties on 25 acres.

Ress, Balthasar ★★→★★★ R'GAU estate (74 good acres), cellars in HATTENHEIM. Also runs SCHLOSS REICHARTSHAUSEN. Variable wines; original artists' labels.

Restsüsse Unfermented grape sugar remaining in (or more often added to) wine to give it sweetness. TROCKEN wines have v little, if any.

Rheinburgengau (Bereich) District name for MITTELRHEIN v'yds around the Rhine gorge. Wines with 'steely' acidity needing time to mature.

Rheinfront, Winzergenossenschaft See Nierstein Winzergenossenschaft.

Rheingau Best v'yd region of Rhine, W of Wiesbaden. 7,000 acres. Classic substantial but subtle RIES. BEREICH name for whole region: JOHANNISBERG.

Rheinhessen Vast region (61,000 acres of v'yds) between Mainz and Worms, bordered by the river NAHE, mostly second-rate, but incl top RIESLING wines from NACKENHEIM, NIERSTEIN, OPPENHEIM, etc.

Rheinhessen Silvaner (RS) New uniform label for dry wines from SILVANER – designed to give a modern quality image to the region.

Rheinpfalz See Pfalz.

Rhodt SUDLICHE WEINSTRASSE village: esp Rietburg coop; agreeable fruity wines.

Richter, Weingut Max Ferd ✱✱✱ Top 37-acre MITTELMOSEL family estate, based at Mülheim. Fine barrel-aged RIES from: BRAUNEBERG (Juffer-Sonnenuhr), GRAACH, Mülheim (Helenenkloster), WEHLEN (usually models).

Rieslaner Cross between SILVANER and RIES; has made fine AUSLESEN in FRANKEN, where most is grown. Also fine from MULLER-CATOIR.

Riesling The best German grape: fine, fragrant, fruity, long-lived. Only CHARDONNAY can compete as the world's best white grape.

Rosewein Rosé wine made of red grapes fermented without their skins.

Rotwein Red wine.

Rüdesheim Rhg w ✱✱→✱✱✱✱ 71 75 76 79 *81* 82 83 84 85 86 87 88 **89 90 91 92 93 94** Rhine resort with excellent vineyards; the three best called Rüdesheimer Berg-. Full-bodied wines, fine-flavoured, often remarkable in 'off' years. Grosslage: Burgweg. Most top RHEINGAU estates own some Rüdesheim v'yds. Best growers: G BREUER, J LEITZ, Dr Nägler, SCHLOSS SCHONBORN.

Rüdesheimer Rosengarten RUDESHEIM is also the name of a NAHE village near BAD KREUZNACH. Do not be misled by the ubiquitous blend going by this name. It has nothing to do with RHEINGAU Rüdesheim. Avoid.

Ruländer PINOT GRIS: grape giving soft full-bodied wine, alias (as dry wine) GRAUBURGUNDER. Best in BADEN and southern PFALZ.

Ruppertsberg Pfz w ✱✱→✱✱✱ 75 76 83 85 86 87 88 89 90 91 92 93 94 Southern village of MITTELHAARDT. First-class v'yds incl Hoheburg, Linsenbusch, Nussbien, Reiterpfad, Spiess. Grosslage: Hofstück. Growers include BASSERMANN-JORDAN, BIFFAR, VON BUHL, BURKLIN-WOLF, DEINHARD.

Ruwer Tributary of MOSEL nr TRIER. V fine delicate but highly aromatic and well-structured wines. Villages incl EITELSBACH, KASEL, MERTESDORF.

Saale-Unstrut Region in former E Germany, 1,000 acres around confluence of these two rivers at Naumburg, nr Leipzig. Terraced v'yds of WEISS-BURGUNDER, SILVANER, GUTEDEL, etc and red PORTUGIESER and SPATBURGUNDER have Cistercian origins. Quality leader: Landesweingut Kloster Pforta.

Saar Tributary of MOSEL S of RUWER. Brilliant austere 'steely' RIES. Villages include AYL, OCKFEN, Saarburg, SERRIG, WILTINGEN (SCHARZHOFBERG). Grosslage: SCHARZBERG. Many fine estates.

Saar-Ruwer (Bereich) District covering these 2 regions.

Sachsen Former E German region (750 acres) in ELBE VALLEY around Dresden and Meissen. MULLER-T dominant, but WEISSBURGUNDER, GRAUBURGUNDER, TRAMINER, RIES give dry wines with more character. Best growers: SCHLOSS PROSCHWITZ, Jan Ulrich, Schloss Wackerbarth, Klaus Zimmerling.

St-Antony, Weingut Excellent 50-acre estate. Rich, intense dry and off-dry RIES from First-class v'yds of NIERSTEIN.

St-Ursula Well-known merchants at BINGEN.

Salm, Prinz zu Owner of SCHLOSS WALLHAUSEN and Villa Sachsen in RHEINHESSEN. President of VDP.

For key to grape variety abbreviations, see pages 6–9.

Salwey, Weingut ★★ Leading BADEN estate at Oberottweil, esp for RIESLING, WEISSBURGUNDER and RULANDER.

Samtrot WURTTEMBERG grape. Makes Germany's closest shot at Beaujolais.

Schaefer, Willi ★★★ The finest grower of GRAACH (but only 5 acres).

Scharzberg Grosslage name of WILTINGEN and neighbours.

Scharzhofberg M-S-R (Saar) w ★★★★ 71 75 76 83 85 86 87 88 89 90 91 92 93 94 Superlative 67-acre SAAR v'yd: austerely beautiful wines, the perfection of RIESLING. Do not confuse with the previous entry. Top estates: EGON MULLER, VON HOVEL, VON KESSELSTATT.

Schaumwein Sparkling wine.

Scheurebe Fruity grape of high quality (and RIESLING parentage) esp used in PFALZ. Excellent for botrytis wine (BA, TBA).

Schillerwein Light red or rosé QBA, speciality of WURTTEMBERG (only).

Schloss Groenesteyn Formerly top-grade RHEINGAU estate (80 acres) in RUDESHEIM. Not on top form.

Schloss Johannisberg Rhg w ★★★ 76 79 83 85 86 87 88 89 90 91 92 93 94 Famous RHEINGAU estate of 86 acres owned by the Princess Metternich and Oetker family. Original Rhine 'first growth'. Wines incl fine SPATLESE, KABINETT TROCKEN. More could be achieved with this truly great v'yd.

Schloss Proschwitz Resurrected princely estate at Meissen, leading former E Germany in quality, esp with dry WEISSBURGUNDER.

Schloss Reichartshausen 10-acre HATTENHEIM v'yd run by RESS.

Schloss Reinhartshausen Fine 175-acre estate in ERBACH, HATTENHEIM, KIEDRICH, etc. Changed hands in '88. The mansion is now a hotel.

Schloss Saarstein ★★ SERRIG estate of 25 acres with consistently fine RIES.

Schloss Salem ★★ 188-acre estate of Margrave of BADEN near L Constance in S Germany. MULLER-T and WEISSHERBST.

Schloss Schönborn ★★★ One of biggest RHEINGAU estates, based at HATTENHEIM. Full-flavoured wines, variable, at best excellent. Also vg SEKT.

Schloss Staufenberg ★★ 69-acre DURBACH estate. KLINGELBERGER is best wine.

Schloss Thorn Ancient OBERMOSEL estate, remarkable ELBLING, RIES and castle.

Schloss Vollrads Rhg w ★★★ 71 76 83 85 86 87 88 89 90 91 93 94 Great WINKEL estate since 1300. 116 acres. Dry austere RIES; TROCKEN and HALBTROCKEN are specialities; recently not impressive. See MATUSCHKA-GREIFFENCLAU.

Schloss Wallhausen ★★→★★★ The 25-acre NAHE estate of the PRINZ ZU SALM, one of Germany's oldest. 65% RIES. Vg TROCKEN.

Schlossböckelheim Nahe w ★★→★★★★ 71 75 76 79 83 85 86 87 88 89 90 91 92 93 94 Village with the finest NAHE v'yds, incl First-class Felsenberg, In den Felsen, Königsfels, Kupfergrube. Firm yet delicate wine. Grosslage: Burgweg. Top growers: CRUSIUS, DONNHOF, STATE DOMAIN.

Schlossböckelheim District name for the whole S NAHE, amalgamated with KREUZNACH to form BEREICH NAHETAL.

Schneider, Weingut Georg Albrecht Impecably-run 32-acre estate. Classic off-dry and sweet RIES in NIERSTEIN, the best from First-class Hipping.

Schoppenwein Café (or bar) wine: ie wine by the glass.

Schubert, von Owner of MAXIMIN GRUNHAUS.

Schwarzer Adler, Weingut ★★→★★★ Franz Keller and his son make top BADEN GRAU-, WEISS- and SPATBURGUNDER on 35 acres at Oberbergen.

Schweigen Pfz w r ★→★★ 85 86 87 88 89 90 91 92 93 94 S PFALZ village. Grosslage: Guttenberg. Best is Fritz Becker, esp for SPATBURGUNDER.

Sekt German (QBA) sparkling wine, best when label specifies RIES, WEISSBURGUNDER or SPATBURGUNDER. Sekt bA is the same but from specified area.

Selbach-Oster ★★★ 15-acre ZELTINGEN estate among MITTELMOSEL leaders.

Serrig M-S-R (Saar) w ★★→★★★ 71 75 76 83 85 86 87 88 89 90 91 93 94 Village for 'steely' wine, excellent in sunny yrs. First-class v'yds: Herrenburg, Saarstein, Serriger Schloss, Würzberg. Grosslage: SCHARZBERG. Top grower: VEREINIGTE HOSPITIEN. Others: SCHLOSS SAARSTEIN, BERT SIMON.

Sichel, Söhne H Famous wine merchants at Alzey, RHEINHESSEN. Owners of BLUE NUN LIEBFRAUMILCH. Recently bought by Langguth of TRABEN-TRARBACH.

Silvaner The third most-planted German white grape, usually underrated, best in FRANKEN. Worth looking for in RHEINHESSEN and KAISERSTUHL, too.

Simmern, Langwerth von ★★★ Top ELTVILLE family estate. Famous v'yds: Baiken, Mannberg, MARCOBRUNN. Some of v best, most elegant R'GAU RIES.

Simon, Weingut Bert ★★ One of largest SAAR estates. 80 acres: KASEL, SERRIG.

Sonnenuhr Sundial. Name of several v'yds, esp one at WEHLEN.

Spätburgunder Pinot Noir: the best red wine grape in Germany, esp in BADEN and WURTTEMBERG and, increasingly, PFALZ – generally improving quality, but most still pallid and underflavoured.

Spätlese Late Harvest. One better (stronger, sweeter) than KABINETT RIESLING. Wines to age at least 5 yrs. Dry Spätlesen can be v fine.

Staatlicher Hofkeller ★★★ The Bavarian STATE DOMAIN. 287 acres of finest FRANKEN v'yds with spectacular cellars under the great baroque Residenz at WURZBURG. Wines currently less spectacular.

Staatsweingut (or Staatliche Weinbaudomäne) The State wine estates or domains; esp KLOSTER EBERBACH, SCHLOSS-BÖCKELHEIM, TRIER.

State Domain See Staatsweingut.

Steigerwald (Bereich) District name for E part of FRANKEN.

Steinberg Rhg w ▩▩▩ 71 75 76 79 83 85 86 87 88 89 90 91 92 93 94 Famous 79-acre HATTENHEIM walled v'yd, planted by Cistercians 700 yrs ago. Now owned by STATE DOMAIN, ELTVILLE. Some glorious wines; some feeble.

Steinwein Wine from WURZBURG's best v'yd, Stein.

Stuttgart Chief city of WURTTEMBERG, producer of some fine wines (esp RIES), recently beginning to be exported.

Südliche Weinstrasse (Bereich) District name for S PFALZ. Quality improved tremendously in last 25 yrs. See Ilbesheim, Schweigen, Siebeldingen.

Tafelwein Table wine. The vin ordinaire of Germany. Frequently blended with other EC wines. But DEUTSCHER TAFELWEIN must come from Germany alone and may be excellent. (See also Landwein.)

Tauberfranken (Bereich) New name for minor Badisches Frankenland BEREICH of N BADEN: FRANKEN-style wines.

Thanisch, Weingut Wwe Dr H ★★★ BERNKASTEL estate, incl part of Doctor v'yd.

Traben-Trarbach M-M w ▩▩ 76 83 85 86 87 88 89 90 91 92 93 94 Major wine town of 800 acres, 87% of it RIESLING. Top vineyards: Ungsberg, Würzgarten. Grosslage: Schwarzlay. Top grower: MAX FERD RICHTER.

Traisen Nahe w ▩▩▩ 71 75 76 79 83 85 86 87 88 89 90 91 92 93 94 Small village incl superlative First-class Bastei and Rotenfels v'yds, making RIES of great concentration and class. Top grower: CRUSIUS.

Traminer See Gewürztraminer.

Trier M-S-R w ★★→★★★ Top wine city of Roman origin, on MOSEL, nr RUWER, now also incl AVELSBACH and EITELSBACH. Grosslage: Römerlay. Big Mosel charitable estates have cellars here among stunning Roman ruins.

Trittenheim M-M w ▩▩ 71 75 76 83 85 87 88 89 90 91 92 93 94 Attractive S MITTELMOSEL light wines. Top v'yds were Altärchen, Apotheke, but now incl second-rate flat land: First-class are Felsenkopf, Leiterchen. Grosslage: Michelsberg (avoid). Top growers: GRANS-FASSIAN, Milz.

Trocken 'Dry'. By law trocken on a label means with a maximum of 9 grams per litre unfermented sugar. The new wave in German winemaking upsets the old notion of sweetness balancing acidity and embraces an austerity of flavour that can seem positively Lenten. It is much harder to make good dry wines in German conditions, and non-initiates should not expect to fall in love at first sip. To be good, trocken wines need substantial body or alcohol; more than most Riesling Kabinett wines have to offer. Best trocken regions are Pfalz, Baden, Württemberg, Franken. Weissburgunder trocken is more satisfying. Halbtrockens are friendlier. Spätlesen (or QbA) often make the best trocken wines. Auslese trocken sounds like a contradiction in terms – and usually tastes like one. Do not be confused by the apparent link with Trockenbeerenauslesen (see entry over page): they are unrelated.

Remember that vintage information for German wines is given in a different form from the ready/not ready distinction applying to other countries. Read the explanation on page 106.

Trockenbeerenauslese Sweetest, most expensive category of German wine, extremely rare, with concentrated honey flavour. Made from selected shrivelled grapes affected by 'noble rot' (botrytis). TBA for short. See also Edel. Edelbeerenauslese would be a less confusing name.

Trollinger Common (pale) red grape of WÜRTTEMBERG; locally v popular.

Ungstein Pfz w ****→▓▓▓** 71 75 76 83 85 86 *87* 88 89 90 91 92 93 94 MITTELHAARDT village with fine harmonious wines. First-class v'yds: Herrenberg, Spielberg, Weilberg. Top growers: Darting, FITZ-RITTER, PFEFFINGEN, Karl Schäfer. Grosslagen: Honigsäckel, Kobnert.

Urzig M-M w ▓▓▓▓ 71 75 76 83 85 86 87 88 89 90 91 92 93 94 Village on red sandstone famous for firm, full, spicy wine unlike other MOSELS. First-class v'yd: Würzgarten. Grosslage: Schwarzlay. Growers incl JJ CHRISTOFFEL, DR LOOSEN, WEINS-PRÜM.

Valckenberg, P J Major merchants and growers at Worms, with Madonna LIEBFRAUMILCH. Also dry Ries. Now part owner of HEYL ZU HERRNSHEIM.

VDP Verband Deutscher Prädikats und Qualitätsweingüter. The pace-making association of premium growers. President: PRINZ ZU SALM.

Vereinigte Hospitien *** 'United Hospitals'. Ancient charity at TRIER with large holdings in PIESPORT, SERRIG, TRIER, WILTINGEN, etc; but wines recently below their wonderful potential.

Verwaltung Administration (of property/estate etc).

Wachenheim Pfz w ▓▓▓→**** 71 75 76 79 83 85 86 *87* 88 89 90 *91* 92 93 94 840 acres, including exceptionally fine RIESLING. First-class v'yds are Belz, Gerümpel, Goldbächel, Rechbächel, etc. Top grower: BÜRKLIN-WOLF. Grosslagen: Mariengarten, Schenkenböhl, Schnepfenflug.

Wagner, Dr ** Saarburg estate. 20 acres of RIES. Fine wines incl TROCKEN.

Waldrach M-S-R (Ruwer) w ▓▓ 76 83 85 88 89 90 *91* 92 93 94 Grosslage: Römerlay. Some charming light wines.

Walluf Rhg w ▓▓▓ 75 76 79 83 85 *87* 88 89 90 *91* 92 93 94 Neighbour of ELTVILLE; formerly Nieder- and Ober-Walluf. Underrated wines. First-class v'yd: Walkenberg. Grosslage: Steinmächer. Growers incl BECKER.

Walporzheim Ahrtal (Bereich) District name for the whole AHR VALLEY.

Wawern M-S-R (Saar) w **→*** 71 75 76 83 85 *87* 88 89 90 91 92 93 94 Small village, fine RIES. 1st-class v'yd: Herrenberg. Grosslage: SCHARZBERG.

Wegeler-Deinhard *** 136-acre RHEINGAU estate. Vineyards: GEISENHEIM, MITTELHEIM, OESTRICH, RUDESHEIM, WINKEL, etc. Consistent quality; dry SPÄTLESE, classic AUSLESE, finest EISWEIN. Also 67 acres in MITTELMOSEL, including major part of BERNKASTELER Doctor, WEHLENER SONNENUHR, etc, 46 acres in MITTELHAARDT (DEIDESHEIM, FORST, RUPPERTSBERG). Only best sites are named on labels. See also GEHEIMRAT 'J'.

Wehlen M-M w ▓▓▓→**** 71 75 76 83 85 86 *87* 88 89 90 91 92 93 94 Neighbour of BERNKASTEL with equally fine, somewhat richer wine. Great First-class v'yd: SONNENUHR. Grosslage: Münzlay. Top growers: HERIBERT KERPEN, DR LOOSEN, J J PRÜM, WEGELER-DEINHARD, WEINS-PRÜM.

Weil, Wiengut Robert **** Outstanding 95-acre estate in KIEDRICH; now financed by Suntory of Japan. Superb QmP, EISWEIN; standard wines also vg since '92. Rapidly acquiring reputation as RHINEGAU's new No 1.

Weinbaugebiet Viticultural region. For TAFELWEIN (eg MOSEL, RHEIN, SAAR).

Weingut Wine estate.

Weinkellerei Wine cellars or winery. See Keller.

Weins-Prüm, Dr **→*** Classic MITTELMOSEL estate; 12 acres at WEHLEN. WEHLENER SONNENUHR is top wine.

Weinstrasse Wine road. Scenic route through v'yds. Germany has several. The most famous is the Deutsche Weinstrasse in PFALZ.

Weintor, Deutsches See Schweigen.

Weissburgunder Pinot Blanc. One of the better grapes for TROCKEN and HALBTROCKEN wines: low acidity, high extract. Also much used for Sekt.

Weissherbst Usually pale pink wine of QBA standard or above, from a single variety, even occasionally BEERENAUSLESE, the speciality of BADEN, PFALZ and WURTTEMBERG. Currently fashionable in Germany.

Werner, Domdechant ■■■ Fine family estate on best HOCHHEIM slopes.

Wiltingen M-S-R (Saar) w ✶✶→✶✶✶✶ 71 75 76 83 85 86 87 88 89 90 91 92 93 94 The centre of the SAAR. 790 acres. Beautiful subtle austere wine. Great First-class v'yd is SCHARZHOFBERG (ORTSTEIL); and First-class are Braune Kupp, Hölle. Grosslage (for the whole SAAR): SCHARZBERG. Top growers: EGON MULLER, LE GALLAIS, VON KESSELSTATT, etc.

Winkel Rhg w ✶✶ 71 75 76 83 85 86 87 88 89 90 91 92 93 94 Village famous for full fragrant wine, incl SCHLOSS VOLLRADS. First-class v'yds incl Hasensprung, Jesuitengarten, Klaus, SCHLOSS VOLLRADS, Schlossberg. Grosslagen: Erntebringer, Honigberg. Growers incl DEINHARD, PRINZ VON HESSEN, VON MUMM, BALTHASAR RESS, SCHLOSS SCHONBORN, etc.

Winningen M-S-R w ■■ Lower MOSEL village nr Koblenz: some fine delicate RIES. Top v'yds. Röttgen, Uhlen. Top grower: Heymann-Löwenstein.

Wintrich M-M w ✶✶→✶✶✶ 71 75 76 83 85 86 87 88 89 90 91 92 93 94 Neighbour of PIESPORT; similar wines. Top vineyards: Ohligsberg, Sonnenseite. Grosslage: Kurfürstlay. Good grower: REINHOLD HAART.

Winzergenossenschaft Wine-growers' cooperative, often making sound and reasonably priced wine. Referred to in this text as 'coop'.

Winzerverein The same as the above.

Wirsching, Hans ✶✶✶ Leading estate in IPHOFEN, and indeed FRANKEN. Wines firm, elegant and dry. 100 acres in top v'yds: Julius-Echter-Berg, Kalb...

Wonnegau (Bereich) District name for S RHEINHESSEN.

Wolff Metternich ✶✶→✶✶✶ Noble DURBACH estate: BADEN's best RIES.

Württemberg Vast S area, little known for wine outside Germany. But some vg RIES (esp Neckar Valley). Half is red: LEMBERGER, Trollinger, SAMTROT.

Würzburg Frank ✶✶→✶✶✶✶ 71 76 79 81 83 85 86 87 88 89 90 91 92 93 94 Great baroque city on the Main, centre of FRANKEN wine: fine, full-bodied, dry. First-class v'yds: Abtsleite, Innere, Leiste, Stein. No Grosslage. See Maindreieck. Growers: BURGERSPITAL, JULIUSSPITAL, STAATLICHER HOFKELLER.

Zell M-S-R w ✶→✶✶ 76 83 88 89 90 91 92 93 94 The best-known lower MOSEL village, esp for its awful Grosslage: Schwarze Katz ('Black Cat'). RIES on steep slate gives aromatic light wines. Top grower: Albert Kallfelz.

Zell (Bereich) District name for whole lower MOSEL from Zell to Koblenz.

Zeltingen M-M w ■■→✶✶✶ 71 75 76 79 83 85 86 87 88 89 90 91 92 93 94 Top MOSEL village nr WEHLEN. Lively crisp RIES. First-class v'yd: SONNENUHR. Grosslage: Münzlay. Many estate-owned v'yds, esp PRUM, SELBACH-OSTER.

Zilliken, Forstmeister Geltz ✶✶✶ Former estate of Prussian royal forester at Saarburg and OCKFEN, SAAR. Racy minerally RIESLINGS, incl EISWEIN.

Zwierlein, Freiherr von ✶✶ 55-acre family estate in GEISENHEIM. 100% RIES.

Luxembourg

Luxembourg has 3,285 acres of v'yds on limestone soils on the Moselle's left bank. High-yielding Elbling and Rivaner (Müller-T) vines dominate, but there are also significant acreages of Ries, Gewürz and (usually best) Auxerrois, Pinot Bl and Pinot Gr. These give light to medium-bodied (10.5–11.5˚) dry Alsace-like wines. The Vins Moselle coop makes 70% of the wines. Domaine et Tradition estates association, founded in '88, promotes quality from noble varieties. The last six vintages were all good; 89 90 92 outstanding. Best from: Aly Duhr et Fils, M Bastian, Caves Gales, Bernard Massard (surprisingly good Cuvée de l'Ecusson classic method sparkling), Clos Mon Vieux Moulin, Ch de Schengen, Sunnen-Hoffmann.

Spain & Portugal

The following abbreviations are used in the text:

Amp	Ampurdán-Costa Brava
Alen	Alentejo
Bair	Bairrada
B Al	Beira Alta
B Lit	Beira Littoral
Cos del S	Costers del Segre
El B	El Bierzo
Gal	Galicia
La M	La Mancha
Mont-M	Montilla-Moriles
Nav	Navarra
Pen	Penedès
Pri	Priorato
Rib del D	Ribera del Duero
R Alt	Rioja Alta
R Ala	Rioja Alavesa
RB	Rioja Baja
Som	Somontano
Set	Setúbal
U-R	Utiel-Requena
VV	Vinhos Verdes
g	vino generoso
res	reserva

Spain and Portugal have had ten years, since they joined the European Community, to modernize their venerable wine industries. Much has been done and there is much to do. The continuing state of ferment is highly productive, and some splendid new wines are appearing both in the few traditional quality areas and in former bulk-wine regions.

Currently in Spain (apart from sherry country), the northeast, Rioja, Navarra, Galicia, Rueda and Ribera del Duero still hold most interest; in Portugal (apart from the port vineyards and Madeira) Bairrada, the Douro, Ribatejo, Alentejo, the central coast and the north. In Portugal especially, newly delimited areas are successfully challenging such old appellations as eg Dão.

The following list includes the best and most interesting types and regions of each country, whether legally delimited or not. Geographical references (see map above) are to demarcated regions (DOs and DOCs), autonomies and provinces.

Spain

AGE, Bodegas Unidas R Alt r w (p) dr sw res ★→★★ 85 86 90 91 93 Large BODEGA with a wide range recently bought by BODEGAS Y BEBIDAS. Siglo red is reliable if unspectacular; avoid its white counterpart. Best are the Siglo Gran Reserva (85) and Azpilicueta Gran Reserva (82).

Albariño High-quality aromatic white grape of GALICIA and its wine. See also Rías Baixas.

Sherry, port and madeira, still the greatest glories of Spain and Portugal, have a chapter to themselves on pages 137–143.

Alella r w (p) dr sw ⋆⋆ Small demarcated region just N of Barcelona. Pleasantly fruity wines. (See Marfil, Marqués de Alella, Parxet.)

Alicante r (w) ⋆ DO. Wines still earthy and overstrong.

Alion Rib del D r Since discontinuing the 3-yr-old VALBUENA, VEGA SICILIA has acquired this second BODEGA to make CRIANZAS: 91 to be released shortly.

Almendralejo E Spain r w ⋆ Wine centre of Extremadura. Much of its wine is distilled to make the spirit for fortifying sherry. See Lar de Barros.

Aloque La M r ✳ DYA A light (though not in alcohol) speciality of VALDEPEÑAS, made by fermenting red and white grapes together.

Alta Pavina, Bodegas Castilla y Leon r ⋆ Non-DO Pinot N since '91: oak-aged, dark and dense.

Alvear Mont-M g ⋆⋆⋆ The largest producer of excellent sherry-like aperitif and dessert wines in MONTILLA-MORILES.

Ampurdán, Cavas del Amp r w p sp res ⋆→⋆⋆ Producers of big-selling white Pescador, red Cazador table wines and commercial sparklers.

Ampurdán-Costa Brava Amp r w p ⋆→⋆⋆ Demarcated region abutting Pyrenees. Mainly coop-made rosés, reds. See also last entry.

Año Year: 4° Año (or Años) means 4 yrs old when bottled. Common on labels in the past, now largely discontinued in favour of vintages, or terms such as CRIANZA.

Antaño, Bodegas Rueda w (r) DYA New BODEGA esp for clean fruity balanced whites. Labels are Viña Mocen (w) and Viña Cobranza (r). To watch.

123

Aragonesa, Compañia Vitivinícola Som r w p res ∗∗→∗∗∗ 89 90 92 New SOMONTANO estate. Varietal wines under Viñas del Vero label: Chard, Ries, Gewürz, Cab... Vines still young, oak excessive: but one to watch.

Bach, Masia Pen r w p dr sw res ∗∗→∗∗∗ 85 88 Spectacular villa-winery nr SAN SADURNI DE NOYA, owned by CODORNIU. White Extrísimo, both sweet and oaky, and dry. Also good red RESERVAS.

Barbier, René Pen r w res ∗∗ 87 88 90 Owned by FREIXENET, known for 'Mediterraneo', fresh white Kraliner, red RB RESERVAS, budget CAVA.

Barón de Ley RB r (w) res ∗∗∗ 85 86 87 Newish RIOJA BODEGA linked with EL COTO: good single-estate wines.

Barril, Masía Pri r br res ∗∗ 87 88 91 93 Tiny family estate in DO PRIORATO: powerful fruity reds – the 83 was 18°! – and superb RANCIO.

Berberana, Bodegas R Alt r (w) res ∗→∗∗∗ 87 90 91 92 Fruity full-bodied reds best: young Carta de Plata, Carta de Oro CRIANZA, velvety RESERVAS.

Berceo, Bodegas R Alt r w p res ∗∗→∗∗∗ 87 89 Cellar in HARO with vg Gonzalo de Berceo GRAN RESERVA.

Beronia, Bodegas R Alt r w res ∗∗→∗∗∗ 81 82 87 89 93 Small modern BODEGA making reds in traditional oaky style and fresh 'modern' whites. Owned by Gonzalez Byass (see page 139).

Bilbaínas, Bodegas R Alt r w (p) dr sw sp res ∗∗ 82 87 88 89 Large BODEGA in HARO. Wide and usually reliable range incl dark Viña Pomal, lighter Viña Zaco, Vendimia Especial RESERVAS and Royal Carlton CAVA.

Binissalem r w ∗∗ Best-known MAJORCA DO. See also Ferrer, José L.

Blanco White.

Bodega Spanish for (i) a wineshop; (ii) a concern occupied in the making, blending and/or maturing of wine; and (iii) a cellar.

Bodegas y Bebidas Formerly 'Savin'. One of largest Spanish wine companies; wineries all over Spain. Mainly good quality and value brands. Also controls various prestigious firms, eg CAMPO VIEJO, MARQUES DE PUERTO.

Calatayud (∗) Aragon DO (of 4): esp Garnacha. Coop San Isidro holds sway.

Campillo, Bodegas R Ala r (p) res ∗∗∗ 82 85 87 88 Affiliated with FAUSTINO MARTINEZ, a young BODEGA with wines of consistently high quality.

Campo Viejo, Bodegas R Alt r (w) res ∗→∗∗∗ 82 87 88 89 Makes the popular and tasty young San Asensio and some big fruity red RESERVAS, esp Marqués de Villamagna. See Bodegas y Bebidas.

Can Rafols dels Caus Pen r w ∗∗ 87 88 89 Young small PENEDES BODEGA: own-estate fruity Cab, pleasant Chard-Xarel-lo-Chenin; gd Cab-Merlot.

Caralt, Cavas Conde de Pen r w sp res ∗∗ 86 88 87 90 91 CAVA wines from outpost of FREIXENET, esp gd vigorous Brut NV; also pleasant still wines.

Cariñena r (w p) ∗ Demarcated region and large-scale supplier of strong everyday wine, dominated by coops. Now being invigorated (and its wines lightened) by modern technology.

Casa La Vina Valepeñas r BODEGAS y BEBIDAS-owned estate, since '80s making sound range of fruity 'Cencibel' wines. Drink young.

Casar de Valdaiga El B r w ∗∗ Fruity red from Pérez Carames, N of LEON.

Castellblanch Pen w sp ∗∗ 88 90 91 PENEDES CAVA firm, owned by FREIXENET. Look for Brut Zéro and Gran Castell GRAN RESERVAS.

Castillo Ygay R Alt r w ∗∗∗∗ (r) 25 34 42 52 68 70 75 78 82 85 87 (Current white vintage is 75!) See Marqués de Murrieta.

Cava Official term for any classic method Spanish sparkling wine, and the DO covering the areas up and down Spain where it is made.

Cenalsa See Principe de Viana, Bodegas.

Cenicero Wine township in RIOJA ALTA with an ancient Roman winepress.

Cepa Wine or grape variety.

Cervera, Lagar de Gal w ∗∗∗ DYA Makers of one of best ALBARIÑOS: flowery and intensely fruity with subdued bubbles and a long finish.

Chacolí Pais Vasco w (r) ∗ DYA Alarmingly sharp, often fizzy wine from the Basque coast, now possessing its own DO, which applies to all 141 acres! It contains only 9–11% alcohol. Best producer: Txomín Etxaníz.

Chaves, Bodegas Gal w ∗∗ DYA Small firm: good, fragrant, acidic ALBARIÑO.

Chivite, Bodegas Julián Nav r w (p) dr sw res ∗∗ 85 87 88 89 90 Biggest NAVARRA BODEGA. Full red, flowery well-balanced white. See Gran Feudo.

Cigales r p ∗→∗∗ Recently demarcated region north of Valladolid, esp for light reds (traditionally known as CLARETES).

Clarete Traditional term, now banned by EC, for light red wine (or dark rosé).

Codorníu Pen w sp ∗∗→∗∗∗ One of the two largest firms in SAN SADURNI DE NOYA making good CAVA: v high tech, 10 million bottles ageing in cellars. Non Plus Ultra is matured. Many prefer the fresher Anna de Codorníu (91), the Première Cuvée Brut and the Chard.

Compañía Vinícola del Norte de España (CVNE) R Alt r w (p) dr sw res ∗∗→∗∗∗ 88 89 90 91 Top RIOJA BODEGA. Monopole (92) is one of the best slightly oaky whites. Recent vintages of the red CRIANZA have not always been up to old high standards. Excellent red Imperial and Viña Real RESERVAS. CVNE is pronounced 'coonay'. See also Contino.

Rioja's characteristic style

To the Spanish palate the taste of luxury in wine is essentially the taste of (American) oak. Oak contains vanillin: hence the characteristic vanilla flavour of all traditional Spanish table wines of high quality – exemplified by the reservas of Rioja (red and white). Fashion swung (perhaps too far) against the oaky flavour of old Rioja whites but the pendulum is swinging back, although to subtler oak flavours than in the old days.

Conca de Barberá Pen w (r p) Catalan DO region growing Parellada grapes for making CAVA. Its best wine is TORRES MILMANDA Chard.

Condado de Huelva DO see Huelva.

Consejo Regulador Official organization for the defence, control and promotion of a DENOMINACION DE ORIGEN.

Contino R Ala r res ∗∗∗ 85 86 87 88 Very fine single-v'yd red made by a subsidiary of COMPANIA VINICOLA DEL NORTE DE ESPANA.

Cosecha Crop or vintage.

Cosecheros Alaveses R Ala r ∗∗ 90 91 92 Up-and-coming RIOJA coop, esp for good young unoaked red Artadi.

Costers del Segre Cos del S r w p sp Small demarcated area around the city of Lleida (Lérida) and famous for the v'yds of RAIMAT.

Criado y embotellado por... Grown and bottled by...

Crianza Literally 'nursing'; the ageing of wine. New or unaged wine is 'sin crianza' or 'joven' (young). Reds labelled 'crianza' must be at least 2 yrs old (with 1 yr in oak), and must not be released before the third yr.

Cumbrero See Montecillo, Bodegas.

De Muller Tarragona br (r w) ∗∗→∗∗∗ Venerable TARRAGONA firm specializing in altar wine, gd PRIORATO, superb sumptuous v old SOLERA-aged dessert wines. Incl Priorato DULCE, PAXARETE. Also fragrant Moscatel Seco.

Denominación de Origen (DO) Official wine region (see page 122).

Denominación de Origen Calificada (DOCa) Classification for wines of the highest quality; so far only RIOJA benefits (since '91).

Diaz e Hijos, Jesús La M r w p res ∗∗ 86 91 Unoaked reds from this small BODEGA near Madrid win many prizes.

Domecq R Ala r (w) res ∗∗→∗∗∗ 81 82 89 91 RIOJA outpost of sherry firm. Inexpensive Viña Eguia and excellent Marqués de Arienzo CRIANZAS and RESERVAS, fragrant and medium-bodied.

Don Darias/Don Hugo Alto Ebro r w ∗ Huge selling, modestly priced wines, v like RIOJA, from undemarcated Bodegas Vitorianas. Sound red, white.

Dulce Sweet.

El Bierzo DO since '90, N of León. See Casar de Valdaiga, Palacio de Arganza.

El Coto, Bodegas R Ala r (w) res ∗∗ BODEGA best known for light, soft, red El Coto and Coto de Imaz.

Elaborado y añejado por... Made and aged by...

Enate Somontano DO r w ∗∗ DYA Bargain modern blends from SOMONTANO in the N: light, clean, fruity.

Espumoso Sparkling (but see Cava).

Evena Nav Gov't research station revolutionizing NAVARRA. Run by J OCHOA.

Fariña, Bodegas Toro r w res ✳✳ 87 89 92   Rising star of new DO TORO: good spicy reds. Gran Colegiata is cask-aged; Colegiata not.

Faustino Martínez R Ala r w (p) res ✳✳→✳✳✳ 82 86 88 89   Bodega with good reds. Light fruity white Faustino V. GRAN RESERVA is Faustino I. Do not be put off by the repellent fake-antique bottles.

Felix Solis Valdepeñas r ✳✳   BODEGA in VALDEPEÑAS making sturdy oak-aged reds, Viña Albali, RESERVAS (87 88) and fresh white.

NB Vintages in colour are those you should choose first for drinking in 1996.

Ferrer, José L Majorca r res ✳✳ 84 87 89 90   Best-known MAJORCA BODEGA at Binissalem, scarcely worth seeking. Second is Vinos Oliver, at Felanitx.

Fillaboa, Granxa Gal w ✳✳✳ DYA   New small firm: delicately fruity ALBARIÑO.

Franco-Españolas, Bodegas R Alt r w dr sw res ✳→✳✳   Old-est'd RIOJA BODEGA now part of group controlled by Marcos Eguizabal. Bordón is fruity red. Semi-sweet white Diamante is a Spanish favourite.

Freixenet Cavas Pen w sp ✳✳→✳✳✳✳   Huge CAVA firm, rivalling CODORNIU in size. Range of good sparklers, notably bargain Cordon Negro in black bottles, Brut Nature (88), Reserva Real and Premium Cuvée DS (85). Also owns Gloria Ferrer in California, Champagne Henri Abelé (Reims) and a sparkling wine plant in Mexico. Paul Cheneau is low-price brand.

Galicia Rainy NW Spain: esp for fresh aromatic, not cheap whites, eg ALBARIÑO.

Generoso (g) Aperitif or dessert wine rich in alcohol.

Gonzalez y Dubosc, Cavas Pen w sp ✳✳   A branch of the sherry giant GONZALEZ BYASS. Pleasant sparkling wines exported as 'Jean Perico'.

Gran Feudo Nav w res ✳✳ 88 89 90   Brand name of fragrant white, refreshing rosé, soft plummy red; the best-known wines from CHIVITE.

Gran Reserva See Reserva.

Gran Vas Pressurized tanks (French cuves closes) for making cheap sparkling wines; also used to describe this type of wine.

Grandes Bodegas Rib del D r ✳→✳✳   Recently reorganized and with its own extensive v'yds, the aim of this BODEGA, in a region notorious for high prices, is to make quality wines that are affordable. Watch this space.

Guelbenzu, Bodegas Nav r res ✳✳→✳✳✳ 89 90 91 92 93   New 89-acre family estate: conc full-bodied red from Tempranillo, Cab, Merlot. Top is 'Evo'.

Haro Wine centre of the RIOJA ALTA, a small but stylish old city.

Hill, Cavas Pen w r sp res ✳✳ 88 89 91   Old PENEDES firm: fresh dry white Blanc Cru, good Gran Civet, Gran Toc reds, delicate RESERVA Oro Brut CAVA.

Huelva Condado de Huelva (DO) r w br ✳→✳✳   W of Cádiz. White table wines and sherry-like GENEROSOS; formerly imp't source of 'Jerez' for blending.

Irache, SL Nav r p (w) res ✳ 87 89 92   Well-known inexpensive everyday reds.

Jean Perico See Gonzalez y Dubosc.

Joven (vino) Young, unoaked wine.

Jumilla r (w p) ✳→✳✳   DO in mountains N of Murcia. Its overstrong (up to 18%) wines are being lightened by earlier picking and better wine-making, esp by French-owned Bodegas VITIVINO (eg Altos de Pío).

Juvé y Camps Pen w sp ✳✳→✳✳✳   Family firm aiming for and achieving top quality CAVA, from free-run juice only, esp Reserva de la Familia (89).

La Rioja Alta, Bodegas R Alt r w (p) dr (sw) res ✳✳✳ 78 81 82 84 85 86 87 88 89   Excellent RIOJAS, esp red CRIANZA Viña Alberdi, velvety Ardanza Reserva, lighter Araña Reserva, splendid Reserva 904 and marvellous RESERVA 890. Now making only RESERVAS and GRAN RESERVAS.

Laguardia Picturesque walled town at the centre of the RIOJA ALAVESA.

Lagunilla, Bodegas R Alt r ✳✳ 88   Modern firm recently bought by BERBERANA. Easy oaky light reds incl Viña Herminia and GRAN RESERVA.

Lan, Bodegas R Alt r (p w) res ✳✳→✳✳✳ 82 86 88 90   Huge modern BODEGA: aromatic red RIOJAS (good Lanciano and Lander), fresh white Lan Blanco, but recent vintages disappointing.

SPAIN/Esp–Mas

Lar de Lares SW r res ✱✱ 84 87 Meaty GRAN RESERVA from Bodegas Inviosa, in remote Extremadura. Quality of younger Lar de Barros has declined.

León r p w ✱→✱✱ 88 91 N region to watch: fruity dry refreshing wines, esp from Vinos de León (aka VILE): eg young Coyanza, more mature Palacio de Guzman, full-blooded Don Suero RESERVA. See also El Bierzo.

León, Jean Pen r w res ✱✱✱ 85 86 87 Small firm; TORRES-owned since '95. Good oaky Chard, deep full-bodied Cab that repays bottle-ageing.

Logroño First town of RIOJA region. HARO has more charm (and BODEGAS).

López de Heredia R Alt r w (p) dr sw res ✱✱→✱✱✱ 76 86 87 89 Startlingly old-est'd BODEGA in HARO known for exceptionally long-lasting, v traditional wines, but variable since '85. Viña Tondonia reds and whites are delicate and fine; Viña Bosconia fine and beefy.

López Hermanos Málaga ✱✱ Large BODEGA for commercial MALAGA wines, incl popular Málaga Virgen and Moscatel Gloria.

Los Llanos Valdepeñas r (p w) res ✱✱ 84 87 88 90 One of the growing number of VALDEPEÑAS BODEGAS to age wine in oak. It markets a RESERVA, GRAN RESERVA and premium Pata Negra Gran Reserva of 100% Cencibel (Tempranillo). Also clean fruity white, Armonioso.

Magaña, Bodegas Nav r res ✱✱→✱✱✱ Tiny young BODEGA: excellent red with Merlot, Cab S. Vintages variable and recently disappointing.

Málaga br sw ✱✱→✱✱✱ Demarcated region around city of Málaga. At their best its dessert wines can resemble tawny port. See Scholtz.

Majorca JOSE FERRER, Miguel Oliver and Jaume Mesquida make the island's only wines of interest (eg Chard) – otherwise, drink ROSADOS or Catalan.

Mancha, La La M r w ✱→✱✱ Vast demarcated region N and NE of VALDEPEÑAS. Mainly white wines, the reds lacking the liveliness of the best Valdepeñas but showing signs of improvement. To watch.

Marfil Alella r w (p) ✱✱ Brand of Alella Vinícola (oldest-est'd producer in ALELLA). Means 'ivory'. Now for lively, rather pricey new-style dry whites.

Marqués de Alella Alella w (sp) ✱✱ 92 93 94 (DYA) Light and fragrant white ALELLA wines from PARXET, some from Chard (incl barrel-fermented 'Allier'), made by modern methods. Also CAVA.

Marqués de Cáceres, Bodegas R Alt r p w res ✱✱→✱✱✱ 82 85 86 87 89 Good RIOJAS made by modern French methods from CENICERO (R Alt) grapes; also surprisingly light, fragrant white (DYA) and another, over-oaked.

Marqués de Griñón La M r w ✱✱✱ 87 88 Enterprising nobleman making v fine Cab nr Toledo, S of Madrid, a region not known for wine. Fruity wines to drink fairly young. Also an excellent white Selección Especial 91 made from Verdejo grapes in RUEDA, plus good RIOJAS and Durius, a red RIBERA DEL DUERO made for him by BODEGAS BERBERANA.

Marqués de Monistrol, Bodegas Pen p r sp dr sw res ✱✱ 85 89 Old BODEGA now owned by Martini & Rossi. Reliable CAVAS.

Marqués de Murrieta R Alt r p w res ✱✱✱→✱✱✱✱ 34 42 52 59 62 64 68 70 78 83 85 89 90 Historic, much-respected BODEGA near LOGROÑO, formerly for some of best RIOJAS. Also known for red CASTILLO YGAY, old-style oaky white and wonderful old-style RESERVA ROSADO. Except Rosado, recent quality disappointing but returning to form with deep brandy-scented 89.

Marqués del Puerto R Alt r (p w) res ✱✱→✱✱✱ 87 88 89 Small firm, was Bodegas López Agos, now owned by BODEGAS Y BEBIDAS. Reliable.

Marqués de Riscal R Ala r (p w) res ✱✱✱ 81 87 88 89 90 91 Best-known BODEGA of RIOJA ALAVESA. Its red wines are relatively light and dry. Old vintages are v fine; some more recent ones poor; currently are right back on form. Baron de Chirel, 50% Cab S, new in '86, is magnificent. Whites from RUEDA, incl a vg Sauv and oak-aged RESERVA Limousin.

Martínez-Bujanda R Ala r p w res ✱✱✱ 82 85 87 89 91 Refounded ('85) family-run RIOJA BODEGA, remarkably equipped. Excellent wines, incl fruity SIN CRIANZA, irresistible ROSADO, noble Valdemar RESERVAS and making waves with a new 100% Garnacha.

Mascaró, Cavas Pen r p w sp ✱✱→✱✱✱ Top brandy maker, good sparkling, lemony refreshing dry white Viña Franca, excellent (88) Anima Cab S.

127

Mauro, Bodegas Valladolid r ∗∗ 87 89 90   Young BODEGA in Tudela del Duero with vg round fruity Tinto del País (Tempranillo) red. Not DO as it is made by Bodegas Sanz in RUEDA.

Méntrida La M r w ∗   DO west of Madrid, source of everyday red wine.

Milmanda ∗∗∗ DYA   See Conca de Barberá, Torres.

Monopole See Compañía Vinícola del Norte de España (CVNE).

Montecillo, Bodegas R Alt r w (p) res ∗∗ DYA   RIOJA BODEGA owned by OSBORNE. Old GRAN RESERVAS (eg 73) are magnificent. Now reds are appealing young but recent vintages fragile.

Montecristo, Bodegas Mont-M ∗∗   Well-known brand of MONTILLA-MORILES.

Monterrey Gal r ∗   Region nr N border of Portugal; strong VERIN-like wines.

Montilla-Moriles Mont-M g ∗∗→∗∗∗   DO nr Córdoba. Its crisp sherry-like FINO and AMONTILLADO contain 14–17.5% natural alcohol and remain unfortified. At best, singularly toothsome aperitifs.

Muga, Bodegas R Alt r (w sp) res ∗∗∗ 81 85 89 90   Small family firm in HARO, known for some of RIOJA's best strictly trad reds. Wines are light but highly aromatic, with long complex finish. Best is Prado Enea (81 outstanding, but 86 87 88 far below par). Whites and CAVA less good.

Navajas, Bodegas R Alt r w res ∗∗→∗∗∗ 85 86 87 89 91 92   Small firm with bargain reds, CRIANZAS, RESERVAS, fruity and full-bodied. Also excellent oak-aged white Viura and cherry and vanilla flavoured CRIANZA ROSADO.

Navarra Nav r p (w) ∗∗→∗∗∗   Demarcated region; mainly rosés and sturdy reds, now well launched on stylish Tempranillo and Cab reds, some RESERVAS up to RIOJA standards. See Chivite, Guelbenzu, Magaña, Ochoa, Principe de Viana.

Nuestro Padre Jésus del Perdón, Coop de La M r w ∗→∗∗ 87 89 92 DYA   Look for bargain fresh white Lazarillo and more-than-drinkable Yuntero; 100% Cencibel (alias Tempranillo) aged in oak.

Ochoa Nav r p w res ∗∗→∗∗∗ 88 89 90   Small family BODEGA now with an excellent white, but better known for well-made red and rosés, incl 100% Tempranillo. Outstanding early vintages; recently disappointing.

Olarra, Bodegas R Alt r (w p) res ∗∗   Vast modern BODEGA in LOGROÑO, one of the showpieces of RIOJA. Interesting 5–6 yrs ago, esp for silky, well-balanced Cerro Añon reds, but quality now disappointing.

Pago de Carraovejas Rib del D r res ∗∗ 92 94   New estate earning reputation for some of the region's most stylish, densely fruity Tinto Fino Cab.

Palacio, Bodegas R Ala r p w res ∗∗∗ 85 87 89 90   Since this old family firm parted company with Seagram in '87 its wines have regained much of their former reputation. Esp Glorioso RESERVA.

Palacio de Arganza El B r p (w) res ∗∗ 83 85   Best-known BODEGA in new EL BIERZO DO. Somewhat variable red Almena del Bierzo is worth trying.

Palacio de Fefiñanes Gal w res ∗∗∗   Famous for untypical ALBARIÑO. No bubbles and oak-aged 3–5 yrs.

Palacio de la Vega Nav r p w ∗   New BODEGA with juicy Tempranillo JOVEN (like primeur) and much promise.

Parxet Alella w p sp ∗∗→∗∗∗   Makers of excellent fresh, fruity, exuberantly fizzy CAVA (only one from ALELLA): top is Brut Nature. Also elegant white Alella, 'MARQUES DE ALELLA'.

Paternina, Bodegas R Alt r w (p) dr sw res ∗→∗∗ 73   Known for its standard red brand Banda Azul. Conde de los Andes label was fine; 64 70 73 were outstanding, but recent vintages, as of their other RIOJAS, are disappointing. Most consistent is Banda Dorada white (DYA).

Paxarete Traditional intensely sweet dark brown almost chocolatey speciality of TARRAGONA. Not to be missed. See De Muller.

Pazo Gal r p w ∗∗ DYA   Brand name of the RIBEIRO coop, whose wines are akin to VINHOS VERDES. Rasping red is local favourite. Pleasant slightly fizzy Pazo whites are safer; Viña Costeira has quality.

Spain entries also cross-refer to Sherry, Port & Madeira, pages 137–143.

Pazo de Barrantes Gal w *** 91 93 New ALBARIÑO from RIAS BAIXAS, from an estate owned by the Conde de Creixels of MURRIETA. Delicate, exotic and of impeccable quality, but v expensive and hard to find.

Penedès Pen r w sp *→*** Demarcated region including Vilafranca del Penedès, SAN SADURNI DE NOYA and SITGES. See also Torres.

Perelada Amp w (r p) sp ** In the demarcated region of AMPURDAN on the Costa Brava. Best known for sparkling, both CAVA and GRAN VAS.

Pérez Pascuas Hermanos Rib del D r (p) res *** 88 89 90 91 Immaculate tiny family BODEGA in RIBERA DEL DUERO. In Spain its fruity and complex red Viña Pedrosa is rated one of the country's best.

Pesquera Rib del D *** 87 88 89 90 91 Small quantities of RIBERA DEL DUERO from Alejandro Fernandez. Robert Parker has rated it level with B'x Grands Crus. Janus is special (even more expensive) bottling.

Piqueras, Bodegas La M r *** 83 85 88 Small family BODEGA. Some of LA MANCHA's best reds: Castillo de Almansa CRIANZA, Marius GRAN RES.

Principe de Viana, Bodegas Nav r w ** 90 92 Large firm (formerly 'Cenalsa'), blending and maturing coop wines and shipping a range from NAVARRA, incl flowery new-style white and fruity red, Agramont.

Priorato Pri br r *** 87 88 89 91 93 DO enclave of TARRAGONA, known for alcoholic RANCIO, and splendidly full-bodied, almost black reds, often used for blending, but at their brambly best one of Spain's triumphs. Lighter blend is good carafe wine. See Barril, De Muller, Scala Dei.

Protos, Bodegas Rib del D r w res **→*** 86 87 89 91 Formerly PENAFIEL's coop and the region's second oldest BODEGA. Originally privatized ('91) as 'Bodegas Ribera del Duero'. Much improved by new oenologist.

Raimat Cos del S r w p sp **→*** (Cab) 83 84 85 86 87 88 89 90 Clean, structured wines from new DO nr Lérida, planted by CODORNIU with Cab, Chard, other foreign vines. Good 100% Chard CAVA.

Rancio Maderized (brown) white wine of nutty flavour.

Raventos i Blanc Barcelona w sp **→*** 85 86 87 Excellent CAVA aimed at top of market, also fresh El Preludi white (91).

Real Divisa, Bodegas R Alt r res ** 85 86 87 90 Picturesque old BODEGA; one of few growing all its own fruit. Esp Marqués de Legarda RESERVAS.

Remelluri'La Granja R Ala r res *** 85 87 88 89 90 Small estate (since '70), making vg traditional red RIOJAS and improving all the time.

Reserva (res) Good quality wine matured for long periods. Red reservas must spend at least 1 year in cask and 2 in bottle; gran reservas 2 in cask and 3 in bottle. Thereafter many continue to mature for years.

Rías Baixas Gal w **→*** NW DO embracing subzones Val do Salnés, O Rosal and Condado de Tea, now for some of the best (and priciest) cold-fermented Spanish whites, mainly from ALBARINO grapes.

Ribeiro Gal r w (p) *→** Demarcated region on N border of Portugal: wines similar in style to Portuguese VINHOS VERDES – and others.

Ribera del Duero Rib del D 91 92 94 Fashionable fast-expanding DO east of Valladolid, now revealed as excellent for Tinto Fino (Tempranillo) reds. Vintages are somewhat variable and prices high. See Peñafiel, Pérez Pascuas, Pesquera, Torremilanos, Vega Sicilia. Also Mauro.

Ribera Duero, Bodegas See Bodegas Protos.

Rioja r p w sp 64 70 75 78 81 82 85 89 90 91 92 93 94 N upland region along River Ebro for many of Spain's best red table wines in some 60 BODEGAS DE EXPORTACION. Tempranillo predominates. Other grapes and/or oak incl depending on fashion and vintage. Subdivided into 3 areas:

Rioja Alavesa N of the R Ebro, produces fine red wines, mostly light in body and colour but particularly aromatic.

Rioja Alta S of the R Ebro and W of LOGROÑO, grows most of the finest, best-balanced red and white wines; also some rosé.

Rioja Baja Stretching E from LOGROÑO, makes coarser red wines, high in alcohol and often used for blending.

Important note:

An extended range of vintages is printed for a number of Rioja bodegas. But remember that the quality of the older reservas and gran reservas is dependent on proper cellarage. Old wines kept for any period in the racks of a warm restaurant soon deteriorate. Riojas do not now last as long as their oakier predecessors – some of the '85s are already drying out – but depending upon the bodega, an older vintage may well be memorable. Currently, the '89, '90 and '91 vintages are the safest choices.

Rioja Santiago R Alt r (p w dr sw) res ★→★★★ 85 86 88 89 91 BODEGA at HARO with brands incl the biggest-selling bottled SANGRIA. Its top reds, Condal and Gran Enologica, are respectable.

Riojanas, Bodegas R Alt r (w p) res ★★→★★★ 64 70 73 75 78 81 82 83 85 86 88 91 Old BODEGA for trad Viña Albina and big mellow Monte Real RESERVAS (82).

Rosado Rosé.

Rovellats Pen w p sp ★★→★★★ 92 Small family firm making only good (and expensive) CAVAS, stocked in some of Spain's best restaurants.

Rovira, Pedro Tar/Pen r p br w dr sw res ★→★★ Large firm with BODEGAS in the DOs TARRAGONA, Terra Alta and PENEDES. A wide range. Recent Australian involvement could improve recent dullness.

Rueda br w ★→★★ Small historic DO west of Valladolid. Trad FLOR-growing, sherry-like wines up to 17° alcohol, now for fresh whites, incl MARQUES DE RISCAL, MARQUES DE GRIÑON. Its secret weapon is the Verdejo grape.

Ruiz, Santiago Gal w ★★★ DYA Small prestigious RIAS BAIXAS co, now owned by BODEGAS LAN: fresh lemony ALBARIÑO. Its ageing, is one of v best.

Salceda, Bodegas Viña R Ala r res ★★→★★★ 85 89 Fruity light balanced reds.

San Sadurní de Noya Pen w sp ★★→★★★ Town S of Barcelona, hollow with CAVA cellars. Standards can be v high, though the flavour (of Parellada and other grapes) is quite different from that of champagne.

San Valero, Bodega Cooperativa Cariñena r p w res ★→★★ 85 87 88 90 Large CARINENA coop with some modern wines. Good red CRIANZA Monte Ducay; fresh ROSADO with slight spritz; and value young unoaked Don Mendo.

Sangre de Toro Brand name for a rich-flavoured red from TORRES.

Sangría Cold red wine cup traditionally made with citrus fruit, fizzy lemonade, ice and brandy. But too often repulsive commercial fizz.

Sanlúcar de Barrameda Centre of the Manzanilla district (see Sherry).

Sarría, Bodegas de Nav r (p w) res ★★→★★★ 85 86 89 90 Quality remains high, though the Duarte family's departure has left the lustre of this model estate's international reputation sadly dimmed.

Scala Dei, Cellers de Pri r w p res ★★→★★★ 87 88 91 One of few BODEGAS in PRIORATO. Full reds with Cab (Negre Crianza, Cartoixa G RESERVA), some oak-aged; lighter Novell is pure Garnacha. Also the region's only white, Scala Dei Blanco; and delicious Tavel-style ROSADO. Less alcohol recently.

Scholtz, Hermanos Málaga br ★★★ Makers of the best MALAGA, incl dry 10-yr-old AMONTILLADO, excellent Moscatel and trad Dulce y Negro. Best of all is the dessert Solera Scholtz 1885. Try it before it disappears.

Seco Dry.

Segura Viudas, Cavas Pen w sp ★★→★★★ CAVA from SAN SADURNI (FREIXENET-owned). Buy the Brut Vintage, Aria or RESERVA Heredad.

Serra, Jaume Pen r w res ★★ 86 88 89 91 Refreshing varietal whites, fruity balanced reds, easy-drinking CAVA (esp 'Cristalino'). Reputation may be enhanced by '95 involvement of charismatic Chilean Ignacio Recabarren.

Sitges Pen w sw ★★ Coastal resort S of Barcelona once noted for dessert wine from Moscatel and Malvasia grapes. One maker, Celler Robert, survives.

Somontano Som Pyrenees foothills DO. Best-known BODEGAS: old French-est'd Lalanne (esp Viña San Marcos red: Moristel-Tempranillo-Cab S; white Macabeo, Chard), Coop Somontano de Sobrarbe now privatized as Bodegas Pirineos (esp Montesierra range and oak-aged Señorío de Lazán), new COVISA (Viñas del Vero).

Tarragona r w br dr sw *→*** (i) Table wines from demarcated region (DO); of little note. (ii) Dessert wines from the firm of DE MULLER.

Tinto Red.

Toro r *→** DO 150 miles NW of Madrid. Formerly for over-powerful (up to 16°) reds, now often tasty and balanced. See Bodegas Fariña.

Torremilanos Rib del D r res *→** 85 86 87 88 89 90 Label of Bodegas López Peñalba, a fast-expanding family firm nr Aranda de Duero. Tinto Fino (Tempranillo) is smoother, more RIOJA-like than most. Aka 'Peñalba'.

Torres, Bodegas Pen r w p dr s/sw res **→**** 87 89 90 91 World-famous family co for many of best PENEDES wines; a flagship for all Spain. Wines are flowery white Viña Sol, Green Label Fransola Sauv and Parellada, Gran Viña Sol, MILMANDA oak-fermented Chard, semi-dry aromatic Esmeralda, Waltraud Ries, red Tres Torres, Gran Sangre de Toro, vg Gran Coronas (Cab) RESERVAS, fresh soft Las Torres Merlot and Santa Digna Pinot. Mas Borras is 100% Pinot N. Also in Chile and California.

Utiel-Requena U-R r p (w) Demarcated region W of Valencia. Sturdy reds and chewy vino de doble pasta for blending; also light fragrant rosé.

Valbuena Rib del D r ▓▓ 84 85 86 88 89 Made with the same grapes as VEGA SICILIA but sold when 5 yrs old. Best at about 10 yrs. Some prefer it to its elder brother. 88 is outstanding. But see Alion.

Valdeorras Gal r w *→** DO E of Orense. Dry and (at best) refreshing wines.

Valdepeñas La M r (w) *→** Demarcated region nr Andalucían border. Mainly red wines, high in alcohol but surprisingly soft in flavour. Best wines (eg LOS LLANOS, FELIX SOLIS and Casa la Viña) now oak-matured.

Valduero, Bodega Rib del D r 86 89 91 New ('84) BODEGA: vg, value RESERVAS.

Valencia r w * Demarcated region exporting vast quantities of clean and drinkable table wine; also refreshing whites, esp Moscatel.

Vallformosa, Masia Pen r w p sp res ** CAVA respectable, reds poor.

Vega de la Reina Rueda w r res ** 73 75 81 85 87 BODEGA making dark oaky reds (this RIBERA DEL D), characterful white Verdejo, rather good Sauv.

Vega Sicilia Rib del D r res **** 41 48 53 59 60 61 62 64 66 67 69 70 72 73 74 75 76 79 80 82 Top Spanish wine: full, fruity, piquant, rare and fascinating. Up to 16% alcohol. Reserva Especial is a blend, chiefly of 62 and 79(!). See also Valbuena, Alion. Now investing in Tokaji, Hungary.

Vendimia Vintage.

Verín Gal r * Town near N border of Portugal. Its wines are the strongest from GALICIA, without a bubble, and with up to 14% alcohol.

Viña Literally, a vineyard. But wines such as Tondonia (LOPEZ DE HEREDIA) are not necessarily made with grapes from only the v'yd named.

Viña Pedrosa See Pérez Pascuas.

Viña Toña Pen w **→*** 93 DYA Clean fresh fruity white of Xarel-lo and unoaked Chard from small Celler R Balada. Justifiably high reputation.

Viñas del Vero Som w p r res **→*** See COMPANIA VITIVINICOLA ARAGONESA.

Vinícola de Castilla La M r p w ▓▓ 83 84 87 89 91 92 One of largest LA MANCHA firms. Red and white Castillo de Alhambra are palatable. Top are Cab, Cencibel (Tempranillo), Señorío de Guadianeja (89) GRAN RESERVAS.

Vinícola Navarra Nav r p w res ** 88 89 Old-est'd, now part of BODEGAS Y BEBIDAS, thoroughly trad. Best: Castillo de Tiebas, Las Campanas (89).

Vinival, Bodegas Valencia r p w * Huge Valencian consortium marketing the most widely drunk wine in the region, Torres de Quart (rosé best).

Vino comun/corriente Ordinary wine.

Vitivino, Bodegas Jumilla r w **→*** 88 89 91 French J-L Gadeau has caused a stir with lively/meaty Altos de Pío from local Monastrell grapes.

Yecla r w * DO north of Murcia. Good red from Bodegas Castaño.

Yllera Rib del D r ▓▓ 86 88 89 Good value RIBERO DEL DUERO red from now privatized Los Curros coop (but bottled in RUEDA so not DO).

To decipher codes, please refer to symbols key at front of book, and to 'How to use this book' on page 5.

Portugal

Portugal entries also cross-refer to Sherry, Port & Madeira, pages 137–143.

Abrigada, Quinta de Central Portugal r w res ** 80 86   Family estate: characterful light whites and cherry-like Castelão Francês (alias PERIQUITA). Best are the oak-aged GARRAFEIRAS.

Adega A cellar or winery.

Alenquer r w   Aromatic reds, whites from IPR just N of Lisbon.

Alentejo Alen r (w) *→**** Vast tract of S Portugal with only sparse v'yds, nr the Spanish border, but rapidly emerging potential for excellent wine. To date the great bulk has been coop-made. Estate wines from ROSADO FERNANDES, HERDADE DE MOUCHAO, QUINTA DO CARMO (now part Rothschild-owned) and ESPORAO have potency and style. Best coops are at BORBA, REDONDO and REGUENGOS DE MONSARRAZ. Growing excitement here.

Algarve Algarve r w *   The wines of the holiday area are covered by DOCs Lagos, Tavira, Lagoa and Portimão. With few exceptions its wines are nothing to write home about.

Aliança, Caves Bair r w sp res **→**** Large BAIRRADA-based firm making classic method sparkling. Reds and whites incl good Bairrada wines and mature DAOS. Aliança Tinta Velha is the best-selling red in Portugal.

Almeirim Ribatejo r w *   Large new IPR east of ALENQUER. Its coop makes the admirably fruity, extremely inexpensive Lezíria.

Almodovar, Casa Agricola Alen w r res ** 84 86 87   The whites of this ADEGA at Vidigueira are better known, but its reds are worth trying.

Amarante Subregion in the VINHO VERDE area. Rather heavier and stronger wines than those from farther north.

Arrábida nr Lisbon r w   IPR W of SETUBAL. Reds mostly from Castelão Francês (or PERIQUITA) some Cab S allowed.

Arruda, Adega Cooperative de nr Lisbon r res *   Vinho Tinto Arruda is a best buy, but avoid the reserva. (Arruda is now an IPR.)

Aveleda, Quinta da Douro w ** DYA   A first-class VINHO VERDE made on the Aveleda estate of the Guedes family. Sold dry in Portugal but sweetened for export.

Azevedo, Quinta de VV w ** DYA   Superior VINHO VERDE from SOGRAPE. 100% Loureiro grapes.

Bacalhoa, Quinta da Set r res *** 85 87 88 89 90 91   American-owned estate near SETUBAL, famous for harmonious fruity mid-weight Cab S vinified by J P VINHOS.

Bairrada Bair r w sp *→*** 78 79 80 81 82 83 84 85 86 87 88 89 90 91 92 93   Demarcated region producing excellent red GARRAFEIRAS. Also good sparkling by the classic method. Now an export hit.

Barca Velha Douro r res **** 78 81 82 83 85   Perhaps Portugal's best red, made in v limited quantities in the high DOURO by the port firm of FERREIRA (now owned by SOGRAPE). Powerful resonant wine with deep bouquet, still unchallenged by younger rivals.

Barrocão, Cavas do Bair r w res *→*** Based in BAIRRADA; blends good red DAOS and sells first-rate old Bairrada GARRAFEIRAS.

Basto A subregion of the VINHO VERDE area on the R Tamego, producing more astringent red wine than white.

Borba Alen r *→** Small DOC area nr Evora, making some of the best wine from ALENTEJO.

Borba, Adega Cooperativa de Alen r (w) res *→** 82 84 87 88 89 90 91   Leading ALENTEJO coop modernized with stainless steel and oak by EC funding. Big fruity vinho de ano red and vg 82 reserva.

Borges & Irmão Merchants of port and table wines at Vila Nova de Gaia, incl GATAO and (better) Gamba VINHOS VERDES, sparkling Fita Azul.

Braga Subregion of the VINHO VERDE area, good red and white.

Branco White.

Bright Brothers The gifted Australian Peter Bright, formerly with JOAO PIRES, has teamed up with his brother to make a quartet of attractive RIBATEJO wines, incl Chard, 'Early Release' Cab (93) and Merlot (93).

Buçaco nr Dão r w (p) res **** (r) 51 53 57 58 60 63 67 70 72 75 77 78 82 (w) 56 65 66 70 72 75 78 82 84 85 86 Legendary speciality of the Palace Hotel at Buçaco nr Coimbra, not seen elsewhere. At best incredible quality, worth the journey. So are the palace and park.

Bucelas w *** Tiny demarcated region N of Lisbon. CAVES VELHAS make aromatic whites with 11–12% alcohol. Reliable, not dramatic.

Camarate, Quinta de Lisbon r ** 82 83 84 85 86 87 89 90 Notable red from FONSECA, S of Lisbon, incl detectable proportion of Cab S.

Campos da Silva Olivera, JC Dão r res ** 84 85 Small ADEGA with v fruity estate DAO, Sete Torres Reserva.

Carcavelos br sw *** normally NV Minute DOC W of Lisbon. Excellent but rare sweet aperitif or dessert wines average 19% alcohol and resemble honeyed MADEIRA. The only producer is now Quinta dos Pesos, Caparide.

Carmo, Quinta do Alen r w res *** 86 87 88 89 Small, beautiful ALENTEJO ADEGA, partly bought in '92 by the Rothschilds of Lafite. 125 acres, plus cork forests. Fresh dry white. Best is the fruity harmonious red.

Cartaxo Ribatejo r w * A district in the RIBATEJO N of Lisbon, now an IPR area making everyday wines popular in the capital.

Carvalho, Ribeiro & Ferreira N Lisbon r w res ***→*** Large merchants blending and bottling SERRADAYRES and excellent GARRAFEIRAS from the RIBATEJO and elsewhere (74 78 85).

Casa da Insua Dão r w ** One of the v few single-estate wines of DAO (but not DOC), made with a proportion of Cab for the proprietors by FONSECA.

Casa de Sezim VV w *** DYA Top estate-bottled VINHO VERDE from a member of the association of private producers, APEVV.

Casal García Douro w ** DYA Big-selling VINHO VERDE, made at AVELEDA.

Casal Mendes VV w ** DYA The VINHO VERDE from CAVES ALIANCA.

Casaleiro Trademark of Caves Dom Teodosio-João T Barbosa, who make a variety of standard wines: DAO, VINHO VERDE, etc.

Castelo Rodrigo NE Portugal r w IPR reds resembling DAO.

Cepa Velha VV w (r) *** Brand name of Vinhos de Monção. Their Alvarinho is one of the best VINHOS VERDES.

Chaves N Portugal r w IPR. Sharp pale fizzy reds from granite soils. Rounder ones from schist.

Clarete Relatively light red wine.

Colares Colares r *** TOTB (the older the better) Small DOC on the sandy coast W of Lisbon. Its antique-style dark red wines, rigid with tannin, are from vines that have never suffered from phylloxera. Drink the oldest available: it needs at least 10 yrs (see Paulo da Silva).

Conde de Santar B Al r (w) res **→*** 78 85 86 Estate-grown DAO, matured and sold by port firm CALEM. Reservas are fruity, full-bodied, v smooth.

Consumo (vinho) Ordinary wine.

Coruche Coruche r w Large IPR of Sorraia river basin NE of Lisbon. Only growth of interest is the botrytis wine made by J P VINHOS.

Corval, Quinta do Pinhão r ** Estate nr Pinhão: good CLARETES.

Côtto, Quinta do Douro r w res *** 82 85 90 Pioneer table wines from port country; vg red Grande Escolha and also Q do Côtto are dense fruity tannic wines that will repay long keeping. Also port.

Cova da Beira r w Largest of the IPRs nr Spanish border. Light reds best.

Dão Dão r w res ** 80 81 82 83 84 85 86 87 88 89 90 91 92 93 DOC region round town of Viseu. Produces some of Portugal's best-known, but often dull table wines: solid reds of some subtlety with age; substantial dry whites. Most sold under brand names. But see Duque de Viseu, Casa da Insua, J M da Fonseca, Porta dos Cavalheiros, etc.

NB Vintages in colour are those you should choose first for drinking in 1996.

DOC (Denominacão de Origem Controlada) Official wine region. There are 18 in Portugal, incl BAIRRADA, COLARES, DAO, DOURO, SETUBAL, VINHO VERDE; and new in '95: BORBA, PORTALEGRE, REDONDO, REGUENGOS, VIDIGUEIRA.

Doce (vinho) Sweet (wine).

Dom Ferraz Brand name for v drinkable wines from DAO, BAIRRADA etc, shipped by D&F Wine Shippers of London.

Douro Douro r w **80 81 82 83 84 85 86 87 88 89 90 91 92** Northern river whose valley produces port and some of Portugal's most exciting new table wines. See Barca Velha, Quinta do Côtto, etc. Watch this space.

Duque de Viseu Dão r **90 91** High quality branded red DAO from SOGRAPE.

Encostas de Aire Central Portugal r w Fruity high-alcohol wines from large IPR.

Esporão, Herdade do Alen w r **87 89 90 91** Owners Finagra SA spent US $10 million on their space-age winery and planting 900 acres. Their light fresh Roupeiro white and 91 red, with a touch of Cab S, are pleasant. Wines now made by Australian David Baverstock.

Espumante Sparkling.

Esteva Douro r *→** DYA V drinkable DOURO red from port firm FERREIRA.

Evelita Douro r ** Reliable middle-weight red made near VILA REAL by REAL COMPANHIA VINICOLA DO NORTE DE PORTUGAL. Ages well.

Evora Alen w r **86 87 88 89 90 91** Large new IPR south of Lisbon.

Ferreirinha Douro r res *** **80 84** Reserva Especial. The second wine to BARCA VELHA, made in less than ideal vintages.

Fonseca, JM da Lisbon r w dr sw sp res **→*** Venerable firm in Azeitão nr Lisbon with one of the longest and best ranges in Portugal, incl dry white PASMADOS, PORTALEGRE and QUINTA DE CAMARATE; red PERIQUITA, PASMADOS, TERRAS ALTAS DAO; and famous dessert SETUBAL. Fonseca also owns ROSADO FERNANDES and makes the wines for CASA DA INSUA.

Fonseca Internacional, JM da nr Lisbon p sp * Formerly part of the last, now owned by Grand Met. Produces LANCERS rosé and a surprisingly drinkable sparkling Lancers Brut made by a continuous process of Russian invention.

Gaeiras Central Coast r ** Dry full-bodied well-balanced red made nr OBIDOS.

Garrafeira Label term. The 'private reserve' wine of a merchant, aged for a minimum of 2 yrs in cask and 1 in bottle, but often much longer. Usually their best, though traditionally often of indeterminate origin but now have to show origin on label.

Gatão VV w ** DYA Standard VINHO VERDE from BORGES & IRMAO; fragrant but sweetened.

Gazela VV w ** DYA VINHO VERDE made at Barcelos by SOGRAPE since the AVELEDA estate went to a different branch of the Guedes family.

Generoso Aperitif or dessert wine rich in alcohol.

Grão Vasco Dão r w res ** **82 83 85 87 88 89 93** One of the best brands of DAO, from a new high-tech ADEGA at Viseu. Fine red GARRAFEIRA (85); fresh young white (DYA). Owned by SOGRAPE.

IPR Indicacões de Proveniência Regulamentada. See below.

Thirty-one new Portuguese wine regions came into play in 1990, there are now 47. These 'IPRs' (Indicacões de Proveniência Regulamentada) are on a six-year probation for DOC status. In EC terminology they are VQPRDs. Those which are really performing are included in this edition.

1992 saw the introduction of 8 new broader 'Vinhos Regionais': Rios do Montes, Trás os Montes, Beiras, Ribatejo, Estramadura, Alentejo, Terras do Sado, Algarve.

J P Vinhos Set r w sp res **→*** One of best-equipped and best-run wineries. Delicious João Pires Branco (Moscato), Catarina (with Chard), dry red and white Santa Marta, red Santo Amaro made by macération carbonique, TINTO DE ANFORA, QUINTA DA BACALHOA, dessert SETUBAL, classic sparkling J P Vinhos Bruto and Cova da Ursa oak-fermented Chard.

Lafões r w IPR between DAO and VINHO VERDE.

Lagosta VV w * DYA VINHO VERDE from the REAL COMPANHIA VINICOLA DO NORTE DE PORTUGAL.

Lancers nr Lisbon p w sp * Sweet carbonated rosé and sparkling white extensively shipped to the US by FONSECA INTERNACIONAL.

Lezíria See Almeirim.

Lima Subregion in N of VINHO VERDE area, for mainly astringent red wines.

Madeira br dr sw **→**** Source of famous aperitif and dessert wines. See pages 137–143.

Maduro (vinho) A mature table wine – as opposed to a VINHO VERDE.

Mateus Rosé Bair p (w) * World's biggest-selling medium-sweet carbonated rosé, made by SOGRAPE at VILA REAL and Anadia in BAIRRADA.

Monção N subregion of the VINHO VERDE area on R Minho: producing the best of them from the Alvarinho grape.

A general rule for Portugal: chose youngest vintages of whites, oldest of red.

Morgadio de Torre VV w ** DYA A top VINHO VERDE from SOGRAPE. Largely Alvarinho grapes.

Mouchão, Herdade de Alen r res *** 74 82 89 Perhaps the best ALENTEJO estate, ruined in the '74 revolution; since replanted.

Moura Alen r w 85 86 87 88 89 90 91 IPR: source of J P VINHOS red and white Santa Marta.

Obidos r w IPR nr coast, S of Alcobaça (central coast). Similar wines.

Pacheca, Quinta da Douro r w ** DOURO table wines, estate-grown-made and -bottled. Unfortunately not free of faults.

Palacio de Brejoeira VV w (r) *** Outstanding estate-made VINHO VERDE from MONCAO, with astonishing fragrance and full fruity flavour made entirely from Alvarinho grapes.

Palmela Set r w Sandy soil IPR NE of SETUBAL. Reds esp long-lived.

Pancas, Quinta de Central Coast r w res ** 87 90 91 Red and white wine to watch from ALENQUER district N of Lisbon.

Pasmados Very tasty FONSECA red from the SETUBAL peninsula (88 90).

Paulo da Silva, Antonio Bernardino Colares r (w) res **→**** 68 70 74 77 79 80 83 84 85 His COLARES Chita is one of the very few of these classics still made (by the ADEGA Regional).

Pedralvites, Quinta de Bair w *→** 93 Pleasant BAIRRADA white with apple and apricot flavours from the Maria Gomes grape, by SOGRAPE.

Penafiel Subregion in the S of the VINHO VERDE area.

Periquita Lisbon r ** 85 86 87 88 90 91 One of Portugal's most enjoyable robust reds, made by FONSECA at Azeitão S of Lisbon. Periquita is an alias of Castelão Francês, a grape much grown in the RIBATEJO.

Pinhel B Al w (r) sp * IPR region E of DAO: similar white, mostly sparkling.

Pires, Vinhos João See J P Vinhos.

Planalto Douro w ** 90 Good white wine from SOGRAPE.

Planalto Mirandês r w Large IPR NE of DOURO. Port grapes in reds. Verdelho in whites.

Ponte de Lima, Cooperativa de VV r w * Maker of one of the best bone-dry red VINHOS VERDES, and first-rate dry and fruity white.

Porta dos Cavalheiros Dão ** 80 83 85 One of the best red DAOS, matured by CAVES SAO JOAO in BAIRRADA.

Portalegre Alen r w 85 86 87 88 89 90 Important new DOC on Spanish border. Strong fragrant reds with potential to age. Alcoholic whites.

Quinta Estate.

Ramos-Pinto, Adriano Douro r ** 91 Rich red Duas Quintas from go-ahead port house.

Raposeira Douro w sp ** Well-known fizz made by the classic method at Lamego. Ask for the Bruto. An outpost of Seagram.

Real Companhia Vinícola do Norte de Portugal Giant of the port trade (see page 142); also produces EVELITA, LAGOSTA, etc.

Redondo Alen r w   Nr Spanish border. One of Portugal's best-kept secrets. Newly granted DOC status.

Reguengos de Monsarraz, Cooperativa de Alen r (w) res ✶✶ 80 81 82 83 84 85 86 87 88 89 90   Important coop making steadily better wines; the best of them red, esp Terras d'el Rei Reserva.

Ribatejo r w 80 81 82 83 84 85 86 87 88 89 90 91   Region on R Tagus north of Lisbon. Several good GARRAFEIRAS etc.

Ribeirinho, Quinta de Bair r sp ✶✶ 80 85   Luis Pato makes some of the best estate-grown BAIRRADA: fruity red and fresh classic method sparkling.

Rosa, Quinta de la Douro r ✶✶ 91 92 93   Firm oak-aged red from v'yds formerly used for port. Also young peppery Quinta das Lamelas. Both made by Australian David Baverstock.

Rosado Rosé.

Rosado Fernandes, José de Sousa Alen r res ✶✶ 75 79 83 86 87 88   Small firm recently acquired by FONSECA, making the most sophisticated of the full-bodied wines from the ALENTEJO, fermenting them in earthenware amphoras and ageing them in oak.

Santarém r w   Central IPR. Reds and whites fruity and strong; reds age.

São Claudio, Quinta de VV w ✶✶✶ DYA   Estate at Esposende: perhaps the best VINHO VERDE outside MONCAO.

São João, Caves Bair r w sp res ✶✶→✶✶✶✶ 78 80 82 83 85   One of the best firms in BAIRRADA, known for fruity and full-bodied reds and PORTA DOS CAVALHEIROS DAOS. Also fizz.

Seco Dry.

Serradayres r (w) res ✶ 90 91   Blended RIBATEJO table wines from CARVALHO, Ribeiro & Ferreira. Recently much improved.

Setúbal Set br (r w) sw (dr) ✶✶✶   Small demarcated region S of the River Tagus, where FONSECA make a highly aromatic Muscat-based dessert wine (80 81 82 83 84 85 86 87 88 89 90 91 92 93) sold at 5 yrs old.

Sogrape Sociedad Comercial dos Vinhos de Mesa de Portugal. Largest wine concern in the country, making VINHOS VERDES, DAO, BAIRRADA, MATEUS ROSE, VILA REAL red, etc, and now owners of FERREIRA port.

Solar das Bouças VINHO VERDE estate. Its dry aromatic wine is a model.

Terra Franca Bair r res ✶✶ 85 87 88 90   Good red BAIRRADA from SOGRAPE, available also as a GARRAFEIRA (85 89).

Terras Altas Dão r w res ✶✶ 85 86 87 88 89 90 91 92   Good DAO from FONSECA.

Tinto Red.

Tinto da Anfora Set r ✶✶ 84 85 86 87 89 90 91   Deservedly popular juicy and fruity red from J P VINHOS.

Tomar r w   Central Portugal IPR for acidic whites, smooth reds.

Torres Vedras r w ✶   IPR area N of Lisbon famous for Wellington's 'lines'. Major supplier of bulk wine; one of biggest coops in Portugal.

Valpaços r   IPR N of DOURO. Wines like CHAVES' (esp from schist soils).

Velhas, Caves Bucelas r w res ✶✶→✶✶✶   Until very recently the only maker of BUCELAS; also good DAO and (80) Romeira GARRAFEIRAS.

Verde Green (see Vinhos Verdes).

Vidigueira Alen w r   Famous for traditionally-made unmatured whites from volcanic soils. Newly awarded DOC status.

Vila Real Douro r ✶→✶✶   Town in the DOURO. Some good reds.

Vinhos Verdes VV and Douro w ✶→✶✶✶ r ✶   DOC between R Douro and N frontier with Spain, for 'green wines': made from grapes with high acidity and (originally) undergoing a special secondary fermentation to leave them with a slight sparkle. Today the fizz is usually just added CO_2. Ready for drinking in spring after harvest, it may be white or red.

For key to grape variety abbreviations, see pages 6–9.

Sherry, Port & Madeira

The original authentic sherries of Spain, ports of Portugal and madeiras of Madeira are listed below. No other wines that use these names have a moral right to them; nor do any compare in quality and value for money with good examples of the originals.

The map on pages 122–123 locates the port (Douro) and sherry (Jerez) districts. Madeira is an island 400 miles out in the Atlantic from the coast of Morocco, a port of call for west-bound sailing ships: hence its historical market in North America.

In this section most of the entries are shippers' names followed by a brief account of their wines. The names of wine types are also included in the alphabetical listing.

Abad, Tomas Small sherry BODEGA owned by LUSTAU. Vg light FINO.

Almacenista Individual matured but unblended sherry; usually dark dry wines for connoisseurs. Often superb quality and value. See Lustau.

Amontillado A FINO which has been aged in cask beyond its normal span to become darker, more powerful and pungent. The best are natural dry wines. In general use merely means medium sherry.

Amoroso Type of sweet sherry, v similar to a sweet OLOROSO.

Barbadillo, Antonio Much the largest SANLUCAR firm, with a range of 50-odd MANZANILLAS and sherries mostly excellent of their type, incl Sanlúcar FINO, superb SOLERA manzanilla PASADA, Fino de Balbaina, austere Principe dry AMONTILLADO. Also young Castillo de San Diego table wines.

Barbeito One of the last independent MADEIRA shipping families, now Japanese controlled. Wines incl rare vintages, eg MALMSEY 1901 and the latest, BUAL 1960.

Barros Almeida Large family-owned port house with several brands (incl Feuerheerd, KOPKE): excellent 20-yr-old TAWNY and many COLHEITAS.

Bertola Sherry shippers, best known for their Bertola CREAM SHERRY.

Blandy Historic family firm of MADEIRA shippers and one of two top names used by MADEIRA WINE CO. Duke of Clarence Rich Madeira is their most famous wine. 10-year-old reservas (VERDELHO, BUAL, MALMSEY) are vg. Many glorious old vintages.

Blázquez Sherry BODEGA at JEREZ owned by DOMECQ. Outstanding FINO, Carta Blanca, v old SOLERA OLOROSO Extra, and Carta Oro AMONTILLADO al natural (unsweetened).

Bobadilla Large JEREZ BODEGA, recently bought by OSBORNE and best known for v dry Victoria FINO and Bobadilla 103 brandy, esp among Spanish connoisseurs. Also excellent sherry vinegar.

Borges, H M Independent MADEIRA shipper of old repute.

Brown sherry British term for a style of budget dark sweet sherry.

Bual One of the best grapes of madeira, making a soft smoky sweet wine, usually lighter and not as rich as MALMSEY. (See panel on page 143.)

Burdon English-founded sherry BODEGA owned by CABALLERO. Puerto FINO, Don Luis AMONTILLADO and raisiny Heavenly Cream are top lines.

Burmester Old, small, family-owned port house with fine soft sweet 20-yr-old TAWNY; also vg range of COLHEITAS. Vintages: 48 55 58 60 63 70 77 80 84 85 89 91.

Caballero Important sherry shippers at PUERTO DE SANTA MARIA, best known for Pavón FINO, Mayoral Cream OLOROSO, excellent BURDON sherries and PONCHE orange liqueur. Also owners of LUSTAU.

Cálem Old family-run Portuguese house with fine reputation, esp for vintage wines. Owns excellent Quinta da Foz (82 84 86 87 88 89 90 92). Vintages: 50 55' 58 60 63' 66 70 75 77' 80 83 85 91. Good light TAWNY; exceptional range COLHEITAS: 48 50 52 57 60 62 65 78 84 85 86.

Casa dos Vinhos da Madeira Vg house (long-time market leader in Canada): fine basic, 5 yr-olds, reserves and 10 yr-olds.

Churchill The only recently founded port shipper, already highly respected for excellent vintages 82 and 85, also 91. Also a vg CRUSTED. Quinta da Agua Alta is Churchill's single-QUINTA port: 83 87 90 92.

'All wine would be port if it could.'
– old English saying

Cockburn British-owned (Allied-DOMECQ) port shippers with a range of good wines incl the v popular fruity Special Reserve. Fine vintage port from high v'yds can look deceptively light when young, but has great lasting power. Vintages: **55 60 63' 67 70' 75 83 85** 91.

Colheita Vintage-dated port of a single yr, but aged at least 7 winters in wood: in effect a vintage TAWNY. The bottling date is also shown on the label. Excellent examples come from KOPKE, CALEM and Krohn.

Cossart Gordon At one time the leading firm of MADEIRA shippers, founded 1745, with BLANDY now one of the two top-quality labels of the MADEIRA WINE CO. Wines slightly less rich than Blandy's. Best known for Good Company Finest Medium Rich but also producing 5-yr-old reservas, old vintages (latest, 74) and SOLERAS (esp BUAL 1845).

Côtto, Quinta do Single-v'yd port from Miguel Champalimaud, best-known of a new wave of grower-bottlers up in the DOURO. Vg vintage 82. See also in Portugal section for table wine.

Cream Sherry A style of amber sweet sherry made by sweetening a blend of well-aged OLOROSOS. It originated in Bristol, England.

Croft One of the oldest firms shipping vintage port: since 1678. Now owned by Grand Met Co. Well-balanced vintage wines tend to mature early (since 66). Vintages: **55 60 63' 66 67 70' 75 77' 82 85'** 91; and lighter vintage wines under the name of their Quinta da Roeda in several other years (**78 80 83** 87). Distinction is their most popular blend. MORGAN is a small separate company (see also Delaforce). Also now in the sherry business with Croft Original (PALE CREAM) and Particular (medium), Delicado (FINO, also medium), and good PALO CORTADO.

Crusted Term for vintage-style port, usually blended from several vintages not one. Bottled young, then aged so it forms a 'crust'. Needs decanting.

Delaforce Port shippers owned by CROFT, best known in Germany. His Eminence's Choice is a v pleasant TAWNY; VINTAGE CHARACTER is also good. Vintage wines are v fine, among the lighter kind: **55 58 60 63' 66' 70 74 75 77' 82 83 85'**; Quinta da Côrte in **78 80 84 87** 91.

Delgado Zuleta Old-established SANLUCAR sherry firm best known for marvellous La Goya MANZANILLA PASADA.

Diez-Merito SA Sherry house famous for FINO Imperial and Victoria Regina OLOROSO. Bought by Rumasa and incorporated into BODEGAS INTER-NACIONALES. Control passed to Marcos Eguizabal (of PATERNINA in RIOJA). Now apparently exists as little more than a trade name. Its excellent DON ZOILO sherry has been sold to the MEDINA group, and Gran Duque de Alba brandy to WILLIAMS & HUMBERT.

Domecq Giant family-run sherry BODEGAS at JEREZ, recently merged with Allied-Lyons as Allied-Domecq, famous also for Fundador and other brandies. Double Century Original OLOROSO, their biggest brand, now replaced by Pedro Cream Sherry, La Ina is their excellent FINO. Other famous wines incl Celebration CREAM, Botaina (old AMONTILLADO) and the magnificent Rio Viejo (v dry amontillado) and Sibarita (PALO CORTADO). Recently: a range of wonderful old SOLERA sherries (Sibarita, Amontillado 51-1a and Venerable Oloroso). Also in RIOJA and Mexico.

Sherry, Port & Madeira entries also cross-refer to Spain and Portugal sections, respectively pages 122–131 and 132–136.

Don Zoilo Luxury sherries, including velvety FINO, recently sold by BODEGAS INTERNACIONALES to the MEDINA group.

Dow Old port name, well-known for relatively dry but splendid vintage wines, said to have a faint 'cedarwood' character. Also vg VINTAGE CHARACTER and Boardroom, a 15-year-old TAWNY. Quinta do Bomfim is single-QUINTA port (**78 79 82 84** 86 87 88 89 90 92). Vintages: **55 60 63' 66' 70' 72 75 77'** 80 83 85' 91. Dow, GOULD CAMPBELL, GRAHAM, QUARLES HARRIS, SMITH WOODHOUSE, WARRE all belong to the Symington family.

Dry Fly A household name in the UK. A crisp nutty AMONTILLADO made in JEREZ for its British proprietors, Findlater Mackie Todd & Co.

Sherry: which to choose

The sherry industry has been so badly depleted recently that a short list of truly excellent wines still being made is needed to keep it in focus. They include: Barbadillo manzanillas; Blázquez Carta Blanca fino; Domecq La Ina fino, Rio Viejo oloroso, Sibarita palo cortado; Gonzalez Byass Tio Pepe fino, Amontillado del Duque, Matusalem and Apostoles dry and sweet olorosos; Harveys 1796 range; Hildugo La Gitana manzanilla fino; Lustau Almacenista range; Osborne Fino Quinta; Páez Don Zoilo fino; Sandeman Don fino, Royal Corregidor sweet oloroso; de Soto Soto fino; Valdespino Inocente fino, Don Tomás amontillado; Williams & Humbert Pando fino and palo cortado.

Dry Sack See Williams & Humbert.

Duff Gordon Sherry shippers best known for El Cid AMONTILLADO. Also good FINO Feria and Nina Medium OLOROSO. Owned by OSBORNE.

Eira Velha, Quinta da Small port estate with old-style vintage wines shipped by MARTINEZ. Vintages: 78 82 87 92.

Ferreira One of the biggest Portuguese-owned port growers and shippers (since 1751), recently bought by SOGRAPE (see Portugal). Largest selling brand in P. Well-known for old TAWNIES and juicily sweet, relatively light vintages: **60 63' 66 70' 75 77' 78** 80 82 85' 87 91. Also Dona Antónia Personal Reserve, splendidly rich tawny Duque de Bragança and single-QUINTA wines Quinta do Seixo (83) and Quinta do Leda (90).

Fino Term for lightest, finest sherries, completely dry, v pale, delicate but pungent. Fino should be drunk cool and fresh: it deteriorates rapidly once opened. TIO PEPE is the classic. Use half bottles if possible.

Flor A floating yeast peculiar to FINO sherry and certain other wines that oxidize slowly and tastily under its influence.

Fonseca Guimaraens British-owned port shipper of stellar reputation, connected with TAYLOR'S. Robust deeply coloured vintage wine, among the v best. Vintages: Fonseca **60 63' 66' 70' 75 77'** 80 83 85' 92; Fonseca Guimaraens 76 78 82 84 86 87 88 91. Quinta do Panascal 78 is a single-QUINTA wine. Also delicious VINTAGE CHARACTER Bin 27.

Forrester Port shippers and owners of the famous Quinta da Boa Vista, now owned by Martini & Rossi. Their vintage wines tend to be round, 'fat' and sweet, good for relatively early drinking. Baron de Forrester is vg TAWNY. Vintages: (Offley Forrester) **55 60 62' 63' 66 67 70' 72 75 77'** 80 82 83 85' 87 89.

Garvey Famous old sherry shippers at JEREZ, now German-owned. Their finest wines are deep-flavoured FINO San Patricio, Tio Guillermo Dry AMONTILLADO and Ochavico Dry OLOROSO. San Angelo Medium amontillado is the most popular. Also Bicentenary PALE CREAM.

Gonzalez Byass Enormous family-run firm shipping the world's most famous and one of the very best FINO sherries: TIO PEPE. Brands include La Concha medium AMONTILLADO, Elegante dry fino and new El Rocío Manzanilla Fina, San Domingo PALE CREAM, Nectar CREAM and Alfonso Dry OLOROSO. Amontillado del Duque is on a higher plane, as are Matusalem and Apostoles: respectively sweet and dry old olorosos of rare quality. The company is now linked with Grand Metropolitan. Also makers of top-selling Soberano and exquisite Lepanto brandies.

Gould Campbell See Smith Woodhouse.

Graham Port shippers famous for some of the richest, sweetest and best of VINTAGE PORTS, largely from their own Quinta dos Malvedos (52 57 58 61 65 68 76 78 79 82 84 86 87 88 90 92). Also excellent brands, incl Six Grapes RUBY, LBV, and 10- and 20-yr-old TAWNIES. Vintages: 55' 60 63' 66' 70' 75 77' 80 83 85' 91.

Guita, La Famous old SANLUCAR BODEGA and its v fine MANZANILLA PASADA. Also vg vinegar.

Hartley & Gibson See Valdespino.

Harvey's Important pillar of the Allied-Domecq empire, along with DOMECQ and TERRY. World-famous Bristol shippers of Bristol Cream and Bristol Milk (sweet), Club AMONTILLADO and Bristol Dry (medium), Luncheon Dry and Bristol FINO (not v dry). More to the point is their very good '1796' range of high quality sherries comprising Fine Old Amontillado, PALO CORTADO and Rich Old OLOROSO. Harvey's also control COCKBURN and have been MADEIRA shippers since 1796 (vg range).

Henriques & Henriques The biggest independent MADEIRA shippers of Funchal, now with the largest, most modern cellars on the island: wide range of well-structured rich, toothsome wines – the 10 year-olds are gold medal winners. Also a good dry aperitif, Monte Seco, and v fine old reservas as well as vintages.

Hidalgo, Vinícola Old SANLUCAR family firm best known for high quality sherries: pale MANZANILLA La Gitana, fine OLOROSO Seco and Jerez CORTADO.

Internacionales, Bodegas Once the pride of the now-defunct Rumasa and incorporating such famous houses as BERTOLA, VARELA and DIEZ-MERITO, the company was taken over by the entrepreneur Marcos Eguizabal. The building, one of the largest in Jerez, and remaining stocks of sherry, have recently been sold to the MEDINA group.

Jerez de la Frontera Centre of the sherry industry, between Cádiz and Seville in southern Spain. The word 'sherry' is a corruption of the name, pronounced in Spanish 'hereth'. In French, Xérès.

Kopke The oldest port house, founded by a German in 1638. Fair quality vintage wines (55 58 60 63 65 66 67 70 74 75 77 78 79 80 82 83 85 87 89 91) and excellent COLHEITAS.

Late-bottled vintage (LBV) Port of a single vintage kept in wood for twice as long as VINTAGE PORT (about 5 yrs), therefore lighter when bottled and ageing quicker. A real LBV will 'throw a crust' like vintage port. Few (eg WARRE, SMITH WOODHOUSE) qualify.

Leacock One of the oldest MADEIRA shippers, now a label of the MADEIRA WINE CO. Basic St John range is v fair; 10-yr-old Special Reserve MALMSEY and 15-yr-old BUAL are excellent.

Lustau One of the largest family-run sherry BODEGAS in JEREZ (now controlled by CABALLERO), making many wines for other shippers, but with a vg Dry Lustau range (esp FINO and OLOROSO) and Jerez Lustau PALO CORTADO. Pioneer shippers of excellent ALMACENISTA and 'landed age' wines; AMONTILLADOS and olorosos aged in elegant bottles before shipping. See also Abad.

Macharnudo One of the best parts of the sherry v'yds, N of JEREZ, famous for wines of the highest quality, both FINO and OLOROSO.

Madeira Wine Company Formed in 1913 by two firms as the Madeira Wine Association, subsequently to include all the British MADEIRA firms (26 in total) amalgamated to survive hard times. Remarkably, three generations later the wines, though cellared together, preserve their house styles. BLANDY and COSSART GORDON are top labels. The Co is now controlled by the Symington group (see Dow).

Malmsey The sweetest and richest form of MADEIRA; dark amber, rich and honeyed yet with madeira's unique sharp tang. (See panel on page 143.)

Manzanilla Sherry, normally FINO, which has acquired a peculiar bracing salty character from being aged in BODEGAS at SANLUCAR DE BARRAMEDA, on the Guadalquivir estuary nr JEREZ.

Manzanilla Pasada A mature MANZANILLA, half-way to an AMONTILLADO-style
wine. At its best (eg LA GUITA) one of the most appetizing of all sherries.

Marqués del Real Tesoro Old sherry firm, famous for MANZANILLA and
AMONTILLADO, bought by the enterprising José Estévez. Shrugging off
the current slump in sales he has built a spanking new bodega – the
first in years. Tío Mateo, for which the SOLERA was acquired from the
now defunct Palomino & Vergara via HARVEY'S, is a vg FINO.

Passing the Port

*Vintage port is almost as much a ritual as a drink. It always needs to be
decanted with great care (since the method of making it leaves a heavy
deposit in the bottle). The surest way of doing this is by filtering it through
clean muslin or a coffee filter-paper into either a decanter or a well-rinsed
bottle. All except very old ports can safely be decanted the day before
drinking. A week may not be too long. At table the decanter is traditionally
passed from guest to guest clockwise. Vintage port can be immensely long-
lived. Particularly good vintages older than those mentioned in the text
include 1904 08 11 20 27 34 35 45 50.*

Martinez Gassiot Port firm, subsidiary of COCKBURN, known esp for
excellent rich and pungent Directors 20-yr-old TAWNY, CRUSTED and
LBV. Vintages: 55 60 63 67 70 75 82 85 87 91.

Medina, José Originally a SANLÚCAR family BODEGA, now a major exporter,
especially to the Low Countries. Through the recent acquisition of
BODEGAS INTERNACIONALES, and huge stocks of CRIANZA sherry, the
dynamic Luís Paéz has probably become the biggest sherry grower
and shipper, with some 25% of total volume.

Miles Formerly Rutherford & Miles, MADEIRA shippers famous for Old
Trinity House Medium Rich etc. The latest vintage is 73 VERDELHO.
Now a label of the MADEIRA WINE CO.

Morgan A subsidiary of CROFT, best known in France.

Niepoort Small (Dutch) family-run port house with long record of fine
vintages (42 45 55 60 63 66 70 75 77 78 80 82 83 85 87 91 92) and
exceptional COLHEITAS.

Noval, Quinta do Historic port house now French (AXA) -owned. Intensely
fruity, structured and elegant vintage port; a few ungrafted vines still
at the QUINTA make a small quantity of Nacional – extraordinarily
dark, full, velvety and slow-maturing wine. Also vg 20-yr-old TAWNY.
Vintages: 55' 58 60 63 66' 67 70' 75 78 82 85' 87 91.

Offley Forrester See Forrester.

Oloroso Style of sherry, heavier and less brilliant than FINO when young,
but maturing to greater richness and pungency. Naturally dry, but
generally sweetened, for sale as CREAM.

Osborne Enormous Spanish firm with well-known brandies but also good
sherries incl Fino Quinta, Coquinero dry AMONTILLADO, 10 RF (or
Reserva Familiale) Medium OLOROSO. Also a range of 'rare' sherries,
top quality are numbered bottles. See also Duff Gordon.

Pale Cream Popular style of pale sherry made by sweetening FINO,
pioneered by CROFT's Original.

Palo Cortado A style of sherry close to OLOROSO but with some of the
character of an AMONTILLADO. Dry but rich and soft. Not often seen.

Pasada Style of FINO or MANZANILLA which is close to AMONTILLADO: a stronger
drier wine without FLOR character.

Pereira D'Oliveira Vinhos Family-owned MADEIRA co est'd 1850. V good
basic range as well as 5 and 10 yr-olds; fine old reserva VERDELHO
1890, BUAL 1908 and Malvasia 1895.

Poças Junior Family port firm specializing in TAWNIES and COLHEITAS.

Ponche An aromatic digestif made with old sherry and brandy, flavoured
with herbs and orange, presented in eye-catching silvered bottles.
See Caballero and de Soto.

Puerto de Santa María Second city and former port of the sherry area, with important BODEGAS.

PX Short for Pedro Ximénez, the grape part-dried in the sun used in JEREZ for sweetening blends.

Quarles Harris One of the oldest port houses, since 1680, now owned by the Symingtons (see Dow). Small quantities of LBV, mellow and well-balanced. Vintages: **60 63' 66' 70' 75 77' 80 83 85' 91**.

Quinta Portuguese for 'estate'. Also used to denote vintage ports which are usually, but not invariably, from the estate's v'yds, made in good but not exceptional vintages.

Rainwater A fairly light, Medium Dry blend of MADEIRA – traditionally popular in N America.

Ramos-Pinto Dynamic small port house specializing in single-QUINTA TAWNIES of style and elegance; now owned by champagne house Louis Roederer.

Real Companhia Vinícola do Norte de Portugal Aka Royal Oporto Wine Co and Real Companhia Velha; the largest port house, with a long political history. Many brands and several QUINTAS, incl Quinta dos Carvalhos which makes TAWNIES and COLHEITAS. Vintage wines generally dismal.

Rebello Valente Name used for the VINTAGE PORT of ROBERTSON. Light but elegant and well-balanced, maturing rather early. Vintages: **55' 60 63' 66' 67 70' 72 75 77' 80 83 85'**.

Robertson Subsidiary of SANDEMAN, shipping REBELLO VALENTE VINTAGE, LBV, Robertson's Privateer Reserve, Game Bird TAWNY, 10-yr-old Pyramid and 20-yr-old Imperial. Vintages: **63' 66' 67 70' 72 75 77' 80 83 85'**.

Rosa, Quinta de la Fine single-QUINTA port of the Bergqvist family at Pinhão. Recent return to traditional methods and stone lagars. Esp 85 88 90.

Rozes Port shippers controlled by Moët Hennessy. RUBY v popular in France; also TAWNY. Vintages: **63 67 77' 78 83 85 87 91**.

Ruby Youngest (and cheapest) port style: simple, sweet and red. The best are vigorous, full of flavour; others can be merely strong and rather thin.

Sanchez Romate Family firm in JEREZ since 1781. Best known in Spanish-speaking world, esp for brandy Cardinal Mendoza. Good sherry: FINO Cristal, OLOROSO Don Antonio, AMONTILLADO NPU ('Non Plus Ultra').

Sandeman A giant of the port trade and a major figure in the sherry one, owned by Seagram. Founder's Reserve is their well-known VINTAGE CHARACTER; TAWNIES are much better. Partners' RUBY is new (94). Vintage wines are at least adequate – some of the old vintages were superlative (**55' 57 58 60' 62' 63' 65 66 67 68 70' 72 75 77 78 80 82 85 88**). Of the sherries, Medium Dry AMONTILLADO is top-seller, Don FINO is vg; also two excellent CREAM SHERRIES: Armada, and rare de luxe Royal Corregidor. Also shippers of MADEIRA since 1790 (elegant RAINWATER, fine Rich).

Sanlúcar de Barrameda Seaside sherry town (see Manzanilla).

Sercial MADEIRA grape for driest of the island's wines – a supreme aperitif. (See panel on the next page.)

Smith Woodhouse Port firm founded in 1784, now owned by the Symington family (see Dow). Gould Campbell is a subsidiary. Relatively light and easy wines incl Old Lodge Tawny, Lodge Reserve VINTAGE CHARACTER (widely sold in USA). Vintages (v fine): **60 63' 66' 70' 75 77' 80 83 85' 91 92**. Gould Campbell Vintages: **60 63 66 70 75 77 80 83 85 91**.

Solera System used in making both sherry and (in modified form) MADEIRA, also some port. It consists of topping up progressively more mature barrels with slightly younger wine of the same sort, the object being to attain continuity in the final wine. Most sherries when sold are blends of several solera wines.

Soto, José de Best known for inventing PONCHE, this family firm, which now belongs to the former owner of RUMASA, José María Ruiz Mateos, also makes a range of good sherries, esp the delicate FINO.

Tawny Style of port aged for many yrs in wood (VINTAGE PORT is aged in bottle) until tawny in colour. Many of the best are 20-yrs-old. Low-price tawnies are blends of red and white ports. Taste the difference.

Taylor, Fladgate & Yeatman (Taylor's) Perhaps the best port shippers, esp for full rich long-lived VINTAGE wine and TAWNIES of stated age (40-yr-old, 20-yr-old, etc). Their VARGELLAS estate is said to give Taylor's its distinctive scent of violets. Vintages: 55' 60' 63' 66' 70' 75 77' 80 83' 85' 92'. QUINTA DE VARGELLAS is shipped unblended in certain (lesser) years (67 72 74 76 78 82 84 86 87 88 91). Also now Terra Feita single-QUINTA wine (82 86 87 88 91). Their LBV is also better than most.

Since January '93, madeiras labelled Sercial, Verdelho, Bual or Malmsey must be at least 85% from that grape variety. The majority, made using the chameleon Tinta Negra Mole grape, which vinified similarly easily imitates each of these grape styles, may only be called Seco (Dry), Meio Seco (Medium Dry), Meio Doce (Medium Rich) or Doce (Rich) respectively. Meanwhile replanting is building up supplies of the (rare) classic varieties.

Terry, Fernando A de Magnificent BODEGAS at PUERTO DE SANTA MARÍA, now part of Allied-Domecq. Makers of Maruja MANZANILLA and a range of popular brandies. The blending and bottling of all HARVEY'S sherries is carried out at the vast modern El Pino plant.

Tio Pepe The most famous of FINO sherries (see Gonzalez Byass).

Valdespino Famous family-owned BODEGA at JEREZ, owner of the Inocente v'yd and making the excellent aged FINO of that name. Tío Diego is their dry AMONTILLADO, Solera 1842 an OLOROSO, Don Tomás their best amontillado. Matador is the name of their popular range. In the US, where their sherries rank No 3 in volume of sales, they are still sold under the name of 'Hartley & Gibson'.

Vargellas, Quinta de Hub of the TAYLOR's empire, giving its very finest ports. The label for in-between vintages. See Taylor Fladgate & Yeatman.

Verdelho MADEIRA grape for fairly dry but soft wine without the piquancy of SERCIAL. A pleasant aperitif and a good all-purpose wine. Some glorious old vintage wines. (See panel above.)

Vesuvio, Quinta de Enormous 19th C FERREIRA estate in the high DOURO. Bought '89 by Symington family. 130 acres planted. Esp 89 90 91 92.

Vintage Character Somewhat misleading term used for a good quality, full and meaty port like a first-class RUBY, made by a version of the SOLERA system. Lacks the splendid 'nose' of VINTAGE PORT.

Vintage Port The best port of exceptional vintages is bottled after only 2 yrs in wood and matures very slowly for up to 20 or more in bottle. Always leaves a heavy deposit and therefore needs decanting.

Warre The oldest of all British port shippers (since 1670), owned by the Symington family (see Dow) since 1905. Fine elegant long-maturing vintage wines, a good TAWNY (Nimrod), VINTAGE CHARACTER (Warrior), and excellent LBV. Their single-v'yd Quinta da Cavadinha is a new departure (78 79 82 84 86 87 88 89 90 92). Vintages: 55' 58 60 63' 66' 70 75 77' 80 83 85' 91.

White Port Port made of white grapes, golden in colour. Formerly made sweet, now more often dry: a fair aperitif but a heavy one.

Williams & Humbert Famous first-class sherry BODEGA, now owned by the Dutch firm of Bols. Dry Sack (medium AMONTILLADO) is its best-seller; Pando an excellent FINO; Canasta CREAM and Walnut BROWN are good in their class; Dos Cortados is its famous dry old OLOROSO. Also the famous Gran Duque de Alba brandy acquired from DIEZ-MERITO.

Wisdom & Warter Not a magic formula for free wine, but an old BODEGA (controlled by GONZALEZ BYASS) with good sherries, especially AMONTILLADO Tizón and v rare Solera. Also FINO Olivar.

Switzerland

Switzerland has no truly great wines, but almost all (especially whites) are enjoyable and satisfying – and very expensive. It has some of the world's most efficient and productive vineyards; costs are high and nothing less is viable. All the most important are in French-speaking areas, along the south-facing slopes of the upper Rhône Valley and Lake Geneva, respectively the Valais and the Vaud. Wines from German- and Italian-speaking zones are mostly drunk locally. Wines are known by place, grape names and legally controlled type names and are usually drunk young. 1988 saw the establishment of a Swiss cantonal and federal appellation system, but controlled indication of orgin is still under discussion.

Recent vintages
1994 Summer close to perfect; but rainy harvest.
1993 Classic year: wines better than expected.
1992 A hot summer with particularly high yields in the east; a rainy harvest in the south.

Aargau Wine-growing canton in E Switz (946 acres). Best for fragrant RIES-SILVANER, rich BLAUBURGUNDER and pleasant country wines.
Aigle Vaud r w ★★→★★★ Well-known for elegant whites and supple reds.
Aligoté White Burgundy variety doing well in the VALAIS and GENEVA.
Amigne Trad VALAIS white grape, esp of VETROZ. Full-bodied tasty, often sweet.
Ardon Valais r w ★★→★★★ Wine commune between SION and MARTIGNY.
Arvine Old VALAIS white grape (also 'Petite Arvine'): dry and sweet, elegant long-lasting wines with characteristic salty finish. Best in SIERRE, SION.
Basel Second-largest Swiss town surrounded almost exclusively by vines. Best: RIES-SILVANER, BLAUBURG'R, CHASSELAS, esp from city v'yd Riehen.
Beerliwein Originally wine of destemmed BLAUBURG'R (E). Today name for wine fermented on skins traditionally rather than in pressure tanks.
Bern Swiss capital and canton of same name. V'yds in W (BIELERSEE: CHASSELAS, PINOT, SPEZIALITATEN) and E (Thunersee: BLAUBURGUNDER, RIES-SILVANER); 625 acres. Prized by Germanic Swiss.
Béroche, La Neuchâtel p w ★→★★ Wine-growing region on Lake Neuchâtel incl communes of Gorgier, Fresens, St-Aubin, Vaumarcus.
Bex Vaud r w ★★ CHABLAIS appellation, esp for red wines.
Bielersee r p w ★→★★ Wine region on N shore of the Bielersee (dry light CHASSELAS, PINOT N) and at the foot of Jolimont (SPEZIALITATEN).

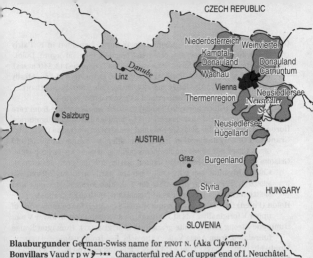

Blauburgunder German-Swiss name for PINOT N. (Aka Clevner.)

Bonvillars Vaud r p w ?→★★ Characterful red AC of upper end of L Neuchâtel.

Bündner Herrschaft Grisons r p w ★★→★★★ Best E Swiss region incl top villages: Fläsch, Jenins, Maienfeld, Malans. Serious BLAUB'R ripens esp well due to warm Foehn wind, cask-aged vg. Also CHARD, SPEZIALITÄTEN.

Calamin Vaud w ★★→★★★ LAVAUX v'yds next to DEZALEY: lush fragrant whites.

Chablais Vaud r w ★★→★★★ Robust full-bodied reds, whites from between L Geneva and Rhône Valley. Best villages: AIGLE, BEX, Ollon, VILLENEUVE, YVORNE, and Rhône-side Port Valais, Vouvry, Vionnaz, Monthey.

Chamoson Valais r w ★★→★★★ Largest VALAIS commune, esp for SILVANER.

Chardonnay Long est'd in French Switzerland, now also in other parts.

Chasselas (Gutedel) Top white grape of W: neutral in flavour, so takes on local character: elegant (GENEVA), refined full (VAUD), potent racy (VALAIS), pleasantly sp (Bienne, L Neuchâtel, Murtensee). In E only in BASEL.

Completer Native white grape, only in GRISONS. Aromatic generous wines which keep well. Also Beerenauslese types from BÜNDNER HERRSCHAFT. ('Complet' was monk's final daily prayer and occasion to drink this wine.)

Cornalin Local VALAIS speciality; dark spicy v strong red. Best: SALGESCH, SIERRE.

Cortaillod Neuchâtel r (w) ★★ Small village S of Lake: esp PINOT N, OEIL DE P.

Côte, La Vaud r p w ★→★★★ Largest VAUD wine area, on N shore of Lake Geneva. Whites with elegant finesse; fruity harmonious reds. Esp from Begnins, Coteau de Vincy, Féchy, Morges etc.

Côtes de l'Orbe Vaud r p w ★→★★ N VAUD appellation between NEUCHATEL and Lake Geneva esp for light fruity reds .

Dézaley Vaud w (r) ★★★ Famous LAVAUX v'yd on slopes above L Geneva, once tended by Cistercian monks. Unusually potent CHASSELAS, develops esp after ageing. Red Dézaley is a GAMAY-PINOT N-MERLOT-SYRAH rarity.

Dôle Valais r ★★→★★★ Appellation for PINOT N, can also be blend of (at least 80%) PINOT/GAMAY (PN must predominate): full supple, often vg. Lightly pink Dôle Blanche is pressed immediately after harvest. Eg from MARTIGNY, SIERRE, SION, VETROZ etc.

Epesses Vaud w (r) ★★→★★★ LAVAUX appellation: supple full-bodied whites.

Ermitage Alias the Marsanne grape; a VALAIS SPEZIALITAT. Concentrated full-bodied dry white, s'times with residual sugar. Esp from FULLY, SION.

Federweisser E Swiss name for white wine from BLAUBURGUNDER.

Fendant Valais w ★→★★★ VALAIS appellation for CHASSELAS. Wide range of wines. Better ones now use village names only (FULLY, SION, etc).

Flétri/Mi-flétri Late-harvested grapes from which sweet and slightly sweet wine (respectively) is made; SPEZIALITAT in VALAIS.

Fribourg Small W Swiss region (279 acres, nr Jura). Esp for CHASSELAS, PINOT N, GAMAY, SPECIALITES from VULLY, Lake Murten, S NEUCHATEL.

Fully Valais r w ★★→★★★ Village nr MARTIGNY: excellent ERMITAGE and GAMAY.

145

Gamay Red Beaujolais grape abounds in W but is forbidden in E. Fairly thin wine. 100% in GENEVA, otherwise blended. (See Salvagnin, Dôle).

Geneva Capital of, and W Swiss wine canton; the 3rd largest (3,340 acres). Key areas: MANDEMENT, Entre Arve et Rhône, Entre Arve et Lac. Mostly CHASSELAS, GAMAY. Also lately RIES-SILV, CHARD, Cab, PINOT, good ALIGOTE.

Gewürztraminer Grown in Switzerland as a SPECIALITAT variety.

Glacier, Vin du (Gletscherwein) Fabled oxidized wooded white from rare Rèze grape of Val d'Anniviers; offered by thimbleful to visiting dignitaries.

Goron Valais r ★ AC for pleasant reds and DOLE that fails to make the grade.

Grand Cru Quality designation. Implication differs by canton: in VALAIS and GENEVA used where set requirements fulfilled, in VAUD, for any top wine.

Grisons (Graubünden) Mountain canton, partly in E (BUNDNER HERRSCHAFT, Churer Rheintal; esp BLAUBURGUNDER) and partly in TICINO (Misox, esp MERLOT). 997 acres, primarily for red, also RIESLING-SILVANER and SPEZIALITATEN. Tiny quantities of Puschlav wine (Italian grapes).

Heida (Païen) Old VALAIS white grape (Jura's Savagnin) for country wine of upper V (originally v'yds at 1,000 m+), so successful now in lower V too.

Humagne Strong native white grape (VALAIS SPEZIALITAT). Humagne Rouge (unrelated, from Aosta Valley) also sold. Esp from CHAMOSON, LEYTRON.

Landwein (Vin de pays) Trad light easy white and esp red BLAUB'R from E.

Lausanne Capital of VAUD. No longer with v'yds in town area, but long-time owner of classics: Abbaye de Mont, Château Rochefort (LA COTE); Clos des Moines, Clos des Abbayes, Dom de Burignon (LAVAUX). Pricey.

Lavaux Vaud w (r) ★→★★★ Scenic wine region on N shore of Lake Geneva. Delicate refined whites, good reds. Best from CALAMIN, Chardonne, DEZALEY, EPESSES, Lutry, St-Saphorin, VEVEY-MONTREUX, Villette.

Légèrement doux Any Swiss wine not completely dry must say this.

Leytron Valais r w ★★→★★★ Commune nr SION/MARTIGNY, esp Le Grand Brûlé.

Mandement r w ★→★★ Largest Geneva wine area incl Satigny; one of best.

Martigny Valais r w Lower VALAIS commune esp for HUMAGNE rouge.

Merlot Grown in Italian Switzerland (TICINO) since 1907 (after phylloxera destroyed local varieties): aromatic, soft. Also used with Cab. See Viti.

Mont d'Or, Domaine du Valais w s/sw ★★→★★★ Well-sited property nr SION: rich concentrated demi-sec wine, notable SILVANER. Controlled by SCHENK.

Morges Vaud r p w ★→★★ Large LA COTE/VAUD AOC: CHASSELAS, fruity reds.

Muscat Grown in VALAIS as a SPEZIALITAT variety.

Neuchâtel City and canton on N shore of lake (W Switz). V'yds from L Neuchâtel to BIELERSEE. Mainly CHASSELAS: fragrant lively (sur lie, sp). Also (increasingly) good PINOT N (esp OEIL DE PERDRIX), PINOT GR, CHARD.

Nostrano Word meaning 'ours', applied to red wine of TICINO, made from native and Italian grapes (Bondola, Freisa, Barbera, etc).

Oeil de Perdrix Pale PINOT rosé. Esp (originally) NEUCHATEL'S; also VALAIS, VAUD.

Perlan Name for usually thin CHASSELAS grown in the GENEVA area.

Pinot Blanc (Weissburgunder) Recent, full-bodied and elegant Swiss wines.

Pinot Gris (Malvoisie) Widely planted white grape for dry and residually sweet wines. Makes v fine late-gathered in VALAIS (called Malvoisie).

Pinot Noir (Blauburgunder) Top red grape. Esp: BUNDNER H, NEUCHATEL, VALAIS.

Rauschling Old white ZURICH grape; esp for discreet fruit, elegant acidity.

Riesling (Petit Rhin) Mainly in the VALAIS. Excellent botrytis wines.

Riesling-Silvaner Swiss for Müller-THURGAU (E's top white; SPECIALITE in W). Typically elegant wines with nutmeg aroma and some acidity.

St-Gallen E wine canton nr L Constance. Esp for BLAUBURG'R (full-bodied), RIES-SILVANER, SPEZIALITATEN. Incl Rhine Valley, Oberland, upper L Zürich.

Salquenen Valais r w ★→★★ Village nr SIERRE. First to use 'GRAND CRU'.

Salvagnin Vaud r ★→★★ GAMAY and/or PINOT N appellation. (See also Dôle.)

Schaffhausen E Swiss canton and town on R Rhine. Esp BLAUBURGUNDER; also some RIESLING-SILVANER and SPEZIALITATEN (eg Perle von Alzey).

Schafis Bern r p w ★→★★ Top BIELERSEE commune and wines of its N shore.

Schenk Europe-wide wine giant, founded and based in Rolle (VAUD). Owns firms in Burgundy, Bordeaux, Germany, Italy, Spain.

Sierre Valais r w ∗∗→∗∗∗ Sunny resort and famous wine town. Known for Fendant, PINOT N, ERMITAGE, Malvoisie. Vg DOLE.

Sion Valais r w ∗∗→∗∗∗ Capital/wine centre of VALAIS. Esp FENDANT de Sion.

Silvaner (Johannisberg, Gros Rhin) White grape esp in hot VALAIS v'yds. Heady, spicy: some with residual sweetness, some vg Spätlese.

Spezialitäten (Spécialités) Wines of unusual grapes: vanishing local Gwass, Elbling, Bondola, etc, or modish Chenin Bl, Sauv, Cab (first grown experimentally). Eg VALAIS: 43 of its 47 varieties are considered 'spezialitäten'.

Süssdruck Dry rosé/bright red wine: grapes pressed before fermentation.

Thurgau E Swiss canton beside Bodensee (632 acres). Top wines from Warth, Seebachtal, Thur, Hüttwilen, Rhine Valley, S shore of the Untersee. Esp BLAUBURGUNDER, also good RIES-SILVANER (ie Müller-T, born in the region).

Ticino Italian-speaking S Switzerland (with Misox), growing mainly MERLOT (good from mountainous Sopraceneri region) and SPEZIALITÄTEN. Trying out Cab (cask-matured Bordeaux style), Sauv, Sém, Chard, Merlot rosé.

Valais Rhône Valley from German-speaking upper-V to French lower-V. Nr perfect climatic conditions. Wide range: 47 grape varieties: FENDANT, SILVANER, GAMAY, PINOT N, plus many SPECIALTIES. Esp white. See Fendent.

Vaud Region of L Geneva and the Rhône. W Switzerland's second largest wine canton incl CHABLAIS, LA COTE, LAVAUX and appellations Bonvillars, Côtes de l'Orbe, VULLY, CHASSELAS stronghold. Also GAMAY, PINOT N etc.

Vétroz Valais w r ∗∗→∗∗∗ Top village nr SION, esp famous for AMIGNE.

Vevey-Montreux Vaud r w ∗∗ Up-and-coming appellation of LAVAUX. Famous wine festival held about every 30 years; next in 1999.

Villeneuve Vaud w (r) ∗∗→∗∗∗ Nr L Geneva: powerful yet refined whites.

Vispertal Valais w (r) ∗→∗∗ Upper VALAIS v'yds esp for SPECIALITIES.

Vully Vaud w (r) ∗→∗∗ Refreshing white from L Murten/FRIBOURG area.

Winzerwy Quality label (E Swiss) for cantons AARGAU, Appenzell, BASEL, BERN, GRAUBUNDEN, ST-GALLEN, SCHAFFHAUSEN, THURGAU and ZURICH.

Zürich Capital of largest E wine canton (same name). Mostly BLAUBURG-UNDER; also PINOT GR and GEWURZ, and esp RIES-SILVANER and RAUSCHLING.

Austria

Austria has now emerged as a vigorous, well-regulated producer of hearty white wines, including aromatic ones in the modern German style (but more potent), liquorous ones closer to Sauternes, and increasingly fine 'international' sorts. Her reds (20% of vineyards) are just starting to make an international reputation but this will come. New laws, passed in 1985 and revised for the 1993 vintage, include curbs on yields (Germany please copy) and impose higher levels of ripeness for each category than their German counterparts. Many regional names, introduced under the 1985 law, are still unfamiliar outside Austria. This is a country to explore.

Recent vintages

1994 Unusually hot summer and fine autumn resulted in v ripe grapes. Another excellent vintage.

1993 Frost damage caused a smaller than average yield which produced excellent wines.

1992 Extremely hot summer may have led to acidity problems in some areas. Very good wines from the Wachau, Kamptal-Donauland and Styria. Good red wine year (esp Burgenland).

1991 Good to average quality along with a few vg wines from Burgenland.

1990 One of the best vintages of the last 50 yrs.

Ausbruch PRADIKAT wine (v sweet) between Beerenauslese and Trockenbeerenauslese in quality. Traditionally produced in RUST.

Ausg'steckt ('hung up') HEURIGEN are not open all year. To show potential visitors wine is being served a green bush is hung up above the door.

Bergwein Legal classification for wines made from grapes grown on slopes with an incline of over 26%.

Blauburger Austrian red grape variety. A cross between BLAUER PORTUGIESER and BLAUFRANKISCH. Dark-coloured but light-bodied.

Blauer Burgunder (Pinot N) A rarity. Vintages fluctuate greatly. Best in BURGENLAND, KAMPTAL, THERMENREGION (BRUNDLMAYER, Fischer, STIEGELMAR).

Blauer Portugieser Light, fruity wines to drink slightly chilled when young. Mostly made for local consumption. Top producers: Fischer, Lust.

Blauer Wildbacher Red grape used to make SCHILCHER wines.

Blauer Zweigelt BLAUFRANKISCH-ST-LAURENT cross: high yields, rich colour. Top producers (Heinrich, Pfaffl, Pöckl, UMATHUM) have gained it recognition.

Blaufränkisch (Lemberger in Germany, Kékfrankos in Hungary) Austria's most widely planted red grape, esp in MITTELBURGENLAND for peppery acidity, fruity taste of cherries. Often blended with Cab. Best: GESELLMANN, Iby, IGLER, Krutzler, Nittnaus, Tibor Szemes, E TRIEBAUMER, WENINGER.

Bouvier Indigenous grape, producing light wines with low alcohol but plenty of aroma, esp good for Beeren- and Trockenbeerenauslese.

Bründlmayer, Willi r w sp **→**→**** 90 92 93 94   Leading LANGENLOIS-KAMPTAL estate. Vg wines: both local (RIES, GRUNER V) and international (CHARD, red) styles. Also Austria's best Sekt.

Burgenland Province and wine area (50,000 acres) in E next to Hungarian border. Warm climate. Ideal conditions, esp for botrytis wines near NEUSIEDLER SEE, also reds. Four wine regions: MITTELBURGENLAND, NEUSIEDLERSEE, NEUSIEDLERSEE-HUGELLAND and SUDBURGENLAND.

Buschenschank The same as HEURIGE; often a country cousin.

Cabernet Sauvignon Increasingly cultivated in Austria; used esp in blends.

Carnuntum r w   Wine region since '94, E of Vienna, bordered by the Danube to the north. Best producers: Glatzer, Pitnauer.

Chardonnay Increasingly grown, mainly barrique-aged. Also trad in STYRIA as 'MORILLON' (unoaked): strong fruit taste, lively acidity. Esp BRUNDL-MAYER, Loimer, MALAT, SATTLER, STIEGELMAR, TEMENT, Topf, WIENINGER.

Deutschkreutz r (w)   MITTELBURGENLAND red wine area, esp for BLAUFRANKISCH.

Donauland (Danube) w (r)   Wine region since '94, just W of Vienna. Incl KLOSTERNEUBURG and Wagram regions S of Danube. Mainly whites, esp GRUNER VELTLINER. Best producers: Chorherren KLOSTERNEUBURG, Leth, Neumayer, Wimmer-Cerny, Zimmermann.

Dürnstein w   Wine centre of the WACHAU with famous ruined castle. Mainly GRUNER V, RIES. Esp from FREIE WEINGARTNER WACHAU, Mittelbach, Schmidt.

Eisenstadt r w dr sw Capital of BURGENLAND and historic seat of Esterházy family. Top producers: Barmherzige Brüder, Esterházy, Tinhof.

Falkenstein w Wine centre in eastern Weinviertel nr Czech border. Good GRUNER VELTLINER. Best producers: Jauk, Luckner, SALOMON.

Federspiel Medium quality level of the VINEA WACHAU categories, roughly corresponding to Kabinett. Fruity, elegant wines.

Feiler-Artinger r w sw **→**→**** 90 91 92 93 94   Vg RUST estate: top PRADIKATS.

Fels am Wagram r w   Large wine region with loess terraces in DONAULAND. Best producers: Leth, Wimmer-Cerny.

Freie Weingärtner Wachau w (r) *→→**** 91 92 93 94   Important wine-growers' cooperative in DURNSTEIN. Excellent GRUNER VELTLINER, RIES.

Gamlitz w   Largest, oldest region of S STYRIA: Lackner-Tinnacher, SATTLER.

Gemischter Satz A blend of grapes (mostly white) grown, harvested and vinified together. Traditional wine, still served in HEURIGEN.

Gesellmann, Engelbert r (w) **→→**** 90 92 93 94   Estate in DEUTSCH-KREUTZ. Vg red and white: both traditional and international styles.

Gols r w dr sw   Largest BURGENLAND wine region (N shore of NEUSIEDLER SEE). Best producers: Beck, HEINRICH, Leitner, Nittnaus, Renner, STIEGELMAR.

Grüner Veltliner 'National' white grape (over a third of total v'yd area). Fruity, racy, lively young wines. Distinguished age-worthy Spätlesen. Best producers: BRUNDLMAYER, FREIE WEING'R WACHAU, HIRTZBERGER, Högel, KNOLL, MANTLER, NIKOLAIHOF, Pfaffl, F X PICHLER, PRAGER, Schmelz, Walzer.

G'spritzter Popular refreshing summer drink, usually white wine-based; made sparkling by adding soda or mineral water. Esp in HEURIGEN.

Gumpoldskirchen w r dr sw   Resort village S of Vienna, famous for HEURIGEN. Centre of THERMENREGION. Distinctive wines from ZIERFANDLER and ROTGIPFLER grapes. Best producers: Biegler, Schellmann.

Heinrich Gernot r w dr sw ★★→★★★ 90 91 92 93 94   Young modern estate in GOLS with Pannobile and (esp) red Gabarinza labels.

Heurige Wine of the most recent harvest, called 'new wine' for one yr, then classified as 'old'. Heurigen are wine houses where growers-cum-patrons serve wine by glass/bottle with simple local food – an institution, esp in VIENNA. (First licence granted by Emperor Josef II in 1784.)

Hirtzberger, Franz w ★★★→★★★★ 90 91 92 93 94   Leading producer with 22 acres at Spitz an der Donau, WACHAU. Esp RIES, GRUNER VELTLINER, NEUBURGER; other grapes vg too.

Horitschon MITTELBURGENLAND region for reds. Best: Anton Iby, WENINGER.

Igler, Hans r ★★→★★★ 90 92 93 94   Top DEUTSCHKREUTZ estate; pioneer reds.

Illmitz w (r) dr sw   SEEWINKEL region famous for Beeren- and Trockenbeerenauslese. Best from KRACHER, Haider, Heiss, Alois und Helmut Lang, Opitz.

Jamek, Josef w ★→★★★ 91 92 93 94   Well-known estate and restaurant at Joching in the WACHAU. Pioneer of dry whites since the '50s.

Jurtschitsch/Sonnhof w (r) dr (sw) ★→★★★ 92 93 94   Domaine run by three brothers: outstanding whites (RIES, GRUNER VELTLINER, CHARD).

Kamptal r w   Wine region since '94, along R Kamp. Top v'yds: LANGENLOIS, STRASS, Zöbing. Best growers: BRUNDLMAYER, Dolle, Ehn, Hiedler, Hirsch, JURTSCHITSCH, Loimer, METTERNICH-SANDOR, Topf.

Kattus ★→★★★   Producer of traditional Sekt in VIENNA.

Kellergassen Picturesque alleyways lined with wine presses and cellars, devoted exclusively to production, storage and consumption of wine, situated outside the town, typical of the WEINVIERTEL region.

Klöch w   W STYRIA wine town famous for Traminer. Best from Stürgkh.

Kloster Und Wine tasting centre in a restored Capuchin monastery near KREMS, run by ERICH SALOMON.

Klosterneuburg r w   Wine district rich in tradition, N of VIENNA, with a famous Benedictine monastery and a wine college founded in 1860. Best producers: Chorherren Klosterneuburg, Zimmermann.

KMW Abbreviation for 'Klosterneuburger Mostwaage' (must level), the unit used in Austria to measure the sugar content in grape juice.

Knoll, Emmerich w ★★→★★★ 91 92 93 94   V traditional estate in Loiben, WACHAU, producing showpiece wines from GRUNER VELTLINER and RIES.

Kollwentz-Römerhof w r dr (sw) ★★→★★★ 90 92 93 94   Innovative wine producer in Grosshöflein nr EISENSTADT: Sauv Bl, Eiswein and reds.

Kracher, Alois w (r) dr (sw) ★★→★★★★ 81 89 90 92 93 94   First class small ILLMITZ producer; speciality: PRADIKATS, some barrique-aged, others not.

Krems w (r) dr (sw)   Ancient town, W of VIENNA. Capital of KREMSTAL. Best from Aigner, Ditz, SALOMON, Weingut Stadt Krems, Walzer, WINZER KREMS.

Kremstal w (r)   Wine region since '94 for GRUNER V and RIES esp. Top growers: Ditz, Geyerhof, MALAT, MANTLER, Nigl, SALOMON, W Stadt Krems, Unger.

Langenlois r w   Major wine town and region in KAMPTAL with 50,000 acres of vines. Best producers: BRUNDLMAYER, Ehn, Hiedler, JURTSCHITSCH.

Lenz Moser Major producer nr KREMS, now in 5th generation. Lenz Moser III invented a high vine system. Also incl wines from Schlossweingut Malteser Ritterorden (wine estate of the Knights of Malta) in Mailberg, WEINVIERTEL and Klosterkeller Siegendorf in BURGENLAND.

Loiben w   Wine region in lower, wider part of Danube Valley (WACHAU) where conditions are ideal for RIES and GRUNER VELTLINER. Best from Alzinger, Dinstlgut Loiben, KNOLL, Mittelbach, FRANZ X PICHLER.

Malat, Gerald w r sp ★★→★★★ 90 91 92 93 94   Modern producer in Furth, S of KREMS: vg trad and 'international' wines. Interesting classic sparkling.

Mantler, Josef w ★★→★★★ 86 90 92 93   Leading trad estate in Gedersdorf nr KREMS. Vg RIES, GRUNER VELTLINER, CHARD, and rare red Veltliner.

Mayer, Franz w With 90 acres, the largest producer in VIENNA. Traditional jug wines (at picturesque HEURIGE Beethovenhaus – yes, he drank here), plus excellent 'ancient-vintage' RIESLING.

Messwein Mass wine: must have ecclesiastical approval and natural must.

Metternich-Sándor, Schlossweingüter w (r) *→** Large wine estate in STRASS; 173 acres of v'yd jointly run with Adelsgütern Starhemberg, Abensberg-Traun and Khevenhüller-Metsch estates.

Mittelburgenland r (w) dr (sw) Wine region on Hungarian border protected by 3 hill ranges. Large quantities of appellation-controlled red (esp BLAUFRANKISCH). Producers: GESELLMANN, Iby, IGLER, Szemes, Weninger.

Mörbisch r w dr sw Region on W shore of NEUSIEDLER SEE. Schindler is good.

Morillon Name given in STYRIA to CHARDONNAY.

Müller-Thurgau See Riesling-Sylvaner.

Muskat-Ottonel Fragrant, often dry, whites; also interesting PRADIKATS.

Muskateller Rare aromatic grape, recently popular again as aperitif. Best in STYRIA and WACHAU. Top growers: Gross, HIRTZBERGER, JAMEK, Lackner-Tinnacher, F X PICHLER, POLZ, SATTLER.

Neuburger Indigenous white grape: nutty flavour; mainly in the WACHAU (delicate flowery), in the THERMENREGION (mellow, well-developed) and in N BURGENLAND (strong, full). Best from Alphart, HIRTZBERGER, Pöckl.

Neusiedler See V shallow (max 1.5m deep) BURGENLAND lake on Hungarian border. Warm temperatures, autumn mists encourage botrytis. Gives name to wine regions of NEUSIEDLERSEE-HUGELLAND and NEUSIEDLERSEE.

Neusiedlersee r w dr sw Region N and E of NEUSIEDLER SEE. Best growrs: Beck, HEINRICH, KRACHER, Nittnaus, Pöckl, UMATHUM.

Neusiedlersee-Hügelland r w dr sw Wine region W of NEUSIEDLER SEE based around OGGAU, RUST and MORBISCH on the lake shores, and EISENSTADT in the foothills of the Leitha Mts. Best producers: FEILER-ARTINGER, KOLLWENTZ, Mad, Prieler, Schröck, ERNST TRIEBAUMER.

Niederösterreich (Lower Austria) With 58% of Austria's v'yds: CARNUNTUM, DONAULAND, KAMPTAL, KREMSTAL, THERMENREGION, WACHAU, WEINVIERTEL.

Nikolaihof w *→*** 90 91 92 93 94 Mautern-Wachau estate: top RIES, GRUNER V.

Nussdorf VIENNA district famous for HEURIGEN and vg Ried Nussberg.

Oggau Wine region on the W shore of NEUSIEDLER SEE.

Pichler, Franz X w ***→**** 90 91 92 93 94 Top RIES, GV, esp Kellerberg.

Polz, Erich and Walter w *→** 91 92 93 94 South STYRIAN (Weinstrasse) growers with top Hochgrassnitzberg label for Sauv and CHARD.

Prädikatswein Quality graded wines from Spätlese upwards (Spätlese, Auslese, Eiswein, Strohwein, Beerenauslese, AUSBRUCH and Trocken-beerenauslese). See Germany, page 103.

Prager, Franz w **→*** 90 91 92 93 94 Together with JOSEF JAMEK, pioneer of WACHAU dry white. His son-in-law Anton Bodenstein carries on the tradition developing new varieties and great PRADIKAT wines.

Retz r w Important region in W WEINVIERTEL. Esp Weinbauschule Retz.

Ried Single v'yd: when named on the label it is usually a good one.

Riesling On its own always means German RIES. WELSCHRIES (unrelated) is labelled as such. Top growers: BRUNDLMAYER, FREIE W WACHAU, HIRTZBERGER, Högl, KNOLL, MANTLER, Nigl, NIKOLAIHOF, F X PICHLER, PRAGER, Schmelz.

Riesling-Sylvaner Name used for Müller-T, which accounts for about 10% of Austria's grapes. Best producers: HIRTZBERGER, JURTSCHITSCH.

Rotgipfler Fragrant, indigenous grape of THERMENREGION. With ZIERFANDLER makes lively, interesting wine. Esp Biegler, Schellmann, Stadelmann.

Rust w r dr sw BURGENLAND region, famous since 17th C for AUSBRUCH. Now also for red and dry white. Esp from FEILER-ARTINGER, Schandl, Heidi Schröck, ERNST TRIEBAUMER, Paul Triebaumer, Wenzel.

St-Laurent Traditional red wine grape with cherry aroma, believed to be related to Pinot N. Esp from Fischer, Mad, STIEGELMAR, UMATHUM.

Salomon-Undhof w Vg producer of RIES, WEISSBURGUNDER, Traminer in KREMS. Erich Salomon also owns/runs KLOSTER UND wine tasting centre.

Sattler, Willi w **→*** 90 92 93 94 Top S STYRIA grower. Esp Sauv, MORILLON.

Schilcher Rosé wine from indigenous BLAUER WILDBACHER grapes (high acidity). Speciality of W STYRIA. Vg: Klug, Lukas, Reiterer, Strohmeier.

Schlumberger Largest sparkling wine maker in Austria (VIENNA); bottle-fermented according to their own 'Méthode Schlumberger'.

Seewinkel ('Lake corner'.) Name given to the S part of NEUSIEDLERSEE incl Apetlon, ILLMITZ and Podersdorf. Ideal conditions for botrytis.

Servus w BURGENLAND everyday light and mild white wine brand.

Smaragd Highest quality category of VINEA WACHAU, similar to Spätlese.

Spätrot-Rotgipfler Typical THERMENREGION (Spätrot and ROTGIPFLER) wine.

Spitz an der Donau w W WACHAU region: vg individual microclimate: fine from Tausendeimerberg, Singerriedel. Esp HIRTZBERGER, Högl, Lagler.

Steinfeder VINEA WACHAU quality category for light, fragrant wines.

Stiegelmar, Georg w r dr sw *→*** 90 91 92 93 94 GOLS grower: consistent for quality wine and unusual specialities.

Strass w (r) Wine centre in the KAMPTAL region for good Qualität white wines. Best producers: Dolle, METTERNICH-SANDOR, Topf.

Styria (Steiermark) The southernmost wine region of Austria. Its Qualitätswein are developing real prestige. Incl SUDSTEIERMARK, SUD-OSTSTEIERMARK and WESTSTEIERMARK (S, SW and W Styria).

Süd-Oststeiermark (SW Styria) w (r) STYRIAN region with islands of v'yds. Best producers: Neumeister, Platzer, Stürgkh, Winkler-Hermaden.

Südburgenland r w Small S BURGENLAND wine region: good red wines. Best producers: Körper-Faulhammer, Krutzler, Wachter, Wiesler.

Südsteiermark (S Styria) w Best wine region of STYRIA: v popular whites (MORILLON, MUSKATELLER, WELSCHRIESLING and Sauv Bl). Top producers: Gross, Lackner-Tinnacher, Muster, POLZ, SATTLER, TEMENT, Wohlmuth.

Tement, Manfred w **→*** 90 92 93 94 Vg estate on S STYRIA Wein-strasse for traditional ('Steirisch Klassik') and international wines.

Thermenregion r w dr sw Wine/hot-springs region, S of VIENNA. Indigenous grapes (eg ZIERFANDLER, ROTGIPFLER) and good reds. Main centres: Baden, GUMPOLDSKIRCHEN Tattendorf, Traiskirchen. Top producers: Alphart, Biegler, Fischer, Reinisch, Schafler, Schellmann, Stadelmann.

Triebaumer, Ernst r (w) dr sw **→*** 90 91 92 93 94 One of the best red wine producers in Austria (RUST). Top label: Mariental.

Umathum, Josef w r dr sw **→*** 90 91 92 93 94 Distinguished NEUSIEDLERSEE producer for vg reds; whites also from Burgunder grapes.

Vienna w (r) The Austrian capital is a wine region in its own right (1,800 v'yd acres in suburbs). Simple lively wines served in HEURIGEN are increasingly well-made: Breyer, MAYER, Schilling, WIENINGER.

Vinea Wachau WACHAU appellation started by winemakers in '83 with three categories of wine: STEINFEDER, FEDERSPIEL and SMARAGD.

Wachau w Danube wine region W of KREMS: some of Austria's best wines, incl RIES, GRUNER V. Top producers: Alzinger, HIRTZBERGER, Högl, JAMEK, KNOLL, Lagler, NIKOLAIHOF, F X PICHLER, Pichler, PRAGER, Schmelz, Schmidl.

Weinviertel (Wine Quarter) w (r) Largest Austrian wine region, between the Danube and the Czech border. Mostly light refreshing whites esp from Falkenstein, Poysdorf, RETZ. Best producers: Hardegg, Jauk, Luckner, Lust, Malteser Ritterorden, Pfaffl, Taubenschuss, Zull.

Weissburgunder (Pinot Bl) Ubiquitous: good dry wines and PRADIKATS. Esp Beck, Fischer, Gross, HEINRICH, HIRTZBERGER, Neumayer, Steiner/Podersdorf.

Welschriesling White grape, not related to RIESLING, grown in all wine regions: light, fragrant, young-drinking dry wines and good PRADIKATS.

Weststeiermark (West Styria) p Smallest Austrian wine region which specialises in SCHILCHER. Esp from Klug, Lukas, Reiterer, Strohmeier.

Wieninger, Fritz w r **→*** 90 91 92 93 94 Vg VIENNA-Stammersdorf grower: HEURIGE, CHARD, reds and esp good GRUNER VELTLINER and RIES.

Winzer Krems Wine growers' co-operative in KREMS: good whites.

Zierfandler (Spätrot) White grape grown almost exclusively in the THERMENREGION. With the ROTGIPFLER produces robust, lively wines which age well. Best producers: Biegler, Schellmann, Stadlmann.

Central & Southeast Europe

Prague ♣

POLA

CZECH
REPUBLIC

GERMANY

SLOV
REPU

Bratislava

AUSTRIA

Budapest

Danube

SLOVENIA

Ljubljana

Drava

CROATIA

Zagreb

Sava

BOSNIA–
HERZEGOVINA

ITALY

Split

Sarajevo

Dubrovnik

*A d r i a t i c
S e a*

To say
that parts
of the region
covered by this
map are somewhat
provisional these days
is an understatement.
But new regional autonomies
and new statehoods are frequently
being followed by higher aspirations
in winemaking and new international
interest and/or investment. So far Hungary
and Bulgaria, and perhaps Moldova, as well as
Czechoslovakia, have taken the lead in what has
become an area to follow with fascination. The
potential of other ex-communist states is still on hold.

In this section references are arranged country by country,
each shown on the map on this page. Labelling in all the
countries involved, except Greece and Cyprus, is broadly based
on the international pattern of place name and grape variety.
Main grape varieties are therefore included alongside areas,
producers and other terms in the alphabetical listings.

Heavily shaded areas are the wine-growing regions

UKRAINE

MOLDOVA

Kishinev

GARY

Tirnave

ROMANIA

Olt

grade

Danube

Bucharest

Prut

Danube

Varna

BIA

BULGARIA

Black Sea

Sofia

Plovdiv

Euros

MACEDONIA

Skopje

Istanbul

ANIA

Thessaloniki

Aegean Sea

GREECE

TURKEY

Patras

Athens

Hungary

Hungary is the unquestioned regional leader in terms of tradition, although neighbouring Austria is now ahead in quality. Magyar taste is for fiery, hearty, full-blooded wines, which their traditional grapes (mainly white) perfectly provide, but which are being superseded in many cases by 'safer' international varieties. Since the end of Communism several French, German and other concerns have bought land or entered into joint ventures, especially in Hungary's most famous region, Tokay. Expect to hear much more of this. Meanwhile visitors to the country will find plenty of original wines in the old style.

Alföld Hungary's Great Plain: much everyday wine (mostly Western grapes) and some better, esp at HAJOS, HELVECIA, KECSKEMET, KISKUNHALAS, Szeged.

Aszú Botrytis-shrivelled grapes and the sweet wine made from them, as in Sauternes (see page 77). Used to designate both wine and rotten berries.

Aszú Eszencia Tokaji br sw **** 57 63 Second commercial TOKAY quality: superb amber elixir, like a great Sauternes with a hint of fino sherry.

Badacsony Balaton w dr sw **→→*** Famous 426-m hill on the N shore of LAKE BALATON whose basalt soil can give rich high-flavoured white wines, among Hungary's best, esp SZURKEBARAT and KEKNYELU.

Balaton Balaton r w dr sw *→**** Hungary's inland sea and Europe's largest freshwater lake. Many good wines take its name. The ending 'i' (eg Balatoni, Egri) is the equivalent of -er in Londoner.

Balatonboglár Balaton r w p *→** Newer progressive area S of Lake B: sound wines, esp whites (Chard, Sém, Muscat). Also cuve close sparkling.

Balatonfüred Balaton w (r) dr sw ** Town on the N shore of LAKE BALATON. Softer, less fiery wines from Western and OLASZRIZLING grapes.

Bársonyos-Csàszàr Northern area for traditional dry whites.

Bikavér Eger r * 'Bulls Blood', the historic name of the best-selling red wine of EGER: at best full-bodied and well-balanced, but dismally variable in its export version today. A three-variety (minimum) blend, mostly KEKFRANKOS and Cab, also Merlot. Now also made in SZEKSZARD.

Csárfás Royal v'yd, still state-owned, at Tarcal; perhaps the finest in TOKAJI.

Csopák Village next to BALATONFURED, with similar wines but drier whites.

Debrö Mátraalja w sw ** Town famous for mellow aromatic HARSLEVELU.

Dinka Widespread but ordinary white grape.

Disznókö Important French insurance (AXA) investment in first-rate TOKAY land at Szombor. 100+ acres.

Edes Sweet (but not as luscious as ASZU) wine.

Eger Eger district r w dr sw *→** Best-known red wine centre of N Hungary; a baroque city of cellars full of BIKAVER. Also fresh white LEANYKA (perhaps its best product today), OLASZRIZLING, Chard and Cab.

Eszencia **** The fabulous quintessence of TOKAY (Tokaji): intensely sweet and aromatic from grapes wizened by botrytis. Properly grape juice of v low, if any, alcoholic strength, reputed to have miraculous properties: its sugar content can be over 750 grams per litre.

Etyek Nr Budapest. Source of modern standard wines, esp Chard, Sauv Bl.

Ezerjó The grape grown at MOR to make one of Hungary's best dry white wines; potentially distinguished, fragrant and fine.

Felsöbabad Regional cellar S of Budapest with authentic (but in Hungary unauthorised) fragrant Pinot N.

Francois President French founded (1882) sparkling wine producer at Budafok, nr Budapest. Vintage wine: President.

Furmint The classic grape of TOKAY (Tokaji), with great flavour and fire, also grown for table wine at LAKE BALATON and in SOMLO.

Gyöngyös Mátraalja w (r) ** Region with promising dry white SZURKEBARAT, Chard, MUSKOTALY, Sauv, and recent French and Australian investment.

Hajós Alföld r ✦ Village in S Hungary known for good lively Cab S reds of medium body and ageing potential. Also good (if unpermitted) Pinot N.

Hárslevelü 'Lime-leaved' grape used at DEBRO and as the second main grape of TOKAY (cf Sém/Sauv in Sauternes). Gentle mellow wine: aromatic full.

Helvécia (Kecskemét) Historic ALFOLD cellars. V'yds ungrafted: phylloxera cannot negotiate sandy soil. Whites and rosés modernist; reds trad.

Hétszölö Noble first-growth 116-acre estate at TOKAJI bought by Grands Millésimes de France and Suntory. Second label: Dessewffy.

Hungarovin Traders/producers with huge cellars at Budafok nr Budapest: mainly 'western varietals', also cuve close, transfer and classic sparkling. Now owned by German Sekt specialists, Henkell.

Izsák Major sparkling wine producer; the majority by cuve close.

Kadarka Red grape for vast quantities of everyday wine in S, but capable of ample flavour and interesting maturity (eg at SZEKSZARD and VILLANY).

Kecskemét Major town of the ALFOLD. Much everyday wine, some better.

Kékfrankos Hungarian for Blaufränkisch; reputedly related to Gamay. Good light or full-bodied reds, esp at SOPRON. Used in BIKAVER at EGER.

Kéknyelü High-flavoured, low-yielding white grape making the best and 'stiffest' wine of MT BADACSONY. It should be fiery and spicy stuff.

Kékoporto Kék means blue, so this grape could be the German Portugieser. Makes concentrated oakable red; esp from VILLANY, s'times in BIKAVER.

Kiskunhalas Huge-scale plains winery, good esp for KADARKA.

Különleges Minöség Special quality: highest official grading.

Lang and Lauder New partnership of famous international Hungarians to make TOKAY at Mád. Also v'yds at EGER.

Leányka or Király Old Hungarian white grape also grown in Transylvania. Makes admirable aromatic faintly Muscat dry wine in many areas. Kiraly ('Royal') Leányka is supposedly superior.

Mátraalja Wine district in the foothills of the Mátra range in N Hungary, incl DEBRO, GYONGYOS and NAGYREDE. Esp for white wines.

Mecsekalja S Hungary district (the warmest), known for good whites of PECS.

Médoc Noir The Merlot grape.

Mezesfehér Widely planted 'white honey' grape; sweet, soft wine esp from EGER and GYONGYOS.

Minöségi Bor Quality wine. Hungary's appellation contrôlée.

Mór N Hungary w ✦✦→✦✦✦ Region long famous for fresh dry EZERJO. Now also Riesling and Sauvignon.

Muskotály The yellow Muscat. Makes light, though long-lived, wine in Tokaji and EGER. A little goes into the TOKAY blend (cf Muscadelle in Sauternes). V occasionally makes an ASZU wine solo.

Nagyburgundi Literally 'great burgundy': indigenous grape, not Pinot N as sometimes thought. Sound solid wine esp around VILLANY and SZEKSZARD.

Nagyréde Mátraalja Foothill winery. Competent and modern.

OBI Official laboratory based in Budapest, responsible for labelling, quality control and export licence. Old notions being modernized.

Olaszrizling Hungarian name for the Italian Riesling or Welschriesling.

Oporto Red grape increasingly used for soft jammy wines to drink young.

Oremus Ancient TOKAJI v'yd of founding Rakóczi family at Sárospatak, being reconstituted by owners of Spain's Vega Sicilia.

Pécs Mecsek w (r) ✦→✦✦ Major S wine city. Esp OLASZRIZLING, Pinot Bl, etc.

Pezsgö Sparkling wine, mostly transfer method, can often be v palatable.

Pinot Noir Normally means NAGYBURGUNDI. But see Felsöbabad.

Puttonyos The measure of sweetness in TOKAY ASZU. A 'putt' is a 20–25 kilo measure (traditionally a hod) of Aszú grapes. The number of 'putts' added per barrel (136 litres) of dry base wine determines the richness of the final product, from 3 putts to 6. (3 = 60 grams of sugar per litre, 4 = 90, 5 = 120, 6 = 150. Aszú ESZENCIA must have 180 gpl. But see Eszencia for the really sticky stuff.)

Royal Tokaji Wine Co Early Anglo-Danish-Hungarian joint venture at Mád (TOKAJI). 150 acres, first or second growth. First wine ('90) a revelation.

Siklós Southern district known for its white wines: esp HARSLEVELU, also Chard, TRAMINI, OLASZRIZLING.

Somló N Hungary w ✴✴ Isolated small v'yd district N of BALATON: white wines (formerly of high repute) from FURMINT and ancient Juhfark grapes.

Sopron W Hungary r ✴✴ Historic enclave S of Neusiedler See (see Austria): light KEKFRANKOS, Austrian-style sweet wines, but now mostly for Cab etc.

Szamorodni Word meaning 'as it comes'; used to describe TOKAY without the addition of ASZU grapes. Can be dry or (fairly) sweet, depending upon proportion of aszú grapes naturally present. Sold as an aperitif.

Száraz Dry, esp of TOKAJI SZAMARODNI.

Szekszárd r ✴✴ District in south-central Hungary with investment from Italy's Antinori. KADARKA red wine which needs age (say 3–4 yrs); can also be botrytised ('Nemes Kadar'). Also good organic wines and (now) BIKAVER. Good Chard emerging too, esp 'Dunavar'.

Szürkebarát Literally means 'grey friar': Pinot Gr, which makes rich (not necessarily sweet) wine in the BADACSONY v'yds and elsewhere.

Tokay (Tokaji) Tokaji w dr sw ✴✴→✴✴✴✴ The ASZU is Hungary's famous liquorous sweet wine (since c1660), comparable to a highly aromatic and delicate Sauternes, from hills in the NE close to the Russian border. The appellation covers 13,500 acres. See Aszú, Eszencia, Furmint, Puttonyos, Szamorodni. Also dry table wine of character.

Tramini Gewürztraminer, esp in SIKLOS.

Villány Siklós r p (w) ✴✴ Southernmost town of Hungary and well-known centre of red wine production. Villányi Burgundi is largely KEKFRANKOS and can be good. Cabs S and F are v promising. See also Nagyburgundi.

Villány-Siklós Wine region named after the two towns.

Zweigelt Indigenous (S) red grape: deep-coloured spicy flavoursome wine.

Bulgaria

Since 1978 Bulgaria has come from nowhere to be the world's second-largest exporter of bottled wines after France, trading 90 percent of its production. Enormous new vineyards and wineries have overwhelmed an old, if embattled, wine tradition. The formerly state-run and state-subsidized wineries learnt almost everything from the New World and offer Cabernet, Chardonnay and other varieties at bargain prices. Controlled appellation ('Controliran') wines, introduced in 1985, have been joined by wood-aged 'Reserve' bottlings, simpler wines of Declared Geographical Origin and Country Wines. Bulgaria is divided into five main wine regions: the Danube, the eastern Black Sea region, Stara Planina, Haskovo and Harsovo.

The recent drop in sales to Russia has led to new emphasis on quality, somewhat higher prices and a ban on planting outside the 27 Controliran regions. There are 410,000 acres of vines in all.

In 1990 the organizing monopoly, Vinprom, was disbanded to give wineries autonomy (30 at first; the number continues to increase, as does privatization). A brisk air of competition is now provoking even greater efforts.

Asenovgrad Main MAVRUD-producing cellar on the outskirts of PLOVDIV – stainless steel being introduced. Mavrud and CAB can last well.

Boyar, Domaine Bulgaria's first independent wine merchants for almost 50 yrs: based in Sofia, set up '91, now marketing in the UK.

Burgas Black Sea resort and source of rosé (the speciality), easy whites (incl a MUSCAT blend) and increasingly reds too.

Cabernet Sauvignon Highly successful (4 times California's acreage). Dark vigorous fruity wine, v drinkable young; top qualities good with age.

Chardonnay Rather less successful. V dry but full-flavoured wine, improves with a yr in bottle. Some recent oak-aged examples are promising.

Controliran Top quality wines (single grape variety) of AC-style status. The system was begun in '78: 27 regions were est'd by late '80s.

Country Wines Regional wines (cf French vins de pays), often a blend of 2 varieties for original taste.

Damianitza MELNIK winery with good Strambolovo MERLOT and Melnik CAB.

Danube Cool northern region, mostly for reds: incl SUHINDOL and SVISHTOV.

Dimiat The common native white grape, grown in the E towards the coast. Agreeable dry white without memorable character.

Euxinograd (Château) Ageing cellar on the coast, in a once-royal palace.

Gamza Good red grape, the Kadarka of Hungary. Aged wines, esp from LOVICO SUHINDOL, can be delicious.

Han Krum Co nr VARNA: modern whites, esp oaked CHARD, lighter Chard, SAUV.

Harsovo Southwest region, esp for MELNIK.

Haskovo Southern region, principal source of MERLOT for export. Incl ASENOVGRAD, ORIACHOVITSA, PLOVDIV, STAMBOLOVO, SLIVEN, and other areas.

Iskra Sparkling wine, normally sweet but fair quality. Red, white or rosé.

Kadarka Widely planted Hungarian grape; spicy in good years.

Karlovo Town famous for its 'Valley of Roses' and pleasant white MISKET.

Klosterkeller Harmless brand for export; mainly Silvaner white.

Korten Subregion of SLIVEN. Korten CAB is more tannic than most.

Lovico Suhindol Neighbour of PAVLIKENI, site of Bulgaria's first coop (1909). Good GAMZA (CONTROLIRAN), CAB, MERLOT, PAMID, blends. First to declare independence after collapse of state monopoly ('90). Privatized '92. Now B's most important winery/coop, giving guidance to contributing v'yds.

Mavrud Grape variety and darkly plummy red from S Bulgaria, esp ASENOVGRAD. Can mature 20 yrs. Considered the country's best.

Melnik City of the extreme southwest and its highly prized grape. Dense red wine that locals say can be carried in a handkerchief. Needs at least 5 yrs and lasts for 15. Also CAB, ripe and age-worthy.

Merlot Soft red grape variety grown mainly in HASKOVO in the south.

Misket Indigenous Bulgarian grape: mildly aromatic wines; white and red Misket often used to fatten up white blends.

Muscat Ottonel Normal Muscat grape, grown in E for mid-sweet fruity white.

Novi Pazar Controlled appellation CHARD winery nr VARNA with finer wines.

Novo Selo Controliran red GAMZA from the north.

Oriachovitza Major S area for Controliran CAB-MERLOT. Rich savoury red best at 4–5 yrs. Recent RESERVE Cab releases have been good, esp 84 86.

Pamid The light soft everyday red of the southwest and northwest.

Pavlikeni Northern wine town with a prestigious estate specializing in GAMZA and CAB of high quality. Also light COUNTRY WINE MERLOT and Gamza blend.

Peruschitza PLOVDIV's winery, nr ASENOVGRAD, esp for reds.

Petrich Warm SW area for soft fragrant MELNIK, also blended with CAB.

Pinot Noir One of B's three main red grapes, along with CAB and MERLOT.

Pleven N cellar for PAMID, GAMZA, CAB. Also Bulgaria's wine research station.

Plovdiv Southern HASKOVO wine town and region, source of good CAB and MAVRUD. Winemaking mostly at ASENOVGRAD.

Preslav Bulgaria's largest white wine cellar, in NE region. Esp for SAUV BL and RESERVE CHARD. Also makes rather good brandy.

Provadya Another centre for good white wines, esp dry CHARD.

Reserve Used on labels of selected and oak-aged wines. Usually with 2–4 yrs in oak vats (often American), may or may not be CONTROLIRAN.

For key to grape variety abbreviations, see pages 6–9.

Riesling (In Bulgaria) normally refers to Italian Riesling (Welschriesling). Some Rhine Riesling is grown: now made into Germanic-style white.

Rkatziteli One of Russia's favourite white grapes for strong sweet wine. Produces bulk dry or medium whites in NE Bulgaria.

Russe NE wine town on the Danube. Some fresh high-tech whites: Welschriesling-MISKET blends, straight medium-dry Welschries, CHARD, MUSCAT and good Aligoté. Now also reds, esp CONTROLIRAN YANTRA VALLEY CAB S.

Sakar SE wine area for CONTROLIRAN MERLOT, some of Bulgaria's best.

Sauvignon Blanc Grown in E Bulgaria, recently released for export.

Schumen Eastern region, especially for whites.

Sliven Big producing S region, esp for CAB. Also MERLOT and Pinot N (Merlot is blended with Pinot in a COUNTRY WINE), Silvaner, MISKET and CHARD.

Sofia The country's capital with large pace-setting winery, but no v'yds.

Sonnenkuste Brand of medium-sweet white sold in Germany.

Stambolovo Wine area esp for CONTROLIRAN MERLOT from HASKOVO.

Stara Planina Balkan mountain region of central Bulgaria, incl KARLOVO.

Stara Zagora S region of ORIACHOVITSA: CAB and MERLOT to RESERVE quality.

Sungarlare E town giving its name to a dry CONTROLIRAN MISKET; also CHARD.

Svishtov CONTROLIRAN CAB-producing winery by the Danube in the north. A front-runner in Bulgaria's controlled appellation wines.

Tamianka Sweet white wine of eponymous aromatic grape. (Aka Tamiîoasa.)

Targovichte Independent cellar nr SCHUMEN. Esp medium and sweet whites.

Tirnovo Strong sweet dessert red wine.

Varna Major coastal appellation for CHARDONNAY (buttery or unoaked, Ch Euxinograd promising), SAUV. Also Aligoté, Ugni Bl (s'times blended).

Yantra Valley DANUBE region, CONTROLIRAN for CABERNET SAUVIGNON since '87.

The Former Yugoslav States

Before its disintegration in 1991 Yugoslavia was well-established as a supplier of wines of international calibre, if not generally of exciting quality. Now there are barely enough for export. Current political disarray and competition from other East European countries makes commercial contacts difficult (except in Slovenia, whose 'Riesling' was the pioneer export, since followed by Cabernet, Pinot Blanc, Traminer and others). All regions except the central Bosnian highlands make wine, almost entirely in giant cooperatives, although small private producers are emerging with the '90s. The Dalmatian (Croatian) coast and Macedonia have good indigenous wines whose roots go deep into the ancient world. In this edition the wines of Serbia, Bosnia-Herzegovina and Macedonia are omitted.

Slovenia

Bela Krajina SAVA area, esp 'Ledeno Laski Ries' (late-harvest frozen grapes).

Beli Pinot The Pinot Bl, a popular grape variety. Belo is white.

Bizeljsko-Sremic SAVA district. Full-flavoured local variety reds and LASKI R.

Crno vino Red (literally 'black') wine.

Cvicek Traditional pale red or dark rosé of the SAVA VALLEY.

Dolenjska SAVA region: CVICEK, LASKI RIZLING and Modra Frankinja (dry red).

Drava Valley (Podravski) Slovene wine region. Mainly whites from aromatic (Welschries, Muscat Ottonel) to flamboyant (Ries and Sauv); also Eisweins and Beerenauslesen as in neighbouring Austria.

Gorna Radgona Winery for sparkling, late-harvest sweet and Eiswein. Many grape varieties used, mostly in blends.

Grasevina Slovenian for Italian RIES. The normal 'Riesling' of the region.

Jerusalem Slovenia's most famous v'yd, at LJUTOMER. Its best wines are late-picked RAJNSKI RIZLING and LASKI RIZLING. Also makes charmat sparklers.

Kakovostno Vino Quality wine (one step down from VRHUNSKO).

Kontrolirano poreklo Appellation. Wine must be 80% from that region.

Koper Hottest area of LITTORAL between Trieste and Piran. Full rich MERLOTS.

Kraski Grown on the coastal limestone or Karst. A region famous for REFOSCO wines eg Kraski Teran and oak-aged Teranton.

Laski Rizling Yet another name for Italian RIES. Best-known Slovene wine, not best-quality. Top export brand: 'Cloburg' from Podravski (DRAVA) region.

Littoral (Primorski) Coastal region bordering Italy (Collio) and the Med. Esp reds: Cab, Merlot (aged in Slovene oak), Barbera and REFOSCO.

Ljutomer (or Lutomer) -Ormoz Slovenia's best-known, probably best white wine district, in NE (DRAVA); esp LASKI RIZLING, at its best rich and satisfying. Ormoz winery also has sparkling and late-harvest.

Malvasia Ancient white grape giving luscious wine.

Maribor Important centre in NE (DRAVA). White wines, mainly from VINAG, incl LASKI RIZLING, RIES, Sauv, Pinot Bl and Traminer.

Merlot Reasonable in Slovenia. Comparable with neighbouring NE Italian.

Namizno Vino Table wine.

Ptui Historic wine town with trad-based coop: wines clean, mostly white.

Radgona-Kapela DRAVA district next to Austrian border, esp late-harvest wines, eg RADGONSKA RANINA, also classic method sparkling.

Radgonska Ranina Ranina is Austria's Bouvier grape. Radgona is nr MARIBOR. The wine is sweet. Trade name is Tigrovo Mljeko (Tiger's Milk).

Rajnski (or Renski) Rizling The Rhine RIESLING: rare in these regions, but grown a little in LJUTOMER-ORMOZ.

Refosco Vg Italian red grape grown in east and in ISTRIA (Croatia) as TERAN.

Riesling Used without qualification formerly meant Italian Riesling. Now legally limited to real Rhine Riesling.

Sauvignon Blanc Vg with the resources to make it well; otherwise horrid.

Sava Valley Central Slovenia: light dry reds, eg CVICEK. Northern bank is for whites, eg LASKI RIZLING, Silvaner and recent Chard and Sauv Bl.

Sipon Name for Furmint of Hungary – locally prized, p'haps has a future.

Slamnak Λ late-harvest LJUTOMER estate RIES.

Slovenijaveno Slovenia's largest exporter. Wines (esp WELSCHRIES) bought in and blended with care for Slovin, Ashewood and Avia brands.

Tigrovo Mljeko See Radgonska Ranina.

Tocai The Pinot Gr, making rather heavy white wine.

Vinag Huge production cellars at MARIBOR. Top wine: Cloburg LASKI RIZLING.

Vipava LITTORAL region with tradition of export to Austria and Germany: good Cab, MERLOT, Barbera, Chard. Vipava winery is the most modern.

Vrhunsko Vino Top quality wine.

Welschriesling A greater export even than LASKI RIZLING.

Zelen Local grape variety – perhaps with a future?

Croatia

Babić Standard red of dalmatia, ages better than ordinary plavac.

Banat Region partly in Romania: up-to-date wineries making adequate RIES.

Baranjske Planote SLAVONIA area for Ries and BIJELI BURGUNDAC.

Bogdanusa Local white grape of the DALMATIAN islands, esp Hvar and Brac. Pleasant, refreshing faintly fragrant wine.

Burgundac Bijeli Chard, grown in SLAVONIA.

Dalmaciajavino Coop at Split: full range of DALMATIAN coastal/island wines.

Dalmatia The coast of Croatia, from Rijeka to Dubrovnik. Has a remarkable variety of characterful wines, most of them potent.

Dingač Heavy sweetish PLAVAC red, speciality of mid-DALMATIAN coast.

Faros Substantial age-worthy PLAVAC red from the island of Hvar.

Graševina Local name for ubiquitous LASKI RIZLING.

Grk White grape, speciality of the island of Korcula, giving strong, even sherry-like wine, and also a lighter pale one.

Istria Peninsula in the N Adriatic, Porec its centre: a variety of pleasant wines, MERLOT as good as any. V dry TERAN is perfect with local truffles.

Kontinentalna Hrvatska Inland Croatia. Mostly for whites (GRASEVINA).

Marastina Strong herbal dry DALMATIAN white, best from Cara Smokvica.

Opol Pleasant light pale PLAVAC red from Split and Sibenik in DALMATIA.

Plavac Mali Native red grape of DALMATIA; wine of body, strength, ageability. See Dingac, Opol, Postup, etc. There is also a white, Plavac Beli.

Portugizac Austria's Blauer Portugieser: plain red wine.

Pošip Pleasant white of the DALMATIAN islands, notably Korcula.

Postup Sweet heavy DALMATIAN red of Peljesac peninsula. Highly esteemed.

Prosek Dessert wine from DALMATIA: 15–16° (can be almost port-like).

Slavonia N Croatia, on Hungarian border between Slovenia and Serbia. Big producer. Standard wines, esp white, incl most of former 'Yugoslav Ries'.

Teran Stout dark red of ISTRIA. See Refosco (Slovenia).

Vugava Rare white variety of Vis in DALMATIA. Linked (at least in legend) with the Viognier of the Rhône Valley.

Former Czechoslovakia

Re-established January '93 as the Czech (Moravia and Bohemia) and Slovak republics. While there was little or no tradition of exporting from this mainly white wine region, good wines have emerged since 1989. Labels will say whether they are blended or single varietal. All are worth trying for value.

Moravia Favourite wines in Prague: variety and value. V'yds situated along Danube tributaries. Many wines from Austrian border: similar grapes, Grüner Veltliner, Müller-T, Sauv, Traminer, St-Laurent, Pinot N, Blauer Portugieser, Frankovka, etc; and similar wines, eg from Mikulov (white, red, dry, sweet classic-method sparkling; esp Valtice Cellars, est'd 1430, and Vino Mikulov), Satov (modern, mostly white, grapes from local farms and coops) and Znojmo (long-est'd, ideal limestone soil; local white grapes, Grüner-V, Müller-T, Sauv, 'Tramín' and sweetish prize-winning 'Rynsky Ryzlink' (82) from Znovín). Other regions: Jaroslavice (oak-aged reds), Prímetice (full aromatic whites), Blatnice, Hustopece, sunny Pálava, Saldorf (esp Sauv, 'Rynsky' Ries) and Velké Pavlovice (good Rulander and award-winning Cab 92 from recently est'd ('91), still expanding H&B). Moravia also has sparkling.

Bohemia Winemaking since 9th C. Same latitude and similar wines to eastern Germany. Best: N of Prague, in Elbe Valley, and (best known) nr Melník (King Karel IV bought in Burgundian vines in 15th C; today Ries, Rulander and Traminer predominate). 'Bohemia Sekt' is growing, eg from Stary Plzenec: tank-fermented (mostly), some oak used, with grapes from SLOVAKIA and MORAVIA too; French advice. Top wineries: Lobkowitz (at Melnik), Roudnice, Litomerice, Karlstein.

Slovakia Warmest climatic conditions and most of former Czechoslovakia's wine. Best in E v'yds neighbouring Hungary's Tokay region. Slovenia uses Hungarian varieties and makes good Tokay too. Key districts: Malo-karpatská Oblast (largest region, in foothills of Little Carpathians, incl Rulander, Ries, Traminer, Limberger, etc), Malá Trna, Nové Mesto, Skalice (small, mainly reds), and (in Tatra foothills) Bratislava, Pezinok, Modra. Best recent vintages: 71 79 81 83 89 92 94.

Romania

Romania has a long winemaking tradition (as long as 6,000 years) and good potential for quality, wasted during decades of supplying the Soviet Union with cheap sweet wine. The present political situation sadly allows little progress. Quantity is still the goal (domestic wine consumption is large). But with cleaner winemaking and earlier bottling, there is certainly the potential to rival the success of Bulgaria. There are 500,000 acres of vines.

Aiud TIRNAVE region with wine school, quality and a 'flor sherry'-style wine.

Alba Iulia Town in warm TIRNAVE area of TRANSYLVANIA, known for off-dry white (Italian RIES, FETEASCA, MUSKAT-OTTONEL), bottle-fermented sparkling.

Aligoté The junior white burgundy grape makes pleasantly fresh white.

Băbească Traditional red grape of the FOCSANI area: agreeably sharp wine tasting slightly of cloves. (Means 'grandmother grape'.)

Banat Plain on border with Serbia. Workaday Italian RIES, SAUV BL, MUSKAT-OTTONEL; light red CADARCA, CABERNET and Merlot.

Burgund Mare 'Big Burgundian'. A clone of Pinot N, not the real thing.

Buzav Hills Good reds (CAB, Merlot, BURGUND M) from continuation of DEALUL M.

Cabernet Sauvignon Increasingly grown, esp at DEALUL MARE, to make dark intense wines, though sometimes too sweet for Western palates.

Cadarca Romanian spelling of the Hungarian Kadarka.

Chardonnay Used at MURFATLAR for sweet dessert wine. Dry and oak-aged too.

Coteşti Warmer part of the FOCSANI area making deep-coloured reds of PINOT N, Merlot, etc, and dry whites claimed to resemble Alsace wines.

Cotnari Region at Moldavia's N v'yd limit; good botrytis. Famous (rarely seen) historical wine: light dessert white from local GRASA, FETEASCA ALBA, TAMAIOASA, rather like v delicate Tokay, gold with tints of green.

Crişana W region incl historical Miniş area (since 15th-C: reds, esp CADARCA, and crisp white Mustoasă), Silvania (esp FETEASCA), Diosig, Valea lui Mihai.

Dealul Mare Important up-to-date v'yd area in SE Carpathian foothills. Red wines from FETEASCA N, CAB, Merlot, PINOT, etc. Whites from TAMAIIOASA, etc.

Dobrudja Sunny dry Black Sea region. Incl MURFATLAR. Quality is good.

Drăgăşani Region on R Olt south of the Carpathian Mts, since Roman times. Both trad and 'modern' grapes (esp Sauv). Good MUSKAT-OTTONEL, reds.

Fetească Romanian white grape with spicy, faintly Muscat aroma. Two types: F Albă (same as Hungary's Leányka, considered more ordinary, but base for sparkling wine and sweet COTNARI) and F Regală (F Alba x Furmint cross, good acidity and good for sparkling).

Fetească Neagră Red Feteasca. Light wines, made coarse by clumsiness, good when aged (blackcurranty and deep red).

Focsani Important MOLDAVIA region incl COTESTI, NICORESTI and ODOBESTI.

Grasă A form of the Hungarian Furmint grape grown in Romania and used in, among other wines, COTNARI. Prone to botrytis. Grasa means 'fat'.

Iaşi Region for fresh acidic whites (F ALBA, also Welschries, ALIGOTE, spumante-style MUSKAT O): Bucium, Copu, Tomesti. Reds: Merlot, CAB; top BABEASCA.

Istria-Babadag Newish wine region N of MURFATLAR (CAB S, Merlot, F ALBA etc).

Jidvei Winery in the cool Carpathians (TIRNAVE) among Romania's N-most v'yds. Good whites: FETEASCA, Furmint, RIES, SAUV BL.

Lechinta Transylvanian wine area. Wines noted for bouquet (local grapes).

Moldavia NE province. Largest Romanian wine area with 12 subregions incl IASI, FOCSANI, PANCIU. Temperate, with good v'yd potential.

Murfatlar V'yds nr Black Sea, 2nd-best botrytis conditions (see Cotnari): esp sweet CHARD, late-vintage CAB. Now also full dry wines and sparkling.

Muskat Ottonel The E European Muscat, a speciality of Romania, esp in cool climate TRANSYLVANIA and dry wines in MOLDAVIA.

Nicoreşti Eastern area of FOCSANI, best known for its red BABEASCA.

Odobeşti The central part of FOCSANI; white wines of FETEASCA, RIES, etc.

Oltenia Wine regions including DRAGASANI. Sometimes also a brand name.

Panciu Cool MOLDAVIA region N of ODOBESTI. Good still and sparkling white.

Perla The speciality of TIRNAVE: a pleasant blended semi-sweet white of Italian RIES, FETEASCA and MUSKAT-OTTONEL.

Pinot Noir Grown in the south: can surprise with taste and character.

Pitesti Principal town of the Arges region S of Carpathians. Trad whites.

Premiat Reliable range of higher quality wines for export.

Riesling Actually Italian Riesling. V widely planted. No exceptional wines.

Sadova Town in the SEGARCEA area exporting a sweetish rosé.

Sauvignon Blanc Romania's tastiest white, esp blended with FETEASCA.

Segarcea Southern wine area near the Danube. Rather sweet CAB.

Tamîîoasa Traditional white grape known as 'frankincense' for its exotic scent and flavour. Pungent sweet wines often affected by botrytis.

Tîrnave Important Transylvanian wine region (Romania's coolest), known for its PERLA and much FETEASCA R. Well-situated for dry and aromatic wines, eg JIDVEI's. Also bottle-fermented sparkling. Germanic-style.

Trakia Export brand. Better judged for Western palates than most.

Transylvania See Alba Iulia, Lechinta, Tîrnave.

Valea Călugărească 'Valley of the Monks', part of DEALUL MARE with go-ahead research station. Currently proposing new AC-style rules. CAB (esp Special Reserve 85), Merlot, PINOT are admirable, as are Italian RIES, Pinot Gr.

Vin de Mesa Most basic wine classification – for local drinking only.

VS and VSO Higher quality wines; VSO requires specified grapes and region.

VSOC Top range wines: CMD is late harvest, CMI late harvest with noble rot, CIB is from selected nobly rotten grapes (like Beerenauslese).

Greece

Since Greece's entry into the EC in 1981 its antique wine industry has started moving into higher gear. Some is still fairly primitive, but a new system of appellations is in place and the past six years have seen much investment in equipment and expertise. Modern, well-made, but still authentically Greek wines are worth tasting.

Achaia-Clauss Well-known wine merchant with cellars at PATRAS, N PELOPONNESE. Makers of DEMESTICA, etc.

Agiorgitiko Widely planted red-wine grape in the NEMEA region.

Agioritikos (Appellation) Good medium white and rosé from Agios Oros or Mt Athos, Halkidiki's monastic peninsula. Source of Cab etc for TSANTALI.

Amintaion Light red or rosé, often pétillant, from MACEDONIA.

Ankiralos Fresh white from the Aegean-facing v'yds of Thessaly.

Attica Region round Athens, the chief source of RETSINA.

Autocratorikos New semi-sparkling medium-dry white from TSANTALI.

Botrys Old-established Athenian wine and spirits company.

Boutari Merchants and makers with high standards in MACEDONIAN and other wines, esp NAOUSSA and SANTORINI. Grand Réserve is excellent (84).

Caïr Label of the RHODES coop. Makes Greece's only classic sparkling wine.

Calliga Modern winery with 800 acres on CEPHALONIA. ROBOLA white and Monte Nero reds from indigenous grapes are adequately made.

Cambas, Andrew Important wine-growers and merchants in ATTICA.

Carras, John Estate at Sithonia, Halkidiki, N Greece. Interesting COTES DE MELITON wines. Ch Carras is a claret-style oak-aged red (75 79 81 83 84 85 87 90) worth 10–20 yrs in bottle. Also non-appellation, eg Ambelos.

Cava Legal term for blended aged red and white. Eg, Cava Boutari (NAOUSSA-NEMEA blend) and Cava Tstantalis (NAOUSSA-Cab).

Cephalonia (Kephalonia) Ionian island: good white ROBOLA, red Thymiatiko.

Corfu Adriatic island with wines scarcely worthy of it. Ropa is trad red.

Côtes de Meliton Appellation (since '81) of CARRAS estate: red (esp Cab and Limnio) and white (again, Greek and French grapes), incl Ch Carras.

Crete Island with potential for excellent wine but current phylloxera problems. Best now from BOUTARI, Kourtaki and indigenous grapes.

Danielis One of the best brands of dry red wine, from ACHAIA-CLAUSS.

Demestica A reliable brand of dry red and white from ACHAIA-CLAUSS.

Emery Maker of good CAVA Emery red and vg Villare white on RHODES.

Epirus Central Greek region with high-altitude vines (1,200 metres): 'Katoyi' Cab is celebrated expensive, 'Zitsa' is dry, demi-sec and sparkling white.

Gentilini Up-market white from CEPHALONIA; a ROBOLA blend, soft and appealing. Now also a v promising oak-aged version. To watch.

Goumenissa (Appellation) Oak-aged red from W MACEDONIA. Esp BOUTARI.

Hatzimichali Small Atalanti estate and its wines. The whites are Greek-grape-based; the reds incl Cab S and Merlot.

Ilios Very drinkable standard RHODES wine from CAIR.

Kokkineli The rosé version of RETSINA: like the white. Drink cold.

Kouros Highly rated white from KOURTAKIS of ATTICA; also red from NEMEA.

Kourtakis, D Athenian merchant with mild RETSINA and good dark NEMEA.

Kretikos White wine made by BOUTARI from CRETAN varieties.

Lemnos (Appellation) Aegean island: sweet golden Muscat RETSINA, KOKKINELI.

Lindos Higher quality RHODES wine (from Lindos or not). Acceptable, no more.

Macedonia Quality wine region in the north, for XYNOMAVRO, esp NAOUSSA.

Malvasia Famous grape said to be from Monemvasia (south PELOPONNESE).

Mantinia (Appellation) Fresh aromatic PELOPONNESE white, now widely made.

Mavro Black – the word for dark (often sweet) red wine.

Mavrodaphne (Appellation) 'Black laurel'. Dark, sweet, port/recioto-like conc red; fortified to 15–22°. Speciality of PATRAS, N PELOPONNESE. To age.

Mavroudi Red wine of Delphi and N shore of Gulf of Corinth: dark, plummy.

Mercouri Family estate in PELOPONNESE for v fine Refosco red. (Refosco grapes brought to Greece in 1870 and known locally as Mercouri.)

Metsovo Town in Epirus (north) producing Cab blend called Katoi.

Minos Popular CRETAN brand; the Castello red is best.

Moscophilero Lightly spicy grape that makes MANTINIA.

Naoussa (Appellation) Above average strong dry XYNOMAVRO red from MACEDONIA in the north, esp from BOUTARI, the coop and TSANTALI.

Nemea (Appellation) Town in E PELOPONNESE famous for its lion (a victim of Hercules), fittingly forceful MAVRO, AGIORGITIKO grapes (unique spicy red).

Patras (Appellation) White wine (eg plentiful dry Rhoditis and rarer Muscats) and wine town on the Gulf of Corinth. Home of MAVRODAPHNE.

Pegasus, Château NAOUSSA estate for superior red (esp 81 86 88).

Peloponnese Southern landmass of mainland Greece, with half of the country's v'yds, incl NEMEA and PATRAS; vines mostly used for currants.

Rapsani Interesting oaked red from Mt Ossa. Rasping until TSANTALI rescue.

Retsina White wine with Aleppo pine resin added, tasting of turpentine and oddly appropriate with Greek food. ATTICA speciality. Much modern retsina is disappointingly mild. (So is commercial Taramasalata.)

Rhodes Easternmost Greek island. Chevalier de Rhodes is a pleasant red from CAIR. Makes Greece's best sparkling. See also Caïr, Emery, Ilios.

Robola (Appellation) Dry CEPHALONIA white: pleasant, soft, quite characterful.

Samos (Appellation) Island nr Turkey with ancient reputation for sweet pale golden Muscat and Malvasia. Esp (fortified) Anthemis, (sun-dried) Nectar.

Santorini Dramatic volcanic island N of CRETE: sweet Visanto (sun-dried grapes, once Orthodox church communion wine), v dry white. Potential.

Semeli, Château Estate nr Athens making good white and red, incl Cab S.

Strofilia Brand of 'boutique' winery at Anavissos. Good whites; reds incl Cab.

Tsantali Producers at Agios Pavlos with wide range of country and appellation wines, incl MACEDONIAN and wine from the monks of Mt Athos, NEMEA, NAOUSSA, RAPSANI and Muscat from SAMOS and LIMNOS. CAVA is a blend.

Vaeni Good red from NAOUSSA producers' coop.

Xynomavro The tastiest of many indigenous Greek red grapes – though its name means acidic-black. Basis for NAOUSSA and other northern wines.

Zitsa Mountainous N Epirius appellation. Delicate Debina white, still or fizzy.

Cyprus

Cyprus exports 75% of its production, mostly strong wines of reasonable quality, especially low-price Cyprus 'sherry', though treacly old Commandaria is the island's finest product. As with Bulgaria, the fall of the old USSR as a major wine market was a serious blow. Quality now has to compete with that in the rest of Europe. Until recently only two local grapes were grown; now others are on trial. The international standards are inevitably being planted, but many growers still believe in the individuality of their own varieties. The island has never had phylloxera.

Afames Village at the foot of Mt Olympus, giving its name to dry tangy red (MAVRO) wine from SODAP.

Alkion A new smooth light dry KEO white (XYNISTERI grapes from Limassol).

Aphrodite Consistent medium-dry XYNISTERI white from KEO.

Arsinöe Dry white wine from SODAP, named after an unfortunate female whom the last entry turned to stone.

Bellapais Fizzy medium-sweet white from KEO, named after the famous abbey nr Kyrenia. Essential refreshment for holidaymakers.

Commandaria Good quality brown dessert wine since ancient times in hills N of LIMASSOL, from 15 specified villages; named after a crusading order of knights. Made by solera maturation of sun-dried XYNISTERI and MAVRO grapes. Best (as old as 100 yrs) is superb, of incredible sweetness, fragrance, concentration. Most is just standard Communion wine.

Domaine d'Ahera Modern-style lighter estate red from KEO. (From Grenache – recent on the island – and local Lefkas grapes.)

Emva Brand name of well-made fino, medium and cream SHERRIES.

Etko See Haggipavlu.

Haggipavlu Wine merchant at LIMASSOL since 1844. Trades as Etko.

Keo The biggest and most go-ahead firm at LIMASSOL. Standard Keo Dry White and Dry Red are vg value. See also Othello and Aphrodite.

Khalokhorio Principal COMMANDARIA village, growing only XYNISTERI.

Kokkineli Rosé: the name is related to 'cochineal'.

Kolossi Crusaders' castle nr Limassol; gives name to table wines from SODAP.

Laona The largest of the small independent regional wineries at Arsos. Good range of wines incl a 'nouveau' and an oak-aged red.

Limassol 'The Bordeaux of Cyprus'. Southern wine port (and its region): location for all four main Cyprus wineries.

Loel Major producer, with Amathus and Kykko brands, Command Cyprus SHERRY and good Negro red.

Mavro The black grape of Cyprus (and Greece) and its dark wine.

Monte Roya Modern regional winery at Chryssoroyiatissa Monastery.

Mosaic KEO's brand of Cyprus SHERRIES. Includes a good dry wine.

Muscat All major firms produce pleasant low-price 15° Muscats.

Opthalmo Black grape (red/rosé): lighter, sharper than MAVRO. Not native.

Othello A good standard dry red wine (MAVRO and OPTHALMO grapes from PITSILIA). Solid and satisfying from KEO. Best at 3–4 yrs.

Palomino Soft dry white made of this (sherry) grape by LOEL. V drinkable ice-cold. Imported to make Cyprus SHERRY.

Pitsilia Region S of Mt Olympus for the best white and COMMANDARIA wines.

Rosella Light dry fragrant rosé from KEO. OPTHALMO from PITSILIA.

St-Panteleimon Brand of medium-sweet white from KEO.

Semeli Good traditional red from HAGGIPAVLU. Best at 3–4 years old.

Sherry Sherry-style wine is an island staple. The best is dry.

SODAP Major wine coop at LIMASSOL.

Thisbe Fruity medium-dry light KEO wine, (XYNISTERI grapes from LIMASSOL).

Xynisteri The native aromatic white grape of Cyprus.

Asia & North Africa

Algeria As a combined result of Islam and the EC, the once massive v'yds of Algeria have dwindled in the last decade from 860,000 acres to under 200,000 (still nearly as many as Germany); many vines are 40+ yrs old and won't be replaced. Red, white and esp rosé wines of some quality are still made in the coastal hills of Tlemcen (powerful), Mascara (good red and white), Haut-Dahra (strong red, rosé), Zaccar, Tessala, Médéa and Ain-Bessem (Bouira esp good). Sidi Brahim is a drinkable red brand. These had VDQS status in French colonial days. Wine is still the third largest export. Algeria is also a cork producer.

China Germans and Russians started making wine on the Shantung (now called Shandong) peninsula in the late 1800s. Since 1980 a modern industry, initiated by Rémy Martin, has produced the adequate white Dynasty and Tsingtao wines (Tsingtao is on same latitude as southern France). New plantings of better varieties in Shandong and Tianjin (further north) promise more interest. Basic table wines are made of the local Dragon Eye and Muscat Hamburg grapes (especially in Tianjin). In Qingdao (with China's only maritime climate) the Huadong winery (since '86, now Allied-Lyons owned) has made very palatable Welschriesling and Chardonnay and is experimenting with Cabernet Sauvignon, Syrah and Gewürztraminer. Dragon Seal Wines (nr Peking, since '87) have Dragon Eye grapes, recent Chardonnay (with oak), and more planned. Other foreign investors and innovators are Seagram (Summer Palace), Pernod Ricard (Beijing Friendship Winery since '87). As of '92 Rémy Martin are making 'Imperial Court', China's first classic method sparkling wine, near Shanghai.

India In 1985 a Franco-Indian firm launched a Chard-based sparkling wine, Omar Khayyám, made at Narayangoan, nr Poona, SE of Bombay. It sets an astonishing standard. Plans are to export up to 2 million bottles and to add still wines of Chard and Cab S. Sweeter Marquise de Pompadour followed, also slightly drier Princess Jaulke, made with advice from Charbaut of Champagne – still improving. Now near Bangalore there is Cab, from Grover V'yds in the Dodballapur Hills.

Japan Japan has a small wine industry mostly in Yamanashi Prefecture, W of Tokyo, but extending as far as cool Hokkaido (N island). Most wine is blended with imports from S America, Eastern Europe, etc. But premium Sém, Chard, Cab and local white Kôshû, are the new surprise. Top producers are Manns, Sanraku (Mercian label) and Suntory. Château Mercian and Suntory lead with high quality Chard, Cab, etc. The most interesting (and expensive) are Suntory's Château Lion red B'x-blend and vg botrytis Sém; Mercian's Kikyogahara Merlot (since '85), and esp Jyonohira Cab of extraordinary denseness and quality. Manns not only have Cab (French oak aged) but emphasize local varieties (Kôshû, Zenkôji – China's Dragon Eye) and local-Euro crosses (adapted to Japan's rainy climate) too. Second-rankers are Sapporo (Polaire label), Kyowa Hakko Kogyo (Ste Neige), Marufuji (big-selling Rubaiyat), Shirayuri Winery (L'Orient label) and Ch Lumière. Regrettably, labelling laws have been so lax that misrepresentation of imported wines as 'Japanese' has been the rule rather than exception. The law now stipulates that if imported wine in the bottle is above 50% it must be indicated on the label (larger percentage printed before the smaller). But local wines are now attracting interest, and Katsunama district is capitalising by introducing Certificate of Origin labels.

For key to grape variety abbreviations, see pages 6–9.

Lebanon The small Lebanese industry, based on Ksara in the Bekaa Valley NE of Beirut, makes wines of real vigour and quality. There are 3 wineries of note. Château Musar (★★★), the heroic survivor of years of civil war, produces splendid claret-like matured reds, largely of Cab S; a full-blooded oak-aged white, from indigenous Obaideh grapes (like Chard), surprisingly capable of ageing 10–15 yrs; and recently a lighter red wine, 'Tradition', which is 75% Cinsaut, 25% Cab S. Ksara is the largest and oldest (Jesuit-founded) winery. Kefraya more dynamic: 'Rouge de K' is Cinsaut-Carignan blend, 'Château Kefraya' is fragrant and from best yrs only; there is rosé and white too; all early-drinking.

Morocco Morocco makes N Africa's best wine (85% red, from Cinsaut, Grenache, Carignan), from v'yds along the Atlantic coast (Rabat to Casablanca, light and hopefully fruity with speciality white – 'Gris' – from red grapes) and around Meknés and Fez (solid full-bodied, best-known). Also further east around Berkane and Angad (tangy, earthy) and in the Gharb and Doukkalas regions. But in 10 years v'yds have declined from 190,000 to 35,000 acres. Main producers are Dom de Sahari (nr Meknés, French investment, a new winery in '93, and Cab, Merlot, along with local grapes), Celliers de Meknés (dominating state-owned coop), Chaudsoleil, and Sincomar. Chanteblee, Tarik and Toulal are drinkable reds. Vin Gris (10% of production), esp de Boulaoune, is the best bet for hot-day refreshment. Cork production is also important.

Tunisia Tunisia now has 22,000 v'yd acres (there were 120,000 10 yrs ago). Her speciality is sweet Muscat, but most wines are reasonable reds and light rosés from Cap Bon, Carthage, Mornag, Tébourba and Tunis. Trying to improve quality; state and coop best. A third is exported.

Turkey Most of Turkey's 1.5 million acres of v'yds produce table grapes; only 3% are for wine. Wines from Thrace, Anatolia and the Aegean are very drinkable. Indigenous varieties (there are over 1,000: 60 are commercial) such as Emir, Narince (for white) and Bogazkere, Oküzgözü (for red) are used along with Ries, Sém, Pinot N, Grenache, Carignan and Gamay. Trakya (Thrace) white (light Sém) and Buzbag (E Anatolian) red are the well-known standards of Tekel, the State producer (with 21 state wineries). Diren, Doluca, Karmen, Kavaklidere and Taskobirlik are private firms of fair quality. Doluca's Villa Neva red from Thrace is well made, as is Villa Doluca. Kavaklidere makes good light Primeurs (white 'Cankaya' and red 'Yakut') from local grapes. But Buzbag remains Turkey's most original and striking wine.

The Old Russian Empire

Over 3 million acres of v'yds make the 16 republics of the former USSR collectively the world's fourth-biggest wine producer. Russia is the largest of the 12 producing wine, followed by Moldova, the Ukraine (incl top Crimea region) and Georgia. Soviet consumers have a sweet tooth, for both table and dessert wines, also for sparkling.

Russia Makes fair Ries (Anapa, Arbau, Beshtau) and sweet sparkling Tsimlanskoye 'Champanski'; also Chard, Sauv, Welschriesling (heavy, often oxidized), processed in state wineries nr Moscow, St Petersburg etc. Best are Don Valley v'yds (Black Sea Coast of the Caucasus), for Ries, Aligoté, Cab.

Moldova With the most temperate climate (same latitude as N France) and now the most modern outlook, Moldova has high potential: esp whites from centre, reds from south, and red and fortified nr the Black Sea (west). Grapes incl Cab, Pinot N, Merlot,

Saperavi (fruity), Ries, Chard, Pinot Gr, Aligoté, Rkatsiteli. Former
Moscow bottling was disastrous. But the 63 Negru de Purkar
released in '92 gave a startling glimpse of Moldova's potential,
reinforced by following vintages (with 4 yrs oak, and v best from
Cab-Saperavi-Rara Negre blends (like 63)). Purkar may be the best
winery. Krikova is also good: esp Kodru 'Claret' blend, Krasny
Reserve Pinot N-Merlot-Malbec and sparkling. Romanesti winery
(since '82) has wines from French varieties; and Yaloveni, fino-
and oloroso-style 'flor sherries'. Good old-vine Cab from Tarakliya.
Abrodsov is classic method sparkling. Investment from Germany,
Italy, UK and Australia (Penfolds since '93) at Hincesti enables
local clean bottling and better winemaking: Ryman's Chard is vg.
Half v'yds are still state farmed: progress (and privatization) is not
smooth, but well worth watching. Plans for an appellation system.

Crimea (Ukraine) Crimea produces first-class dessert wines.
Sotheby's auction house disclosed as much in '90, with sales of old
wines from the Tsar's Crimean cellars at Massandra, nr Yalta
(Muscats and port- and madeira-like wines of v high quality).
Alupka Palace fortified (European grapes, since 1820s), classic
method sparkling from Novi Svet and Grand Duchess (the latter
from Odessa Winery founded by Louis Roederer in 1896) are also
adequate. Reds have good potential (eg Alushta from Massandra).
All are still produced under state monopoly. Ukraine also makes
Aligoté and Artemosk sparkling, mostly from Romanian varieties.

Georgia Uses antique methods to make v tannic wines for local
drinking, slightly newer techniques for export blends (Mukuzani,
Tsinandali); Georgians are disinclined to modernize. Kakhetià (E)
is famed for tannic red and white. Imeretia (W) makes milder, highly
original, earthenware-fermented wines. Kartli is central region.
Sparkling is v cheap, drinkable. When equipment (incl bottles and
stoppers) and techniques improve Georgia will be an export hit.

Israel

Israeli wine, since the industry was re-established by Baron Edmond
de Rothschild in the 1880s, has been primarily of kosher interest until
recently, when Cab, Merlot, Sauv, Chard were introduced. Traditionally
v'yds were planted in coastal Samson and Shomron regions but new
cooler Golan Heights vines (north) have resulted in great improvements.
Sixty percent of the annual 25 million bottle production is white.

Barkan Newish winery with promising Emerald Ries and Sauv Bl.
Baron Small family grower. Vg whites, esp dry Muscat and Sauv Bl.
Binyamina (Formerly Eliaz) Medium-sized winery for light-style wines.
Carmel Coop, est 1882, with Israel's two largest wineries (at Zichron-
Yaacov and Rishon-le-Zion). Top wines are 'Carmel Rothschild', esp
Cab, Chard, 'Selected Vineyards' Cab, Emerald Ries. Also new Merlot.
Galil/Galilee Region incl Golan Heights (Israel's top v'yd area).
Gamla & Golan Both labels of the Golan Heights winery. Soft fruity
Cab S, oaky Chard and grassy Sauv Bl. (See Yarden.)
Samson Central coastal plain v'yds (SE of Tel Aviv to W of Jerusalem).
Segal Family-owned winery sometimes known as Askalon. Cab S-
Carignan blends under Segal and Ben Ami labels.
Shomron V'yds in the valleys around Zichron-Yaacov, nr Haifa.
Yarden Young ('83) modern winery in the Golan Heights, involving
Californian oenologists and setting highest standards for Israel.
Full-bodied oaky Cab (85 89 90), complex Merlot, barrel-fermented
Chard and crisp Sauv; recently some classic method sparkling.

England & Wales

Well over a million bottles a year are now being made from over 450 vineyards, amounting in total to some 2,700 acres. Almost all are white and generally Germanic or similar to Alsace in style (some more Loire-like), many from new German varieties designed to ripen well in cool weather. Acidity is often high, which means that good examples have a built-in ability (and need) to age. Four years is a good age for many, and up to eight for some. Experiments with both oak-ageing and bottle-fermented sparkling are promising; especially the latter. The English Vineyards Association (EVA) seal is worn by tested wines. Since 1991 non-hybrid English wines may be labelled as 'Quality Wine', taking them into the European Community quality bracket for the first time. But as the (excellent) hybrid Seyval Blanc is so important here, few growers apply. NB Beware 'British Wine', which is neither British nor indeed wine, and has nothing to do with the following.

Adgestone nr Sandown (Isle of Wight) Prize-winning 8.5-acre v'yd on chalky hill site. Est'd '68. Wines with good structure and longevity.

Astley Stourport-on-Severn (Hereford and Worcester) 4.5 acres; some fair wines. Madeleine Angevine and Kerner are prize-winning.

Avalon Shepton Mallet (Somerset) Organically grown grapes. 2.3 acres.

Bagborough Shepton Mallet (Somerset) New v'yd to note. 3 acres.

Bardingley Staplehurst (Kent) 2.5-acres. Interesting red (some oak-aged).

Barkham Manor E Sussex 34 acres since '85. Wide range. Modern winery.

Barton Manor East Cowes (Isle of Wight) 15.5-acre v'yd: trophy-winning, consistently interesting wines incl barrel-aged and bottle-fermented sparkling. Considerable recent investment. New owners since '91.

Bearstead Maidstone (Kent) 4 acres planted '86. Improving, esp Bacchus.

Beaulieu Abbey Brockenhurst (Hampshire) 4.6-acre v'yd, established '58 by Gore-Browne family on old monastic site. Good rosé.

Beenleigh Manor Totnes (Devon) Esteemed Cab S and Merlot grown under 0.5 acres of polythene. Wine made at SHARPHAM. 90 is trophy winner.

Biddenden nr Tenterden (Kent) 20-acre v'yd planted '69: Wide range incl Ortega, Huxelrebe, Bacchus, bottle-fermented sparkling. Gd cider too.

Bishops Waltham Southampton (Hampshire) 13 acres for fair Wurzer and Schönburger.

Bookers Bolney (E Sussex) 4 acres of Müller-T; other varieties planted '92.

Bothy Abingdon (Oxfordshire) Just 3 acres so far, for esp good Huxelrebe-Perle and fragrant Ortega-Optima (**90 91**).

Boyton Stoke-by-Clare (Suffolk) Small 2-acre v'yd: Huxelrebe (90), Müller-T.

Boze Down Whitchurch-on-Thames (Oxfordshire) 5.8 acres. Wide range; red and sweet now looking good. Worth watching.

Breaky Bottom Lewes (Sussex) 5.5-acre v'yd. Semi-cult following. Good dry wines, esp award-winning Seyval (**89 90**), Müller-T. Sparkling is next.

Brenchley Tonbridge (Kent) 17 acres of Seyval Bl, Schönburger, Huxelrebe, now with some style. One to watch.

Bruisyard Saxmundham (Suffolk) 10 acres of Müller-T. Since '76. Incl oak-aged and sparkling wine.

Cane End Reading (Berkshire) 12 acres; mixed vines. Good sweet late-harvest Bacchus in '90. Interesting style.

Carden Park Chester (Cheshire) 9-acre v'yd in large 'leisure park' nr Welsh Marches. Good Seyval Bl, some oak-aged. New sparkling in '94.

Carr Taylor Vineyards Sussex 21 acres, planted '73. Esp for Reichensteiner. Pioneer of classic method sparkling wine in UK: Kerner-Reichensteiner (vintage, NV), Pinot N rosé. Some lively, intense, balanced wines.

Chapel Down Winery Burgess Hill (W Sussex)   New winery venture, blending from bought-in grapes, esp classic-method sparkling. Barrel-fermented 'Epoch I' red is good, as are 'sur lie' still and sparkling.

Chiddingstone Edenbridge (Kent)   28-acre v'yd with stress on dry French-style wines. Some barrique-ageing.

Chilford Hundred Linton (Cambridge)   18 acres: fairly dry wines since '74.

Chiltern Valley Henley-on-Thames (Oxfordshire)   3 acres of own v'yds high up on chalk, plus neighbouring growers': incl prize-winning oak-aged unusual sweet late-harvest Noble Bacchus, Old Luxters Dry Reserve.

Crickley Windward Little Witcombe (Gloucestershire)   5.5 acres beginning to show well, esp 91 Schönburger Reserve.

Denbies Dorking (Surrey)   250-acre v'yd (England's biggest); first harvest '89. Impressive new winery with good tour facilities, improving wines, esp 92 dessert Botrytis.

Elham Valley Canterbury (Kent)   Boutique winery/2-acre v'yd: impressive hand-crafted medium-dry Müller-T, and sparkling Kerner-Seyval Bl.

Elmham Park East Dereham (Norfolk)   4.5-acre v'yd, est '66. Light flowery wines, Madeleine Angevine esp good. Also apple wine.

Fonthill Salisbury (Wiltshire)   9 acres. Incl good Seyval, and Dornfelder rosé.

Gifford's Hall Bury St Edmunds (Suffolk)   12 acre-v'yd for interesting wines (incl oak-aged) and visitor facilities.

Hagley Court Hereford   7.5 acres planted '85, wines now worth watching.

Halfpenny Green W Midlands   28 v'yd-acres; esp good Madeleine Angevine.

Hambledon nr Petersfield (Hampshire)   The first modern English v'yd, planted in '51 on a chalk slope with advice from Champagne.

Harden Farm Penshurst (Kent)   18 acres. Member of Winegrowers coop.

Headcorn Maidstone (Kent)   5-acre medal-winning v'yd: Seyval Bl, etc.

Helions Helion's Bumpstead, Haverhill (Suffolk)   One acre, 50:50 Müller-T and Reichensteiner; good aromatic dry wine.

Hidden Spring Horam (E Sussex)   9 acres. Success esp with oak-aged Dry Reserve and Dark Fields red.

High Weald Winery Kent   No vines, but winemaker (proprietor Christopher Lindlar) for several growers. Buys in grapes for 'English V'yd' blend.

Highfield Tiverton (Devon)   1.5 acres. Good wines, esp Siegerrebe.

La Mare Jersey (Channel Islands)   Only (but long-est'd) CI v'yd. Fair wines.

Lamberhurst (Kent)   One of the best: 11 acres est'd '72. Consistent range of award winners (83 85 90), reds, sparkling, oak-aged. Medium-dry 91 Bacchus esp good. Winemaker for many other growers.

Leeford nr Battle (Sussex)   25-acre v'yd; more planned. Various labels incl Saxon Valley, Battle, Conquest.

Llanerch S Glamorgan (Wales)   5.5 acres est'd '86. Wines sold under Cariad label. Individual style developing, worth its awards. Good rosé.

Loddiswell Kingsbridge (Devon)   6 acres plus one under plastic tunnels.

Lymington Hampshire 6 acre-v'yd est'd '79.

Manstree Exeter (Devon)   3-acres; esp sparkling: 'Essling' (90) is a winner.

Meon Valley Southampton (Hampshire)   25 acres of mixed varieties: wines variable, but reds can be interesting.

Mersea Colchester (Essex)   Small v'yd. Wine quality gets better and better.

Monnow Valley Monmouth (Wales)   4 acres. Wines attracting increasing attention, esp 92 Huxelrebe-Seyval Bl.

Moorlynch Bridgewater (Somerset)   15 acres of an idyllic farm. Good wines: have been variable, now improving.

New Hall nr Maldon (Essex)   87 acres of mixed farm planted with Huxelrebe, Müller-T and Pinot N, etc. Some vinified elsewhere.

Northbrook Springs Bishops Waltham (Hampshire)   13 acres of young vines with improving range of wines.

Nutbourne Manor nr Pulborough (W Sussex)   18.5 acres: elegant and tasty Schönburger and Bacchus.

Nyetimber West Chiltington (W Sussex)   12-acre v'yd of Chard, Pinot N, Pinot Meunier specializing in bottle-fermented sparkling. First vintage 95.

Oatley Bridgewater (Somerset)   4.5 acres of young vines now producing good wines. 92 Kernling worth trying.

Partridge Blandford (Dorset)   5 acres. 92 dry Bacchus is trophy-winning.

Penshurst Tunbridge Wells (Kent)   12 acres since '72, incl good Seyval Bl and Müller-T. Fine modern winery.

Pilton Manor Shepton Mallet (Somerset)   15-acre hillside v'yd (est'd '66). Wines regaining form, esp Westholme Late Harvest, a '92 prize-winner.

Plumpton Agricultural College nr Lewes (Sussex)   One-acre experimental v'yd at college for winemakers.

Priory Vineyards Little Dunmow (Essex)   10 acres; now some good wines.

Pulham Diss (Norfolk)   12.6-acre v'yd planted '73; Müller-T is top wine.

Queen Court Faversham (Kent)   Brewery-owned: esp Müller-T, Schönburger.

Rock Lodge nr Haywards Heath (Sussex)   8-acre v'yd since '65. Fumé (oak-aged Ortega-Müller-T blend) and Impresario sparkling recommended.

St-George's Waldron, Heathfield (E Sussex)   15 acres, planted '79. Müller-T etc. Well-publicized; wide range, popular styles.

St-Nicholas Ash (Kent)   5 acres. Esp good for Schönburger.

Sandhurst Cranbrook (Kent)   Mixed farm with 16 acres of vines, 80 of hops, plus apple orchards, sheep, etc. Wines improving, esp 91 Seyval Bl, 92 Bacchus (both oak-aged). Sparkling Pinot N-Seyval available from '94.

Scott's Hall Ashford (Kent)   Boutique v'yd: oak-aged white, sparkling rosé.

Seddlescombe Organic Robertsbridge (E Sussex)   The UK's main organic v'yd. 6 acres for range of wines with quite a following.

Sharpham Totnes (Devon)   5 acres. Now own winery: getting interesting.

Shawsgate Framlingham (Suffolk)   17 acres incl good Seyval Bl-Müller-T blends. Wins awards.

Staple nr Canterbury (Kent)   7 acres planted '77. Excellent quality. Müller-T and Huxelrebe especially interesting.

Staplecombe Taunton (Somerset)   2.5 acres for some good wines.

Staverton (Woodbridge) Suffolk   1.5 acres of improving v'yds, esp Bacchus.

Tenterden Tenterden (Kent)   12 acres, planted '79. Wines v dry to sweet, Müller-T, oak-aged Seyval (vg 81, 91 Trophy winner), rosé, sparkling.

Thames Valley Twyford (Berkshire)   25-acre v'yd: all styles of wine. Serious oak-matured white, red; classic method sparkling; also late harvest sweet: botrytis Clock Tower Selection won '92 Gore-Browne trophy.

Three Choirs Newent (Gloucestershire)   60 acres (more planned), est'd '74. Müller-Thurgau, Seyval Bl, Schönburger, Reichensteiner, and esp Bacchus Dry, Huxelrebe. Recent new £1-million winery. English 'Nouveau' is popular.

Throwley Faversham (Kent)   4.5 acres. Excellent bottle-fermented sparkling from Pinot N and Chard. 91 Ortega also vg.

Wickham Shedfield (Hampshire)   9.5-acre v'yd (since '84): starting to show some style. Vintage Selection is worth trying, esp 91.

Wissett Halesworth (Suffolk)   10 acres beginning to show up well. Esp for Auxerrois-Pinot blends and Müller-T.

Wooldings Whitchurch (Hampshire)   Young 7-acre v'yd. Vg Schönburger.

Wootton Shepton Mallet (Somerset)   6-acre v'yd of Schönburger, Müller-T, Seyval Bl, Auxerrois, etc. Consistently good fresh fruity wines since '71.

Wyken Bury-St-Edmunds (Suffolk)   Range starting to look gd, esp Bacchus.

The current trend towards 'low-alcohol' wines and beers, from which most alcohol has been removed artificially, should be a golden opportunity for wines that are naturally lower in alcohol than the 12 or 13 degrees expected in most table wines. Germany is the prime exponent; England is another. Their best wines, with plenty of fruity acidity, do not need high alcohol to make an impact. Today's logical choice – at least at lunch-time.

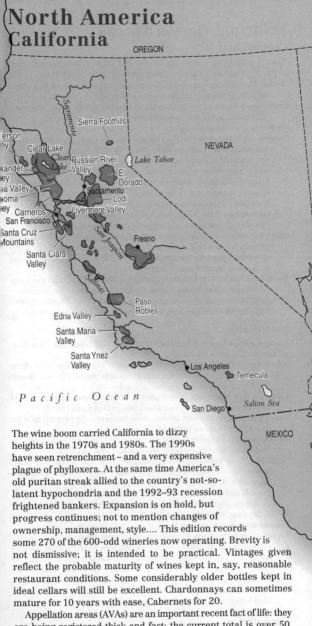

North America
California

OREGON

Sacramento

Sierra Foothills

NEVADA

Clear Lake

Clear Lake

erson
ey

kander
ey

a Valley

oma
ey

Russian River
Valley

El
Dorado

Sacramento

Lodi

Lake Tahoe

Carneros

San Francisco

Santa Cruz
Mountains

Livermore Valley

San Joaquin

Santa Clara
Valley

Salinas

Fresno

Edna Valley

Santa Maria
Valley

Paso
Robles

Santa Ynez
Valley

Los Angeles

Temecula

P a c i f i c   O c e a n

San Diego

Salton Sea

MEXICO

The wine boom carried California to dizzy
heights in the 1970s and 1980s. The 1990s
have seen retrenchment – and a very expensive
plague of phylloxera. At the same time America's
old puritan streak allied to the country's not-so-
latent hypochondria and the 1992–93 recession
frightened bankers. Expansion is on hold, but
progress continues; not to mention changes of
ownership, management, style…. This edition records
some 270 of the 600-odd wineries now operating. Brevity is
not dismissive; it is intended to be practical. Vintages given
reflect the probable maturity of wines kept in, say, reasonable
restaurant conditions. Some considerably older bottles kept in
ideal cellars will still be excellent. Chardonnays can sometimes
mature for 10 years with ease, Cabernets for 20.

Appellation areas (AVAs) are an important recent fact of life: they
are being registered thick and fast; the current total is over 50,
with nine in Napa alone. But it is still too soon to use them as a guide
to style. Listed below are the regions usually referred to. Grapes
and brand names, though, remain the key to California wine.

Principal vineyard areas

Central Coast

A long sweep of coast with scattered though increasing wine activity, from San Francisco Bay south to Santa Barbara.

Hecker Pass Pass through the SANTA CRUZ MTS S of San Francisco Bay with a dwindling cluster of small old-style wineries.

Livermore Valley E of San Francisco Bay long famous for white wines (esp Sauvignon) but now largely built-over.

Monterey See Salinas Valley.

Salinas Valley/Monterey The Salinas Valley runs SE inland from Monterey. After frenzied expansion in the '70s, many vines were torn up. What are left make wines of singular character. Currently refining its internal divisions: Arroyo Seco AVA (esp Chard and Ries), Santa Lucia Highlands AVA (Chard, has hopes for Pinot N), San Lucas AVA (steady commercial wines), and coastal Carmel Valley (tiny, sometimes impressive Cab and Chard).

San Luis Obispo Edna Valley just S of San Luis Obispo (1,000 acres, esp Chard) and scattered v'yds nr Paso Robles (6,000 acres, esp Zin).

Santa Barbara Santa Maria Valley is dominant, esp for vg Chardonnay and distinctive Pinot N. The smaller Santa Ynez Valley also has cool foggy conditions: good for Burgundian varieties at seaward end, Bordeaux varieties in warmer inland areas.

Santa Cruz Mts Wineries (though few v'yds) are scattered round the Santa Cruz Mts S of San Francisco Bay, from Saratoga down to HECKER PASS.

Temecula (Rancho California) Small area in S California, 25 miles inland, halfway between San Diego and Riverside. Mainly white/sparkling.

North Coast

Encompasses Lake, Menodocino, Napa and Somoma counties, all north of San Francisco.

Alexander Valley/Russian River (Sonoma) Top quality area from Alexander Valley (N of Napa Valley) towards the sea (Russian River). Incl Dry Creek Valley. Most varieties thrive.

Carneros, Los Important cool region N of San Francisco Bay, shared between NAPA and SONOMA counties. Esp for Chard and Pinot N.

Lake Clear Lake AVA: warm climate, most impressive for Sauv Bl, good for Cab S. Small Guenoc Valley AVA similar.

Mendocino Northernmost coastal wine country; a varied climate coolest in Anderson Valley nr the coast, warm inland around Ukiah.

Napa The Napa Valley, N of San Francisco Bay. The oldest and most-honoured of California wine valleys busily fragmenting itself: Stag's Leap AVA (Cab), CARNEROS AVA (shared with SONOMA, good Chard, Pinot N and sparkling), Mt Veeder (Cab), Howell Mountain AVA (Cab, Zinfandel, Chard), Atlas Peak AVA (Sangiovese) and new AVAs on the valley floor, Rutherford and Oakville.

Russian River See Alexander Valley.

Sonoma County N of San Francisco Bay, between rival NAPA and the sea. California's most divided wine area. Includes historic Sonoma Valley AVA ('Valley of the Moon', versatile, partly in CARNEROS, see Napa); far west, RUSSIAN RIVER VALLEY AVA (increasingly devoted to Chard, Pinot N, sparkling, encompassing Chalk Hill and Sonoma-Green Valley AVAs); warmer inland, ALEXANDER, Dry Creek and Knights Valley AVAs (Cab S, Zin, increasingly Rhône varieties).

The Interior

Amador County in the SIERRA FOOTHILLS E of Sacramento. Grows vg Zinfandel, esp in Shenandoah Valley AVA.

Lodi Town and district at the N end of the SAN JOAQUIN VALLEY, its hot climate modified by a westerly air-stream.

San Joaquin Valley The great central valley of California, fertile and hot, the source of most of the jug and dessert wines in the state. (Incl LODI AVA and the Clarksburg AVA on the Sacramento River delta.)

Sierra Foothills Encompasses AMADOR (Shenandoah Valley, Fiddletown AVAs), El Dorado (AVA of the same name), Calaveras counties, among others. Zin is universal grape; Rhône and Italian varieties seen more and more.

Recent vintages

The Californian climate is far from being as consistent as its reputation. Although, on the whole, grapes ripen regularly, they are subject to spring frosts in many areas, sometimes a wet harvest-time and too often drought.

Wines from the San Joaquin Valley tend to be most consistent year by year. The vintage date on these, where there is one, is more important for telling the age of the wine than its character.

Vineyards in the Central Coast region are widely scattered; there is little pattern. The Napa and Sonoma valleys are the areas where comment can usefully be made on the last dozen or more vintages of the top varietal wines: Cabernet Sauvignon and Chardonnay.

Chardonnay

NB These ageing assessments are based on well-balanced wines with fruit flavours dominant. Very rich and oaky examples tend to be v short-lived: 2 yrs at most. Marker wines for good ageing qualities incl eg Chappellet, Clos du Bois Calcaire, Dehlinger, Freemark Abbey, Matanzas Creek, Shafer, Silverado, Simi, Sonoma-Cutrer, Trefethen.

1994	Excited murmuring in the cellars as the first major players went to bottle.
1993	A bit uneven, but the majority are above average, the best worth keeping.
1992	Comfortable growing year; agreeable wines with full flavours, good but not long-keeping balance.
1991	The best are opening up and showing signs of potential longevity.
1990	Healthy and trouble-free. Coming along as an irreproachable vintage but not a grand one.
1989	Ups and downs after rainy harvest, but the ups reach some of the decade's highest peaks. Some of the best wines still special.
1988	Lacks focus now. Drink up.
1987	Most are stepping onto the downslope. The v best continue in excellent form.
1986	Solid and worthy; a handful still have time left. Little to wait for.
1985	Except for the best, the great majority are a little past it.
1983	Good once, but only the very best (Trefethen, Freemark Abbey) carry on.

Cabernet Sauvignon

NB As with Chardonnays, over-rich and over-oaky wines usually collapse quickly. The markers for the assessments below are not Reserves, but fine standard Cabernets from eg Beaulieu, Beringer (Knights Valley), Caymus, Chappellet, Clos du Val, Fetzer (Barrel Select), Freemark Abbey, Hafner, Jordan, Laurel Glen, Louis Martini (Monte Rosso), Parducci, Raymond, Shafer, Silverado.

1994	Rivals '91 for focus, length; fruit flavours less restrained, textures less austere than that year. Textbook demo of California capacity to charm early, impress later.
1993	As the first few come to market, they still look approachable early.
1992	Well focussed, well balanced; pleasing now yet promising for a long term.
1991	After latest harvest ever, leanest, raciest, best focussed wines in years. Still slightly reticent.
1990	Picture-perfect California vintage: ripe, enveloping, still showing more fruit than maturity.
1989	Many beautifully dark, flavoury wines with solid structure for ageing; some got caught in rains.
1988	Bland, lacking focus and structure.
1987	Evolving as perhaps the best of the decade overall.
1986	Quickly approachable vintage. Baby fat is now fleshy.
1985	Lean, firm to hard, deep-flavoured. Slow-maturing but impressive (frailer ones with some decline).
1984	Showy early: ripe and fragrant. Still in good form.
1983	Awkward hard wines. Closed, but alive and perhaps still able to develop. Wait a while longer.
1982	Few or none worth a search now; even the best only tottering along.
1981	Promptly picked examples have substance and depth. Probably at peak.
1980	High reputation but merely good and solid. Over-tannic. Ready to drink.
1979	Apparently lightish, but the best keep going sturdily.
1978	Wonderful early; most faded now; the best few holding.
1977	Attractive wines now mainly crumbling.
1976	Drought made v concentrated wines. Good ones are v ripe and potent now.
1975	Delicate, charming; mature.
1974	Blockbuster wines: some flopped, the best are ripe and ready.
1970	Wonderful vintage, but has about run its course.

California wineries

Acacia Napa ✦✦✦ (Chard) 87 88 89 91 92 93 (Pinot N) 85 87 88 89 90 91 92
Specialist in single-v'yd CARNEROS Chard (Marina) and Pinot (Lund, St-
Clair, Madonna): depth, durability but recent phylloxera trouble.
Owned by CHALONE. 45,000 cases.

Adelaida Cellars San Luis Obispo ✦✦ Soft Paso Robles Chard, supple Cab,
vigorous Zin, and Rhône varieties to follow soon.

Alderbrook Sonoma ✦✦ (Chard) 86 87 88 89 90 91 Indelibly flavoured,
age-worthy Dry Creek Sém, Sauv. Recent new owners making fuller
Chard and have introduced Zin.

Alexander Valley Vineyards Sonoma ✦✦ Long-lived, rich (s'times front-
rank) Cab leads list. Also dark sturdy Pinot, mild Ries. Steady after
recent wobble. 40,000 cases.

Almaden San Joaquin ✦ Famous pioneer name, now a CANANDAIGUA-owned
everyday brand, operated from Madera. 1 million+ cases.

S Anderson Vineyard Napa ✦✦→✦✦✦ (Chard) 90 91 92 93 (Cab S) 90 91'
Robust Chard; robuster classic sparkling. Début Cab (from neighbouring v'yd) is stunning.

Arrowood Sonoma ✦✦→✦✦✦ (Chard) 88 89 90 91 92 93 (Cab S) 87 88 89 90
91 Long-time CHATEAU ST JEAN winemaker Dick A makes leaner wines
on his own behalf. Chard for oak-lovers. 15,000 cases.

Atlas Peak Napa ✦✦ Huge international (incl Antinori) investment in E
hills. Sangiovese and Sangiovese-Cab 'Consenso' extremely promising.

Au Bon Climat Sta Barbara ✦✦✦ (Chard) 90 91 92 93 (Pinot N) 87 88 89 90
91 92 93 Jim Clendenen listens to his private drummer: ultra-toasty
Chard, flavourful Pinot N, light-hearted Pinot Bl. Also for QUPE and
VITA NOVA (Santa Maria Valley) wines. 5,000 cases.

Beaucanon Napa ✦✦ Owners of Bordeaux Ch Lebegue turning out
consistently supple stylish Cab S, Merlot, Chard from own 250 acres.
Aim is for pleasant drinking.

Beaulieu Vineyard Napa ✦✦✦ (Cab S) 36 45 49 58 65 70 80 83 85 89 90 Long-
time growers and makers of famous age-worthy Georges Delatour
Private Reserve Cab (87 88 89 not so special). Also Rutherford Cab,
Beautour Cab and crackerjack dry oak-free Sauv Bl. Emphasis is now
on the approachable.

Belvedere Sonoma ✦✦ Bold appellation-named Chard, Cab S and Zin are
top of line; separate Grove Street series is value. 250,000 cases.

Benziger All SONOMA wines. Family sold off GLEN ELLEN Private Reserve and
M G Vallejo labels to HEUBLEIN. Oak flavours foremost in Cab, Merlot,
Ch'ard, Sauv, Sém. Also red and white 'A Tribute' Meritage blends.

Benziger of Glen Ellen Sonoma ✦✦ Fast-growing brand built by BENZIGER,
now HEUBLEIN-owned. Value-for-money but misnames Proprietor's
Reserve line of easy quaffers. Also M G Vallejo label, priced one step up.

Beringer Napa ✦✦→✦✦✦ (Chard) 90 91 92 93 (Cab S) 78 79 80 81 84 85 86
87 89 90 91 Century-old winery restored to front rank. Well-defined
Cabs (NV Private Reserve, Knights Valley) far outshine fat, ultra-oaky
Chards; Zin more than just worthy; Sauv lately distressingly veg in
flavour. Separate Napa Ridge is for everyday wines.

Boeger El Dorado ✦✦ Steady SIERRA Cab, Zin, savoury Barbera (esp 91).

Bonny Doon Sta Cruz Mts ✦✦✦ Rabid francophile led charge towards
Rhône varieties: esp red Cigare Volant (Grenache-Mourvèdre), white
Cuvée des Philosophes (Marsanne-Roussanne), Le Sophiste and
Viognier. Now trying Italian. All worth tasting. Never a dull moment.

Bouchaine Carneros ✦✦ (Chard) 89 90 91 92 (Pinot N) 91 92 Specialist in
CARNEROS Chard (recently less oaky), Pinot N and so far vg bone-dry
Gewürz. Cellar investment bodes well.

NB Vintages in colour are those you should choose first for drinking in 1996.

Brander Vineyard Sta Barbara ✴✴ Impressive intense Sauv from regional leader Sta Ynez Valley. Good Cab F-S Bouchet, 87 Merlot. Ripe and oaky. 8,000 cases.

Bronco Wine Company ✴→✴✴ High-capacity label-rescuing winery. Owns LAURIER, Grand Cru, Hacienda, Napa Creek, RUTHERFORD VINTNERS, prestigious LAURIER and part of Montpellier labels; also Forest Glen (well-made coastal varietals). C C Vineyard and J F J Bronco are labels for generic wines.

Bruce, David Sta Cruz Mts ✴✴ (Pinot N) 85 87 88 89 90 91 92 Long-time source of eccentric bruiser (now moderated) Chard. Pinot N (now from RUSSIAN RIVER) is forte (superior 87 89 91, vg 88 90). 32,000 cases.

Buehler Napa ✴✴ (Chard) 91 92 (Cab) 87 89 90 91 In E hills: has turned sharp corner: flavoury Cabs, Zins. Vg RUSSIAN RIVER fruit-first Chard has finesse.

In 1970, California Chardonnay plantings produced roughly 370,000 cases of wine. In 1995 the potential was approximately 18,600,000 cases.

Buena Vista Carneros ✹✹ (Chard) 90 91 92 93 (Cab S) 81 83 85 86 87 89 90 91 Historic name now German-owned. An utterly reliable source of taste-the-grapes Chard, Sauv, Cab S, Merlot, Gewürz, Ries, mainly from own 1,100-acre v'yd in CARNEROS. 110,000 cases.

Burgess Cellars Napa ✴✴ (Zin) 81 84 85 87 88 90 91 Emphasis on dark weighty well-oaked wines; Zin much the best. 30,000 cases.

BV Abbreviation of BEAULIEU VINEYARD used on its labels.

Bynum, Davis Sonoma ✹✹ (Chard) 90 91 92 93 (Pinot N) 87 88 90 91 92 Reliable, sometimes stylish wines go beyond special selection Chard, Cab S to include correct Pinot N, enticing dry Gewürz. 28,000 cases.

Byron Vineyards Sta Barbara ✴✴→✴✴✴ (Chard) 91 92 93 (Pinot) 84 85 86 87 88 89 90 91 92 R MONDAVI-owned source of tasty polished Pinot and vg Chard from estate v'yds. Also some Cab, Sauv and Pinot Bl from nearby.

Cain Cellars Napa ✴✴✴ (Cain Five) 85 86 87 89 90' Focal point is lovely supple Cain Five, blended from Cab varieties grown in estate v'yd on Spring Mt. Cain Cuvée is declassified C Five; white is MONTEREY Sauv Musqué.

Cakebread Napa ✴✴✴ (Chard) 90 91 92 93 (Cab S) 80 81 84 85 86 87 88 89 90 91 Bold style rules in memorable Sauv, excellent Chard and Cab.

Calera Monterey ✴✴✴ (Chard) 89 90 91 92 (Pinot N) 82 84 85 87 89 90 91 Heady, dark, often tannic estate Pinot Ns are much in fashion: each named after a section of the hilly chalky v'yd (Jensen, Selleck, Reed). Also smoky well-knit Chard; now Viognier. 10,000 cases.

Callaway Temecula ✴✴ (Chard) 88 89 90 91 92 93 Mild easy whites incl lees-aged Chard, oak-aged Fumé. 150,000 cases. Reds coming.

Cambria Sta Barbara ✴✴ KENDALL-JACKSON property for smoky Chard and enticing Pinot N from own grapes. Growing fast.

Canandaigua Est'd NY firm with major role in California budget wines: has acquired GUILD (COOKS, Dunnewood), Paul Masson, Taylor's California Cellars, and, mostly recently, ALMADEN and INGLENOOK.

Carey Cellars Sta Barbara ✹✹ (Chard) 89 90 91 92 93 Impressive since acquisition by FIRESTONE: vg tropical Chard, also Sauv and Cab and Merlot of the capsicum persuasion.

Carmenet Sonoma ✴✴→✴✴✴ (Cab S blend) 87 88 89 90 91 CHALONE-owned mountain v'yd and winery above SONOMA town: classy plummy Cab-based blend. Also Edna Valley white based on Sauv Bl. 27,000 cases.

Carneros Creek Carneros ✴✴→✴✴✴ (Chard) 90 91 92 93 (Pinot N) 85 87 88 89 90 91 92 Resolute explorer of climates and clones in CARNEROS focuses on Pinot N. Well-oaked Reserve, lightheartedly fruity Fleur and reliable estate bottlings. Also deftly oaked Chard. 25,000 cases.

Caymus Napa ✴✴✴ (Cab S) 73 74 75 78 79 81 85 86 87 89 90 91 Dark firm herbaceous estate Cab Special Selection is the celebrated core; slightly lighter Napa Valley covers the flanks. Also dark Zin, ultra-ripe Pinot. Good value second label: Liberty School. 35,000 cases.

Chalk Hill Sonoma ** From large estate nr Windsor, me-too Chard latterly joined by similarly oaky Sauv. Still groping for a style for Cab.

Chalone Monterey *** (Chard) 86 87 88 89 90 91 92 93 Unique hilltop estate high in Gavilan Mts; source of smoky, woody, flinty Chard and dark tannic Pinot N, both slow-to-open burgundy-imitations. Also Pinot Bl and Chenin styled after Chard. 25,000 cases. Also owns ACACIA, CARMENET, EDNA VALLEY V'YD, Gavilan. Links with (Lafite) Rothschilds.

Chappellet Napa *** (Chard) 86 87 88 91 92 93 (Cab S) 75 76 78 82 84 86 87 88 89 90 91' Beautiful amphitheatrical hill v'yd: lean racy Cab to age, understated Chard and California's best dry Chenin Bl – all long-lived. 30,000 cases.

Chateau De Baun Sonoma ** Young winery doing well by Chard and Pinot N from RUSSIAN RIVER estate v'yd. Esp value Pinot-based Ch Rouge.

Chateau Montelena Napa *** (Chard) 85 88 89 90 91 92 Understated firm age-worthy Chard and epically tannic potent Cab to age forever.

Château Potelle Napa ** French-owned new producer of balanced quietly impressive NAPA Chard (with fruity and toasty Reserve versions), also Cab S and Mt Veeder Zin. 22,000 cases.

Château St Jean Sonoma *** (Chard) 88 90 91 92 93 Intensely flavoured, richly textured, individual-v'yd Chards (Robert Young, Belle Terre, McCrea), Fumé Bls (Petite Etoile), and sweet botrytised Ries and Traminers (Robert Young, Belle Terre). Now reds (Cab, Pinot) again. Idiosyncratic classic sparkling (separate winery). Owned by Suntory.

Château Souverain Sonoma ** (Chard) 92 93 (Cab S) 85 87 88 89 90 91 Reliable Chard, Cab S and Dry Creek Zin, all distinctive, lately with lots of oak. 150,000 cases. Same owner as BERINGER.

Château Woltner Napa *** (Chard) 90 91 92 93 Ex-owners of Ch La Mission Haut Brion now encamped on NAPA hillside making 4,000 cases of wine a year. Pricey Chards from 3 separate blocks of their v'yd.

Chimney Rock Napa ** (Cab S) 86 87 88 89 90 91 92 Recently impressive Cab S from Stag's Leap District. Sound Chard, Sauv. 15,000 cases.

Christian Brothers Madera (San Joaquin Valley) One-time NAPA institution, now shrunken to brandy-only label for HEUBLEIN.

Cline Cellars Carneros ** Rhône Rangers (blends and varietals), eg Côtes d'Oakley.

Clos du Bois Sonoma **→*** (Chard) 88 90 91 92 93 (Cab S) 85 87 89 90 91 92 Sizeable Allied-Hiram Walker firm at Healdsburg has consistent Cab, Chard, Gewürz. Single-v'yd Chard (Calcaire, Flintwood), Cab S (Briarcrest), Cab S blend (Marlstone), from ALEXANDER and Dry Creek valleys, can be memorable. 320,000 cases.

Clos Pegase Napa **→*** (Chard) 87 88 89 90 91 92 93 (Cab S) 87 88 89 90 91 92 Post-modernist winery-cum-museum (or vice versa) improving faster than already good reputation. 40,000 cases.

Clos du Val Napa *** (Chard) 89 90 91 92 93 (Cab) 73 74 75 77 78 79 80 81 82 83 84 85 86 87 88 89 90 91 French-run. Supple polished Cab, Merlot, bold Zin from Stag's Leap District; improving Chard, Pinot from CARNEROS, and ageable Sém. 55,000 cases.

Codorníu Napa *** CARNEROS arm of great Catalan cava co is competing well with local Champenois.

Concannon Livermore ** WENTE BROS now own this historically famous source of Sauv. Also Chard and Cab S. 85,000 cases.

Conn Creek Napa **→*** (Cab S) 83 85 86 87 88 89 90 91 Best known for supple, almost juicy Cab: as of '93 concentrating on this and blends. Owned by Château Ste Michelle (see Washington). 30,000 cases.

Cooks Penny-saving 'Cooks Champagne' etc, belong to CANANDAIGUA.

Corbett Canyon San Luis Obispo ** (Chard) 90 91 92 93 (Pinot N Res) 85 86 87 89 90 91 92 93 Recently memorable Reserve Pinot is best. Reserve lots small, good value. Coastal Classics line abundant. 300,000 cases.

Corison Napa *** Long-time CHAPPELLET winemaker on her own making supple flavoury Cab S promising to age well.

Cosentino Napa ** (Cab) 85 86 87 88 89 90 91   Irrepressible winemaker-owner always chasing newer, loftier goals, esp with power-house Cab, Cab-blend, Pinot N. 8,000 cases.

Crichton Hall Napa **   Deep distinct NAPA Chard. Recently Merlot, Pinot too.

Culbertson Temecula **   Specialist in classic sparkling: labelled Thornton. Recently 'Brindiamo' table wines too.

Cuvaison Napa *** (Chard) 89 90 91 92 93 (Merlot) 85 86 87 88 89 90 91 92   Lean crisp CARNEROS Chard is steadily top rank. Dark ripe Merlot, and up-valley Cab following suit. Pinot is new: début 91 pretty good.

Dehlinger Sonoma **→*** (Chard) 90 91 92 93 (Pinot) 82 84 85 87 88 90' 91 92   Firm fruit-filled toasty-oaky Chard and dark full complex focal-point Pinot (regular and Reserve) from RUSSIAN R estate. Both long-lived.

DeLoach Vineyards Sonoma *** (Chard) 88 90 91 92 93 (Zin) 81 87 88 90 91 92 93   V'yd terroirs define rich Chard, lean Pinot N, juicy Sauv and vg single-v'yd Zins (Papera, Pelletti). Steadily growing family winery with RUSSIAN RIVER vines.

de Lorimier Sonoma **   ALEXANDER VALLEY estate winery: vg soft toasty Chard, better Sauv-Sém and Cab family blends show promise. 5,000 cases.

Diamond Creek Napa *** (Cab S) 76 77 78 79 80 81 82 83 84 85 86 87 89 90 91   Austere long-ageing Cabs from hilly v'yd nr Calistoga go by names of v'yd blocks, eg Gravelly Meadow, Volcanic Hill. 3,000 cases.

Domaine Carneros Carneros (***)   Showy US outpost of Taittinger in CARNEROS echoes austere style of its parent in Champagne. Recent Blanc de Blancs leads the way. 25,000+ cases.

Domaine Chandon Napa **→***   Californian outpost of Moët & Chandon is most broadly known for reliable Brut and Blanc de Noirs; luxury cuvée is Etoile, but NV Reserve really star of show. Shadow Creek is second (non-Napa) label. 500,000 cases.

Domaine Napa Napa ** (Chard) 87 89 90 91 (Cab) 83 85 86 87 89 90   French owner/grower of consistently supple balanced wine. Look esp for intense, tense Sauv and vg Cab S.

Dominus Napa **** 83 84 85 86 87 88 89 90 91 92   Christian Moueix of Pomerol is now sole owner of v fine ex-INGLENOOK v'yd. Massively tannic Cab-based blend up to 88, now looks (esp 90 91) amazingly like fine B'x.

Dry Creek Vineyard Sonoma **   Unimpeachable source of dry tasty whites, esp Chard and Fumé Bl, but also Chenin Bl. Cab S and Zin rather underrated.110,000 cases.

Duckhorn Vineyards Napa ** (Merlot) 81 82 83 84 85 86 87 88 89 90' 91   Known for dark, tannic, almost plummy-ripe reds, eg single-v'yd Merlot (Three Palms, Vine Hill). Also Sauv. 18,000 cases.

Dunn Vineyards Napa *** (Cab) 80 81 82 83 84 85 86 87 88 89 90 91 92   Ex-CAYMUS winemaker Randall Dunn makes dark tannic austere Cab from Howell Mt, slightly milder from valley floor. 4,000 cases.

Durney Vineyard Monterey ** (Cab) 83   New owners reviving Carmel Valley estate after death of eponymous founder. Esp dark robust Cab, Chard.

Eberle Winery San Luis Obispo **   Burly ex-footballer makes Cab and Zin in his own image. Also look for their polar opposite: Muscat Canelli.

Edna Valley Vineyard San Luis Obispo **→*** (Chard) 87 90 91 92 93   Characterful Chard from a joint venture of local grower and CHALONE. Pinot N starts well but fades quickly in most vintages. 48,000 cases.

Estancia MONTEREY white and SONOMA red made at FRANCISCAN.

Etude Napa *** (Pinot N) 87 89 90 91 92 93   Winemaker-owned cellar of Tony Soter (long time at CHAPPELLET, now respected consultant). Top CARNEROS Pinot (87 89 90 91), excellent Cab: both burnished, supple.

Far Niente Napa *** (Chard) 90 91 92 93 (Cab S) 85 87 89 90 91   V oaky Chard, more restrained Cab at high prices. 36,000 cases.

To decipher codes, please refer to symbols key at front of book, and to 'How to use this book' on page 5.

Farrell, Gary Sonoma ✳✳→✳✳✳ (Pinot) 88 90 91 92 93 Winemaker's label for brilliant well-oaked full-flavoured Pinots (Howard Allen Ranch, RUSSIAN RIVER). Also vg Chard, Sauv and increasingly good Russian River Zin.

Ferrari-Carano Sonoma ✳✳→✳✳✳ (Chard) 88 90 91 (Cab) 87 88 89 Shifting styles make wines hard track: red steadiest, esp Cabs, Sangiovese. Chard is ultra-buttery. From own 1,000 acres of topflight SONOMA v'yds.

Fetzer Mendocino ✳✳→✳✳✳ (Chard) 90 91 92 93 (Cab S) 87 88 89 90 91 92 Reliable source of modest (Sun Dial, Valley Oaks) to expensive (Barrel Select Reserve) ranges. Bel Arbors is value second label. 1.5M cases. Brown-Forman Distillers are owners.

Ficklin San Joaquin ✳✳ First in California to use Douro grapes. Tinta, since 1948, still California's best 'port', . Sometimes vintages.

Field Stone Sonoma ✳✳ Sturdy, increasingly steady: Petite Sirah. Also Cab.

Firestone Sta Barbara ✳✳✳→✳✳✳ (Chard) 89 90 91 92 93 (Merlot) 86 89 90 91 92 93 Fine Chard overshadows but does not outshine delicious Ries. Merlot good; Cab one of region's best; also Sauv, Gewürz. Owns CAREY.

Fisher Sonoma ✳✳ Mountain estate for often fine Chard; NAPA grapes dominate steady Cab. 10,000 cases.

Flora Springs Wine Co Napa ✳✳✳ (Chard) 90 91 92 93 (Cab S) 85 86 87 88 89 90 91 Old stone cellar. Fine Sauv Soliloquy parallels oak-fermented Chard, flavoury Reserve Cab and luxury Cab blend Trilogy: all are topline. Regular bottlings are good value. 18,000 cases.

Fogarty, Thomas Sta Cruz Mts ✳✳ Fine Gewürz from VENTANA sets the pace; whole line is well made.

Foppiano Sonoma ✳✳ Long-est'd wine family annually turns out fine reds, esp transcendent Petite Sirah. Reserve label for Chard, Cab (fine 85 87) is Fox Mountain; good value second label is Riverside Farms.

Forman Napa ✳✳✳ The winemaker who brought STERLING its first fame in the '60s now makes excellent Cab and Chard on his own. 15,000 cases.

Foxen Sta Barbara ✳✳✳ Tiny winery nestled between Sta Ynez and Sta Maria valleys. Frequently brilliant Pinot N.

Franciscan Vineyard Napa ✳✳ (Chard) 89 90 91 92 93 (Cab) 73 74 79 80 85 86 87 89 90 91 92 Big v'yd at Oakville: increasingly stylish Chard, Cab, MERITAGE. Sister labels: MOUNT VEEDER, ESTANCIA, Pinnacles (MONTEREY).

Franzia San Joaquin ✳ Penny-saver wines (eg Franzia label); varietals under William Bates brand. All say 'Made and bottled in Ripon'. 5M cases.

Freemark Abbey Napa ✳✳✳ (Chard) 84 87 88 89 90 91 92 93 (Cab S) 70 73 74 75 77 78 79 80 81 85 87 88 89 90 91 Underrated today, but consistent for inexhaustible stylish Cabs (esp single-v'yd Sycamore and Napa Valley) of great depth. Merlot soon. Vg almost-bold Chard. Late harvest Ries Edelwein infrequent but always among finest.

Fritz, J Sonoma ✳✳ V'yd-first Chard, Sauv the anchors; small winery also offers startlingly fine Dry Creek Zin (87 88 90 91 92).

Frog's Leap Napa ✳✳→✳✳✳ (Cab S) 82 84 85 87 89 90 91 92 Small winery, charming as its name (and T-shirts). Lean, racy Zin, Cab. Sauv usually understated; toasty Chard quite the reverse. Now Merlot too, and organic to boot.

Gainey Vineyard, The Sta Barbara ✳✳ Steadily attractive Chard, Sauv, Cab and esp Pinot N 'Sanford & Benedict V'yd'. 12,000 cases.

Gallo, E & J San Joaquin ✳→✳✳✳ (Cab S) 80 81 82 (Zin) 81 84 The world's biggest winery: pioneer in quantity and quality. Family-owned. Standby gulpers (hearty 'Burgundy', 'Chablis Blanc') still set national standards. Paying great and growing attention to SONOMA varietals: Cab and Chard the flagships at both mid and luxury prices. Also Merlot, Zin.

Gan Eden Sonoma ✳✳ Kosher producer of serious Chard and Cab won wide critical acclaim for early vintages. 25,000 cases.

Geyser Peak Sonoma ✳✳ Since brief marriage with Penfolds of Australia, extensive v'yds of Henry Trione in ALEXANDER and RUSSIAN RIVER valleys (lovely grapes) make oaky Aussie-style wine: modestly priced and highly characterful. 500,000 cases.

Glen Ellen Proprietor's Reserve HEUBLEIN penny-saver brand purchased '94 from BENZIGER.

Gloria Ferrer Sonoma **→*** Substantial classic sparkling winery of Spain's Freixenet has scored well, esp for Cuvée Royale and Cuvée Carneros. Smoky, silky CARNEROS Pinot N commands attention.

Green and Red Napa ** Tiny winery. Vigorous Tuscan-tasting Zin and rustic Chard worth a hunt.

Greenwood Ridge Mendocino ** (Pinot) 89 90 91 92 Est'd specialist in racy Anderson Valley Ries now offers attention-getting Cab (83 84 90), melony Sauv (88 92) and well-made Zin (92). Pinot N is less convincing. 3,000 cases.

Grgich Hills Cellars Napa *** (Chard) 88 89 90 91 92 93 (Cab S) 80 81 83 84 85 86 87 88 89 90 Winemaker Grgich and grower Hills join forces on a stern deftly-oaked Chard, impressively long-ageing rich Cab, Sauv Bl, and – too little noticed – Spätlese-sweet Ries. Also plummy thick SONOMA Zin. 40,000 cases.

Groth Vineyards Napa *** (Chard) 90 91 92 93 (Cab S) 82 83 84 85 86 87 88 89 90 91 Estate at Oakville challenges leaders with polished refined Cab (and weightier, woodier Reserve). Also vg Chard. 30,000 cases.

Guenoc Vineyards Lake County **→*** Ambitious winery/v'yd venture just N of NAPA county line. NB for Zin (81 84 85 88), Petite Sirah, Cab S. Chard surprisingly fine. Property once belonged to Lillie Langtry, hence Reserve Langtry label for MERITAGES (red and white). 75,000 cases.

Guild It and its many labels, esp COOKS, Dunnewood, bought by and absorbed into CANANDAIGUA.

Gundlach-Bundschu Sonoma **→*** (Chard) 87 90 91 92 93 (Cab) 82 85 86 87 88 89 90 91 Pioneer name solidly revived by newest generation. Rhine-farm V'yd signals memorably individual Gewürz, Cab, Merlot, Zin, Chard. 50,000 cases.

Hafner Sonoma ALEXANDER V winery for polished ageable Cab. Also Chard.

Hagafen Napa ** First and perhaps still finest of the serious kosher producers. Cab, Chard, Johannisberg Ries. 6,000 cases.

Handley Cellars Mendocino ** (Chard) 87 90 91 92 93 Winemaker-owned small producer of refined Chard and Gewürz (90 92), classic sparkling and refreshing Brightlighter (Gewürz-based). 12,000 cases.

Hanna Winery Sonoma ** 600 acres of RUSSIAN RIVER and ALEXANDER valleys with middle-of-the-road Chard, Cab, Sauv.

Hanzell Sonoma *** (Chard) 88 89 90 91 92 93 (Pinot N) 86 87 88 89 90 91 92 The late founder revolutionized California Chards, Pinot Ns with new oak in late '50s. Two owners later Hanzell remains a throwback source of its original ripe full-flavoured style. 2,000 cases.

Haywood Vineyard Sonoma ** Source of intense Zin and conventional Chard under German (Racke) ownership, made at BUENA VISTA. 34,000 cases before sale. Vintner Select Cab and Chard is bought-in wine.

A vigorous strain of phylloxera is forcing Napa and Somona to replant about half of their 60,000 acres of vineyard on new rootstocks. Napa is expected to pass its halfway mark in 1997, Sonoma about two years later.

Heitz Napa **** (Cab S) 69 70 73 74 75 77 78 79 80 81 84 85 87 88 89 90 91 An individualist winemaker has set lofty standards for his peers with his dark deep emphatic Cabs, esp Martha's Vineyard but also Bella Oaks, Napa Valley and newer Trailside. Other wines can be eccentric. 40,000 cases.

Hess Collection, The Napa **→*** (Chard) 90 91 92 93 (Cab S) 85 87 89 90 91 A Swiss art collector's winery-cum-museum in former Mont La Salle winery of CHRISTIAN BROTHERS. Steady Cab, Chard. Non-Napa Hess Selection label is vg value. 15,000 cases, aiming for 50,000.

Heublein Vast drinks firm with ambivalent interest in wine (see Beaulieu, Christian Bros, Glen Ellen Proprietor's Reserve, M G Vallejo).

Hidden Cellars Mendocino-Lake ** Ukiah producer of oaky, steady Zin ('Pacini' best) and Chard. 20,000 cases.

Hill Winery, William Napa *** (Chard) 90 91 92 93 (Cab S) 81 83 85 87 89 90 91 All but one v'yd high in Mayacamas Mts: steady Chard, ever more stylish Cabs and Merlot. 12,000 cases. Same owners as ATLAS PEAK, CALLAWAY, CLOS DU BOIS.

Hop Kiln Sonoma ** Source of refined Napa Gamay 'Valdiguie'. Gewürz is full-flavoured and large-scale. 10,000 cases.

Husch Vineyards Mendocino ** Reliable Chard, Sauv, Cab; sometimes outstanding Pinot N and Gewürz from Anderson Valley. 15,000 cases.

Inglenook Napa **→*** (Chard) 86 90 91 (Cab) 55 56 62 68 78 81 87 88 89 Great old NAPA name in perpetual transition. (The winery now belongs to F F Copola.) The label has three separate lines from penny-savers to underrated and recently improved Napa: esp supple Cab, heartier Cask (Reserve) Cab and thoroughly tannic Reunion Cab. Also Merlot, Gravion (Sauv Bl-Sém) and Reserve Chard. 60,000 cases of Napa. Fresh start in '95 under new CANANDAIGUA ownership.

Iron Horse Vineyards Sonoma *** (Chard) 91 92 93 (Cab) 88 89 90 91 92 Substantial RUSSIAN RIVER property increasingly for v successful classic sparkling with real finesse, but continues with Chard and Pinot from same estate v'yd. Cab and Sauv from affiliated ALEXANDER v v'yd can be memorable. Laurent-Perrier joint venture on the way. 40,000 cases.

Jade Mountain Napa Sharing winery with WHITE ROCK and pursuing lofty goals using Rhône varieties, esp Syrah.

Jekel Vineyards Monterey ** (Chard) 90 91 92 93 Jekel's ripe juicy Ries is most successful wine from SALINAS v'yds. Also good Chard, intensely regional (capsicum-flavoured) Cab. 60,000 cases.

Jepson Vineyards Mendocino ** Chard, Sauv Bl, classic sparkling, and pot-still brandy from estate in Ukiah area. 30,000 cases.

Jordan Sonoma *** (Chard) 91 92 93 (Cab S) 80 81 84 85 86 87 88 89 90 91 92 Extravagant ALEXANDER VALLEY estate models its Cab on supplest Bordeaux. But it lasts. (Chard is less successful.) Separate classic sparkling called simply 'J' is deft, soft, luxurious. 75,000 cases.

Judd's Hill Napa Tiny property nr PHELPS. 1,500 cases of vg Cab S.

Karly Amador ** Among more ambitious sources of SIERRA FOOTHILLS Zin.

Keenan Winery, Robert Napa ** (Chard) 90 91 92 93 (Cab) 81 85 86 87 88 89 90 91 Winery on Spring Mountain has veered away from overweight heavily oaked to more restrained Cab, Merlot, Chard. 12,000 cases.

Kendall-Jackson Lake County **→*** (Chard) 90 91 92 93 (Cab) 86 87 88 89 90 91 92 Hugely successful maker of popular rather sweet Chards; Sauv, v oaky Cab (primary label reds more trad). Now developing an empire of smaller estate or regional wineries incl CAMBRIA, Camelot (Central Coast), Edmeades, LA CREMA, R PEPI, J Stonestreet (N Coast).

Kenwood Vineyards Sonoma **→*** (Chard) 90 91 92 93 (Cab S) 87 88 89 90 91 Substantial producer of vg crisp Sauv and focussed Zin. Soft Chard (incl single-v'yd Beltane) and plummy Cab S (single-v'yd Jack London Ranch) can challenge the best. 150,000 cases.

Kistler Vineyards Sonoma *** (Chard) 88 89 90 91 92 93 Chards much in smoky buttery style (esp single v'yd). Pinot N and Cab more recent.

Konocti Cellars Lake County ** Excellent value Sauv, good Chard, but intrigue is refreshing Cab Franc. 40,000 cases.

Korbel Sonoma ** Long-established classic sparkling specialists place extra emphasis on fruit flavours, lots of fizz. Natural, Brut and Blanc de Blancs are best. 1.5 million cases.

Krug, Charles Napa ** (Chard) 90 91 92 93 (Cab S) 73 74 78 79 81 84 85 88 89 90 91 92 Historically important winery with generally sound wines. Cabs at head of list. CK-Mondavi is jug brand. 200,000 cases.

For key to grape variety abbreviations, see pages 6–9.

Kunde Estate Sonoma ★★ Long-time growers turned winemakers ('88). Good (Chard) to brilliant (Sauv) early results. Cab, Cab Reserve, Merlot and Zin still finding a footing.

La Crema Sonoma ★★ (Chard) 89 90 91 92 93 (Pinot N) 88 89 90 91 92 Deftly oaked Chard; often deep-flavoured Pinot. Now KENDALL-JACKSON-owned.

Lakespring Napa ★★ Sound Cab, Chard, Sauv, flossier Merlot. 15,000 cases.

Landmark Sonoma ★★ (Chard) 83 85 87 89 90 91 92 Long-time Chard specialist moving from crisp and fresh to overripe too-toasty-buttery.

Laurel Glen Sonoma ★★★ (Cab S) 81 82 85 86 89 90 91 92 Fine, firm, distinctly regional Cab from steep hilly v'yd in Sonoma Mountain AVA. Counterpoint is good value second label. 5,000 cases.

Laurier Sonoma ★★ (Chard) 90 91' 92' Crown-jewel label of BRONCO WINE CO. Currently aiming high with Chard. Pinot N began with 93.

Lava Cap El Dorado ★ Where bold styles rule, these are understated, intriguing Zins, Cabs and others.

Lazy Creek Mendocino ★★ 'Retirement hobby' of a long-time restaurant waiter yields serious Anderson Valley Gewürz and Chard. Also Pinot N.

Leeward Winery Ventura (Chard) 89 90 91 92 93 Ultra-toasty Central Coast Chards are the mainstay. 18,000 cases.

Lohr, J Central Coast ★★ Wide range of steady varietals from wineries at San José and Paso Robles (SAN LUIS OBISPO), v'yds in PR and Clarksburg.

Long Vineyards Napa ★★★ (Chard) 89 90 91 92 93 (Cab) 80 81 82 83 84 85 86 87 90 Tiny neighbour of CHAPPELLET: lush Chard, flavoury Cab.

Lyeth Vineyard Sonoma ★★ Former winery, now a brand owned by J C Boisset (Burgundy). Christophe is more modest label for bought wines.

Lytton Springs Sonoma ★★ Now RIDGE-owned: ink-dark hard heady Zins.

MacRostie Sonoma ★★ Veteran winemaker producing silky CARNEROS Chards, increasingly buttery-toasty. Recently Pinot N and Merlot too.

Madrona El Dorado ★★ Loftiest v'yds in SIERRA FOOTHILLS, good for steady Chards (among others). 10,000 cases.

Maison Deutz San Luis Obispo ★★→★★★ Californian arm of Champagne Wm Deutz shows a firm sense of style: grapes from Arroyo Grande AVA.

Mark West Vineyards Sonoma ★★ V satisfactory Gewürz from coolest part of RUSSIAN RIVER. Also sturdy to rustic Chard, Pinot and, at times, classic Bl de Noirs sparkling. Now owned by Associated Vintners Group.

Markham Napa ★★→★★★ (Chard) 89 90 91 92 93 (Cab S) 88 89 90 91 92 Recently good to excellent, esp Merlot and B'x-style blend 'Laurent'.

Martin Bros San Luis Obispo ★★ (Chard) 87 88 89 90 Family winery aims to establish Paso Robles as California's Piedmont with Nebbiolo, and is developing Italian theme with Aleatico, 'Vin Santo', Cab-Sangiovese and 'Primitivo' Zin. Oaked Chard is only non-Italian white left.

Martini, Louis M Napa ★★→★★★ (Cab S) 52 55 59 64 68 70 74 78 79 80 83 85 87 88 89 90 91 92 Historic family-owned winery with high standards, esp single v'yd Cab (Monte Rosso), Merlot (Los Vinedos del Rio) and reserve Cab. Zins s'times surpassing.

Masson Vineyards Monterey ★→★★ Now the 'fighting varietal' spoke in CANANDAIGUA's growing wheel of California wineries and labels.

Matanzas Creek Sonoma ★★★ (Chard) 89 90 91 92 93 (Merlot) 89 90 91 Fine ripe fruity toasty-oaky Chard, Sauv, and renowned ultra-fleshy Merlot.

Maurice Car'rie Temecula ★★ Setting standards for its region with reliable, approachable Chard, Sauv and others.

Mayacamas Napa ★★★ (Chard) 76 79 85 87 90 91 (Cab S) 69 73 78 81 85 87 88 89 90 Vg small v'yd with rich Chard and firm (but no longer steel-hard) Cab. Some Sauv, Zin. 5,000 cases.

McDowell Valley Vineyards Mendocino ★★ Now a grower-label for family with hearts set on Rhône varieties, esp ancient-vine Syrah and Grenache (Les Vieux Cépages). 40,000 cases.

Meridian San Luis Obispo ★★ Fast-growing latecomer property. Impressive single-v'yd Edna Valley Chard (87 89 90 91); Pinot N (88) and Paso Robles Syrah (88) and Cab. 300,000 cases.

Meritage Trademarked name for reds or whites using Bordeaux grape varieties. Aiming for 'varietal' status and gaining ground.

Merry Vintners Sonoma (**) Busy consulting winemaker (LAURIER, Liparita, etc) takes time to make small lots of well-oaked Chards for her own label.

Merryvale Vintners Napa ** St-Helena partnership: solid Chard, better Cab. Sauv-Sém white MERITAGE is best. Second label: Sunny St Helena.

Michel-Schlumberger Sonoma ** Dry Creek Valley winery with reinvigorating Alsace input; esp evident with newly subtle Cab S.

Mill Creek Sonoma ** Cab, Merlot, Chard, Sauv. 15,000 cases.

Mirassou Central Coast ** Fifth-generation grower in Sta Clara; pioneer in Monterey (SALINAS VALLEY). Value Cab, Chard, Pinot Bl, Gewürz, Pinot N and v pleasant classic sparkling. 350,000 cases.

Mondavi, Robert Napa **→**** (Chard) 85 90 91 92 93 (Cab) 71 73 74 75 79 81 84 85 87 89 90 91 Winery with brilliant quarter-century record of innovation in styles, equipment, technique. Famous successes: Sauv ('Fumé Bl'), Cab, Chard, even Pinot N. 'Reserves' are marvels, regularly among NAPA's best. Less pricey California appellation varietals: Mondavi-Woodbridge. 500,000 cases. See also Opus One.

Mont St John Napa ** Old NAPA wine family makes good value Pinot N, Chard from own CARNEROS v'yd; buys in for solid Cab. 20,000 cases.

Monte Volpe Mendocino * Greg Graziano looks to his heritage and wins with tart, juicy Barbera, rich Sangiovese and luscious Moscato.

Monterey Peninsula Monterey ** Small winery in Monterey town: chunky long-living reds, esp Zin, Cab, from SALINAS grapes and others.

Monterey Vineyard, The Monterey ** Seagram-owned label for Chard, Pinot N, Cab: Classic and more costly Limited Release. 550,000 cases.

Monteviña Amador ** Major force in revitalizing hearty-style SIERRA FOOTHILL Zins. Now, under ownership of SUTTER HOME, also turning to a major exploration of Italian varieties. 50,000 cases.

Monticello Cellars Napa ** (Cab S) 83 85 86 87 88 89 90 91 Ultra-modern winery nr Napa City. Grows its own sternly oaky Chard, buys in grapes for graceful Monticello and darkly tannic Corley Reserve Cabs.

Morgan Monterey **→*** (Pinot) 89 90 91 92 Winemaker-owner. Rich earthy Pinot becoming flagship ahead of toasty Chard. Fine SONOMA Sauv.

Mount Eden Vineyards Sta Cruz Mts ** (Chard) 88 90 91 92 93 Expensive big-scale Chard from old Martin Ray v'yds and gentler one from MONTEREY. Also Pinot N, Cab. 4,000 cases.

Mount Veeder Napa *** (Chard) 90 91 92 93 (Cab) 74 81 87 89 90 91 Once oaky Chards and austere Cabs are gentler and better balanced since acquired by FRANCISCAN. Now MERITAGE (88 89 90 91). About 8,000 cases.

Mumm Napa Valley Napa *** G H Mumm-Seagram joint venture out of the box fast with fine leanish Vintage Reserve (85 86 87) and Brut. Also distinctive single-v'yd Winery Lake cuvée. Luxury DVX newest.

Murphy-Goode Sonoma ** Large ALEXANDER v estate. Pinot Bl interesting, Sauv important. Pretty good (oaky) Cab S and Merlot. 40,000 cases.

Nalle Sonoma **→*** (Zin) 85 86 88 89 90 91 Winemaker-owned Dry Creek cellar gets to the very heart of Zin. Wonderfully berryish young; that and more with age. 2,500 cases.

Napa Ridge Sonoma (!) * New name for famous old Italian Swiss Colony winery at Asti. Related to BERINGER. Pinot N (and others) to watch.

Navarro Vineyards Mendocino **→*** (Chard) 83 85 86 88 89 90 91 Firm fine Chard, outstanding dry Gewürz and Ries from cool Anderson Valley. Pinot N begins to find a footing. 12,000 cases.

Newton Vineyards Napa *** (Chard) 92 (Cab S) 83 85 86 88 89 90 91 Luxurious estate growing more so; formerly ponderous style now reined back to the merely opulent for Chard, Cab, Merlot.

Niebaum-Coppola Estate Napa ** Movie-man Coppola's luxuriously wayward hobby much invigorated by new winemaker (Tony Soter of ETUDE) and acquisition of INGLENOOK winery and 220-acre v'yd (but not name). MERITAGE-like Rubicon is the (improving) wine.

Opus One Napa ★★★★ (Cab S) 80 81 83 85 87 88 89 90 91 Joint venture of R MONDAVI and Baronne Philippine de Rothschild. Spectacular new winery opened '92. Wines are showpieces too. 10,000 cases.

Parducci Mendocino ★★ (Cab S) 85 87 90 91 92 Long-est'd v'yds and winery: ever reliable Cab, Cab-Merlot, Zin, Barbera. No-oak Chard, off-dry Sauv.

Rigorous pest management during the past 20 years is apparently causing Botrytis cinerea to disappear from some of its old Napa haunts. Some vineyards once favoured for late harvest wines can no longer produce them.

Pecota, Robert Napa ★★ Drink-young Cab, Sauv, Chard, Gamay.

Pedroncelli Sonoma ★★ (Chard) 90 91 92 93 (Cab S) 83 85 89 90 91 Old family firm with above-average sturdy vinous Cab, Zin (esp Reserves). Chard and Sauv growing stylish. 125,000 cases.

Pepi, Robert Napa ★★→★★★ (Chard) 87 89 90 91 92 (Cab S) 84 85 87 89 90 91 Originally Sauv specialist; that still good but Cab S 'Vine Hill', winning Sangiovese 'Colline di Sassi' more important.

Phelps, Joseph Napa ★★★ (Chard) 87 89 90 91 92 93 (Cab S) 75 81 85 87 89 90 91 92 Deluxe winery and beautiful v'yd: impeccable standards. Vg Chard, Cabs (esp Backus Vineyard, vg 90), Rhône varieties (under Vin du Mistral label) and splendid late-harvest Ries, Gewürz. Reserve red Insignia Cab has tamed tannin and is now consistently impressive.

Philips, R H Yolo, Sacramento Valley ★★ Large producer worth seeking out esp for some of California's most stylish tributes to the Rhône.

Pine Ridge Napa ★★→★★★ (Chard) 90 91 92 93 (Cab S) 80 81 84 85 86 87 89 90 91 92 Winery nr Stag's Leap makes consistently well-oaked Chard, Cab (several) and Merlot. 50,000 cases.

Piper Sonoma Sonoma ★★→★★★ Venture of Piper-Heidsieck: mostly RUSSIAN RIVER grapes. Vg classic sparklers esp with bottle-age. 125,000 cases.

Preston Sonoma ★★→★★★ (Cab S) 86 87 89 90 One of California's few 'terroiristes' concentrating on wines best suited to his Dry Creek v'yds: esp top Sauv and Zin, with promising Barbera, Syrah and Marsanne experiments.

Quady Winery San Joaquin ★★ Imaginative Muscat dessert wines from Madera: incl celebrated orangey 'Essencia', dark 'Elysium' and Moscato d'Asti-like 'Electra'. 'Starboard' is a play on port; better name than wine.

Quail Ridge Napa ★★ (Chard) 90 91 Specialist in barrel-fermented Chard. Also Cab. Recently added vg Sauv and Merlot. New owners in '95.

Quivira Sonoma ★★ Sauv, intensely berryish Zin and MERITAGE-like blend Cab Cuvée all from Dry Creek Valley. Recently more oaky.

Qupé Sta Barbara ★★→★★★ Never-a-dull-moment cellar-mate of AU BON CLIMAT. Marsanne, Pinot Bl, Syrah are all well worth trying.

Rafanelli, A Sonoma ★★ (Cab) 84 88 89 90 91 92 (Zin) 82 86 87 89 90 91 92 Hearty, somewhat rustic Dry Creek Zin; Cab of striking intensity.

Rancho Sisquoc Sta Barbara ★★ Highly personal little winery shows vivid quality of Sta Maria Valley grapes, incl Ries, Chard, even Silvaner.

Ravenswood Sonoma ★★★ A critical success for (or despite) great bruiser reds, heady and tannic. 15,000 cases.

Raymond Vineyards and Cellar Napa ★★→★★★ (Chard) 89 90 91 92 93 (Cab S) 75 77 80 81 83 84 85 87 89 90 91 92 Old NAPA wine family now with Japanese partners. Emphatically fruity Chard and Sauv Bl; dark sturdy keeper Cabs, esp Reserve. 110,000 cases.

Ridge Sta Cruz Mts ★★★★ (Cab S) 83 85 86 87 88 89 90 91 Winery of highest repute among connoisseurs draws from NAPA, SONOMA, SAN LUIS OBISPO and its own mountain v'yd for concentrated v tannic Cabs and Zins, needing long maturing in bottle. Most notable efforts from single v'yds, esp Monte Bello, York Creek (Spring Mt) Cabs, Geyserville, Dusi Zins. Now also extremely smoky Chard. 40,000 cases.

Rochioli, J Sonoma ★★ Owners of v'yd famed for Pinot N now making vg example of their own. Also fine Sauv Bl.

Roederer Estate Mendocino ★★★ Anderson Valley branch of Champagne house (est '88). Resonant Roederer style apparent esp in luxury cuvée l'Ermitage. Still stuns the Champenois. Potentially 90,000 cases.

Rombauer Vineyards Napa ★★ Well-oaked Chard, dark Cab (esp Reserve-style 'Meilleur du Chai'). 15,000 cases.

Count on typical Napa Valley and other North Coast Cabernet Sauvignons to last eight years in good form. Do not expect any but famously durable ones to stay at their peak beyond fifteen.

Roudon-Smith Sta Cruz Mts ★★ Chard, Cab. 10,000 cases.

Round Hill Napa ★★ Formerly diverse range now narrowed to Cab, Chard, Merlot, Sauv, but in 3 price ranges: bargain California, regular Round Hill, separate top-of-the-line Rutherford Ranch. 350,000 cases.

Rutherford Hill Napa ★★ (Chard) 88 89 90 91 (Cab) 82 85 87 88 89 90 Larger stable-mate of FREEMARK ABBEY. Flavoury Chards (Jaeger, XVS), sturdy Cabs (XVS) can be more rewarding than the 75%-of-production Merlots.

Rutherford Ranch See Round Hill. Value.

Rutherford Vintners Napa ★★ One time NAPA Cab specialist, now BRONCO brand.

St Clement Napa ★★→★★★ (Chard) 89 90 91 92 93 (Cab) 77 79 86 87 88 90 91 Firm Chard, Cab, Merlot. Distinctive ageable Sauv. Japanese-owned.

St Francis Sonoma ★★ (Chard) 90 91 92 93 (Cab S) 86 88 89 90 91 Gaining speed after slow start. Firm v tasty SONOMA VALLEY estate Chard (esp 90). Steady Merlot. Also Cab. 34,000 cases.

St Supery Napa ★★ French-owned; supplied by 500-acre estate v'yd in Pope Valley. Good Sauv Bl, accessible Cab. Also Chard – and now Merlot. 50,000 cases, able to expand tenfold.

Saintsbury Carneros ★★★ (Chard) 81 85 89 90 91 92 (Pinot N) 85 86 87 88 89 90 91 92 CARNEROS' finest (and slowest-ageing) Pinot N. Lighter Pinot Garnet, and less-oaky-than-formerly Chard also vg. 35,000 cases.

Sanford Sta Barbara ★★★ (Chard) 88 89 90 91 92 93 (Pinot N) 81 85 87 89 90 91 92 Specialist in clean-fruity intense age-worthy Pinot N (esp Barrel Select). Also exceptionally bold Chard, firmly regional Sauv Bl and a little Pinot N 'Gris'. 40,000 cases.

Santa Barbara Winery Sta Barbara ★★ (Chard) 89 90 91 92 93 (Pinot) 90 91 92 Former jug-wine producer, now among regional leaders, esp for Reserve Chard. Also Pinot N, Zin, Cab. 28,000 cases.

Santa Cruz Mountain V'yd Sta Cruz Mts ★★ Huge, tannic, heady Pinot N and Cab dominate. 2,500 cases.

Santa Ynez Valley Winery Sta Barbara ★★ Sauv, Chard and Merlot.

Santino Amador ★★ Stylish SIERRA FOOTHILLS Zins (Fiddletown, Grand Père); also crackerjack white Zin. Italian varieties too.

Scharffenberger Mendocino ★★ First to try MENDOCINO for serious classic sparkling. Now Clicquot-owned and doing well. 25,000 cases.

Schramsberg Napa ★★★★ Dedicated specialist: California's best sparkling. Historic caves. Reserve splendid; Bl de Noir outstanding, deserves 2–10 yrs. Luxury cuvée J Schram from '87 (now on 89) is America's Krug.

Schug Cellars Sonoma ★★ (Chard) 89 90 91 92 (Pinot N) 91 German-born and trained owner-winemaker developing refined Chard and Pinot N from CARNEROS. Relocated from NAPA to Carneros in '91. 10,000 cases.

Sebastiani Sonoma ★★ Substantial old family firm works on several different market levels: SONOMA appellations at top (esp 'Sonoma Cask'), North Coast varietals in middle, August Sebastiani Country wines in jugs. Also Vendange cheapo label. 4 million cases.

Seghesio Sonoma ★★ (Chard) 89 90 91 92 93 (Zin) 85 86 88 89 90 91 92 Long-time jug-wine producer recently turned to bottling its own wines with striking results. Vg Chard, Pinot N; often exceptional Zins (esp 'Old Vines' reserve bottling) and fresh juicy Sangiovese 'Vitigno Toscano'.

Sequoia Grove Napa ★★→★★★ (Chard) 91 92 (Cab) 82 87 89 90 91 Vg Chards age well. NAPA Cabs (2 labels): dark and firm.

Shadow Creek See Domaine Chandon.

Shafer Vineyards Napa ★★★ (Chard) 90 91 92 93 (Cab S) 80 84 85 86 87 89 90 91 92 Polished Chard (new 80 acres in CARNEROS), stylish Cab (esp Hillside Select) and Stag's Leap District Merlot.

Sierra Vista El Dorado ★★ Steady SIERRA FOOTHILLS Chard, Cab, Zin, Syrah.

Silver Oak Napa ★★★ Cabs, very American-oaked, eg pricey Bonny's V'yd.

Silverado Vineyards Napa ★★→★★★ (Chard) 84 85 87 90 91 92 93 (Cab S) 85 86 87 89 90 91 92 Showy hilltop Stag's Leap District winery. Cab, Chard, Sauv all consistently refined; Cabs from '81 on ageing well.

Simi Sonoma ★★★ (Chard) 80 84 85 88 90 91 92 93 (Cab) 74 81 85 87 90 91 Restored historic winery has flowered under expert direction of Zelma Long. Wonderfully long-lived Chard, Sauv. Seductive Cab rosé for picnics. Vg Cab recently austere. New Sauv-Sém Sendal. 130,000 cases.

Smith & Hook Monterey ★★ (Cab S) 86 88 90 91 Specialist in dark intensely regional Cabs – so herbaceous you can taste dill. Also Merlots. Lone Oak is second label for Cab, Chard. 10,000 cases.

Smith-Madrone Napa ★★ Soft, round, durable Spring Mt Ries; Cab, Chard.

Sonoma-Cutrer Vineyards Sonoma ★★★→★★★★ (Chard) 81 84 87 88 90 91 92 Ultimate specialist in Chard. Advanced techniques display characters of individual v'yds, as in Burgundy. Les Pierres is No 1 ager; Russian River Ranches is quickly accessible. 75,000 cases.

Spottswoode Napa ★★★→★★★★ (Cab S) 83 85 86 87 89 90 91 Seductive resonant luxury Cab from tiny estate v'yd right in St Helena town. Also supple polished Sauv. 3,500 cases.

Stag's Leap Wine Cellars Napa ★★★→★★★★ (Chard) 85 88 90 91 92 93 (Cab S) 75 77 78 83 84 86 89 90 91 Celebrated v'yd and cellar for Cabs (NAPA, Stag's Leap V'yd, and recently controversial top-of-line Cask 23). Also vg Chard, Ries, improving Sauv. 40,000 cases.

Zinfandel, after many interim theories, is again thought to have originated somewhere between southern Hungary, Slovenia and Croatia.

Stags' Leap Winery Napa ★★ Neighbour to above with more tannic, austere Cab and muscular Petite Syrah. 25,000 cases.

Sterling Napa ★★★ (Chard) 85 88 90 91 92 93 (Cab S) 78 80 81 85 87 88 89 90 91 Proficient (also scenic) winery owned by Seagram. Strong tart Sauv and Chards. Burly Cab, Reserve (Cab-based) and vg v'yd designated Three Palms Merlot. Winery Lake Vineyard Pinot N still promises more than it performs. 150,000 cases.

Stony Hill Napa ★★★ (Chard) 75 81 85 88 90 91 92 Hilly v'yd and winery for many of California's v best whites over past 30 yrs. Founder Fred McCrea died in '77, widow Eleanor in '91; son Peter carries on powerful tradition. Chard less steely, more fleshy than before, esp SHV non-estate version. Oak-tinged Ries and Gewürz understated but ageworthy. 6,000 cases.

Stratford Napa ★★ Merchant label for reliable Cab, Merlot and Chard.

Strong Vineyard, Rodney Sonoma ★★ (Chard) 87 89 90 91 92 93 (Cab) 87 88 90 91 92 Formerly Sonoma V'yds, draws mostly on RUSSIAN RIVER VALLEY for steady Chards (esp Chalk Hill V'yd) and Pinot N; ALEXANDER VALLEY for Cabs (esp single-v'yd Alexander's Crown) and Sauv. 375,000 cases.

Sutter Home Napa ★★ (Zin) 68 73 77 83 85 89 90 91 92 Best known for sweet white Zin; most admired for sometimes heady Amador Zin. Also bargain-priced Cab, Chard. 3 million cases.

Swan, Joseph Sonoma ★★ (Zin) 77 78 79 80 81 82 83 84 85 86 87 90 91 Ultra-bold Zins, Pinots of late Joe Swan, now directed by his son-in-law.

Swanson Napa ★★→★★★ Estimable age-worthy Chards lead list; Cab and Merlot are worth note. Also pursuing Italian (esp Sangiovese) and Rhône reds. Less oak would be a good idea.

Taft Street Sonoma ★★ After muddling along, has hit an impressive stride with esp good value RUSSIAN RIVER Chards, Merlots. 18,000 cases.

Talbott, R Monterey   Wealthy owner doing well with Chards from Santa Lucia Highlands AVA, Carmel Valley.

Tanner, Lane Santa Barbara   Owner-winemaker with often superb single-v'yd Pinots (Sanford & Benedict, Sierra Madre) to drink now or keep.

Torres Estate, Marimar Sonoma (★★★)   Sister of Catalan hero makes ultra-buttery Chard; estate in W RUSSIAN RIVER VALLEY promises lovely Pinot.

Trefethen Napa ★★★ (Chard) 79 81 82 83 84 85 86 87 90 91 92 93 (Cab) 75 78 79 80 84 85 87 89 90 91   Respected family winery. Vg dry Ries, tense Chard for ageing (late-released Library wines show how well). Cab shows increasing depths. Low-priced Eshcol blends value.

Tudal Napa ✻✻ (Cab S) 80 84 86 87 89 90 91   Tiny estate winery N of St Helena; steady source of dark firm ageable Cabs.

Tulocay Napa ★★ (Pinot N) 82 85 89 90 91 92   Tiny winery at Napa City. Chard and esp Pinot can be v accomplished. Cab is also worth attention.

Turnbull Wine Cellars Napa ★★ (Cab) 81 83 84 85 86 87 89 90 91   Rich full minty Cab from estate facing ROBERT MONDAVI winery; SONOMA Chard.

Ventana Monterey ★★   '78 winery, showcase for owner's v'yds: watch for Chard and esp Sauv from Musqué clone.

Viader Napa ★★ 90 91   Argentine Delia Viader fled to California to do her own thing: fine Cab-based blend from estate in hills above St Helena.

Viansa Carneros ★★   Sam SEBASTIANI's reliable NAPA-SONOMA Chard, Sauv and Cab, now concentrating on everything Italian: Nebbiolo, Sangiovese, Sangio-Cab ('Thalia'), etc to good effect. No wine made in '91.

Vichon Winery Napa ★★→★★★ (Chard) 90 91 92 93 (Cab) 82 85 86 87 89 90 91   MONDAVI-owned. Subtle agreeable Chevrignon (Sauv-Sém). Stern oaky NAPA Cab and Chard. Coastal Selection is value second line.

Villa Mt Eden Napa ★★ (Chard) 90 91 92 93 (Cab) 75 85 86 89 90 91   Oakville estate reputed for rich, nearly plummy Cab – still the wine to seek. Bought and expanded by Château Ste Michelle group (see Washington). Grand Reserve is label for NAPA, Cellar Select for California appellations.

Vine Cliff Napa ★★★   New well-heeled family winery in E hills above Oakville. Likeable early Chard, flavoursome portentous Cab.

Vita Nova Sta Barbara ★★   Label from stable of AU BON CLIMAT. To watch esp for Bordelais red blend.

Weibel Mendocino ★→★★   Mainly tank-made sparklers; also range of accessible table wines. 200,000 cases. Serious money problems.

Wente Bros Livermore and Monterey ★→★★★   Historic specialists in whites, esp LIVERMORE Sauv and Sém. MONTEREY sweet Ries can be exceptional. A little classic sparkling. 300,000 cases.

White Rock Napa ★★★   French owner placing faith in promise-the-earth v'yd nr Stag's Leap District. Esp finessy Cab-based simply 'Claret' (90 91).

White Oak Sonoma ✻✻ (Chard) 88 90 91 92 93 (Zin) 87 88 90 91   Dominant Zin and underrated, vibrantly fruity ALEXANDER VALLEY Chard and Sauv.

Whitehall Lane Napa ★★   Recently bought from Japanese owners by San Francisco family. Obligatory Chard, Cab, weighty Knights Valley Merlot.

Wild Horse Winery San Luis Obispo ★★→★★★ (Pinot) 86 87 89 90 91 92   Reaches into STA BARBARA for impressive Pinot. Good Merlot. Also Chard, Cab.

William Wheeler Sonoma ★★   French owners (J-C Boisset). Chard is the mainstay. 19,000 cases. Now a label only, winery up for sale.

Williams & Selyem Sonoma ★★★→★★★★ (Pinot) 85 87 88 89 90 91 92   Intense smoky pricey Pinot of emphatic character, esp Rochioli and Allen v'yds.

Zaca Mesa Sta Barbara ★★   Deliberately down-sized from 80,000 to 35,000 cases and refocussed on buttery Chard, well-wooded Pinot and Rhône varieties (esp Syrah) for future.

ZD Napa ★★→★★★ (Pinot) 86 87 90 91 92   Lusty Chard scarred by American oak is the ZD signature wine. Pinot N is often finer. 18,000 cases.

NB Vintages in colour are those you should choose first for drinking in 1996.

The Pacific Northwest

America's main quality challenge to California lies in Oregon and Washington, on the same latitudes of the Pacific Coast as France is on the Atlantic. As in California, the modern wine industry started in the 1960s. Each of the northwestern states (Oregon, Washington, Idaho) has developed a distinct identity. The small production of British Columbia fits in here, too.

Oregon's vines (6,050 acres) lie mainly in the cool temperate Willamette and warmer Umpqua valleys between the Coast and Cascade Ranges, in sea-tempered climates giving delicate flavours.

Washington's vineyards (11,300 acres) are mostly east of the Cascades in a dry, severe climate scarcely curbed by the Yakima and Columbia rivers. Idaho's are east of Oregon along the Snake River. Both regions have hot days and cool nights which preserve acidity and intensify flavours.

Most of Oregon's 96 wineries are small and highly individual. Vintages are as uneven as in Burgundy, whose Pinot Noir is the state's most celebrated (also controversial) grape. Pinot had a rare run of good vintages with '88, '89, '90 and '91; '92 was hot and heady; '93 again was excellent, and '94 looks promising.

The Washington industry, with 95 wineries, is remarkably consistent over a wide range. Cabernet and Merlot grow excellently, as well as all the classic white varieties. A run of fine vintages, '88, '89, '90, '91, '92, '94 has coincided with maturing winemaking talent. '93 was a record crop. Value remains good.

Oregon

Adelsheim Vineyard Willamette ✱✱✱ (Chard) 90 (Merlot) 88 92 (Pinot) 88 90 91 92 Nicely oaked Pinot, Chard best early. Pinots Gr, Bl: clean, bracing.

Amity Willamette ✱✱ (w) 90 91 92 Excellent Gewürz and Ries, patchy Pinot.

Argyle (Dundee Wine Co) ✱✱→✱✱✱ Willamette (w) 90 (sp) 87 88 Since '87, Australia's NW outpost, led by Brian Croser of Petaluma. Dry Ries, Chard; vg classic sparkling.

Beaux Freres Willamette ✱✱✱ Big, extracted, oaky, somewhat controversial Pinot (91 92), now Chard (92). Partly owned by critic Robert Parker.

Bethel Heights Willamette ✱✱✱ (Pinot N) 88 90 91 92 Deftly made, rising-star Pinot N ('Early Release', Vintage and Selected) from estate nr Salem; top quality. Also adequate Chard.

Bridgeview Vineyards Rogue Valley ✱ (w) 91 (Pinot N) 91 92 Starting to command attention, esp whites: good Gewürz, also Chard and Pinot.

Cameron Willamette (Pinot) ✱✱ 85 91 Nr KNUDSEN-ERATH. Eclectic producer of Pinot N, Chard: some great, others conversation pieces. Vg Pinot Bl.

Château Benoit Willamette ✱ Most consistent successes Müller-T and Ries. Pioneer sparkling wines. Currently solid, unexciting.

Chehalem N Willamette ✱✱ (Pinot N) 90 91 92 93 Small premium estate winery, since '90. Big Pinot N. Also Chard, Pinot Gr and 'Cerise' (Passetoutgrains-style Gamay-Pinot N). To watch, esp for Pinot N.

Cristom N Willamette ✱✱ r 92 First vintage '91. Vg Pinot, Chard. Rising star.

Domaine Drouhin Willamette ✱✱✱✱ Bold enterprise of great Beaune name; superb quality. Fine Pinot (88 89 90 91 92), tiny amount of estate Chard.

Domaine Serene Willamette New as of 92 vintage. Meaty Pinot N from former PANTHER CREEK winemaker.

Elk Cove Vineyards Willamette ✱✱ Pinot N was somewhat erratic; steadier now and can rival best (esp estate 'La Bohème', 90 91 92 93). Also fresh Ries (and late-harvest 86 92), well-oaked Chard and Pinot Gr.

Eola Hills Nr Salem (Willamette) ** Consistently good Chardonnay (4 acre v'yd-designated) and Pinot Noir.

Evesham Wood Willamette ** Tiny family winery nr Salem showing talent. Esp Pinot Gr and Gewürz (92 93); Pinot N (91 92) often vg too.

Eyrie Vineyards, The Willamette *** Pioneer ('65) winery with Burgundian convictions. Oregon's most famous Pinot (87, though recent vintages wavering) and v oaky Chard (91). Also Pinots Gr (irreplaceable with salmon), Meunier, dry Muscat.

Foris Vineyards S Oregon * Pinot N, Chard etc from warmer Rogue Valley. Oustanding Merlot and Gewürz in 92.

Henry Estate Umpqua Valley * Distinctive Pinot (American oak), good Gewürz.

Hinman Vineyards S Willamette *→** Eugene winery focusing on quality: Pinot Gr, Gewürz, Ries all vg. Sliven Ridge is the premium label.

King Estate S Willamette ** Huge by Oregon standards. First wines: 92 93 Pinot Gr (vg), Chard and Pinot N.

Knudsen-Erath Willamette **→*** (Pinot) 91 92 93 Oregon's second-largest winery (est '72). Big turnaround in last 3 yrs: value Pinot improving, dry Ries and Gewürz v fine. Pinot Gr 93 is among O's best; good Chard.

Lange Winery Yamhill County (Willamette) * Small family winery, occasionally brilliant Pinot N and Pinot Gr. Inconsistent.

Laurel Ridge Winery Willamette *→** Washington County winery with v'yds in Yamhill. Reliable classic method sparkling and Sauv Bl.

Montinore Vineyards Willamette ** Ambitious winery with, for Oregon, huge 465-acre v'yd nr Forest Grove. New French winemaker since '92. Chard and Pinot N improving (Pinot N 91).

Oak Knoll Willamette ** Started with fruit wines but has turned into one of Oregon's larger Pinot N producers. Recently inconsistent.

Panther Creek Willamette *** (Pinot N) 89 90 91 92 Tiny McMinnville winery: excellent beefy Pinot N, luscious Melon de Bourgogne.

Ponzi Willamette Valley *** (Pinot N) 90 91 92 Small winery almost in Portland, well-known for Ries. Also Pinot Gr, Chard and delicate full, (French) oaky, cellarable Pinot N.

Rex Hill Willamette *** (Pinot N) 83 88 90 91 92' Well-financed successful assault on top Pinots, Chards. Esp single v'yd. Ries too.

St-Innocent Willamette ** Up-coming Eola Hills winery: Chard, Pinot N.

Shafer Vineyard Cellars Willamette ** Small producer of frequently good Pinot N, delicate Chard. Currently rather inconsistent.

Sokol Blosser Willamette ** (Pinot N) 90 91 92 One of the larger Oregon wineries; aim is popular taste with easy, accessible Chard, Pinot (vg 91 92). Also Ries, Sauv, Merlot (seldom grown in Oregon): recently rough.

Tualatin Vineyards Willamette ** (Pinot) 92 93 (Chard) 91 92 Large estate winery: v consistent Chard best, plus Gewürz, Ries. Pinot improving.

Tyee Willamette ** Recent arrival: family-owned and run, now well-established. Early vintages of Gewürz, Chard, Pinot N are well made.

Valley View Vineyards S Oregon ** Rogue Valley estate since '90. Focus is top Cab (90 91 92), Merlot, Chard (91 92), Sauv (92): always improving.

Van Duzer Eola and Amity Hills (N Willamette) * William Hill-owned (see California). Exciting Ries, vg Pinot N, Chard since '90.

Willamette Valley Vineyards Willamette ** New, large, nr Salem. Moderate to high quality Chard, Ries, Pinot N. Founders' Reserve wines best.

Yamhill Valley Vineyards Willamette * Young estate near college town of McMinnville focuses on Pinot Gr, Chard and Pinot N (avoid 91 92).

Washington and Idaho

Arbor Crest Spokane (Washington) ** Expanding winery has had ups and downs. Ups are Chard, Sauv Bl and late-harvest Ries.

Barnard Griffin Prosser (Washington) *** Small producer of well-made Merlot (91), Chard (esp barrel-fermented, 93) and Sauv.

Caterina NE Wash * Spokane wines (Cab, Merlot, Chard, Sauv) to watch.

Château Ste Michelle (ubiquitous in Washington) ✭✭✭   Regional giant growing ever larger. Château Ste M and COLUMBIA CREST made 750,000 cases before '91 acquisition of SNOQUALMIE, then the state's second-largest producer. Major v'yd holdings, first-rate equipment and skilful winemakers keep Chard (91 92 93 94), Sém, Sauv Bl, Ries, Cab (83 85 87 89 91 92 93 94) and Merlot in the front ranks. First serious efforts at sparkling are attractive. Newest reds and Chards v exciting.

Chinook Wines Yakima Valley (Washington) ✭✭✭   Owner-winemakers Kay Simon and Clay Mackey buying in Yakima Valley grapes for sturdy Chard, Sauv and Merlot. Excellent Sém too (92).

Columbia Crest Columbia Valley (Washington) ✭✭✭   Separately run CHATEAU STE MICHELLE label for delicious well-made accessible wines priced one cut lower – most of them from big River Run v'yd. Reserve line is best Cab, Merlot (88 90 91 92 93 94) and Chard. Reds value.

Columbia Winery Woodinville (Washington) ✭✭✭→✭✭✭✭ (Cab) 79 85 86 87 88 89 92 93 94 Pioneer ('62, as Associated Vintners): still a leader. Balanced stylish understated single-v'yd wines, esp Merlot (Milestone), Cabs (Otis, Red Willow), Syrah (Red Willow). Oak-fermented Woodburne Chard, elegant Pinot, vg fruity long-lived Sém. Reds consistently among finest.

Covey Run Yakima Valley (Washington) ✭✭ (Chard) 91 92 93 94 Mostly estate. Intriguing Aligoté and Caille de Fumé; intense heady Merlot, Cab.

De Stefano ✭ Small winery for classic sparkling. 'De Stefano' since late '94.

DeLille Cellars Woodinville (Washington) Exciting new winery for vg red 'Bordelais' blends: Chaleur Estate (needs 5 yrs age), 'D2' (more forward, affordable). Massive expertise and potential. Another LEONETTI?

Gordon Brothers Columbia Valley (Washington) ✭✭   Tiny cellar for consistent Chard (Reserve 91), Merlot and Cab (89).

Hedges Cellars Puget Sound (Washington) ✭✭   Esp for Washington's first (vg) Cab-Merlot blend. Began as négociant label, now with own v'yd.

Hogue Cellars Yakima Valley (Washington) ✭✭✭ (Cab) 85 87 88 89 90 91 92 93 94 Leader in region, known for off-dry whites (esp Ries, Chenin, Sauv), but recently for stylish balanced Chard, Merlot, Cab. Value.

Kiona Vineyards Yakima Valley (Washington) ✭✭ (Cab) 83 85 86 Good v'yd for substantial Cabs and (Austrian) Lembergers; fruity Chard and Ries. Also v fine late harvest Ries (88) and Gewürz.

Latah Creek Spokane (Washington) ✭ Small cellar, mainly for off-dry Chenin Bl, Ries. Erratic, esp with drier oak-aged types and reds.

Leonetti Walla Walla (Washington) ✭✭✭ (r) 83 85 86 87 88 91 92 93 94 Harmonious individualistic Cab, fine big-scale Merlot: bold, ageworthy.

McCrea Seattle (Washington) ✭✭   Small winery for delicious Chard and Grenache. Experiments with Rhône blends are in progress.

Neuharth W Washington ✭ Olympic Peninsula winery uses Yakima Valley grapes for supple balanced Cab (Chard fair, though not equal to reds).

Preston Wine Cellars Columbia Valley (Washington) ✭ Wide range. Some eccentric, some conventional/sound. Occasionally wonderful Cab, Merlot.

Quilceda Creek Vintners Puget Sound (Washington) ✭✭✭ (Cab) 83 85 86 87 88 89 90 91 92 93 94 Leading ripe well-oaked Cab S from Columbia Valley grapes is the speciality.

Ste Chapelle Caldwell (Idaho, nr Boise) ✭✭→✭✭✭   Top-drawer winemaking keeps intensely flavoured, impeccably balanced Chard, Ries (Washington and local v'yds) in forefront. Reds on the rise. Attractive sparkling.

Salishan Vancouver (Washington) ✭ Promising Pinot N and occasionally brilliant dry Ries from nr Willamette Valley.

Silver Lake nr Seattle (Washington) ✭✭   Fine regular and reserve Chard and Sauv; also fine Cab, Merlot.

Snoqualmie ✭✭ Consistent quality. Whites best.

Staton Hills Yakima Valley (Washington) ✭✭   Recently inconsistent, s'times excellent Cab; gd off-dry white (Ries, Chenin, Gewürz). Also sparkling.

Stewart Vineyards Yakima Valley (Washington) ✭✭   Estate v'yds well-suited to whites, esp Chard and Ries. Latterly some promising Cabs.

Thomas, Paul Bellevue (Washington) ★   Started as (still is in part) a fruit winery; now: full-flavoured Chard, Sauv, Chenin Bl. Reds show promise.

Thurston Wolfe Yakima Valley (Wash) ★★★   Tiny eclectic Yakima-based winery: excellent Lemberger (red), late harvest Sauv, Black Muscat.

Washington Hills Cellars Yakima Valley (Washington) ★★   Newly est'd. Winemaker Brian Carter making solid attractive Sém, Fumé and Cab. Value. Apex label is premium line for Sauv, Cab, late harvest white.

Waterbrook Walla Walla (Wash) ★★ (r) 85 87 89 **90** 91 92 93 94   Young winery has now hit its stride: stylish big and oaky Cab, Merlot, Sauv.

Will, Andrew Seattle ★★★   Exciting Cab and Merlot from E Washington grapes.

Woodward Canyon Walla Walla (Washington) ★★★ (r) 81 82 83 84 85 86 87 88 89 90 91 92 93 94   Small top-notch cellar: well-oaked ultra-bold Cab, buttery Chard. Also Charbonneau blends (Merlot-Cab, Sauv-Sém).

British Columbia

A small but locally significant wine industry has developed since the '70s in the Okanagan Valley, 150 miles east of Vancouver, in climatic conditions not very different from eastern Washington.

CedarCreek ★★ 92 94   Fine Merlot, good Ehrenfelser and Ries.

Gray Monk ★★ 92 94   Good Okanagan Auxerrois, Gewürz and Pinot.

Mission Hill ★→★★★ 92 94   Caused a gold medal stir in '94. Esp for Chard.

Summerhill ★★ 91 92 94   Entered British Columbia with a bang. Zesty sparkling Ries and ice wine, and fresh still Ries.

East of the Rockies & Ontario

Producers in New York (there are now 101 in 6 AVAs) and other eastern states, as well as Ohio (43 in 4 AVAs) and Ontario (30), traditionally made wine from hardy native grapes, varieties of Vitis labrusca whose wine has strong 'foxy' flavour, off-putting to non-initiates. To escape the labrusca flavour, growers then turned to more nuanced French-American hybrids. Today consumer taste plus cellar and vineyard technology have largely bypassed these, although Seyval Blanc and Vidal keep their fans. European varieties, esp Chardonnay and Riesling, are now firmly established. Success is mixed (the winter of 1993/94 took its toll), but progress, from Virginia to Ontario, is accelerating, particularly on Long Island.

Allegro ★★ 91 92   Est'd Pennsylvania producer of noteworthy Chard, Cab.

Aurora (Aurore) One of the best white French-American hybrids; the most widely planted in New York. Good for sparkling.

Baco Noir One of the better red French-American hybrids: high acidity but clean dark wine which usually needs ageing.

Bedell ★★★ 91 92 93 94   LONG ISLAND winery known for excellent Merlot.

Biltmore Estate ★★ 92 93   North Carolina winery on 8,500-acres with 253-room mansion, America's largest. Chard and sparkling.

Canandaigua Wine Co ★→★★★   FINGER LAKES winery with many California properties. Major producer (second largest in the US, behind Gallo) of labrusca, and table and sparkling wines. Owns Manischewitz, the best-selling kosher sweet wine. See California.

Catawba Old native American grape, perhaps the second most widely grown. Pale red and 'foxy' flavoured. Appears in crowd-pleasing dry, off-dry and sweet wines, still and sparkling.

Cave Spring ★★★ 91 93 Ontario boutique: sophisticated Chard and Ries.

Cayuga White Hybrid created at Cornell Uni. Delicate fruity off-dry wine.

Chaddsford ★★ 91 93 94 Pennsylvania producer since '82; esp for burgundy-style Chard.

Chamard ★★ 91 93 Connecticut's best winery, owned by Tiffany's chairman. Top Chard. AVA is Southeastern New England.

Chambourcin Red grape of French origin; under-appreciated Loire-like reds and agreeable rosé.

Château des Charmes ★★→★★★ 91 93 Show-place château-style Ontario winery (opened '94). Good Chard, Aligoté, Cab, sparkling.

Chelois Popular red hybrid. Dry medium-bodied burgundy-style wine.

Clinton Vineyards ★★ 92 93 Hudson River winery known for clean dry Seyval Bl and spirited Seyval sparkling.

Concord Labrusca variety, by far the most widely planted grape in New York. Heavy 'foxy' sweet one-dimensional red wines, but mostly grape juice and jelly. Long a staple of kosher wines.

Debonné Vineyards ★★ 91 93 Popular Ohio estate (in Lake Erie AVA): hybrids, eg CHAMBOURCIN and VIDAL; and vinifera, eg Chard, Ries.

De Chaunac Red wine hybrid found in New York and Canada. Avoid.

Finger Lakes Beautiful historic upstate NY cool-climate region, source of most of the state's wines (52 producers), and the seat of its 'vinifera revolution'. GLENORA and WAGNER are the outstanding wineries.

Firelands ★★ 90 91 93 Ohio estate on Isle St George in LAKE ERIE AVA, growing Chard and Cab.

Frank, Dr Konstantin (Vinifera Wine Cellars) ★★ 90 93 Small, influential winery. The late Dr F was a pioneer in growing European vines in the FINGER LAKES. Vg new Chateau Frank sparkling and promising Pinot N.

Glenora Wine Cellars ★★★ 91 93 94 Aggressive FINGER LAKES producer of outstanding sparkling wine and good Chard and Ries.

Gristina ★★ 93 94 Promising young winery on LONG ISLAND'S NORTH FORK AVA with Chard, Cab and Pinot N.

Hamptons (Aka South Fork) LONG ISLAND AVA. The top winery is moneyed SagPond.

Hargrave Vineyard ★★★ 90 93 94 LONG ISLAND'S pioneering winery, v'yds since '72 on NORTH FORK. Good Chard, Cab S and Cab F.

Henry of Pelham ★★★ 91 93 Elegant Ontario Chard, Ries and distinctive Baco Noir.

Hillebrand Estates ★→★★★ 91 94 Aggressive Ontario producer attracting attention with Chard and Bordeaux-style red blend.

Hudson River Region America's oldest winegrowing district (21 producers) and New York's first AVA. Straddles the river, two hours' drive N of Manhattan.

Inniskillin ★★★ 91 93 Outstanding (VINCOR-owned) producer that spear-headed birth of modern Ontario wine industry. Skilful burgundy-style Chard and Pinot N. Vg Riesling, Vidal ice wine and Auxerrois. Interesting winery tours.

Knapp ★★ 90 91 93 Versatile FINGER LAKES winery. Tasty Bordeaux-style blend, Cab, Ries, Bl de Bls sparkling.

Lake Erie The biggest grape-growing district in the east; 25,000 acres along the shore of Lake Erie, incl portions of New York, Pennsylvania and Ohio. 90% is CONCORD, most heavily in New York's Chautauqua County. Also the name of a tristate AVA: NY's sector has 6 wineries, Pennsylvania's 5, Ohio's 20.

Lakeridge ★★ Popular Florida winery nr Disneyland. Esp for Muscadine. Spumante-like sparkling from local Carlos grapes flies off the shelf. Rarely uses vintage dates.

Lamoreaux Landing ★★→★★★ 93 94 Young, stylish, talented FINGER LAKES house: promising Chard and Ries.

Lenz ★★★ 92 93 94 Classy winery of NORTH FORK AVA. Fine austere Chard in the Chablis mode, also Gewürz, Merlot and sparkling wine.

Long Island The most talked about new wine region E of the Rockies and a hothouse of experimentation. Currently 1,300 acres all vinifera (47% Chard) and 2 AVAs (NORTH FORK and HAMPTONS). Most of its 18 wineries are on the North Fork. Best varieties: Chard, Cab, Merlot. A long growing season; relatively little frost.

Maréchal Foch Workmanlike red French hybrid. Depending on vinification yields boldly flavoured or nouveau-style wines.

Michigan Potentially America's finest cool-climate Ries area. Ch Chantal's can be stunning, Ch Grand Traverse's vg. Watch Fenn Valley, Tabor Hill, Bowers Harbor (for sparkling version).

Millbrook ✶✶✶ 90 91 93 The No 1 HUDSON RIVER REGION winery. Money-no-object viticulture and savvy marketing has lifted spiffy, whitewashed Millbrook in big old barn into New York's firmament. Burgundian Chards are splendid, Cab F can be delicious.

Niagara Quintessential labrusca greenish-white grape, sometimes called 'white Concord'. Makes lovely aromatic sweet wine and wants to be gobbled right off the vine.

North Fork LONG ISLAND AVA (of 2). Top wineries: BEDELL, GRISTINA, HARGRAVE, LENZ, PALMER, PELLEGRINI, PINDAR. 2½ hrs drive from Manhattan.

Ontario Main E Canada wine region, on Niagara Peninsula: 30 producers. Heavy investment and glimmerings of great future. Ries, Chard, even Pinot N, show incipient longevity. Ice wine is flagship.

Palmer ✶✶✶ 91 93 94 Superior LONG ISLAND (NORTH FORK) producer and byword in the Darwinian metropolitan market. Surviving with class, perpetual-motion marketing and flavourful Chard, Sauv Bl and Chinon-like Cab F.

Pellegrini ✶✶ 91 93 94 LONG ISLAND's most enchantingly designed winery (on NORTH FORK), opened '93. Opulent Merlot, stylish Chard, B'x-like Cab. Early hints of inspired winemaking.

Pindar Vineyards ✶✶→✶✶✶ 93 94 Huge 285-acre mini-Gallo winery of NORTH FORK, LONG ISLAND. Wide range of toothsome blends and popular varietals, incl Chard, Merlot, and esp good Bordeaux-type red blend, Mythology.

Ravat (Vignoles) French-American white hybrid of intense flavour and high acidity, often made in yummy prize-winning 'late harvest' style.

Sakonnet ✶✶ 92 94 Largest New England winery, based in Little Compton, Rhode Island (Southeastern New Eng AVA). Its regional reputation, resting on Chard, VIDAL and dry Gewürz, has blossomed since '85.

Stonington ✶✶ 91 93 Casual Connecticut estate in Southeastern New England AVA. Peppy wines. Good Burgundian-style Chard.

Swedish Hill Creditable Ries from FINGER LAKES. Also Chancellor and late-harvest Vignoles.

Tomasello ✶✶ 91 Progressive New Jersey winery. Good Blanc de Noirs sparkling and CHAMBOURCIN.

Vincor International ✶→✶✶ 93 Canada's biggest winery (formerly Brights-Cartier), in Ontario, BC, Quebec, New Brunswick. Mass-market and premium wines; varietals, blends, Canadian and imported grapes. Owns INNISKILLIN. Also Jackson-Triggs and Sawmill Creek labels.

Vidal Mainstay French-American hybrid making full-bodied personable dry whites.

Vineland Estates ✶✶ 91 92 Good Ontario producer whose VIDAL ice wine, dry and semi-dry Ries and Ries ice wine are admired.

Wagner Vineyards ✶✶✶ 91 93 Jewel of a winery in the FINGER LAKES – arguably New York's best – for succulent barrel-fermented Chard, dry and sweet Ries, RAVAT ice wine and NIAGARA. Charming to visit.

Westport Rivers ✶✶ 90 93 Massachusetts house est'd '89. Good Chard and fledgling sparkling. (Southeastern New England AVA.)

Wiemer, Hermann J ✶✶→✶✶✶ 90 92 93 Creative German-born FINGER LAKES winemaker. Interesting Ries incl vg sparkling and 'late harvest'.

Other Eastern states

Virginia Ambitious new wine state (since '72). Acquiring status. Whites,
esp Chard, lead. 46 wineries (in 6 AVAs) produce good Ries, Viognier,
Cabs and Merlot from 1,394 acres of grapes. Monticello has some of
the top producers: Prince Michel (though its good 'Le Ducq' B'x blend
is made mostly with Napa grapes) and its second property, Rapidan
River, Barboursville (inspired Malvaxia Reserve), Montdomaine.
Others are Horton (for Viognier), Ingleside Plantation, Linden, Naked
Mountain, Meredyth, Oasis (for 'Champagne'), Piedmont, Tarara and
Williamsburg Winery. Ch Morrisette and Wintergreen bear watching.

Missouri A blossoming industry with 30 producers in 3 AVAs: Augusta (first
in the US), Hermann, Ozark Highlands. In-state sales catching fire. Best
wines: Seyval, Vidal, Vignoles (sweet/dry). Top estate is Stone Hill, in
Hermann (since 1847), with rich red from Norton (or Cynthiana) grape;
Hermannhof (1852), is drawing notice for the same. Mount Pleasant,
in Augusta, makes rich 'port' and nice sparkling. To watch: Augusta
Winery, Blumenhof, Les Bourgeois, Montelle, Röbller, St James.

Maryland 9 wineries and 2 AVAs. Basignani makes good Merlot, Chard,
Seyval. Catoctin, a mountain-v'yd boutique-winery, is developing solid,
modest-priced Cab, Chard. Elk Run's Chard and Cab can be delicious.
Best-known Boordy Vineyards gets good marks for Seyval (esp Reserve),
Vidal, Cab. Woodhall understands Seyval, Cab. Fiore's Chambourcin is
interesting. Catoctin AVA is main Cab, Chard area. Linganore is 2nd AVA.

The Southwest

Texas

In the past fifteen years a brand-new Texan wine industry has sprung
noisily to life. It now has 450 growers and 26 wineries (10 in Hill Country).
The best wines (nearly all varietals) are comparable with N California's.

Bell Mountain Hill Country AVA with just one winery.
Bell Mountain Vineyards TEXAS HILL COUNTRY winery at FREDERICKSBURG. 52
acres. Erratic but known for Cab S.
Cap*Rock Since '90. Cab, Chard, Chenin, Sauv, sparkling all promising.
Cordier Estates (Ste-Genevieve V'yds) Largest producer by far: 1,000 acres
for Sauv and varietals. Links with B'x Cordier and University of Texas.
Escondido Valley Latest (4th) Texas AVA, in western Trans-Pecos region.
Fall Creek Vineyards TEXAS HILL COUNTRY estate: fine Sauv, Chard. Also Cab S
and surprising Emerald Ries and Carnelian.
Fredericksburg Texas Hill Country AVA.
Hill County Cellars Nr Austin: exemplary Chard.
Leftwich Tiny amount of good Chard from Lubbock v'yds; winery nr Austin.
Llano Estacado The pioneer (since '76); nr Lubbock with 220 acres (210
leased). Known for Chard and Cab S.
Pheasant Ridge Lubbock estate founded '78. Now 36 acres. Esp for reds.
Texas High Plains AVA centred on Lubbock.
Texas Hill Country One of 3 Hill Country AVAs (S of Lubbock, W of Austin).

New Mexico etc

At present **New Mexico** is known for one wine, Rio Grande Valley's remarkable
Gruet sparkling, but other sparklers (Dom Cheurlin) and Anderson Valley
Winery varietals have proved the potential. There are now two AVAs and 19
wineries. **Colorado** and **Arizona** are both focusing on vinifera grapes:
Colorado for Merlots and Meritages (Plum Creek Cellars and Grande River
V'yds at Palisade are both vg), Arizona with Pinot N and Cab from hot, high
altitude, terra rossa v'yds. **Oklahoma and Utah** will be the next to emerge.

South America

Argentina

Argentina has the world's fifth-largest wine production, most of it uncritically consumed within South America. But things are stirring. Modernization is now rapid; exports have increased by four times over the last decade, while the domestic market is beginning to demand higher standards. Quality vineyards (all irrigated) are concentrated in Mendoza province in the Andean foothills at about 2,000 feet. San Juan, to the north, is the second largest vineyard area. San Rafael, 140 miles south of Mendoza city, is slightly cooler. Salta to the north and Rio Negro, south, also produce interesting wines. Denomination of Origin regulations now exist for Luján de Cuyo and San Rafael; others are on the way. Malbec is the most planted grape; Cabernet, Pinot Noir etc are on the increase – reds generally being better than whites. Star-ratings are local, and provisional.

Arizu, Leoncio ✦✦✦ Makers of Luigi Bosca wines: Malbec, Cab and Syrah from small Mendoza (Maipu) bodega; all vg. Also interesting Chard, Sauv, Pinot N and Riesling.

Bianchi, Bodegas ✦→✦✦ Well-known premium producer at San Rafael owned by Seagram. Don Valentin Cab, Bianchi Borgoña and Malbec-Barbera blend are best-sellers. 'Particular' is their top Cab. Also Sauv.

Canale, Bodegas ✦✦→✦✦✦ Premier Rio Negro winery: Cab and Sém both won Bordeaux gold medals, Merlot good too. Also good whites, esp Torrontes.

Catena ✦✦✦✦ Modern California-influenced Mendoza winery, one of Argentina's best. Top oak cask Chard; excellent Malbec.

Esmeralda ✦✦→✦✦✦ Producers of a good Cab and Chard, St Felician, at Mendoza. NB 89 Malbec, Syrah.

Etchart Salta and Mendoza wineries. Delicate aromatic but dry Torrontes white and sound range of reds (mainly Cab S). French consultant, M Rolland, makes top red, Arnold B Etchart (**90**).

Finca Flichman ✦✦ Old Mendoza firm now owned by a bank (investing heavily in wine). Top Caballero de la Cepa Cab and Chard, plus Syrah, Merlot and other single-varietals.

Goyenechea, Bodegas ✦→✦✦ Basque family firm in San Rafael making old-style wines (esp Cab, Syrah, Malbec, Merlot and Aberdeen Angus red), but now modernizing.

Lagarde ✦→✦✦✦ Old bodega revived. Good Cabs and Malbecs.

Lopez, Bodegas ✦✦→✦✦✦ Family firm best known for their Château Montchenot red and white and Château Vieux Cab.

M Chandon ✦✦✦→✦✦✦✦ Producers of Baron B and M Chandon sparkling wine under Moët & Chandon supervision. Also still reds and whites including vg Castel Chandon, less exciting Kleinburg (whites), smooth Comte de Valmont, Beltour and Clos du Moulin (reds). Chard Renaud Poirier is first of varietal range.

Martins ✦✦ Recent notable Merlot and Malbec from Mendoza.

Nacari, Bodegas ✦✦ Small La Rioja cooperative. NB its Torrontes white.

Navarro Correas ✦✦✦ 3 wineries: vg Malbec, notable Syrah, sparkling and Spätlese-style Ries.

Norton, Bodegas ✦✦→✦✦✦ Old firm, originally English, now Austrian-owned, being thoroughly updated. Reds (esp Malbec) are best. Perdriel is premium brand. Also good sparkling.

Orfila, José ✦→✦✦✦ Long-established bodega at St Martin, Mendoza. Top wines: Cautivo Cab and white Extra Dry (Pinot Bl). Now making sparkling wine in France for local sale.

Peñaflor ✶ Argentina's biggest wine co, reputedly the world's third largest. Bulk wines, for top jugs, but see Trapiche (esp Medalla), Andean V'yds, Fond de Cave (Chard, Cab). Aim is to export. Also 'Sherry': Tio Quinto.

H Piper ✶✶→✶✶✶ Sparkling wine made under licence from Piper-Heidsieck.

Rural, Bodegas La ✶✶→✶✶✶ ('San Filipe' is label.) Family-run winery at Coquimbito (Mendoza) making some of Argentina's best Ries and Gewürz and some good reds. Filipe Rutini Cab is top wine. Also a charming wine museum.

San Telmo ✶✶→✶✶✶ Modern winery with a Californian air and outstanding fresh full-flavoured Chard, Chenin Bl, Merlot and esp Malbec and Cab 'Cruz de Piedra-Maipu'. 568 acres.

Santa Ana, Bodegas ✶→✶✶✶ Said to be S America's biggest. Old-est'd family firm at Guaymallen, Mendoza. Wide range incl good Syrah, Merlot-Malbec, Pinot Gr 'blush' and sparkling (Chard-Chenin) 'Villeneuve'.

Suter, Bodegas ✶ Swiss-founded firm (distributed by Seagram) making best-selling Etiquetta Marron white and good classic 'JS' red.

Toso, Pascual ✶✶→✶✶✶ Old Mendoza winery at San José, making one of Argentina's best reds, Cabernet Toso. Also Ries and sparkling wines (incl one classic method).

Trapiche ✶✶→✶✶✶ Premium label of PENAFLOR and a spearhead of technical advance. Single-grape wine range incls Merlot, Malbec, Cab, Pinot N, Chard and Torrontes. Also 'Oak Cask' selection, rosé Cab, native grapes.

Vistalba, Viña y Cava ✶✶✶→✶✶✶✶ (Ex Perez Cuesta) Small bodega for outstanding reds, esp Syrah and Malbec.

Weinert, Bodegas ✶✶✶✶ Small winery. Classic reds led by good Cab-Merlot-Malbec Cavas de Weinert. Also promising Sauv Carrascal.

Chile

Conditions are ideal for wine-growing in central Chile, the Maipo Valley near Santiago, and in places for 300 miles south. But the country's potential has only started to emerge in the past eight years. So far wines are good – very few fine, but foreign investors, especially French, are optimistic. Cabernets led the way with easy-drinking flavours, rapidly gaining in quality. Other varieties, especially Sauvignon and Chardonnay, now show equal promise. Stainless steel and new oak have brought international standards. A new region (Casablanca), between Santiago and Valparaíso on the coast, is proving especially good for whites. Many long-time grape-growers are no longer supplying large bodegas but branching out, even exporting, alone. Principal regions, from north to south, are Aconcagua, Maipo, Rapel, Maule, Bio-Bio.

Aconcagua N'most quality wine region. Incl CASABLANCA, Panquehue.

Agrícola Aquitania 60-acre joint venture of Bordeaux's Paul Pontallier and Bruno Prats with Felipe de Solminihac near COUSINO MACUL. Cabernet only, from '94. Their label is Paul Bruno.

Bio-Bio Southernmost 'quality' wine region. V rainy.

Bisquertt Colchagua (RAPEL) winery (350 acres), for generations owned by family of same name. Began exporting in '91.

Caliterra Former venture of ERRAZURIZ and Franciscan of California in Curicó (MAULE). Now solely owned by Errázuriz. Good value Chard, Cab.

Cánepa, José Big modern bodega, of Italian origin, MAIPO-based, handling wine from several areas. Vg frank and fruity Cab from Lontué, Curicó, and 100 miles south; recently particularly good Chard (some oak-aged), RIES and Sauv. Top wines from Domaine Caperana in Isla de Maipo.

Carmen, Viña One of the oldest Chilean wineries, dating from 1850 and acquired by Ricardo Claro (also owners of SANTA RITA) in '88. Extensive v'yds and new MAIPO winery make good Sauv, Chard and Cab.

Carta Vieja 1,160 acres in Maule. Del Pedregal family-owned for 6 generations. Top selection Cab and Chard are good.

Casa Lapostolle Moneyed (Grand Marnier) new French winery in Colchagua, MAULE. Cab, Chard, Sauv etc from '94.

Casablanca Second bodega of VINA SANTA CAROLINA. For premium wines.

Chateau Los Boldos Label of French-owned Santa Amalia winery at the foot of the Andes in MAULE. Cab, Sauv and some Chard for export only.

Concha y Toro Biggest, most outward-looking wine firm with bodegas and v'yds all over Chile, mainly in MAIPO and RAPEL, totalling 4,210 acres. Remarkable dark deep Cab, Merlot, Petit Verdot. Brands are Marqués de Casa Concha, Casillero del Diablo. Chard and Sauv now well est'd. New top wine: Don Melchor Cab. Banfi (USA) are minority shareholders.

Cono Sur Young company with 650 acres of v'yd at Chimbarongo in RAPEL. Best-known for Chard, Cab and esp Pinot Noir (Reserva 93).

Cousiño Macul Distinguished and beautiful old estate nr Santiago (MAIPO). V dry Sém and Chard. Don Luis light red, Don Matias dark and tannic, are good Cabs. Antiguas Reservas is top export Cab.

Domaine Oriental French-owned modern winery in Maule Valley, Talca.

Domaine Rabat Since 1927 in MAIPO and Colchagua (RAPEL); offers Cab, Chard, Sauv Bl. Different labels from each estate incl Domaine Rabat, Santa Adela. Joined forces with Grand Marnier in '94.

Echeverría Grower from Curicó (MAULE) producing good Sauv, Chard, Cab.

Errázuriz Historic firm in Aconcagua Valley, N of Santiago, modernized and making v rich full-bodied wines, esp Cabernet Don Maximiano.

Exposición Label of Talca Coop (MAULE). Growers cover 3,210 v'yd acres.

Lomas de Cauquenes Brand name for best wines from the coop, formed by Cauquenes (MAULE) growers after 1939 earthquake. 260 members farm 3.7 million acres of unirrigated land and 120,000 of irrigated.

Maipo Oldest wine region, nr Santiago. Relatively warm. Many good v'yds.

Maule S'most top quality region. Incl Curicó, Lontué, Talca etc.

Montes Label of Discover Wines 250-acre estate, nr Curicó (MAULE), emerging as quality leader with good fresh Sauv, Chard, Fumé Bl aged in American oak, fruity Merlot, good Montes Cab, excellent Montes Alpha (90, French oak). Nogales and Villa Montes are unoaked, less expensive.

Porta Viña, New winery in Rancagua (RAPEL). First-rate Chard and Cab.

Portal del Alto Viña, Small bodega with excellent Cab-Merlot blend. 250 acres: half in Maipo, half in San Fernando (RAPEL).

Rapel Central quality region. Incl Colchagua, Rancagua, Cachapoal etc.

Robles, Los Label of coop of Curicó, MAULE. Wines incl Cab and Merlot. 'Flying winemaker' Peter Bright is consultant.

San Carlos, Viña New Colchagua bodega with good range. Esp full-bodied Sém, Cab-Malbec blend.

San Pedro Long established at Molina, Curicó (MAULE). One of the biggest exporters, with 2,250 acres in the Lontué Valley. Gato Negro and Gato Blanco are top sellers. Best are Castillo de Molina and Santa Helena Seleccíon de Director. Jacques Lurton of Bordeaux is consultant.

Santa Carolina Viña, Architecturally splendid old Santiago bodega with 'Reserva Especial'. Recent modernization. Concentrating on Casablanca Valley (ACONCAGUA) and quality. Other labels: CASABLANCA, Ochagavía.

Santa Ema 550-acre MAIPO estate in family since 1955. Esp Cab, Merlot (90), Sauv and Chard. Reserva Cab (French oak) is their pride.

Santa Emiliana Co-owned with CONCHA y TORO. V'yds in RAPEL and CASABLANCA. Second label popular in Canada and USA: Walnut Crest.

Santa Inés Successful small family winery in Isla de MAIPO. Labels are De Martino, Santa Inés.

Santa Mónica Rancagua (RAPEL) winery; the best label is Tierra del Sol. Producing quality wine, esp Sémillon and Cab.

Santa Rita, Viña, Long-established bodega in the MAIPO Valley south of Santiago. Medalla Real Cab and '120' are best-sellers abroad. New top wine is excellent Casa Real Cab.

Segu Ollé Linares (MAULE) estate owned by two Catalan families. Labels: Caliboro and Doña Consuelo: Cab (92), and vg Merlot (94).

Tarapacá Ex-Zavala Santiago producer rated in Chile for red wines. New owner, new plantations and conversion to imported oak underway.

For key to grape variety abbreviations, see pages 6–9.

Torreón de Paredes Recent family-owned RAPEL bodega (253 acres). Modern; no expense spared. Good Reserva Cab.

Torres, Miguel Enterprise of Catalan family firm (see Spain) at Curicó (MAULE) sets a modern pace. Good Sauv (Bellaterra is oak-aged) and Chard, vg Ries. Cab is more 'elegant' than other Chileans.

Undurraga Famous MAIPO family winery; first to export to the USA. Old and modern styles: good clean Sauv, oaky yellow Viejo Roble, fruity Pinot.

Valdivieso A household word in Chile for sparkling wines since '24. Now owned by the distillers Mitjans, it is also making good Chard, Cab, Merlot from MAIPO and Lontué (MAULE), some labelled 'Saint Morellón'.

Vascos, Los Family estate in Colchagua Province, RAPEL. 550 acres. Some of Chile's better Cab (B'x- and California-influenced). Also stylish Sauv-Sém. Made headlines in '88 by link with Lafite-Rothschild (50% owners).

Villard Recent venture of Frenchman Thierry Villard. Top quality Chard, Sauv Bl, Cab and Merlot from CASABLANCA and RAPEL.

Vinícola Mondragón CANEPA's 2nd bodega. Labels: Rowan Brook, Peteroa, Montenuevo etc.

Other South American wines

Brazil New plantings of better grapes are transforming Brazilian wines. International investments, esp in Rio Grande do Sul and Santana do Liuramento, esp from France (eg Moët & Chandon) and Italy (Martini & Rossi), are significant. The new sandy Frontera region (neighbouring Argentina and Uruguay) and the Sierra Gaucha hills (for Italian-style sparkling) are some to watch. Exports are beginning. Large home market increasing too. Equatorial v'yds (eg nr Recife) can have two crops a year – or even five in two years. This is not a recommendation.

Mexico Oldest American wine industry is reviving, with investment from abroad (eg Freixenet, Martell, Domecq) and California influence via UC Davis. Best in Baja California (85% of total), Querétaro and on the Aguascalientes and Zacatecas plateaux. Top Baja C producers are L A Cetto (Valle de Guadaloupe, the largest, esp for Cab, Nebbiolo, Syrah), Bodegas Santo Tomas (since 1888, Mexico's oldest), Monte Xanic (with Napa-award winning Cab), Bodegas San Antonio, and Cavas de Valmar. Marqués de Aguayo is the oldest (1593), now only for brandy.

Peru Viña Tacama near Ica (top wine region) exports some promising wines, especially the Gran Vino Blanco white; also Cab S and classic method sparkling. Chincha, Moquegua and Tacha regions are slowly making progress. But phylloxera is a serious problem.

Uruguay Winemaking since 1700s, influenced along the way by France, Spain, Germany and Italy. Great efforts currently being made, with French advice and grapes, to improve wine from the 30,000 acres of warm, humid v'yds (eg along Rio de la Plata and the Brazilian border, esp Bella Unión). 50% is planted with hybrids. Regions with promise are Cerro Chapeau, Carpinteria, El Carmen, Montevideo. Simple varietals (mainly white) have been sighted in European supermarkets.

Australia

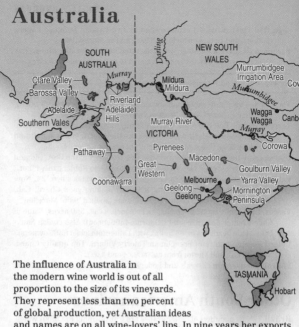

SOUTH AUSTRALIA

Clare Valley
Barossa Valley
Adelaide
Southern Vales
Riverland
Adelaide Hills
Pathaway
Coonawarra
Great Western

Murray
Murray River

VICTORIA

Pyrenees
Macedon
Goulburn Valley
Melbourne
Geelong
Yarra Valley
Mornington Peninsula

Darling

NEW SOUTH WALES

Mildura
Mildura

Murrumbidgee Irrigation Area
Murrumbidgee

Wagga Wagga
Corowa
Murray

Cow
Canbe

TASMANIA
Hobart

The influence of Australia in the modern wine world is out of all proportion to the size of its vineyards. They represent less than two percent of global production, yet Australian ideas and names are on all wine-lovers' lips. In nine years her exports have grown from 8 to 140 million litres and the number of wineries has climbed to nearly 800. It is not just the climate that has done this, but radical research, uninhibited experiment and generous pooling of techniques. Even growers in the south of France are listening carefully. Australia has mastered easy-drinking wine and is well on the way to making some of the world's very best.

Her long-term classics are Shiraz, Semillon and Riesling. In the '70s they were joined by Cabernet and Merlot, Chardonnay, Pinot Noir and other varieties. At the same time, cool fermentation and the use of new barrels accompanied a general move to cooler areas. For a while excessive oak flavour was a common problem. Moderation is now the fashion – and sparkling wine of startling quality is a new achievement.

A massive planting programme is underway with the aim of doubling production. Value for money is generally high. Long may the boom continue.

Wine areas

Adelaide Hills (SA) Spearheaded by PETALUMA: 22 wineries at v cool, 450-metre sites in the Mt Lofty ranges.

Adelaide Plains (SA) Small area just north of Adelaide, formerly known as Angle Vale. The top Adelaide Plains wineries include Lauriston and PRIMO ESTATE.

Barossa (SA) Australia's most important winery (though not v'yd) area; grapes from diverse sources (local, to MURRAY VALLEY; high quality cool regions: from adjacent hills, to COONAWARRA far S) make diverse wines. Local specialities: SHIRAZ, SEMILLON, GRENACHE etc.

Bendigo/Ballarat (Vic) Widespread small v'yds, some of vg quality, re-creating glories of the gold rush. 20 wineries incl BALGOWNIE, JASPER HILL, HEATHCOTE.

Canberra District (ACT) 16 wineries now sell 'cellar door'. Quality is variable, as is style.

Clare Watervale (SA) Small, high quality area 90 miles north of Adelaide, best for Riesling; also SHIRAZ and CABERNET. 26 wineries spill over into new subdistrict, Polish Hill River.

Coonawarra (SA) Southernmost and finest v'yd of state: most of Australia's best CAB, successful CHARD, RIES and SHIRAZ. New arrivals incl Balnaves, Majella, PARKER ESTATE, PENLEY ESTATE.

Geelong (Vic) Once-famous area destroyed by phylloxera, re-established mid-'60s. Very cool dry climate: firm table wines from good quality grapes. Names incl BANNOCKBURN, IDYLL, SCOTCHMAN'S HILL.

Goulburn Valley (Vic) V old (eg CHATEAU TAHBILK) and relatively new (eg MITCHELTON) wineries in temperate mid-Victoria; full table wines.

Granite Belt (Qld) High altitude, (relatively) cool region just N of NSW border; 15 wineries. Esp spicy SHIRAZ and rich SEM-CHARD.

Great Western (Vic) Temperate region in central W of state. High quality (esp sparkling). 9 wineries, 7 of relatively recent origin.

Hunter Valley (NSW) Great name in NSW. Broad, soft, earthy SHIRAZ and SEM that live for 30 yrs. CAB not important; CHARD increasingly so.

Margaret River (WA) Temperate coastal area with superbly elegant wines 174 miles S of Perth. 39 operating wineries; others planned.

Mornington Peninsula (Vic) Exciting wines in new cool coastal area 25 miles S of Melbourne. 400 acres. 35 commercial wineries on dolls-house scale incl DROMANA, STONIERS, T'GALLANT.

Mount Barker/Frankland River (WA) New, remote cool area in S of state; GOUNDREY and PLANTAGENET are biggest/best wineries, from 37 in all.

Mudgee (NSW) Small isolated area 168 miles NW of Sydney. Big reds, full CHARDS; from 21 wineries.

Murray Valley (SA, Vic & NSW) Vast irrigated v'yds nr Mildara, Swan Hill (Vic and NSW), Berri, Loxton, Morgan, Renmark and Waikerie (S Aus). Principally 'cask' table wines. 40% of total Australian wine production.

NE Victoria Historic area incl Corowa, Rutherglen, Wangaratta. Weighty reds and magnificent sweet dessert wines. 29 wineries.

Padthaway (SA) Large v'yd area (no wineries) developed as an over-spill of COONAWARRA. Cool climate; some good PINOT N and excellent CHARD (esp LINDEMANS and HARDY'S), also Chard-Pinot sparkling wines.

Perth Hills (WA) Fledgling area 19 miles E of Perth with 11 wineries and a larger number of growers on mild hillside sites.

Pyrenees (Vic) Central Vic region with 8 wineries: rich minty reds and some interesting whites, esp Fumé Bl.

Riverina (NSW) NV Large-volume irrigated zone centred around Griffith; good quality 'cask' wines (esp white), great sweet botrytised SEM.

Southern Vales (SA) Covers energetic McLaren Vale and Reynella on S outskirts of Adelaide. Big reds now rapidly improving; also vg CHARD.

Swan Valley (WA) The birthplace of wine in the west, on the N outskirts of Perth. Hot climate makes strong low-acid table wines, but good dessert wines. Declining in importance viticulturally.

Tasmania 45 v'yds now offer wine for commercial sale: over 700,000 litres. Great potential for CHARD, PINOT N and RIES in cool climate.

Upper Hunter (NSW) Est'd in early '60s; irrigated vines (mainly whites), lighter and quicker-developing than Lower Hunter's. Often value.

Yarra Valley ('Lilydale') Superb historic area nr Melbourne: 43 wineries. Growing emphasis on v successful PINOT NOIR and sparkling.

For key to grape variety abbreviations, see pages 6–9.

Grape varieties in Australia

In 1993 Australia crushed 545,000 tonnes of grapes producing 393 million litres of wine. The most important varieties are:

Cabernet Sauvignon (37,900 tonnes)   Grown in all of Australia's wine regions, doing best in COONAWARRA. Flavour ranges from herbaceous, green pepper in coolest regions to blackcurrant and mulberry in Coonawarra, and dark chocolate and redcurrant in warmer areas such as SOUTHERN VALES and BAROSSA. Used both as single varietal and blended with Merlot or more traditionally with SHIRAZ. Should reach 72,600 tonnes in '96.

Chardonnay (55,300 tonnes)   Has come from nowhere since '70, with production forecast to increase to 89,200 tonnes in '96. Best known for fast-developing buttery, peachy, at times syrupy, wines, but cool regions such as PADTHAWAY, S Victoria and ADELAIDE HILLS can produce elegant, tightly structured, ageworthy examples. Oak too, is becoming less heavy-handed.

Grenache (19,200 tonnes)   As everywhere, produces thin wine if over-cropped but given half a chance can do much better. Growing interest in old Dryland BAROSSA plantings, with increasing amounts being diverted from fortified to table wine making.

Mourvèdre (8,500 tonnes)   Called Mataro in Australia and has fulfilled the same role and has a similar destiny to GRENACHE.

Muscat Gordo Blanco (67,900 tonnes)   An up-market version of Sultana: scented spicy wine v useful in cheap table and sparkling blends.

Pinot Noir (10,000 tonnes)   Mostly used in sparkling. Growing awareness of exciting quality of table wines from S Victoria, TASMANIA and (potentially) ADELAIDE HILLS; plantings are increasing rapidly.

Riesling (34,800 tonnes)   For long the mainstay of the quality Australian wine industry, with a special place in the BAROSSA, Eden and CLARE valleys. Usually made bone-dry; can be glorious with 20 years bottle-age. Newer Botrytis Rieslings sparingly made but can be superb. Will hold its place in the sun.

Sauvignon Blanc (9,600 tonnes)   Another recent arrival, with strong growth forecast. Usually not as distinctive as that of New Zealand, and made in many different styles from bland to pungent.

Semillon (39,800 tonnes)   Before the arrival of CHARDONNAY, Semillon was the HUNTER VALLEY'S answer to South Australia's RIESLING. Traditionally made without oak and extraordinarily long-lived, but now unfortunately often an oaky Chard substitute. Far from passé, with production projected to increase to 54,700 tonnes in '96.

Shiraz (56,400 tonnes)   Until the arrival of CAB in the '60s, unchallenged as Australia's red grape. Hugely flexible, with styles ranging from velvety/earthy in the HUNTER, spicy peppery and Rhône-like in central and southern Victoria; and rummy sweet and luscious in BAROSSA and environs (eg PENFOLDS Grange). Recently discovered by overseas markets, with demand exceeding supply.

Wineries

Alkoomi Mount Barker ★★→★★★ (Ries) 82' 84' 86' 87' 88' 90' 92' 93' 94 (Cab S) 77' 80' 83' 84' 86' 87' 90' 91   25-year veteran producing 25,000 cases of fine steely RIES and potent long-lived reds, incl rare Malbec.

All Saints NE Vic ★★→★★★   Once famous old family winery bought in '92 by BROWN BROTHERS: excellent Muscat and 'Tokay'.

Allandale Hunter Valley ★→★★   Small winery without v'yds, buying selected local grapes. Quality variable; can be good, esp CHARD.

Allanmere Hunter Valley ✸✸→✸✸✸✸ (Chard) 85' 86' 88' 90' 91' **93' 94** Expat English doctor's small winery: excellent SEM, CHARD; smooth reds.

Angove's Riverland (SA) ✸→✸✸ Large long-est MURRAY VALLEY family business in Adelaide and Renmark. Value CAB and whites, esp CHARD.

Arrowfield Upper Hunter ✸✸ Light CAB, succulent Reserve CHARD from large irrigated v'yd; also wooded SEM. Majority owned by Japanese firm.

Bailey's NE Vic ✸✸→✸✸✸✸ Rich old-fashioned reds of great character, esp Bundarra SHIRAZ (formerly Hermitage), and magnificent dessert Muscat (✸✸✸✸) and 'Tokay'. Now part of ROTHBURY group.

Balgownie Bendigo/Ballarat ✸✸ Once fine pioneer now owned by MILDARA BLASS: recent vintages v disappointing. Look for pre-'91 CABS.

Bannockburn Geelong ✸✸✸ (Chard) 80' 85' 86' 87' 89' 90' 91' 92' (Pinot N) 84' 86' 88' 89' 91' 92' Intense complex CHARD and PINOT N made using Burgundian techniques. 6,000 cases.

Basedow Barossa Valley ✸✸→✸✸✸ Reliably good range of red and white; esp SEM 'White Burgundy'. Acquired by GRANT BURGE in '94. (NB 94 CHARD.)

Bass Phillip Gippsland (Vic) ✸✸✸→✸✸✸✸ (Pinot) 84 85 86 89 91 92 93 Tiny amounts of stylish, eagerly sought PINOT N in three quality grades; v Burgundian in style.

Berri-Renmano Coop Riverland (SA) ✸→✸✸ See Renmano.

Best's Great Western ✸✸→✸✸✸✸ (Shiraz) 62' 64' 70' 77' 78' 84' 85' 87' 88' 90' 91' 92' Conservative old family winery in GREAT WESTERN with very good mid-weight reds, and CHARD not half bad.

Blass, Wolf (Bilyara) Barossa ✸✸✸ (Cab blend) 75 78 80 82 83 84 86 87 88 90 91' 92 BAROSSA's ebullient German winemaker. Dazzling labels, extraordinary wine-show successes, mastery of blending varieties and areas, and lashings of new oak all continue, though indications are that less extreme sensations are on the way.

Botobolar Mudgee ✸✸ Marvellously eccentric little organic winery which exports successfully to the UK.

Bowen Estate Coonawarra ✸✸✸ (Shiraz) 78 81 82 84 87 90 91 (Cab) 79 80 82 84 86 90' 91' Small winery; intense, CAB and spicy SHIRAZ.

Brand Coonawarra ✸✸→✸✸✸ (Shiraz) 77' 78' 82 84 85 87 90 91 92 (Cab S) 70 71 74 79 81 82 84 87 90 91 Family estate now owned by McWILLIAMS. Fine bold and stylish CHARD, CAB and SHIRAZ under Laira label.

Briar Ridge Hunter Valley ✸✸ Old name for SEM and SHIRAZ owned by experienced new partners. To watch.

Bridgewater Mill Adelaide Hills ✸✸→✸✸✸ Second label of PETALUMA; suave wines, SAUV BL and SHIRAZ best.

BRL Hardy See Hardy's.

Brokenwood Hunter Valley ✸✸✸ (Shiraz) 75 79 80 82 83 86 87 89 91 93 (Cab) 75 77 80 81 83 86 87 89 91 Exciting CAB, SHIRAZ since '73 – Graveyard SHIRAZ outstanding. New winery ('83) added quality CHARD, SEM.

Brown Brothers Milawa (Vic) ✸→✸✸✸ (Chard) 80 82 84 86 88 90 91 92 94 (Noble Ries) 70 72 74 76 78 82 84 85 88 Old family firm with new ideas: v wide range of delicate single-grape wines, many from cool mountain districts. CHARD, RIES. Dry white Muscat outstanding. CAB blend is best red. See also All Saints.

Burge Family Barossa ✸✸ Resurgent winery; watch for Old Vine GRENACHE, CHARD and 'Tawny Ports'. 3,000 cases.

Buring, Leo Barossa ✸✸→✸✸✸ (Ries) 70 71 73 75 79 82 84 86 87 88 90 91 92 'Chateau Leonay', old RIES specialists, now owned by LINDEMANS. Steady Reserve Bin is great with age (even great age), esp show reserve releases.

Campbells of Rutherglen NE Vic ✸✸ Smooth ripe reds and good dessert wines, the latter in youthful fruity style.

Cape Clairault Margaret River ✸✸ Progressive producer of SEM, SAUV BL and CAB, in reasonable quantities, with good progress in quality.

NB Vintages in colour are those you should choose first for drinking in 1996.

Cape Mentelle Margaret River ✳✳→✳✳✳✳ (Zin) 81 83 84 87 88 90 91 92 93 (Cab S) 78 81 82 83 86 88 90 91 92 Idiosyncratic robust CAB can be magnificent, CHARD even better; also Zin and v popular SEM. David Hohnen also founded Cloudy Bay, NZ. Both bought in '90 by Veuve Clicquot.

Capel Vale SW (WA) ✳✳✳ (Ries) 84 86 88 89 90 91 93 94 (Chard) 85 86 87 89 90 91 93 Outstanding whites, incl RIES, Gewürz. Also vg CAB.

Cassegrain Hastings Valley (NSW) ✳✳ Relatively new winery on NSW coast: grapes both from local plantings and HUNTER VALLEY. CHARD is best.

Chambers' Rosewood NE Vic ✳✳✳→✳✳✳ Good cheap table and great dessert wines, esp 'Tokay'.

Charles Melton Barossa ✳✳✳ Tiny winery with bold luscious reds, esp Nine Popes, an old-vine GRENACHE and SHIRAZ blend. To watch.

Chapel Hill McLaren Vale (SA) ✳✳✳→✳✳✳✳ (r) 90 91 92 Once tiny, now booming: extra-rich fruity-oaky CHARD, SHIRAZ, CAB; big show successes.

Chateau Hornsby Alice Springs (N Territory) ✳ A charming aberration and magnet for tourists to Ayer's Rock.

Chateau Rémy Great Western/Avoca ✳✳ (Cab S) 82 84 86 88 90 91 92 Owned by Rémy Martin. Sparkling based on CHARD and PINOT N is much improved. Also good Blue Pyrenees CAB S.

Chateau Reynella S Vales ✳✳→✳✳✳✳ ('Vintage Port') 67 70 71 72 75 77 79 81 82 87 88 Historic winery serving as HQ for BRL HARDY group. VG 'Basket pressed' red table wines, superb vintage 'Port'.

Chateau Tahbilk Goulburn Valley ✳✳→✳✳✳ (Marsanne) 70 72 74 75 80 82 86 88 89 90 92 94 (Shiraz) 68 71 76 79 80 81 84 86 88 91 92 (Cab) 62 64 65 66 71 76 79 81 83 86 88 90 92 Beautiful historic family estate: ageable reds, RIES, Marsanne. Private Bins outstanding; value for money ditto.

Chateau Yaldara Barossa ✳→✳✳✳ A plethora of brands incl Acacia Hill, Ch Yaldara, Lakewood and The Farms: oaky, slightly sweet, cheap – apart from eccentrically expensive The Farms.

Coldstream Hills Yarra Valley ✳✳✳→✳✳✳✳ (Chard) 86 88 90 91 92 93' 94 (Pinot N) 87 88 90 91 92 94' (Cab S) 85 86 88 90 91 92' Estate winery est'd '85 by wine critic James Halliday. Delicious PINOT N to drink young and Reserve to age, lead Australia. Vg CHARD (esp Reserve wines), delicate CAB and Cab-Merlot.

Conti, Paul Swan Valley ✳→✳✳✳ One of the doyens of the SWAN VALLEY, s'times exceptionally elegant SHIRAZ and intensely grapey Frontignac.

Coriole S Vales ✳✳→✳✳✳ (Shiraz) 70 74 75 77 80 84 88 89 90 91 92 Esp old-vine SHIRAZ Lloyd Reserve, nicely balanced by oak best. Others worthy.

Craiglee Macedon (Vic) ✳✳✳ (Shiraz) 79 80 84 85 86 88 90 91 92 93 94 Recreation of famous 19th-C estate: fragrant peppery SHIRAZ, CHARD.

Craigmoor Mudgee ✳✳ Oldest district winery, now part of ORLANDO group. Fair CHARD and SEM (the two are also blended), and CAB-SHIRAZ.

Croser Adelaide Hills ✳✳✳→✳✳✳✳ 87 88 90 92 93 Now Australia's top sparkling CHARD-PINOT N blend. Offshoot of PETALUMA with Bollinger as partner. Lean, fine, with splendid backbone from Pinot N.

Cullens Willyabrup Margaret River ✳✳✳ (Chard) 81 82 85 86 87 88 90 92 93 94 (Cab S-Merlot) 80 81 82 84 86 87 89 90 91 92 Mother-daughter team pioneered the region with strongly structured (esp Reserve) CAB-Merlot, substantial but subtle SAUV and bold CHARD: all real characters.

Dalwhinnie Pyrenees ✳✳→✳✳✳ (Chard) 80 82 84 86 88 90 91 92 94 (Cab S) 80 82 85 86 88 90 91 92 3,500-case producer of concentrated rich CHARD, SHIRAZ and CAB S, arguably the best in PYRENEES.

d'Arenberg S Vales ✳✳→✳✳✳ Old firm with new lease of life; sumptuous SHIRAZ, GRENACHE, fine CHARD and sound RIES at misleadingly low prices.

De Bortoli Griffith (NSW) ✳→✳✳✳ (Noble Sem) 82 84 85 87 88 90 91 92 Irrigation-area winery. Standard reds and whites but magnificent sweet botrytised Sauternes-style Noble Sem. See also next entry.

De Bortoli Yarra Valley ✳✳→✳✳✳ (Chard) 88 90 91 92 93 94 (Cab S) 88 90 91 92 Formerly Ch Yarrinya: bought by De Bortoli and now YARRA's largest producer. Main label is good; 2nd label, Windy Peak, vg value.

202

Delatite Central Vic *** (Ries) 82 83 86 87 90 92 93 94 Rosalind Ritchie makes appropriately willowy and feminine RIES, Gewürz, PINOT N and CAB from this v cool mountainside v'yd.

Diamond Valley Yarra Valley **→*** (Pinot N) 81 82 85 86 87 88 90 91 92 94 Outstanding PINOT N in significant quantities; other wines good.

Domaine Chandon Yarra Valley *** The showpiece of the YARRA VALLEY, leading Oz in fizz. Sparkling wine from grapes grown in all the cooler parts of Australia, with strong support from owner Moët & Chandon. Immediate success in UK under Green Point label.

Drayton's Bellevue Hunter Valley ** ('Hermitage') 73 75 79 81 85 86 87 91 93 Traditional 'Hermitage' and SEM, occasionally good CHARD; recent quality improvements after a lapse.

Dromana Estate Mornington Peninsula **→*** (Chard) 86 88 90 91 92 94 (Cab-Merlot) 85 86 88 90 92 Top producer led energetically by Gary Crittenden: light, fragrant CABS, Pinots, CHARDS. 2nd label: Schinus Molle.

Eaglehawk Clare *→** Formerly Quelltaler. Once known for Granfiesta 'Sherry'. Recently good RIES and SEM. Owned by MILDARA BLASS.

Evans Family Hunter Valley *** (Chard) 82 84 86 87 88 91 93 94 Excellent CHARD from small vineyard owned by family of Len Evans and made at ROTHBURY ESTATE. Fermented in new oak. Repays cellaring.

Evans and Tate Swan Valley *** (Sem) 82 83 84 88 89 91 92 93 94 (Cab) 81 82 84 86 88 90 91 92 Fine elegant SEM, CHARD, CAB, Merlot from MARGARET RIVER, Redbrook. Going from strength to strength; now over 50,000 cases.

Forest Hills Mount Barker ** Pioneer in region, now in common ownership with VASSE FELIX. RIES and CHARD usually vg.

Freycinet Tasmania **→*** (Pinot N) 90 91 92 93 East coast winery producing voluptuous rich PINOT N, good CHARD and CAB.

Geoff Merrill S Vales *→*** (Sem-Chard) 82 84 86 87 88 89 90 91 (Cab) 80 82 84 85 86 88 90 91 Ebullient maker of Geoff Merrill, Mt Hurtle and Cockatoo Ridge wines. A questing enthusiast; best wines excellent, others can fail to hit.

Giaconda Central Vic *** (Chard) 86 88 90 91 92 93 94 (Pinot) 88 89 91 92 93 V small ultra-fashionable winery nr Beechworth: popular CHARD, PINOT N.

Goundrey Wines Great Southern (WA) *** (Ries) 82 85 88 90 91 93 94 (Cab S) 77 81 83 85 87 88 89 90 91 Recent expansion and quality upgrade. Now in top rank: esp good CABERNET, CHARD and SAUV BL.

Grant Burge Wines Barossa **→*** Rapidly expanding output of silky-smooth reds and whites (vg CHARD 93) from the best grapes of Burge's large v'yd holdings. Burge was founder of KRONDORF. 70,000 cases.

Green Point See Domaine Chandon.

Grossett Clare *** (Ries) 82 84 86 88 90 92 93 94 (Gaia) 86 90 91 92 Fastidious maker: elegant RIES, recent spectacular Gaia CAB-Merlot.

Hanging Rock Macedon (Vic) **→*** (Shiraz) 87 88 90 91 92 Eclectic range: budget Picnic wines; huge Heathcote SHIRAZ; complex sparkling.

Hardy's S Vales, Barossa, Keppoch, etc *→*** (Eileen Chard) 86 90 91 92 93' 94 ('Vintage Port') 45' 51' 54 56 69 71 73 75' 81' 87 88' Historic company using and blending wines from several areas. Best are Eileen Hardy and Thomas Hardy series and (Australia's greatest) 'Vintage Ports'. Hardy's bought HOUGHTON and CH REYNELLA and, more recently, STANLEY. Ch Reynella's beautifully restored buildings are now group headquarters. '92 merger with BERRI-RENMANO and public ownership (BRL Hardy) makes this Australia's second-largest wine co.

Heemskerk Tasmania *** (Ries) 84 86 88 90 91 92 93 94 (Chard) 82 84 86 87 88 90 91 92 94 A major commercial operation: herby CABERNET, promising CHARD, also PINOT N and steely RIES. High profile Jansz sparkling wine, sold to Tasmanian JAC group in '94.

Heggies Adelaide Hills ** (Ries) 79 80 82 84 86 88 90 91 92 93 94 (Chard) 85 87 88 90 91 92 93 (Botrytis Ries) 84 86 88 90 91 92 Vineyard at 500 metres in eastern Barossa Ranges owned by S SMITH & SONS. Excellent RIES and Botrytis Ries are separately marketed.

Henschke Barossa **** (Shiraz) 52 56 59 61 62 66 67 72 78 80 82 84 86 88 90 91 92 (Cab S) 78 80 81 84 85 86 88 90 91 92 125-year-old family business, perhaps Australia's best, known for delectable SHIRAZ (esp Hill of Grace), vg CAB and red blends, but Eden Valley RIES and SEMILLON also excellent. New high-country Lenswood v'yds on ADELAIDE HILLS add excitement.

Hill-Smith Estate Adelaide Hills **→**** Another separate brand of S SMITH & SONS, perhaps best of all; CHARD, SAUV and CAB-SHIRAZ can be vg value.

Hillstone Adelaide Hills ** Recent small winery using excellent fruit for intense vivid CHARD, PINOT N; also CAB-Merlot, SAUV BL.

Hollick Coonawarra **→**** (Chard) 84 86 87 90 91 92 93 94 (Cab-Merlot) 84 85 86 89 90 91 92 Hollick family plus former TOLLANA maker: gd CHARD, RIES; much-followed reds, esp Ravenswood. Terra is trendy 2nd label.

Houghton Swan Valley *→**** (Supreme) 81 82 84 86 87 89 91 93 94 The most famous old winery of WA. Soft ripe Supreme CHARD is top wine; a national classic. Also excellent CAB, Verdelho, etc. See Hardy's.

Howard Park Mount Barker *** (Ries) 86 87 88 90 91 93' 94' (Cab S) 86 88 89 90 91 92 John Wade (formerly WYNNS, now PLANTAGENET'S wine-maker) handcrafts tiny quantities of scented RIES, CHARD and spicy CAB. Major winery expansion under way. Second label: Madfish Bay.

Huntington Estate Mudgee **→**** (Cab S) 75 77 79 81 83 84 86 89 91 92 Small winery; best in MUDGEE. Fine CABS, vg SHIRAZ. Invariably under-priced.

Idyll Geelong ** Small winery making Gewürz and CAB in v individual style. A pioneer exporter.

Jasper Hill Bendigo *** (Shiraz) 80 82 85 86 90 91 92 94 Emily's Paddock SHIRAZ-Cab F blend and George's Paddock Shiraz from dryland estate v'yds are intense, long-lived and much admired; BENDIGO's best maker.

Kaiser Stuhl Barossa * Now part of PENFOLDS; a huge winery taking fruit from diverse sources. Diminishing importance as a brand.

Katnook Estate Coonawarra *** (Chard) 80 82 84 86 90 92 (Cab S) 80 81 82 85 86 90 91 Excellent and pricey CAB and CHARD; also SAUVIGNON.

Krondorf Wines Barossa **→**** Part of MILDARA BLASS group with niche market brands: Show Reserve wines are best, esp CHARD.

Lake's Folly Hunter Valley **** (Chard) 81 82 85 86 87 89 91 92 93 94 (Cab S) 69 72 75 77 78 81 83 85 87 89 91 92 93 Small family winery of Max Lake. The pioneer of HUNTER CABERNET. Cab is v fine, complex. CHARD exciting and age-worthy.

Lark Hill Canberra District **→**** Most consistent CANBERRA producer, making esp attractive RIES, pleasant CHARD.

Leasingham Clare *→*** Important medium-sized quality winery bought by HARDY'S in '87. Good RIES, SEM, CHARD and CAB-Malbec. Various labels.

Leconfield Coonawarra **→**** (Ries) 84 86 88 90 91 92 94 (Cab S) 80 82 84 88 90 91 92 COONAWARRA CAB of great style. RIES and CHARD well made by former TYRRELL winemaker.

Leeuwin Estate Margaret River **** (Chard) 80 82 83 85 86 87 89 90 91 (Cab) 79 81 82 84 85 87 88 89 90 Leading W Australia estate, lavishly equipped, making superb (and v expensive) CHARD; vg RIES, SAUV and CAB.

Lindemans originally Hunter Valley, now everywhere *→**** (Hunter Sem) 66 67 70 72 75 79 86 87 91 92 94 (Hunter Shiraz) 59 65 66 70 73 75 79 82 83 86 87 91 (Padthaway Chard) 83 85 86 87 88 90 91 92 93 94 (Coonawarra Red) 76 78 80 82 85 86 88 90 91 92 One of the oldest firms, now a giant owned by PENFOLDS. Owns BURING in BAROSSA, ROUGE HOMME in COONAWARRA, and imp't v'yds at PADTHAWAY. Vg CHARD and Coonawarra reds (eg Limestone Ridge, Pyrus). Pioneer of new styles, yet still makes fat, old-style 'Hunters'. Bin-number Classics can be vg. Dominant performer at wine shows.

Little's Hunter Valley ** Popular little winery with wide range of wines; energetic exporters.

Marsh Estate Hunter Valley ** Substantial producer of good SEM, SHIRAZ and CAB of steady quality.

McWilliams Hunter Valley & Riverina ∗→∗∗∗ (Elizabeth Sem) 74 79 80 **81 82** 84 86 87 88 89 91 94   Famous family of HUNTER V winemakers at Mt Pleasant: 'Hermitage' and SEM – 'Elizabeth' is the only bottle-aged (6 yrs) Sem sold, vg value. Also pioneers in RIVERINA with, incl CAB s and sweet white Lexia. Recent show results demonstrate high standards.

The taste of oak

The fashion of deliberately flavouring wine with oak began in California in the '60s and has been widely exaggerated and misused ever since. Formerly, barrels were used for their virtues as strong movable containers with enough porosity to allow very gradual oxidation of their contents. New barrels were needed for transport, but were used for storage only for the very finest, most concentrated wines, whose expected life was decades – by which time any oak flavour would be lost. The slower oak grows, the better its physical properties and the less pungent its aroma/flavour. American oak is very pungent; Baltic oak the opposite. Of the famous French oak forests, 'Limousin' (western) is relatively pungent and coarse, usable only for red wines; central 'Allier', 'Nevers', (top-grade) 'Tronçais' are most delicate, best for white or red wines; 'Bourgogne', 'Champagne', 'Vosges' (eastern) are intermediate. Barrels are put together over a fire which helps bend the staves. How much this burns (or 'toasts') the oak affects the wine as much as its origin.

Mildara Coonawarra & Murray Valley ∗→∗∗∗ (Coonawarra Cab) 63 **64** 68 70 71 78 79 80 82 85 86 88 90 91 92   'Sherry' and brandy specialists at Mildara on the Murray River, also make fine CAB s and RIESLING at COONAWARRA. Now own BALGOWNIE, BLASS, KRONDORF and YELLOWGLEN too.

Miramar Mudgee ∗∗ Some of MUDGEE's best whites, esp CHARD.

Mitchells Clare ∗∗∗ (Ries) 78 84 86 90 92 93 94 (Cab S) 78 80 82 84 85 90 92   Small family winery for excellent CAB and v stylish dry RIES.

Mitchelton Goulburn Valley ∗∗→∗∗∗   Big modern winery, acquired by PETALUMA in '92. A wide range incl a vg wood-matured Marsanne, SHIRAZ, CAB from COONAWARRA; classic RIES from GOULBURN VALLEY is one of Australia's v best. Many enterprising blends and labels.

Montrose Mudgee ∗∗ Reliable underrated producer of vg CHARD and CAB blends. Now part of the ORLANDO group.

Moondah Brook Estate Gingin (WA) ∗∗   HOUGHTON v'yd 80km NW of Perth; v smooth flavourful CHARD, Chenin Bl, Verdelho and CAB.

Moorilla Estate Tasmania ∗∗→∗∗∗ (Ries) 81 82 83 88 89 90 91 93 94' Senior winery on outskirts of Hobart on Derwent River: vg RIES (94' superb), Traminer and CHARD; PINOT N disappointing.

Morris NE Vic ∗∗→∗∗∗∗   Old winery at Rutherglen for Australia's greatest dessert Muscats and 'Tokays'; also recently vg low-price table wine.

Moss Wood Margaret River ∗∗∗∗ (Sem) 83 85 86 87 88 91 92 93 94 (Chard) 80 85 89 90 92 93 (Cab) 74 77 80 81 83 86 87 90 91 92 93   To many the best MARGARET RIVER winery (only 29 v'yd acres). SEM, CAB, Pinot, CHARD, all with rich fruit flavours, not unlike top California wines.

Mount Avoca Pyrenees ∗→∗∗∗   Solid alcoholic and at times distinctly rustic wines with considerable impact; the best age well.

Mount Helen Strathbogie Ranges (Vic) ∗∗   High-altitude v'yd owned by TISDALL/MILDARA BLASS; after a period of inactivity, being re-launched.

Mount Hurtle See Geoff Merrill.

Mount Langi Ghiran Great Western ∗∗→∗∗∗ (Shiraz) 82 84 85 86 88 89 90 91 92 93   Superb rich peppery Rhône-like SHIRAZ, vg CAB and also RIES.

Mount Mary Yarra Valley ∗∗∗∗ (Pinot N) 78 79 82 83 85 86 87 89 90 91 92 (Cab S-Cab F-Merlot) 76 78 79 80 82 84 85 86 88 90 91 92   Dr John Middleton is a perfectionist making tiny amounts of suave CHARD, vivid PINOT N, and (best of all) CAB S-Cab F-Merlot. All age impeccably.

Mountadam Barossa ∗∗∗ (Chard) 82 84 87 89 90 91 92 93   High Eden Valley winery of David and Adam Wynn. CHARDONNAY is rich, voluptuous and long. Other labels include David Wynn, Eden Ridge.

Orlando (Gramp's) Barossa ★★→★★★ (St Hugo Cab) 80 82 84 85 86 88 90 91 92 Great pioneering co, bought by management in '88 but now owned by Pernod Ricard. Full range from huge-selling Jacob's Creek 'Claret' to excellent Jacaranda Ridge CAB from COONAWARRA. See Wyndham Estate.

Parker Estate Coonawarra ★★★→★★★★ New estate making exceptional CAB, esp Terra Rossa First Growth.

Penfolds orig Adelaide, now everywhere ★★→★★★★ (Grange) 52 53 55 62 63 66 67 71 75 76 80 82 83 85 86 88 90 (Bin 707) 64 65 66 78 80 83 84 86 88 90 91 (Bin 389) 66 70 71 82 83 86 87 88 90 91 92 Ubiquitous and excellent: in BAROSSA, CLARE, COONAWARRA, RIVERINA, etc. Consistently Australia's best red-wine co. Bought LINDEMANS in '90. Its Grange (was 'Hermitage') is deservedly ★★★★. Bin 707 CAB not far behind. Other bin-numbered wines (eg Cab-SHIRAZ 389, Kalimna Bin 28 Shiraz) can be outstanding. Grandfather 'Port' often excellent. Penfolds/Lindemans group was taken over by SOUTHCORP, already owner of SEPPELT, in '90.

Penley Estate Coonawarra ★★→★★★ High profile, no-expense-spared newcomer: with fine fruit-and-oak CAB; also SHIRAZ-Cab and CHARD.

Petaluma Adelaide Hills ★★★★ (Ries) 79 80 82 84 86 88 90 91 93 94 (Chard) 77 80 81 86 90 92 93 (Cab S) 79 82 85 86 88 90 91 92 A rocket-like '80s success with COONAWARRA Cab S, ADELAIDE HILLS CHARD, CLARE RIES, all processed at winery in Adelaide Hills. Reds have become richer from '84 on, most recent vintages are outstanding. Also: BRIDGEWATER MILL. Now owns TIM KNAPPSTEIN and MITCHELTON. See also Croser.

Peter Lehmann Wines Barossa ★★→★★★ Defender of BAROSSA faith, Peter Lehmann makes vast quantities of wine (some sold in bulk), with v fine 'special cuvées' under own label; now public listed and flourishing. NB Stonewell SHIRAZ (tastes of brambles and rum) and dry RIESLING.

Pierro Margaret River ★★★ (Chard) 86 87 89 90 91 93 94 Highly rated maker of expensive, tangy SEM, SAUV and sophisticated barrel-fermented CHARD.

Piper's Brook Tasmania ★★★ (Ries) 79 82 84 85 89 91 92 93 94 (Chard) 82 84 86 87 88 91 92 93 Cool-area pioneer with vg RIES, PINOT N, excellent CHARD from Tamar Valley. Lovely labels. 2nd label: Tasmanian Wine Co.

Pirramimma S Vales ★→★★★ Big supply of good standard; reds best.

Plantagenet Mount Barker ★★★ (Chard) 86 88 89 90 91 93 (Shiraz) 77 79 82 83 85 88 89 90 91 92 (Cab S) 77 81 82 85 86 88 90 91 92 The region's largest producer: wide range of varieties, especially rich CHARDONNAY, SHIRAZ and vibrant potent CABERNET SAUVIGNON.

Primo Estate Adelaide Plains ★★★ Joe Grilli is a miracle worker given the climate; successes incl vg botrytised RIES, tangy Colombard, rich Joseph CAB and Merlot. Latest potent red: Moda Amarone.

Quelltaler See Eaglehawk.

Redman Coonawarra ★→★★ (Cab S) 69' 70 71 76 79 87 90 91 92 93 The most famous old name in COONAWARRA; makes two wines: 'Claret' and CABERNET. Quality reviving after a disappointing period.

Renmano Murray Valley ★→★★ Huge coop now part of BRL HARDY (see Hardy's). 'Chairman's Selections' value. Exceedingly voluptuous CHARD.

Reynold's Yarraman Estate Upper Hunter ★★ Former stone prison building to watch: winery of ex-HOUGHTON/WYNDHAM winemaker Jon Reynolds.

Rockford Barossa ★★→★★★ Small producer, wide range of thoroughly individual wines, often made from v old low-yielding v'yds; reds best. Sparkling Black SHIRAZ has super-cult status.

Rosemount Upper Hunter, McLaren Vale, Coonawarra ★★→★★★ Rich unctuous HUNTER 'Show' CHARD is international smash. This, McLaren Vale Show Syrah and COONAWARRA CAB lead wide range, which gets better every yr.

Rothbury Estate Hunter Valley ★★★→★★★★ (Cowra Chard) 81 86 90 91 92 93 94 (Shiraz) 73 75 79 80 81 83 89 91 93 Estate with over 500 acres. Now a public listed co under chairmanship of Len Evans. Trad HUNTER Reserve SHIRAZ and SEMS to keep for ever. Rich buttery COWRA CHARD is vg and value too. Hunter Chard now oak-fermented. New: Chard and SAUV v'yds in Marlborough, NZ. Also owns BAILEY'S, ST HUBERTS, SALTRAM.

Rouge Homme Coonawarra ✱✱ (Shiraz-Cab S) 78 79 80 81 85 86 90 91 92 Separately branded and promoted arm of LINDEMANS with keenly priced CHARD and SHIRAZ-CAB leaders.

Rymill Riddoch Run Coonawarra ✱✱→✱✱✱ Descendants of John Riddoch carrying on the good work of the founder of COONAWARRA. Strong dense SHIRAZ and CAB esp noteworthy.

St Hallett Barossa ✱✱✱ (Old Block) 80 82 83 84 86 87 88 90 91 92 Rejuvenated winery. 100-yr-old vines give splendid Old Block SHIRAZ. Rest of range (eg CHARD, SAUV-SEM) is smooth and stylish.

St Huberts Yarra Valley ✱✱→✱✱✱ (Chard) 82 84 86 87 88 90 91 92 93 94 (Cab) 77 79 82 84 86 88 90 91 92 Acquired by ROTHBURY in late '92; accent on fine dry CHARD and smooth 'berry' CAB. Second label: Rowan.

St Leonards NE Vic ✱✱ Excellent varieties sold only 'cellar door' and by mailing list, incl exotics, eg Orange Muscat.

St Sheila's SA p sw sp 36 22 38 Full-bodied fizzer. Ripper grog.

Saltram Barossa ✱→✱✱✱ Merged with ROTHBURY in '94. Pinnacle Selection is best label (esp COONAWARRA CAB); also good are Mamre Brook wines. Metala is assoc Stonyfell label for old-style Langhorne Creek Cab-SHIRAZ.

Sandalford Swan Valley ✱→✱✱✱ Fine old winery with contrasting styles of red and white single-grape wines from SWAN and MARGARET RIVER areas. Wonderful old fortified Verdelho.

Scotchman's Hill Geelong ✱✱ Newcomer making significant quantities of v stylish PINOT N and good CHARD at modest prices.

Seaview S Vales ✱✱→✱✱✱ Old winery now owned by SOUTHCORP. CHARD, SHIRAZ-CAB and CAB s frequently rise above their station in life, while sparkling wines are among Australia's best – now based on PINOT N and Chard.

Seppelt Barossa, Great Western, Keppoch, etc ✱✱✱ ('Hermitage') 70 78 81 84 85 86 89 90 91 92 (Salinger) 84 86 88 90 91 92 Far-flung producers of Australia's most popular sparkling (Great Western Brut); also good dessert and new range of Victoria-sourced table wines, PADTHAWAY and BAROSSA (in S Australia). Top sparkling is highly regarded 'Salinger'. Now part of SOUTHCORP, Australia's biggest wine co.

Seville Estate Yarra Valley ✱✱✱ (Chard) 82 86 87 90 91 92 94 (Shiraz) 85 86 88 90 91 92 93 Tiny winery with CHARD, SHIRAZ, PINOT N and vg CAB. Sadly, Botrytis RIES is no more.

Shaw & Smith S Vales ✱✱✱ Trendy young venture of flying winemaker Martin Shaw and Australia's first MW Michael Hill-Smith. Crisp SAUV, vg unoaked CHARD, complex barrel-fermented Chard are the 3 wines.

Southcorp The giant of the industry, despite its naff name: owns PENFOLDS, LINDEMANS, SEPPELT, SEAVIEW, WYNNS etc etc.

S Smith & Sons (alias Yalumba) Barossa ✱✱→✱✱✱ Big old family firm with considerable verve, using computers, juice evaluation, etc, to produce full spectrum of high-quality wines, incl HILL-SMITH ESTATE. HEGGIES and Yalumba Signature Reserve are best. Angas Brut, a good value sparkling wine, and Oxford Landing CHARD are now world brands.

Stafford Ridge Adelaide Hills ✱✱→✱✱✱ 20-acre estate of former HARDY's wine-maker, Geoff Weaver, at Lenswood. V fine SAUV, CHARD, RIES, CAB-Merlot.

Stanton & Killeen NE Vic ✱✱ Small old family firm. Rich Muscats, also strong Moodemere reds.

Stoniers Mornington Peninsula ✱✱✱ (Chard) 88 90 91 92 93 94 (Pinot) 86 88 90 91 92 93 94 Has overtaken DROMANA ESTATE for pride of place on the Peninsula. CHARD, PINOT are consistently vg; Reserves outstanding.

Taltarni Great Western/Avoca ✱✱✱ (Shiraz) 78 79 81 82 84 86 88 89 90 91 92 (Cab S) 79 81 82 84 86 88 89 90 91 92 Dominique Portet, brother of Bernard (Clos du Val, Napa), son of André (ex-Ch Lafite), makes huge but balanced reds for long ageing, good SAUV and adequate sparkling.

Tarrawarra Yarra Valley ✱✱✱ (Chard) 87 88 90 91 92 93 (Pinot N) 88 91 92 94 Multimillion dollar investment: limited quantities of idiosyncratic expensive CHARD, robust long-lived PINOT N. Tunnel Hill is second label.

Taylors Wines Clare ✱→✱✱✱ Large inexpensive table range on the improve.

Tim Knappstein Wines Clare *** Tim K, an exceptionally gifted winemaker, makes RIES, Fumé Bl, Gewürz, CAB. New Lenswood range from ADELAIDE HILLS produces flashy SAUV, vg CHARD and PINOT N (see Petaluma).

Tisdall Wines Goulburn Valley ** Went into hibernation after '93 acquisition by MILDARA BLASS; now cautiously being revived with low-key re-launch.

'Tokay' NE Vic speciality. Aged intense sweet strong Muscadelle; less aromatic than Muscat but at best superb. Under EC rules the name will have to go.

Tollana Barossa **→*** Old company once famous for brandy. Has latterly made some fine CAB, CHARD, RIES. Acquired by PENFOLDS in '87.

Tolley Pedare Barossa ** Century-old family-run winery crushing 3,000 tonnes of grapes per annum. Gewürz consistently among best in Australia; wooded SEM, CHARD and CAB honest and reliable.

Tulloch Hunter Valley * Old name at Pokolbin for dry reds, CHARD, Verdelho. Now part of PENFOLDS group but a shadow of its former self.

Tyrrell Hunter Valley *** (Sem Vat 1) 70 75 76 77 79 86 87 89 90 92 94 (Chard Vat 47) 72 73 77 79 82 84 85 89 90 92 93 94 (Shiraz Vats) 73 75 77 79 80 81 83 85 87 89 91 92 Some of best trad HUNTER wines, 'Hermitage' and SEM. Pioneered CHARD with big rich Vat 47 – still a classic. Also delicate Pinot.

Vasse Felix Margaret River **→*** (Cab S) 76 78 79 83 85 88 89 91 92 With CULLENS, pioneer of the MARGARET RIVER. Elegant CABS, notable for mid-weight balance, bought by the late Robert Holmes à Court in '87.

Virgin Hills Bendigo/Ballarat **** 74 75 78 79 80 82 83 85 87 88 90 91 Tiny supplies of one red (CAB-SHIRAZ-Malbec) of legendary style and balance.

Wendouree Clare **** 78 79 83 86 89 90 91 Treasured maker (in tiny quantities) of some of Australia's most powerful and concentrated reds based on SHIRAZ, CAB S and Malbec; immensely long-lived.

Westfield Swan Valley *→** John Kosovich's CAB, CHARD and Verdelho show particular finesse for a hot climate, but he is now developing a new v'yd in the much cooler Pemberton region.

Wirra Wirra S Vales *** (Ries) 76 79 81 84 86 89 91 92 93 94 (Chard) 82 84 88 90 91 92 (Cab S) 77 80 84 87 90 91 92 High quality, beautifully-packaged wines making a big impact. Angelus is superb, top of range CAB.

Woodleys Barossa * Well-known for low-price 'Queen Adelaide'.

Wyndham Estate Branxton (NSW) *→** Aggressive large HUNTER and MUDGEE group with brands: CRAIGMOOR, Hunter Estate, MONTROSE, Richmond Grove and Saxonvale. Acquired by ORLANDO in '90.

Wynns Coonawarra *** (Shiraz) 53 54 55 63 65 70 82 85 86 88 90 91 92 (Cab S) 57 58 59 60 62 82 85 86 88 90 91 92 Since its acquisition by PENFOLDS in '85 has produced even better wines: RIES, CHARD, SHIRAZ and CAB – all very good, esp John Riddoch Cab, and Michael 'Hermitage'.

Yalumba See S Smith & Sons.

Yarra Burn Yarra Valley ** Estate making SEM, SAUV, CHARD, sparkling Pinot, PINOT N, CAB; has found going tough, but perseveres.

Yarra Ridge Yarra Valley **→*** Expanding young (50,000 case) winery, v successful CHARD, CAB, SAUV BL, Pinot, all with flavour and finesse at modest prices. Controlling interest acquired by MILDARA BLASS in '93.

Yarra Yering Yarra Valley ***→**** (Dry Reds) 78 79 80 81 82 83 84 85 87 90 91 Best-known Lilydale boutique winery. Esp racy powerful PINOT N, deep herby CAB (Dry Red No 1) and SHIRAZ (Dry Red No 2).

Yellowglen Bendigo/Ballarat **→*** High-flying sparkling winemaker owned by MILDARA BLASS. Recent dramatic improvement in quality, with top end brands like Vintage Brut, Cuvée Victoria and 'Y'.

Yeringberg Yarra Valley *** (Marsanne) 83 84 86 88 90 91 92 93 94 (Cab S) 74 75 76 79 80 81 82 84 86 87 88 90 91 92 Dreamlike historic estate still in the hands of the founding family, now again producing v high quality Marsanne, Roussanne, CHARD, CAB, PINOT, in minute quantities.

For key to grape variety abbreviations, see pages 6–9.

New Zealand

Over the last 12 years New Zealand has made a world-wide name for table wines (mainly white) of startling quality, well able to compete with those of Australia or California. In 1982 it exported 12,000 cases; in 1994 some 867,000. There are now over 18,000 vineyard acres. White grapes prevail. Formerly dominant Müller-Thurgau has now been overtaken by the best varieties: in 1993 Chardonnay supplanted it as number one; in '94 Sauvignon Blanc overtook Chardonnay. Next in line are Cabernet Sauvignon and Pinot Noir respectively, with Riesling gaining ground.

Intensity of fruit flavours and crisp (sometimes too crisp) acidity are the hallmarks of New Zealand. No region on earth can match Marlborough Sauvignon Blanc for pungency. Barrel fermentation and/or ageing add to its complexity (or at least flavour). Marlborough also makes very fine sweet Rieslings with botrytis, and has proved its worth with excellent sparkling. 1989 was perhaps the first vintage to produce really worthy reds. The principal areas and producers follow.

Allan Scott Blenheim ★→★★ Established '90. Ries, Chard and good Sauv Bl. Neighbour of famous CLOUDY BAY.

Ata Rangi Martinborough ★★★ V small but respected winery, est '80 primarily for reds. Outstanding Pinot N, also Cab-Merlot-Petit Syrah (Célèbre). Now also good Chard.

Auckland (r) 89 90 91 93 94 (w) 89 91 92 93 94 Largest city in NZ. Location of head offices of major wineries; many medium and small in outskirts, many bringing in fruit from other regions. Incl Henderson, Huapai, Kumeu and Waiheke Island wine regions.

Babich Henderson (nr Auckland) ★★ Large old Auckland family firm, highly respected in NZ for consistent quality and value. Also uses MARLBOROUGH, GISBORNE and HAWKES BAY grapes. Good Chards (esp Irongate, Stopbank), Sauv Bl (92 is big medal-winner, vg and value), Sém-Chard blend, Gewürz, Cab S and Cab-Merlot. Pinot N still not performing quite so well.

Bloomfield Vineyards (Wairarapa) ★ Small vineyard specializing mostly in red varieties. Cab S, Merlot, Cab F, Pinot Noir.

Brajkovich See Kumeu River.

Brookfields Hawkes Bay ★★ One of the area's top v'yds: outstanding Cab-Merlot, good Chard, Sauv Bl, Cab S, Pinot Gris.

Cairnbrae Wines (Marlborough) ★ Small winery producing quality range of Sauv Bl, Sém, Chard and Ries.

Canterbury (r) 89' 90 91 92 94 (w) 89' 90 91 94   Promising smallish South Island region. Long dry summers favour Pinot N, Chard and Riesling.

Central Otago (r) 90 93 94 (w) 90 93 94   Smallest and coolest region, in S of South Island, Chard and Pinot are best.

Cellier Le Brun Renwick, nr Blenheim ★★→★★★   Small winery est'd by son of Champagne family: some of NZ's best classic method sparkling incl vintage, NV, rosé (vg 89 90), Blanc de Blancs (**90** exceptional).

Chard Farm Central Otago ★★   Scenically NZ's No 1 winery, producing Pinot N, Chard, Ries. Also NZ's only ice wine.

Chifney Wines Martinborough ★   Vg Cab S and good Chard.

Church Road Hawkes Bay ★★   Owned by MONTANA but run independently: classy Chard and Cab from old (McWilliams) estate. Also Twin Rivers sp.

Clearview Estate Hawkes Bay ★   New '92. Already good Chard and Cab S.

Cloudy Bay Blenheim ★★★★   Offshoot of W Australia's Cape Mentelle, with Veuve Clicquot a major shareholder. Top name worldwide for Sauv, Chard. Richly subtle Cab-Merlot 89 shows equal promise, as does new release Pelorus classic sparkling: rich and dense (**87 88 89 90 91**).

Collard Brothers Henderson (nr Auckland) ★★→★★★   Well-established small family winery using grapes from four main areas: top-award Chard from each. Also Sauv (esp Rothesay), Chenin, Ries, Cab-Merlot, Sém. Consistent quality (esp HAWKES BAY).

Cooks Hawkes Bay ★★   Large firm merged with CORBANS and McWilliams in '85. Good steady Chard (esp Winemakers Reserve). Also Cab-Merlot and late-harvest Sauv Bl-Sém.

Coopers Creek Huapai Valley (NW of Auckland) ★★   Small winery augmenting own grapes with GISBORNE, HAWKES BAY and MARLBOROUGH fruit. Exporting good Chard, Sauv Bl, Ries, dry and late-harvest. Also Cab S-Merlot and popular blends: Coopers Dry (white), Coopers Red.

Corbans Henderson (nr Auckland) ★★   Old-est'd, now one of biggest: Has grown to incorporate COOKS, McWilliams and (new premium brands) STONELEIGH (at MARLBOROUGH) and Longridge (HAWKES BAY). Vg Sauv, Chard, Ries, Cab. Corbans White Label collection is good low-priced. Additional premium wines: Robard & Butler label, classic Amadeus sparkling.

Cross Roads (Hawkes Bay)   Small winery with good Chard (Reserve) and Riesling as well as Sauv Bl and Cab S.

De Redcliffe Mangatawhiri (SE Auckland) ★→★★★   Small progressive winery and resort 'Hotel du Vin'; good Chard, Ries, Sauv, Sém, Cab-Merlot.

Delegat's Henderson (nr Auckland) ★★   One of NZ's largest family-owned/run wineries: v'yds in HAWKES BAY. Good Chard, Sauv; Proprietor's Reserve Cab-Merlots (**89 90 91 93 94**) outstanding. Also Chard and Sauv from MARLBOROUGH sold under successful Oyster Bay label.

Deutz Auckland ★★★   The Champagne firm in a pioneer joint venture with MONTANA. 'Classic method' is brisk, lively and vg.

Domaine Chandon (Blenheim) ★★   Start-up of Moët & Chandon in NZ. Still tiny.

Dry River (Martinborough) ★★→★★★   V small winery, but a perfectionist over a wide range: Ries, Chard, Pinot Gr, Gewürz, Pinot N etc.

Esk Valley Bayview (Hawkes Bay) ★★   Former large family firm, now merged with VILLA MARIA/VIDAL. Small range incl vg dry Chenin, Chard, Sauv, and some of NZ's best reds, esp 90 91 Merlot and Merlot-Cab F, Cab-Merlot Private Bin.

Eskdale (Hawkes Bay) ★★   Boutique winery for v tasty Cab, Chard, Gewurz.

Gibbston Valley (Otago) ★★   Pioneer Alan Braay was Otago's first viticulturist. Now successfully makes Pinot, Gewurz, Pinot Gr, Sauv, Chard.

Giesen Estate Burnham (S of Christchurch) and Canterbury (S Island) ★★★   German family winery leading the region. Good Chards (Reserve School Road), Sauv, botrytised Ries, Cab-Merlot from own/some MARLB'H grapes.

Gisborne (r) 89' 90 91 92 94 (w) 89 90 91 92 94   Site of 3 large wineries, CORBANS, MONTANA, PENFOLDS, and centre of large viticultural area incl MATAWHERO and Tolaga Bay. Good for Müller-T, Sém and esp Chard and Gewürz. Replanting due to '86 phylloxera led to improved grapes.

Glenmark Wines (Waipara) ** Small, consistent medal-winner, esp Ries.

Glover's (Nelson) * Tiny winery for excellent Pinot N, Cab S and Sauv Bl.

Goldwater Waiheke I ** Small v'yd at sea edge, esp for drink-soon Cab-Merlot; also MARLB'H Chard (outstanding own-grown 92 93 Delamore).

Grove Mill Blenheim ** Excellent new winery bursting onto the scene with 89 Chard; Lansdowne in 90 91 93 94 even better. Vg Riesling, Blackbirch Cab, Drylands botrytis Sauv. Also Gewürz, Sauv, Pinotage.

Hawkes Bay (r) 89 90 91' 94 (w) 89 91' 92 93 94 Long-est'd,expanding wine region on east coast of N Island. Known for high quality grapes: some of NZ's best reds (esp Cab, Merlot), also big meaty Chards.

Highfield Estate Marlborough *→** Bought by international partnership in '91. Sauv, Chard, Ries, Merlot all promise well. Sparkling planned.

Hunters Marlborough *** Well-est'd small progressive winery using only MARLBOROUGH grapes. Highly reputed for outstanding Sauv Bl (oaky 'Fumé' style), and reliably good Chard. Ries since '89. Also Cab S and Pinot N. Links with DOMAINE CHANDON.

Jackson Estate Blenheim ** Large private v'yd. First vintage 91: impressive Sauv (91 92 94), also Chard, Ries (esp sweet botrytis, one of NZ's best).

Kumeu River Kumeu (NW of Auckland) *** Family-run winery (son Michael is NZ's first MW). Bold, rich Chard and Sauv Bl, vg Cab-Merlot. Second label under family name, Brajkovich.

Landfall Wines Gisborne * New organically-run winery with good Chard (Revington Vineyard, 89 90), Sauv Bl and Pinot N.

Lincoln Vineyards Henderson (nr Auckland) * Medium-sized family winery; esp for Chard, Chenin Bl and Cab. Other varietals: Sauv Bl, Ries, Müller-T, Merlot.

Marlborough (r) 89 91 94' (w) 89 91' 94 Now NZ's largest (and sunniest) wine region: at N end of South Island on stony plain formed by Wairau River. Well-suited to white varieties Chard, Sauv Bl and Ries. Promising Pinot N; Cab tends to greenness. Potential here for vg sparkling. Many top growers.

Martinborough (r) 89' 90 91 94 (w) 89' 90 91 94' New smallish quality appellation in S Wairarapa (North Island). Stony soils, similar to MARLBOROUGH. Home of some of NZ's best Pinot Noir.

Martinborough Vineyards Martinborough *→** Noted for Pinot N (89 91 94). Also Chard, Sauv, Ries, Gewürz.

Matawhero nr Gisborne ** Small winery known esp for Gewürz. Also conc aromatic Chard, Sauv-Sém. Reds are Cab-Merlot, Pinot N, Syrah.

Matua Valley NW of Auckland **→*** One of NZ's best, most consistent wineries. Wide range incl Chard (from Ararimu & Judd Estate, GISBORNE), Sauv Bl and Fumé Blanc. Top-class Cab S (v fine Ararimu). Vg MARLBOROUGH wines under Shingle Peak label.

Merlen Wines Marlborough *→** German-born Almuth Lorenz makes excellent Chard and Ries (90 91 92 94). Also Sauv, Gewürz.

Mills Reef Bay of Plenty ** Producer (since '89) of ripe fat Chard (Elspeth), also Sauv Bl from HAWKES BAY grapes, Ries, Cab, Merlot.

Millton nr Gisborne ** Small organic producer. Good Chard (Clos de Ste-Anne 89 outstanding) and Ries (dry and late harvest, vg 91). Splendid barrel-fermented Chenin Bl (87 90 92) like fine Anjou.

Mission Greenmeadows (Hawkes Bay) ** Oldest continuing wine estate in NZ, French mission-founded and still run by the Society of Mary. Good Sém-Sauv, Ries and Cab-Merlot; Reserve Cab is best wine by far.

Montana Auckland and Hawkes Bay ** NZ's largest wine enterprise: wineries in GISBORNE, MARLBOROUGH; incorporating Penfolds label (in NZ only). Pioneer v'yds in Marlborough, also uses Gisborne and HAWKES BAY grapes. Marlborough labels: Sauv, Chard (vg, outstanding Show Reserves), Ries, Cab and Pinot. Gisborne Chard also big-selling and sound. Original Lindauer sparkling joined by vg cuvée DEUTZ. An input of French know-how in recent Cordier joint venture should improve HAWKES BAY reds.

Morton Estate Tauranga (Bay of Plenty) **→*** Expanding winery bought by Mildara (of Australia) in '89: excellent Chard (range is best black label, white then yellow labels). Also Fumé Bl, Gewürz, Ries and good classic method sparkling (89 90 91).

Nautilus (Marlborough) *→* Owned by Australia's Yalumba: young winery producing vg Chard (92 93 94) from MARLBOROUGH, Sauv from HAWKES BAY.

Nelson (r) 89' 90 91 93 94 (w) 89' 90 91' 93 94 Neighbour of MARLBOROUGH, with v'yds hilly not flat, wineries boutique, not large: quality excellent.

Neudorf Nelson * Charming small-scale winery: award-winning Chard (89 90 91 92 93 94), good Ries, Sauv Bl and Pinot N.

Ngatarawa nr Hastings (Hawkes Bay) ** Boutique winery in old stables of est'd HAWKES BAY family. Well-made, elegant Glazebrook label Cab-Merlot. Also vg Chard (Alwyn) and good Sauv Bl.

Nobilo NW of Auckland *→** NZ's largest family winery: own plus GISBORNE, HAWKES BAY, MARLBOROUGH fruit. Good Chard (Marlb'h and Dixon V'yd), vg pungent Sauv, Sém; long recognized for ageable red: eg Cab, Pinotage. White Cloud is off-dry commercial line.

Oyster Bay See Delegats.

Palliser Estate Martinborough * Ambitious new winery: first vintage '89. Good Chard, Sauv Bl, Ries; also promising Pinot N (91).

Pask, C J Hawkes Bay ** Rising star of the area: outstanding Chard, and Sauv Bl since 91. Also good Cab S, Pinot N and Cab-Merlot.

Pegasus Bay N Canterbury ** New 100-acre estate venture in warm Waipara sub-region. Pinot N, Cab F, Chard, Ries all bode well.

Robard & Butler See Corbans. NB Amberley Riesling.

Rongapai Waikato (S of Auckland) ** German-influenced winery esp for botrytised Ries and Chard. Now with Pinot, Merlot, Cab and Cab-Merlot.

Rothbury NZ ** Off-shoot of Australia's Rothbury Est. Ries, Chard both good.

Sacred Hill (Hawkes Bay) ** Up and coming for Chard, Sauv and Cab S.

St Nesbit Karaka (S of Auckland) **→*** A lawyer's passion. One barrique-matured red blend: Cab S-Cab F-Merlot (vg 91). Also rosé (when main vintage below standard).

Seifried Estate Upper Moutere (nr Nelson) *→*** Small winery started by an Austrian: esp Chard, Sauv, Ries (dry and late-harvest).

Selak's Kumeu (NW of Auckland) ** Small stylish winery. Esp Chard (Founders Selection best), vg Sauv, classic sparkling. Grapes: local, MARLBOROUGH, GISBORNE, HAWKES BAY. Reds less good.

Stoneleigh See Corbans.

Stonyridge Waiheke Island ***→**** Boutique winery concentrating on two reds in Bordeaux style: Larose is exceptional, one of NZ's best (esp 87 93, also good 91 93), Airfield is second label (92).

Te Kairanga Martinborough ** Largest winery in region, with underground facilities. Chard, Sauv Bl, Pinot N coming together.

Te Mata Havelock North (Hawkes Bay) ***→***** Image-leader for HAWKE'S BAY; consistently fine Chard (esp Elston) and Sauv from nearby v'yds, plus one of NZ's v best Cab blends, 'Coleraine' Cab-Merlot (85 88 89 90 91 94) from proprietor's home v'yd. Awatea is second label.

Vavasour nr Blenheim *** First vintage 89. The 91 Chards were top quality; Dashwood Chard also good. Vg Fumé Bl, Sauv, Cab S-Merlot, Cab S-Cab F Reserve.

Vidal Hastings (Hawkes Bay) ** Atmospheric old winery, merged with VILLA MARIA. Vg HAWKES BAY Chards (90 91 92 94), Cab, Cab-Merlot, Fumé Bl. Reserves best; Private Bin fair value.

Villa Maria Mangere (S Auckland) ** Important co including VIDAL and ESK VALLEY. Ihumatao (nr Auckland airport), GISBORNE and HAWKES BAY grapes. V wide range; esp Reserve oak-fermented Chard, Sauv (and wooded 'Fumé'), Gewürz, Cab and Cab-Merlot.

Waipara Springs N Canterbury ** Recent producer of model Sauv Bl, Chard (93) and Pinot N (90 91 good). To follow (most is exported).

Wairau River Marlborough * Small winery, full-flavoured Sauv and Chard.

South Africa

World-wide acceptance of South Africa's wines only began in 1994, but found an industry already mature in its ideas. Exports immediately soared to four million cases (half to the UK). The foundations for quality were laid in the 1970s and confirmed in the 1980s, with the introduction of Chardonnay, Pinot Noir, Sauvignon and modish modern barrels. White wines have been the great success to date; many reds retaining a rather lean dry character when compared with eg Australia. This is South Africa's traditional taste; export demand will no doubt modify it.

Allesverloren r ★→** (Cab) 89 91 Old 395-acre family estate, best known for 'Port' (86 88). Also hefty well-oaked but not always long-lived CAB and Shiraz (88 89) from hot wheatlands district of Malmesbury.

Alphen ★ Gilbeys brand name for wines from STELLENBOSCH area.

Alto r ★★→*** (Cab) 86 87 89 Atlantic-facing mountain v'yds S of s'BOSCH. Solid CAB, Cab-Merlot, Shiraz. Best since mid-'80s (with new French oak).

Altydgedacht r w ★→** (Cab S) 87 88 89 Durbanville estate, best for CAB; also gutsy Tintoretto blend of Barbera and Shiraz.

Avontuur r w★ (r) 89 90 91 93 200-acre ST'BOSCH v'yd, bottling since '87. Soft B'x-style blend, Avon Rouge (87); CAB, Merlot, promising CHARD.

Backsberg r w ★★→*** (r) 89 91 92 (Merlot) 90 92 (Chard) 90 91 92 93 Prize-winning 395-acre PAARL estate. Pioneered oak-fermented CHARD in mid-'80s, with US advice. Delicious B'x blend Klein Babylonstoren is best (92); also vg oaked SAUV John Martin.

Bellingham r w ★★→*** Big-selling brand of DGB. Sound reds (93), popular whites (94), esp sweet, soft, CAPE RIES-based Johannisberger (exported as Cape Gold), CHARD, and Chard-Sauv blend 'Sauvenir'.

Bergkelder Big STELLENBOSCH co, member of Oude Meester group, making/distributing many brands (FLEUR DU CAP, GRUNBERGER), 17 estate wines. First to use French oak (now 10,000 barrels), top for fine oaked reds.

Bertrams r ★★ (Cab) 89 90 91 94 (Shiraz) 89 Gilbeys brand of varietals, esp Shiraz, PINOTAGE. Also Robert Fuller Reserve B'x-style blend.

Beyerskloof r ★★★ (Cab S) 89 90 91 93 New small STELLENBOSCH property, devoted to vg tannic deep-flavoured CAB S.

Blaauwklippen r w ★★→*** (r) 89 90 91 STELLENBOSCH winery with some of the Cape's best bold reds, esp CAB Reserve. Also S Africa's top Zin (89 91); patchy but improving CHARD; good off-dry RIES.

Bloemendal r w ★→** (Cab) 89 91 (Chard) 90 91 92 Sea-cooled Durbanville estate. Fragrant CAB; still CHARD no more. Now good Chard Cap Classique.

Boberg Controlled region for fortified wines comprising PAARL and TULBAGH.

Bon Courage w sw ★→** ROBERTSON estate; vg dessert GEWURZ and CHARD.

Boplaas r w ★★ Estate in dry hot Karoo. Earthy deep 'Vintage Reserve Port' esp since '87 (91 94), fortified Muscadels. Links with Grahams in Portugal.

Boschendal w sp ★★→*** (Chard) 89 91 94 617-acre estate in PAARL area. Good CHARD and METHODE CAP CLASSIQUE (Chard and Pinot); also Cape's first 'blush' off-dry Blanc de Noirs. Improving Merlot (91).

Bouchard-Finlayson r w (★★★) (Chard) 91 93 (Pinot) 93 First French-Cape partnership, between Paul Bouchard of Burgundy and Peter Finlayson at Hermanus, Walker Bay. Maiden release 91. PINOT N firm, even hard.

Breede River Valley Fortified and white wine region E of Drakenstein Mts.

Buitenverwachting r w sp ★★★ (Chard) 90 91 93 Exceptional, German-financed, recently replanted CONSTANTIA v'yds. Vg SAUV (plain, oaked Bl Fumé), CHARD, B'x blend (89 90), Merlot (91). Lively clean METHODE CAP CLASSIQUE (Pinots Gr and Bl). Restaurant worthy of a Michelin star.

NB Vintages in colour are those you should choose first for drinking in 1996.

Cabernet Sauvignon Most successful in COASTAL REGION. Range of styles: sturdy long-lived to elegant fruity. More use of new French oak since '82 giving great improvements. Best recent vintages: 82 84 86 87 89 91.

Cabrière Estate **→*** Franschhoek growers of good NV CAP CLASSIQUE under Pierre Jordan label (Brut Sauvage, CHARD-PINOT N and Belle Rose Pinot N). Now also bottling v promising 'new clone' Pinot N 94.

Cape Independent Winemakers Guild Young group of winemakers in the vanguard of quality. Holds an annual auction of progressive-style wines.

Cavendish Cape ** Range of remarkably good 'Sherries' from the KWV.

Chardonnay S Africa came to Chard relatively late, beginning mid-'80s. Now offering many styles, incl unwooded and blended – with SAUV, among others. Currently nearly 200 labels, and growing; a decade ago, 3.

Chateau Libertas * Big-selling CAB S brand made by SFW.

Chenin Blanc Work-horse grape of the Cape; one vine in three. Adaptable, sometimes vg. KWV makes good value example. See also Steen.

Cinsaut The principal bulk-producing French red grape in S Africa; formerly known as 'Hermitage'. V seldom seen with varietal label.

Claridge r w **→*** (r) 91 92 (Chard) 91 92 93 Good barrel-fermented CHARD and CAB-Merlot from small new winery at Wellington nr PAARL.

Clos Malverne r ** 89 90 91 Small STELLENBOSCH winery. Individual dense CAB S, PINOTAGE (92) from own v'yds and purchased grapes.

Colombard French white grape, as popular in Cape as in California. Crisp lively flowery, usually short-lived wine; often in blends, or for brandy.

Constantia Once the world's most famous sweet Muscat-based wine (both red and white), from the Cape. See Klein Constantia.

Craighall Brand for successful Chard-SAUV (94), CAB-MERLOT, by Gilbeys.

De Wetshof w sw **→*** (Chard) 91 93 94 Pioneering ROBERTSON estate. Powerful CHARD (varying oakiness: Finesse lightly, Bataleur heavily) and fresh dry RHINE RIES. Also dessert GEWURZ, Rhine Ries under Danie de Wet label and own-brand Chards for British supermarkets.

Delaire Vineyards r w ** (Chard) 91 92 93 (r) 90 91 92 Full-flavoured CHARD, Bordeaux blend named Barrique (91 92), and elegant off-dry RHINE RIES, from young winery at Helshoogte Pass above STELLENBOSCH.

Delheim r w dr sw **→*** (r) 89 91 Big winery with mountain v'yds nr STELLENBOSCH. Elegant barrel-aged CAB s-Merlot-Cab F Grand Reserve (88 91). Value Cab (89 91), PINOTAGE, Shiraz; variable PINOT N; improving CHARD, SAUV. Sweet wines: GEWURZ, outstanding botrytis STEEN.

Die Krans Estate ** Karoo semi-desert v'yds making rich full Vintage Reserve 'Port'. Best is 91. Also traditional fortified sweet Muscadels.

Dieu Donné Vineyards r w ** Franschhoek estate. Good CHARD 92 93. CAB 93.

Douglas Green *→** Cape Town merchants marketing range of sound wines incl 'Sherries' and 'Ports' mostly from KWV.

Drostdy * Good range of 'Sherries' from BERGKELDER.

Drostyhof r w * Well-priced range incl CHARD made at TULBAGH cellars.

Edelkeur **** Excellent intensely sweet noble rot white by NEDERBURG.

Eikendal Vineyards r w **→** (red, Merlot) 90 91 93 (Chard) 91 92 93 Swiss-owned 100-acres v'yds and winery in STELLENBOSCH. Vg CHARD; CAB s-Merlot blend Classique. Fresh whites incl semi-sweet CHENIN BL.

Estate wine Official term for wines grown and made on registered estates. Regulations relaxed in '94; estates may now buy in up to 40% of their production. Estate status is not lost if bottling takes place off property.

Fairview Estate r w dr sw **→*** (r) 90 91 (Chard) 90 91 92 93 94 Enterprising PAARL estate with wide range. Best are Reserve Merlot (89 91), Bordeaux blend Charles Gerard Reserve (90), Shiraz Reserve (90 91 93). Also lively Gamay, good CHARD, plus sweet CHENIN BL. Experiments in progress to obtain softer, fruitier wines. Also v interesting Sémillon and Shiraz-Merlot blend.

Fleur du Cap r w sw **→*** (r) 90 91 92 Value range from BERGKELDER at STELLENBOSCH: vg CAB (89) esp since '86. Also Merlot (90 92), Shiraz (86 88), improving CHARD (93), fine GEWURZ, botrytis CHENIN.

Gewürztraminer The famous spicy grape of Alsace, best at NEDERBURG and SIMONSIG. Naturally low acidity makes it difficult to handle at the Cape.

Glen Carlou r w **→*** (r) 89 90 91 (Chard) 90 91 92 PAARL property. Good B'x blends Grande Classique (90 91), Les Trois, Merlot; gd CHARD Res (91 92 93). V promising 'new clone' PINOT N from '94.

Graça * Huge-selling slightly fizzy white blend in Portuguese-style bottle.

Graham Beck Winery w sp ** Avant-garde ROBERTSON winery (57 acres); first METHODE CAP CLASSIQUE Brut Royale NV and CHARD well-received.

Grand Cru (or Premier Grand Cru) Term for a totally dry white, with no quality implications. Generally to be avoided.

Grangehurst Wines ** Among crop of new STELLENBOSCH wineries, buying grapes from range of suppliers. Vg start: PINOTAGE 93, CAB-Merlot Res 93.

Groot Constantia r w **→*** Historic gov't-owned estate nr Cape Town. Superlative Muscat in early 19th C. Renaissance in progress; so far fine CAB (esp CAB-Merlot blend Gouverneur's Reserve 89 91), Shiraz (89), Merlot (90 91), Weiser (Rhine) Ries-Gewürz Botrytis blend (92), dessert Muscat.

Grünberger ▮ BERGKELDER brand: range of dry and semi-sweet STEEN whites.

Hamilton Russell Vineyards r w ***→**** (Pinot N) 89 90 91 93 (Chard) 89 90 91 92 93 Cape's top PINOT 'Burgundy' v'yds and cellar. Small yields, French-inspired vinification in cool Walker Bay. Many awards. Priciest wines in S Africa. From '93 also Chard-Sauv Bl blend.

Hanepoot Local name for the sweet Muscat of Alexandria grape.

Hartenberg r w ** STELLENBOSCH estate, recently modernized; rich Shiraz.

Jordan Vineyards **→*** New property in SW STELLENBOSCH hills: vg SAUV 94, CHARD 93. Reds later. Californian trained husband and wife team.

J P Bredell *** Stellenbosch v'yds. Rich, dark, deep Vintage Reserve 'Port' from Tinta Barocca and Souzão grapes.

Kanonkop r *** (r) 86 89 90 91 Outstanding N STELLENBOSCH estate. Individual powerful CAB (89 91) and B'x-style blend Paul Sauer (86 89 91). Benchmark PINOTAGE (89 91 94), oak-finished since '89 (v improved).

Klein Constantia r w sw *** (r) 88 89 90 (Chard) 90 91 92 93 Old subdivision of famous GROOT CONSTANTIA neighbour. Emphatic CHARD, SAUV, fine powerful CAB, B'x-style blend Marlbrook first released in '88 (88 89 90), also Shiraz. From 86, Vin de Constance revives the 18th-C Constantia legend (annual release, now 91). Top dry botrytis Sauv 'Bl de Blancs' (87 93) is Cape's answer to Ygrec. Revamped since early '80s.

KWV The Kooperatieve Wijnbouwers Vereniging, S Africa's national wine coop created in 1917: vast premises in PAARL, a range of good wines, esp Cathedral Cellars reds, RIES, 'Sherries', sweet dessert wines. In '92 gave up widely criticized quotas, freeing growers to plant v'yds at will.

La Motte r w *** (r) 89 91 Lavish new Rupert family estate nr Franschhoek. Lean but stylish, intensely flavoured reds: CAB S (89 91), Merlot, B'x-style blend Millennium (90 91), among top three for Cape Shiraz (89 91). Racy SAUV.

L'Avenir ** Well-appointed new STELLENBOSCH property, promising CAB (93).

Laborie r w ** KWV-owned showpiece PAARL estate. White and red blends.

Landgoed Afrikaans for 'estate': on official seals and ESTATE WINE labels.

Landskroon r w *→** Family estate owned by Paul and Hugo de Villiers. Good dry reds, esp Shiraz, CAB S, Cab F.

Late Harvest Term for a mildly sweet wine. 'Special Late Harvest' must be naturally sweet. 'Noble Late Harvest' is highest quality dessert wine.

Le Bonheur r w *** (r) 87 89 STELLENBOSCH estate often producing classic tannic minerally CAB; big-bodied SAUV BL revived with 93.

Leroux, JC ** Old brand revived as BERGKELDER's sparkling wine house. SAUV (charmat), PINOT (top METHODE CAP CLASSIQUE is well-aged). Also CHARD.

To decipher codes, please refer to symbols key at front of book, and to 'How to use this book' on page 5.

Lievland r w ∗∗→∗∗∗ (r) 87 89 90 STELLENBOSCH estate making top Cape Shiraz (89 90 92), vg CAB S, Merlot, and (outstanding 92) Cab S-F-Merlot. Also range of whites incl intense RIES, off-dry and promising Sauternes-style dessert wine.

Longridge Winery ∗→∗∗∗ New ('95) STELLENBOSCH winery, purchasing grapes, wines from variety of producers. Incl CHARD, CAB, Shiraz.

L'Ormarins r w sw ∗∗∗ (r) 84 86 87 89 (Chard) 89 90 One of two Rupert family estates nr Franschhoek. CAB (86 89) and vg claret-style Optima (87 88 89), also Shiraz (87 89). Fresh lemony CHARD, forward oak-aged SAUV, outstanding GEWURZ-Bukketraube botrytis dessert wine.

Louisvale w ∗∗→∗∗∗ (Chard) 90 91 92 93 STELLENBOSCH winery. Attractive CHARD, now also good Cab-Merlot (from '94) and SAUV BL-Chard.

Meerlust r w ∗∗∗ (r) 86 87 89 90 91 Old family estate nr STELLENBOSCH; Cape's only Italian winemaker. Outstanding Rubicon (Médoc-style blend) (86 89 91), Cab (86 91), Merlot (87 89 91), PINOT N (87 89 91). CHARD still in pipeline.

Méthode Cap Classique Term for classic method sparkling wine in S Africa.

Middelvlei r ∗∗ 89 90 STELLENBOSCH estate: good PINOTAGE (90), CAB (89 90), Shiraz (90).

Monis ∗→∗∗ Well-known wine co of PAARL, with fine 'Special Reserve Port'.

Morgenhof r w dr s/sw ∗ Fresh start at this expensively refurbished s'BOSCH estate. New French owner and change of winemaker (from '92). Improving reds; dry white (excellent 93 Sauv), s/sw whites; 'Port'.

Mulderbosch Vineyards w ∗∗∗ Enthusiastic reception for new penetrating impressive SAUV from mountain v'yds nr S'BOSCH: one oak-fermented, the other fresh bold (93 is exceptional). Also CHARD, B'x-style blend.

Muratie Ancient STELLENBOSCH estate, esp 'Port' and good CAB (93).

Nederburg r w p dr sw s/sw sp ∗∗→∗∗∗∗ (r) 89 91 (Chard) 90 91 92 93 Well-known large modern PAARL winery (650,000 cases pa, 50 wines). Bicentenary in '92. Own grapes and suppliers'. Sound CAB, Shiraz, CHARD, RIES, blends in regular range. Limited Vintages, Private Bins often outstanding. Fresh approach with late '80s top reds: emphasis on richer fruitier flavour, more barrel-ageing. '80s pioneer of botrytis dessert wines: CHENIN, GEWURZ, SAUV, Muscat, even Chard consistently good. Stages Cape's biggest annual wine event, the Nederburg Auction. See Edelkeur.

Neethlingshof r w sw ∗∗→∗∗∗∗ (r) 87 89 90 91 (Chard) 91 Rising estate: replanted with classic grapes, cellar revamped at huge cost since '85. Run jointly with nearby Stellenzicht: 250,000-cases pa. Vg CAB S (89 90), Merlot, CHARD joining fresh SAUV BL, excellent GEWURZ (91 93) and blush Bl de Noir. National champion Botrytis Noble Late Harvest from RIES (92 93), and Sauv Bl.

Neil Ellis Wines r w ∗∗∗ (r) 89 90 91 92 (Chard) 91 92 93 Good wines from Devon Valley nr STELLENBOSCH (16 widely spread coastal v'yds). Spicy structured CAB S; excellent Whitehall SAUV (94); full bold CHARD.

Nuy Cooperative Winery r w dr sw sp ∗∗ Small Worcester Coop, frequent local-award winner. Outstanding dessert wines; fortified Muscadels (91), regularly excellent Cape COLOMBARD (91). Good S African RIES.

Oak Village Wines ∗ Export brand, blend of good coop cellar wines from STELLENBOSCH, incl CAB-Shiraz, SAUV-CHENIN BL blends.

Overgaauw r w ∗∗ (r) 84 86 87 89 90 91 Old family estate nr STELLENBOSCH; CHARD, CAB S, Merlot (90 91), and Bordeaux-style blend Tria Corda (88). Also 'Vintage Port' 85 from 5 Portuguese varieties.

Paarl Town 30 miles NE of Cape Town and the surrounding demarcated district, among the best in the country, particularly for 'Sherry'.

Paul Cluver w ∗∗ Label launched '92. Good SAUV, RHINE RIES, CHARD (93): grapes from cool upland Elgin Coastal region. Wines made by NEDERBURG.

Pinot Noir Like counterparts in California and Australia, Cape producers struggle for fine, burgundy-like complexity. They are getting closer. Best are HAMILTON RUSSELL, MEERLUST, RUSTENBERG. Very promising from CABRIERE ESTATE and GLEN CARLOU, both 'new clone' growers.

Pinotage S African red grape cross of PINOT N and CINSAUT, useful for high yields and hardiness. Can be delicious but overstated flamboyant esters often dominate. Experiments/oak-ageing show potential for finesse.

Plaisir de Merle r w ★★★ New SFW-owned cellar nr PAARL producing its first reds from own v'yds in '93: Cab-Merlot is outstanding, supple, also CHARD (93). Paul Pontallier of Château Margaux is consultant.

Pongracz ★★→★★★ Successful good value NV METHODE CAP CLASSIQUE from PINOT N (75%) and CHARD, produced by the BERGKELDER, named after the exiled Hungarian ampelographer who upgraded many Cape v'yds.

Premier Grand Cru See Grand Cru.

Rhebokskloof r w ★→★★ (r) 90 (Chard) 92   200-acre estate behind PAARL mountain: sound small range. CAB is promising. Has the Cape's first American winemaker.

Rhine Riesling Produces full-flavoured dry and off-dry wines but reaches perfection when lusciously sweet as 'Noble LATE HARVEST'. Generally needs 2 yrs or more of bottle-age. Also called Weisser Riesling.

Riesling S African Ries (actually Crouchen Bl) is v different from RHINE RIES, providing neutral easy-drinking wines. Known locally as Cape Ries.

Robertson District inland from Cape. Mainly dessert wines (notably Muscat); white table wines on increase. Few reds. Irrigated v'yds.

Roodeberg ★ Red blend from KWV: equal PINOTAGE-Shiraz-Tinta Barocca-CAB.

Rooiberg Cooperative Winery ★ Successful big-selling ROBERTSON range of more than 30 labels. Good CHENIN BL, COLOMBARD.

Rozendal r ★★★ (r) 83 84 86 87 89 91 92   Small STELLENBOSCH v'yd cellar, making excellent CAB-Merlot blend.

Ruiterbosch ★★ Individual wines from unusual cool-climate coastal area nr Indian Ocean. Striking SAUV BL, RHINE RIES. Made at BOPLAAS cellars.

Rust en Vrede r ★★★ Well-known estate just E of STELLENBOSCH: red only. Good CAB (89 90), Shiraz (89 90), vg Rust en Vrede blend (86 89 91).

Rustenberg r w ★★★ (red except Pinot N) 89 91 92   The most beautiful old STELLENBOSCH estate, founded 300 yrs ago, making wine for last 100. Grand reds, esp Rustenberg Gold CAB (86 89 91), Médoc-style blend. Also lighter Cab-CINSAUT-Merlot and Cab (89 91 92). Variable PINOT (91 92).

Sauvignon Blanc Adapting well to warm conditions. Widely grown and marketed in both wooded and unwooded styles. Also v sweet.

Saxenburg Wines r w dr sw ★★ (r) 91 92   STELLENBOSCH v'yds and winery; recently prize-winning. Distinctive powerful reds: robust deep-flavoured PINOTAGE (92); Cab (91), Shiraz (91 92).

Simonsig r w sp sw ★★→★★★ (r) 89 90 91 (Chard) 88 89 90 91 92   Malan family S'BOSCH estate with a wide range: vg CAB, Shiraz (89 91), CHARD, PINOTAGE (89 92 93), dessert-style GEWURZ (90 92). First release in '92 of widely acclaimed Cab-Merlot Tiara (90 91 93). Also popular oak-matured white Vin Fumé and first Cape METHODE CAP CLASSIQUE (esp 91).

Simonsvlei r w p sw sp ★ One of S Africa's best-known coop cellars, just outside PAARL. A prize-winner with PINOTAGE.

Steen S Africa's commonest white grape, said to be a clone of CHENIN BL. It gives strong tasty lively wine, sweet or dry: short-lived if dry, lasts better when off-dry or sweet. Normally better than S African RIES.

Stein Name often for commercial blends of s/sw white. Not to be despised.

Stellenbosch Town and demarcated district 30 miles E of Cape Town (oldest town in S Africa). Heart of wine industry, with the 3 largest companies. Most top estates, esp for red wine, are in mountain foothills.

Stellenbosch Farmers' Winery (SFW) The world's fifth largest winery, S Africa's biggest after KWV: equivalent of 14M cases pa. Range incls NEDERBURG; top is ZONNEBLOEM. Wide selection of mid-/low-price wines.

Stellenryck Collection r w ★★★ Top quality BERGKELDER range. RHINE RIES, Fumé Blanc, CAB (87 89) among S Africa's best.

Swartland Wine Cellar r w dr s/sw sw sp ★ Vast range from hot, dry wheatland: big-selling low-price wines, esp CHENIN and dry, off-dry or sweet, but (recently) penetrating SAUV, also big no-nonsense PINOTAGE.

Talana Hill r w ** (r) 88 89 (Chard) 91 92 93 New STELLENBOSCH winery: good CHARD and Bordeaux-style blend Royale (91 92).

Tassenberg * Popular PINOTAGE-based blend by SFW, known fondly as 'Tassies'. Traditional student party and braaivleis (barbecue) wine. Oom Tas, a dry Muscat, is white equivalent.

Thelema r w *** (Cab S) 89 90 91 92 (Chard) 90 91 92 93 94 Outstanding v'yds and winery at Helshoogte, above s'BOSCH. Impressive minty CAB, B'x blend (starting with vg 91 92), excellent CHARD, and unoaked SAUV.

Theuniskraal w * TULBAGH estate: whites incl S Afrian RIES, GEWURZ.

Tulbagh Demarcated district N of PAARL best known for white THEUNISKRAAL, TWEE JONGEGEZELLEN and dessert wines from DROSTDY. See also Boberg.

Twee Jongegezellen w sp ** Old TULBAGH estate, helped pioneer cold fermentation in '60s, night harvesting in '80s; still in Krone family (18th-C founder). Esp whites, best known: popular dry TJ89 (mélange of a dozen varieties), Schanderl off-dry Muscat-GEWURZ. Recently METHODE CAP CLASSIQUE Cuvée Krone Borealis Brut (CHARD, PINOT N).

Uiterwyk r w * Old estate W of s'BOSCH. CAB 'Carlonet' (89 90), Merlot, whites.

Uitkyk r w ** (r) 89 90 Old estate (400 acres) W of STELLENBOSCH esp for Carlonet (big gutsy CAB, 89 90), Carlsheim (SAUV) white. Recently CHARD.

Van Loveren r w sw sp ** Go-ahead ROBERTSON estate: range incl muscular CHARD (90 91 93), good Pinot Gr (92 93); scarcer Fernão Pires, Hárslevelü.

Veenwouden ** Promising Merlot (93) from new PAARL property owned by Geneva-based opera tenor, Deon Van der Walt.

Vergelegen w ** One of Cape's oldest wine farms, founded 1700. Long neglected, now spectacularly restored. Les Enfants series marked '92 re-launch with wine from bought-in grapes; good CHARD (93 94) and SAUV. Impressive CABERNET and Merlot in pipeline.

Vergenoegd r w sw *→** Old family estate in S s'BOSCH supplying vg 'Sherry' to KWV and bottling CAB S, Shiraz. New B'x-style blend 'Reserve' (89 90).

Villiera r w *** PAARL estate with popular NV METHODE CAP CLASSIQUE 'Tradition'. Top SAUV BL (93 94), good RHINE RIES, fine B'x-style blend CAB-Merlot 'Cru Monro' (90 91 92). Recently exceptional Merlot (89 91).

Vredendal Cooperative r w dr sw * S Africa's largest coop winery in hot Olifants River region. Big range: mostly white, reds incl Ruby Cab.

Vriesenhof r w **→*** (Cab) 89 91 (Chard) 91 92 93 Highly rated CAB and B'x blend Kalista (89 91). Since '88, vg CHARD. Also Pinot Bl.

Warwick r w **→*** (r) 89 90 92 STELLENBOSCH estate run by one of Cape's few female winemakers. CAB and vg Médoc-style blend Trilogy (89 90 92), Cab F (89 90 92) and Chard (92 94).

Weisser Riesling See Rhine Riesling.

Welgemeend r **→*** (r) 87 89 90 92 Boutique PAARL estate: Médoc-style blends (87 90 92), delicate CAB, and Amadé (Grenache-Shiraz-PINOTAGE).

Weltevrede w dr sw *→** (Chard) 89 90 91 93 Progressive ROBERTSON estate. Blended, white, fortified. Vg CHARD, Gewürz (93), White Muscadel (91).

Wine of Origin The Cape's appellation contrôlée, but without French crop yield restrictions. Demarcated regions are described on these pages.

Woolworths Wines Best S African supermarket wines, many specially blended. Top are CHARDS, young reds incl Merlot, B'x-style blends.

Worcester Demarcated wine district round BREEDE and Hex river valleys, E of PAARL. Many coop cellars. Mainly dessert wines, brandy, dry whites.

Yonder Hill ** Small new STELLENBOSCH mountainside property, launching with vg Merlot and CAB-Merlot blend (93).

Zandvliet r *→** (Shiraz) 86 87 89 Estate in the ROBERTSON area making fine light Shiraz and recently a CAB S and Chard.

Zevenwacht r w **→*** (Cab S) 84 86 87 88 89 STELLENBOSCH wines only available via shareholders, restaurants. Impressive CAB, Rhine Ries (93).

Zonnebloem r w ** (Cab S) 82 84 86 87 89 (Chard) 90 91 Good quality range from SFW incl CAB S, Merlot (88 91 92), Bordeaux-style blend Laureat (89 90) launched '92, Shiraz, PINOTAGE (87 89 91), SAUV BL, CHARD (91 93) and, new '94, a Sauv-Chard blend.

A little learning...

The jargon of laboratory analysis is often seen on the back-labels of New World wines. It has crept menacingly into newspapers and magazines. What does it mean? This hard-edged wine-talk, unsympathetic as it is to most lovers of wine, is very briefly explained below.

The most frequent technical references are to the ripeness of grapes at picking; the resultant alcohol and sugar content of the wine; various measures of its acidity; the amount of sulphur dioxide used as a preservative; and occasionally the amount of 'dry extract' – the sum of all the things that give wine its character.

The **sugar** in wine is mainly glucose and fructose, with traces of arabinose, xylose and other sugars that are not fermentable by yeast, but can be attacked by bacteria. Each country has its own system for measuring the sugar content or ripeness of grapes, known in English as the **'must weight'**. The chart below relates the three principal ones (German, French and American) to each other, to specific gravity, and to the potential alcohol of the wine if all the sugar is fermented.

Sugar to alcohol: potential strength

Specific Gravity	°Oechsle	Baumé	Brix	% Potential Alcohol v/v
1.065	65	8.8	15.8	8.1
1.070	70	9.4	17.0	8.8
1.075	75	10.1	18.1	9.4
1.080	80	10.7	19.3	10.0
1.085	85	11.3	20.4	10.6
1.090	90	11.9	21.5	12.1
1.095	95	12.5	22.5	13.0
1.100	100	13.1	23.7	13.6
1.105	105	13.7	24.8	14.3
1.110	110	14.3	25.8	15.1
1.115	115	14.9	26.9	15.7
1.120	120	15.5	28.0	16.4

Residual sugar is the sugar left after fermentation has finished or been artificially stopped, measured in grams per litre.

Alcohol content (mainly ethyl alcohol) is expressed in percent by volume of the total liquid. (Also known as 'degrees'.)

Acidity is both fixed and volatile. **Fixed acidity** consists principally of tartaric, malic and citric acids which are all found in the grape, and lactic and succinic acids which are produced during fermentation. **Volatile acidity** consists mainly of acetic acid, which is rapidly formed by bacteria in the presence of oxygen. A small amount of volatile acidity is inevitable and even attractive. With a larger amount the wine becomes 'pricked' – to use the graphic Shakespearian term. It starts to turn to vinegar.

Total acidity is fixed and volatile acidity combined. As a rule of thumb for a well-balanced wine it should be in the region of one gram per thousand for each 10°Oechsle (see above).

pH is a measure of the strength of the acidity, rather than its volume. The lower the figure the more acid. Wine normally ranges in pH from 2.8 to 3.8. Winemakers in hot climates can have problems getting the pH low enough. Lower pH gives better colour, helps prevent bacterial spoilage and allows more of the SO_2 to be free and active as a preservative.

Sulphur dioxide (SO_2) is added to prevent oxidation and other accidents in winemaking. Some of it combines with sugars etc and is known as **'bound'**. Only the **'free' SO_2** that remains in the wine is effective as a preservative. **Total SO_2** is controlled by law according to the level of residual sugar: the more sugar, the more SO_2 needed.

A few more words about words

In the shorthand essential for this little book (and often in bigger books and magazines as well) wines are often described by adjectives that can seem irrelevant, inane – or just silly. What do 'fat', 'round', 'full', 'lean' and so on mean when used about wine? Some of the more irritatingly vague and some of the more common 'technical' terms are expanded in this list:

Acid
To laymen often a term of reproval, meaning 'too sharp'. But various acids are vital to the quality and preservation of wine (especially white) and give it its power to refresh. For those on the advanced course malolactic, or secondary, fermentation is the natural conversion of tart malic (apple) acid to lactic, replacing the immediate bite of a wine with milder, more complex tastes. The undesirable acid is acetic, smells of vinegar and is referred to as 'volatile'. Too much and the wine is on the way out.

Astringent
One of the characters of certain tannins, producing a mouth-drying effect. Can be highly appetizing, as in Chianti.

Attack
The first impression of the wine in your mouth. It should 'strike' positively, if not necessarily with force. Without attack it is feeble or too bland.

Attractive
Means 'I like it, anyway'. A slight put-down for expensive wines; encouragement for juniors. At least refreshing.

Balance
See Well-balanced.

Big
Concerns the whole flavour, including the alcohol content. Sometimes implies clumsiness, the opposite of elegance. Generally positive, but big is easy in California and less usual in, say, Bordeaux. So the context matters.

Bitterness
Another tannic flavour, usually from lack of full ripeness. Much appreciated in N Italy but looked on askance in most regions.

Body
The 'weight', the volume of flavour and alcohol in wine. See Big and Full.

Botrytis
See page 77.

Charming
Rather patronizing when said of wines that should have more impressive qualities. Implies lightness and possibly a slight sweetness. A standard comment regarding Loire Valley wines.

Corky
A musty taint derived (far too often) from an infected cork. Can be faint or blatant, but is always unacceptable.

Crisp
With pronounced but pleasing acidity on the palate; fresh and eager.

Deep/depth
This wine is worth tasting with attention. There is more to it than the first impression; it fills your mouth with developing flavours as though it had an extra dimension. (Deep colour simply means hard to see through.) All really fine wines have depth.

Earthy
Used of a sense that the soil itself has entered into the flavour of the wine. Often positive, as in the flavour of red Graves.

Easy
Used in the sense of 'easy come, easy go'. An easy wine makes no demand on your palate (or your intellect). The implication is that it drinks smoothly, doesn't need maturing, and all you remember is a pleasant drink.

Elegant
A professional taster's favourite term when he or she is stuck to describe a wine whose proportions (of strength, flavour, aroma), whose attack, middle and finish, whose texture and whose overall qualities call for comparison with other forms of natural beauty.

Extract	The components of wine (apart from water, alcohol, sugar, acids, etc) that make up its flavour. Usually the more the better, but 'over-extracted' means harsh, left too long extracting matter from the grape skins.
Fat	Wine with a flavour and texture that fills your mouth, but without aggression. Obviously inappropriate in eg a light Moselle, but what you pay your money for in Sauternes.
Finesse	See Elegance.
Finish	See Length.
Firm	Flavour that strikes the palate fairly hard, with fairly high acidity or tannic astringency giving the impression that the wine is in youthful vigour and will age to gentler things. An excellent quality with high-flavoured foods, and almost always positive.
Flesh	Refers to both substance and texture. A fleshy wine is fatter than a 'meaty' wine, more unctuous if less vigorous. The term is often used of good Pomerols, whose texture is notably smooth.

Own Goal

The 100-point scoring system for wine lumbers along in America, looking increasingly ridiculous. It never looked more ridiculous than when The Wine Spectator used it to indicate its editorial preferences for – of all things – corkscrews. Apart from the fact that one point is enough for any corkscrew, it solemnly pretended that a Screwpull was worth (let's say) 91 (not 89 or 92) points, while some other model was rated a measly 84.

This professedly precise measure of quality, designed to scalpel nuances, is now routinely used for entire vintages with all their internal variations. To our uproarious confusion the '89s are supposedly worth 91, the '90s 94, but the poor '91s only 80.

The last word on the effects of this lemming approach to wine came from the New York retailer who said 'If a wine scores less than 90 I can't sell it; if it scores more I can't buy it'.

Flowery	Often used as though synonymous with fruity, but really means floral, like the fragrance of flowers. Roses, violets, etc are sometimes specified.
Fresh	Implies a good degree of fruity acidity, even a little nip of sharpness, as well as the zip and zing of youth. All young whites should be fresh: the alternative is flatness, staleness. . . ugh.
Fruity	Used for almost any quality, but really refers to the body and richness of wine made from good ripe grapes. A fruity aroma is not the same as a flowery one. Fruitiness usually implies at least a slight degree of sweetness. Attempts at specifying *which* fruit the wine resembles can be helpful. Eg grapefruit, lemon, plum, lychee. On the other hand writers' imaginations freqently run riot, flinging basketfuls of fruit and flowers at wines which could well be more modestly described.
Full	Interchangeable with full-bodied. Lots of 'vinosity' or wineyness: the mouth-filling flavours of alcohol and 'extract' (all the flavouring components) combined.
Heady	The sense that the alcohol content is out of proportion.
Hollow	Lacking a satisfying middle flavour. Something seems to be missing between the first flavour and the last. Characteristic of wines from greedy proprietors who let their vines produce too many grapes. A very hollow wine is 'empty'.

Honey	A smell and flavour found especially in botrytis-affected wines, but often to a small and seductive degree in any mature wine of a ripe vintage.
Lean	More flesh would be an improvement. Lack of mouth-filling flavours; often astringent as well. Occasionally a term of appreciation of a distinct and enjoyable style.
Length	The flavours and aromas that linger after swallowing. In principle the greater the length the better the wine. One second of flavour after swallowing = one 'caudalie'. Twenty caudalies is good; 50 terrific.
Light	With relatively little alcohol and body, as in most German wines. A very desirable quality in the right wines but a dismissive term in eg reds where something more intense/weighty is desired.
Maderized	Means oxidized until it smells/tastes like madeira. A serious fault unless intentional.
Meaty	Savoury in effect with enough substance to chew. The inference is lean meat; leaner than in 'fleshy'.
Oaky	Smelling or tasting of fresh-sawn oak, eg a new barrel. Appropriate in a fine wine destined for ageing in bottle, but currently often wildly overdone by winemakers to persuade a gullible public that a simple wine is something more grandiose. Over-oaky wines are both boring and tiring to drink.
Plump	The diminutive of fat, implying a degree of charm as well.
Rich	Not necessarily sweet, but giving an opulent impression.
Robust	In good heart, vigorous, and on a fairly big scale.
Rough	Flavour and texture give no pleasure. Acidity and/or tannin are dominant and coarse.
Round	Almost the same as fat, but with more approval.
Structure	The 'plan' or architecture of the flavour, as it were. Without structure wine is bland, dull, and won't last.
Stylish	Style is bold and definite; wears its cap on its ear.
Supple	Often used of young red wines which might be expected to be more aggressive. More lively than an 'easy' wine, with implications of good quality.
Well-balanced	Contains all the desirable elements (acid, alcohol, flavours, etc) in appropriate and pleasing proportions.

Masters of Wine

The Institute of Masters of Wine was founded in London in 1953 to provide an exacting standard of qualification for the British wine trade. A small minority pass its very stiff examinations, even after rigorous training, both theoretical and practical. (They must be able to identify wines 'blind', know how they are made, and also know the relevant EC and Customs regulations.) In all, only 188 people have qualified to become Masters of Wine. Thirty 'Masters' are women.

In 1988 the Institute, aided by a grant from the Madame Bollinger Foundation, opened its examinations for the first time to non-British candidates. The first to pass was a New Zealander (see Kumeu River, page 211). Now candidates come from the USA, Australia, Germany, France, etc. 'Master of Wine' (MW) should eventually become the equivalent of a Bachelor of Arts degree in the worldwide wine trade.

What to drink in an ideal world

Wines approaching their peak in 1996

Red Bordeaux
Top growths of 87, 85, 83, 81, 79, 78, 75, 70, 66, 62, 61, 59
Other crus classés of 87, 86, 85, 83, 82, 81, 79, 78, 70, 66, 61
Petits châteaux of 93, 90, 89, 88, 86, 85, 83, 82

Red Burgundy
Top growths of 92, 89, 87, 85, 83, 82, 80, 79, 78, 76, 72, 71, 69, 66, 64
Premiers Crus of 92, 89, 88, 87, 85, 83, 78, 76, 71
Village wines of 93, 92, 91, 90, 89, 88, 85

White Burgundy
Top growths of 90, 89, 88, 86, 85, 83, 79, 78...
Premiers Crus of 93, 92, 91, 90, 89, 88, 86, 85, 83, 78...
Village wines of 94, 93, 92, 90, 89, 88

Rhône reds
Hermitage/top northern Rhône reds of 88, 86, 85, 83, 82, 79, 78, 71, 70, 69...
Châteauneuf-du-Pape of 90, 89, 88, 86, 85, 83, 82, 81

Sauternes
Top growths of 86, 85, 83, 82, 81, 79, 78, 76, 75, 71, 70, 67...
Other wines of 90, 89, 88, 86, 85, 83, 82, 81, 79, 76, 75...

Alsace
Grands Crus and late-harvest wines of 90, 89, 88, 86, 85, 83, 81, 78, 76, 67...
Standard wines of 93, 92, 91, 90, 89, 88, 85...

Sweet Loire wines
Top growths (Anjou/Vouvray) of 93, 90, 88, 86, 85, 78, 76, 75, 71, 64...

Champagne
Top wines of 86, 85, 83, 82, 81, 79, 78, 76, 75...

German wines
Great sweet wines of 90, 89, 88, 86, 85, 83, 76, 71, 67...
Auslesen of 92, 90, 89, 88, 86, 85, 83, 79, 76, 71...
Spätlesen of 92, 91, 90, 89, 88, 86, 85, 83, 79, 76...
Kabinett and QbA wines of 93, 92, 91, 90, 89, 88, 85, 83...

Italian wines
Top Tuscan reds 90, 88, 86, 85, 82, 79, 78
Top Piedmont reds 89, 88, 87, 86, 85, 83, 82, 79, 78, 74, 71...

California wines
Top Cabernets/Zinfandels of 88, 86, 85, 84, 82, 81, 80, 79, 78, 77, 76, 75, 74, 70
Most Cabernets etc of 92, 90, 89, 88, 87, 86, 85...
Top Chardonnays of 91, 90, 89, 88, 87, 86, 85, 83, 81...
Most Chardonnays of 93, 92, 91, 90, 89, 88...

Australian wines
Top Cabernets and Shiraz of 89, 88, 86, 84, 82, 80, 79, 75...
Most Cabernets etc of 91, 90, 89, 88, 87, 86...
Top Chardonnays of 92, 90, 89, 88, 87, 86
Most Chardonnays of 93, 92, 91...
Top Sémillons and Rieslings of 92, 91, 90, 88, 86, 82, 79...

Vintage Port
83, 82, 80, 70, 66, 63, 60, 55, 48, 45...

QUICK REFERENCE VINTAGE CHARTS

These charts give a picture of the range of qualities made in the principal 'classic' areas (every year has its relative successes and failures) and a guide to whether the wine is ready to drink or should be kept.

Symbol	Meaning	Symbol	Meaning
I	drink now	—	needs keeping
/	can be drunk with pleasure now, but the better wines will continue to improve	ℵ	avoid
		0	no good
		10	the best

FRANCE

	RED BORDEAUX MEDOC/GRAVES	POM/ST-EM	WHITE BORDEAUX SAUTERNES & SW	GRAVES & DRY	ALSACE	
94	5-8 —	5-9 —	4-6 —	5-8 ↖	4-8 ↖	94
93	4-7 ↖	5-8 ↖	2-5 /	5-7 /	6-8 ↖	93
92	3-7 ↖	3-5 ↖	3-5 ↖	4-8 ↖	7-9 ↖	92
91	3-6 ↖	2-4 ↖	2-5 ↖	6-8 ↖	5-7 /	91
90	7-10 ↖	8-10 ↖	7-10 ↖	7-8 ↖	7-9 /	90
89	6-9 ↖	7-9 ↖	7-9 ↖	6-8 ↖	7-10 ↖	89
88	6-9 ↖	7-9 ↖	6-10 ↖	7-9 ↖	8-10 ↖	88
87	3-6 I	3-6 I	2-5 ℵ	7-10 ↖	7-8 I	87
86	6-9 ↖	5-8 ↖	7-10 ↖	7-9 I	7-8 I	86
85	7-9 ↖	7-9 ↖	6-8 ↖	5-8 I	7-10 ↖	85
84	3-5 I	2-5 ℵ	4-6 ℵ	5-7 ℵ	4-6 ℵ	84
83	6-9 ↖	6-9 I	6-10 ↖	7-9 I	8-10 I	83
82	8-10 ↖	7-9 I	3-7 ↖	7-8 I	6-8 I	82
81	4-7 I	6-9 I	5-8 ↖	5-9 I	3-5 ↖	81
80	4-7 I	3-5 ℵ	5-9 I	5-7 ℵ	3-5 ℵ	80
79	5-8 ↖	5-7 I	6-8 ↖	4-6 ℵ	7-8 I	79
78	6-8 ↖	6-8 I	4-6 I	6-8 ↖	7-8 I	78
76	6-8 I	7-8 I	7-9 ↖	4-8 ℵ		76

	BURGUNDY COTE D'OR RED	COTE D'OR WHITE	CHABLIS	RHONE RHONE (N)	RHONE (S)	
94	5-7 —	5-8 ↖	6-8 /	6-9 ↖	5-7 ↖	94
93	6-9 ↖	4-6 /	4-7 /	3-6 /	4-9 ↖	93
92	4-7 /	6-8 ↖	5-8 ↖	4-6 /	3-6 /	92
91	5-7 /	4-6 ↖	4-6 ↖	6-9 ↖	4-5 /	91
90	7-10 ↖	7-9 ↖	7-10 ↖	6-9 ↖	7-9 ↖	90
89	6-9 ↖	6-9 ↖	7-10 ↖	6-8 ↖	5-8 ↖	89
88	7-10 ↖	7-9 ↖	7-9 ↖	7-9 ↖	5-8 ↖	88
87	5-8 ↖	4-7 I	5-7 I	3-6 ↖	3-5 I	87
86	5-8 I	7-10 ↖	7-9 I	5-8 ↖	4-7 /	86
85	7-10 ↖	5-8 ↖	6-9 I	6-8 ↖	6-9 ↖	85
83	4-7 I	6-8 I	7-9 I	7-10 ↖	5-8 I	83
82	4-7 I	6-8 I	6-7 I	5-8 I	5-8 I	82
81	3-6 ℵ	4-8 I	6-9 I	5-7 I	5-9 I	81

Beaujolais 94 and 93 Crus will keep, 92 vg, 91 superb. **Mâcon-Villages** (white) Drink 94, 93, 92 now. **Loire** (Sweet Anjou and Touraine) best recent vintages: 93, 90, 89, 88, 85, 84, 83, 82, 79, 78, 76. **Upper Loire** (Sancerre and Pouilly Fumé): 94, 93 and 90 are good now. **Muscadet** DYA.

GERMANY   ITALY   USA

	RHINE	MOSEL	TUSCAN REDS	CALIFORNIA CABS	CALIFORNIA CHARDS	
94	5-7 /	6-10 ↖	5-7 ↖	6-9 —	4-7 /	94
93	5-8 ↖	6-9 ↖	7-9 ↖	6-8 /	5-8 ↖	93
92	5-9 ↖	5-9 ↖	3-6 ↖	6-8 ↖	5-7 I	92
91	5-7 /	5-7 /	4-6 ↖	8-10 ↖	5-7 I	91
90	8-10 ↖	8-10 ↖	7-10 /	8-9 ↖	5-7 I	90
89	7-10 ↖	8-10 ↖	5-8 ↖	6-9 /	5-9 I	89
88	6-8 ↖	7-9 /	6-9 I	6-8 ↖	6-8 I	88
87	4-7 I	5-7 I	4-7 I	7-10 /	7-9 I	87
86	4-8 I	5-8 I	5-8 I	5-8 ↖	6-8 ℵ	86
85	6-8 ↖	6-9 ↖	7-10 ↖	7-9 I	7-9 I	85
83	6-8 I	7-10 ↖	5-7 I	4-8 ↖	4-7 I	83
82	4-6 ℵ	4-7 ↖	5-8 I	5-8 I	5-6 ℵ	82
81	5-8 ℵ	4-8 I	4-7 I	4-7 I	6-8 ℵ	81